Helion & Company Limited
Unit 8 Amherst Business Centre
Budbrooke Road
Warwick
CV34 5WE
England
Tel. 01926 499 619
Email: info@helion.co.uk
Website: www.helion.co.uk
Twitter: @helionbooks
https://helionbooks.wordpress.com/

Published by Helion & Company 2026

Text © Kevin Wright 2026

Illustrations are reproduced under the Creative Commons license, or derive from the author's personal collection.

Cover: US Army Air Force B-17G Flying Fortresses of the 381st Bombardment Group at RAF Ridgewell photographed on a training mission over England. Combat Cameramen favoured the open waist gunner's position as the best place to get photographs outside of the aircraft during bombing missions. Closest to the camera is B-17G 43-37675 named *Patches (Flak Magnet)*. (USAAF/NARA)

Designed and typeset by Mach 3 Solutions
(www.mach3solutions.co.uk)
Cover design Paul Hewitt, Battlefield Design
(www.battlefield-design.co.uk)

ISBN: 978-1-806720-57-6

British Library Cataloguing-in-Publication Data
A catalogue record for this book is available from the British Library

We always welcome receiving book proposals from prospective authors.

CONTENTS

Note: In order to simplify the use of this book, all names, locations and geographic designations are as provided in *The Times World Atlas*, or other traditionally accepted major sources of reference, as of the time of described events.

ABBREVIATIONS AND ACRONYMS

AAVS	Aerospace Audiovisual Service		**MATS**	Military Air Transport Service
AA-VS	Aerospace Audio-Visual Service (became AAVS on 1 May 1981)		**MPS**	Motion Picture Squadron
			NARA	National Archives and Records Administration (US)
AEC	Atomic Energy Commission			
APCS	Air photographic and Charting Service		**NCA**	National Command Authority
AVS	Audiovisual Squadron		**PS**	Photographic Squadron
CCU	Combat Camera Unit		**SAC**	Strategic Air Command
COMDOC	Combat Documentation		**TAC**	Tactical Air Command
DoD	Department of Defense		**TDY**	Temporary Duty
FWS	Fighter Weapons School		**USAAF**	United States Army Air Force
MAC	Military Airlift Command			

INTRODUCTION AND ACKNOWLEDGEMENTS

US military cameramen and women have documented events from World War Two through Korea, Vietnam, the Cold War, the 1991 Gulf War, and since 2001. If you have ever watched documentaries about wars and military conflicts involving the United States, you have undoubtedly seen their work. Unfortunately, it becomes far too easy to take their efforts for granted.

During World War Two, the Army Air Force's photographers, working in small units around the world, earned the accolade of 'Combat Camera', one that has stayed with them officially and unofficially ever since.

Most military photographers' work occurs beyond the public's gaze. Much of their effort goes into producing training and briefing materials for military eyes alone. Unlike civilian press photographers, military photographers' images usually go unacknowledged, at best annotated as 'US Air Force' or 'official photograph'. Many of the events and topics covered by military photographers are, by their very nature, ephemeral, which makes creating a single detailed history nearly impossible.

Thus, this book explores a tiny fraction of the history and work of US Air Force photographers and videographers from the formative years of the US Army Air Force in World War Two onwards. Much of it concentrates on the period covered by the existence of the USAF's Aerospace Audiovisual Service (AAVS), from the mid-1960s up to the 1991 Gulf War. However, for every topic mentioned here, thousands of others go uncovered, and their stories remain untold.

I have talked with many fascinating people who have worked in Combat Camera. There are many people to thank for helping me. First, Robert Zoucha, for getting me started on this project and introducing me to others who gave me their time and shared their experiences. Sadly, just as this book was going to press, we learned of the recent death of Combat Camera 'Godfather' Ken Hackman. Ken had been very kind with his time, talking with me about the history of USAF Combat Camera and his own personal experiences about 18 months before his death. I hope the words in this book will be seen as some small tribute to his leadership, professional skills, and longstanding support for the Combat Camera community. I would also like to thank Greg Krager for his regular assistance pointing me in the right direction. I am also indebted to Dave van de Brake, Hans Deffner, David Gephardt, Rose Reynolds, Charles Reger and Ron Bogard for their kind contributions. I thank Nick Spark at Periscope Films for his assistance, David Holmes for some of the 7th CCU images, and Zach Drury for several World War Two unit histories.

I have also trawled through many archives, including oral history interviews, news and film archives, NARA, and the Library of Congress. Many APCS/AAVS movie and video productions are gradually being recovered and digitised. Much is being done by organisations such as Periscope Films and The Nuclear Vault, which make them publicly available via their YouTube channels.

WATCH THE MOVIE

Dealing with movie and video imagery, which is so essential to this story, is naturally more challenging. Throughout these pages, you will see many QR codes. Scan them with your phone or other mobile device, to see the original material for yourself. Using them will significantly enhance your experience.

Above all, this book is dedicated to the US Air Forces' combat photographers and all the men and women who have supported their work in every possible way but who rarely get the recognition they deserve. Any errors, misunderstandings or omissions are entirely down to me.

Kevin Wright

1

WORLD WAR TWO: HOLLYWOOD MEETS THE MILITARY

As war raged across Europe and North Africa, the American public's knowledge came through cinemas and newspapers fed by war correspondents and imagery from the combatant countries. In the United States, short movies were commissioned to raise domestic public awareness of the US armed forces, especially some of its newer branches, like the US Army Air Corps, soon to be the US Army Air Force, the Airborne troops and the US Army's Armoured Forces.

In the wake of the attack on Pearl Harbour in December 1941, the immediate requirements of mass mobilisation saw an exponential increase in the demands made on the news media and film industry. Still and movie images from Europe and the Pacific fed the news, but the need went far beyond printed public news press and movies. The sudden need to recruit and train immense numbers of individuals for the armed forces and massively expand military production created vast demands on every part of US society. The requirement for training materials, public information and propaganda exploded far beyond anything the existing capacity of the film and news media could hope to meet.

That immediate necessity meant there was no time to build this capability from scratch. Instead, Hollywood was harnessed as the dominant location where film expertise resided, and its talents and techniques were marshalled to support the US war effort. The expertise of Warner Brothers (and soon other studios) was quickly called upon to produce what was primarily a recruitment film for the US Army Air Force, *Winning Your Wings.* Filmed in just two weeks and credited with recruiting thousands of young men to become aircrew, it was followed by a series of other movies.

The Army Air Force Film Unit

In 1945, *Flying Magazine* recorded the early development of the 'Army Air Force Film Unit'. Formed on 1 July 1942, as the First Motion Picture Unit, it took over the Hal Roach Studio in Culver City, CA, in October 1942 to be the home of the 'Army Air Forces First Picture Unit'. It became the 18th AAF Base Unit (Motion Picture Unit) within a few days.[1]

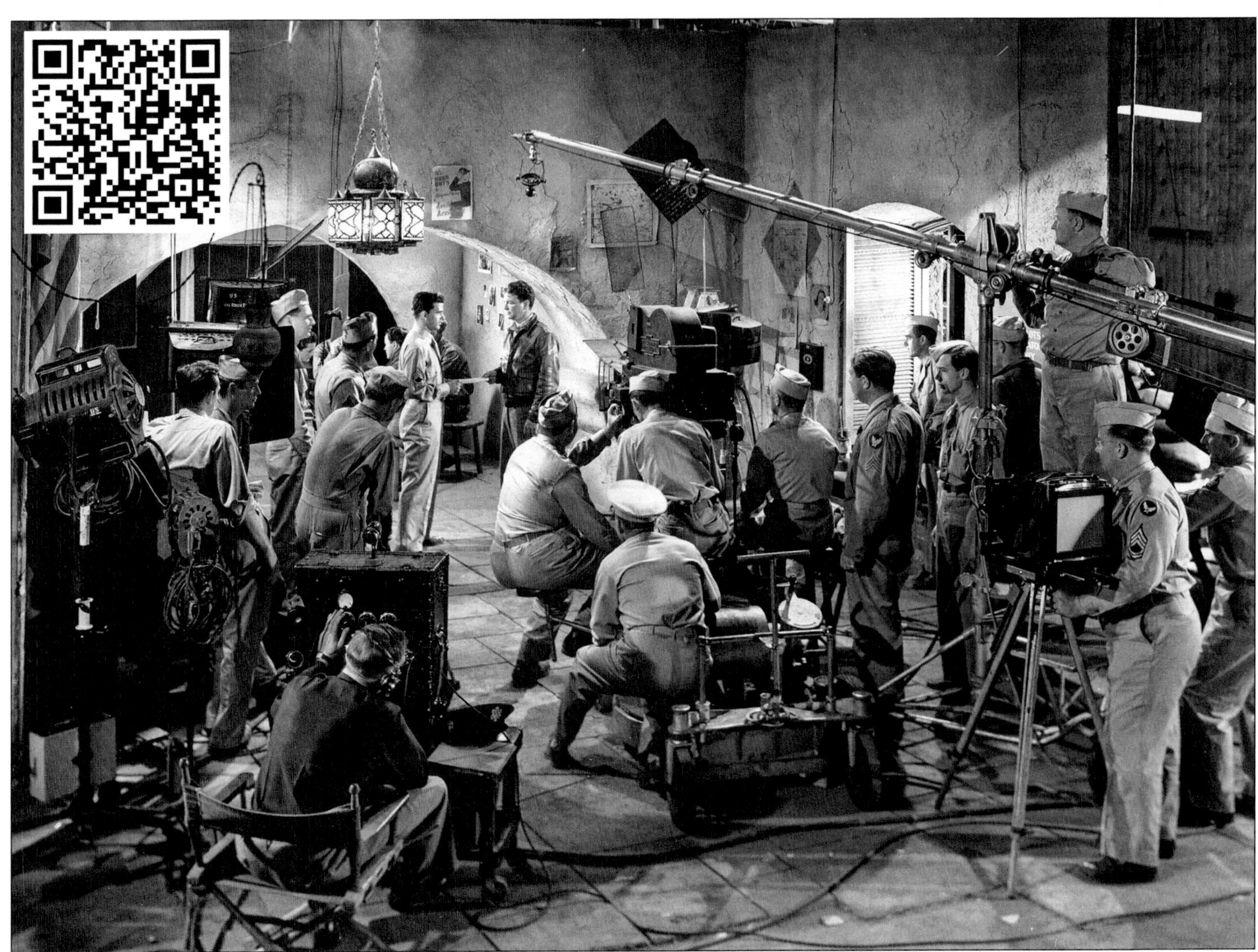

First Motion Picture Unit: Army Air Forces was a 20-minute documentary showing the Unit's work and some of its photographic techniques. (YouTube/NARA)

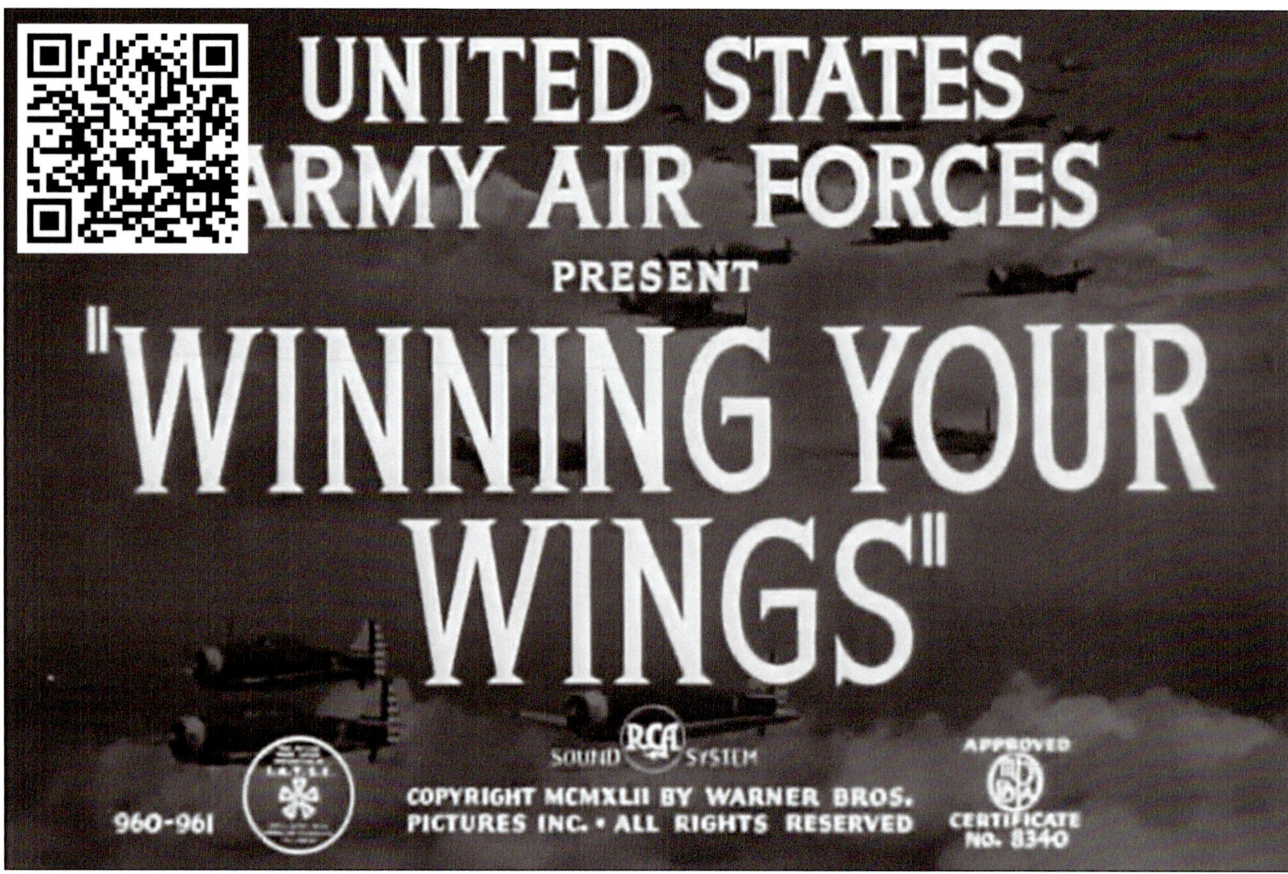

A still from the title sequence of *Winning Your Wings*. (YouTube/NARA)

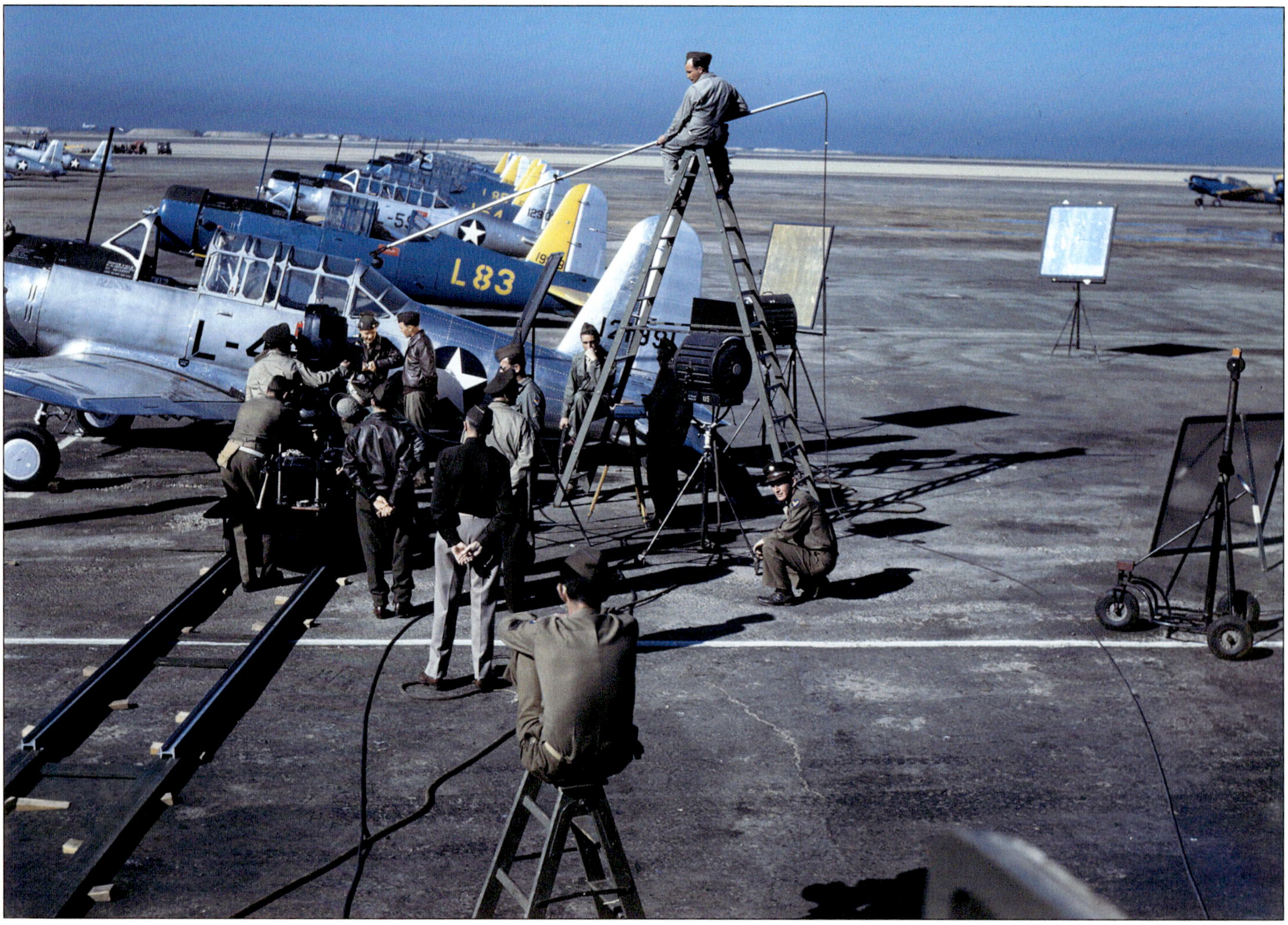

First Motion Picture Unit crew filming actors as part of a training film in front of a BT-13 aircraft. (NARA)

Among a wide range of activities, the unit created aircraft recognition films. It noted that US pilots and anti-aircraft crews in the Pacific area had difficulty telling the P-40 Warhawk and Japanese Zero fighters apart, especially head-on. 'Both a Warhawk and a captured Jap Zero were flown over the San Diego area and photographed from all angles and in all manoeuvres. After the film was shown throughout the Pacific theatre, no further confusion over the two planes was reported'. Although likely an over-optimistic assertion, it made the point about the value of such aircraft recognition training films.

The unit also had pilots and aircraft available to its 'flight echelon'. The 1945 *Flying Magazine* article briefly described the aircraft section's activity was given:

Personnel of the echelon are now commanded by Maj Frank Clarke, formerly a movie stunt pilot, who once flew a plane off a Los Angeles office building. Among Its members are the daring pilots who provided thrills in hundreds of movies. Another member of the echelon is Maj Elmer Dyer, a noted aerial photographer who filmed the air sequences for 'Hell's Angels,' 'Only Angels Have Wings' and many other movies. Attached to the echelon are from 12 to 20 planes, based on Metropolitan Airport, most of them twin-engined Beech Kansas trainers [Beech AT-11 Kansan] converted into camera planes.

The piece continued:

The echelon started with one plane, a Hudson bomber borrowed from Lockheed. Since then, 'Havocs,' have been transferred to the echelon; *Fortresses* and *Liberators* have been borrowed from other commands for long-range missions. The Vultee *Vigilant* high-wing observation plane has been converted into a camera plane for photographing ground operations, and the Boeing P-I2 (obsolete biplane fighter) is used for acrobatic flying.

When a training film has been ordered by the Motion Picture Division of the Army Air Forces In Washington, the production office of the unit first 'breaks it down' and assigns writers to do the scenario. Research experts are sent to Army air bases and technical schools to familiarize themselves with operational conditions. A crew of technicians, actors, a director, and all their equipment is then dispatched to the 'location.' The planes and equipment to be illustrated in the picture are obtained from other commands, and students and instructors are filmed in their daily routines. When the location shots are obtained, the shooting company returns to the Culver City headquarters for interior scenes. A musical background is provided, and the film is edited.

Other films destined for the visual education of embryonic pilots, ground crew members, aerial gunners, radio operators, navigators, and flight engineers are animated cartoons which

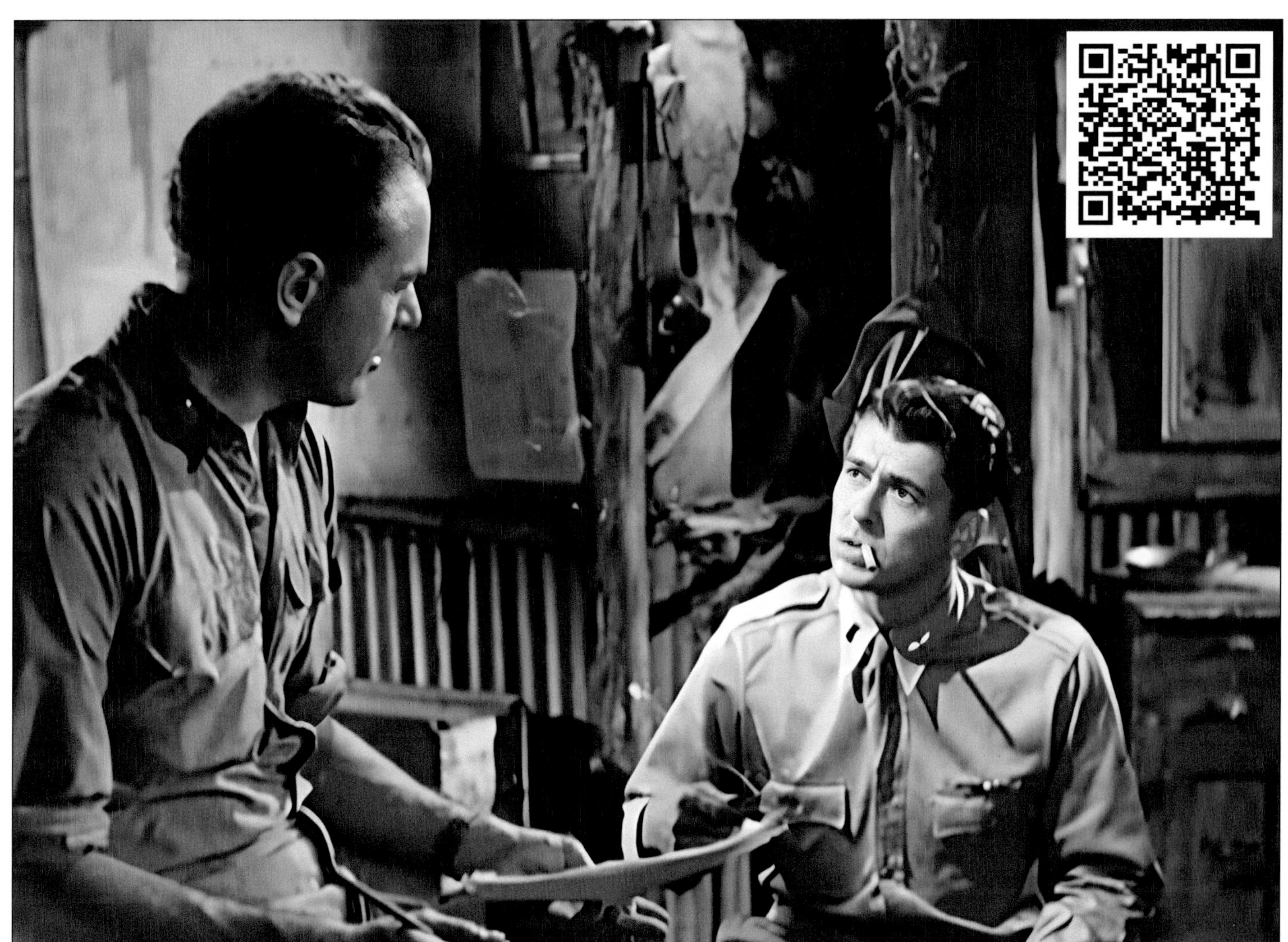

Recognition of the Japanese Zero Fighter, starring future President Ronald Regan, was an official training film aimed at helping aircrews and anti-aircraft gunners distinguish it from the US Curtis P-40 Warhawk. (YouTube/NARA)

drive home their points graphically and often humorously. For instance, animation brings to life an oil gauge in a plane which crashed because the pilot failed to warm his motors. The oil gauge tells the pilot he should not have tried to take off without warming up the motor.[2]

Placed under the command of Lt Col Paul Mantz, the unit was initially comprised of a mix of 'stunt' pilots, aerial photographers, technicians working with directors, writers and actors. Many of these films today are best remembered because of the young, then unknown, actors who took part in them, like Ronald Regan, James Stewart, Clark Gable and many others. However, the unit was not just in the movie business; it had the dual role of producing training films for every part of the USAAF and as the cadre responsible for training future combat photographers.

Combat Photographer Training

There were notable differences between the individuals initially recruited to join the MPU and Combat Camera Units and those recruited to other parts of the USAAF. They were mainly slightly older than the average recruits, had generally attained better levels of education, and most had directly volunteered for their roles.[3] Those with previous experience behind the camera, or with relevant technical expertise, were particularly valued.

Working in such a hurry, it was no surprise that training and facilities in the early days took time to acquire and develop. Initially, recruits went to Camp Letts, a basic 10-acre Boy Scout site in South

Los Angeles, nearly five miles from 'Fort Roach'. An initial intake of 200 recruits was divided into 12 platoons, with the nucleus of 12 Combat Camera Units (CCUs) later increasing to 16 as a CCU was assigned to each existing Air Force. Units each numbered around 23 men, with 15 NCOs as combat-rated cameramen. Units could be increased in size when circumstances warranted it. Each was also expected to be able to operate largely independently, split into smaller detachments operating at widely dispersed locations. Officers were initially not permitted to fly on combat missions, although the regulation was not always followed.

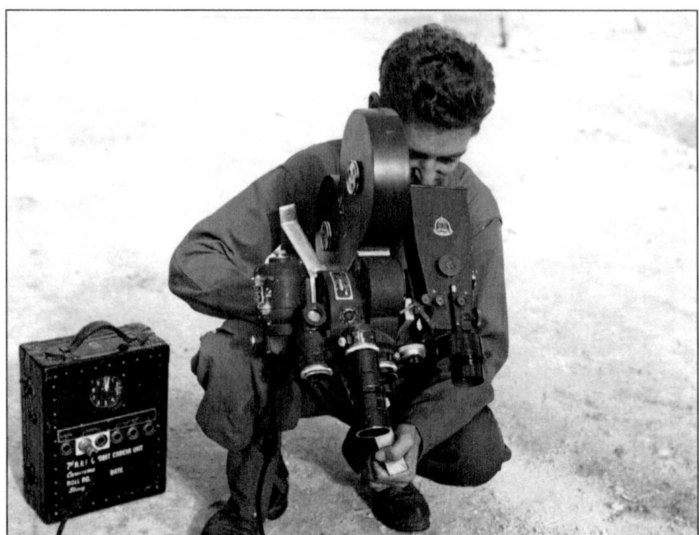

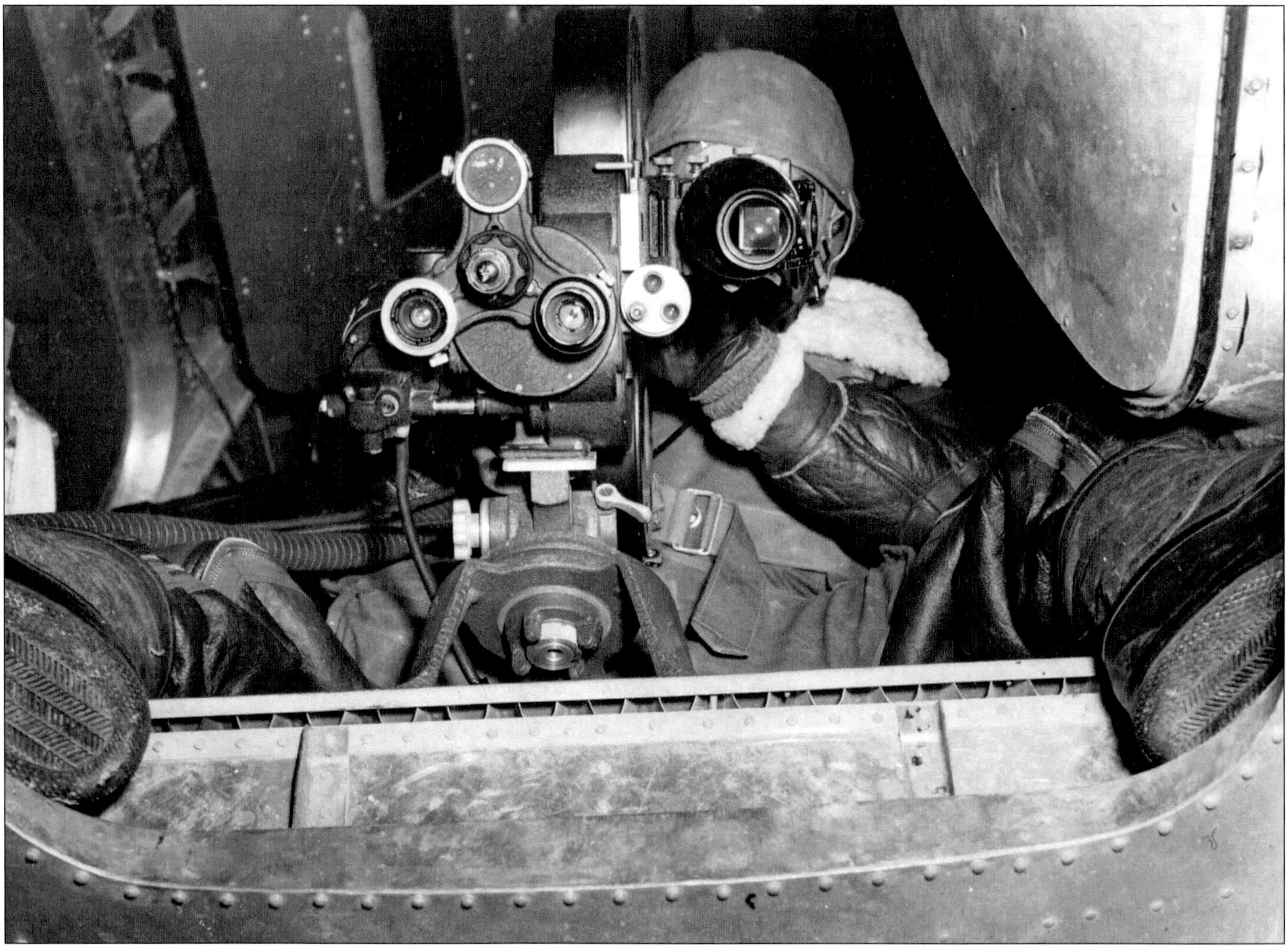

The 35mm Eyemo camera was a 'workhorse' for World War Two cameramen built in several versions with special attachments. (7th CCU, Via David Holmes)

Combat Camera recruit training lasted 17 weeks, the first 11 weeks consisting mainly of theory. There, they were taught by instructors like Sgt Mack McGovern, who attempted to instil in them the skills of operating as newsreel and documentary calibry cameramen. They were encouraged to film interesting footage whenever opportunities arose but to avoid becoming part of the scene and incurring personal injury. They were taught to handle a range of cameras, including the Bell and Howell Filmo series cameras, the Eyemo 35mm movie camera and the unusual-looking Spider Eyemo that soon became strongly associated with World War Two cameramen. Trainees learned to use the 35mm Mitchell Government Camera for high-speed work and alternative 16mm equipment like the Kodak, Victor and Auricon cameras.

The new cameramen were also trained to operate and maintain the Gun Sight Aiming Point (GSAP) camera which could be fitted and synchronised with mounted guns.[4] They were also taught to use film slates and captioning sheets to provide important information for those editing and working with the footage they created, once it was processed.

For their final weeks of training, the men went to Las Vegas Army Airfield to receive training as Gunner/Photographers. They also learned some aircraft recognition, first aid, and how to operate .50 calibre machine guns (with five weeks practical gunnery) that would all too soon prove vital skills for many combat cameramen. Successfully passing their final practical and theory tests led them to earn their Sergeant stripes and become full NCOs. The first course graduates joined the 4th Combat Camera Unit, the first to deploy overseas.[5] Later, as the training machine matured, it moved to the Pacific Military Academy from Camp Letts, and the recruits formed a Cameraman Replacement Pool to be posted wherever needed.

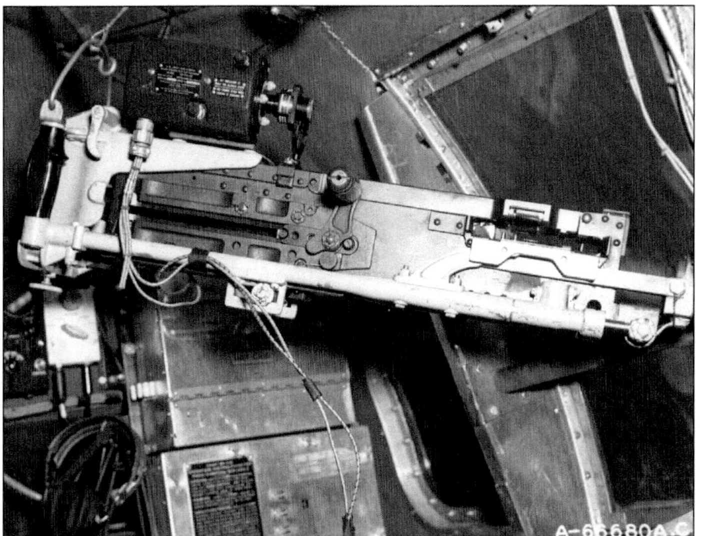

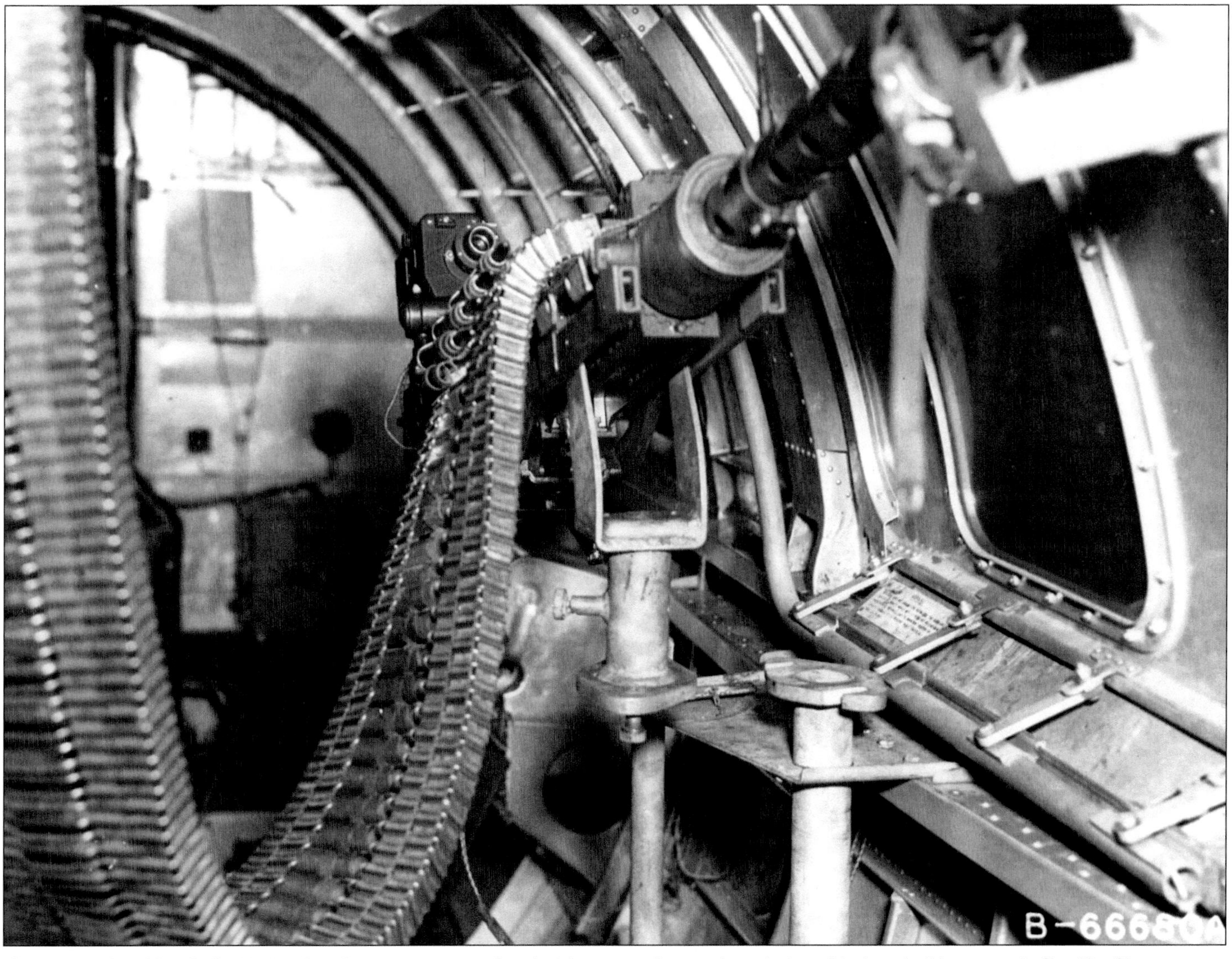

The AN N6 GSAP (Gun Sight Aiming Point) gun camera was fitted with a 35mm lens and used 16mm black and white or movie film. The film cassette contained 50 feet of film. Fitted onto a .50 calibre machine gun, it was activated when the trigger was pulled. For training purposes, it could be used without firing live ammunition. The P-51, P-47 and P-38 could also carry the AN N6. (USAAF)

Bomber Operations in England

Whilst the Motion Picture Unit was frantically producing movie training material, other units were being established and readied for service overseas. Our best available account of a unit from World War Two comes from an exemplary unit history of the 4th Combat Camera Unit's wartime activities in the European Theatre. Many of its operating principles and experiences would still have been familiar to the Combat Camera squadron members of the AAVS, deployed nearly 50 years later during the 1991 Gulf War.

Established on 16 August 1943, and drawn from the First Motion Picture Unit, six officers and 23 enlisted men initially comprised the new unit. Having been trained and equipped, the unit was shipped off to Scotland, eventually being assigned to the Ninth Air Force operating from bases in the east of England, north of London. Attached to the HQ of the USAAF's Ninth Air Force, at Marks Hall adjoining Earls Colne airfield in Essex, the Unit had its first experience of war. On 10 December 1943, while they were preparing for operations, a sudden German raid on Earls Colne airfield killed 11 men and destroyed some of their accommodation.

The 4th CCU created detachments at the Earls Colne airfield with the B-26s of the 455th Bomb Squadron, the 323rd Bomb Group and those of the 451st BS and 322nd BG a few miles away at Andrewsfield. Their early B-26 missions were far from easy, with inadequate flying clothing and film and camera equipment failures, as they began working in the extreme cold of high-altitude missions. However, once adequately equipped, they began accumulating large amounts of film.

One of the 4th CCU's first films was *Double-Header Attack*. This film can still be viewed today. As the unit history records, it received feedback on the reel in a style of critique that would become familiar to later generations of service photographers and videographers:

This, the first shipment received from the 4th Combat Camera Unit, is one of the best bombing mission coverages we have seen. Photography in almost all scenes is very good; sound in the recorded sequence is excellent. The film contains views of heavy flak, cloud effects, formations, exceptionally clear target areas and bursts, damaged B-26s in flight, fighter cover, bombs-away shots within the bomb bay, and a perfect take of a belly landing made by a crippled ship.

The photographer's unit reports added a little more detail to some of the sequences, 'Sgt Mallinson, shooting through the bomb bay at the 100-pounders pouring out, saw a malfunction of the release mechanism which prevented three bombs from falling, though partially free and possibly armed. He called the crew's attention to them and helped replace and secure the lethal cargo'.

Lt Smith reported his experiences of a raid during the same week:

Finally, the bomb bay doors opened. From the astrodome, using a wide-angle lens, I held the camera as I watched the flights behind us. Suddenly, single puffs of heavy black smoke magically mushroomed into sight, then drifted behind. More and more puffs blossomed into view, and I saw them flash uncomfortably close to our ship. Then I heard a 'harraumph' and knew that we had been hit …The air was filled with puffs of black smoke, and it didn't seem possible that our ship could come through. On looking down towards the bomb bay door, I suddenly realised that the bombs were gone and the doors closing. Transferring the cable to the two-inch lens camera, I got what I could of the strikes through the closing doors. The bombs were dropping squarely on their aiming point on the runway intersection.[6]

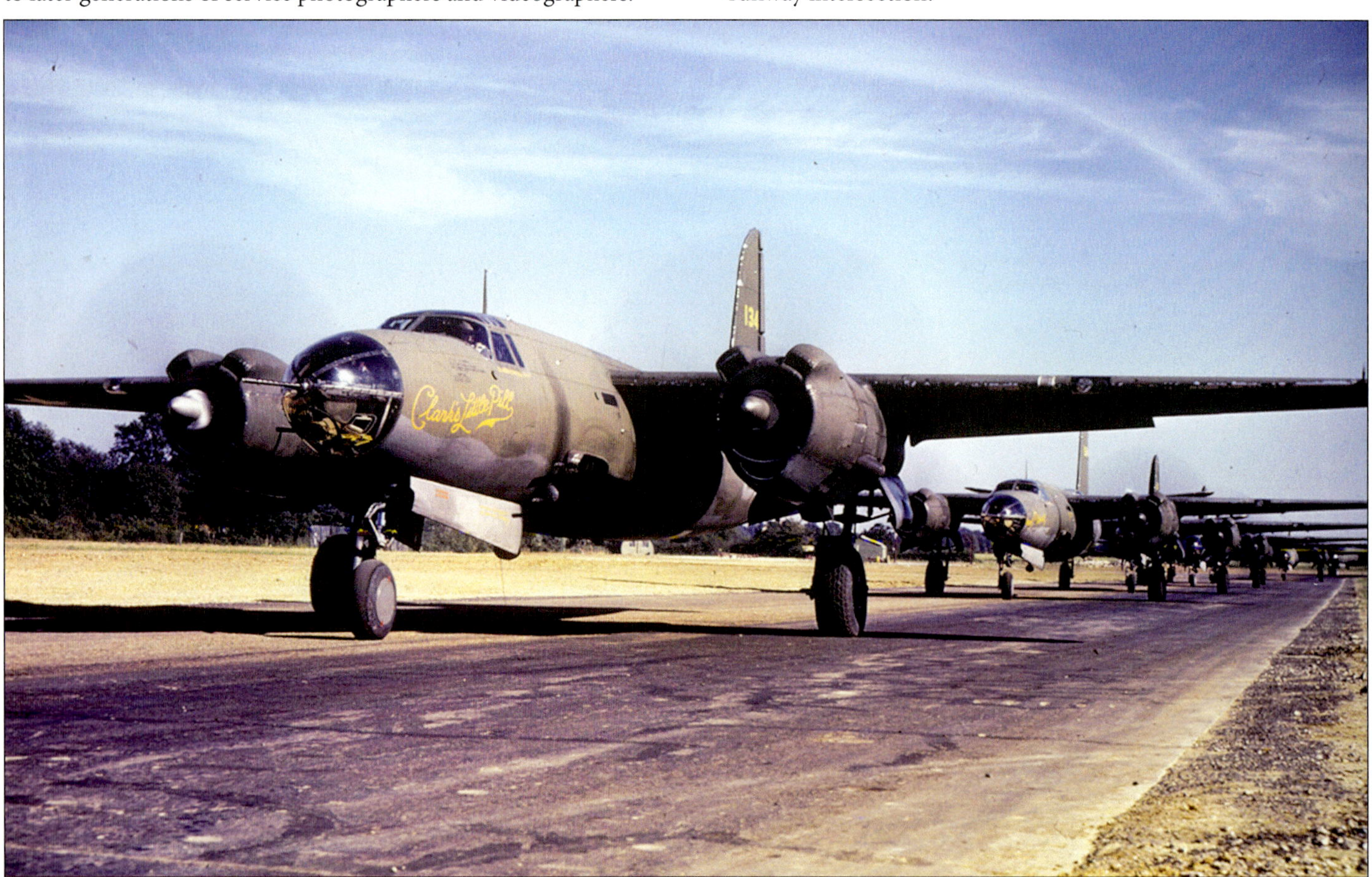

A lineup of 322nd Bomb Group B-26s, including *Clark's Little Pill* taxying at Andrewsfield airfield. The aircraft flew attack missions across western Europe, often carrying 4th CCU cameramen to film the action. (USAAF)

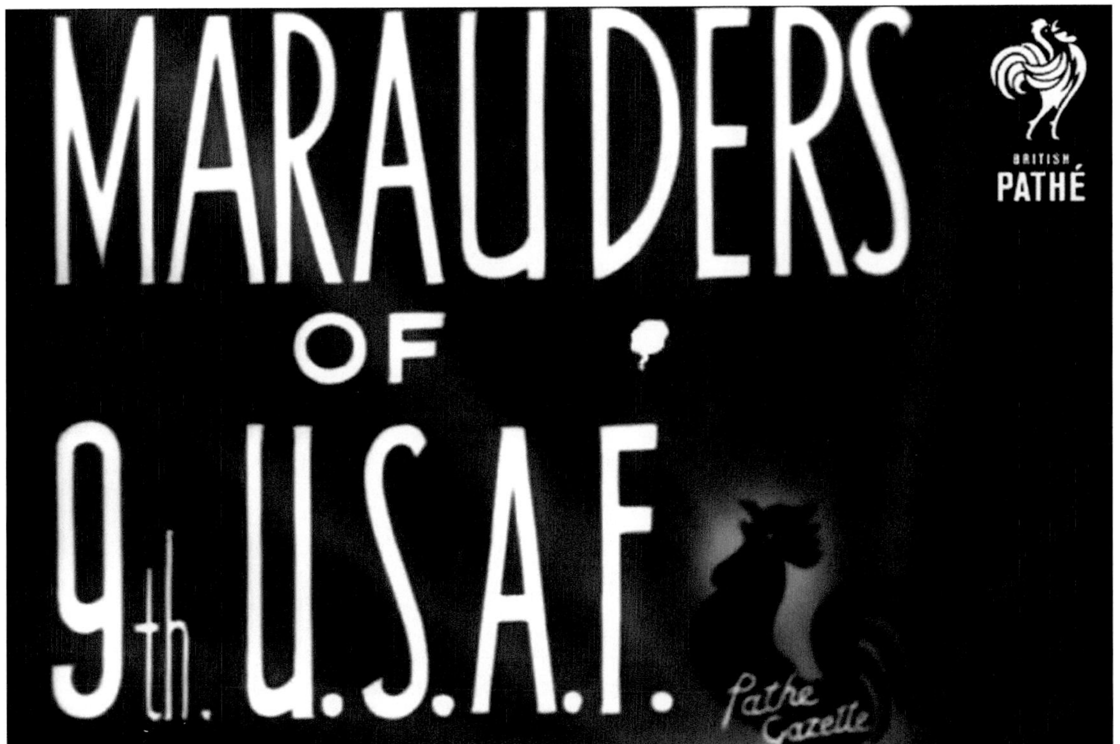

British version.
(YouTube/British Pathe)

US version. (YouTube
ZenosWarbirds)

Cameramen on Ninth Air Force B-26 Marauders, flew missions from bases close to the 4th CCUs HQ at Earls Colne, in Essex. Their footage was used for a documentary about a 'Double-Header' mission. The film received wide distribution in the US and a more extended version was produced for British audiences. (YouTube/British Pathe and YouTube ZenosWarbirds)

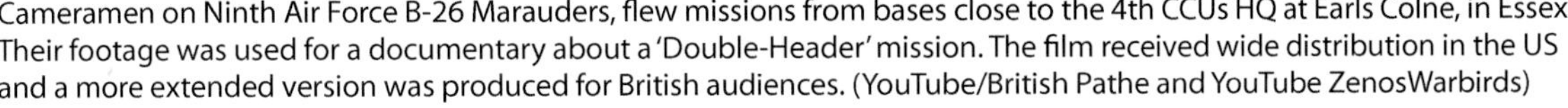

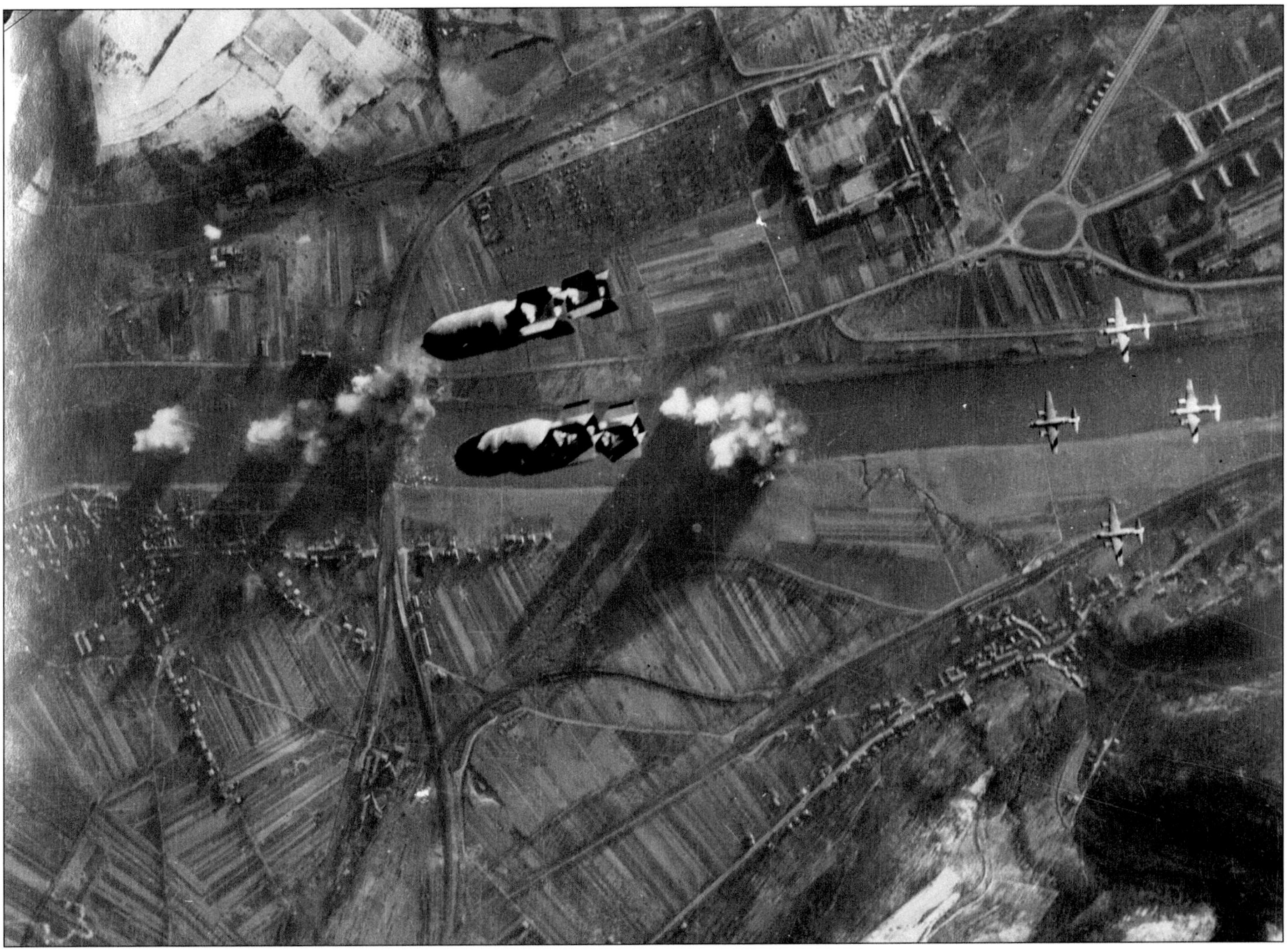

Capturing images of bombs dropping from the bomb bay or from another aircraft in the formation was a high priority for combat cameramen. This image is even more unusual, showing explosions on the ground as other bombs are released from the camera ship. The picture was taken during a raid on a railroad bridge across the Moselle River at Trier-Pfalzel on 24 December 1944, by 69 B-26s of the 323rd and 394th Bomb Groups. (NARA)

The reel was widely distributed in the US as part of newsreels. In Britain, it was used in cinemas with an English narrator and additional footage.

Unit members filmed a wide range of activities, including General Eisenhower inspecting fighter and bomber bases, training US paratroops in southern England, and preparations for D-Day and continuing air operations. The exposed footage was couriered to laboratories in London for rapid processing and onward distribution.

The Mighty Eighth

The deployment of the Eighth Air Force's B-17 Flying Fortress and B-24 Liberator heavy bombers and the assembly of a massive aerial armada in England attracted much public attention in Britain and across the US. From their first raids in the summer of 1942 through to the war's end, the Eighth conducted thousands of sorties deep into the heartland of Germany, at times suffering staggering losses. The high-quality coverage of many B-17 and B-24 missions provided by Combat Camera Units remains a remarkable, often moving tribute to their immense courage and those they filmed in action, even today.

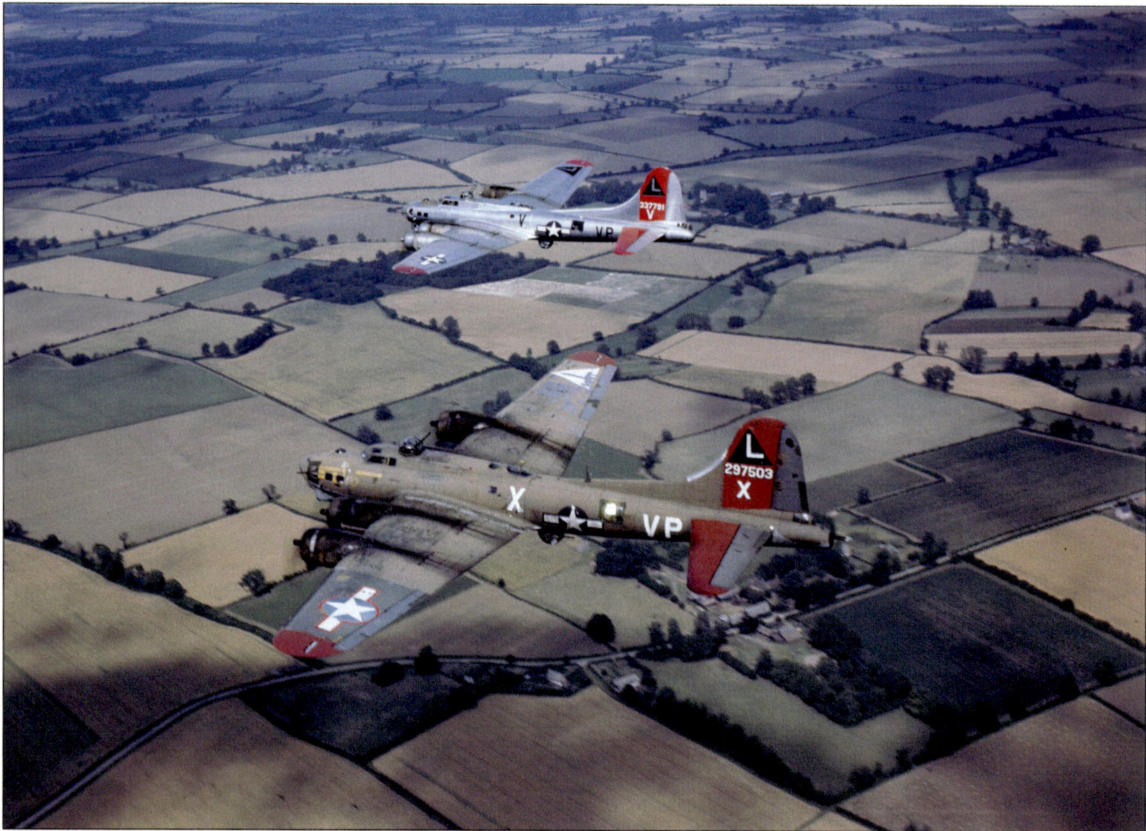

Early 4th CCU unfinished film of paratrooper training somewhere over England in 1943. (NARA)

Footage from the 4th CCS shows Gen Dwight Eisenhower inspecting 9th Air Force fighter and bomber bases. (NARA)

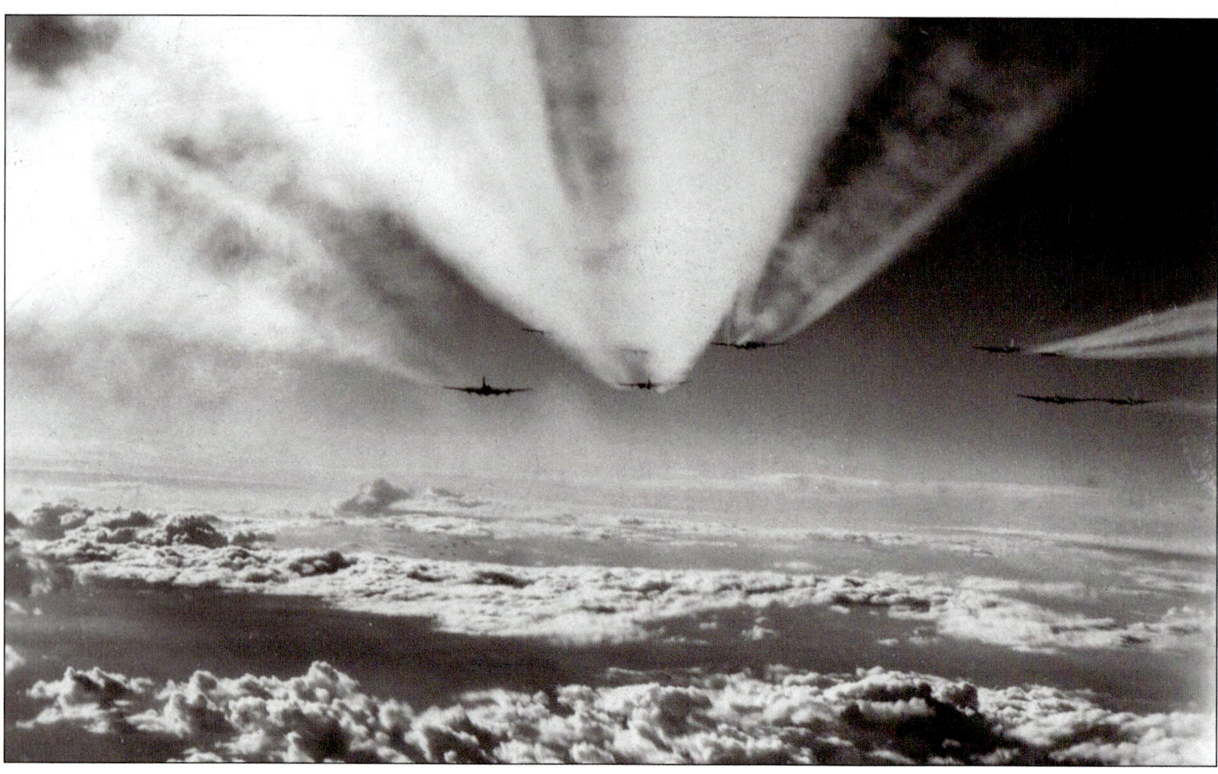

Above: A rare colour shot. Two B-17Gs from the 381st Bomb Group based at RAF Ridgewell, part of a practice formation over southern England. (NARA)

Left: Often made more visible by their contrails, huge armadas of bombers, their crews, and cameramen from the Eighth and Ninth Air Forces daily set off to hit targets in occupied Europe. (NARA)

MEMPHIS BELLE: A STORY OF A FLYING FORTRESS

The story of the B-17 named *Memphis Belle* and its completion of 25 bombing missions over enemy territory is famous. It was always going to be a big story. That milestone was eagerly anticipated and carefully prepared for by the US movie industry, and the Army Air Force for promotion purposes. There were big plans for the first B-17 and the crew to complete 25 missions. They would then be sent back to the United States and used on a tour to promote the purchase of war bonds, accompanied by a documentary on the aircraft. Filmed by Hollywood director William Wyler from the First Motion Picture Unit, it became a landmark of its time. It was such a fascinating story that it received the full Hollywood treatment in another film produced in 1990. *Memphis Belle* flew that 25th mission on 17 May 1943, with the 'documentary movie' released in April 1944.

There had been several candidates likely to be the first B-17 to reach 25 missions. Several aircraft and crews were being filmed by the 4th CCU, taken from angles that did not render the individual aircraft readily identifiable. Cameras had been following Captain Oscar O'Neill (his bomber was named *Invasion II*), also from the 401st BS, part of the 91st Bomb Group at Bassingbourn, until O'Neill's B-17 and five others from the Squadron were shot down over Bremen, Germany, on 17 April 1943. At Chelveston, not far from Bassingbourn, photographer Dan McGovern believed another aircraft, named *SNAFU/We the People* from the 305th Bomb Group, would be selected as the subject of the documentary, but that did not come to pass.

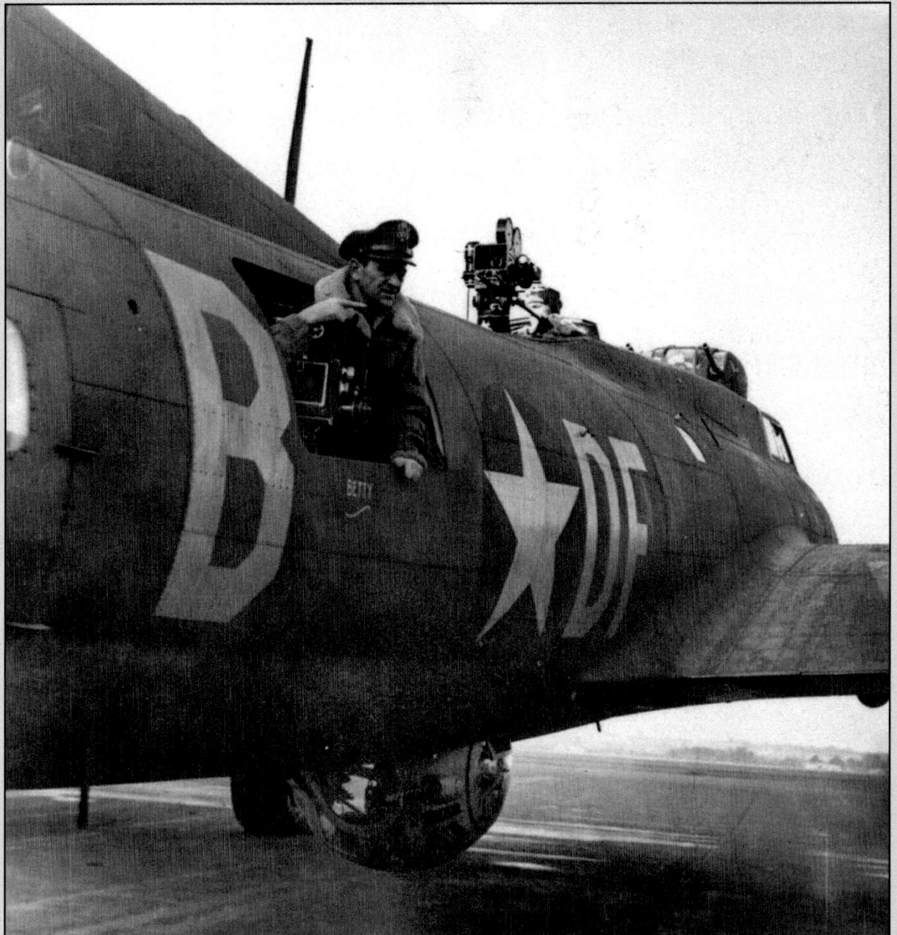

In the end, *Memphis Belle* was not the first aircraft to reach 25 missions; several aircraft reached that mark ahead of it. The first was another 91st Bomb Group aircraft, *Delta Rebel II*, just over two weeks earlier, on 1 May 1943, *Hells Angel* (303rd BG) on 13 May 1943, and *SNAFU/We the People* on 14 May 1943.

The project absorbed a lot of material and resources, and unusually, a lot of the original 16mm film, and reels of outtakes, have been preserved and digitised by NARA. In addition to the film itself, there are some 36 reels of unedited film, in colour. As well as B-17 action elements, there is footage of King George VI visiting to see the aircraft and of the *Memphis Belle* on tour in the US when she returned home.[7]

Left: Major William Wyler stands in the waist gunner position on *Memphis Belle* during filming at RAF Bassingbourn. Maj Wyler, from the First Motion Picture Unit, was an experienced Hollywood director and producer working with the 4th CCU, including its CO, cinematographer Capt William Clothier. Both Wyler and Clothier flew several missions on *Memphis Belle*. (NARA)

Below: Taken from the original print, the *Memphis Belle* crew returned from their 25th operational mission on 17 May 1943. (NARA)

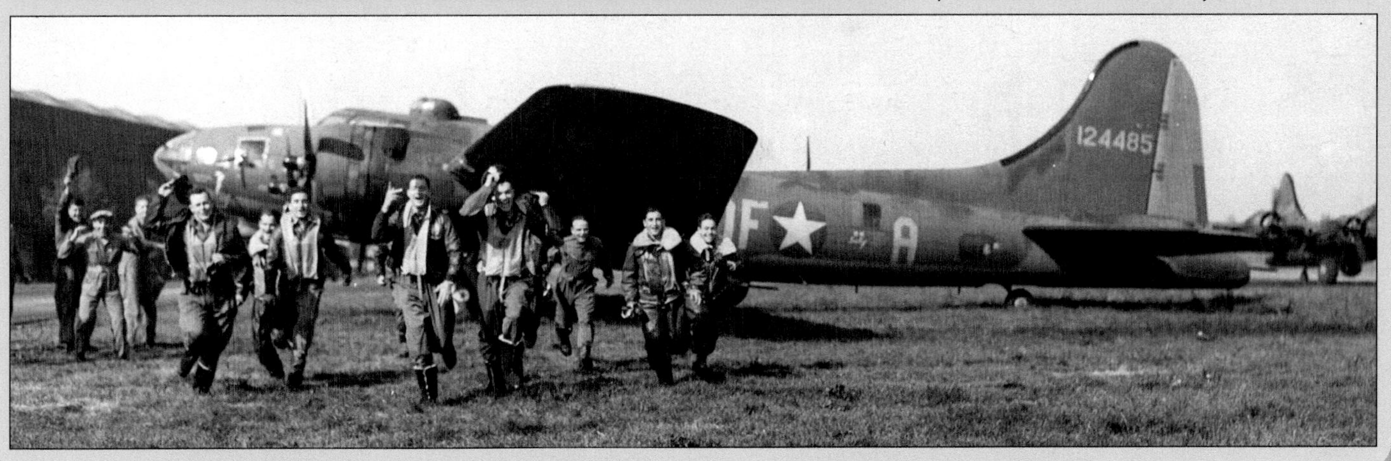

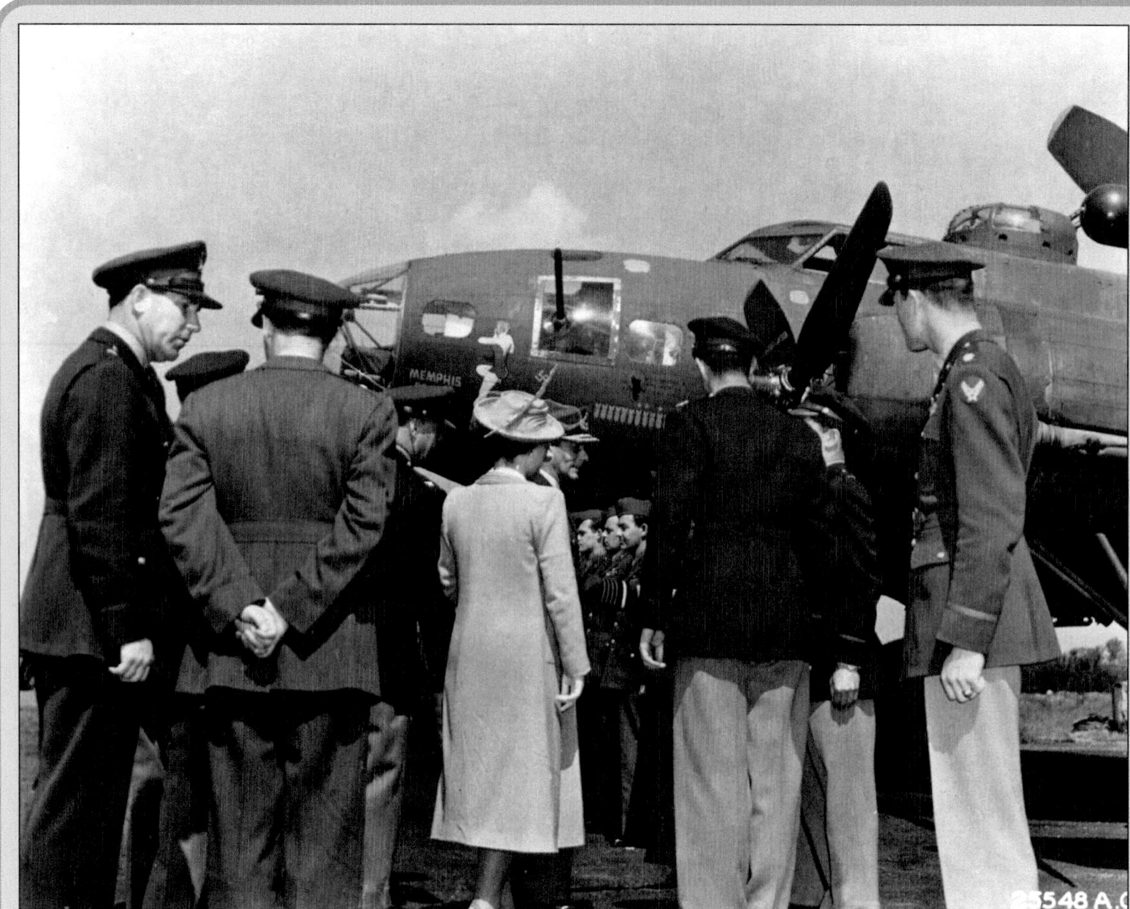

Link to *Memphis Belle* outtakes.

Left: Soon after completing their 25th mission, the crew were congratulated on their achievement in a well-publicised visit by King George VI and Queen Elizabeth. (NARA)

Below: After completing 25 missions, *Memphis Belle* returned to the US to take part in a public tour to boost the sales of War Bonds. (NARA)

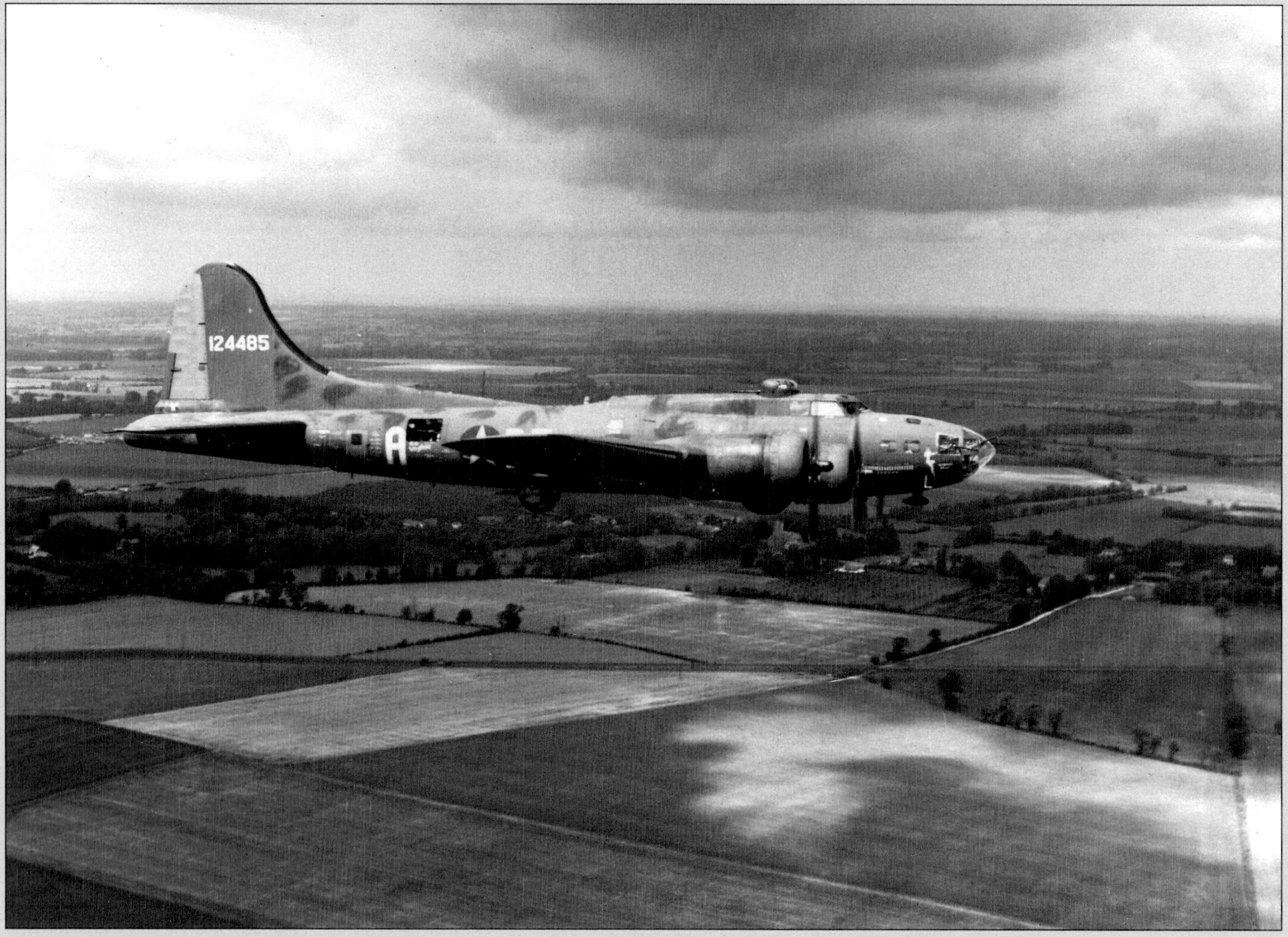

Technical Sergeant Dan McGovern, who had been instrumental in organising the training of Combat Cameramen back in California, was posted to the 305th Bombardment Group at RAF Chelveston in Northampton, England, in June 1943. The 8th CCU comprised six officers and 21 enlisted men, who were soon divided into eight separate operating detachments under the command of distinguished Hollywood cinematographer Major Teddy Tetzlaff.[8]

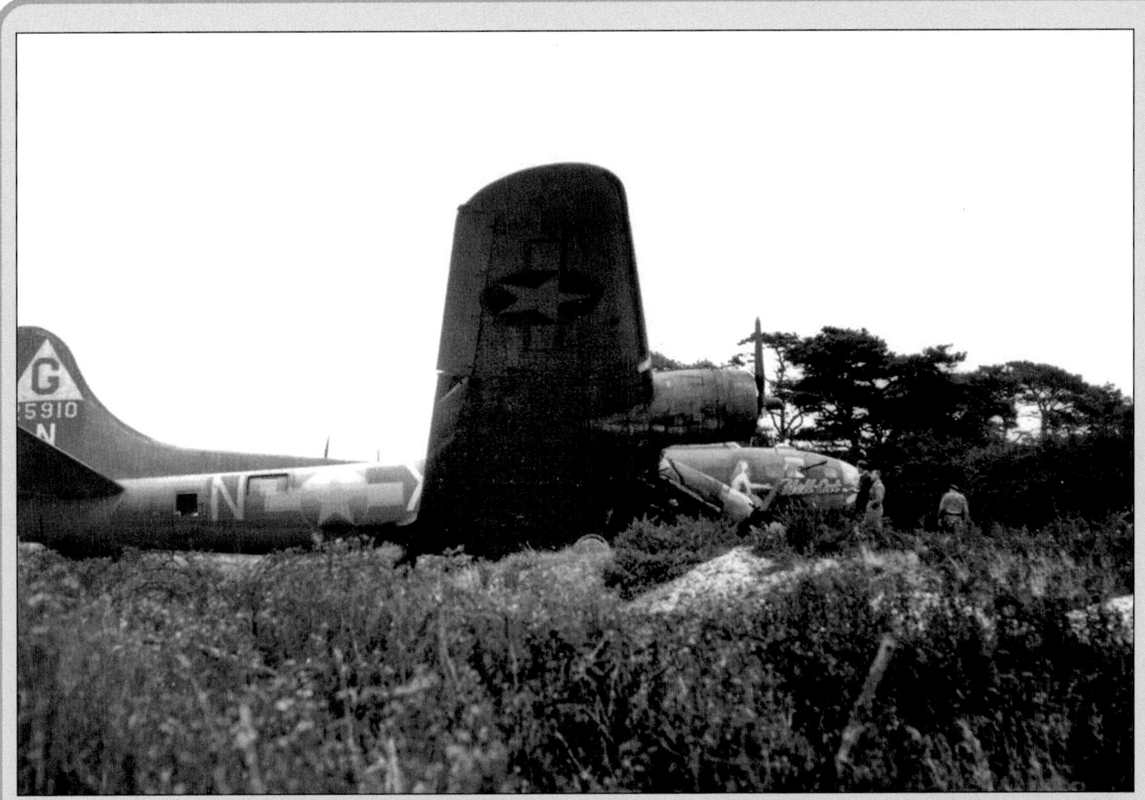

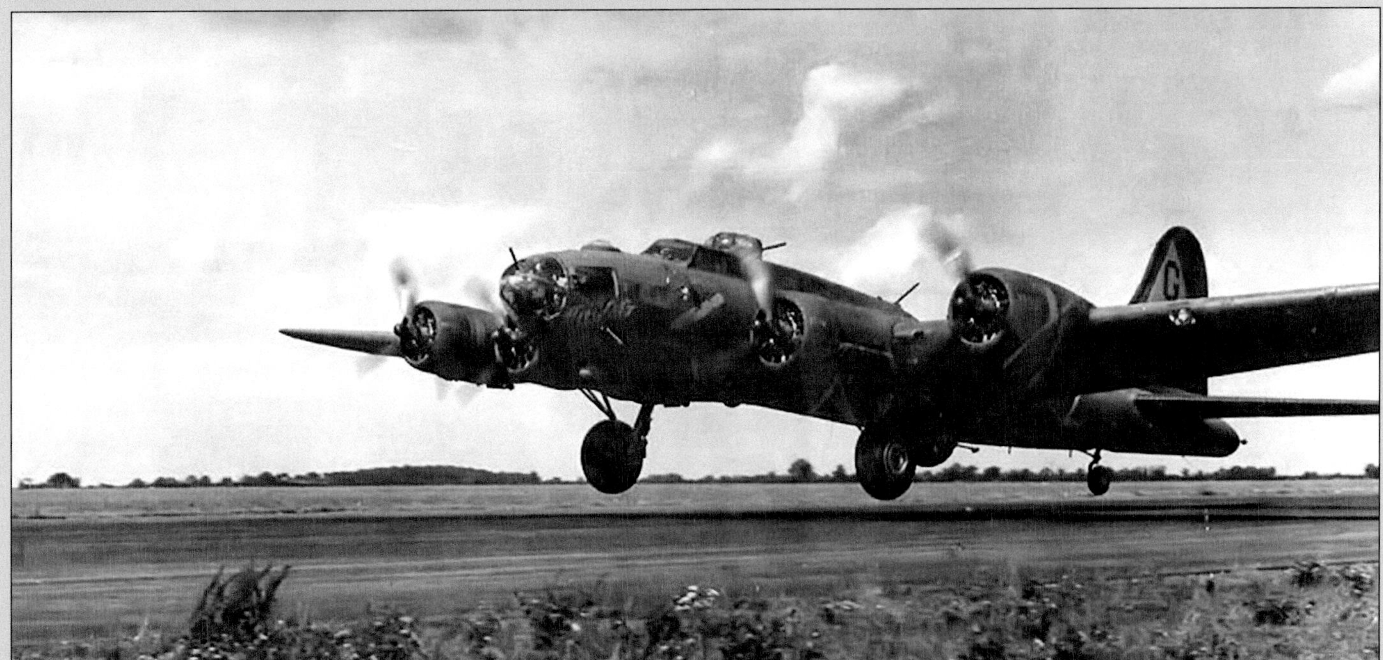

Combat Photographer Tech Sgt Dan McGovern flew missions with the 305th Bombardment Group. On 15 September 1943, he was flying with the crew of B-17F 42-5910 named *Hellcat*. The Wing's mission was to hit a Luftwaffe repair depot and airfield about 80 miles west of Paris at Romilly Sur Seine. Fitted with experimental external bomb racks, the aircraft suffered from poor performance as a result. Unable to climb to the height of the other bombers and experiencing increased fuel consumption, they fell behind their formation. Forced to return prematurely to England, they encountered anti-aircraft fire, an engine lost power, and everything had to be dumped from the B-17, including McGovern's cameras.

They inadvertently flew underneath an incoming Luftwaffe raid on England and were fired upon by British anti-aircraft defences, until a British searchlight signalled them to head westwards. A second engine failed, and the pilot managed to make an emergency landing at the RAF's small Hawkinge grass airstrip, eight miles from Dover. The partially lowered undercarriage collapsed on landing. The crew all survived with some minor injuries, but the aircraft was written off. (NARA)

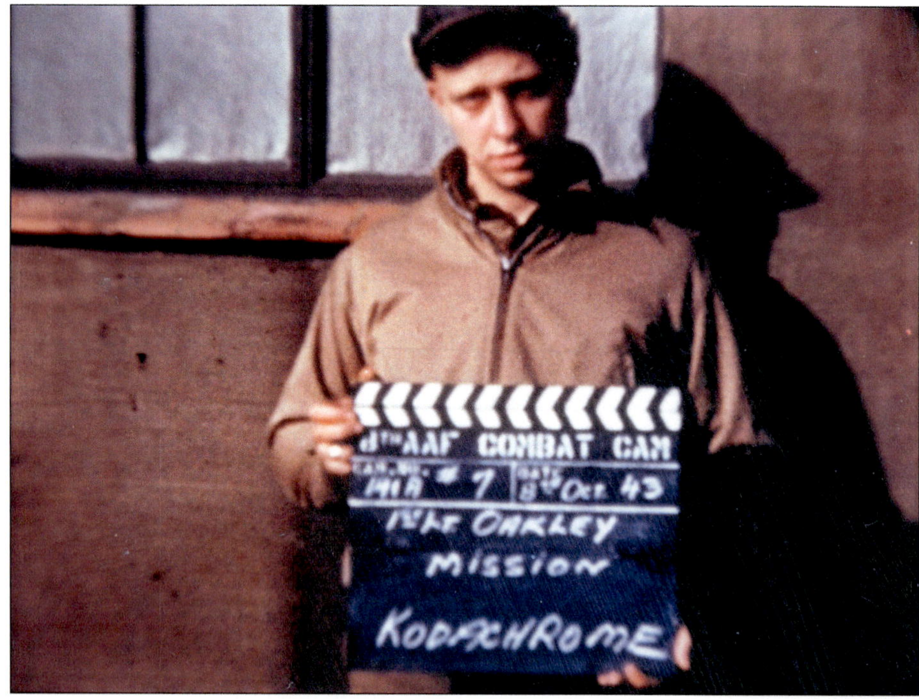

The all-important 'slate', is known to generations of combat cameramen to record when their images were taken. This one is for First Lt Oakley, on an 8th AAF mission on 8 October 1943. On that day, 344 B-17s, in three elements, attacked the Bremen shipyards and other local targets. Twenty-seven aircraft were lost, two more were written off on their return, with 215 B-17s damaged. One hundred and two crewmen were killed, 51 wounded, and 166 became PoWs.[9] (NARA)

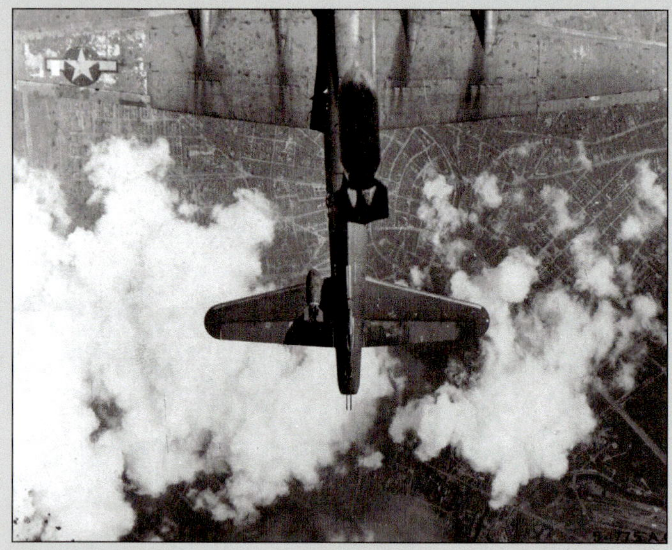

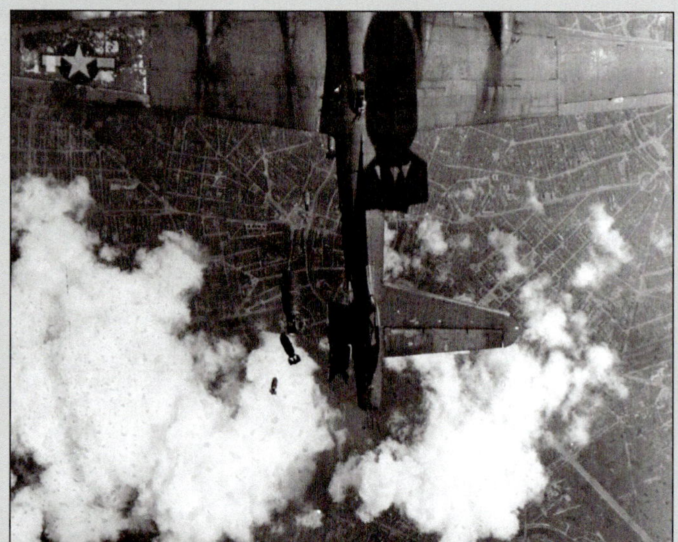

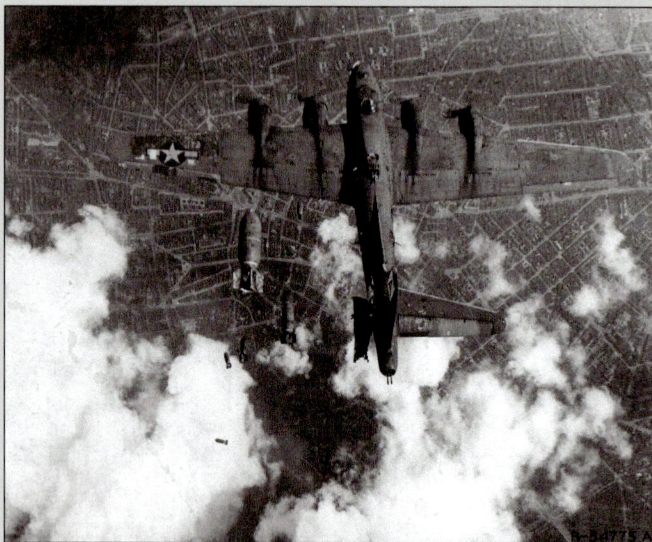

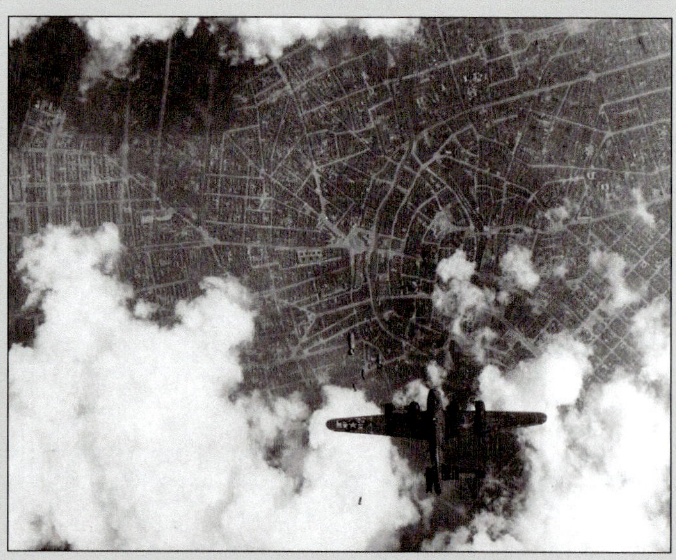

Sometimes, tragic incidents were captured by combat cameramen. Directly above Berlin Cathedral on 19 May 1944, B-17G Flying Fortress *Miss Donna Mae II* drifted under another B-17 during their bomb run over the city. A 1,000 lb bomb from above tore off the left stabiliser and sent *Donna Mae II* into an uncontrollable spin. All 11 on board were killed. (NARA)

Advancing Across Europe

In the run-up to D-Day, unit members began preparations for the approaching invasion of Europe. They were to switch from filming bomber and combat missions to operating alongside frontline troops as the planned invasion advanced, liberating France. Two detachments went into near seclusion along the English south coast to join units forming the spearhead of D-Day forces. One had a vast assortment of cameras and, with 12 personnel loaded in a one-and-a-half ton truck, was attached to the 922nd Aviation Engineers Battalion (AEB) and another to the 834th AEB. A specially equipped A-20 Havoc was assigned to the 4th CCU to film air operations. The aircraft, loaned by the 416th BG with a crew from nearby Wethersfield, would become a key part of 4th CCU operations for the rest of the war.

USAAF cameras were in action from the very start of the Normandy invasion:

The pictures we made over the invasion fleet and of fighting for the coast were the first to reach the world. Cinemas in London showed our films the same afternoon, and they were running in New York the next day at noon. Our streamlined laboratory and courier system scooped the world. It was four days before any other agency landed motion pictures of the invasion in the US.[10]

On the day of the invasion, having landed on the Normandy beaches, cameramen pushed inland with the advancing engineers to photograph the construction of the first landing strip in France. From there, USAAF C-47s flew blood and plasma supplies in and removed the unit's exposed film. With such high levels of activity in the preceding months, several cameramen accumulated large numbers of combat sorties, including SSgt Fay Steel, who reached 58 sorties with the B-26s and earned himself leave back in the US.[11]

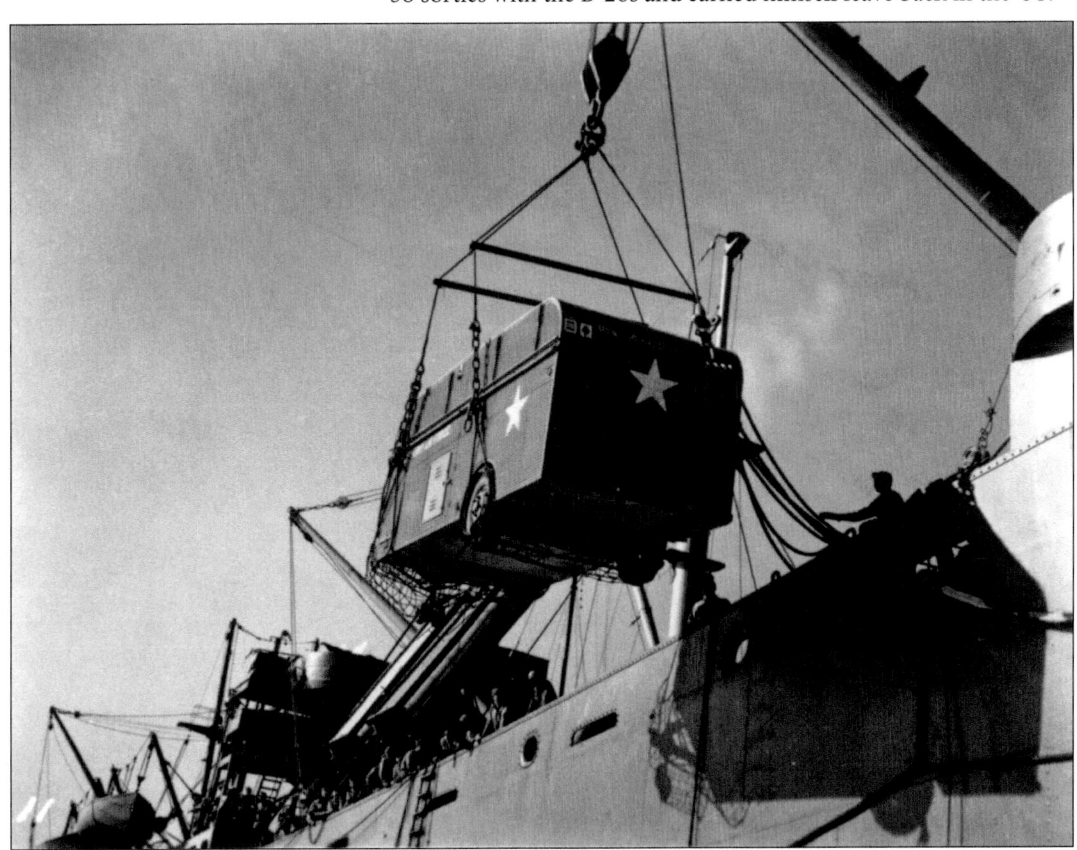

Right: A large amount of the 4th CCU's photographic equipment was carried by ship to land in Normandy after D-Day, including this equipment caravan. (4th CCU)

Below: The 4th CCU was loaned an A-20 and crew by the 416th BG at nearby RAF Wethersfield to film air operations, pictured at Laon Airfield. (NARA)

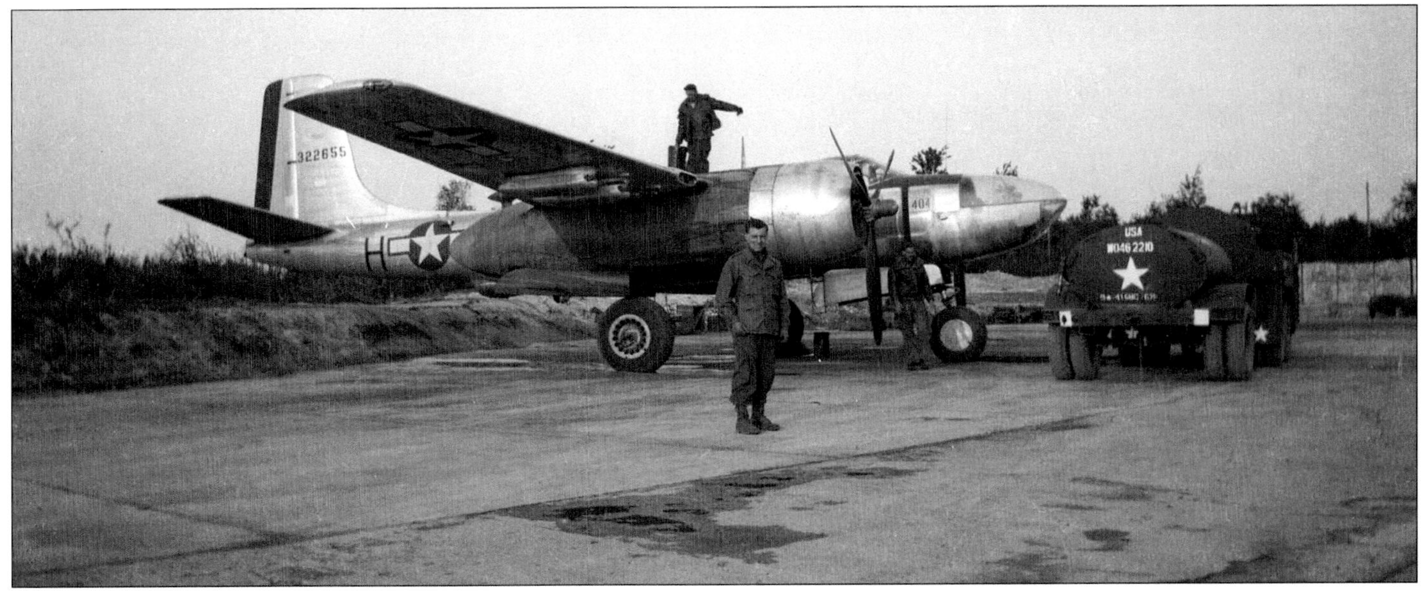

Following D-Day, 4th CCU members advanced across Europe with the Army Air Force. Non-flying photographers were at the forefront of the advance, sometimes becoming isolated from the units they worked with. In December 1944, the sudden German offensive in the Ardennes, the Battle of the Bulge, caught almost everyone unprepared. The 4th CCU's photographers were quickly attached to the 82nd Airborne. At the same time, from Florennes air base in Belgium, others filmed events from the air in an A-20 to photograph 'fighter missions, bomb strikes and the destruction of German transportation'. Six photographers flew from Laon/Athies Aerodrome, covering the counterattack with the 323rd Bomb Group in B-26s, with two more flying over 'The Bulge' with the 474th Fighter Group in their P-38s.

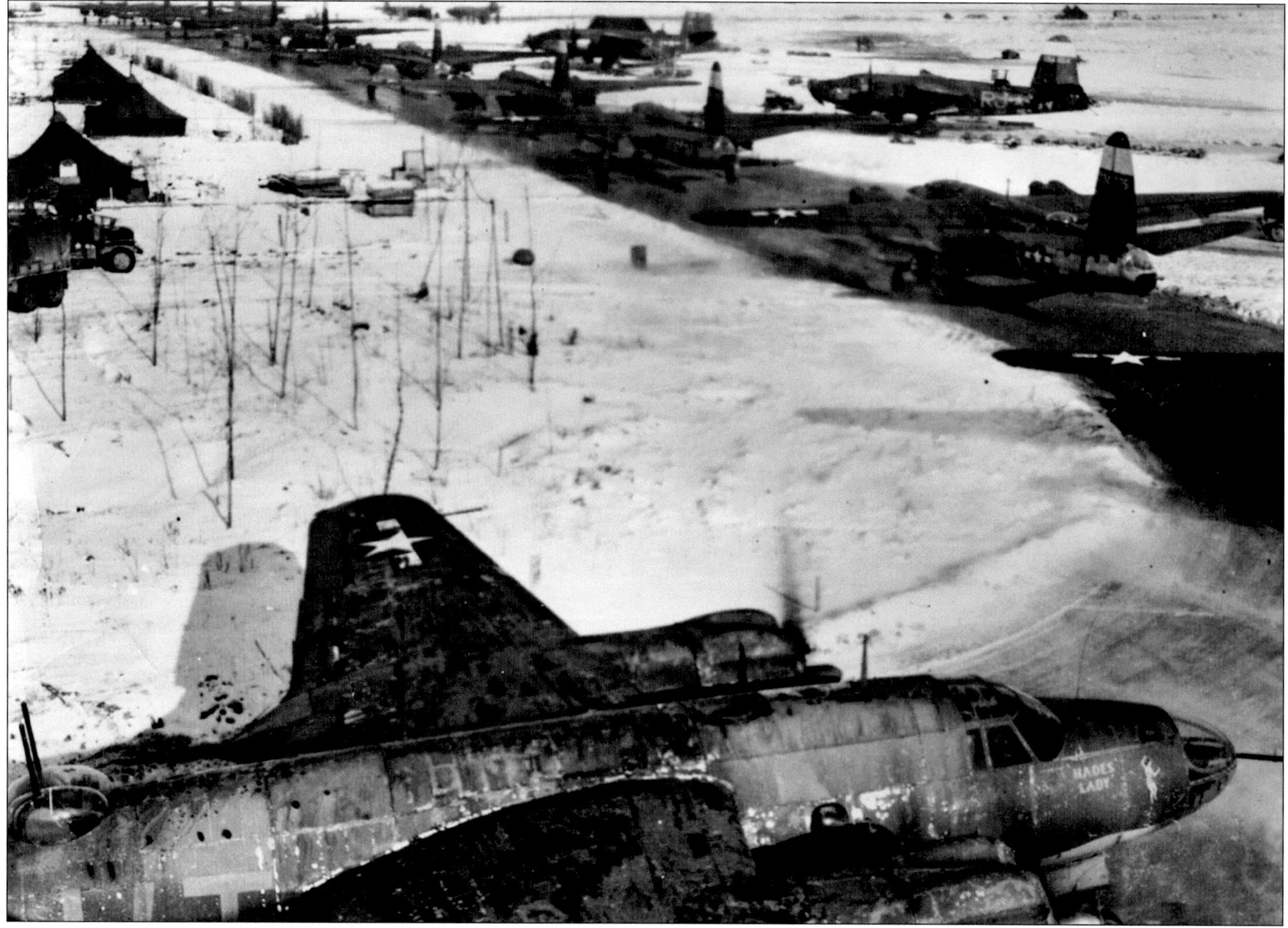

During the Battle of the Bulge in December 1944, six 4th CCU Combat Photographers flew out of Laon airfield with the B-26s of the 323rd BG. (NARA)

COMBAT DOCUMENTATION AT POLTAVA

Not all the combat photographer's work was about covering successful air and ground attacks. In late 1943, USAAF commanders sought to undertake 'shuttle bombing' missions, with bombers flying from England or Italy to drop their bombs at the extreme of their operational range on far distant targets. Then, instead of returning to their home bases, the aircraft were to recover at airfields in the western Soviet Union.

Despite Stalin's reluctance, the first such missions took place in early June 1944, when the Soviets permitted the use of their airfields at Piryatin, Mirgorod and Poltava in the Ukraine for the first time under the codename Operation Frantic Joe. On 22 June 1944, a second CCU mission, Operation Frantic II, was launched successfully from England that included 114 B-17s and 70 P-51s, with the US fighters recovering to Piryatin and the bombers to Mirgorod and Poltava. Seventy-three B-17s, six transports, three 'photo-ships' and a single P-38 landed at Poltava. Just after midnight, 'In a perfectly timed and well-executed attack, the Germans destroyed 47 'Forts' on the ground and more than 400,000 gallons of gasoline. It took three weeks to put the airfield back into full operation'. More than 1,000 US personnel were at the camp. In total, 50 US and one Soviet aircraft were destroyed, and a further 24 US and 25 Soviet aircraft were damaged.

The next day, Combat Photographers filmed the damage extensively, which was later used in the 'restricted distribution' Army Air Forces Digest 54, of 30 October 1944, featuring films from European and Pacific Combat Camera Units to reinforce the need for dispersal and camouflage.[12]

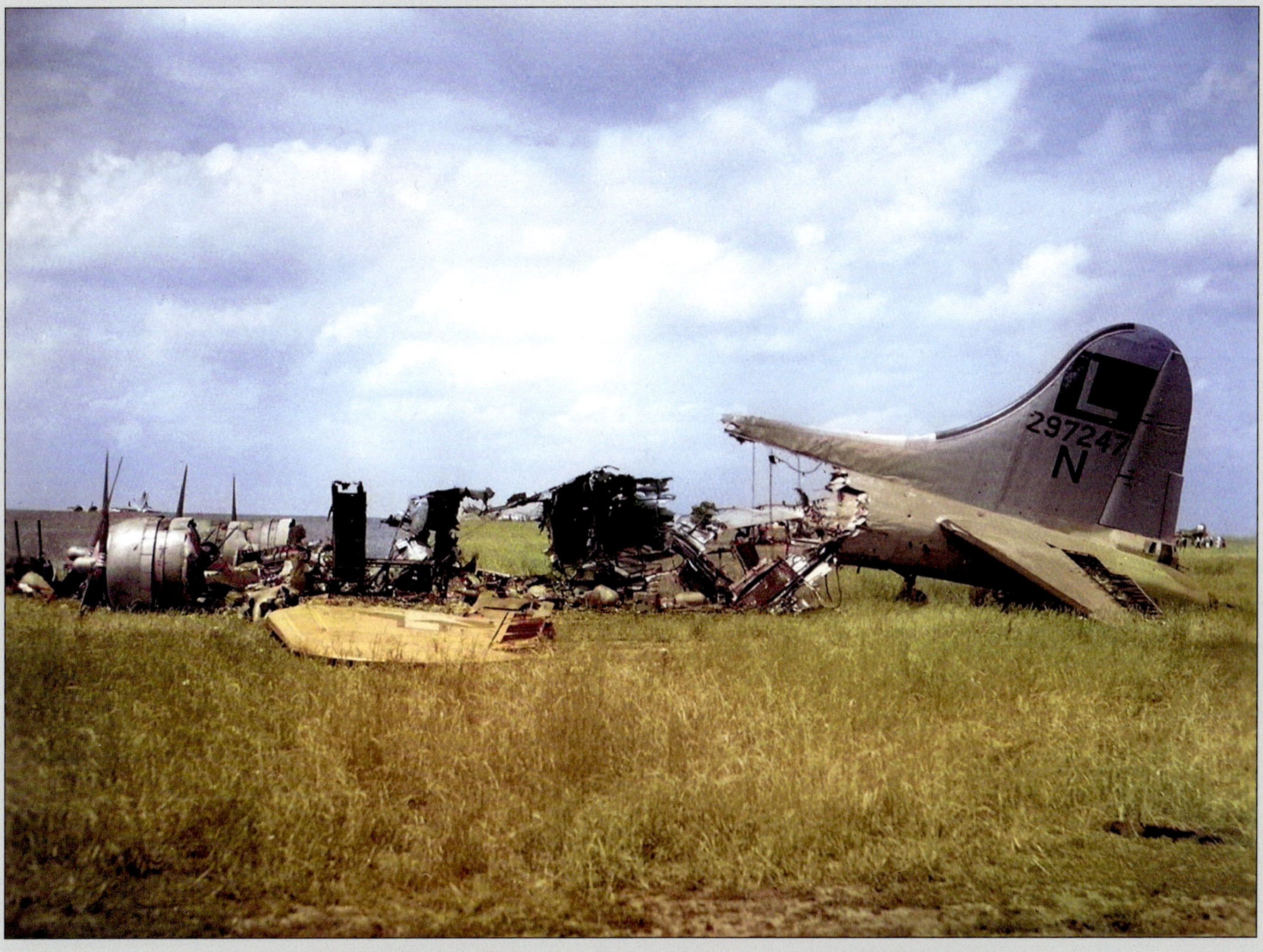

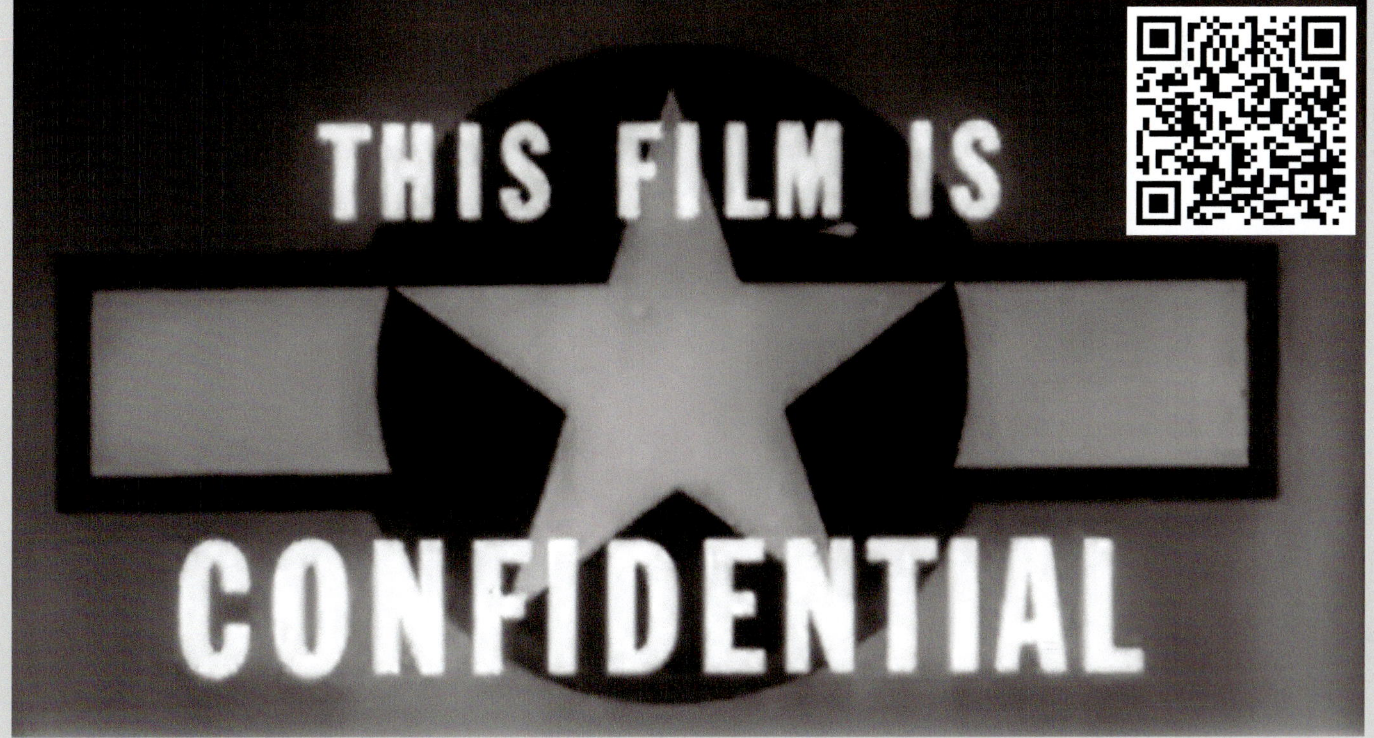

A destroyed B-17 on the ground at Poltava airfield in the Ukraine was hit in a German air raid in June 1944. (NARA)

USAAF Combat Camera Units, *Weekly Digest* No 54, October 30, 1944. Watch from 4 minutes, 19 seconds. (YouTube/PeriscopeFilm)

Special Film Project 186 (SFP 186)

From February 1945, and as the collapse of Nazi Germany became inevitable, the 4th CCU began preparations for their part in a landmark project. Major John Craig brought news of the plan from Washington DC that became known as Special Film Project 186 (SFP 186): 'The mission was the filming, in colour and for the purposes of public release, the Air Force's part in the European victory'. It was to be filmed entirely in colour.[13] This new requirement meant that some of the material already shot by the Unit had to be re-filmed. With the war's end approaching, the pressure was on to collect high-quality footage.

Substantial amounts of the movie footage taken as part of SFP 186 have continued to be used in many documentaries ever since. SFP 186 footage covers a vast range of material, from aerial actions to the post-war recording of bomb damage in major cities, footage from the death camps, and German PoWs. A simple search of YouTube using 'SFP 186' yields a tremendous amount of material filmed by the combat photographers as part of the project.

Col Owen Crump (First Motion Picture Unit) became the CO for the project, assisted by Lt Col Clothier and Major Robert Mack. They held 'numerous conferences with the directing officers of the Ninth Air Force, and outlines of the anticipated operations were prepared'. New camera equipment was made available, and 16 camera crews were assembled. They joined Bomber Group and RAF units in England and the continent to cover their coordinated activities.

Lt Col Crump, his Team #1, and others worked on the ground, recording damage in the Belgian cities of Antwerp and Namur and as they drove through Belgium into the Netherlands, including Maastricht. On their way through Germany, they filmed the damage in Aachen, Duren, and ravaged Cologne. Other teams moved forward with the advancing armoured units as they moved deep into Germany.

Aircraft gun camera footage was necessary for intelligence use, and some of the images could be released for public consumption.

Combat Camera teams worked alongside Ninth AF Fighter Group unit ground crews to supervise loading the gun cameras with Kodachrome magazines and filming ground activities for SFP 186. Other camera crews flew intensively on medium-level A-26 and B-26 bomber operations, striking at enemy targets. To help the movement of exposed film back for processing and provide essential supplies, the 4th CCU had two L-5s, a C-64 Norseman and two extra A-20s attached to them. By the end of March 1945, they had shot 19,650ft of 16mm Kodachrome film and another 6,460ft of 35mm Monopack colour film.[14]

As Allied forces advanced, the cameras tried to keep pace with them on the ground and in the air. Three cameramen were briefly taken prisoner as they outpaced US ground forces. In contrast, others persuaded German troops in an isolated location to surrender. Capt Haglund and Sgt Stindt were the first CCU personnel to document the meet-up between US and Russian troops near the Elbe.[15] In the air, unit teams fitted mountings for 35mm underwing external cameras on a 354th Fighter Group P-51 that proved adept at flying at low level to capture details of bomb damage.[16] During those last few weeks of the war, the 4th CCU began to record broader technical intelligence activities, such as a story of an Me262 flown by an escaping Belgian test pilot, who landed the aircraft at a US-occupied airfield near Frankfurt.

As the war ended, the filming continued, but the emphasis shifted. There were PoWs, the concentration camp at Dachau, and Hitler's redoubt at Berchtesgaden, in the Nazi heartland of Bavaria, to be documented. In early June 1945, US cameramen were permitted to transit the Russian occupation zone to film in Berlin. Eight days of movie and still image documentation was done at the Braunsweig Air Research Center. Said to be the 4th CCU's most ambitious project of the time was their filming of '64 P-47 aircraft of the 371st Fighter Group, as they practised strafing and firebombing a deserted German village and pillbox'.[17]

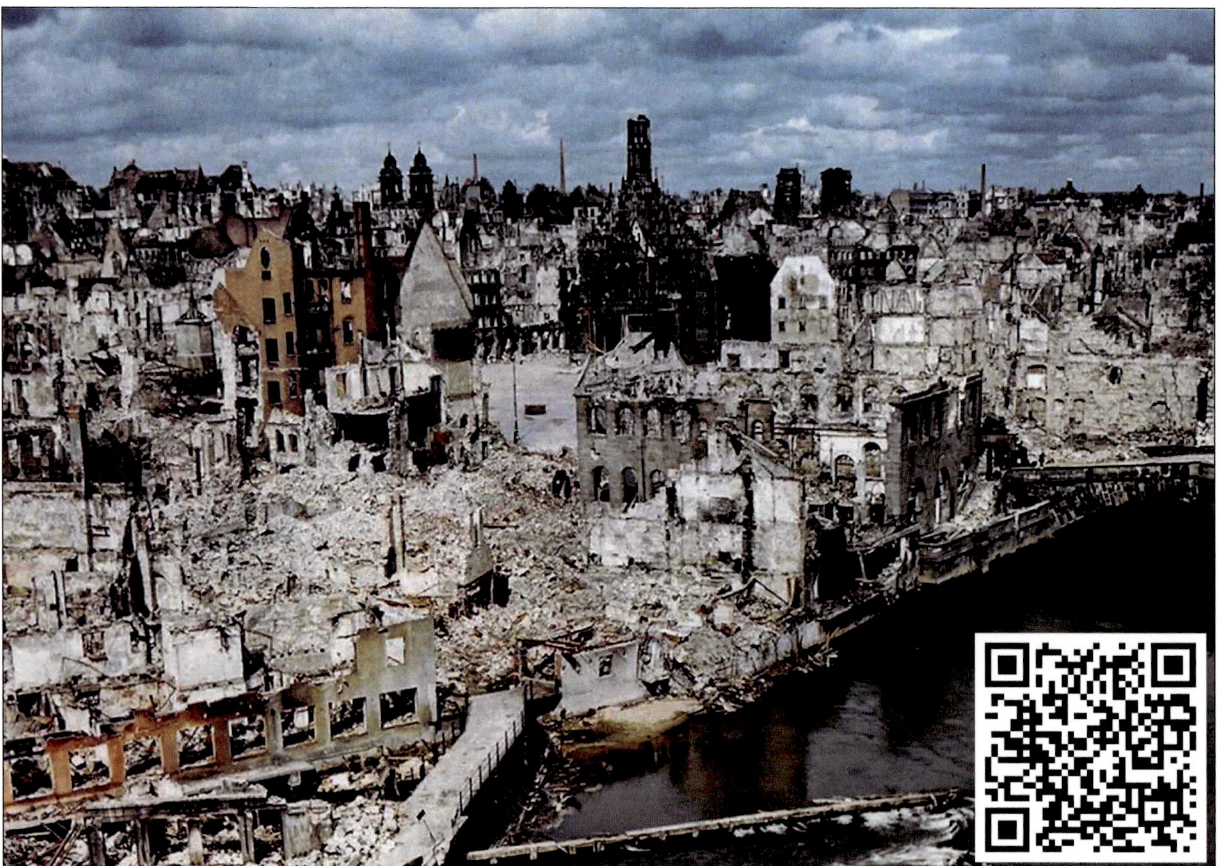

SFP186 covered not only military-related images, but also documented many aspects of life and destruction in Germany towards the end of the war and soon afterwards. (YouTube/NARA)

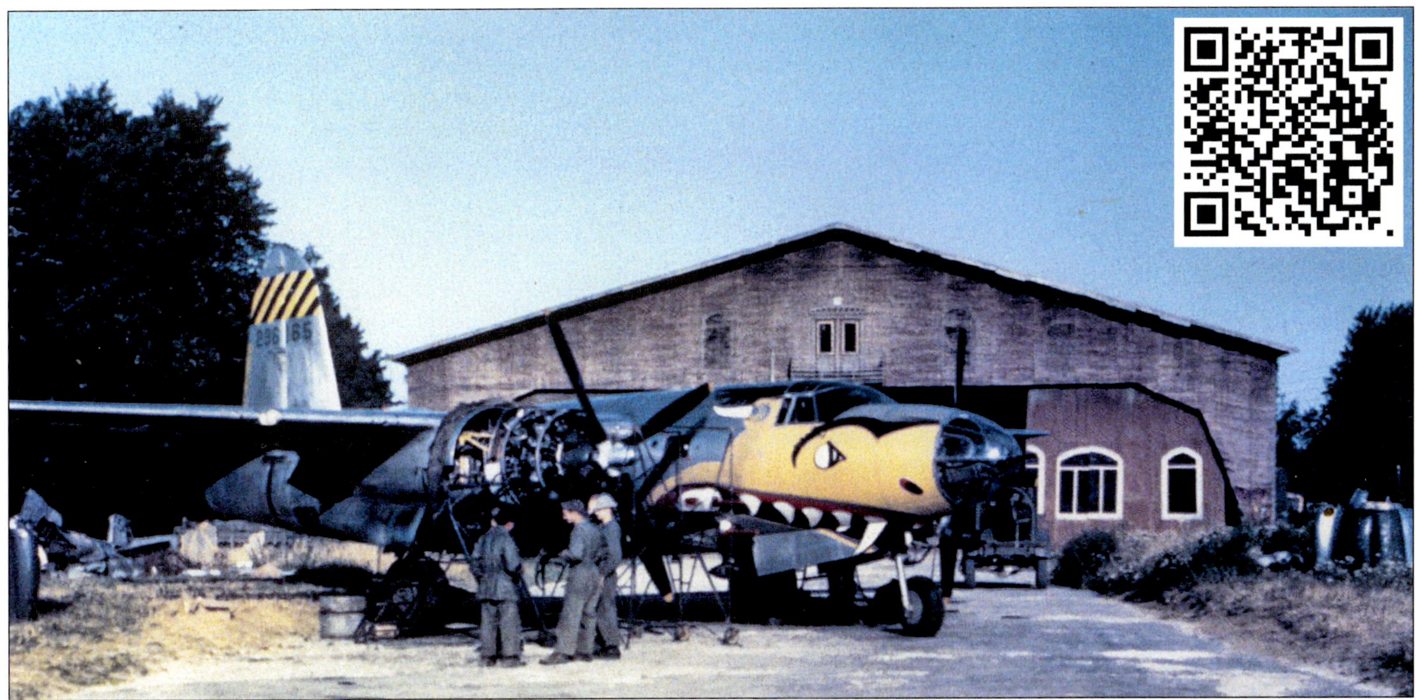

As part of SFP-186, 4th CCU cameramen flew on missions in B-26s to bomb targets in occupied western Europe. (YouTube/World War Footage)

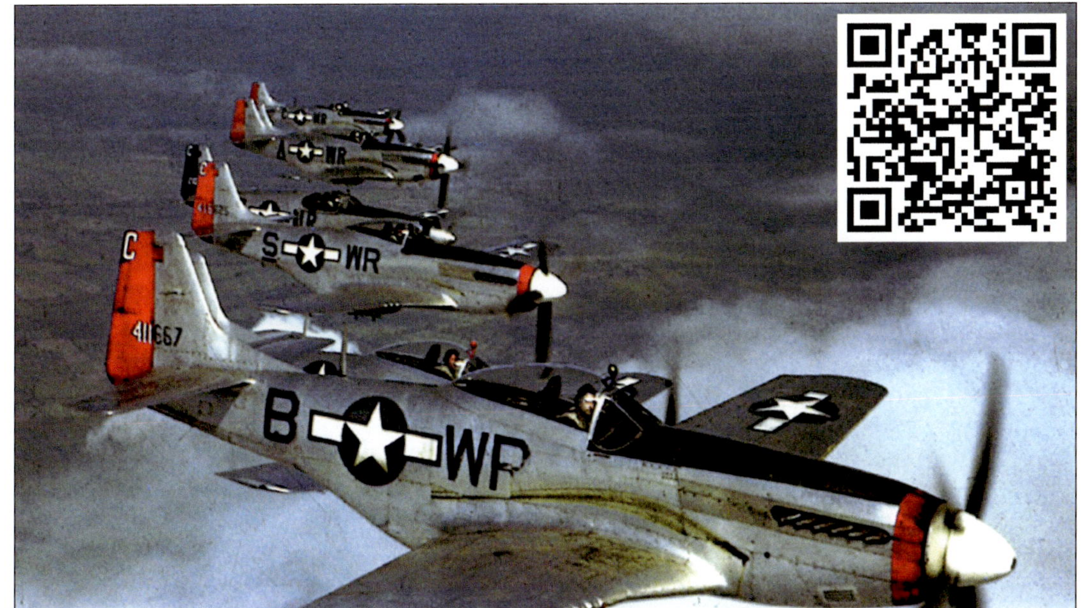

Right: A formation of four 354th FS/355th FG P-51Ds was filmed for SFP 186, and some very unusual close-up images of their aircraft were taken in-flight. (YouTube/World War Footage)

Below: Three reels filmed by the 4th CCU captured P-47 flying operations in Europe, including a specially arranged post-war gunnery exercise.

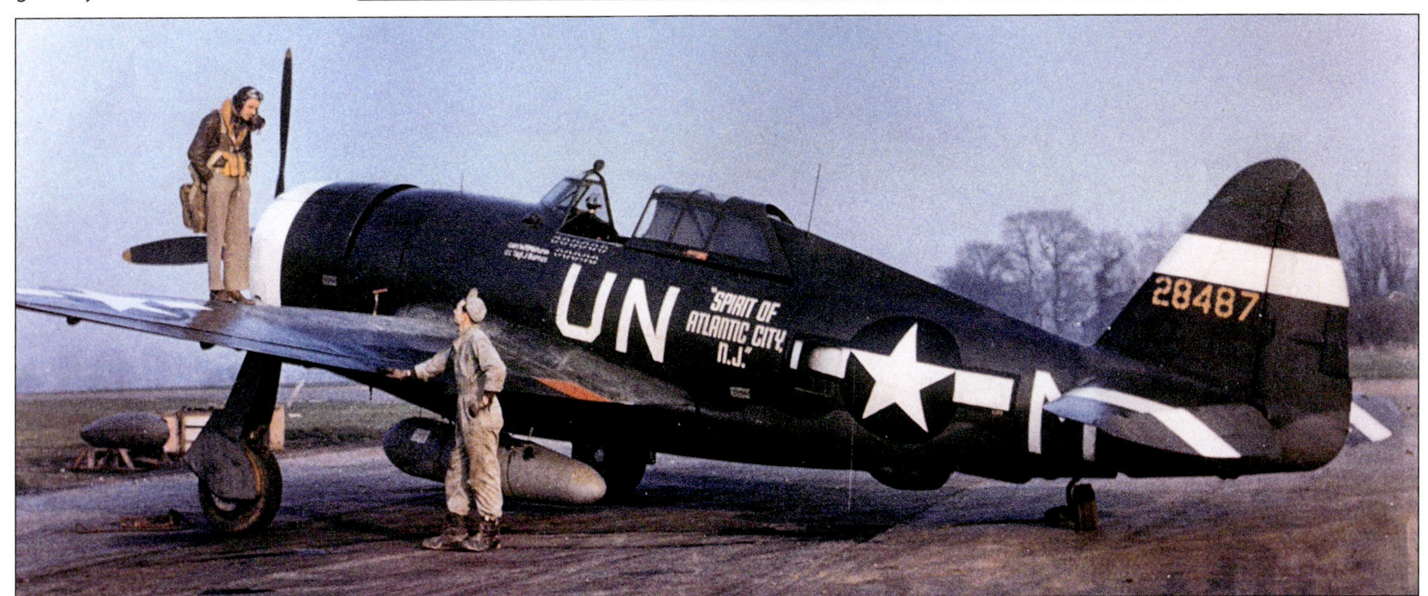

Units serving in the European Theatre of Operations were rapidly demobilised to return home, and the men of the 4th CCU were no exception. By August 1945, just a few unit members remained in Germany. Being cameramen, however, they managed to document themselves while packing for their return to the US.

While many would return home for demobilisation in November 1945, others continued their careers in the military, some going to use their photographic skills during Operation Casey Jones, a large-scale photographic survey of all of Europe for map-making and intelligence purposes.[18]

(YouTube/World War Footage)

(YouTube/NARA)

(YouTube/World War Footage)

Links to Three film reels from SFP186, taken just after the end of the war, showing USAAF P-47 Thunderbolts in action against ground targets.

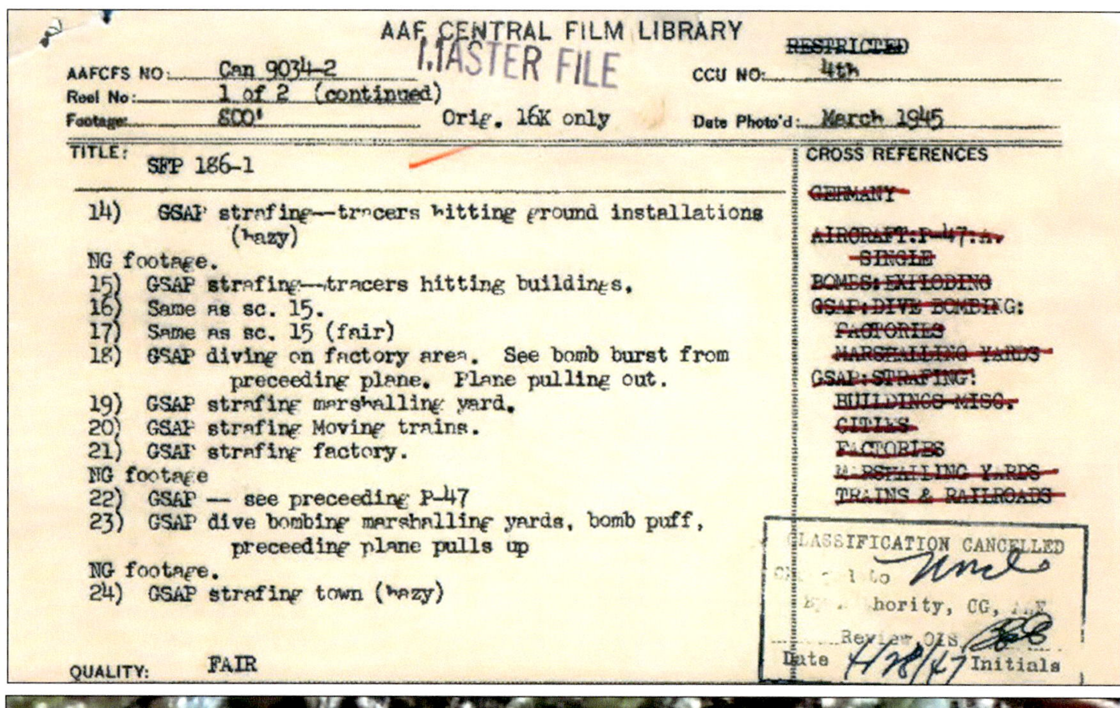

AAF CENTRAL FILM LIBRARY — MASTER FILE — RESTRICTED

AAFCFS NO: Can 9034-2   CCU NO: 4th
Reel No: 1 of 2 (continued)
Footage: 800'   Orig. 16K only   Date Photo'd: March 1945

TITLE: SFP 186-1

14) GSAP strafing—tracers hitting ground installations (hazy)
NG footage.
15) GSAP strafing—tracers hitting buildings.
16) Same as sc. 15.
17) Same as sc. 15 (fair)
18) GSAP diving on factory area. See bomb burst from preceeding plane. Plane pulling out.
19) GSAP strafing marshalling yard.
20) GSAP strafing Moving trains.
21) GSAP strafing factory.
NG footage
22) GSAP — see preceeding P-47
23) GSAP dive bombing marshalling yards, bomb puff, preceeding plane pulls up
NG footage.
24) GSAP strafing town (hazy)

QUALITY: FAIR

CROSS REFERENCES
GERMANY
AIRCRAFT: P-47: A. SINGLE
BOMBS: EXPLODING
GSAP: DIVE BOMBING: FACTORIES MARSHALLING YARDS
GSAP: STRAFING: BUILDINGS MISC. CITIES FACTORIES MARSHALLING YARDS TRAINS & RAILROADS

CLASSIFICATION CANCELLED
Changed to Uncl
By Authority, CG, AAF
Review, O?S
Date 4/28/47   Initials

After a film was developed, a record card was prepared for each can, and a quality assessment was made of its contents. It must have been very frustrating for cameramen to sometimes see the negative or off-hand evaluations of their footage, especially when it was gained under combat conditions with the enemy firing at them. (NARA)

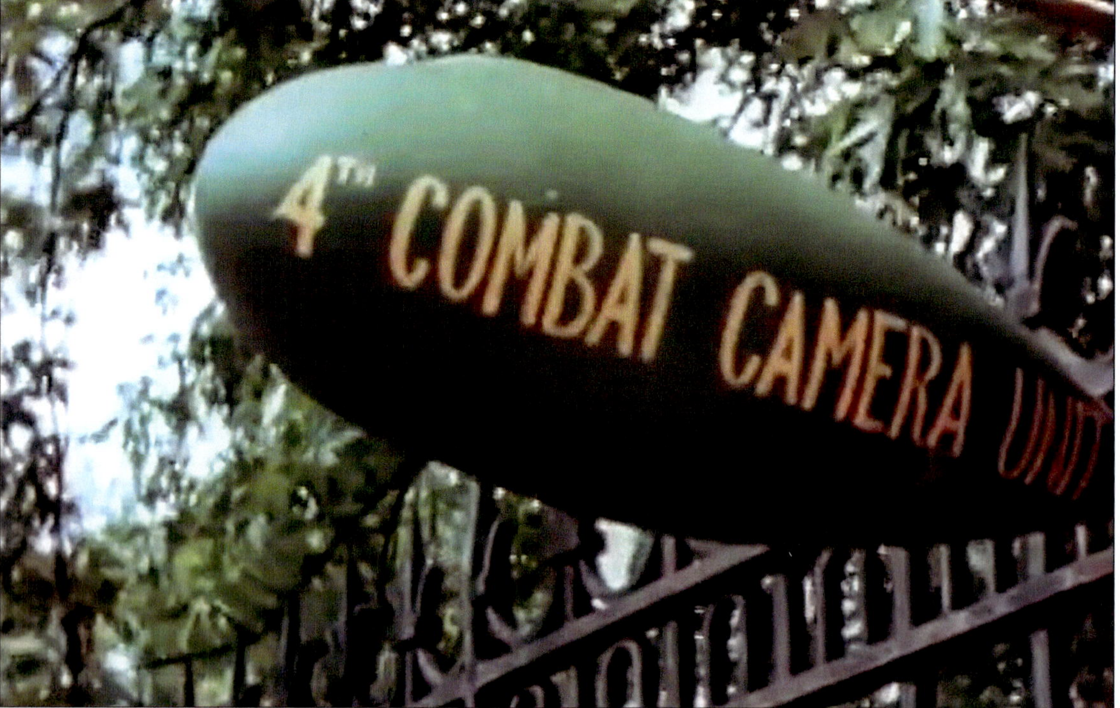

In August 1945, members of the 4th CCU began packing equipment for their return to the US and filmed some of the preparations. (YouTube/World War Footage)

2

COMBAT CAMERA IN THE PACIFIC

Aerial warfare in the Pacific theatre was very different to that in Europe. Most bomber missions involved long over-water transits, passing over or between some of the hundreds of remote Pacific islands. Many of the islands consisted of sparsely settled rugged terrain. Human settlement and target concentrations were few, apart from those on the Japanese home islands. Until the war's final phases, most of these were so distant from Allied airfields that they required B-29s to reach them.

The 13th Air Force, Fifth Air Force in Australia and Seventh Air Force in Hawaii were assigned to the newly created Far East Air Forces (FEAF) on 3 August 1944. The 6th Combat Camera Unit was assigned to the 13th Air Force. It was particularly active with the B-17s, B-24s, B-25s and B-26s of the XIIIth Bomber Command spread across permanent and temporary airfields around the Pacific. The 7th Air Force was primarily responsible for the air defence of Hawaii. Its Combat Camera Unit history reflects that its activities were not mainly in the firing line. The Fifth Air Force, headquartered in Australia, operated a mix of fighters, A-20 and B-25 medium bombers, and B-24 heavy Bomb Groups, all heavily engaged in operations against the Japanese-occupied islands adjacent to Australia.

Yank

Yank Down Under was a weekly wartime magazine published by the US Army aimed at troops serving in and around Australia. Its 7 April 1944 edition featured a cover picture and article about the men and activities of the 5th Air Force Combat Camera Unit.[1]

In May 1943, six combat photographers and an advance team arrived in New Guinea. Their 'equipment lagged behind; not many big strikes were being flown. So they made documentary films and training shorts until August. From that month on, they have been filming air shows that surpass Hollywood's wildest dreams'. Cpl Michael Gerardi's work, from the rear of a B-25, was described in the article:

When the Unit is shooting combat, they get what they can; the film is later edited, and a narration is written to fit the final screening. The boys usually shoot from the tail, one of the side windows, or the turret. Cameramen use hand-wound Eyemo's, Akeley's, and, for colour, a Victor B-I. What still photography is done is shot with 4x5 Speed Graffix.

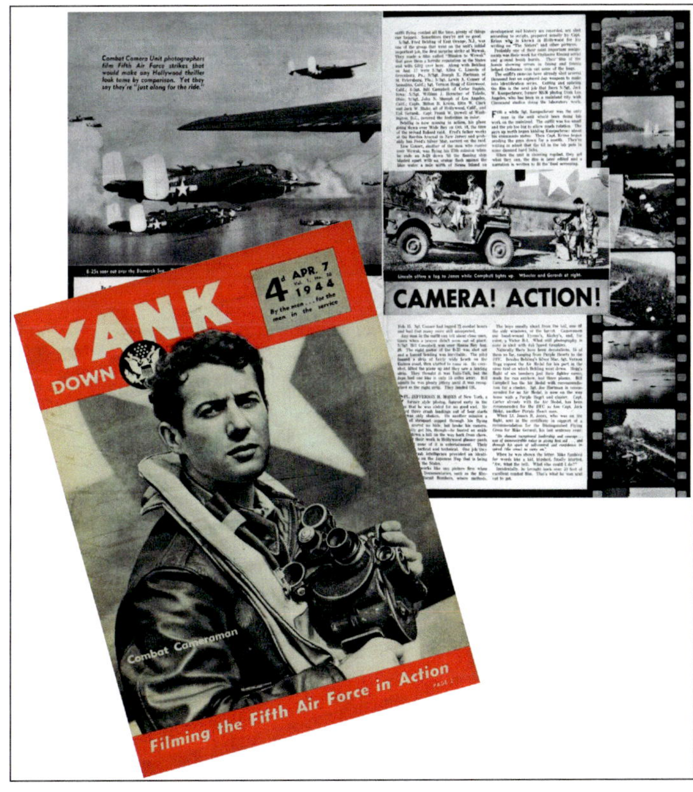

The Yank Downunder was a widely distributed weekly US Army magazine produced in Australia. (Author's collection)

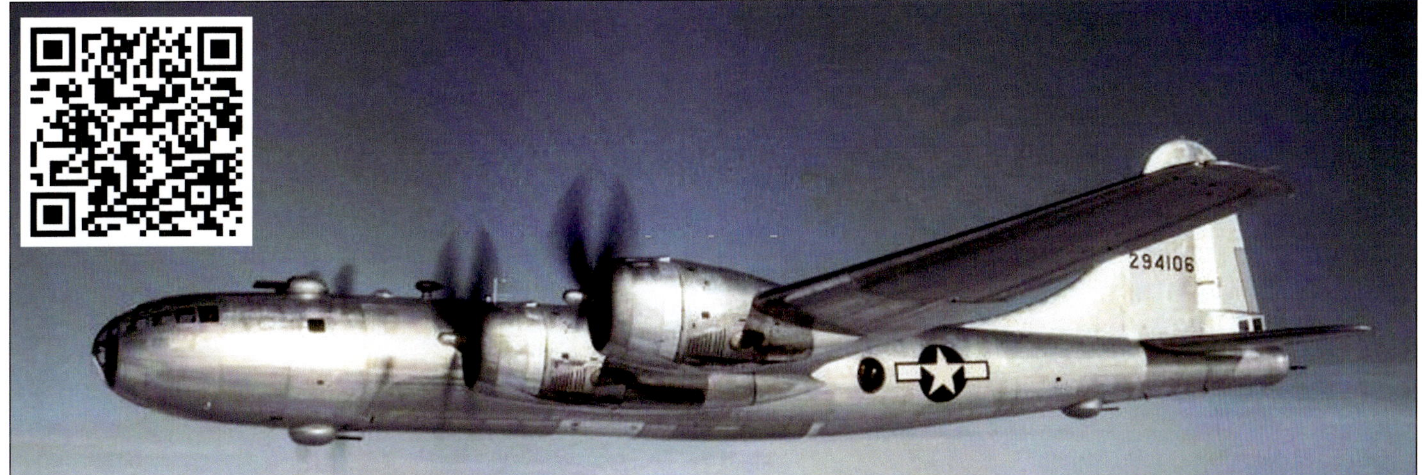

The Last Bomb is a very detailed film documenting aspects of USAAF mass B-29 raids and P-51 attacks on mainland Japan from US Pacific islands in 1945. Filmed in colour, it was a resource-intensive, high-quality production. It includes studio scenes and gives an excellent insight into these extremely long-range bombing missions. (YouTube/NARA)

Handheld cameras were vital for the combat cameraman's work. They enabled them to take internal images of the aircraft's crews but, more importantly, collected action images during the mission, especially attacks by enemy fighters, other aircraft in their formation, bomb releases, and subjects on the ground.

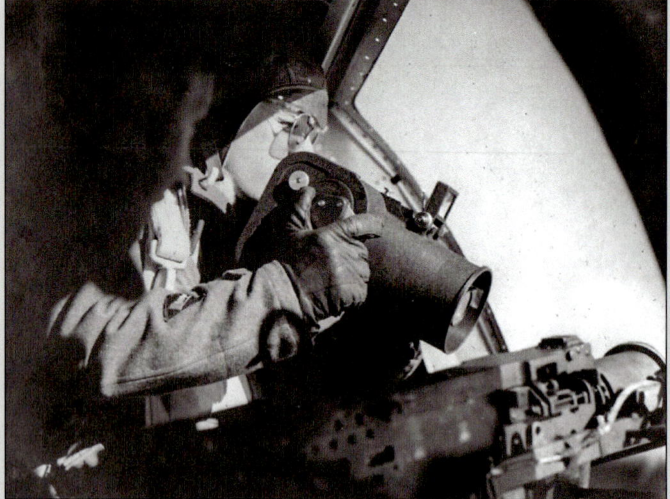

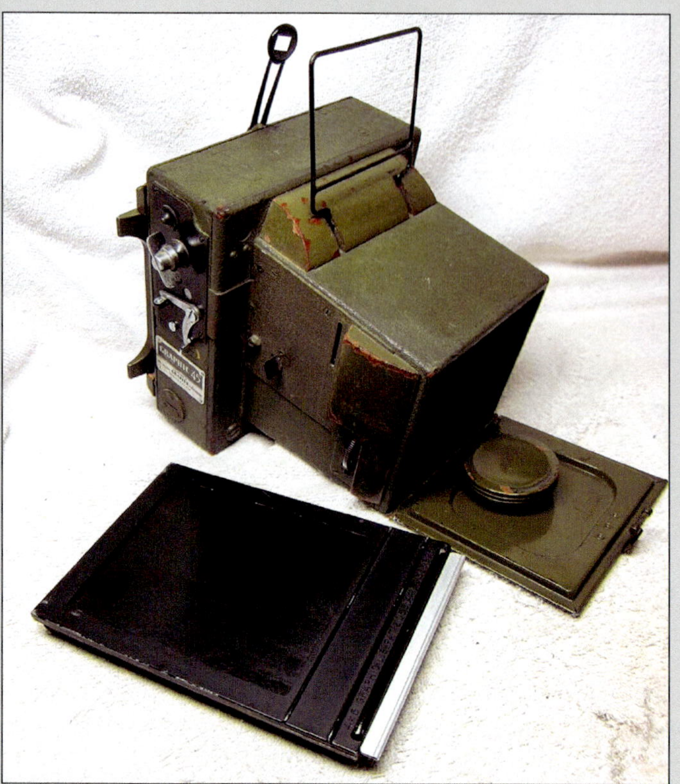

Above: Camera equipment came in many forms, including the Folmer Graflex K-21 5x7 camera. One of the favoured positions for the cameramen was the waist gunner position by the .50 calibre machine guns. (NARA)

Right: The Graflex 4x5 camera was widely used by US military photographers during World War Two and after. When the war suddenly ended in August 1945, the company sold the surplus it had accumulated to the public as the 'Graphic 45', still painted in olive drab. (GPlates)

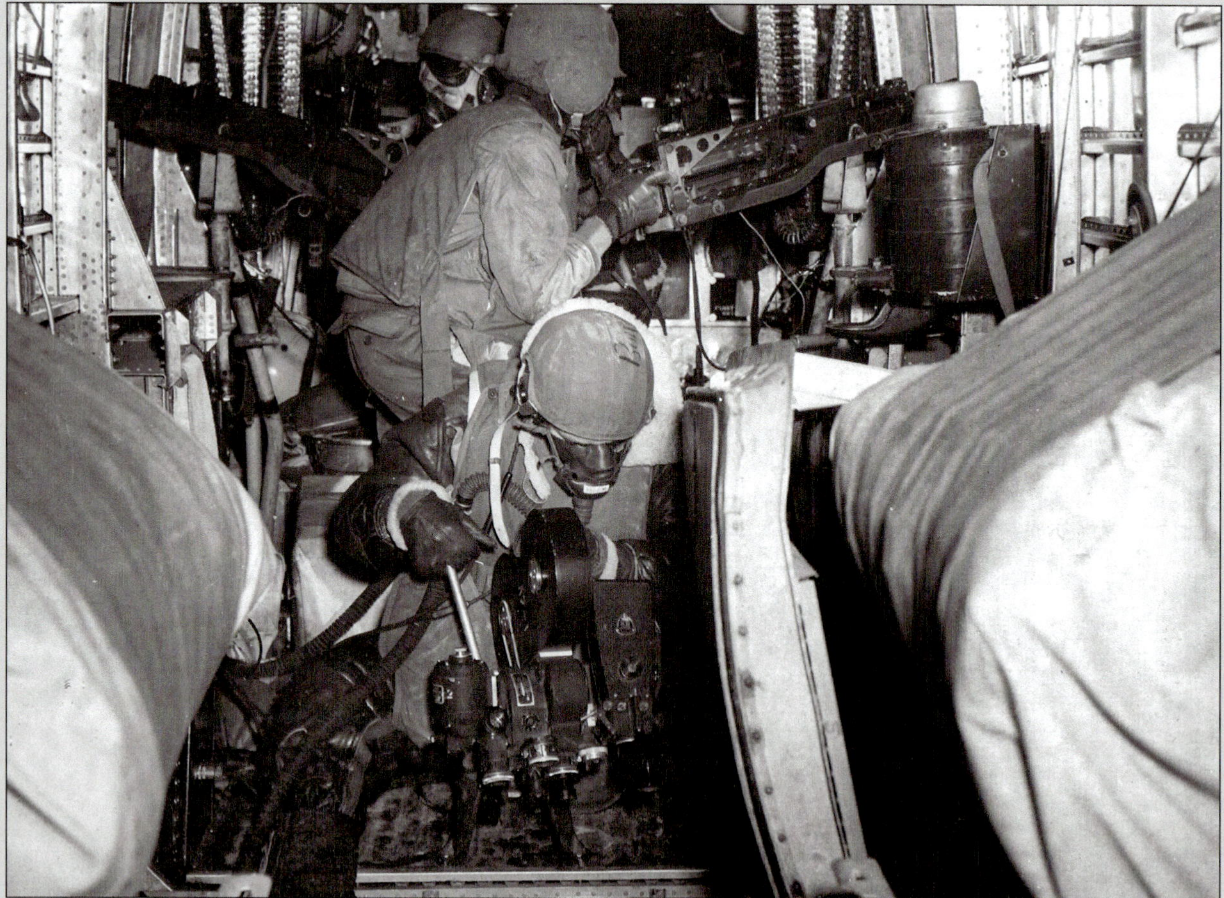

On a high-altitude mission, connected to oxygen, and just behind the two waist gunners on a B-25, the lifted floor hatch enabled the cameraman to shoot bombs dropping from the aircraft. (NARA)

Going in, a cameraman is always busy. A five-hour mission is four hours and 55 minutes of boredom, four minutes of worry over equipment and a minute of shooting. Mike checked his exposure, ensured the two-inch lens was set on infinity, ran off a couple of feet in case of a jam, unconsciously listened to the motors, and waited. They started their run-in with Gerardi's lens shooting where they had been while the pilot worried about where they were going. They were going right through a curtain of 20mm stuff that hammered the fuselage and then rattled around inside like in a sardine can.

Several of the crew on the aircraft were injured to some extent from that enemy fire. Garardi gave first aid to one of the gunners, wounded in the arms and legs. He was also bleeding from a shrapnel injury to his own leg. Badly damaged, the aircraft crash-landed on an airfield at Lae, unable to lower its undercarriage.

The piece continued; 'The unit works like any picture firm when possible. Documentaries, such as the filming of the Biscuit Bombers, are shot according to scripts, prepared usually by Captain Krims, known in Hollywood for his writing on 'The Sisters' and other pictures'. The 'Biscuit Bombers' recorded air supply drops from C-47s to remote groups of isolated Allied troops fighting the Japanese over impossible terrain.[2]

The 5th Combat Camera Unit began to take shape after 21 February 1943, with one of its early projects, *The Biscuit Bombers*, 'An account of the exploits of the air transports on their perilous missions dropping sorely needed supplies to our and Australian troops'. For that mission, Sgt Silbert devised a special external camera mount. A Bell & Howell A-3 Eyemo camera was bolted to a board which was:

Firmly attached to the plane by chains and was extended about 18 inches outside of the escape window and tilted in such a manner as to allow coverage of the 'Biscuit Bombs' as they were pushed from the plane. Due to the terrain over the target, the pilot had to climb during this action, thus setting the proper angle for filming the 'bombs' hitting the target.

Moreover, all of this was done in extremely close proximity to Japanese troops just a few hundred feet away.[3]

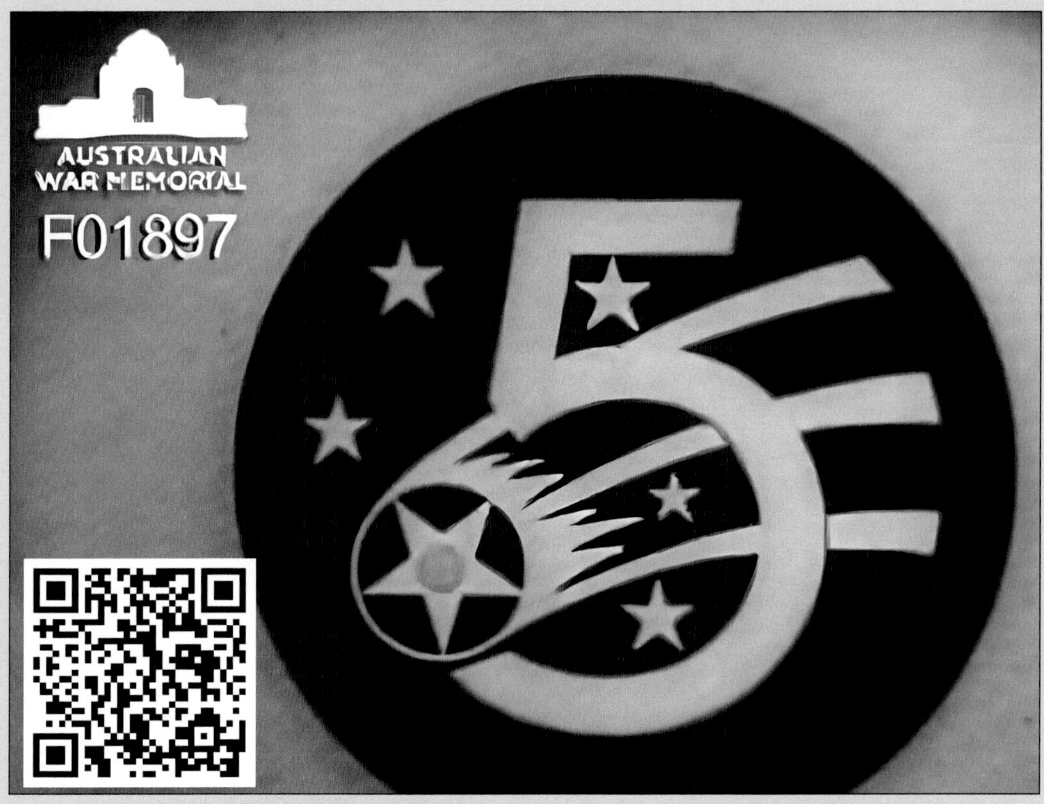

Mission to Wewak. (YouTube Australian War Memorial)

Probably one of their most important assignments was their work for Ordnance filming aerial and ground bursts. Their film of the bursts showed errors in fusing and timing, which helped Ordnance iron out some of the bugs.

Cpl Moses of New York, described as 'a former style photographer' in *Yank*, 'figured early in the game that he was slated for no good end. He scored three crash landings out of four starts… On another mission, a piece of shrapnel zipped through his flying jacket, scored no hit, but broke his camera'. However, casualties among the unit were significant. On 17 August 1943, Combat Photographers SSgt Fred Behling and Lewis Consor were involved in filming one of the 5th CCU's early successful films, *Mission to Wewack*, which received wide distribution. It documented a surprise attack on a Japanese airfield and positions at Wewack in New Guinea.[4] Behling was lost during a mission a few months later, on 18 October.

Behling's loss is described in more detail in the 5th CCU's unit history:

In October 1943, the second mass daylight raid was to have been carried out by B-24s, B-25s, and escorting P-38s and P-47s. Four cameramen were sent out on this mission. These men were concentrated in one squadron of the four flights of nine planes each for complete coverage of the strike at enemy shipping. Though the risk of losing a large percentage

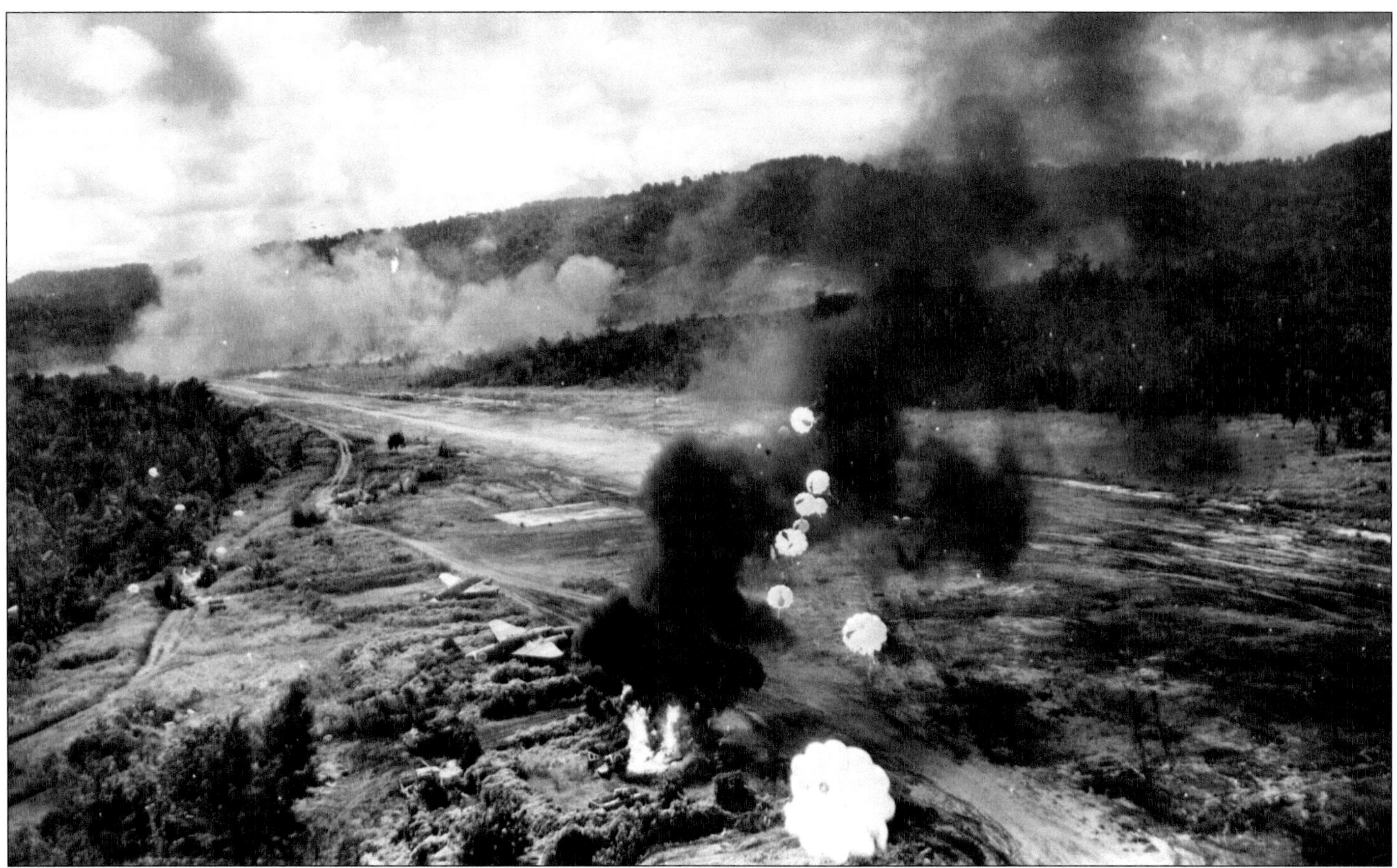

A shot of a later raid on Wewak airfield in November 1943, parachute retarded bombs are being dropped from a B-25 at low level. (NARA)

of highly skilled technicians (extremely difficult to replace) was high, the coverage would have been worth the gamble. Unfortunately, to make matters worse, the B-25 squadron did not receive the message to turn back because of unfavourable weather. This was received and obeyed by the B-24s and the fighter escort. Thus, when they burst out of the weather front directly over Rabaul, they found themselves alone with the Jap ack-ack, navy, and air force. This was the only squadron of the four delegated to attack shipping, and though one section of three planes had to turn back due to failure of armament the moment before the attack, the remaining six pressed their attack with determination. All hell broke loose; one plane was hit and crashed in the harbour, leaving five to carry on. They carried on, destroying a corvette and an undetermined number of smaller ships. The Unit's alert photographers duly recorded this. Much to the dismay of the five remaining planes, they escaped the frying pan to fall into the fire, for when they fought their way clear of the harbour, 60-odd fighters immediately set upon them. The plane to which SSgt Behling was assigned was hit and crash-landed in the sea. Not being content with destroying the plane, those Zeros that could not catch the fleeing B-25s vented their rage by strafing the downed ship time and time again. The remaining planes put up such determined resistance that after losing more than two dozen planes, the enemy turned tail and desisted from further attacks. A Japanese motorboat was seen inspecting the still-floating wreck the following day. For this deed of bravery and courage, SSgt Behling, though missing in action and presumed dead, received the Silver Star for gallantry in action.

After this mission, 5th CCU's flying activities were curtailed forcibly for some time.[5]

Lewis Consor 'Was flying his 27th mission when he rode on an A-20 down 'til the flaming ship blasted apart with an orange flash against the blue water a mile north of Neusa Island on February 15, 1944. SSgt Consor had logged 73 combat hours and had that many more still unreported'. Several other photographers were injured during missions or when the aircraft they were flying in were hit by enemy fire and were forced down over the sea, jungle terrain or island beaches.

Joe Longo

The most detailed personal account of what it was like flying as a Combat Cameraman comes from then SSgt Joe Longo, who flew with the 6th Combat Camera Unit in the Pacific theatre. He was instrumental in forming the International Combat Camera Association many years later. [6]

Having joined the infantry, Joe Longo was posted to Nouméa, New Caledonia, where he contracted fever. Afterwards, he transferred to the Air Corps. He was attached to a headquarters company in Guadalcanal, where he said, 'I found myself looking for something to do. I was a fish out of water, infantry trained, ready to go into combat and now in an Air Force unit'.

There:

I found out that there was a unit called the 6th Combat Camera Unit. I talked to a couple of the guys, and it sounded like they were leading a pretty interesting, exciting life. So, I applied for a transfer. They said, 'No, we are full up now,' because those Combat Camera Units in the Air Force, at the time, were made up, I believe, of 21 men. Their roster was filled, and I returned to doing little to nothing with the headquarters bunch.

One day, he got a message: 'Those people at the Combat Camera Unit want to see you'. There, Longo was asked if he still wanted

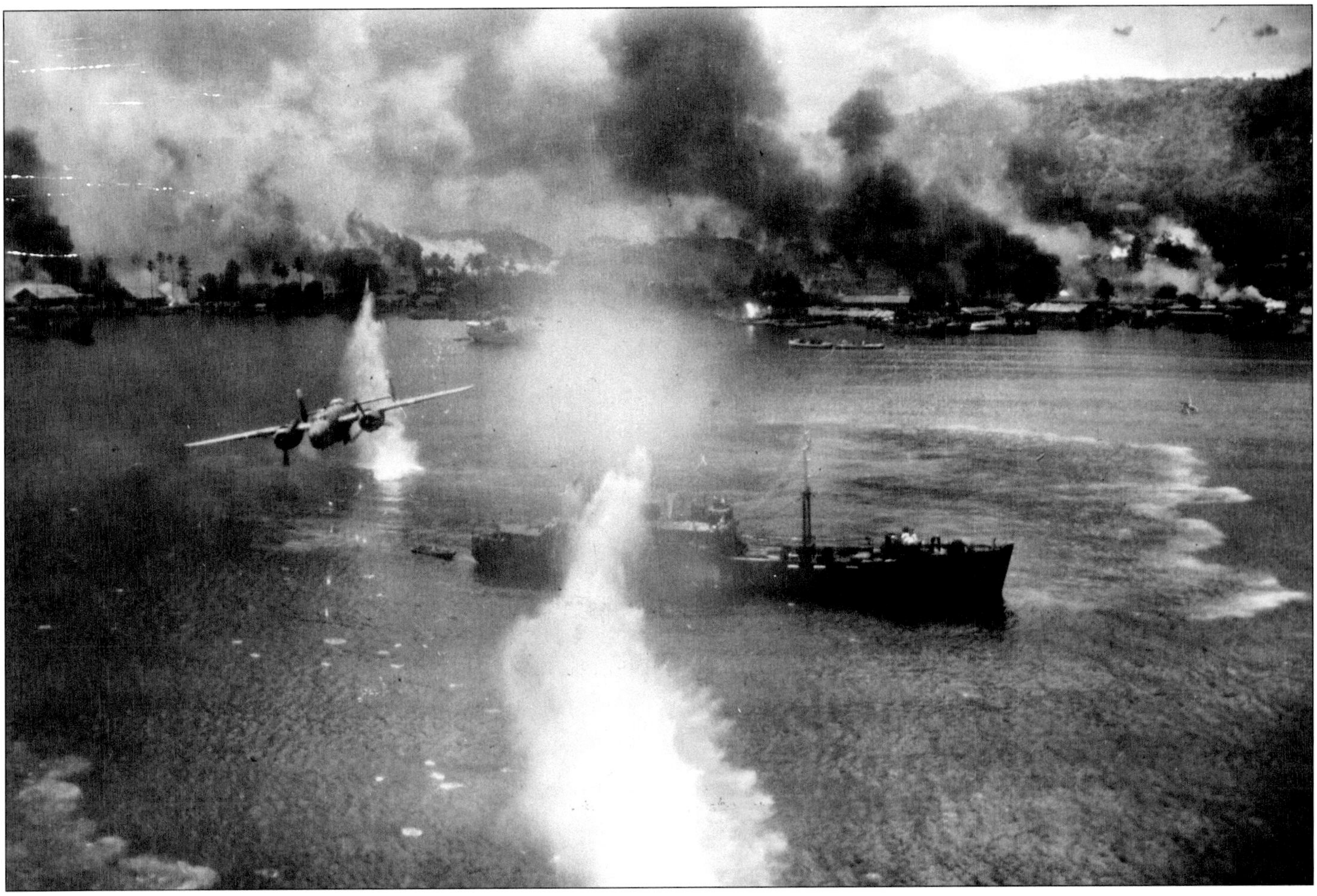

A dramatic shot captured by a 6th CCU cameraman of the B-25 attack on Rabaul harbour in October 1943. (NARA)

to join the unit. Asked what he knew about photography, he told them he had taken pictures for the high school newspaper and had always been interested in it. Asked if he knew how to use a .50 calibre machine gun:

> I said, of course, because coming out of the infantry, that was one of the basic weapons…They gave me a two-week trial, and I went up with an instructor once. Then, the second time, I was on my own. We were flying out of the Admiralty Islands then, and I was flying with the 307th Bomb Group. The film reports returned from the two or three missions I went on was OK, so I guess I made the cut. From then on, I just stayed with it. They wanted me, but I found out later that they had lost two regular men on very hot targets. The vacancies came along within three days of each other, so I replaced one of them.

COMDOC. The fitting of a 75mm cannon to some B-25s made them ideal for coastal patrols to strafe Japanese freighters that moved between the hundreds of Pacific islands. From December 1943, the photo of this attack near Wewak was one of the first publicly released demonstrating this recently acquired capability. (NARA)

From then on, it was just routine. We would take on all the duties thrown at us, mostly flying in B-24s and B-25s. Toward the end, I racked up almost 35 missions and went on TDY (temporary duty) with an Australian Beaufighter Squadron. My first one or two missions were considered 'milk runs' because they did not know whether I could cut it.

The primary mission of the 6th Combat Camera Unit was to cover all the activities of the 13th Air Force. They would get intelligence data from new targets or send a lot of it back to the States, where it was edited, cut into stories and released

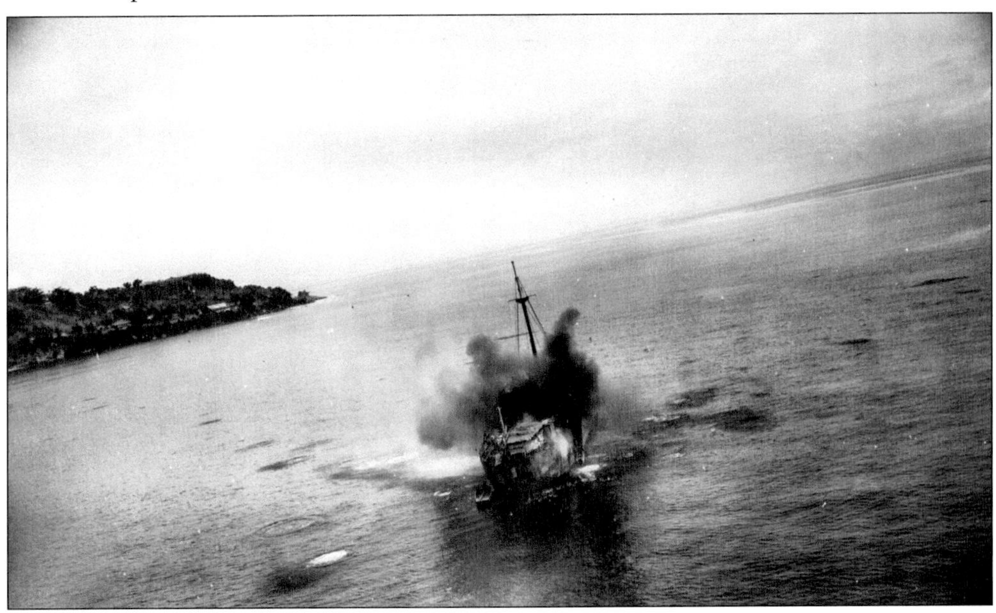

to the newsreels so that the people at home could find out what they were doing. These relied on us military combat cameramen for the pictures. That was our job. Long after I got home, I saw a couple of stories I had shot. I looked for my name on the credits, but there were never personal credits in combat photography.

We were doing shipping strikes and ran into very little ack-ack and fighter activity. However, the third and fourth missions were over Borneo on the Celebes; one particularly hot target was Balikpapan. It was on the southern coast of Borneo and was the 'Ploesti of the Pacific.' The Japanese needed it to get their fuel to send up their fighters and keep their air force going. So it was a very hot target. Three-quarters of the men who flew those missions were lost. They had two Air Forces in on that: the 5th Air Force, General Kenny's outfit, and then ours, the Jungle Air Force, the 13th. We always felt self-conscious because the 13th Air Force was very small. We only had the two heavy groups, whereas, on the 5th, they came on with all the big bombers. They were the Eighth Air Force of the Pacific, and they got most of the publicity and all that. That irked us.

It was on that mission to Borneo; I think that was when I found out what it was all about. At that time, the Japanese were using phosphorus bombs launched from their aircraft. They would come in and lob this weapon at us. If it hit the aircraft, it burned through our control wires and everything else. We could get burned real bad if we tried to do anything about it.

I remember this one mission. I was wearing a flak helmet for safety's sake but I could not get the camera close to my eye, so I was missing lots of shots. When I returned, I went to one of the Crew Chiefs and the armoury shop, which made me a 'sport finder.'[7] When those fighters come in at you, they come real fast. On the camera, we had that little viewfinder hole to look through, and we would miss attacking aircraft because if they were coming in at maybe 180, maybe 200 miles an hour. We only had a very short time to shoot it. That is another reason I would raise the camera's speed to get more exposures. However, only looking through the viewfinder was not good because we would miss much of the action. After that, I took the helmet off and sat on it most of the time. When shooting out of the waist, I used the 'sport finder' to get good peripheral vision. Then, you could follow them out as they came in and wind the camera up again.

We had a 'throw around camera,' a K-20, a fixed-focus still camera. Much of the time, we often got good shots of bomb damage or even fighter action with it. We often passed that camera around to whoever thought they might get some good

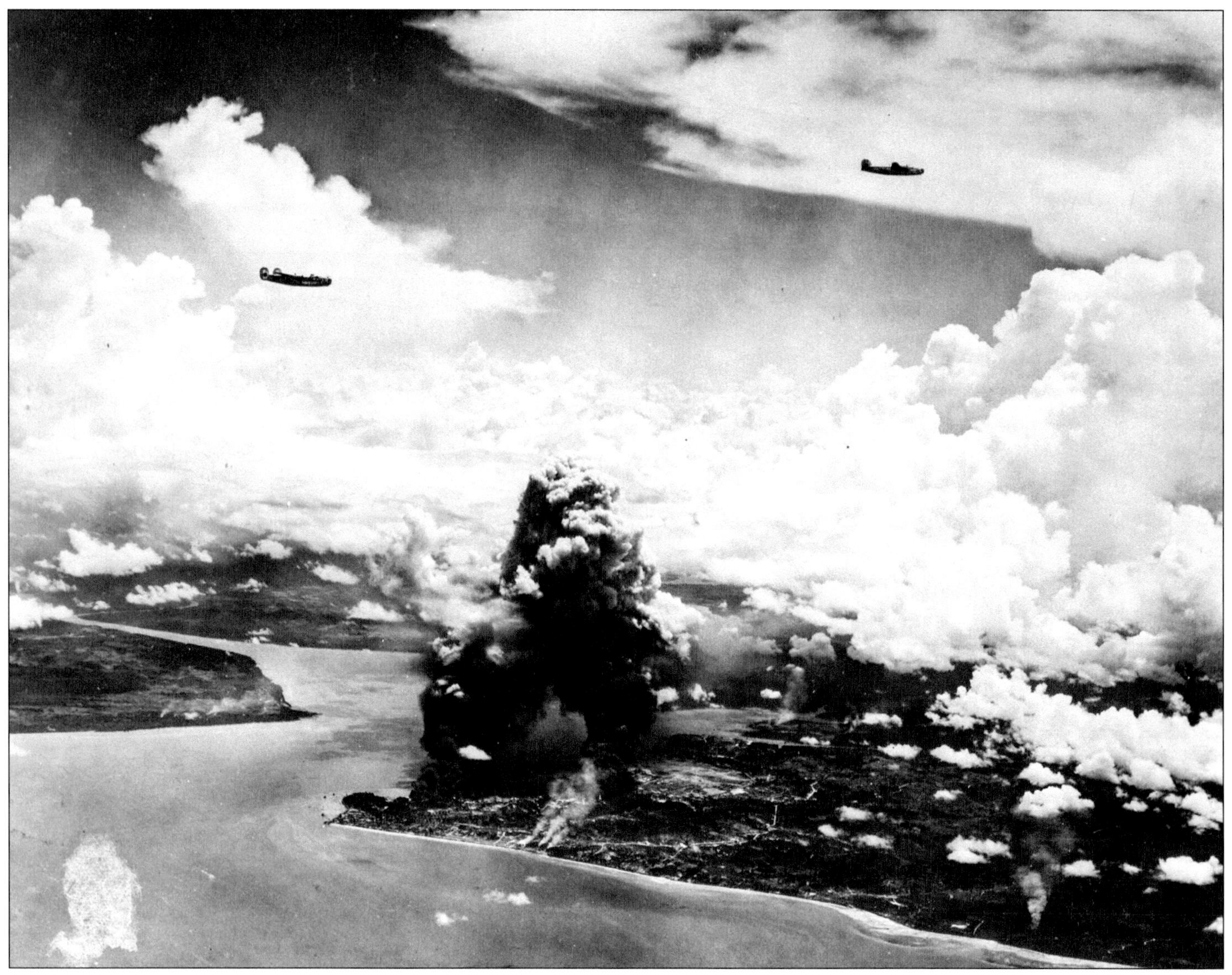

Combat Cameraman captures a strike by B-24s on the vital Japanese Balikpapan refinery on 26 June 1945, part of a 150 aircraft mission by B-24s, B-25s and P-38s. (NARA)

shots. The aircraft crew liked that because they felt they were being photographers. We never got bad stuff; we would maybe get five, six good shots out of a whole film role.

After I turned in some decent footage, they thought I was seasoned enough to go out alone. In a B-24, we had two, sometimes three, cameras. The main camera was used at the camera hatch, and the others were situated behind the right and left waist windows where the two gunners sat. I will never forget we were at 14 or 15,000 feet, and the bombardier came through over the intercom and said, 'Cameramen, get ready.' I went back to the rear hatch, put one foot on one side, one foot on the other and held on. There was nothing but the Pacific Ocean below me, and right away, I am saying, 'Jesus, suppose you had to get lost in that maze of water, they would never find you'.

Anytime there was any action, you would usually shoot over the waist gunner's shoulders. Sometimes, you would have to take that position over if they were hit. This is why they wanted somebody who could handle .50 calibre machine guns. Sometimes, they deliberately went one man short, and being a gunner that became our primary job.

The Bell & Howell, with its 400-foot magazine, set over the camera hatch, gave us about four minutes running time. Depending on your altitude would determine if you would see your bombs hitting their target. We tried to check beforehand but never really had a set formula. Had I been doing it longer, I probably would have worked out that at 15,000 feet, a string of 500-pound bombs would take a specific time to hit the target. However, I usually worked it out pretty well. We had lots of help from the bombardier, who would give me five or

10 seconds warning before he would say, 'Cameramen, start your camera.' From that position, I would be hunched over the hatch and looking through the viewfinder. You see the target coming up, and he would say, 'Bombs away,' and those bombs would come right into your frame. The first time I saw it, it was marvellous because we were at really low-level. And then the concussion from the explosion, which I did not expect.

As the B-24 pulls around, you go to the waist window with another smaller camera with one lens, called a 'Bomb Spotter,' a 35mm camera, and you record the damage from the side. When you run out of that 100-foot load, it runs at 24 frames per second, almost 90 feet a minute, though I always shot mine a little faster to reduce the vibration. You then had to reload the camera real fast because you were waiting to get hit by fighters. When going through flak, it was a good idea always to shoot where it was coming from. When we got back, the intelligence people could see its location and send in another aircraft group to knock out those flak guns.

We flew lots of hours, 11, 12 and 13-hour missions. There were a couple of missions where the two outboard engines quit because they were out of fuel. We just made it back. After we landed, the fella who had driven me to the aircraft in the morning would return and help me with my gear. We would return to our unit, and I would have the captions made up and ship the film back to headquarters. We would not hear anything more about it for two, three or four weeks. Then we would get a critique, saying 'footage good,' or 'this is shaky.' That used to bother me when some clown was telling you your footage was shaky. You are up at 15,000 feet with a virtual carpet of flak, and the aircraft commander is trying to hold

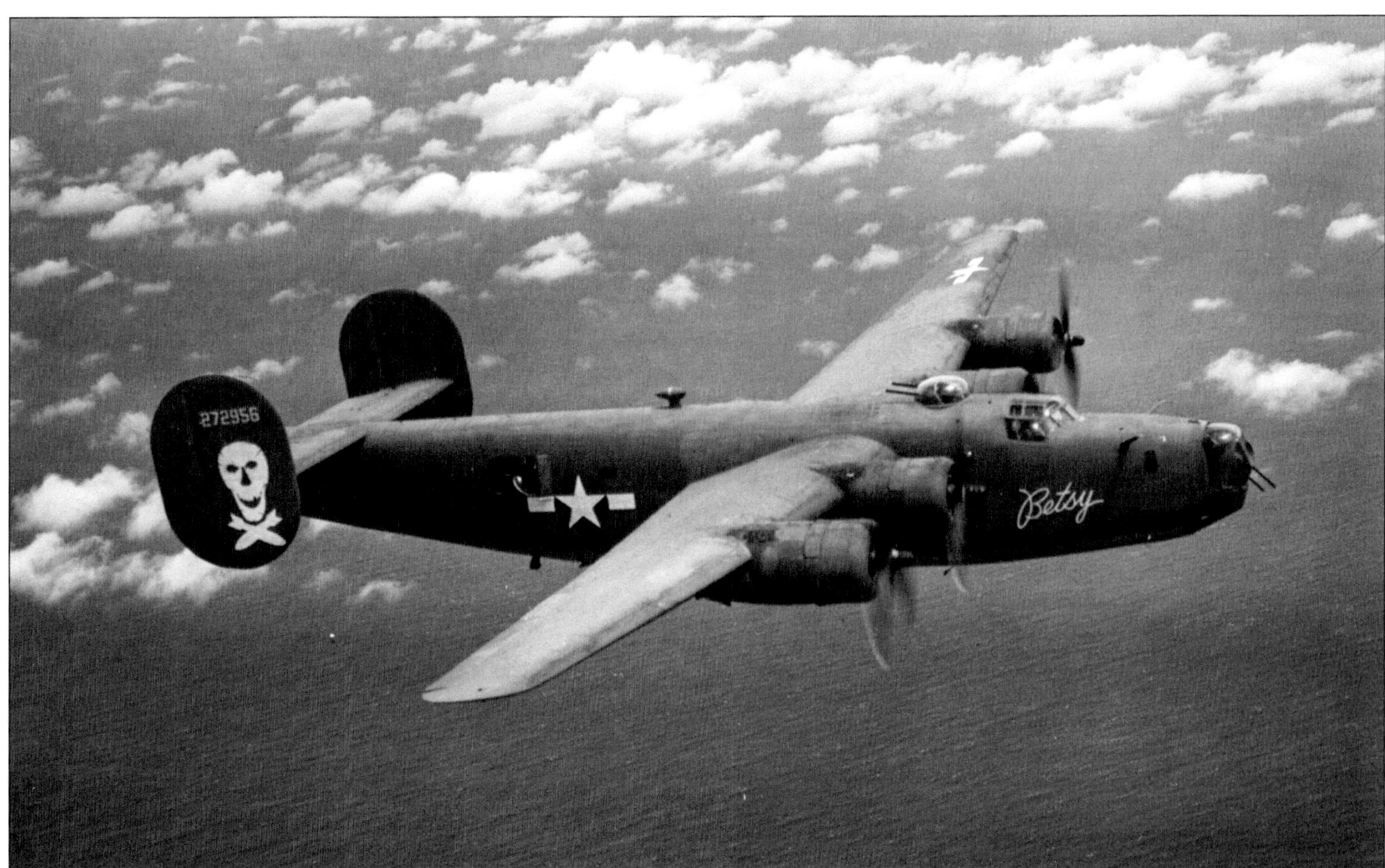

Photographed on a mission to Wewak, B-24 *Betsy*. It was taken by a cameraman from another B-24 in the formation, who would carry a movie camera, and probably a K-22 or other still camera to photograph action and sometimes the crew. (NARA)

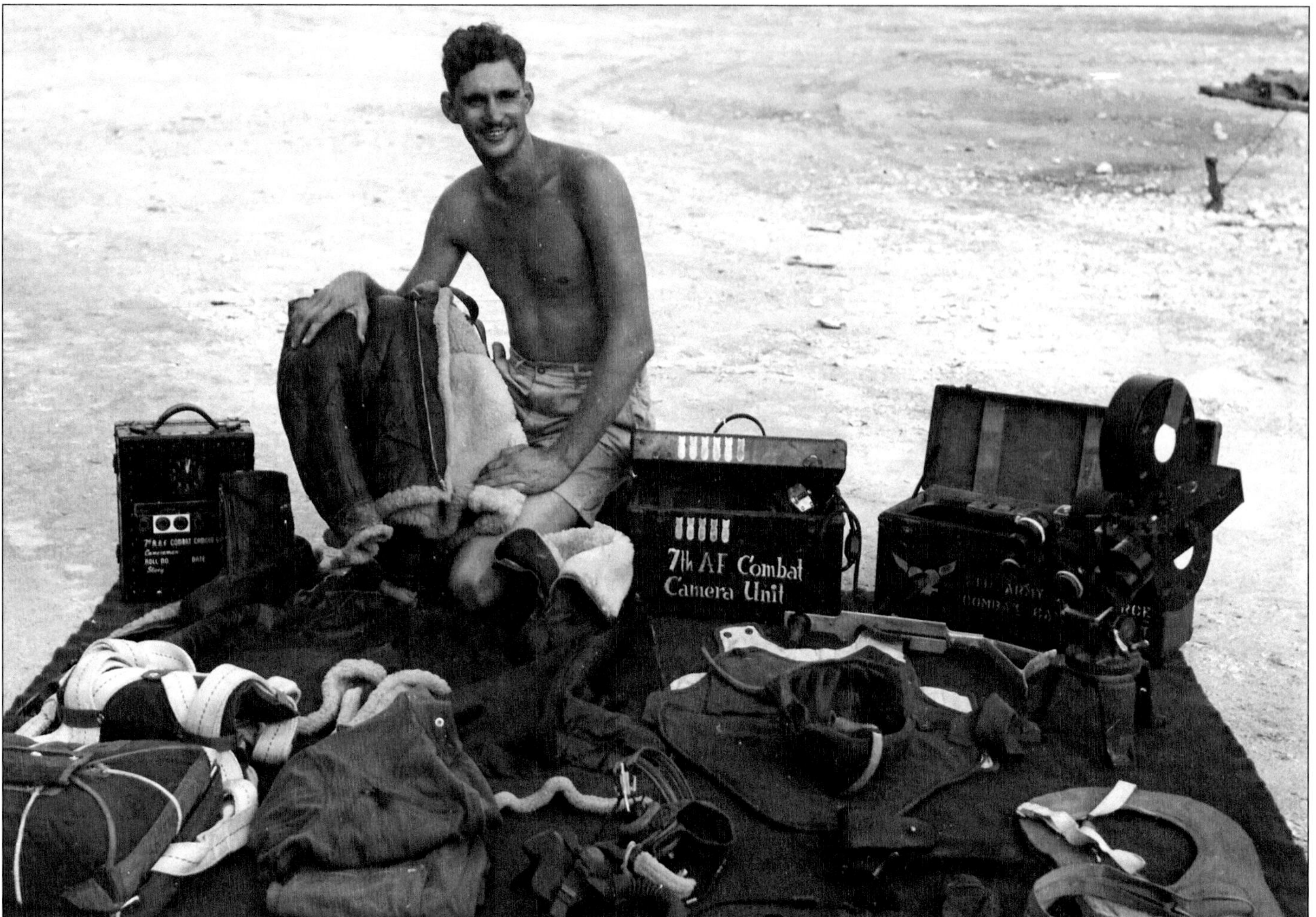

A 7th CCU cameraman lays out his special high-altitude equipment. Such missions required crews to wear heavy flying kit, and carry and operate their cameras in the extreme cold. |(NARA, Via David Holmes)

that airplane still. Then this guy complains about the footage being shaky. That hurt. That really did.

When you are doing your job, it is tense and stressful. However, once it was over, it was over. With the Army and the ground crew, you went forward into battle, cared for the wounded, came back, and maybe had a hot meal. Bingo, you are right back out again. It was constant.

I think it is useful to know how we got our assignments because there were only 11 Combat Cameramen in our unit, all on flying status. One or two would be stationed with a fighter unit to help mount cameras in the P-38s for that gun camera stuff. Some would be with a B-25 outfit in a forward area. My post was with the 13th Bomber Command. We would get a call from the intelligence section saying a new target would be hit. So we would go along to the aircrew briefing. The Operations Officer giving the briefing would roll up the shade, and you would see the target. From that, you would determine how many aircraft were going and pick the best camera spot. As a cameraman, you could be in any aircraft you wanted. All you had to do was report to the aircraft commander, and he would have to take you on board. You do not want to be forward in the formation, and you do not want to be behind. It was always a good idea to get off to the side, but that was not too good because, by that time, the ack-ack guns would be trained on you. So it was very tough, but that made the best camera position.

You always kept your cameras loaded because you never knew what to expect. Sometimes, you might help on a rescue mission. When I was sure that everything was quiet, I would go around, all through the aircraft, and shoot cutaways of the pilot, hands on his controls. And I would also do a shot of the bombardier over the bombs, get a silhouette -stuff so they could edit and make it look like there is a story to it. I only shot what was happening in the aircraft on my first one or two missions. However, after that, I said, 'Well, why not make a story out of it?' They did this very successfully with the 8th Air Force. They passed cameras around, and all these guys were shooting film. The editors loved that because they could cut a sequence and cutaways with the bombardier and the fighter attacks. So I always busied myself. I never came back with much film unused.

When I got off the fixed camera, the one in the hatch, I just let that camera roll out. I would lock it off, and the aircraft would bank off the target. That is when I would climb over the fixed camera and get ready in the waist window. I always liked to shoot over the shoulder of the waist gunner, and you would get cutaway shots of them. On the intercom, you could hear any fighter attacks.

Somebody might say, 'Boy, the flak is so thick up here, you can walk on it'. That is not an original thing to say, but it would be a good shot if you could get a piece of sky with an aircraft in the background and the black puffs of smoke. You are always looking for good shots.

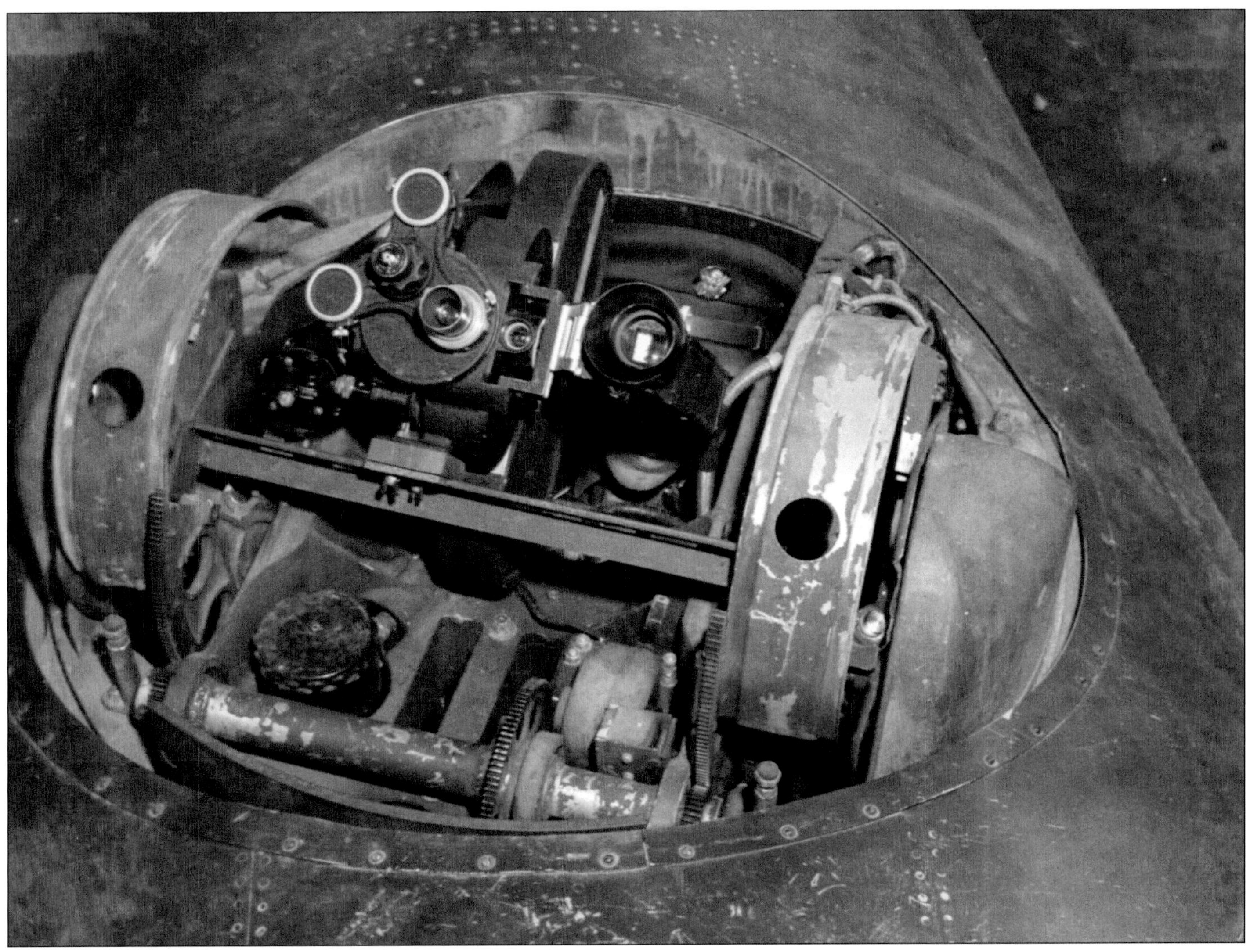

The guns have been removed from this upper turret of a B-26 in the Pacific and replaced with a powered Bell & Howell Eyemo camera. (NARA)

I liked to get good cloud formation shots. Anytime I could, if there was a good cloud formation and the aircraft looked really good, I would photograph them. You were sometimes so close that the pilot knew he was being photographed, and he would bring his B-24, a lumbering piece of equipment, and get it snug right under your wing. Sometimes, he would give you a thumbs up, laugh or smile, which was a great shot. And then somebody would say, 'Where will we use this?' I said, 'Don't worry, somebody will find a good use for this shot.'

I was doing something like that on a target in Borneo. I think it was Tarakan or Brunei Bay. I am not sure now. It was a great shot with great clouds. I was sitting behind the pilot, shooting the back of his head up to the formation and the left. Four B-24s were stacked beautifully, one above the other. They filled the frame just right with a 50mm lens. I had a yellow filter on it that brought out the clouds. I said, 'This is one of the picture shots.' So I was shooting, and I kept shooting. And then I took the camera down and started to wind it. Suddenly, I heard over the intercom, 'Geez, did you see that?' Right away, I looked up and saw where the airplane I had been shooting was. It was gone; I just caught a glimpse of a couple of pieces of metal. In the time that I had taken to lower the camera to wind it, the B-24 was gone. Here I was taking a calendar shot, if you will. Danger came at any time in any way. There was no downtime. In the air, you do not get a second shot at reality.

As combat cameramen, we flew with different crews all the time, which was a disadvantage because we did not have the camaraderie or the spirit that the regular crews had. However, in the air, you all became part of a crew and part of a family. We were afraid, but fear took a different shape in those days, and I think you can attribute that to youth. When looking through the camera viewfinder, everything happens in front of you. However, somehow, those three or four pieces of glass you are looking through separate you from it, and you are invincible. Or you don't think about it. When you saw your footage when it came back, you would say, 'I cannot believe I did that.' I was very lucky. I never got hit. I came close. People around me got hit. And when you put that camera down, and you are suddenly faced with the stark reality of combat, and you see that guy lying on the ground, they are hurt, then it sinks in.

I had to bail out once. We were shot up and lost the hydraulics. The pilot brought the aircraft as close as he could to the beach. Luckily, we were not even a mile offshore when I bailed out, and we got picked up right away. However, had that been over the sea, getting picked up over that vast ocean was very unlikely. That is the thing that worried me.

Like the other Combat Camera Units, the Fifth was quickly rundown after the Japanese surrender in August 1945. It gradually completed a much-reduced task list. The Fifth CCU was inactivated in February 1946.

COMDOC AT YONTAN

As US forces island hopped closer to their home islands, the Japanese military became increasingly desperate. On 24–25 May 1945, Japanese forces dispatched five Ki-21 'Sally' bombers with commandos onboard to raid Kadena and Yontan airfields on Okinawa. These were effectively 'suicide' attacks as no provision was made for their post-attack extraction.

Four aircraft were shot down close to the airfield. A fifth managed to belly land around 100 metres from the Yontan airfield control tower. The 10–12 Japanese commandos on the aircraft, together with some survivors from another plane, began their mission of destroying the American aeroplanes. The following day, the 7th CCU cameramen recorded the raid's effects, including the loss of 27 aircraft and at least another 10 damaged.

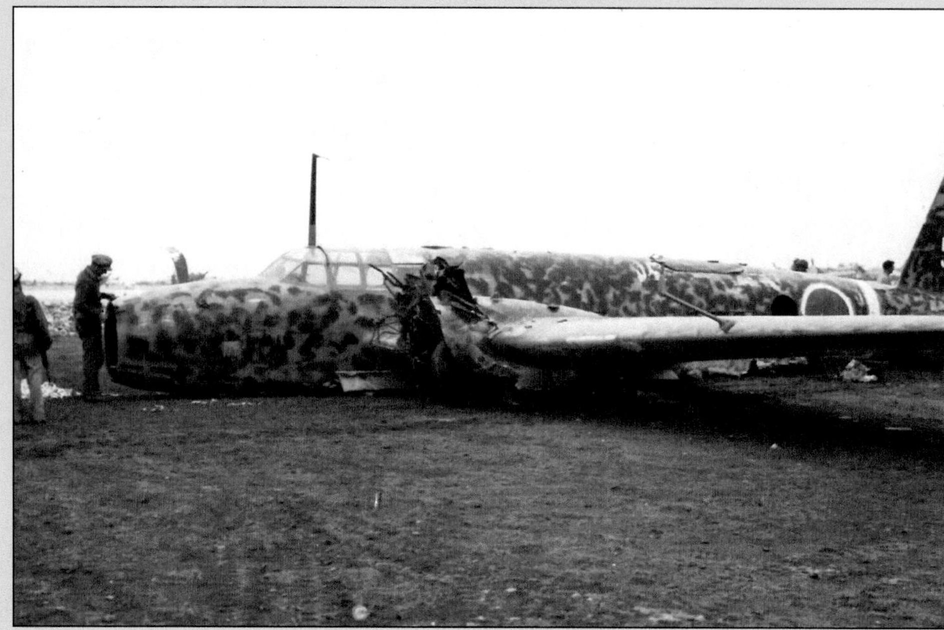

The Japanese 'Sally' that landed intact near the Yontan control tower. Japanese commandos set about destroying as many US aircraft as they could with grenades and explosive charges. (7th CCU via David Holmes)

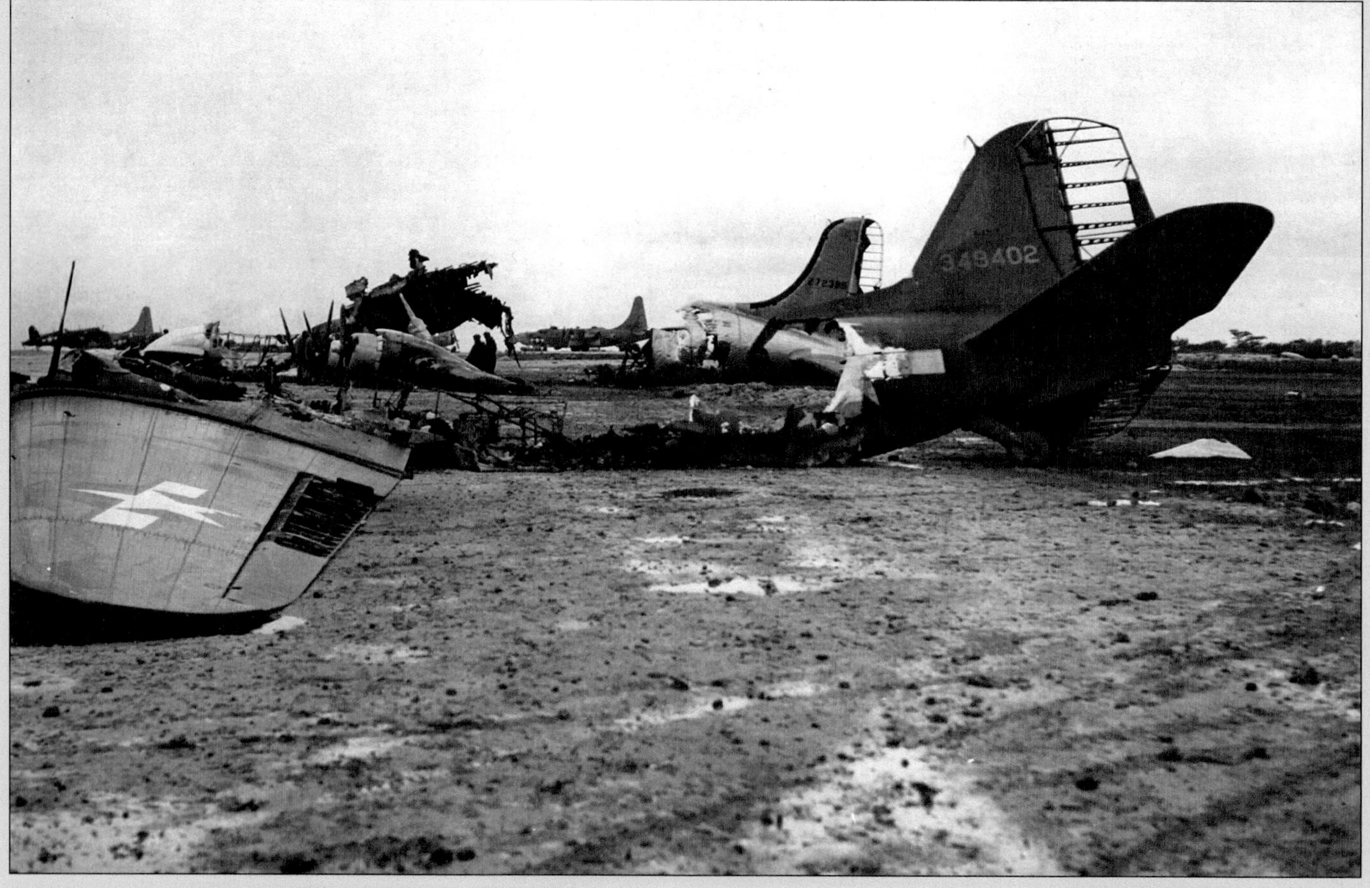

The remains of a destroyed US Navy C-47 (R4D-6) at Yontan, still wearing its former USAAF serial. (7th CCU via David Holmes)

3

NUCLEAR AFFAIRS

The First Atomic War

The decision to use these highly destructive weapons on Japan was of immense seriousness. But once made, there was considerable interest in determining the scale and type of destruction these little-understood bombs wrought.

The initial response was to send cameramen to the scene to capture details of the carnage. However, there was a lot of uncertainty about the possible effects of residual radiation. Lt Dan McGovern was one of the USAAF cinematographers assigned to the region for this task. He travelled to Japan to support a USAAF-led group of high-profile civilian journalists to Tokyo via Astugi AB. He was soon instructed to get images of Allied POWs being released from camps close to Hiroshima and Nagasaki; they chose a camp very close to Nagasaki. With a sound man and some civilian journalists, the 14 men headed to the city in a C-46. They overflew it to view the devastation before landing unannounced at the nearby Omura Air Base. On 9 September 1945, a month after the bomb had been dropped, they arrived in Nagasaki.[1]

There, McGovern and his team filmed the devastation and visited PoW Camp 'Fukuoka No 14', which mainly held Dutch and British prisoners; most of the US servicemen had, on their own initiative, already started to self-evacuate from the city to find American forces. Some of the former prisoners recounted having heard a 'strange sizzling' and then the brilliant flash of the bomb, a huge heated pressure wave passing over them, to be soon followed by a choking dust and then the muddy 'black rain' of fallout. After documenting interviews with some of the released PoWs, the men headed to the centre of the devastation at Ground Zero. There, they encountered the dead, severely burned and those suffering from what was described as a 'strange malady', radiation sickness. After a sobering day in the city, the group returned to Tokyo.

Not long after McGovern returned from Nagasaki, he was seconded to the US Strategic Bombing Survey (USSBS) team to thoroughly document the destruction wrought on Japan for the next nine months. Having secured most of the photographic and cinematic resources freed up by the completion of filming for *The Last Bomb*, McGovern, as part of his new assignment, returned to Nagasaki in November 1945. As well as their own footage, they also obtained priceless additional material from a large Japanese film team, that had been on the scene within a few days of the bombs

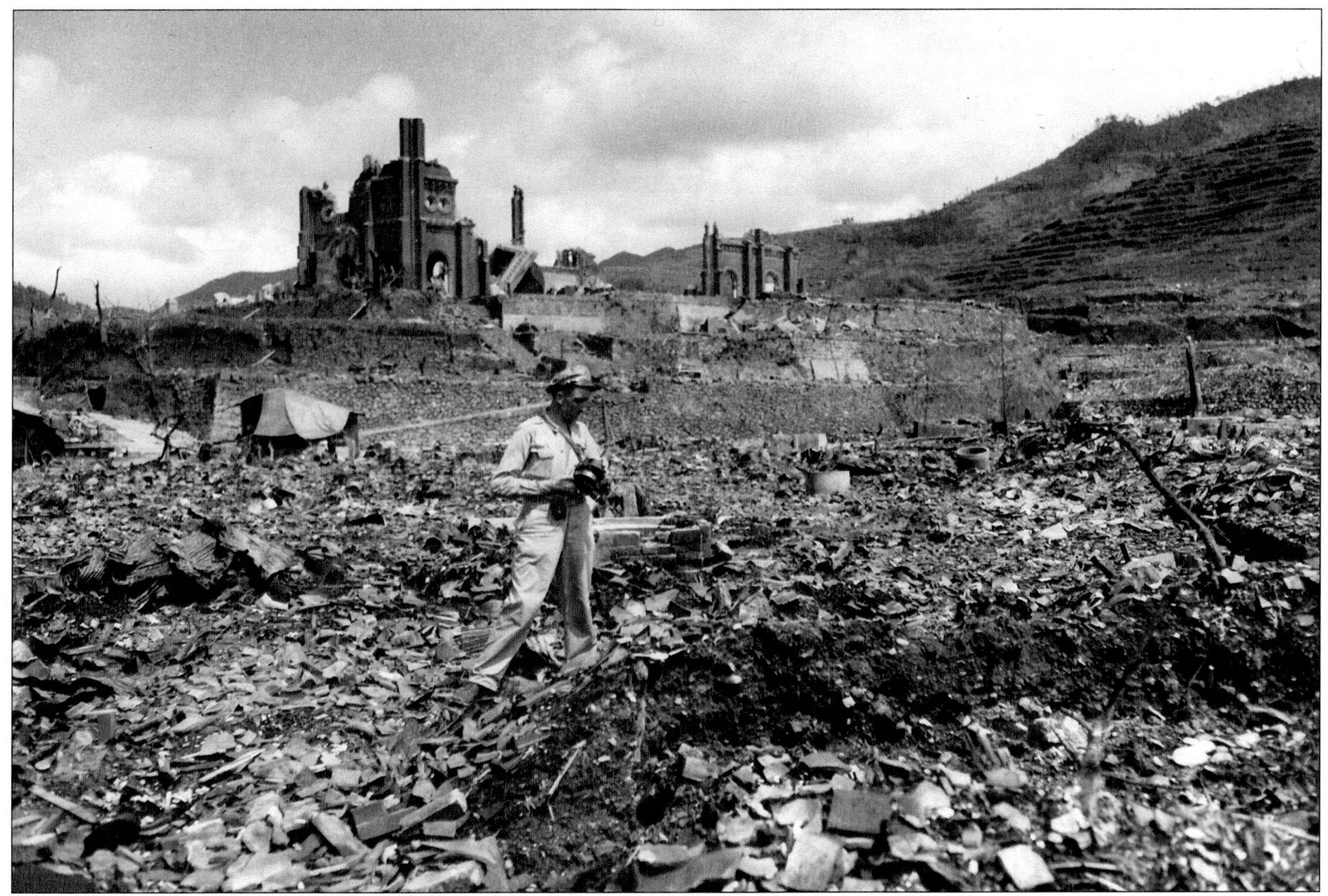

The original caption from this image, now held by NARA, reads, '1st Lt DA McGovern, NY, USAAF, member of the Newsreel Pool, stands at the exact spot where the Atomic Bomb dropped at Nagasaki, Japan. This spot is now called 'Zero.' In the distant background may be seen the Urakami Cathedral, 8 September 1945. (NARA)

being dropped on Hiroshima and Nagasaki. They had amassed some 26,000ft of material. The US occupation forces effectively procured that footage, with several US military organisations vying to get control of it. With support from the US Navy, McGovern and the USSBS eventually gained the material and agreement to film more.

They were authorised to obtain additional footage for themselves. The Japanese film team was permitted to continue their work, now working directly for the Americans, with McGovern overseeing all the post-filming production. An enlarged USSBS team grew to six cameramen, with a C-47 available for air transport. However, they completed most of their travel around Japan using a commandeered train. Hiroshima and Nagasaki remained at the centre of their attention. In addition to the atomic-related work, McGovern also ensured that they covered elements of the defeated Japanese forces. One subject was the Japanese Air Force unit at Chofu, west of Tokyo. There, they got young Japanese soldiers to dress as Kamikaze pilots and reenact their pre-mission rituals. Many Japanese Navy ships that had been sunk or were severely damaged by US sea mines in shallow waters, were also filmed by his cameramen.[2]

The two-hour 44-minute film *Effects of the Atomic Bomb on Hiroshima and Nagasaki*, directed by McGovern, was completed in early 1946 and previewed at McArthur's HQ on 4 May 1946. The film was meticulous in its coverage and analysis. Before long, all the associated footage from the USSBS, including the *Effects*' film, was shipped back to the United States. Before its planned public release, it was shown to a select military audience at the US Navy Support Facility at Anacostia. McGovern was told immediately afterwards that the film would not be publicly released, mainly because officials from the Manhattan Project who were present at the screening saw highly sensitive technical details being disclosed, mostly related to the height of the weapons' detonation.[3] The decision to security classify the film meant it was removed from any potential public viewing. Some reels were discreetly declassified during the 1950s and 1960s but did not reach public attention. It was only in 1970 that snippets of the material were seen for the first time at a showing in New York. Only in recent years, with digitisation, has this incredible film become widely accessible.[4]

McGovern also collected another 100,000ft of high-quality colour production film that he hoped Warner Brothers would turn into a complete motion picture, which he had already decided should be titled *Japan in Defeat*. Although the film was processed and sent to the US, it never achieved the production status McGovern wanted, it appears mainly due to a lack of studio commercial and public interest. However, some of McGovern's footage has recently achieved some public attention. Sequences from a 2004 documentary, narrated by Brian Cox, show material from Nagasaki, Astugi AB, and McArthur's arrival and the early phase of occupation. Although the footage used is un-attributed, these almost certainly come from McGovern's team and the Japanese Nippon Eigasha cameramen.

Nuclear Testing

While there were efforts to hide the footage assembled by McGovern, the Atomic Energy Commission and the Department of Defense would later expend vast resources over the next 20 years documenting almost every aspect of the extensive US nuclear test programme. The programme consisted of just over 200 atmospheric and underwater detonations. What later became the 1352nd Motion Picture Squadron, in May 1962, was based at Lookout Mountain Air Station in California, a facility it shared with the Atomic Energy Commission. Together, they produced over 600 edited films from 1948 to 1969. Many of these productions were about nuclear-related topics, including test documentation and training films. Each major test explosion series was extensively documented and turned into movies. These produced an overall picture of the tests' major objectives and outcomes. The US Department of Energy partially declassified many in the late 1990s. There must have been many thousands of feet more filmed on how specific items of specially constructed test buildings and equipment reacted to different magnitudes of a nuclear explosion.

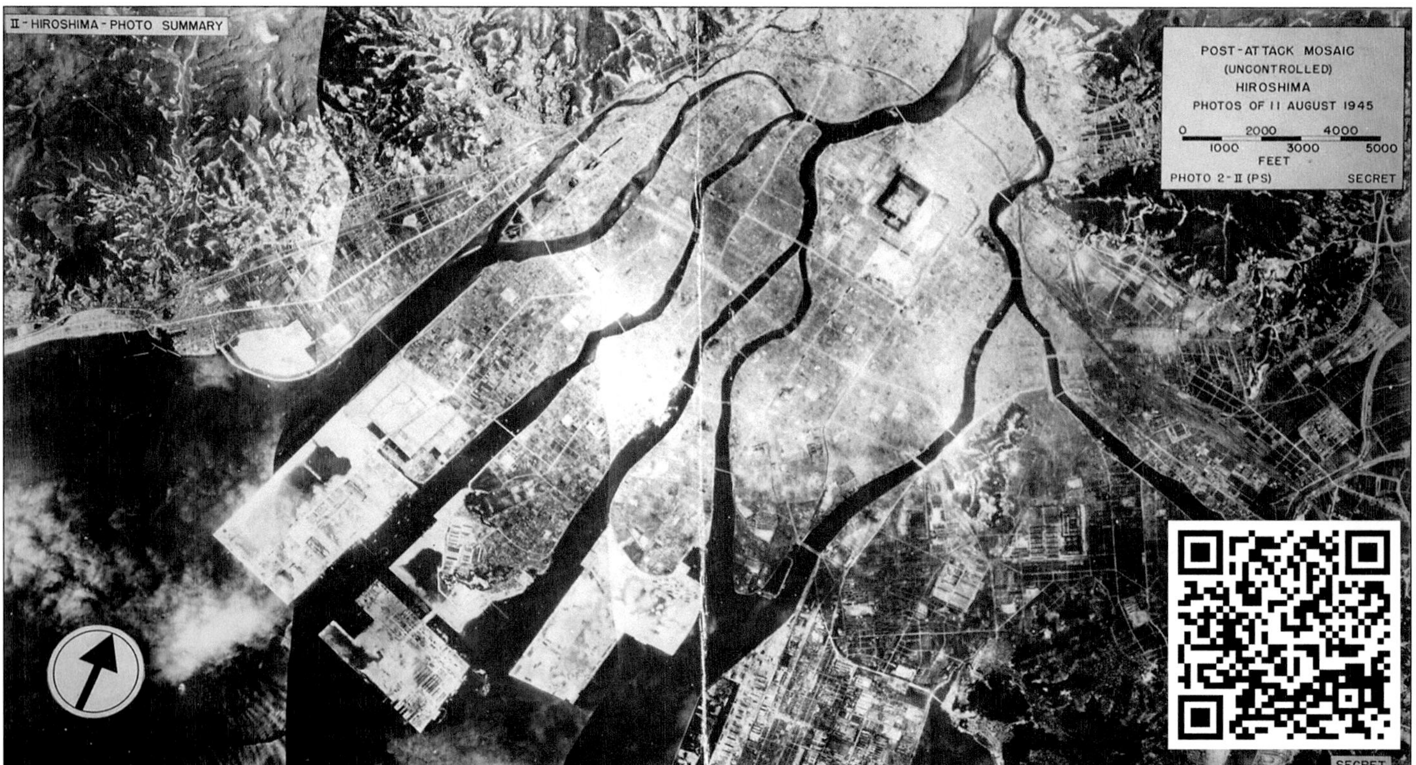

Effects of Atomic Bomb on Hiroshima And Nagasaki. (YouTube/Rebels to Reels)

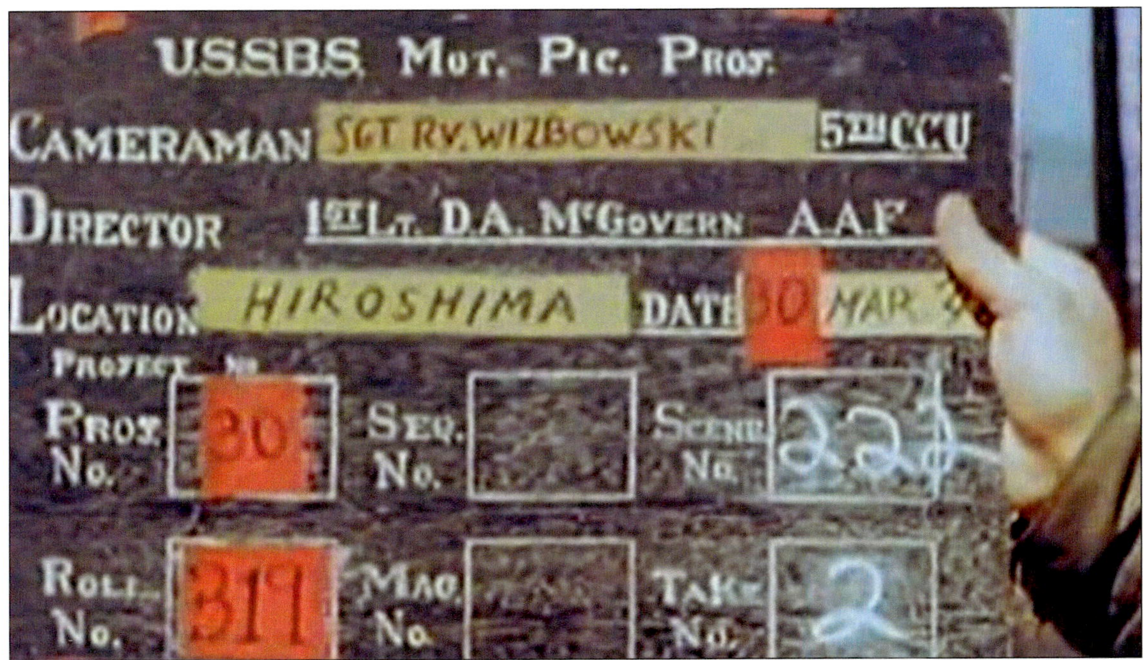

A slate from 30 March 1946 on McGovern's film. This high-quality unedited footage illustrates the blast effects on selected buildings in Hiroshima. (YouTube/NARA)

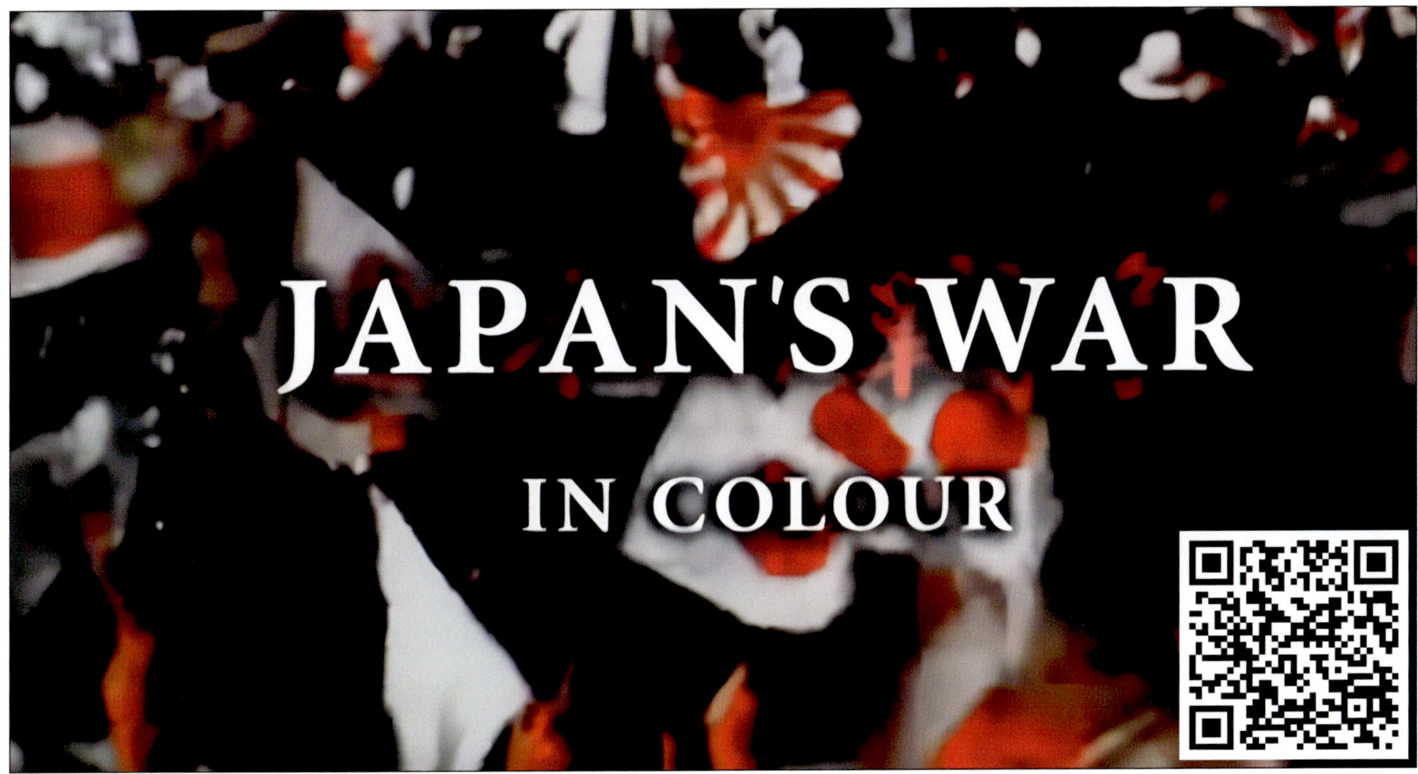

Japan's War in Colour contains sequences from one hour and nine minutes onwards from Nagasaki, Astugi airfield and elsewhere. Other high-quality B-29 and P-51 sequences almost certainly come from USAAF Combat Camera Units. (YouTube/World War II Colour Films)

The film documentation of the nuclear tests was elaborate. These included recording the preparation of the weapon, loading it onto an aircraft or its installation in a test tower. The inside of the test control centre, the monitoring instrumentation, weapon delivery, detonation and subsequent debris spread and the mushroom 'cloud'. Cameras were set up to capture the effects of detonations on people, vehicles, parked aircraft, buildings, ships, protected accommodation and an extensive array of other subjects. *Target Nevada* (SFP 281), filmed between 1949 and 1951, recorded features of some of the 20 atom bomb tests conducted in the Nevada desert. It documents Air Force support of the AEC-led tests that included 14 USAF air-dropped weapons by 'USAF Special Weapons Command' from Indian Springs AF Base.

The extreme effects created by nuclear weapon detonation meant cameras often had to be placed at safe distances from ground zero. Other, usually very high-speed cameras, intended to monitor the effects of heat, light, radiation and blast effects on structures and equipment, had to be placed in locations where they could effectively capture their subject and survive the detonation effects. Particularly for the high-speed cameras, their operation had to be carefully timed to ensure they captured the action at the appropriate stage of the detonation before exhausting their film.

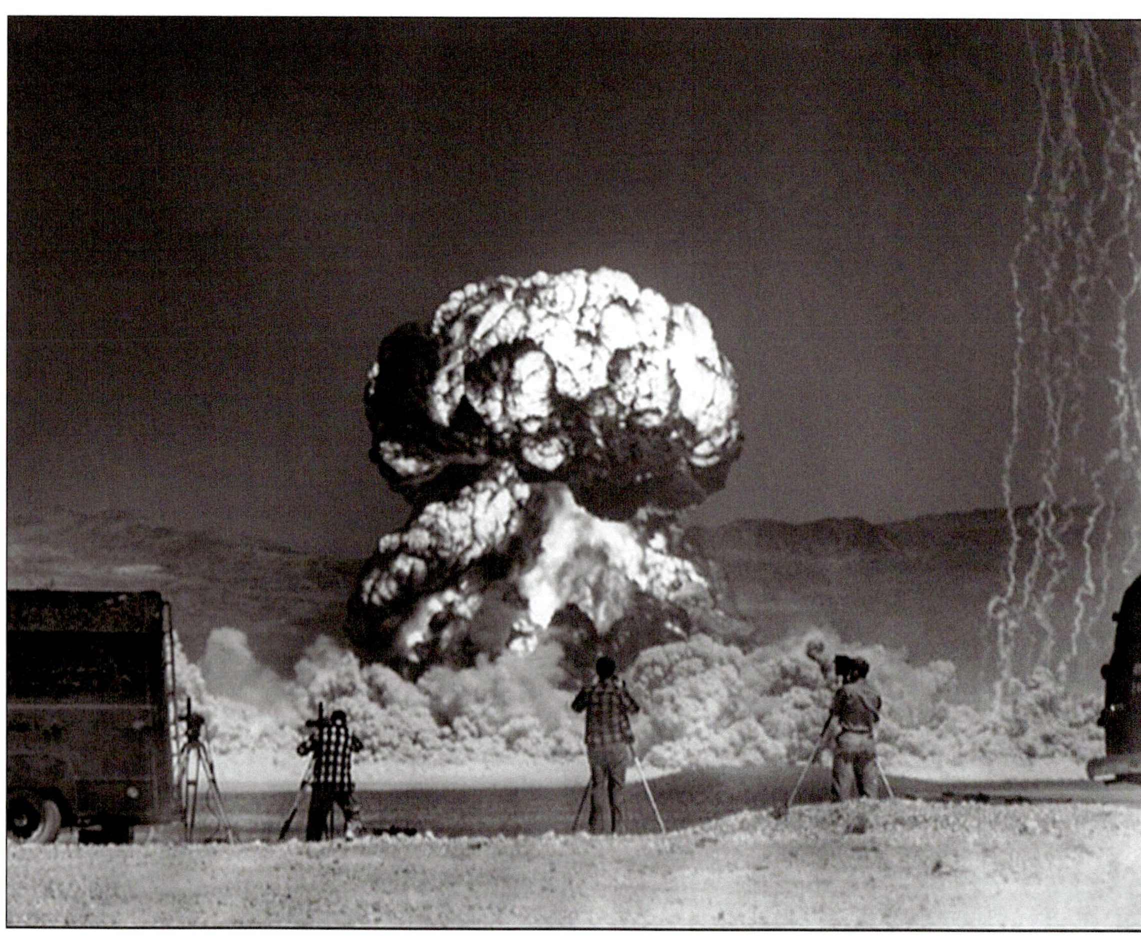

The Nevada Proving Grounds were the location for large numbers of atmospheric nuclear tests in the 1950s and underground tests up to 1992. (AEC)

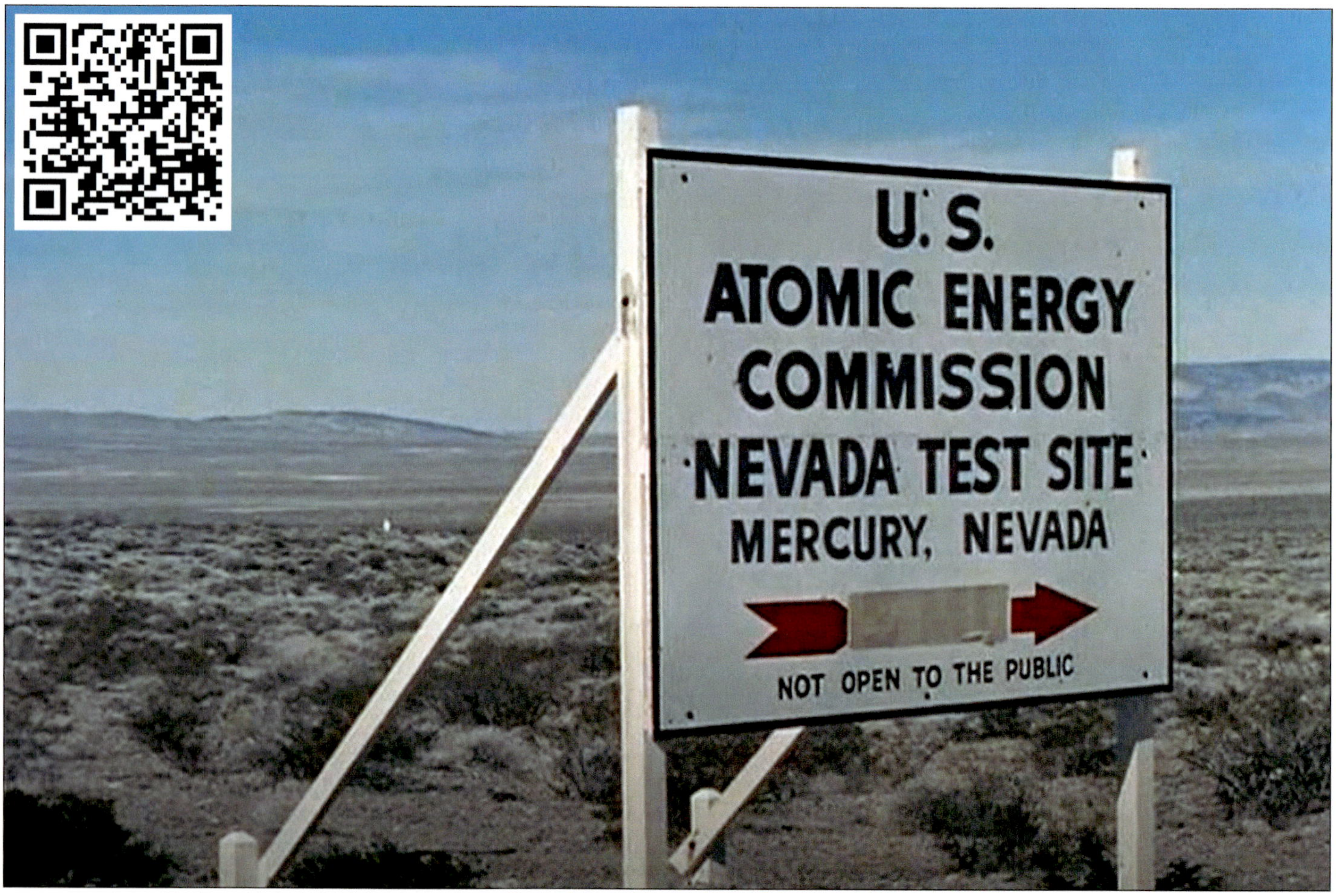

Target Nevada records a series of nuclear tests conducted in the Nevada desert during 1951. It includes some high-speed footage of the damage caused by blast waves on equipment. (YouTube/Nuclear Vault)

While the vast majority of the film material captured was highly classified and used by the AEC and DoD for their purposes, some information was released for public consumption to explain why this very exhaustive test programme was taking place. Significant amounts of the film imagery collected would also be reused in later films produced by the armed services and other federal agencies.

One of the most detailed public releases covered Operation Ivy, the 1952 tests at Enewetak Atoll in the Marshall Islands. In the hour-long film, the introduction makes clear that this is just a 'a non-secret portion of a secret film'. A fascinating production, it documents the 'Mike Shot', then the largest detonation of the time, the first multi-megaton H-bomb test measured at 10.9 Megatons. It was filmed by a large team of cameramen and edited and produced at Lookout Mountain by an Atomic Energy Commission and Department of Defense Team.

Nuclear Training Films

As well as documenting the process and effects of nuclear weapons for scientific, technical and personnel purposes, training films were produced to cover a myriad of topics revolving around the assembly, storage and deployment of atomic weapons.

Another dimension of related activity was corporate-produced films, that covered the work of commercial companies working on new missiles and weapons, like Thor and Minuteman. The materials and equipment these companies produced were often filmed by AAVS personnel at military installations, test locations such as Vandenberg AFB, or at individual operational Missile Wing and Squadron bases, with the footage produced by commercial studios. These films ranged from descriptions of whole programmes to major sub-contractors wanting to illustrate their part in a specific

The efforts to measure the effects of nuclear weapons are particularly well described in a film about the 11 test explosions of Operation Upshot Knothole at the Nevada testing grounds in 1953. (YouTube/Nuclear Vault)

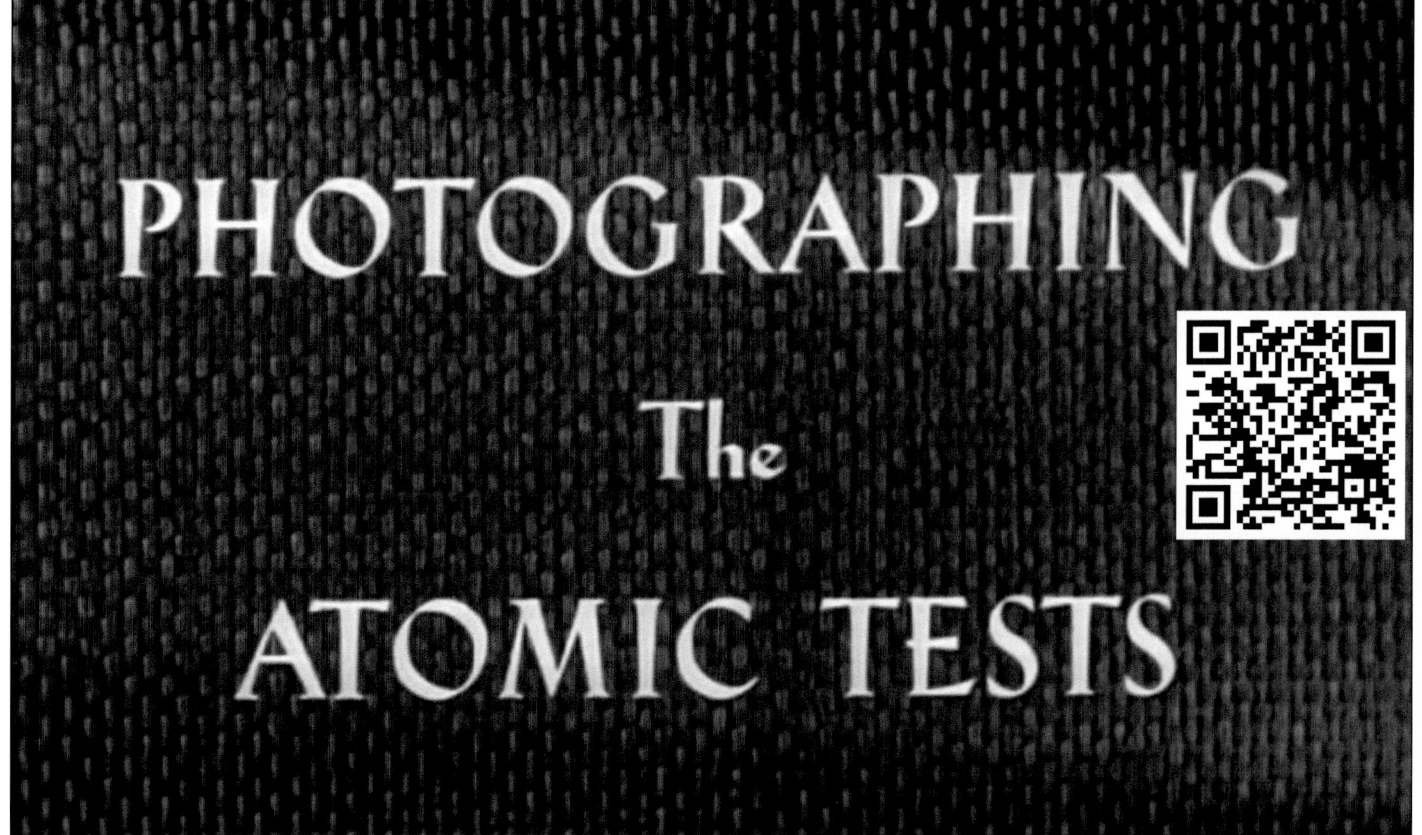

A detailed, high-quality, 10-minute documentary explains some of the camera and film preparations involved in documenting the three 1948 'Sandstone' nuclear tests on Eniwetok Atoll and the subsequent processing and post-production work on the footage at the Lookout Mountain AFS studios. (YouTube/AtomCentral)

programme. One example is the manufacture of rocket fuel by the Thiokol Chemical Corporation, involved in developing missile propulsion technology and fuel for the Minuteman missile.

These films were sometimes also adopted for Air Force use. This was the case with a Boeing-produced film nominally describing the introduction of the Minuteman missile to FE Warren AFB in approximately 1962. It illustrated the construction and handover programme for the launch silos and support facilities to the Air Force and favourably portrayed the company's considerable role in the construction of the USAF's strategic missile programme.

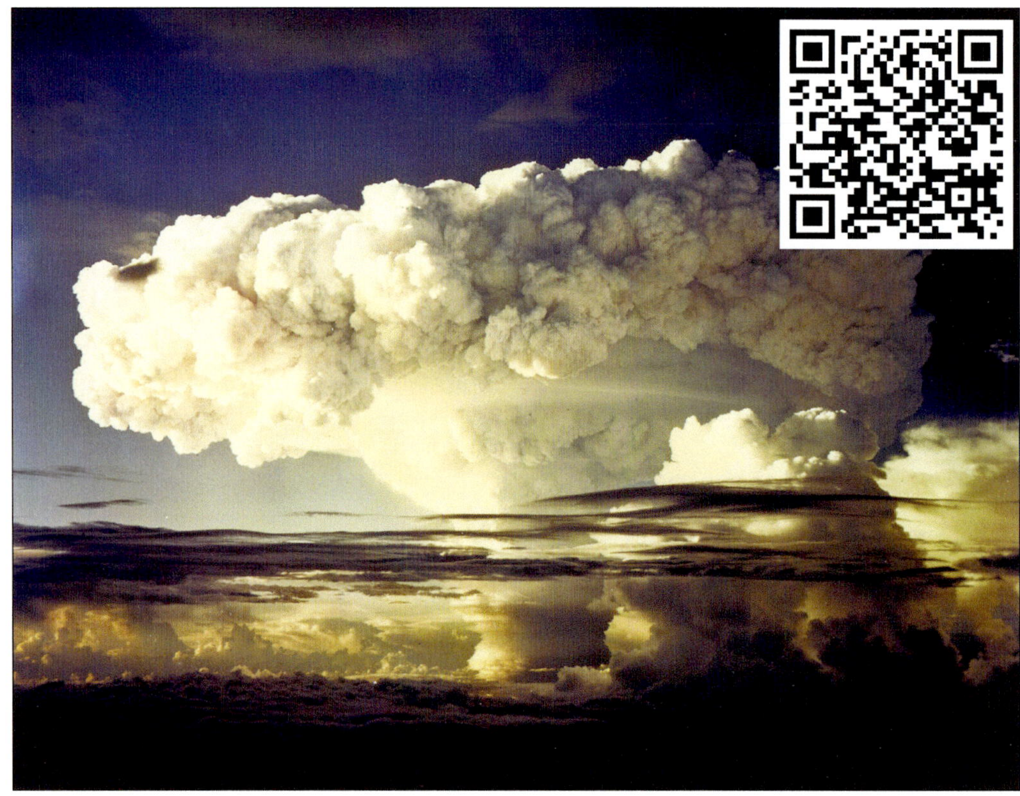

Left: Operation Ivy was a two weapon atmospheric nuclear test series at Enewetak Atoll in October and November 1952. Explosion Mike was the first US hydrogen bomb. (YouTube/PeriscopeFilm)

Below: For many major projects, like the Minuteman missile, USAF Photographic Squadrons often worked with major contractors to produce corporate films illustrating the development of their products. (YouTube/PeriscopeFilm)

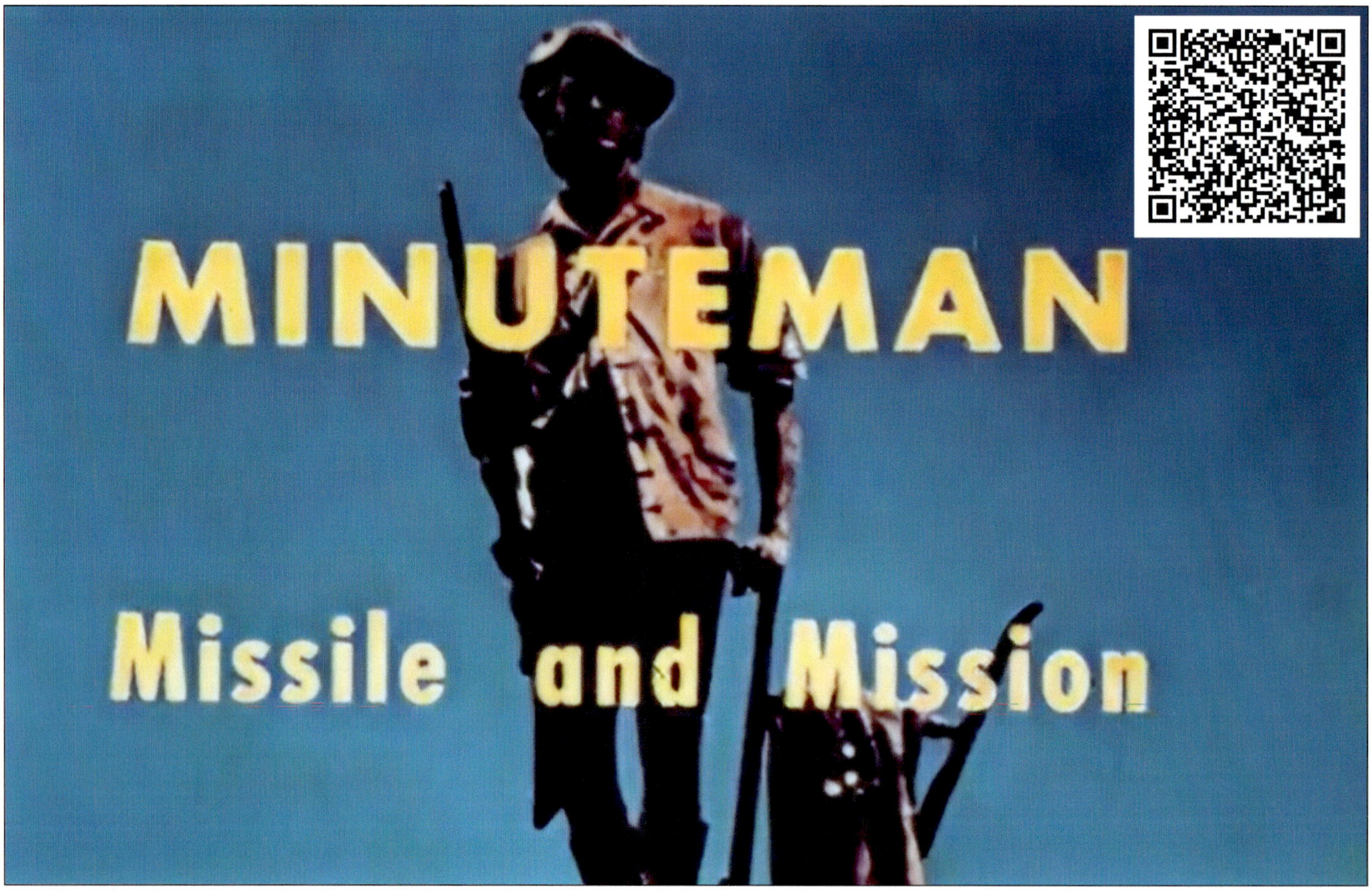

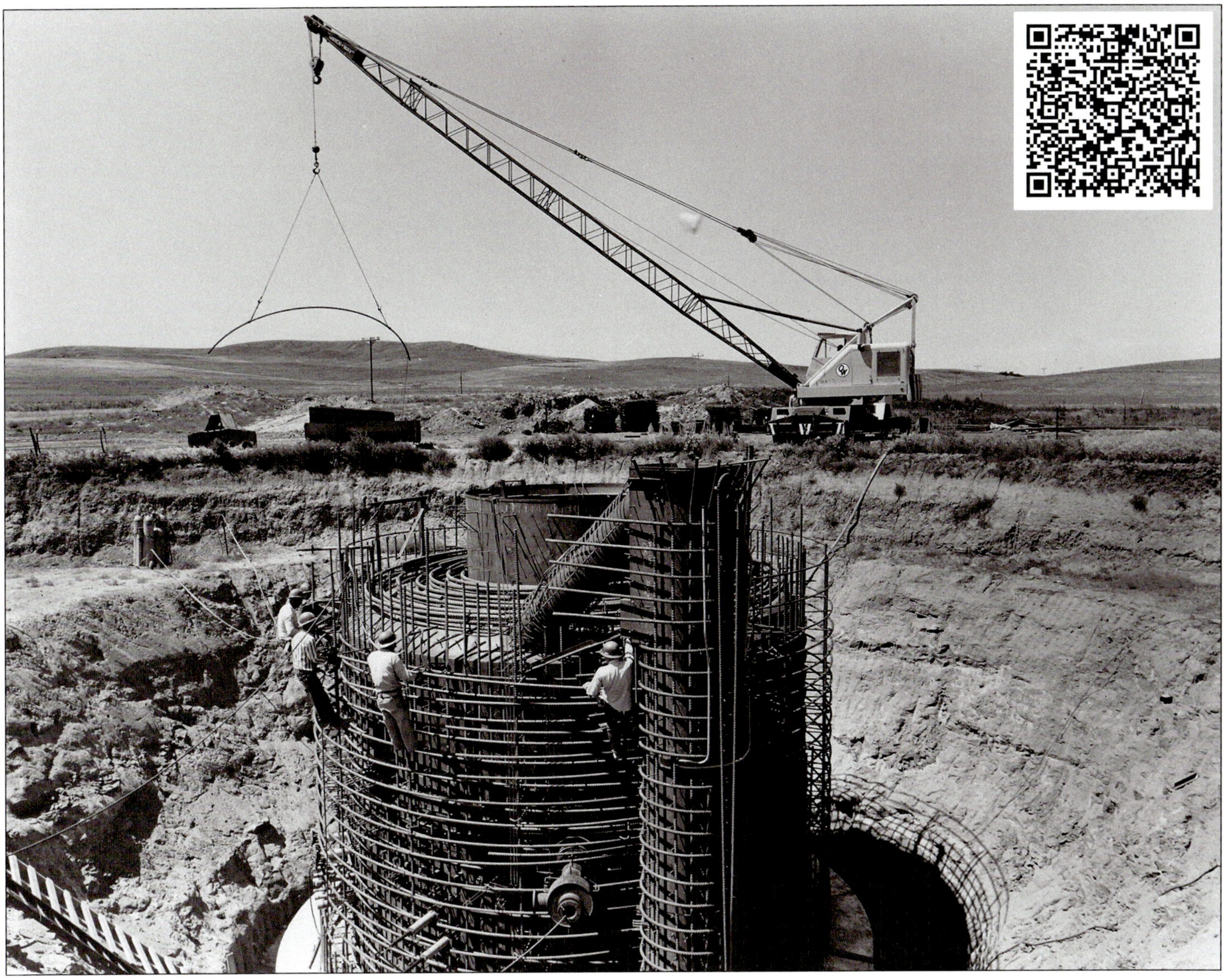

Minuteman in the West. The construction of Minuteman missile silos and launch facilities were major civil engineering tasks. Senior USAF commanders and Boeing representatives wanted regular briefings on their progress. (YouTube/PeriscopeFilm)

The possible impacts and effects of nuclear weapons in bomber mission planning and execution were vital considerations for the crews involved. A 1960 Air Force film, *Nuclear Effects During SAC Delivery Missions* (TF I-5363) declassified in 1985, addresses these issues in some detail. It describes how bomber routes were planned and de-conflicted and the effects crews could expect to encounter when airborne during and after the detonation of the weapons. (YouTube/PeriscopeFilm)

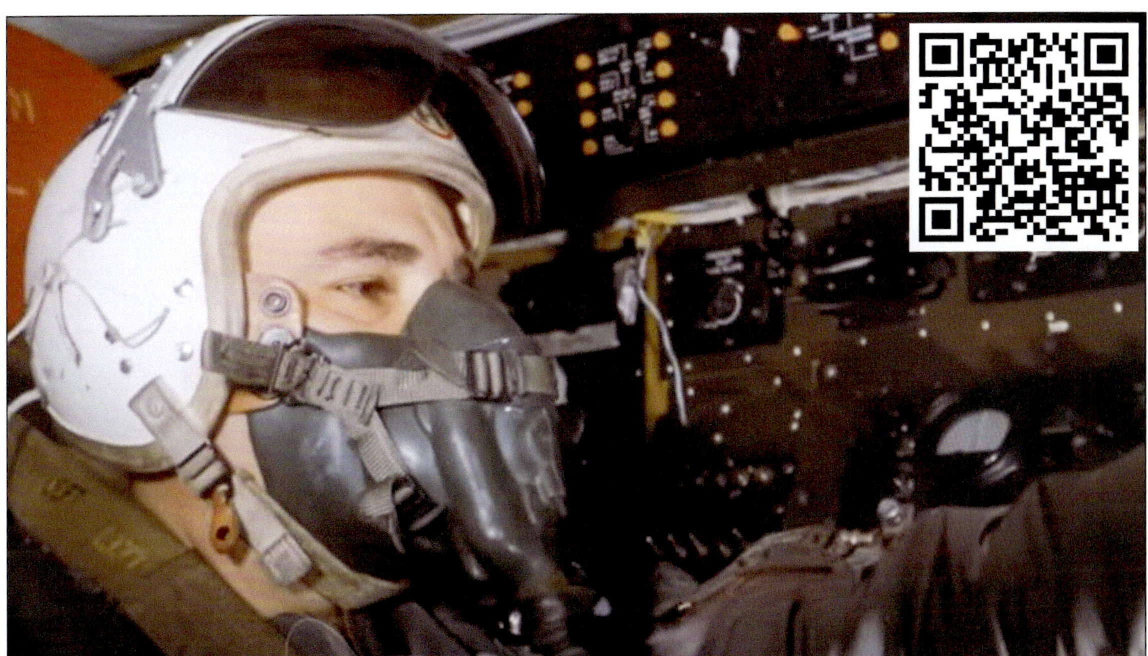

In documentary and movie footage over the years, considerable attention has been aired covering missile silo operations and the SAC War Operations Room and Command Post at Offutt AFB. The extensive maintenance requirements of nuclear missiles are often forgotten at the unclassified level. Another undated, 30-minute AAVS presentation titled *Primed for Defense -The Minuteman* captures some of the general issues involved in concentrating on a missile site assigned to Whiteman AFB. It describes the missile's design, deployment, day-to-day operations and some of the procedures involved in dealing with faults that can develop in operational missiles.

However, films like *Primed for Defense* only scratch the surface of the photographic material produced. Because of the security classifications in place, it is difficult to gather any reliable figure of just how much material has been made for internal Air Force use, over the life of the Minuteman missile so far. However, reference to a 423-page list of films offered to the US National Archives (NARA) by the US Department of Defense, between 1990 and 1996, identifies 96 references to classified and unclassified Minuteman missile-related films. Many of these document missile test launches from Vandenberg AFB, with others covering particular components of the system and its development from the late 1950s into the early 1970s.[5] Trying to assess the scale of AAVS input to coverage of the Minuteman system over its lifetime, has to be tempered with observations that this list reflects only surplus, no longer considered useful, material that the DoD was prepared to transfer out of its control to NARA. Therefore, the size of the AAVS effort in producing film material for just this single, though very important, missile system is likely to be several orders of magnitude larger.

AAVS training materials did not just cover offensive nuclear operations. In 1968, the 1358th Motion Picture Squadron from Wright-Patterson AFB produced a film entitled *Survive to Fight*. This film dealt with the necessary preparations made at an unnamed fighter base for installations to survive and continue to function after a nuclear attack.

Broken Arrows

It was not just wartime nuclear detonations for which SAC and AAVS made training materials. Preparations were also made for peacetime incidents involving nuclear weapons – 'Broken Arrow' events. A 1962 film goes through the planning for and associated training exercise for a declared emergency aboard an incoming B-52 with nuclear weapons on board and the measures to mitigate its possible effects. Many such films would have required updating as the organisations involved and their procedures evolved.

During the Cold War, several Broken Arrow incidents involved missiles or bombs on board SAC aircraft. Most such events are usually at least classified as 'Secret'. However, in the case of armed aircraft crashes in major incidents, such as over Palomares in Spain on 17 January 1966, the events are difficult to hide entirely from public gaze. In such eventualities, emergency response teams are dispatched to the scene to deal with incidents and their aftermath. Other than the bare minimum, few further details are rarely released.

In another incident, on 13 March 1961, B-52F 57-0166 took off from Mather AFB in California. It was on a Chrome Dome mission and carried two Mk 39 hydrogen bombs. Soon after take-off, the pilot, Major Raymond Clay, felt too much hot air was coming from the cockpit vents. He and his copilot, 1st Lt Bingham, tried to turn off the heat.

The air vents refused to close, and it became incredibly hot in the cockpit. Almost seven hours into the flight, their base instructed them to continue their mission as long as possible. At 14 hours, the cockpit temperature reached 160 degrees Fahrenheit. One of the pilot's windows shattered in the extreme heat. Clay again requested permission to end the mission.

Passing through an overcast sky, the B-52 flew off course and fell approximately 30 minutes behind schedule. At 22 hours into the flight, Lt Bigham realised one of the aircraft's main fuel tank gauges was broken. The reading had not changed for at least 90 minutes, but nobody had noticed. The crew requested Mather to send a tanker. Forty minutes later, approaching the tanker, the B-52 ran out of fuel,

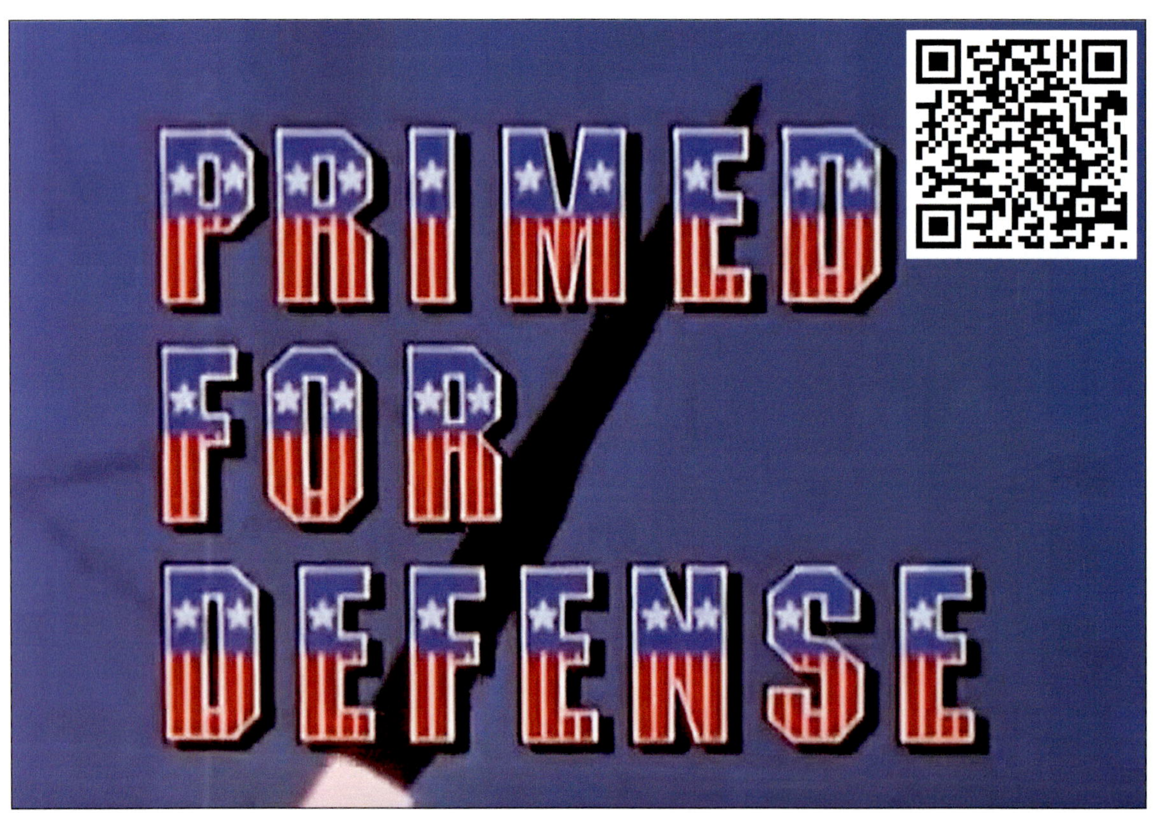

Primed for Defense was intended to give an unclassified glimpse into the complex operations of the Minuteman missile. (YouTube/Association of Air Force Missileers)

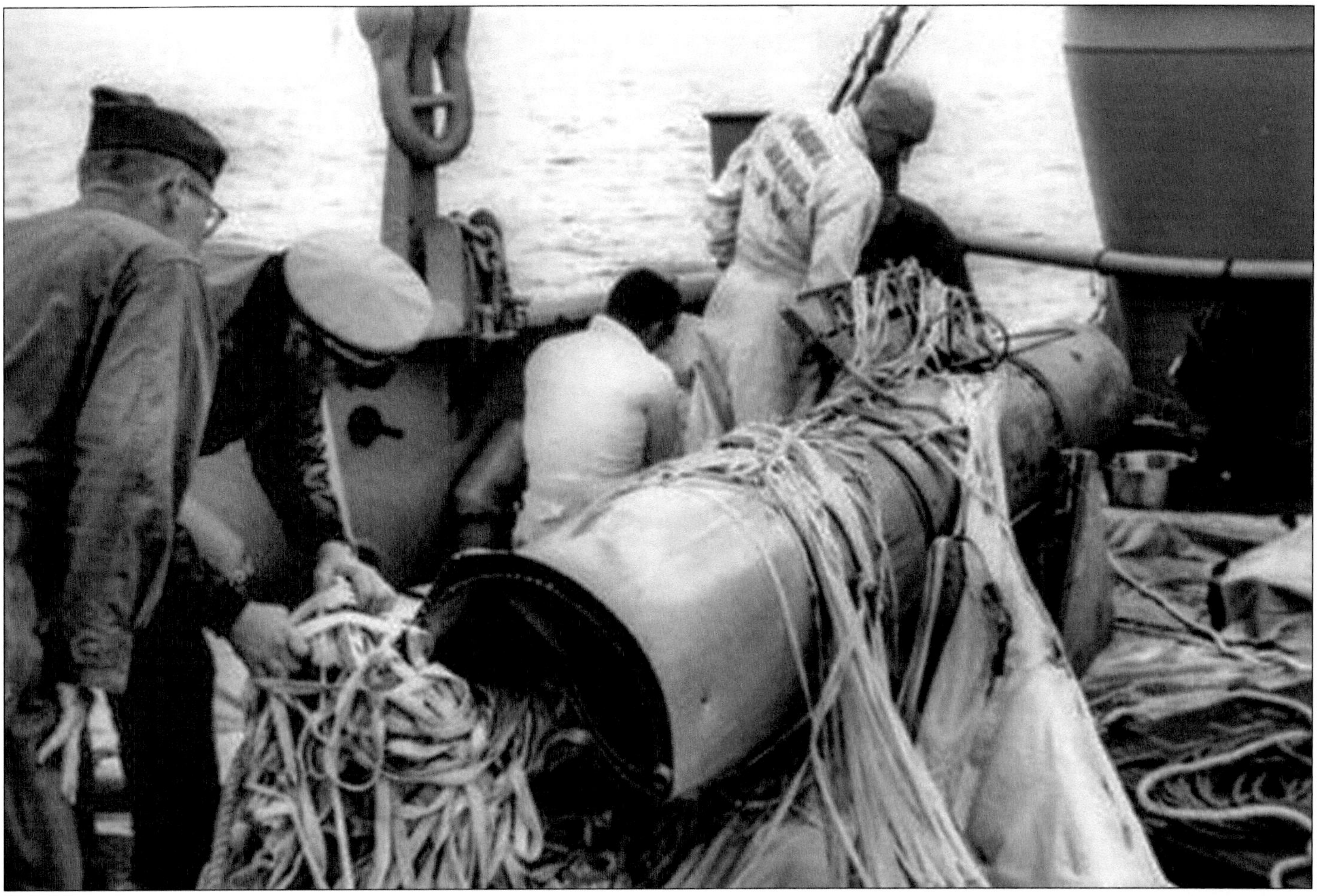

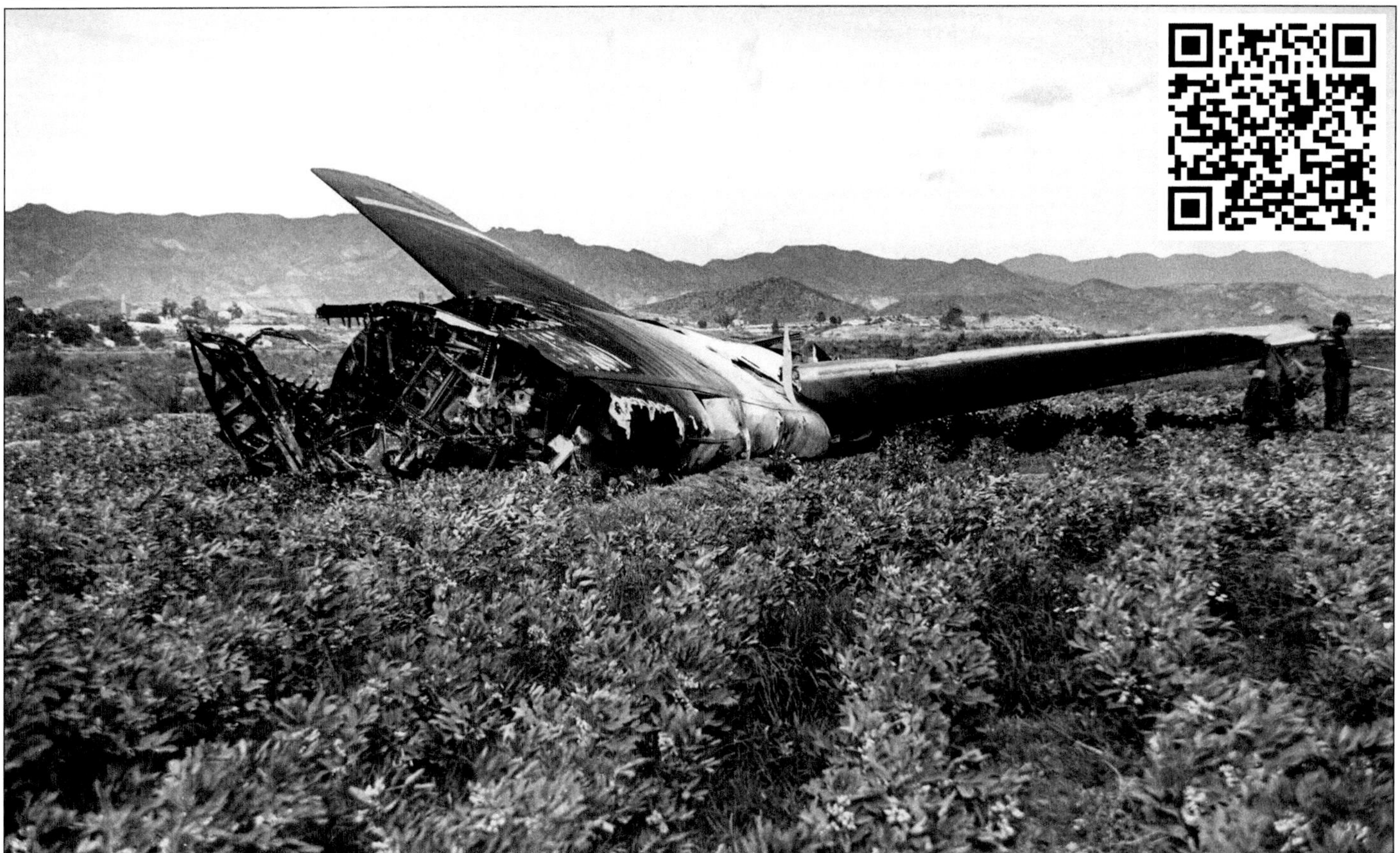

The collision between a KC-135A and B-52G on a 'Chrome Dome' mission on 17 January 1966, near Palomares, Spain, killed four tanker crew members and three from the B-52. It produced significant local contamination and search for the four missing Mk 28 nuclear weapons received international news coverage. The final Mk 28 from the incident was eventually recovered after four months by a Spanish fishing boat during a massive search. (YouTube/NAS Archive)

and all eight engines flamed out at once. At 7,000 feet, the crew began bailing out. Major Clay stayed in the cockpit and successfully banked the bomber away from Yuba City, just 40 miles from their base. Sure that the bomber would miss the town, Clay ejected at 4,000 feet.

The B-52 made a complete 360-degree turn and crashed nose-first into a field. The high explosives of both hydrogen bombs shattered on impact and, very luckily, did not burn or detonate. The weapons harmlessly broke into pieces. All eight crew members survived the crash, but an Air Force fireman rushing to the scene was killed when his truck overturned.[6]

Very unusually, the Department of Energy has declassified and released a film of the crash site without sound, although several scenes remain deleted. The film was shot by a 1365th PS member of the APCS; it contains images of Lt Gen JW Wilson and his Disaster Response Team from SAC HQ examining documents, looking over radios, cameras and radiation monitoring devices as they headed by aircraft to the incident. Boarding an Air Force bus, a film slate identifies the 1365th PS photographer as 'Grimaldi'. On-scene images show Air Force personnel and civilians looking over and recording the crash site. Most of the aircraft was reduced to tiny fragments, but the film shows the B-52's '0166' tail number. Some airborne imagery of the site is taken from a low-flying helicopter.

For Public Consumption

Some of the material gathered for internal documentation and training was used in highly produced public information material. These aimed to reassure the public or favourably depict the strength of the US Air Force and its role. This was particularly so during phases of the Cold War when the fears of nuclear confrontation were at their highest. Were such productions simply public information films, or could they more realistically be viewed as propaganda when they showed the flawless functioning of an organisation like SAC and its plan in an incredibly complex situation? Indeed, that label was applied to films like SFP-1236 'SAC Command Post', a high production value colour film. However, its exact production date and explanation for the subsequent lack of public distribution remain unclear.

The 'US National Security Archive', at George Washington University has identified that at least some of the filming for this production took place after June 1963. They suggest the film was intended to counter the controversy caused by the movie *Dr Strangelove*, the 1958 book *Red Alert* by British author Peter George, and a similar book by Eugene Burdick and Harvey Wheeler. *Fail-Safe*, published in 1962, was about a US-Soviet crisis caused by the accidental transmission of attack orders to SAC bombers. Or perhaps SFP-1236 was simply an attempt to put SAC's side of the story? Whatever the reality, it provides a fascinating window into an otherwise closed world.[7]

The 1966 US Air Force film *The Strength of SAC* (SFP-1448) took a different approach. It sought to illustrate the vast range of tasks undertaken by all those assigned to Strategic Air Command, emphasising their importance in fulfilling its nuclear deterrent role.

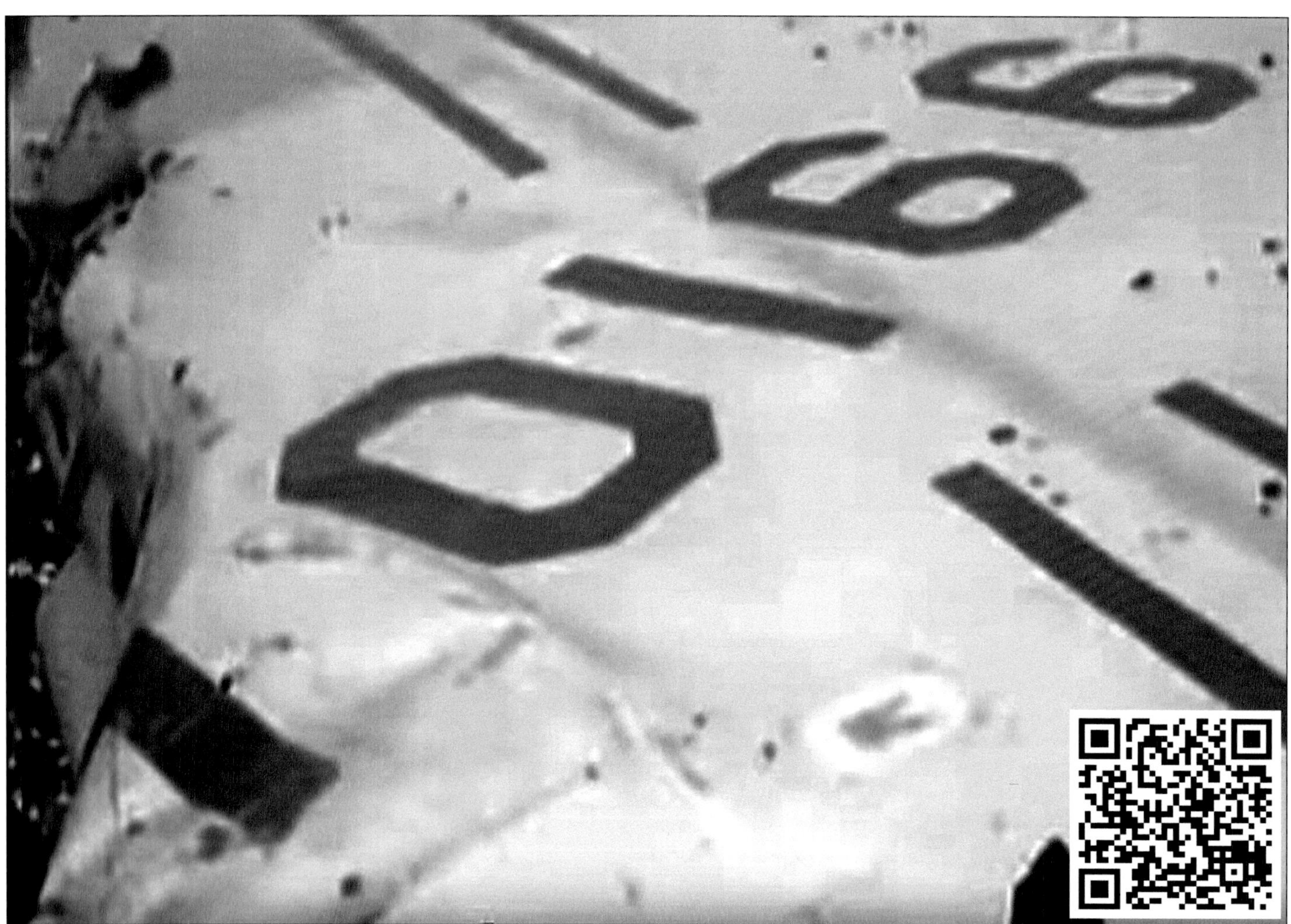

Combat cameramen were always important to the teams that documented and investigated Broken Arrow events. However, it is very rare for footage of them to be de-classified. It makes the material from the 13 March 1961 crash of B-52F 57-0166 even more valuable. (YouTube/Nuclear Vault)

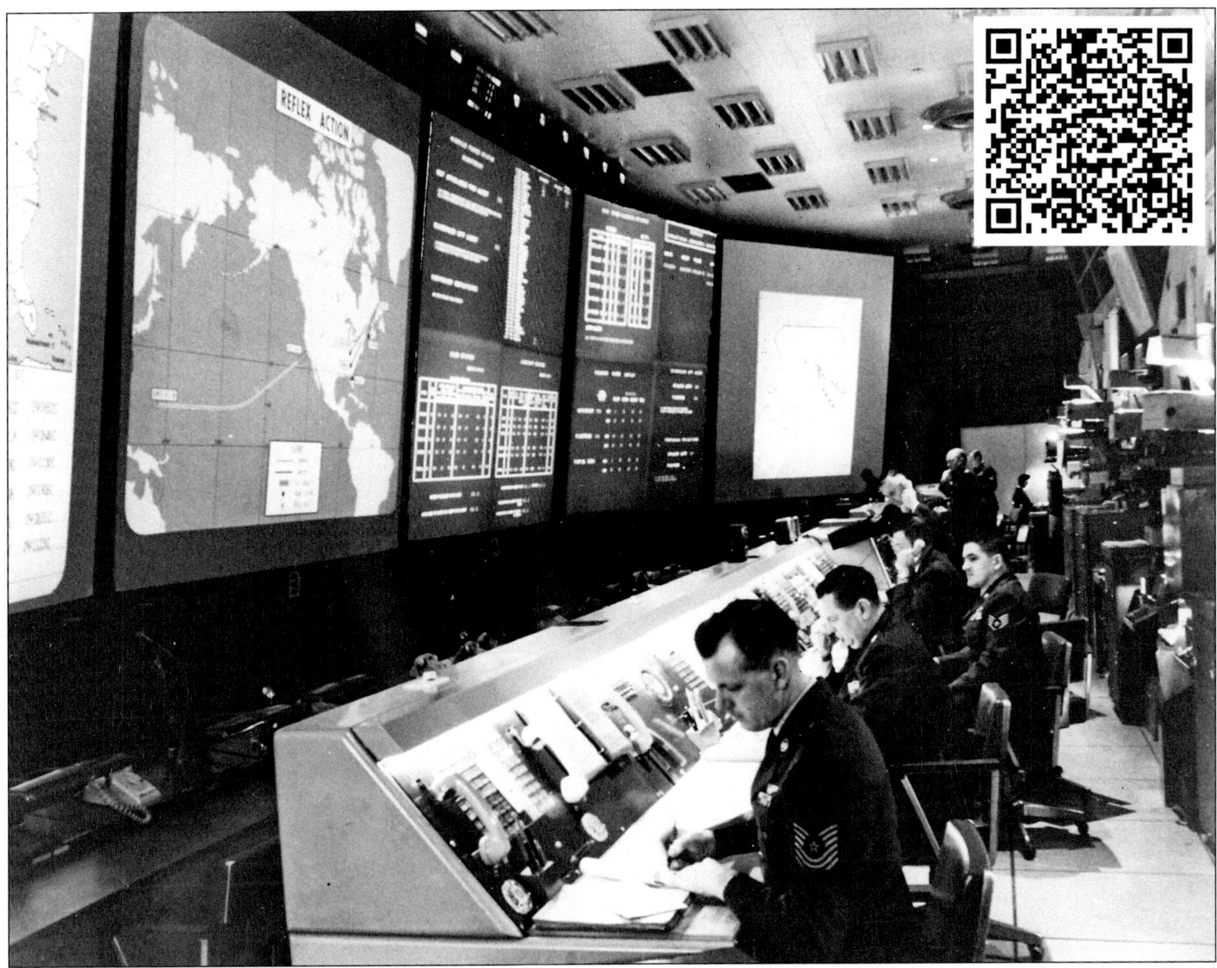

From 1963–64, *SAC Command Post*, was a high production value film showing how SAC's command and control system worked. Some saw this unclassified film as an attempt to counter the then very popular satirical movie *Dr Strangelove*. (YouTube/Nuclear Vault)

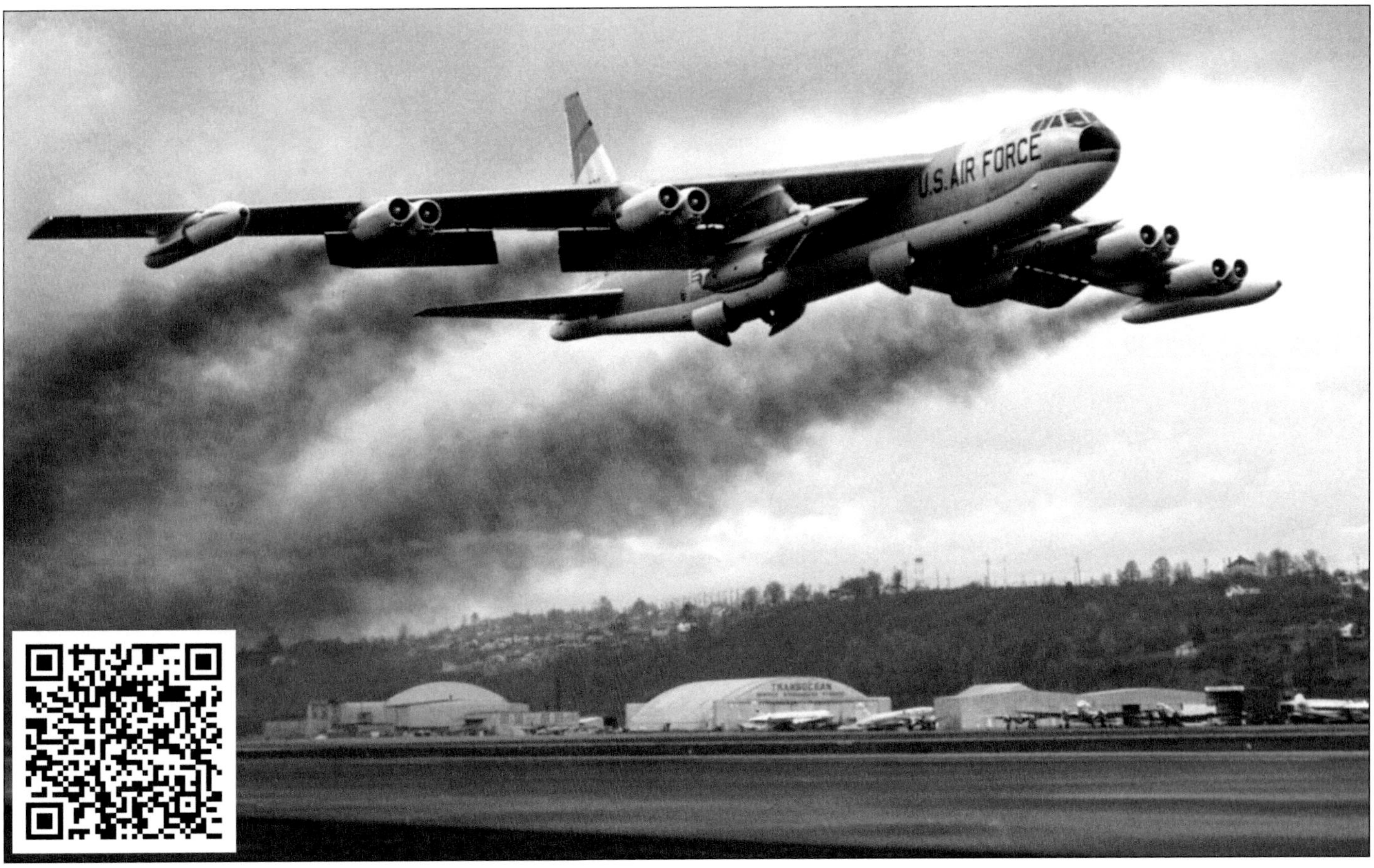

The Strength of SAC. (YouTube/PeriscopeFilm)

4

ACTION IN KOREA

Frequently referred to as a 'forgotten conflict', the North Korean invasion caught US forces and everyone else largely unprepared. The US and its allies, working under the authority of the United Nations, began to assemble and dispatch military forces to shore-up South Korea as quickly as they could.

During the Korean War, US military capabilities were quickly strengthened. After the 1945 victory over Japan, virtually all the remaining elements of the US Air Force's photographic capabilities disappeared. What remained was primarily invested in a few strategic and tactical reconnaissance squadrons and the mapping units of the APCS. Combat Camera capabilities had been almost totally neglected, with very few USAF personnel engaged in combat documentation tasks.

This capability gap can be directly explained by the immediate contraction of US forces in the immediate post-war period. The end of World War Two saw the rapid demobilisation of the Combat Camera Units, as the USAAF quickly divested itself of many wartime capabilities, including any expected need for combat documentation and mass training films.

Constituted in September 1947, the now independent US Air Force was still a 'new' service and in a constant state of reorganisation. The Air Force's vital photographic reconnaissance capabilities had suffered before the Korean War. Strategic reconnaissance resided with a few specialist F-13s. These were B-29s modified for photographic tasks over the Pacific towards the end of the Second World War. Their camera equipment came from that time and, under the control of Strategic Air Command, was now mainly devoted to reconnaissance tasks over the Arctic and Europe. Later in the Korean War, a few dedicated F-13/RB-29 aircraft were used for reconnaissance operations against the Soviet and Chinese coastlines, as were a few specialised RB-45C, RF-80, and RF-86 missions. The 67th Tactical Reconnaissance Group performed tactical reconnaissance

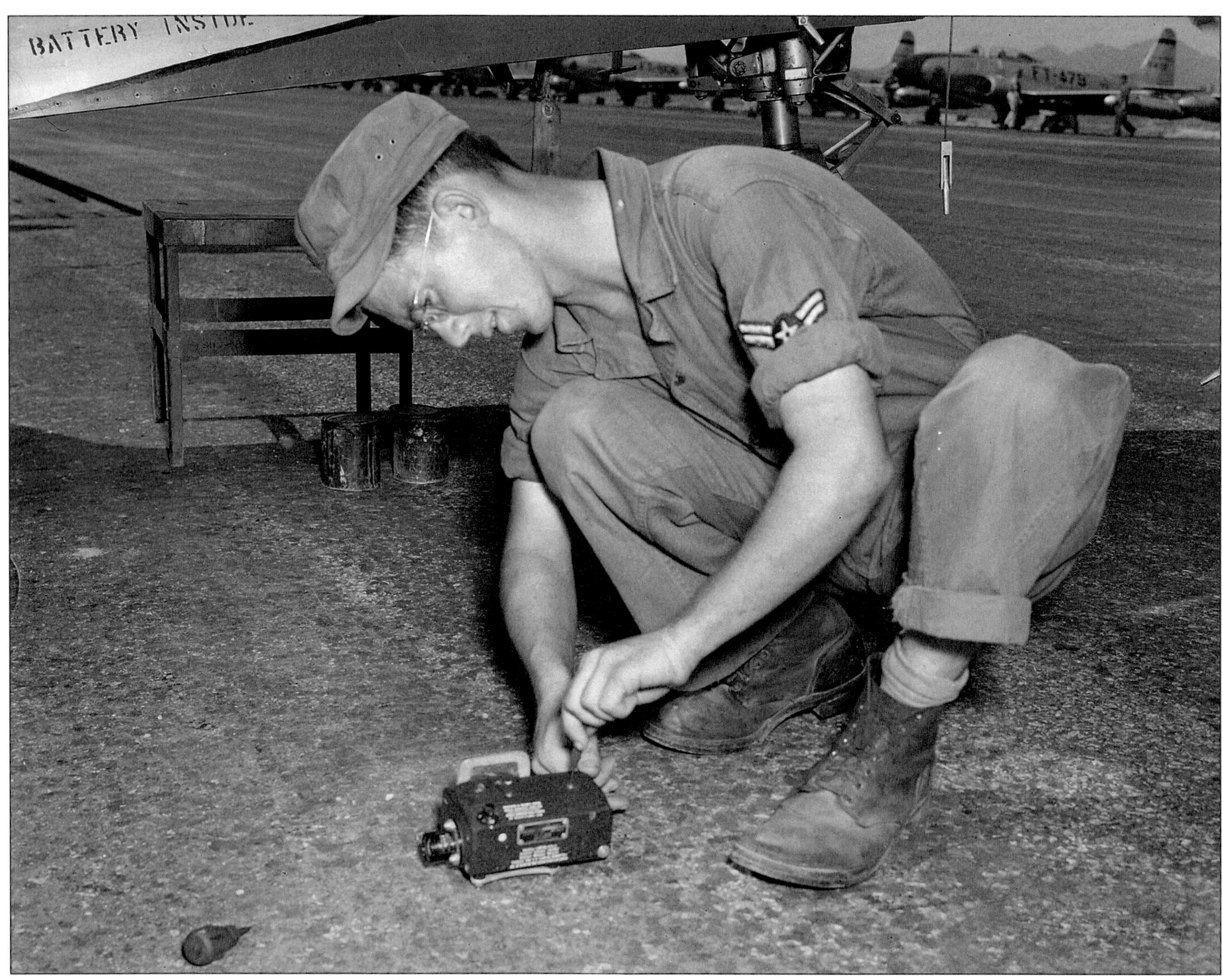

Apart from the F-80s in the background, this could be an image from 1945 of a camera technician working on a gun camera. (NARA)

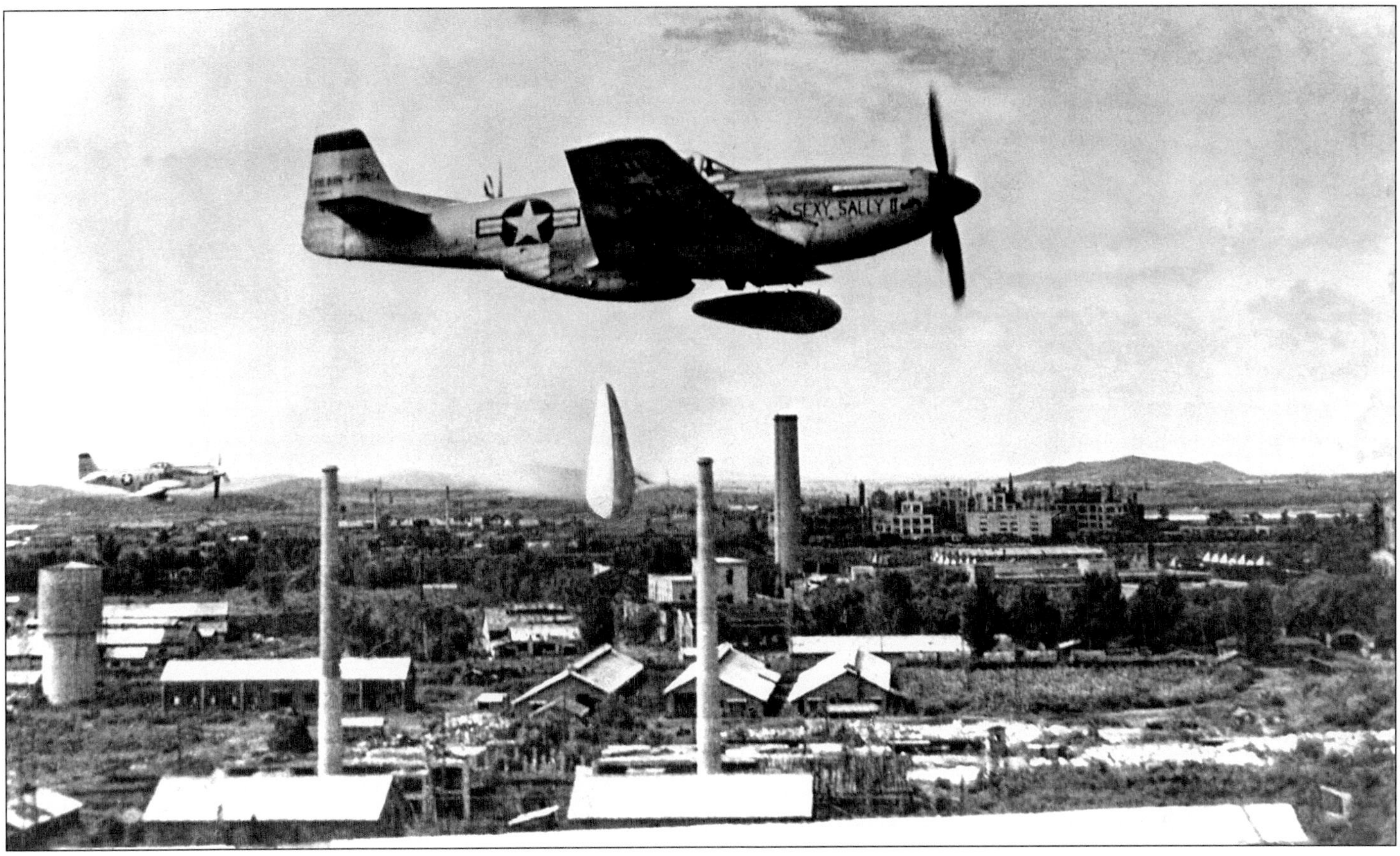

An 18th FBW P-51D releases two napalm bombs over an industrial target in North Korea in 1951. (NARA)

missions using RB-26s, RF-51s, and RF-80s. The reconnaissance imagery collected concentrated on pre and post-strike imagery and some gun camera film. The reconnaissance units struggled with a lack of trained personnel and insufficient and often inadequate equipment.

The Air Pictorial Service was created on 1 April 1951, but on 16 April 1952, it was re-designated as the Air Photographic and Charting Service (APCS) within the Military Air Transport Service. The 6204th Photo Mapping Flight was, in mid-July 1950, located at Clark AB in the Philippines. It deployed the flight's two RB-17 aircraft, complete with combat crews and maintenance personnel, to Johnson AB, Japan. Their RB-17s had been flying peacetime missions and were not equipped for combat. However, by late August 1950, once they had found the necessary gunners and equipment, the detachment began flying photo-mapping missions over Korea. By the end of November 1950, it had photographed the entire North Korean area at least once.

The Air Force largely neglected extensive combat documentation. However, the Navy, Army and Marine Corps were more active in that field. The available USAF combat documentation imagery

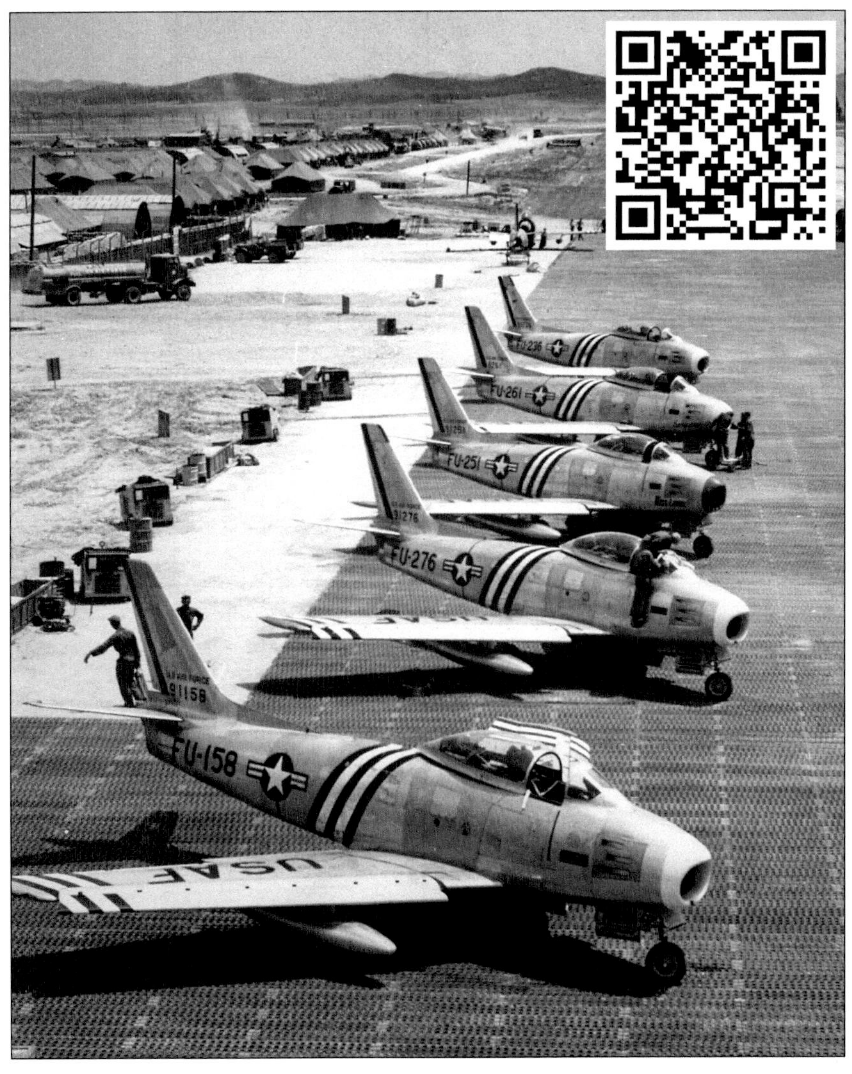

Korea was the first war in which jet fighters were engaged in combat in large numbers by the protagonists. A short unedited film of F-86s being armed and prepared for operations at Taegu AB in South Korea. (NARA)

from the Korean War was primarily aerial shots of B-29s dropping bombs, some gun camera films, air-to-air still imagery and ground-based photography. However, it was not of the systematic nature created in World War Two or would later be achieved during the Vietnam period. Most imagery from this 'Forgotten War' came from civilian photojournalists and the other US services.

Jo Longo in Korea

World War Two cameraman Jo Longo has provided one of the few available detailed accounts of combat cameramen and their work during the Korean War. He said:

> When I got out of the service the first time, I was in the inactive reserve and then recalled to active duty because they really needed combat cameramen, World War Two guys, because I guess, they didn't have any other more recently trained personnel. So they called me back, and I was stationed on the West Coast. I got a call one morning to do some air-to-air refuelling of aircraft on their way to the combat zone.

Longo accompanied them to Asia. Once there his orders kept getting extended, 'I wound up in Korea, at an Air Force installation there'.

Longo said things had not changed much in Korea since World War Two:

> We had different uniforms. In 1947, the Air Force changed from brown to blue. But that didn't mean anything because we were so under-supplied and under-stocked in Korea that I was still wearing flight clothes from some guy who had worn them in the 8th Air Force in England. They just never got around to us. We were a rag-tag bunch. The equipment was the same; we used the same cameras against the enemy; the emphasis was on more of a ground operation.

> Our B-29s flew out of Japan but were limited in what they could do. It was harder to shoot fighter strikes because the Koreans were using MiGs. They flew almost twice the speed of the Japanese Zeros had come in at, making the job even more difficult. Plus, the fact that you were shooting out of a fuselage bubble. The B-29 was a larger aircraft, and you could move around it slightly more easily. But shooting out of a B-29 was very difficult because you didn't have much of a shooting area. In the B-24, the waist window had an almost 18 x 24-inch opening there. And you could have a lot of peripheral vision. In Korea, we relied on the many mounted cameras to get the bomb strikes and a small handheld camera for the rest of the action. A head-on fighter attack was very difficult. They'd come right at you and even in the nose, which was a good area to shoot out of because there was a lot of plexiglass; you could see these fighters coming in. They were challenging to capture when they came in at you at jet speed, fast and firing heavy ammunition. I think I was more frightened in my short tour in Korea than I had been in the Pacific during World War Two from 1942 to 1945.

After Korea, while reconnaissance and mapping capabilities were reconstructed, combat camera-related activities soon moved emphasis to concentrate on the development of nuclear weapons and doctrine, the missiles and aircraft of Strategic Air Command. Tactical Air Command and Aerospace Defense Command were not completely neglected as the Air Force sought to demonstrate the ever-growing reach of air power as Cold War rivalry deepened further.

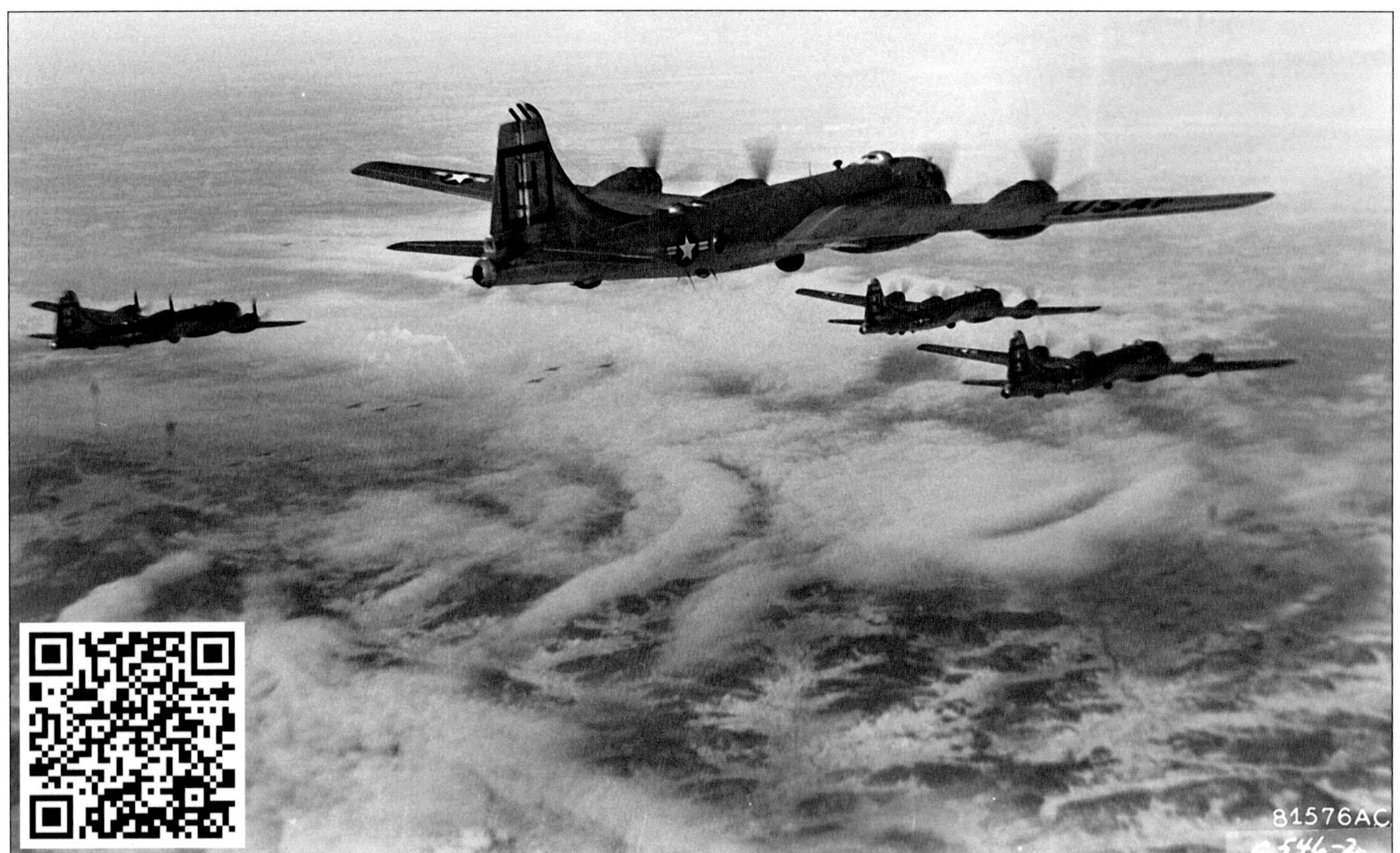

In much the same way as World War Two, a formation of B-29s drop their bombs over North Korea. A one-minute reel shows high quality in-flight imagery of B-29s from the 98th Bomb Wing striking targets in North Korea in 1951. (NARA/ YouTube Combat Camera Archive)

MIG-15S V F-86S

In the air war over Korea, the performance of the MiG-15 came as an initial shock to USAF fighter pilots. Intelligence on the Soviet aircraft was considered vital. Gun camera film of aerial victories against them was at a premium. Most valuable of all was the defection of a North Korean MiG-15 pilot with his aircraft to Kimpo AB in South Korea a few months after the end of the war.

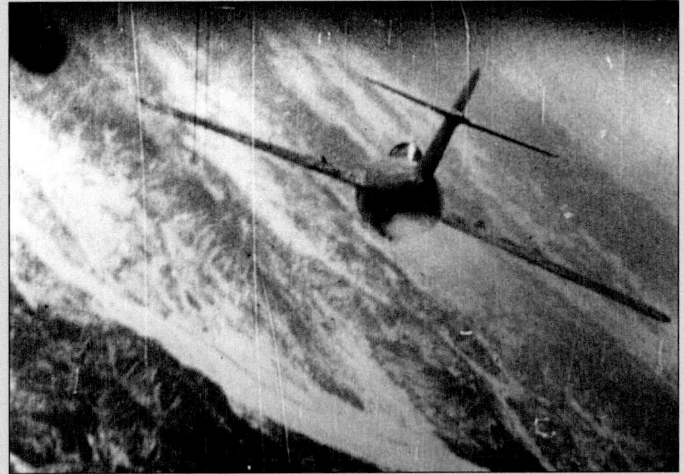

The gun camera of a US Air Force F-86 Sabre captured a MiG-15 over Korea. The same camera could have filmed Japanese or German shootdowns a few years earlier. (USAF)

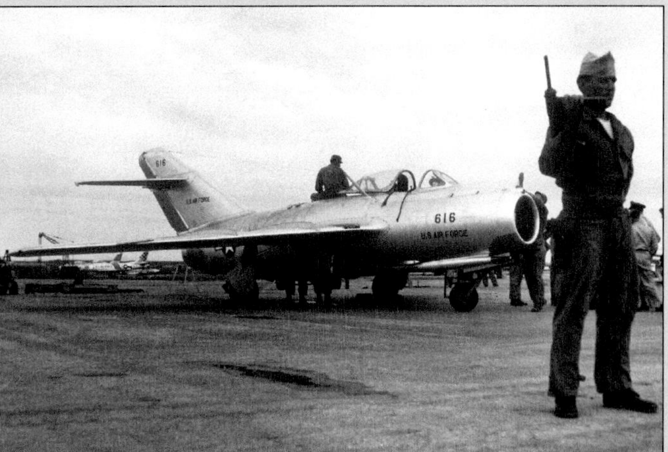

In September 1953, 21-year-old Senior Lt Kum Sok No brought his MiG-15 to Kimpo AB in South Korea. With its North Korean markings removed, the aircraft is under guard prior to being shipped to the US for evaluation. (USAF)

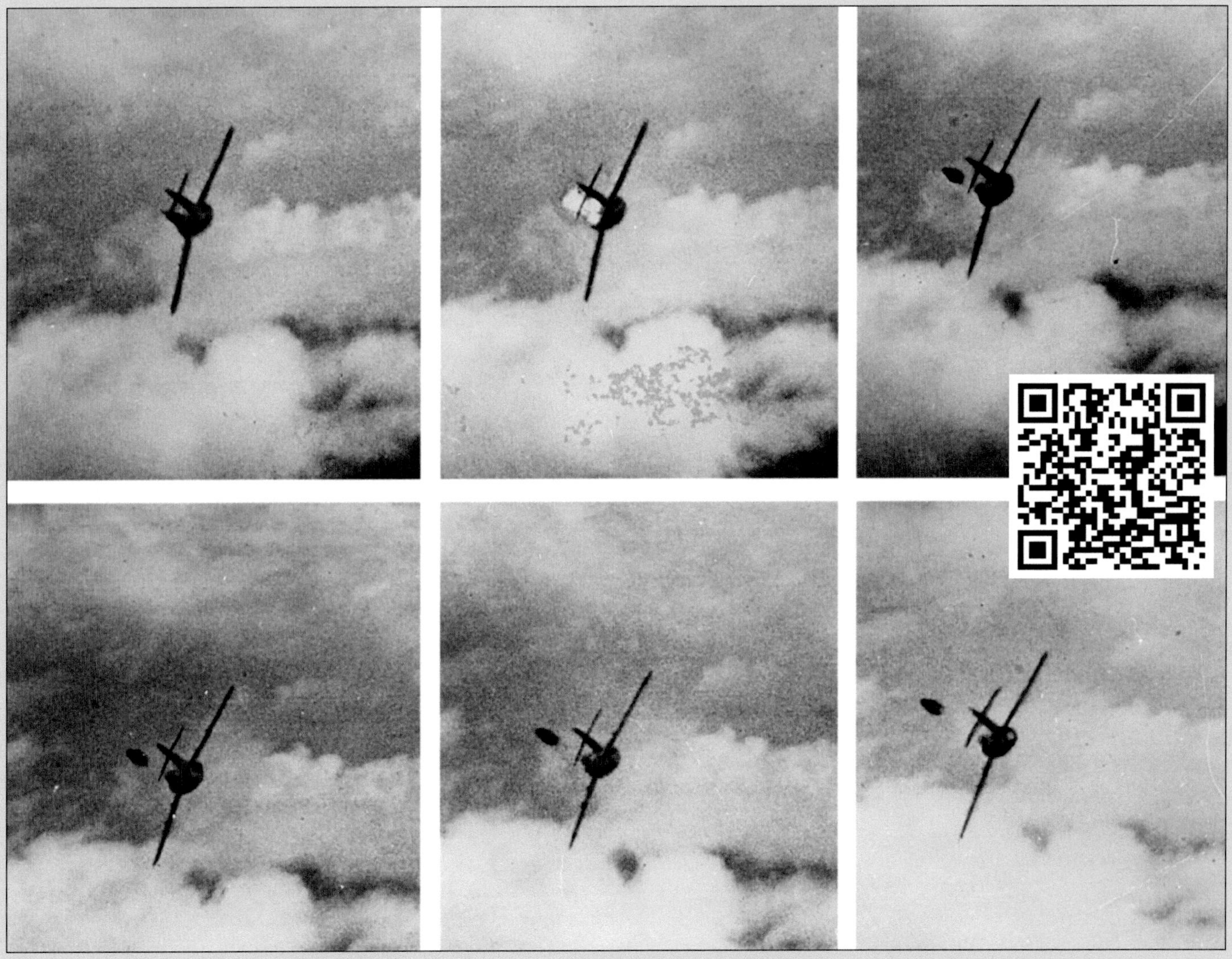

Two reels of gun camera footage. The first shows an F-84 strafing ground targets. The second is of several F-86 engagements and the destruction of enemy MiG-15s. (NARA) (YouTube/NARA)

5

ROCKETS AND MOVIES

1365th Photo Squadron

In July 1960, the APCS formalised the reorganisation of its photographic squadrons. Although never totally fixed, these changes essentially set the core unit structure for the 1960s and into the 1970s, even though the war in SE Asia would, sometimes, put that structure under significant pressure. The basic still- and motion-picture capacity of APCS would, after 1 July 1960, consist of two large photographic squadrons. The 1365th, at Orlando AFB, serviced the eastern United States and Europe. The 1352nd was at Lookout Mountain Air Force Station, meeting the needs of the western half of the United States and the Pacific area.[1] Detachments were to be established where necessary to meet specific needs. The rapid advances in military technology, including the vast growth of the US missile and space programmes and growing reconnaissance capabilities, put significant demands on the APCS. The introduction of SAC's missile force and the high readiness levels at its bases saw the establishment of some 1365th Photo Squadron Detachments at Offutt, Westover and Barksdale AFBs to document SAC combat and training activities. These Detachments and AA-VS Squadrons also contributed to 'Semiannual Film Reports' that provided news items on major developments and events within Strategic Air Command.

For three years between January 1959 and 1962, a detachment of the 1365th Photo Squadron operated from Patrick AFB at the Air Force Missile Test Center. It made still and film recordings of the Air Force's ballistic missile and satellite programmes, including documenting the tests and launches of Thor, Atlas, Titan and other rockets from Florida. M-45 tracking mounts, previously used as mobile anti-aircraft gun mounts, were adapted to enable better and smoother camera tracking. These were fitted with various high-speed cameras and different focal length lenses up to 180 inches. In the APCS history, the cameramen were credited with 'developing an advanced technique that established a new standard for this type of photographic documentation.'[2]

In Europe, the Squadron provided footage of the 1959 Berlin crisis to brief senior commanders. Later, during the month-long Cuban missile crisis from October 1962, the 1365th deployed camera teams widely across the southeastern United States. Their greatest effort was expended at the airbases in central and southern Florida, where the buildup of aircraft, men, supplies, and equipment was concentrated. Smaller teams were also sent to Bermuda and the Azores to photograph the aerial surveillance of Cuba-bound shipping. Responding to the emergency, remote camera pods were fabricated in short order and hung on other aircraft – a critical situation that provided an excellent opportunity to test their effectiveness.

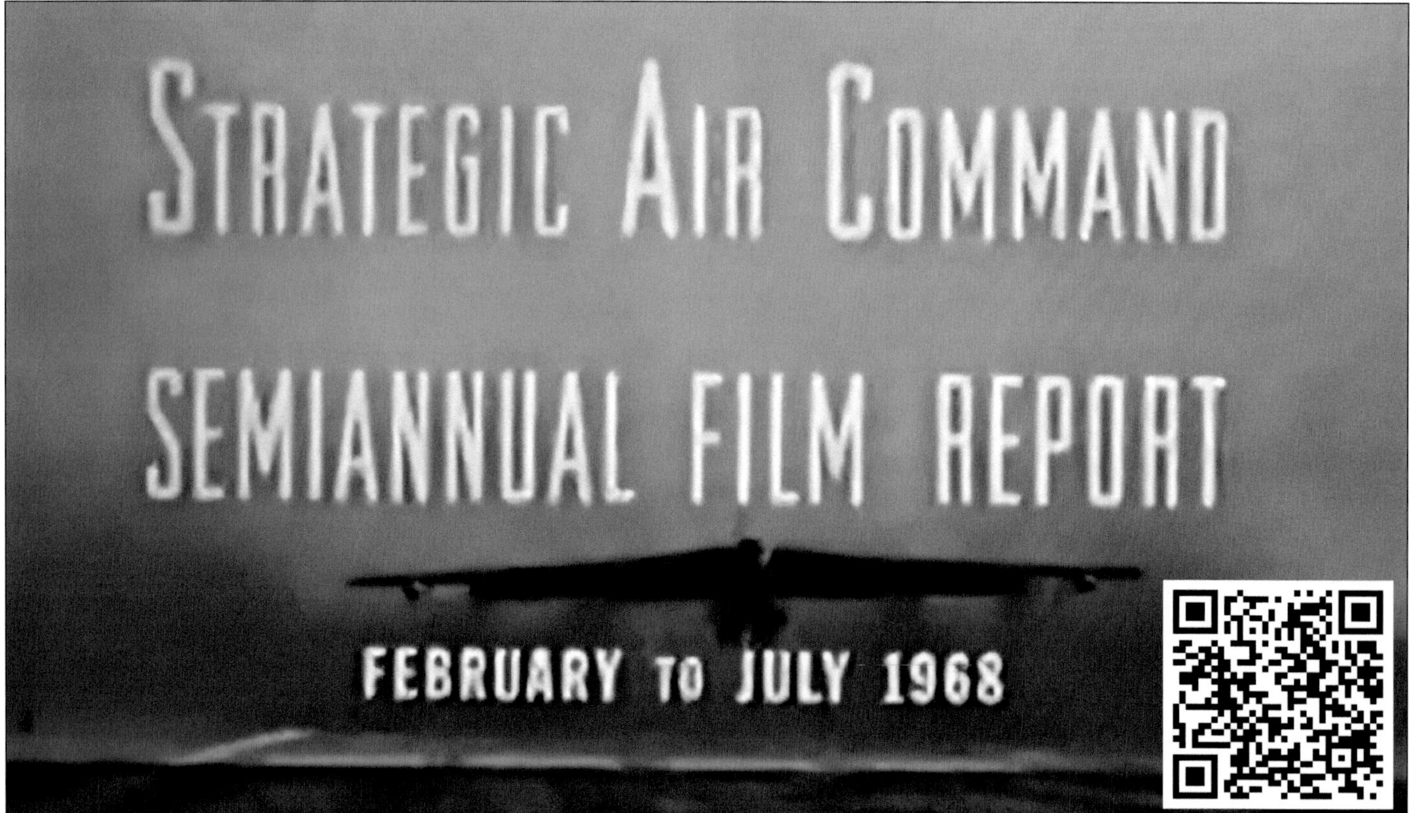

SAC 'Semiannual Film Reports' were regularly produced from material filmed by APCS/AAVS Detachments at SAC bases, for wider distribution. They covered a wide range of segments as a form of news service. This recording for the first half of 1968 covered SAC's automated command and control system, tests of missile silo doors, the crash of a nuclear-armed B-52 near Thule, the renaming of Grissom AFB and B-52 operations in SE Asia, among others. (YouTube/Nuclear Vault)

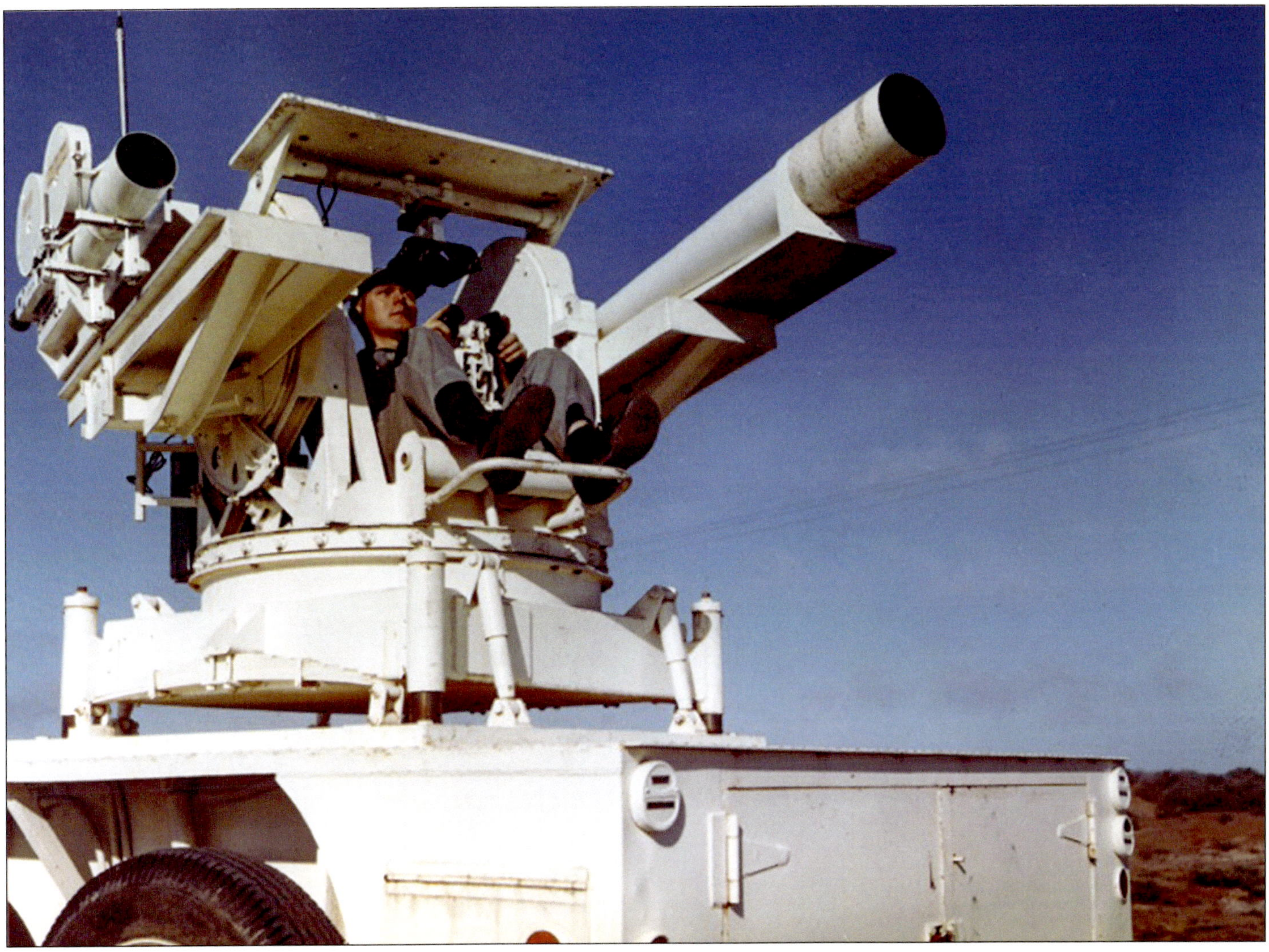

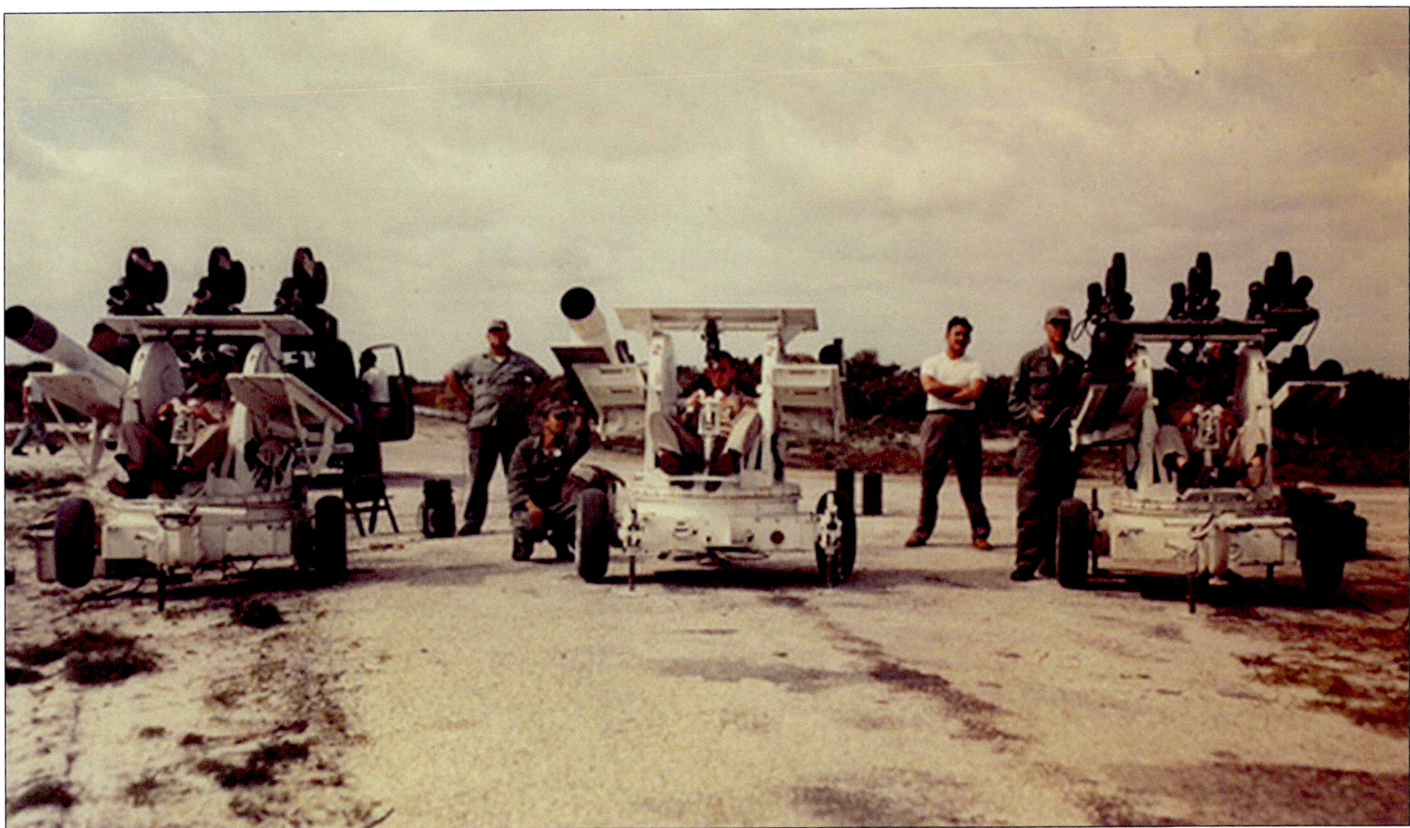

The M-45 trailer-based tracking mount, adapted from an old anti-aircraft gun trailer, has proved invaluable over the years. They have been fitted with many types of high-speed and long focal-length lenses during their careers. (NARA, USAF)

In 1958, the 1365th Photo Squadron produced a film 'Supersonic Thunderbirds' (SFP 637). The demonstration team had been formed in 1953 and converted to the F-100 in June 1956. This 1958 film shows aerial display footage from the Thunderbird's aerobatic routine in their F-100s. It mainly consists of footage shot from the ground, but there are also short in-flight and cockpit sequences. It was shown at the World Congress of Flight in Las Vegas in April 1959 and at international film festivals in Berlin and Edinburgh a few months later. The film and some outtakes have been digitised and are publicly available. The outtakes reel is mostly aerial footage, much of it of good quality, but was not used in the finished film.

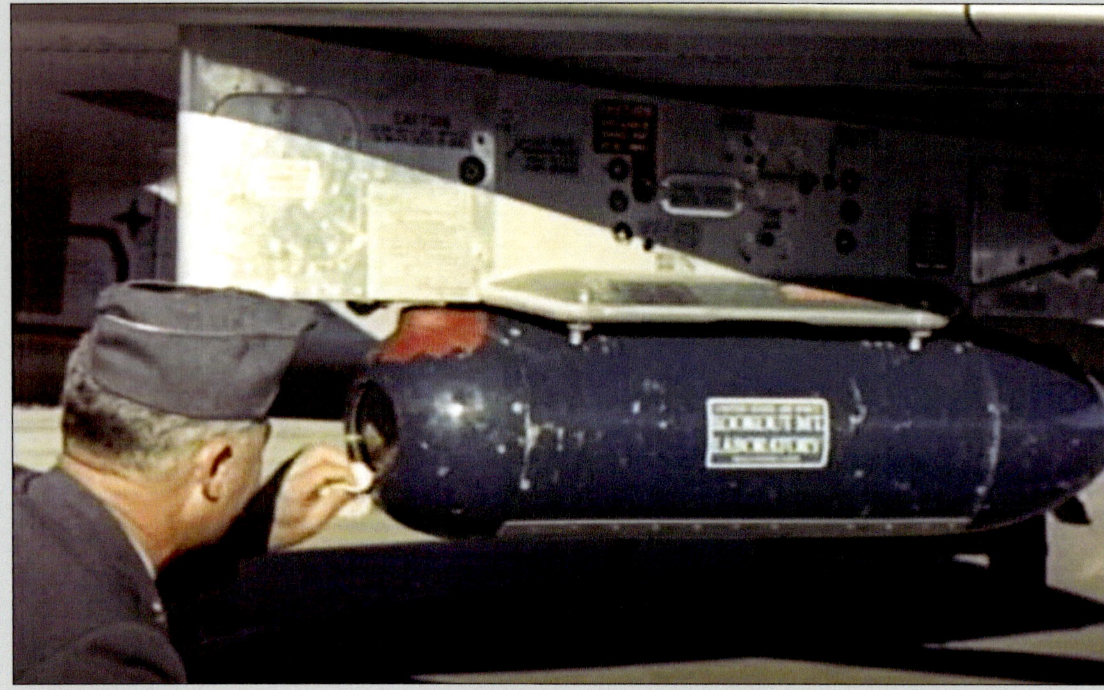

Supersonic Thunderbirds was the first film that used a pod-mounted camera and was fitted in a practice bomb dispenser. (NARA)

AA-VS technicians experimented with an externally mounted camera enclosed in a protective pod. The first attempt used a discarded T-1A practice bomb dispenser. It had a hole cut in the nose and a standard motion picture camera mounted inside.[3]

Col William Barksdale described the USAF's first use of the podded camera for aerial movie photography to make this film. Although the design was relatively crude, it provided the first in-flight pictures of the Thunderbird display team. The camera faced directly ahead but could not record the action behind the aircraft, 'Until 1956, most air-to-air production photography was accomplished with handheld cameras from the rear seats of T-33 aircraft. Not only was the field of view severely limited, but the resulting film was not steady, and the camera picked up reflections from the interior of the aircraft's plastic canopy'.

Outtakes from *Supersonic Thunderbirds*. (YouTube/ Classic airliners & vintage pop culture)

Intended for public consumption, *Supersonic Thunderbirds* was shown at the World Congress of Flight in Las Vegas in April 1959 and film festivals in Berlin and Edinburgh. (YouTube/ Classic airliners & vintage pop culture)

The May 1960 edition of *Air Force Magazine* contained an article on the 1365th Photo Group. The unit comprised a team of writers, animators and technicians who were said to have produced over 400 reels a year on a wide range of topics. A description of the production process at that time explains how once a script was written and approved, it was first reviewed by the Command that had commissioned the film. It was then passed through the Group, HQ APCS and eventually to the Pentagon. If approved, it would be put out to tender, with the lowest bidder winning. At that time, 'about 200 bonafide producers were considered qualified to bid on Air Force films'. After that, any professional actors required were hired, access for the film crews and actors to bases and locations was arranged, and a shooting schedule was created. After shooting was completed, a showing of the rough cuts was arranged at Orlando. Distribution was arranged once the final product was approved and copies were made.[4]

As the war in SE Asia escalated, the role of the 1365th PS evolved, too. It became the Air Force's own motion picture special effects unit. Another seven-minute film, *The Unique 65th*, produced by the 1365th PG, unfortunately undated, gives a resume of some of the unit's work at the time. It showcases 'Solarama', a studio model technique to show perspectives of Earth from space or the movement of space vehicles.

It also described the 'blue screen', which was then a pioneering technique. It included an explanation of why the war in Southeast Asia had increased demands on the Photo Squadrons, making it necessary to expand the numbers of motion picture photographers,

associated sound recording trades, and processing and editing technicians being trained to backfill spaces caused by those going to serve in Vietnam.

The film's final segment examines the introduction of new TV technology to AA-VS and its role in producing the monthly 'USAF News Review' using footage from around the world. The Squadron made 750 copies of each programme and distributed them to USAF installations worldwide.

1369th Photo Squadron, Vandenberg AFB

Vandenberg AFB, on the Californian coast, was transferred to the US Air Force in late 1956. Its coastal position was ideal for missile test launches aimed at US ranges far across the Pacific at Eniwetok and Kwajalein, in the US Marshall Islands. It soon also became where prototype launch facilities were constructed for the US ballistic missile types that eventually entered operational service, and some that did not. Although primarily a test establishment, it served briefly as an operational missile base. From 1 April 1956, it became home to SAC's 576th Strategic Missile Squadron, the Command's first ICBM unit equipped with Atlas missiles. From their first alert on 31 October 1959, the unit was operational until the squadron was inactivated on 2 April 1966. After that, Vandenberg concentrated on its primary task as a missile test and space launch facility.

The range of photographic work undertaken at Vandenberg, especially from the early days, was astounding. Initially operating as Detachment 1 of the 1352nd Photo Group, from 1 July 1962,

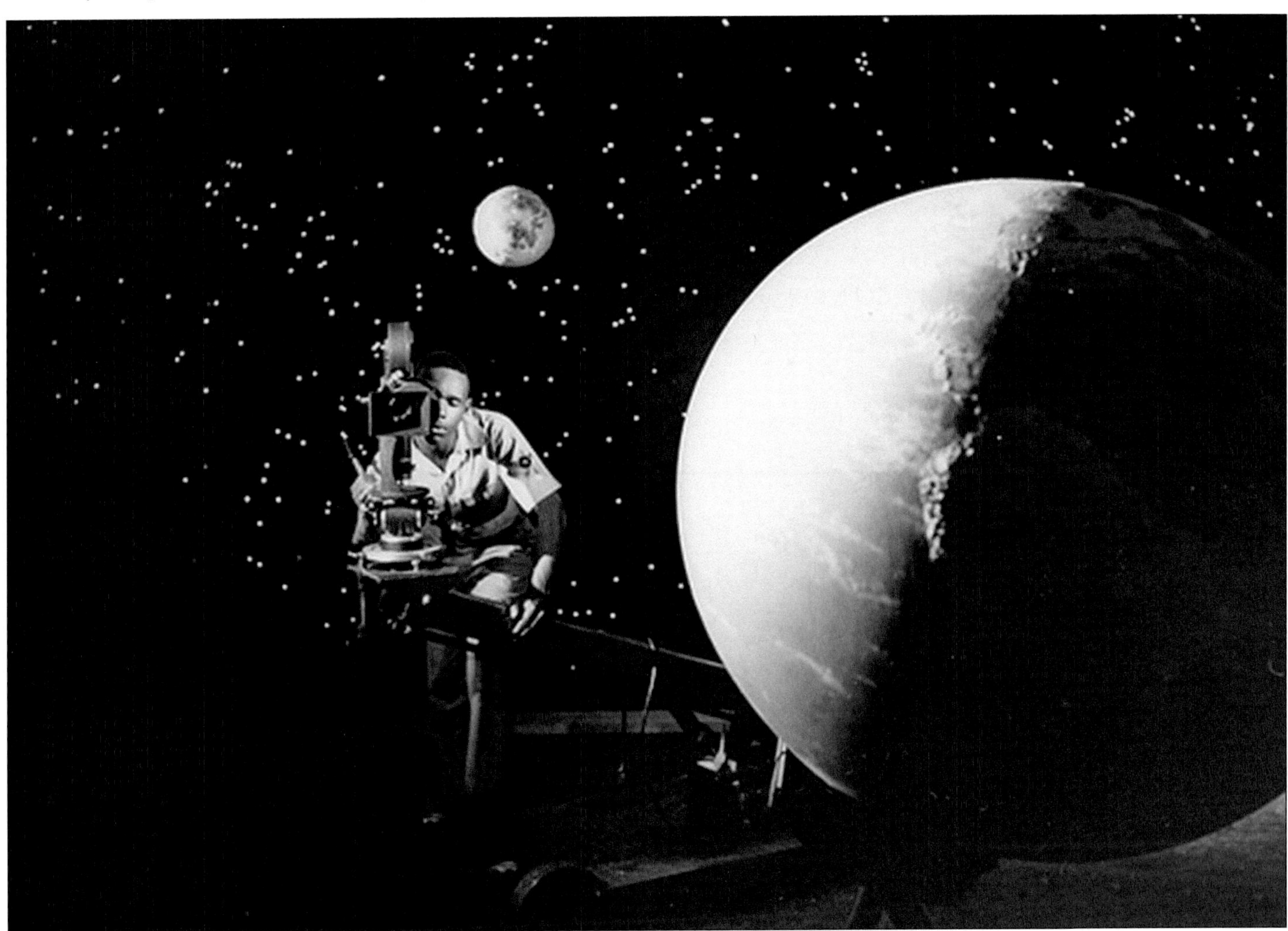

As the US missile and NASA's space programmes rapidly expanded, the 1365th PS developed a model that enabled the shooting of imagery of Earth as if from space. (NARA)

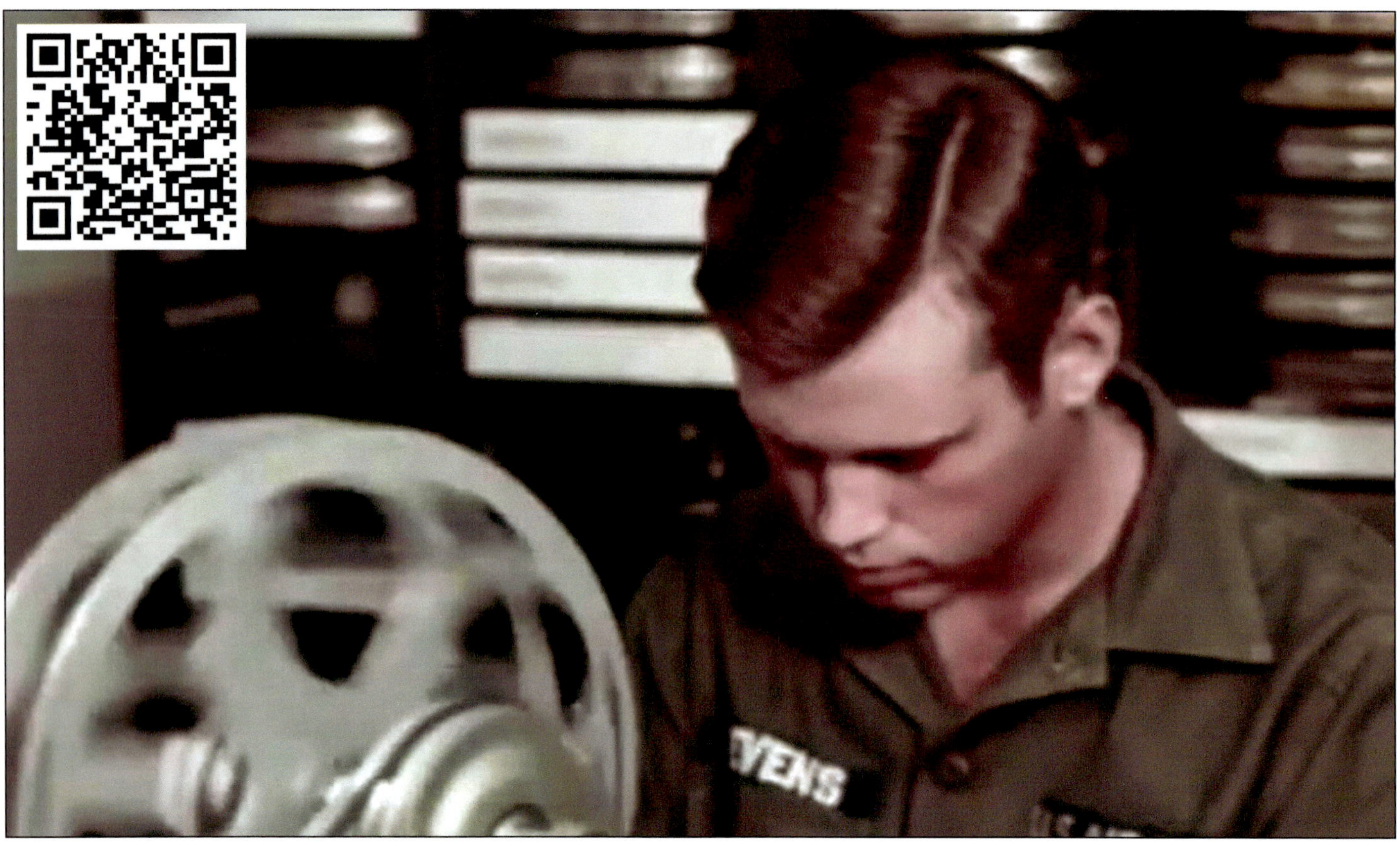

The Unique 65th demonstrates some of the then-advanced special effects used by the 1365th Photographic Squadron in making US Air Force training films. (YouTube/PeriscopeFilm)

An unheralded group of Air Force "moving-picture magnates" contributes to the defense of the nation in an atmosphere of . . .

HOLLYWOOD WITHOUT THE ULCERS

Lt. Col. Carroll V. Glines, USAF

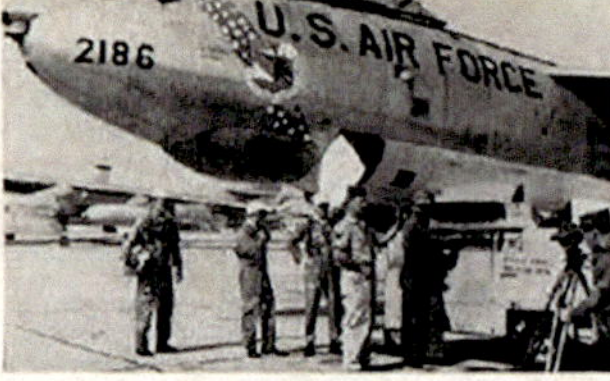

B-47 crew simulates alert for benefit of service camera crew at McCoy AFB, Fla. Photographic personnel belong to Orlando's "Hollywood" group. Actually, most footage in Air Force films is taken by private concerns that work under the supervision of APCS.

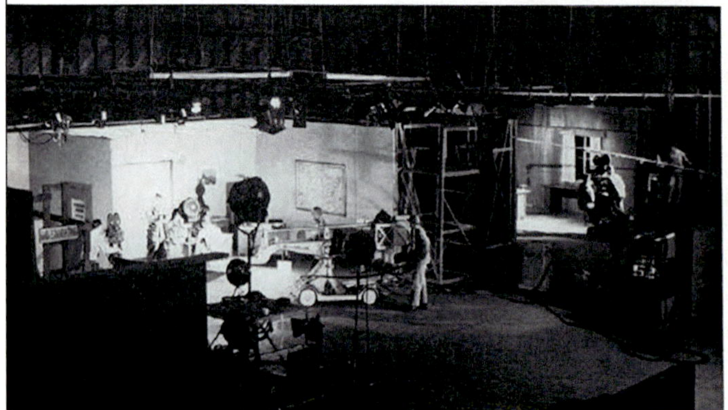

Months of preparation and minutes of noisy activity past, cameras simultaneously record two scenes in Air Force film production. Grouping of scenes and sequence of shooting are important factors on the financial side of service moviemaking, which is carried out by the 1365th Photographic Group of USAF's Air Photographic and Charting Service.

"QUIET on the set!"

"Roll 'em!"

"Speed!"

"Action!"

The reels are in motion on another moving picture—but one significantly different from most Hollywood productions. The producer, in this case, is the United States Air Force.

Almost from his first day in the service, the recruit sees Air Force films. Throughout his military career, he gains much of his total knowledge of his job, his responsibilities, and the mission of the Air Force via this medium.

The complex job of planning and writing most Air Force films is handled by a small group of experienced writers, animators, and technicians. They are the men of the 1365th Photographic Group, USAF Air Photographic and Charting Service (APCS), headed by Lt. Col. James P. Warndorf, USAF. Colonel Warndorf makes his headquarters at Orlando AFB, Fla. The Group is divided into three divisions: Projects, Art and Animation, and Scenario.

The Group turns out more than 400 reels a year for the Air Force. It is not an easy job. The subject matter varies from "Abdominal Colostomy Closure" to "The Zero Reader," and runs the gamut of security classifications from Unclassified, which can be shown to civilian audiences, to Top Secret, NOFORN (No Foreign Nationals), which can be shown only to American military personnel with the highest kind of need to know.

"We have many, many problems that the private producers never have to face," APCS's Maj. Peter Boyko says, "and yet we enjoy a freedom from the pressure of 'box-office draw' which gives Hollywood its biggest headaches. Our writers can work in comparative relaxation here in Orlando. Yet, we still have schedules to meet, and we must please the commanders who asked for the films in the first place. You might say it's Hollywood without the ulcers."

Major Boyko, an old hand at film production, until recently headed APCS's Commercial Projects Division.

While there may be a few similarities between the Air Force's "Hollywood" and the movie capital, these similarities do not include working conditions. The divisions of the Group occupy several one-story buildings on the base, all of which were built during World War II. The writers of the Scenario Division, for example, are assigned a series of "cells" in an E-shaped building. In these cubicles, recently renovated, are born excellent motion pictures that vastly influence the quality of the widespread global Air Force.

The process of getting a training film made for the Air Force is uncomplicated but requires a good deal of work by a number of people.

Production of a film, from conception by a potential Air Force user to final preapproval screening in the Pentagon, takes about a year. The films average some thirty minutes each and are produced in both color and black-and-white.

"As soon as we get the requirement for a film we assign the project to one of our stable of twenty-eight writers," Major Boyko explains. "We call in the technical adviser, usually from the command that originated the request, to explain the technical aspects of the subject matter. The writer then translates the purpose of the film and the technical points into a screenplay, always remembering the type of audience for which the film is intended."

"The job is not always as simple as it sounds," says one script writer who is a prolific author of short stories in his off-duty time. "Sometimes the purpose of the film is not clear. Sometimes the technical adviser wants to keep things too technical for film purposes. Or sometimes we writers have a rough time finding a story line that we can build on."

"More often than not," he continues, "after many hours of discussion with the technical adviser, the writer can see several ways to portray the basic idea and we then choose the best one."

After a script is written and approved by the Group, it goes through a series of reviews. The command that requested the film reviews it to make sure it gets the point across. It is next reviewed by members of the Group staff, then APCS Headquarters, and finally by interested Pentagon staff offices. At any one of these reviews, someone may suggest a change or two or, in fact, flatly disapprove of the whole presentation.

When a script is finally approved, it is scheduled into production and Invitations for Bids (IFBs) are sent out by the Air Materiel Command. Motion picture companies look over the script, figure costs, gauge profit margins, and submit bids. About 200 bona fide producers are considered qualified to bid on Air Force films. The lowest bidder gets the contract. He is invited to a conference at Orlando, where the entire script is carefully reviewed by the Projects Division, the "buyers" from AMC, requesting-command representatives, and the private producer. At this time, also, the Air Force makes arrangements for the concern's crew to visit bases or missile sites necessary to film the story. A shooting schedule is then set.

The next step, if the film requires professional actors, is to call the technical adviser to the producer's studio to choose those who will play the parts listed in the script. At least three actors are sent from a casting agency for each part. This done, scripts are given to the ones chosen, and the shooting sequence is announced.

On the appointed day the producer's studio, which he may own himself or have leased from another firm, is alive with noisy activity. Sets have already been built, "grips" wrestle with props and dolly tracks, the director makes last-minute arrangements, and actors stand by mumbling their lines to themselves —just as on any movie set anywhere.

Then, a few familiar commands from the director . . . cameras begin to turn . . . actors move through

(Continued on following page)

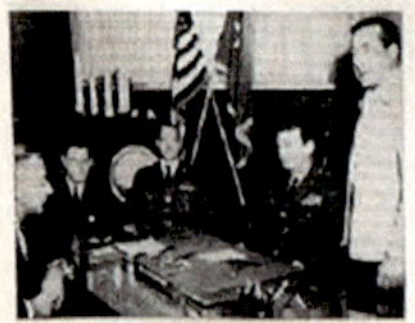

In Maj. Gen. Bernard Schriever's office, when he headed BMD, a civilian director, right, discusses new film with Louis Dana, STL; APCS project officer; Generals Ben Funk and Schriever.

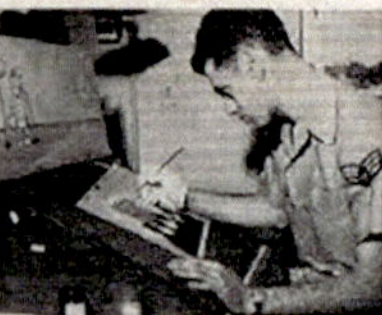

Artist-animator at Orlando prepares art work to be used in portion of Air Force film on the subject of flying safety, an important part of service-wide drive in this regard.

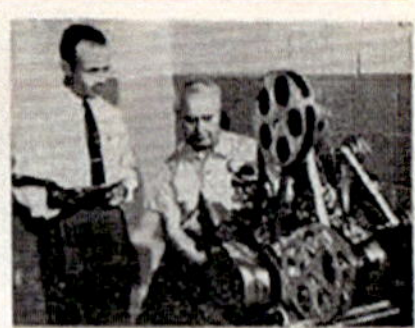

Celluloid files. Here two civilian producers look through Air Force Film Archives, Wright-Patterson AFB, Ohio, for documentary shots to be used in movies which are now in the works.

Air Force Magazine described the process the 1365th Photo Group used to develop training and information films for the Air Force. (NARA)

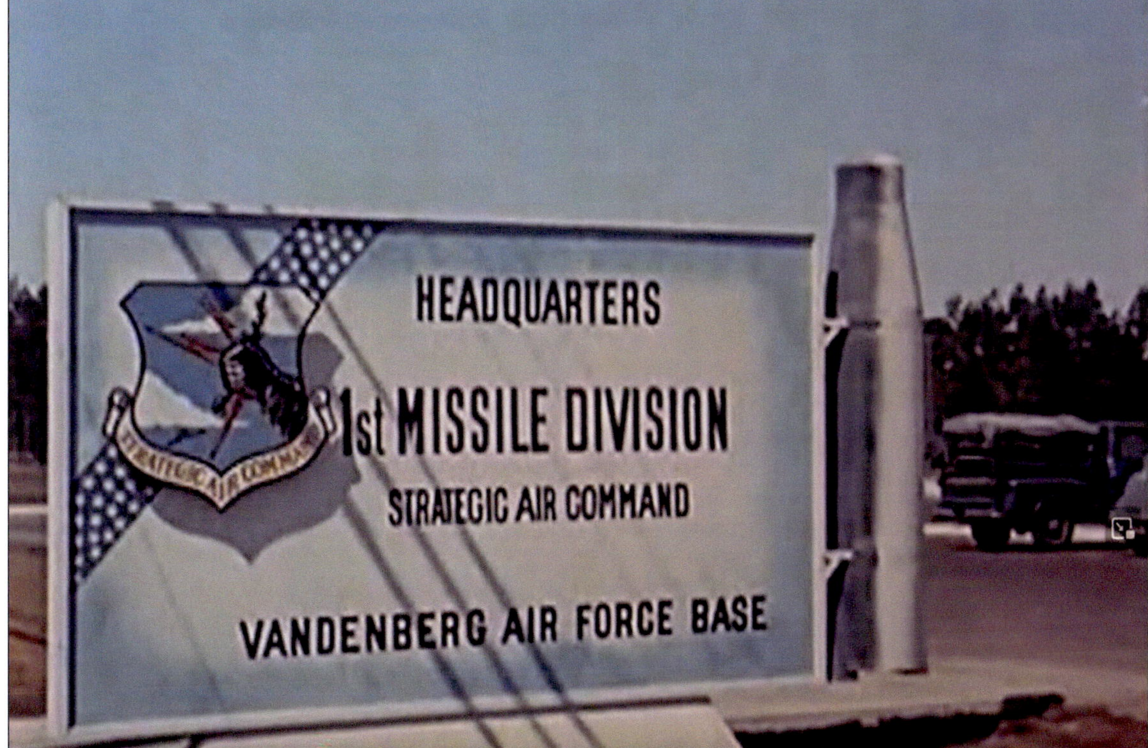

This 1959 film from Vandenberg AFB documents the early training, testing and preparation for the fielding of SAC's ballistic missile forces and the training of RAF Thor missile crews. (YouTube/ Canaveral Space Force Museum)

it became a fully fledged squadron with activation of the 1369th Photo Squadron on 1 January 1962. By June 1963, the unit provided photographic and film coverage for all the activities at Vandenberg AFB and the Point Arguello Naval Missile Facility. This included work by the Air Force, US Army Corps of Engineers, weapons systems contractors and consisted of documenting:

Engineering, sequential surveillance, and tracking photography of operational training and R&D launches, flight readiness firings, fuelling operations, missile weapon checkout tests; documentary and tracking photography downrange on re-entry vehicle projects; documentary photography of missile site construction and systems equipment installation for data analysis, human engineering studies, public information programmes, training films, briefing films, and briefing slide presentations; technical manual photography; and to include combat documentation as required by APCS when not in conflict with the primary mission. Operate and maintain motion picture and still photographic film processing laboratories.[5]

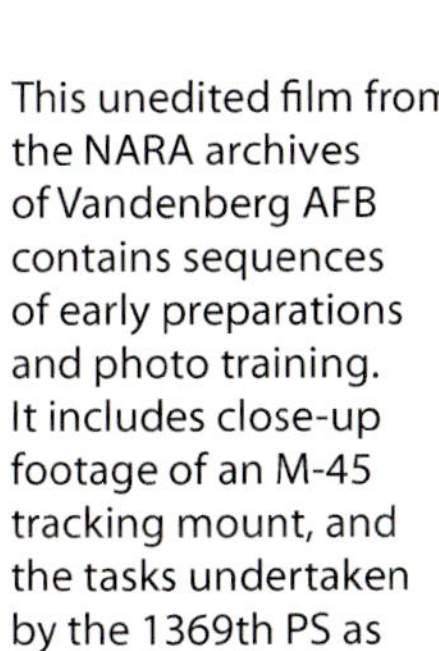

This unedited film from the NARA archives of Vandenberg AFB contains sequences of early preparations and photo training. It includes close-up footage of an M-45 tracking mount, and the tasks undertaken by the 1369th PS as their workload rapidly increased. (NARA)

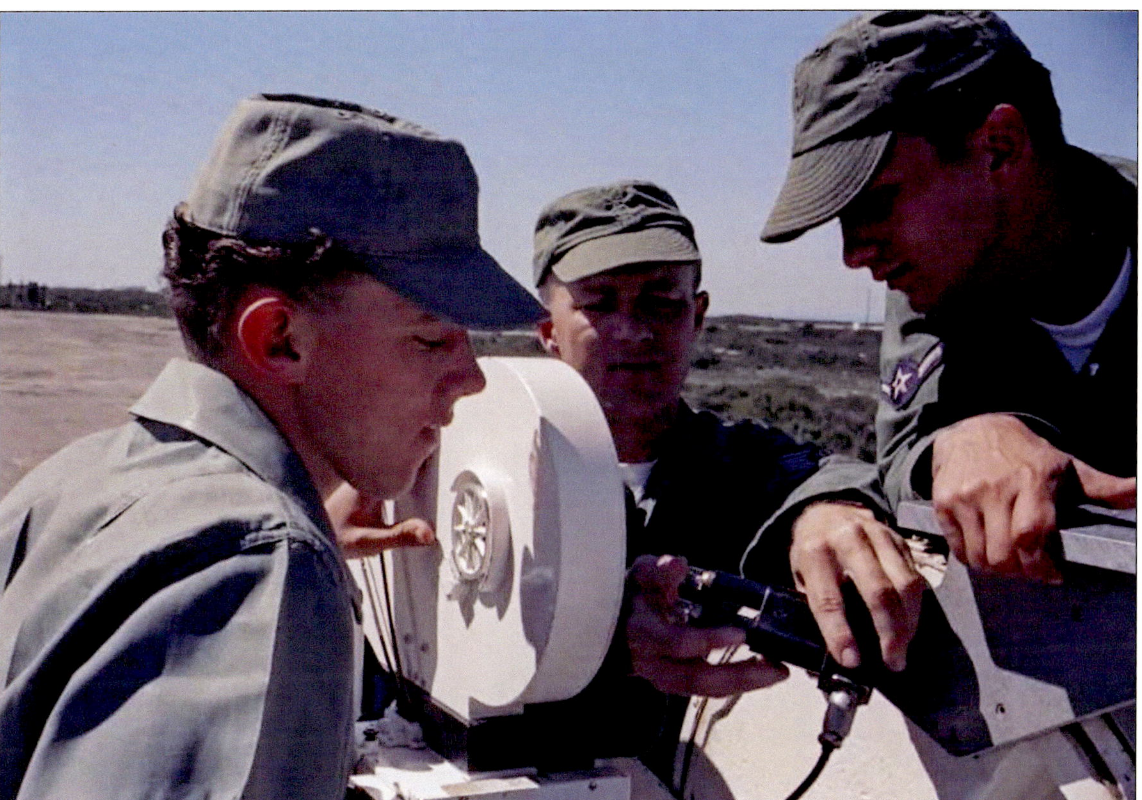

The Squadron's workload included documenting all the construction work at the site. The ongoing construction projects at Vandenberg were significant. These included constructing prototype launch platforms and silo designs for the new missile types entering service, plus the support facilities necessary to enable and monitor test launches. Some of these constructions were huge and very expensive civil engineering projects in their own right, the progress of which senior SAC and USAF commanders wanted to be kept apprised. Over 44,000 images of the work at Vandenberg, mainly centred on the Atlas missiles, have been donated to the San Diego Air and Space Museum Archives. These have been digitised and are available electronically. These remarkable images vividly illustrate developments and events. Most were taken by trained photographers rather than just individuals with cameras.[6]

Typical of the period are the details in the 1369th Squadron's history for the first half of 1963, when some 65 launches of Atlas, Thor, early Minuteman and Titan missiles were documented. The period included work on a massive 2,383 still camera and 828 motion picture projects. The Squadron generated 1.1 million feet of movie film and 224,000 still images during those six months.[7]

However, photo operations were not without problems. There was an extremely high demand for the resources and personnel available to the squadron, who were unimpressed by the poor advanced planning and coordination arrangements at Vandenberg. Security forces sometimes refused to allow cameramen access to the high-security areas they needed to do their work, because of inadequate prior coordination. The unique nature of some projects meant bespoke camera solutions sometimes had to be developed, which did not always function as intended, producing inadequate or useless imagery. The foggy weather, typical of the Vandenberg area, caused condensation problems for cameras, lenses and the film stock that 'resulted in the loss of an appreciable amount of valuable footage'.[8]

Eddie Carroll was assigned to the 1369th PS at Vandenberg in 1967 to monitor missile launches. He explained that during his time:

> Most of the missile launches were done at night, so if we came in at 08:30, they would tell us to take the afternoon off, get some rest because we would have an 03:15 shoot. So, at about midnight, we would gather at the Squadron and get our equipment together. We had several vehicles that we would use to move the heavy equipment, including the large cameras and telephoto lenses. We would get set up on the launch site and set up the close, the remote and instrumentation cameras. Then get on the radio net and wait for the launch commands.

He continued,

> There were only about 150 of us worldwide, so there was a great demand for our services. Logistically, our California base was at Norton AFB. Still, we would feed Japan, Hawaii, Vietnam, South Korea, and any of the needs that came out of the Pacific theatre. So I spent a great deal of time away on a temporary duty.[9]

Recording Missile Launches

The 1369th PS at Vandenberg spent considerable time and effort recording all aspects of the many ballistic missile projects developed by US contractors in the late 1950s and early 1960s.

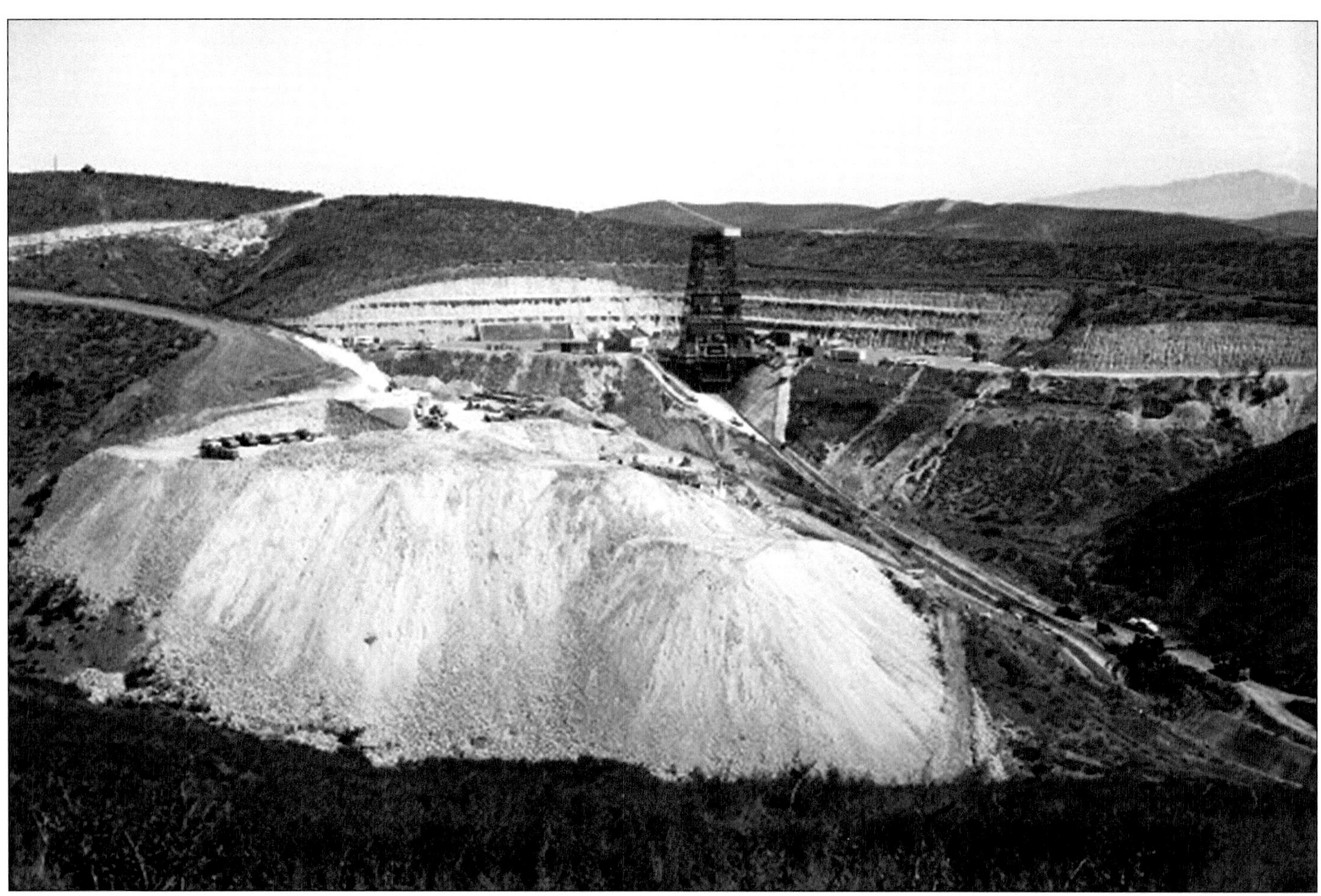

Construction projects at Vandenberg AFB that were associated with ICBM development were huge. Work is in progress at Sycamore Canyon on building an Atlas missile launching platform. (SDSM)

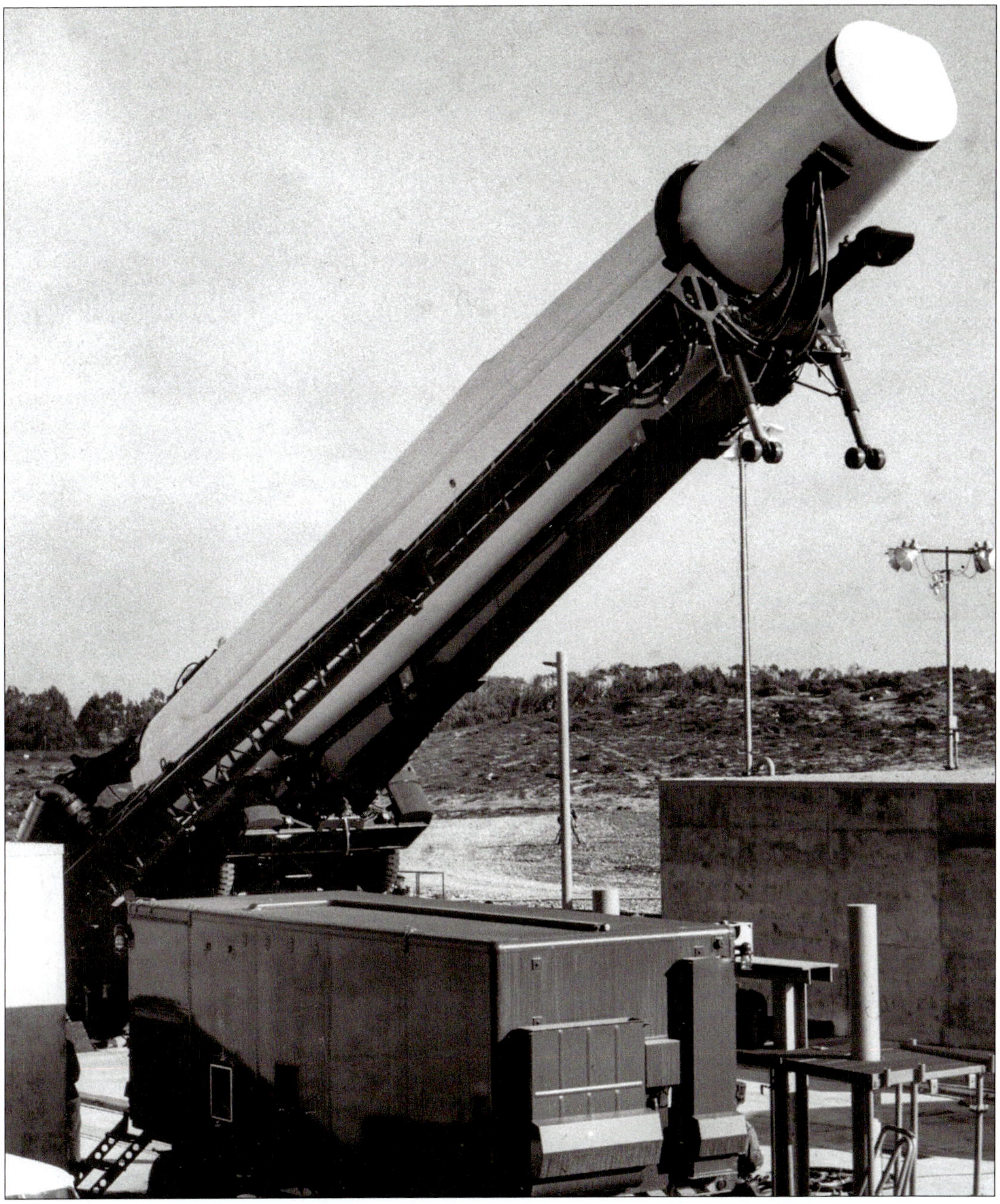

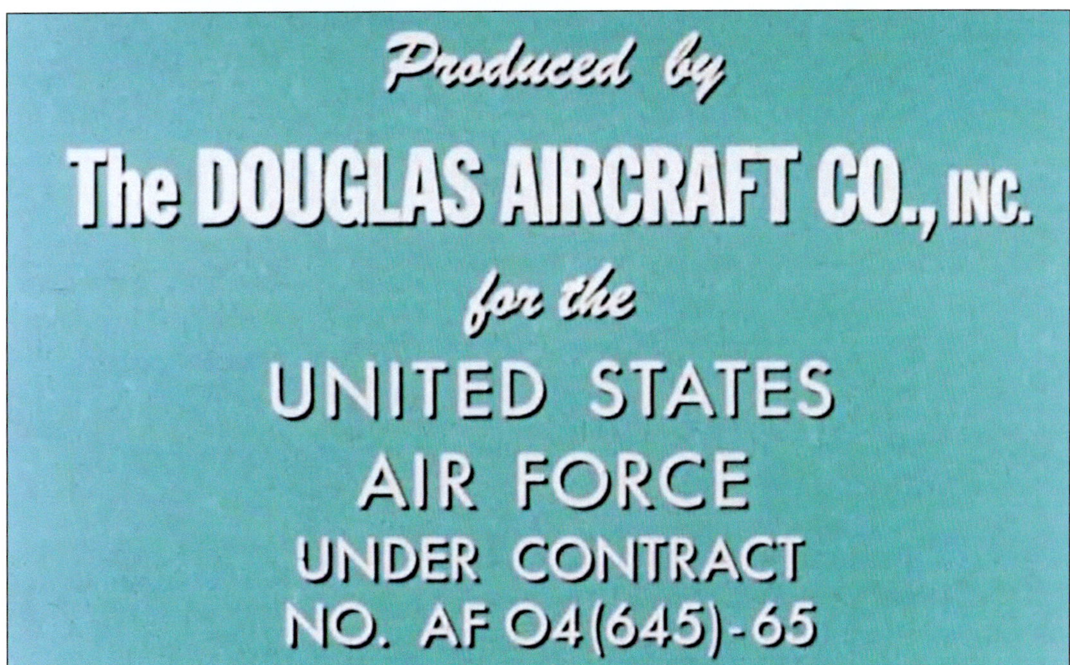

A Douglas SM-75 PGM-17A Thor missile is being erected, ready for launch. (NMUSAF)

Major weapons systems contractors like Douglas, Martin and Boeing regularly worked with the USAF Photo Squadrons to produce films about the missile systems they produced. This 1960 film from Douglas, *WS-115A, The Thor Intermediate Range Ballistic Missile*, is a good example of the genre. (YouTube/Space Systems Command)

The Thor and Jupiter missiles were classed as Intermediate-Range Ballistic Missiles with an approximate 1,500-mile (2,400km) range. They needed to be based comparatively close to the enemy, hence their deployment to Italy, Turkey and the UK. Both used highly volatile liquid fuels. They were sat in the open and had to be erected from their horizontal storage positions before being fuelled and launched from special pads. The time it took to do this, their forward location and open positions made them highly vulnerable and tempting targets for a Soviet pre-emptive strike. Thor missiles were first deployed in 1958, with Jupiter in Italy and Turkey in 1961. Both types were withdrawn from Europe in 1963.

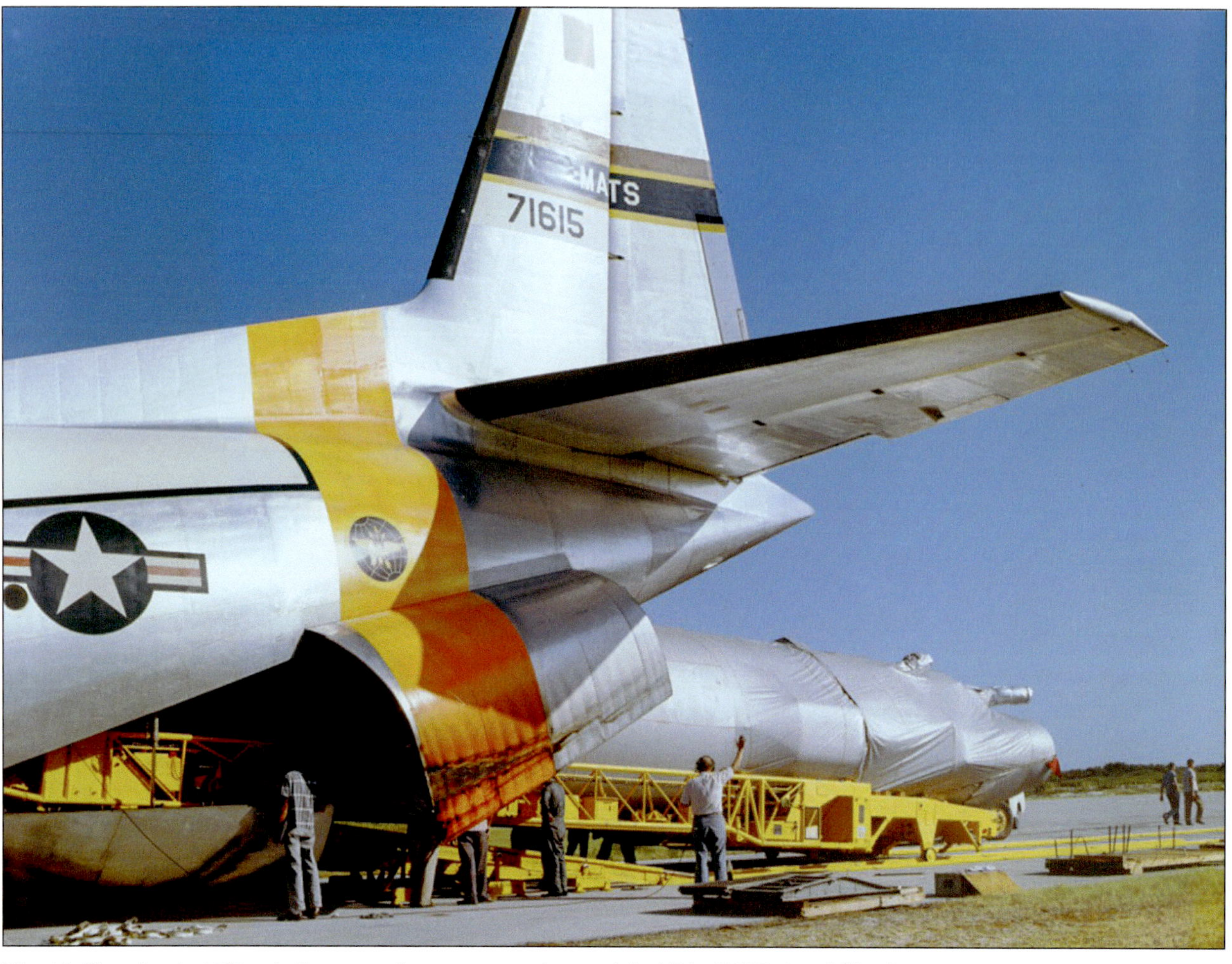

Like this Thor shot in 1960, missiles were often transported around the US by USAF aircraft like the C-133. (Jim McNearny)

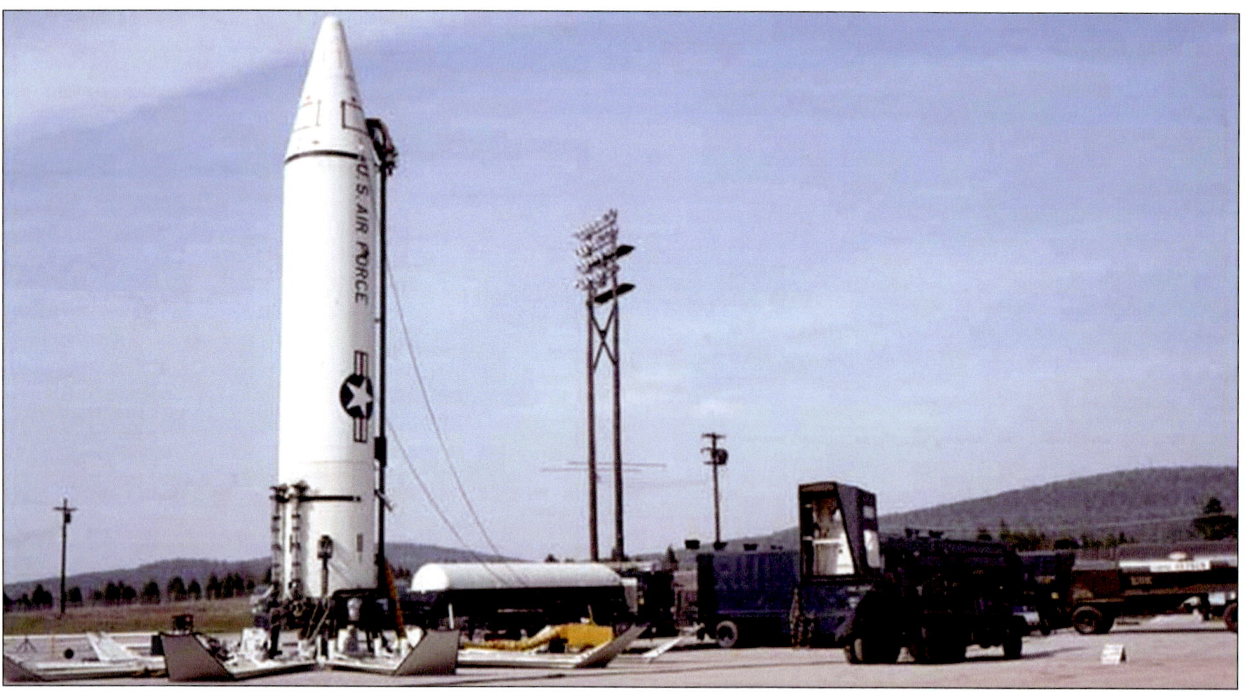

SAC Jupiter medium-range missiles were based in Turkey and Italy. When sitting upright above ground, they were very vulnerable to conventional or nuclear attack. (USAF)

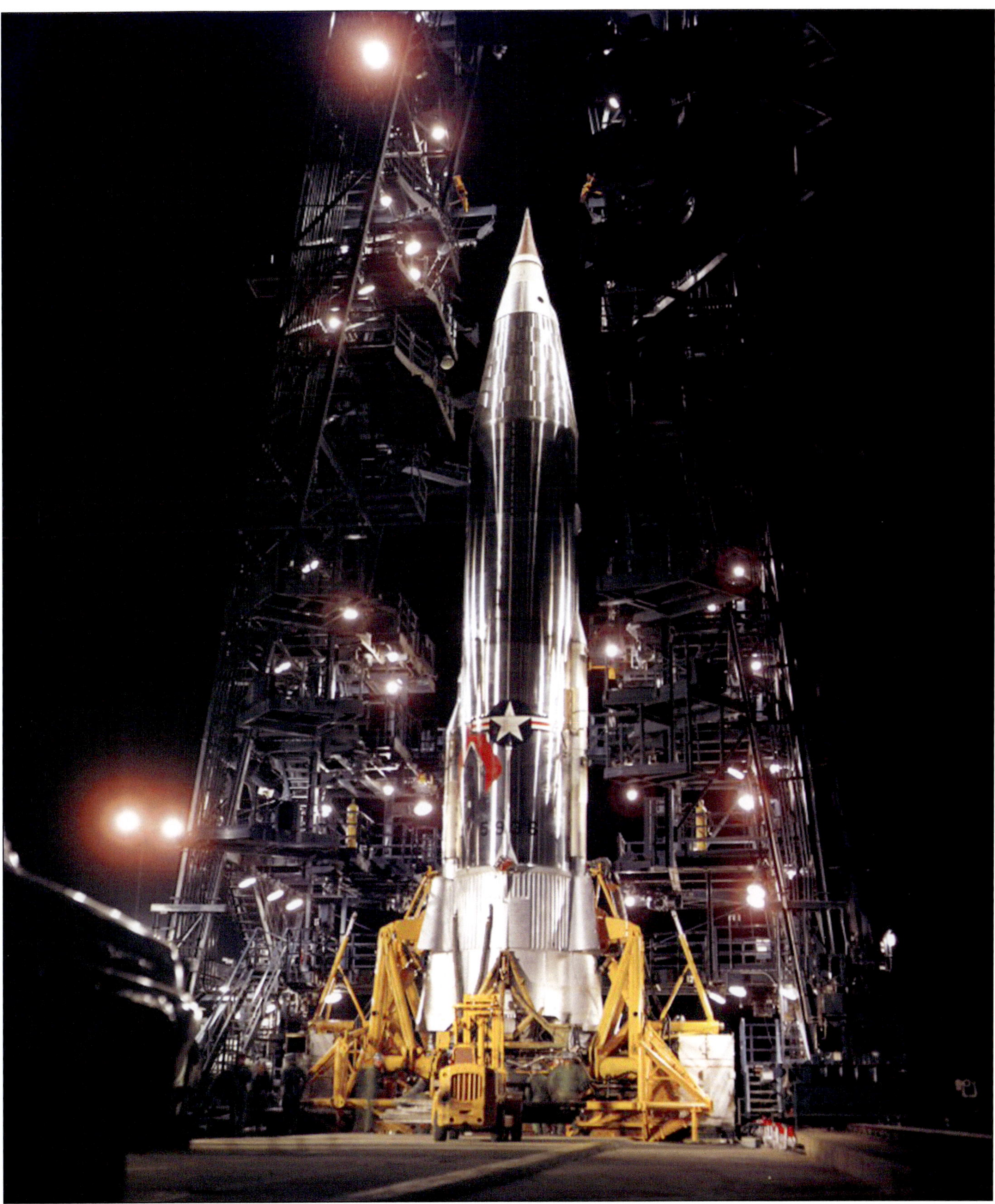

An atmospheric shot of an Atlas missile being prepared for a night launch from Vandenberg. Night launches complicated collecting high-quality imagery of the event. (USAF/1369th PS)

The Convair/General Dynamics Atlas missile was the first true intercontinental missile to enter service, but was just an interim weapon. Three versions of this liquid-fuelled weapon were operational between October 1959 and April 1965. The Atlas D had a range of approximately 9,000 miles (14,500km). These were stored upright above ground and fuelled just before launch but were vulnerable with minimal protection. The Atlas E was deployed to FE Warren AFB, Forbes AFB in Kansas and Fairchild, Washington. They were stored laid down in semi-hardened 'coffins' with the missile raised to the vertical for firing. The Atlas F was the most widely deployed and kept stored vertically in silos. On a launch order, they would have been fuelled and raised to the surface by a massive lift and fired. It could be launched in roughly 10 minutes, which saved about five minutes in the missile launch process over the D and E variants. Around 350 Atlases of all versions were built. Deployment peaked at 79 missiles in 1963. All were withdrawn by April 1965 as early Titan and Minuteman weapons became operational. Many Atlas missiles were later re-purposed for space launches.

Mighty Titan

The Titan I was built as a fallback design in case the development of the Atlas failed, but was itself nearly cancelled in several rounds of budget cuts. Some 62 flight tests took place between 1959–62. Liquid-fuelled again, it took 15 minutes to fuel-up and then taken to the surface by elevator to be launched above ground. The 101 missiles built meant 54 were deployed to the six operational Strategic Missile Squadrons at any one time; two at Lowry AFB Colorado, one each at Beale AFB, at Ellsworth in South Dakota, Larson AFB WA, and another at Mountain Home AFB in Idaho. The Titan I had a 7,000-mile (11,250km) range but was only in service between 1961 and 1965, withdrawn as the Minuteman and Titan II became available.

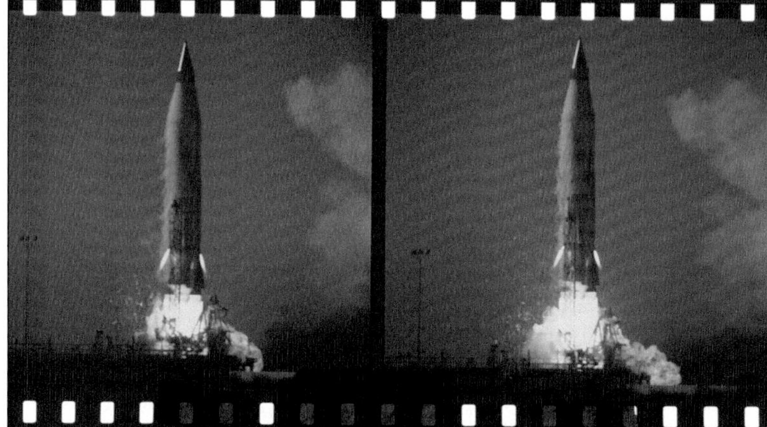

Two shots from a negative strip. A high-speed camera was used to record this Atlas missile launch from Vandenberg AFB in September 1958. (USAF/1369th PS)

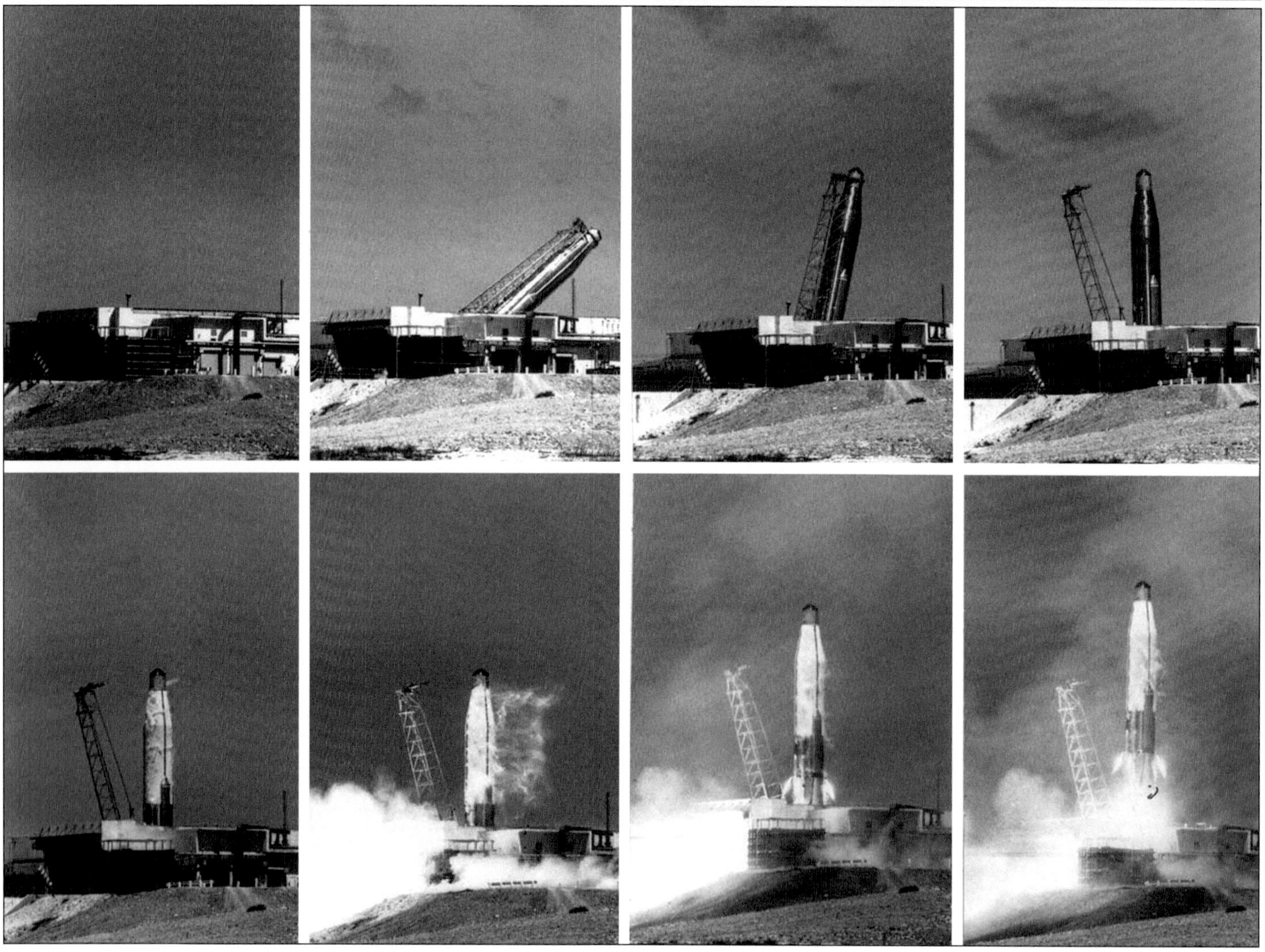

A time-lapse set of images showing an Atlas E being erected from its concrete 'coffin' to the vertical and launched took around 15 minutes. (USAF/1369th PS)

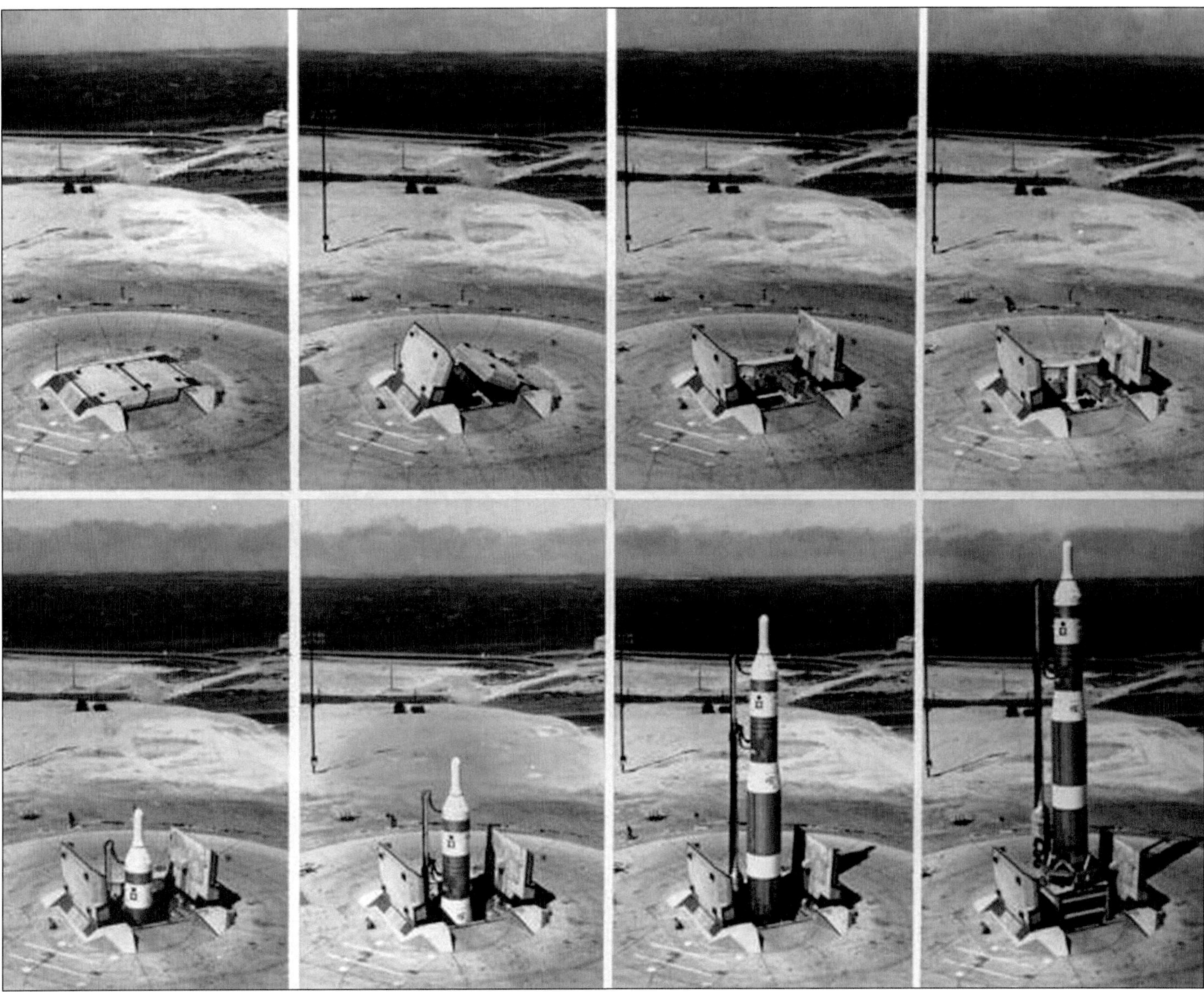

A launch preparation for a Titan 1 missile test. Silo buried, when ordered, the missile was fuelled and its 116-ton weight lifted to the surface by a massive elevator for launch. (USAF/1369th PS)

The Titan II was a real step forward in ICBM operations, primarily enabled by the development of less volatile and corrosive fuels. These could remain in the missile's fuel tanks for more than just a few hours without them needing to be launched or de-fuelled. Titan II was still liquid-fuelled, but its new fuel was safer and could be stored on the missile for long periods. This meant it could also be stored 'ready to go' and rapidly launched from its silo buried deep below ground, and almost invulnerable to Soviet attack. Viewed as an interim platform, it was estimated to be in service for just five to seven years. The Titan II had a 10,000-mile (16,100km) range and was valued because it carried large payloads of up to nine megatons, much greater than its contemporaries, and so was useful for hitting deeply buried Soviet command and control facilities. In 1967, the Titan II fleet peaked at 63 missiles. They were rescheduled for retirement in 1971. Once their internal guidance and other systems were updated, they were retained. Their gradual phase-out did not begin until July 1982, with the last nine Titan IIs retired in 1987.

Lookout Mountain Air Force Station

Lookout Mountain AFS was a small site in a residential area of Hollywood known as Laurel Canyon at 8935 Wonderland Avenue in north Los Angeles. During World War Two, it was used as the Los Angeles Flight Control Center but was quickly abandoned at the end of the war. It became the centre for filming and producing official Air Force and Atomic Energy Commission (AEC) training and information films, many of which remain classified.

In early 1948, the location was acquired by the US Air Force and AEC and developed by the Army Corps of Engineers into a major self-contained movie and production facility. It comprised a complete film stage, two screening rooms, and labs for processing 16mm and 35mm motion picture film and still images. There were animation and editorial work facilities, a helicopter pad, underground climate-controlled film storage vaults, a bomb shelter and standard office space.

The selection of Lookout Mountain AFS as a location was logical. Being close to Hollywood meant a ready supply of the necessary specialised and skilled labour was available. Close to the West coast, made it easier to reach the Pacific island test sites, and later the launches from Vandenberg AFB missile launch site. It also became the location for processing film materials from tests at the Nevada National Security Site. Lookout Mountain was staffed by personnel from the US Air Force, the Atomic Energy Commission (later Department of Energy) and civilians recruited from major picture studios such as MGM, Warner Brothers and RKO Pictures.

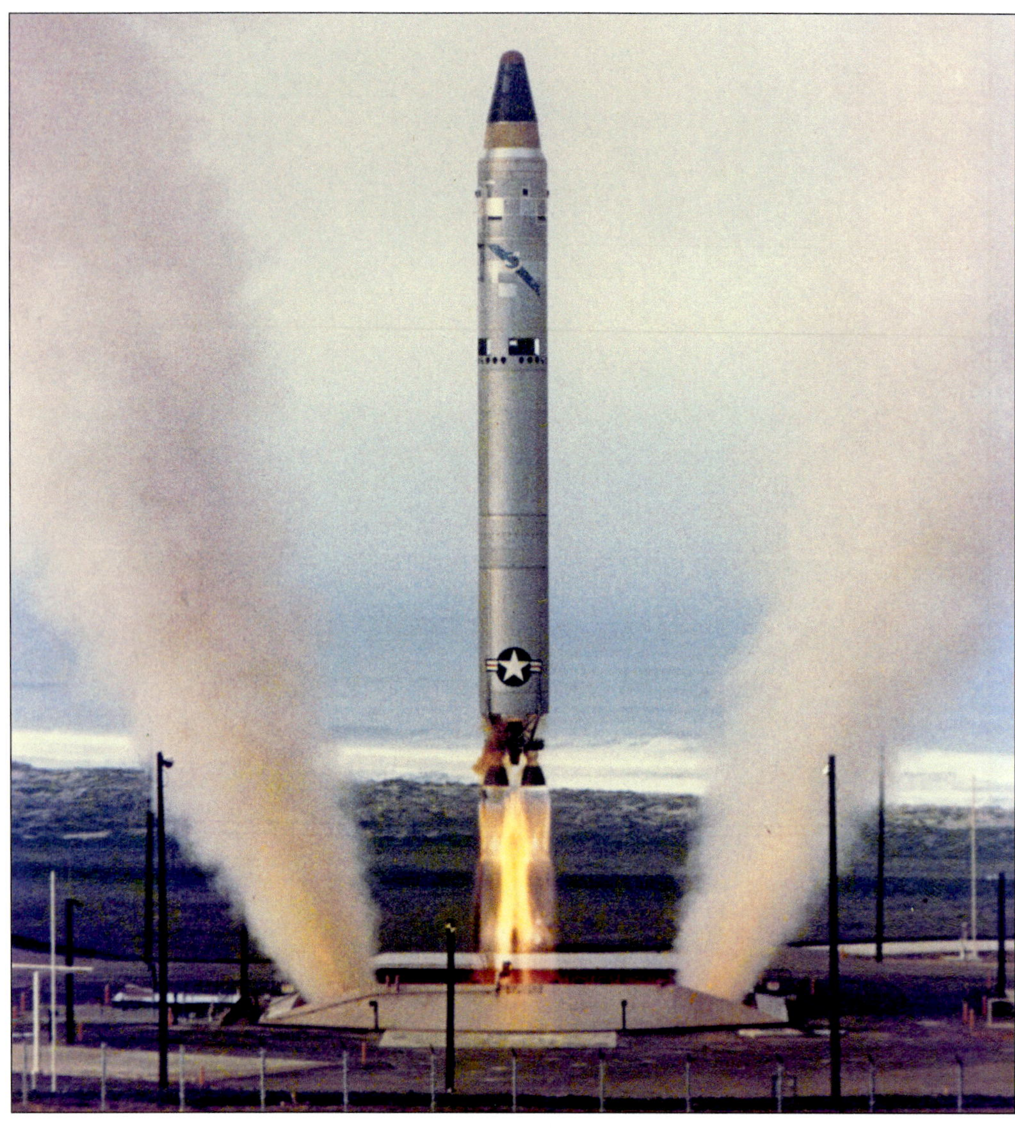

A SAC Titan II missile test launch from Vandenberg AB in 1978. The missile was capable of carrying a nine-megaton warhead. (USAF)

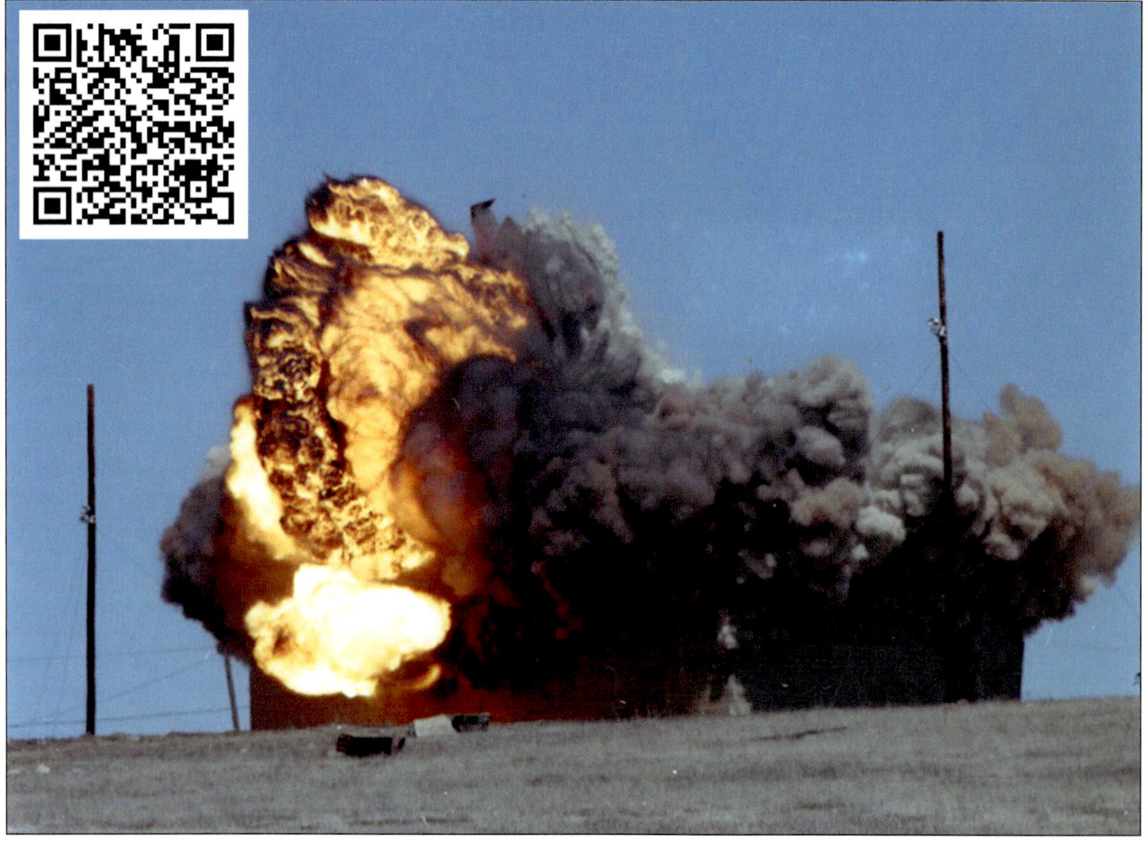

Launch failures. As well as the many successful missile launches, the cameras of the 1369th PS also captured the many failed launches, as this footage shows, and why remote cameras and long focal length lenses were necessary to help identify technical failures. (SDASM Archive) (YouTube/PeriscopeFilm)

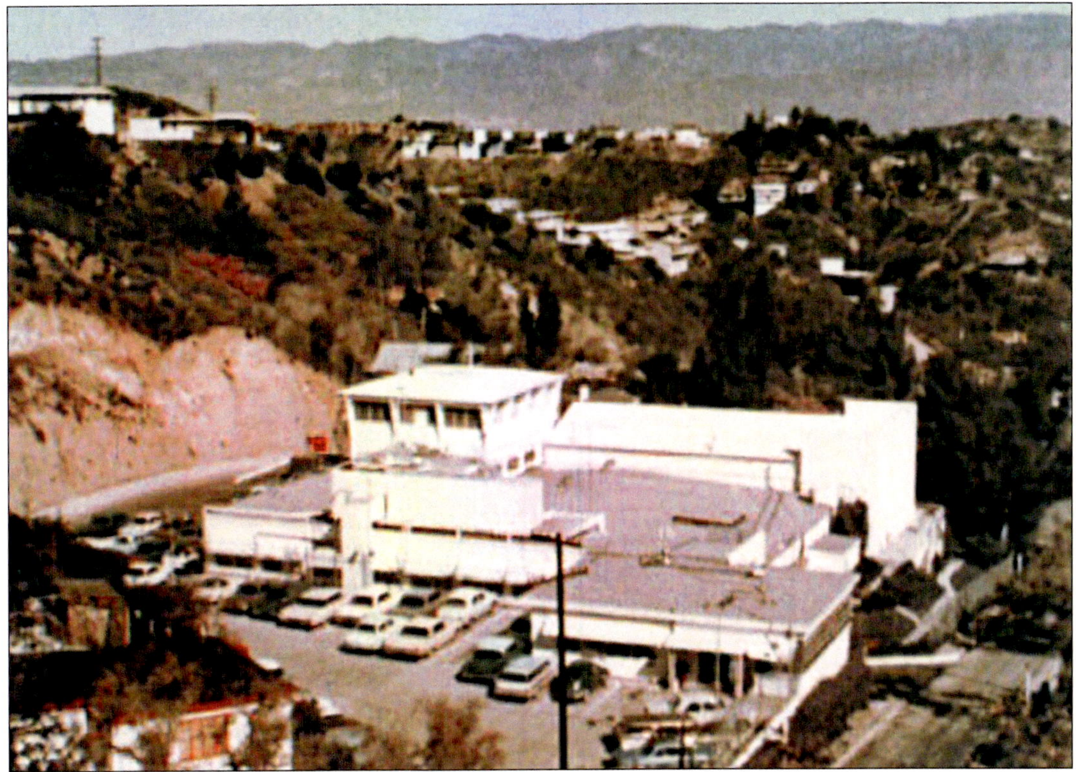

Lookout Mountain Air Force Station, a 20-minute film tagged as 'for official use only', gives an excellent overview of the range of work carried out there. (USAF) (YouTube/PeriscopeFilm)

Up to 250 staff members were also retained, including producers, directors, and cameramen. Many facility staff required Top Secret security clearances for nuclear-related work.[10]

After its transfer from SAC, US Air Force work at Lookout Mountain from 1 April 1951, was initially managed by the 4881st Motion Picture Squadron of the Military Air Transport Service (MATS), the Air Pictorial Service (APS). In April 1952, after the APS became the Air Photographic and Charting Service (APCS), the Lookout Mountain unit was re-designated as the 1352nd Motion Picture Squadron from 1 May 1952. In July 1960, the 'Squadron' was elevated to 'Group' status and was responsible for parenting units distant from Lookout Mountain. By 1962, these included the 1369th Photographic Squadron at Vandenberg AFB, providing photographic coverage for all the units there. Detachment 1 of the 1352nd PS worked from Elmendorf AFB, supporting Alaskan Air Command.

Detachment 2 was based at Ent AFB in Colorado and primarily worked with Air Defense Command, NORAD, and other major Air Force units in the region. Detachment 3 was based at Hickam AFB in Hawaii. Their main commitment was working with the 6954th Test Wing on its reconnaissance satellite film recovery mission. It also maintained a presence at Clark AB (Det 3-1) in the Philippines and Yamoto AS in Japan (DET 3-2).[11]

Over the next 18 years, the Squadron produced many films. The large majority of the classified movies about nuclear activities remain so. However, the unit's extensive facilities enabled it to make many high-quality, full-production films for the US Air Force. A unit history for the first half of 1960 indicates some of the staff and projects on which the Squadron worked. Some 60 percent of the

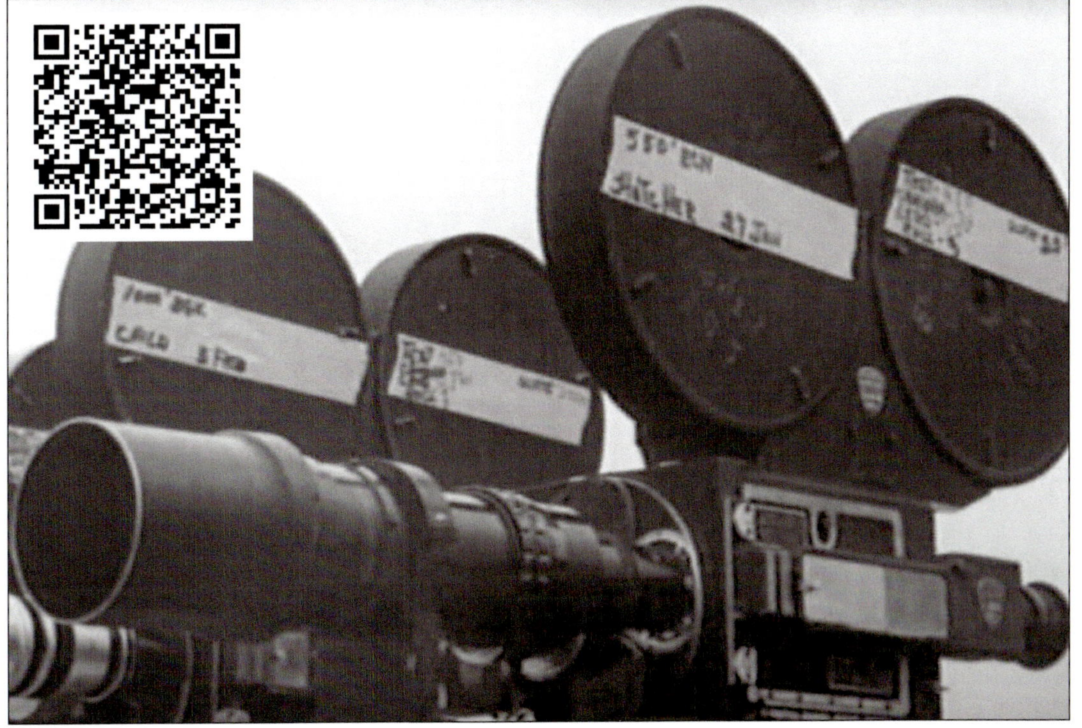

SFP-651 Air Force Photographic Highlights was a 1959 production intended to demonstrate the work of Air Force cameramen. The seven-minute film is high-quality and covers the first Air Force launch of an Atlas Missile. It shows in some detail the M-45 camera mounts and the various camera configurations used on them, including 24- and 48-inch lenses. Other sequences cover the X-15 and F-104 missile launches, Thunderbirds filming, nuclear testing, and an Air Force graduation. (Internet Archive)

unit effort at the time was in support of the USAF ballistic missile programme, producing a mix of classified and unclassified motion pictures as Film Reports (FR), Training Films (TF), Special Film Projects (SFP) and Film Training Aids (FTA). The unit covered some 10 launches from Vandenberg.

Examples of the movies produced at Lookout Mountain included documentation of Exercise Mobile Yoke (a large TAC deployment to SE Asia), medical support for missile operations, the Discoverer satellite, the MB-1 rocket for the F-101 Voodoo, nuclear flash, 'Crowflight' High Altitude Sampling Flights (HASP) carried out by the U-2 and another on the air transportation of the Atlas missile to name just some of the many hundreds of movies produced there.

Most were a combination of live-action and stock footage, many with staged material filmed on location or at Lookout Mountain with added sound, narration and any necessary animation and titling. To support this work, the 'writing division' had a staff of seven writers and a chief, an animation division dealing with titling and graphic displays, and a sound element division.

The Still Photo Division had a staff of 14 at that time, a mix of military and civilian personnel. Up to then, one of the most significant projects ever handled by the Division was '52/935', which covered the ongoing construction work and operations at Vandenberg AFB. This 'book' was created for General Wade of SAC's First Missile Division and involved 17,500 prints prepared in just 10 working days.[12]

By 1969, the ceasing of above-ground nuclear testing, the domination of television as the moving image medium and the war in SE Asia all compounded to see Lookout Mountains' value to the Air Force quickly decline. Said to have authored over 600 edited films,

the facility was closed, sold off, and its remaining responsibilities transferred elsewhere.

Filming Falling Stars

Discreetly hidden in plain sight for over 27 years, the 6594th Test Group flew a unique and initially very secret mission from Hickam AFB in Hawaii. Between August 1960 and June 1984, they regularly caught 'falling stars', or more accurately, 'buckets' of exposed US satellite reconnaissance film, jettisoned from space orbit high over the Northern Pacific. Over those 24 years, the unit completed exactly 40,000 mid-air recoveries, approximately 300 operationally, the remainder in training missions. They played a unique role in supporting Cold War space-based intelligence collection. C-119J aircraft briefly performed the recovery task from 1960, for just over a year, to be replaced by the role-specific modified JC-130B and later JC-130H Hercules.[13] This activity was of such great importance that virtually every aspect was filmed by photographers attached to the unit for documentation and training purposes.

The first photo reconnaissance, 'Corona', plus later 'Gambit' and 'Hexagon' satellites, maintained polar orbits. De-orbiting and recovery were initiated as they passed over Kodiak, Alaska, heading southwards. Between 600,000ft and 550,000ft, the Corona satellites began de-orbiting by pitching downwards and ejecting the nose cone from the priceless bucket of exposed reconnaissance film. After the parachute cover and heat shield separated, the deceleration chute deployed between 65,000ft and 60,000ft. The main parachute opened between 60,000ft to 55,000ft. If all went well, it ended with a successful aerial retrieval between 15,000ft to 12,000ft. If not, it ended in the Pacific.

The 'recovery rig' on the C-119J and later JC-130s was similar. The JC-130s carried a crew of a pilot, copilot, navigator, flight engineer, direction-finding equipment operator, telemetry and winch operators, four equipment riggers and an in-flight photographer. The rear crew opened the aircraft's cargo doors, inserted two 34-foot-long poles into actuators, and lowered them below the aircraft as they passed very close over the descending chute. They were fitted with a 'trapeze-like' arrangement of parachute recovery line, equipped with eight hooks secured and woven into the rig. This first pass over the descending capsule assessed the parachute's condition and descent rate. To successfully 'catch' the payload bucket, the retrieving aircraft's rate of descent had to match that of the parachute exactly. The payload parachutes usually descended between 1,500ft to 2,000ft a minute. There were risks of crew hypoxia from operating at these altitudes for prolonged periods, which meant the aircrew pre-breathed 100 percent oxygen for 45 minutes before the Estimated Time of Parachute Deployment (ETPD).

For every live load recovery, there were roughly 133 practice recoveries. Training was intensive, and there was stiff competition between Squadron crews to be the most successful. One training recovery technique involved flying at 18,000ft and 'throwing' a 210lb training package from the aircraft whilst another aircraft circled below to capture it again. Aircraft could also play this game of 'aerial catch' by themselves. Carrying training packages, they climbed up to 18,000ft and threw one out. The pilot quickly reduced power, applied flap, and descended to make the recovery.

Meanwhile, the rear crew rapidly rigged the 'trapeze' ready for the catch. The onboard cameraman filmed all of these activities, watching the rigging of the aircraft but, more importantly, filming the approach and capture of the training capsule. From the processed imagery, pilot and crew performance was reviewed and graded.

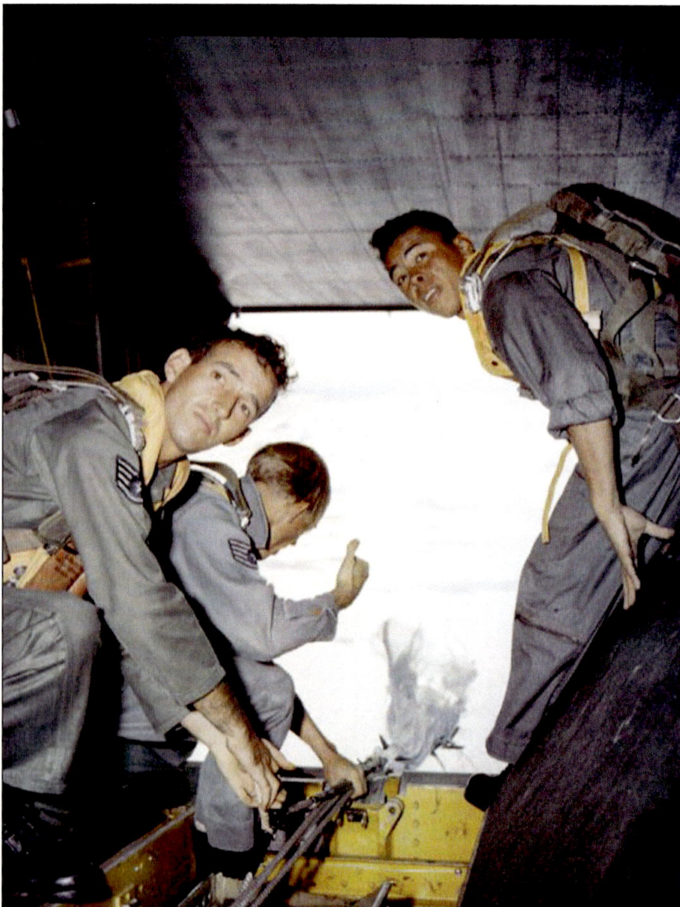

With the recovery parachute safely captured, the C-119 crew is ready to winch the package back onto the aircraft. (NARA)

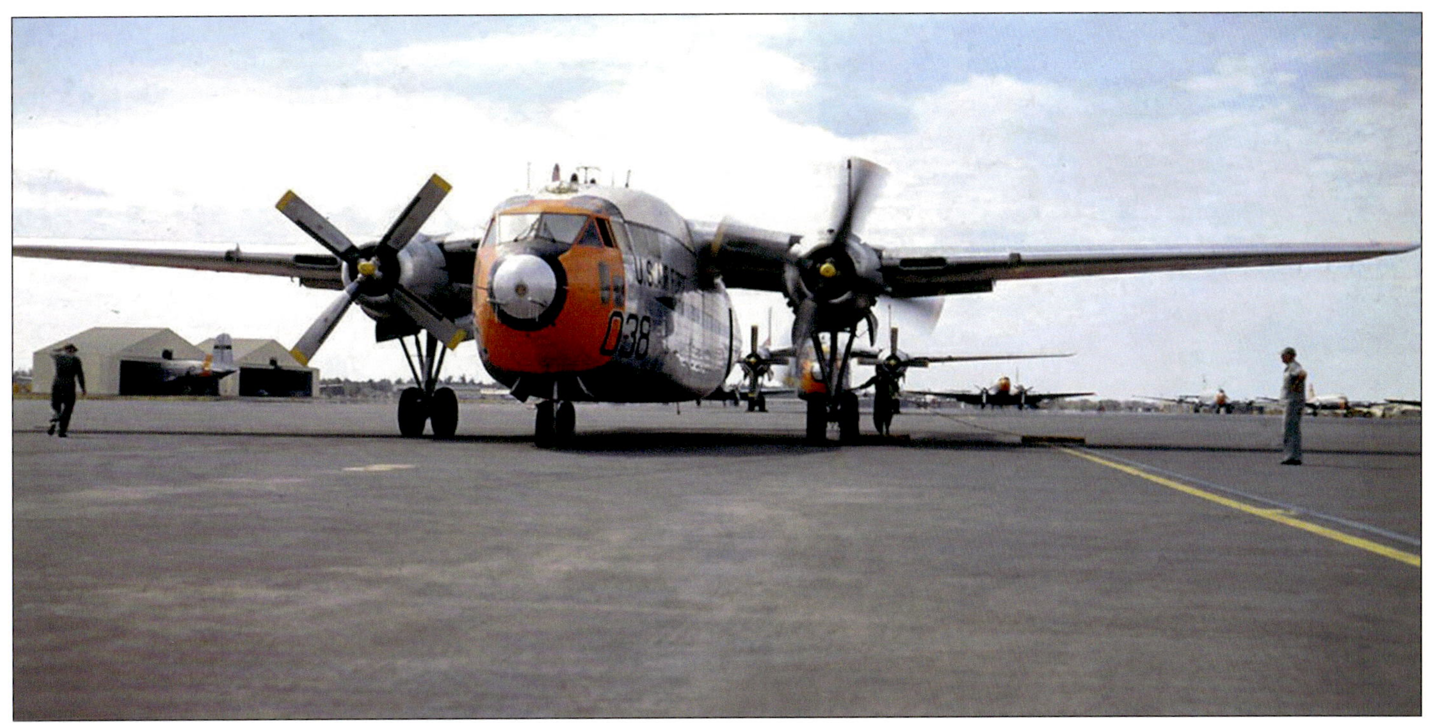

Part 1. (YouTube/Adamsfl)

Part 2. (YouTube/Adamsfl)

One of the most remarkable films produced at Lookout Mountain by the 1352nd Photo Group was *Catch a Falling Star* (SFP-1100). It documents, in considerable detail, using aerial and set-produced imagery, the process of recovering the early Corona satellites, most likely filmed in the summer of 1961. (USAF/1352 PG)

Catching packages in flight required skilled and calm airmanship. The final approach was an 'extremely visual process', dependent on the pilot. Ideally, the top of the parachute was six feet below the aircraft as it passed over it, and the hooks then entangled the chute's nylon load-lines. On capture, the parachute collapsed, often tearing, trailed out behind the plane, and the payload cable fed out. Once stabilised, the crew winched the bucket aboard and secured it.

In July/August 1961, as the 6593rd Test Squadron was converting to the JC-130B, APCS photographers extensively recorded the final days of the JC-119 performing the satellite film recovery task. The 1352nd Air Photo Group at Lookout Mountain AFS edited the images, adding sound, actors, and narration that described the whole process from launch to recovery in a full-length produced film, *Catch A Falling Star*. It is the best publicly available imagery of this very specialised mission.

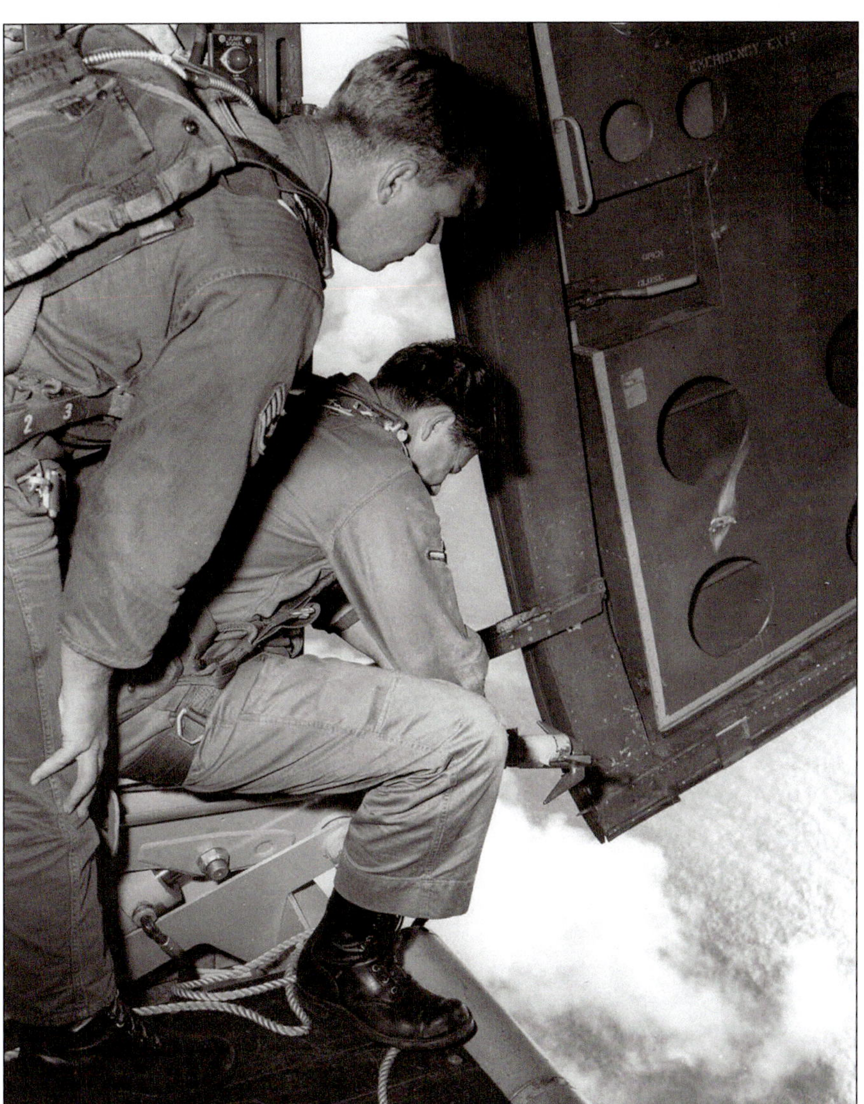

Rigging the aircraft for a recovery involved opening the C-119's rear door and fixing the trapeze to catch the load. (USAF)

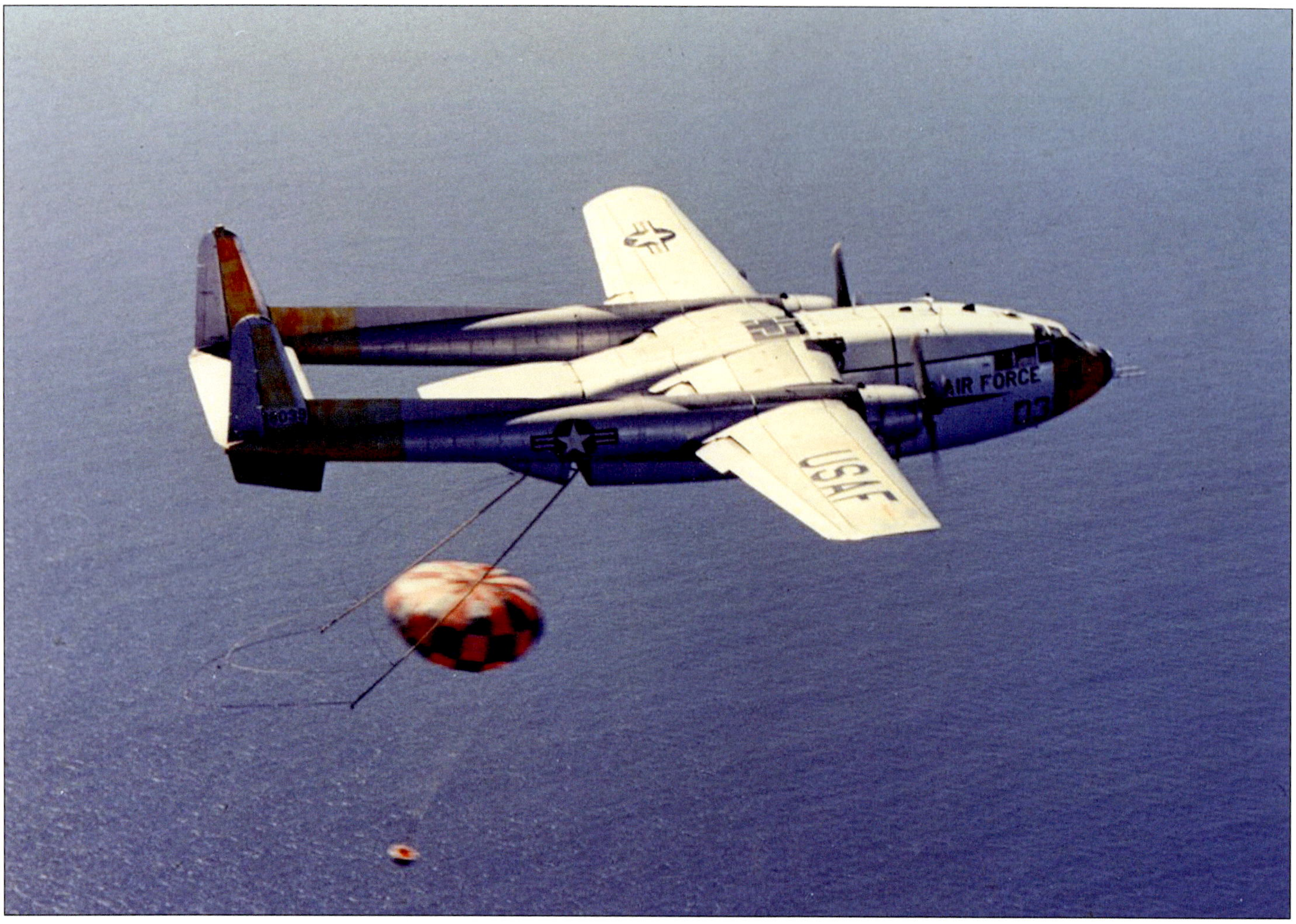

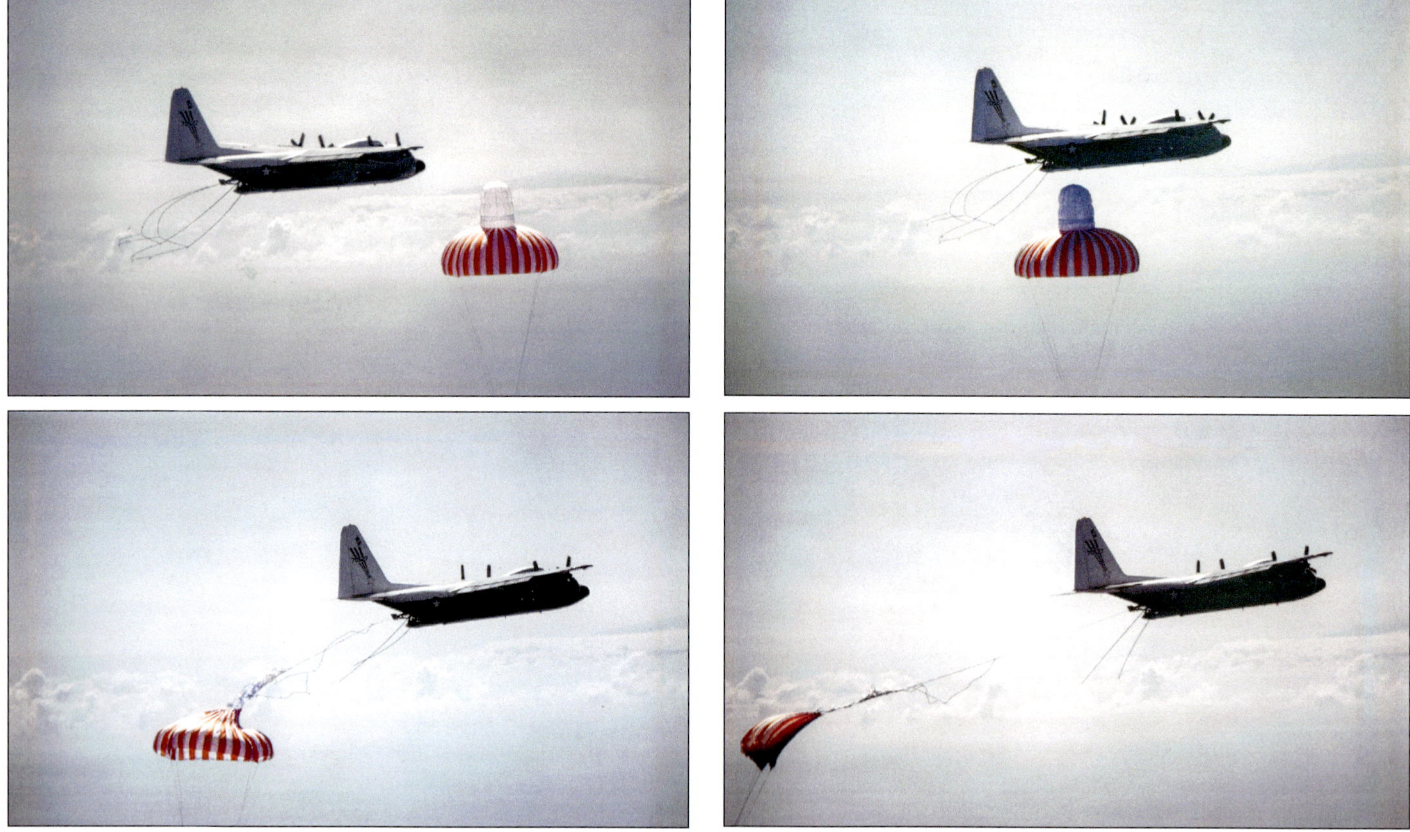

A C-119J is about to capture a training 'bucket'. (USAF)

Sequence showing a practice Mk8 'Hexagon' satellite photo 'bucket' recovery. The JC-130B was flying at 135 knots, and both aircraft and package descending at 1,500 feet per minute. (USAF via Al Blankenship)

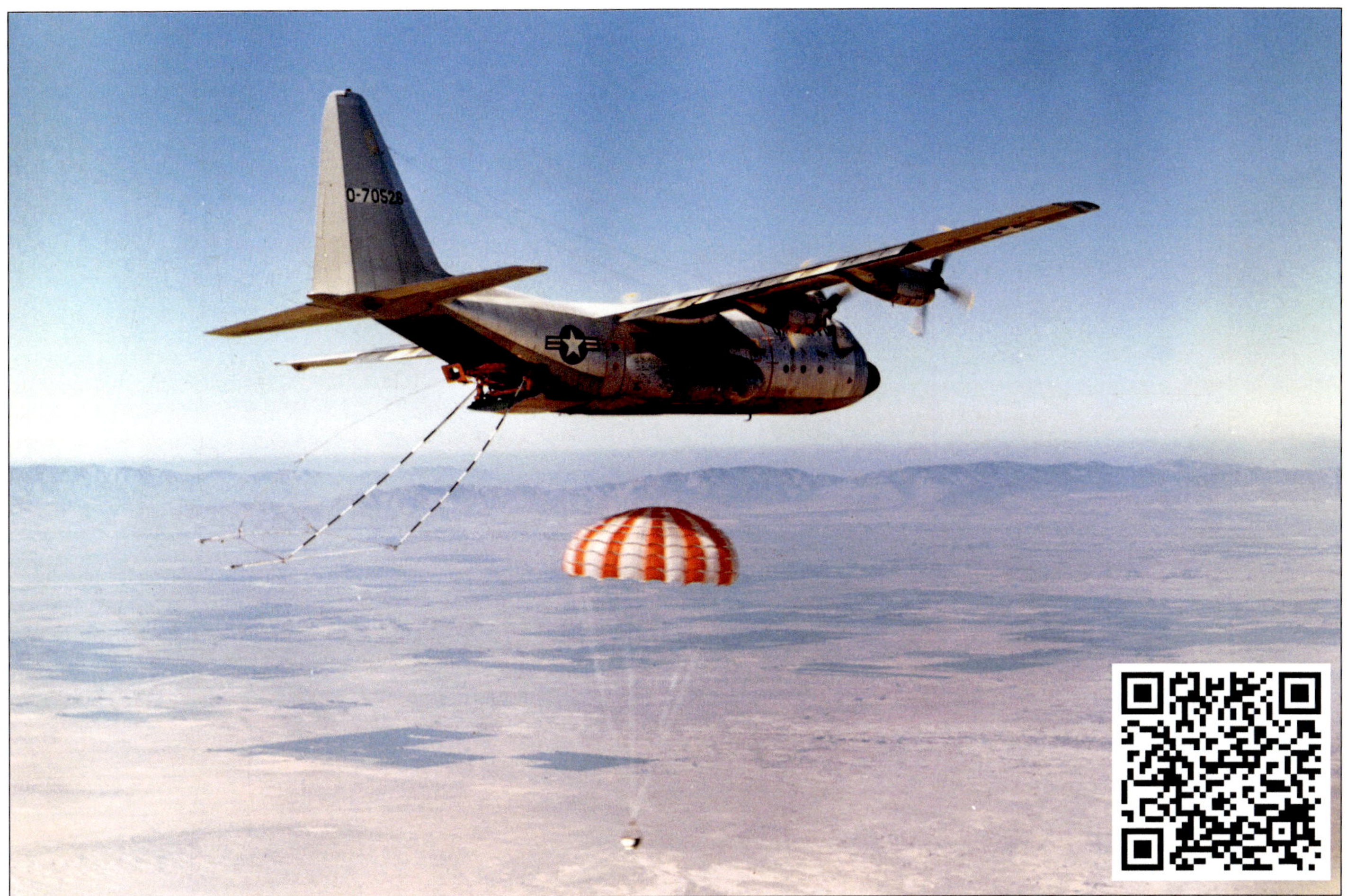

An unedited reel shows a load recovery exercise for a JC-130 with internal rear compartment and cockpit footage. (NARA) (YouTube/Buyout Footage Historic Film Archive)

Life on Det 3

We get a detailed snapshot of the photo support provided to the 6594th Test Group in 1962 by Hickham AFB's Detachment 3 of the 1352nd PS unit history. As it described:

Coverage consists of remotely operated rapid sequence still and high-speed motion picture of photography of live, test and training aerial recovery missions. During this period, the Recovery Control Group has continued its extensive training and development programme. This programme has brought about the need for modification of JC-130B electrical circuitry for multiple camera operation, including the installation of high-speed Milliken cameras. Photographs of these operations are used for engineering evaluation of the recovery equipment function during recovery operations and photo critique by pilots to maintain recovery proficiency. Analysis of photographs has resulted in the development and procurement of improved parachutes and recovery poles for more positive payload recovery. Det 3 aircrew cameramen have flown 16 live recovery missions this period and have averaged 43 practice missions each month, compiling 2,142 man hours, logging a total of 1,440 flying hours, and producing 5,000 feet of 35mm B&W and 19,471 feet 16mm B&W motion picture film, 53,678 exposures 70mm B&W film, 943 enlargements and 1,234 8x10 viewgraphs.[14]

A later Det 3 history from the first half of 1964 records the significance of its work on satellite recovery operations, not just for documentation purposes but also to meet technical needs. 'The employment of high-speed cameras to record special tests has become more and more important to the 6593rd Test Squadron. In their attempts to improve recovery procedures, many special rigs have been used. This experimental equipment frequently has flaws revealed by the Milliken DBM-5 cameras'.

The unit also became involved in Project 'Ashcan'. This involved a radioactive sampling device being lifted into the high atmosphere (up to 100,000ft) by balloon, which was then jettisoned to order and captured by a JC-130 like a satellite recovery. High-speed P-2 strike cameras and the Millikens would record the catches.

However, there were frustrations for the cameramen, as was explained:

Due to the nature of the recovery programme, we are frequently hampered by a lack of information due to security… The major problem which occurs is that due to a lack of knowledge, we are seldom able to recommend improved photo procedures. No member of Det 3 has seen any 'live' recovery film in over two years due to what we consider to be an excess of 'need to know' criteria.[15]

Support for the satellite recovery missions absorbed considerable resources, as the report for the second half of 1964 recorded. Training missions were flown nearly daily, engaging the Detachment's three motion picture photographers and the two still photographers. They devoted the 'majority of their time processing the 70mm film exposed by the hi-speed P-2 strike cameras'.

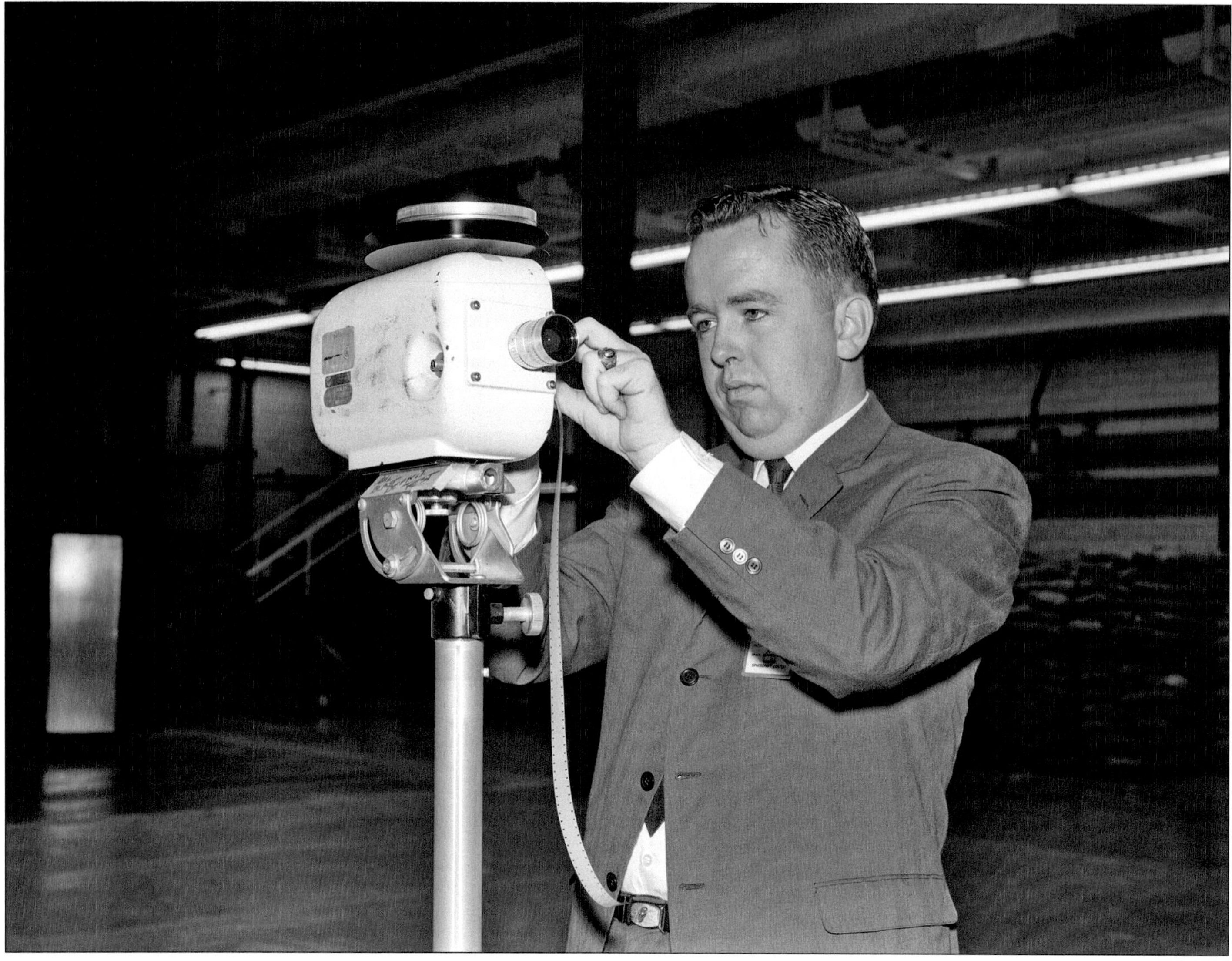

The Milliken DBM-5 high-speed camera was used for many specialised tasks, including recording Falling Star missions. (DVIDS via NASA)

The film from operational satellite recovery missions was not processed locally but was immediately airlifted back to the US. Even without those tasks, there were still significant pressures on the Detachment. These operational responsibilities:

Required seven motion picture cameramen plus a maintenance man on a full-time basis. Each mission of this type consisted of four to six days of ground alert time and one day in the air. Alerts frequently began in the very early morning hours and, in effect, demanded the full attention of the crews assigned. Twenty-four such missions were accomplished in the reporting period [six months]. This amounted to almost a constant alert status for the motion picture branch. Due to the heavy workload in this area, all motion picture cameramen, plus the Commander, Operations Officer and NCOIC, were fully qualified to fly such missions and had done so on frequent occasions.[16]

As Dave van de Brake described:

In 1984, I got picked up by the 6594th Test Group. I started doing instrumentation photography with them, where you're on the command deck and have your crew position. When we're winching in this satellite bucket at the end of this orange and white chute, sometimes you needed to jump up with your camera and catch that action because the higher-ups want to see our guys in action.

The unit provided support to crewed and uncrewed space missions, too. The unit history for the 1352nd Photo Group history for the first half of 1969 recorded 'documenting 365 practice aerial recovery missions and covering the splashdown of Apollo 10 on May 26, 1969, and soon after loading the recovered capsule into a MAC C-133 in Hawaii'.[17]

While all these tasks were ongoing in the mid-1960s, escalating developments in Southeast Asia would profoundly reshape the work of the USAF's Photographic Squadrons. Their involvement would take them firmly back into the combat documentation role.

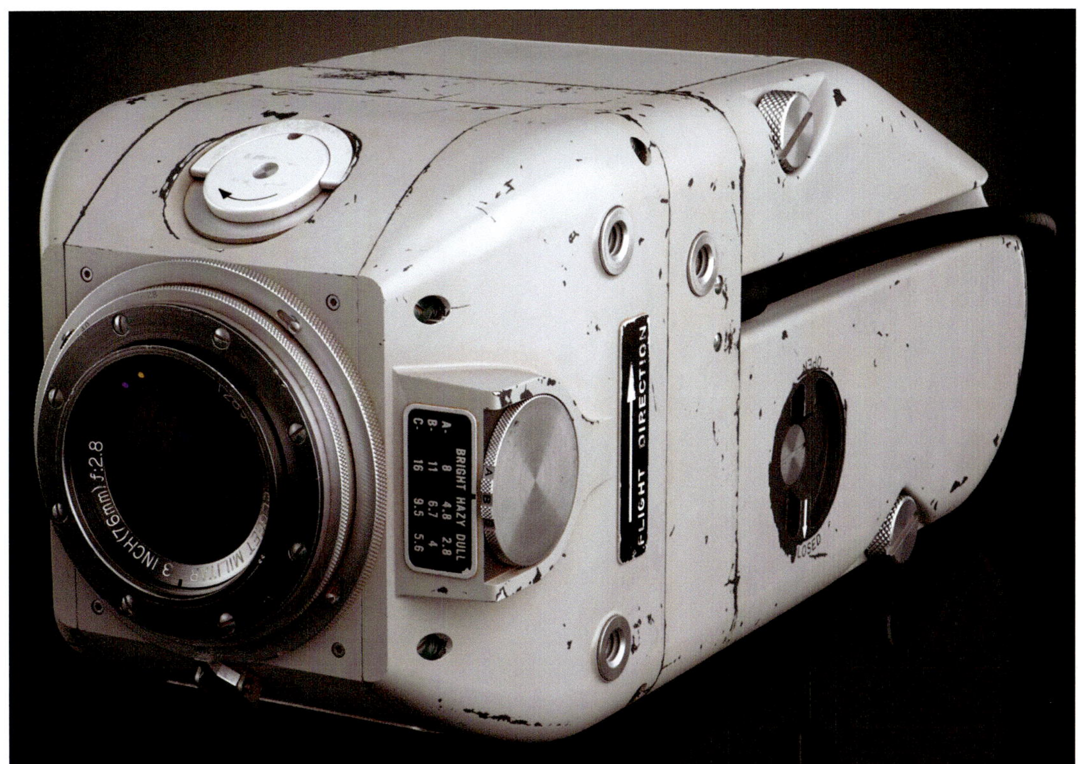

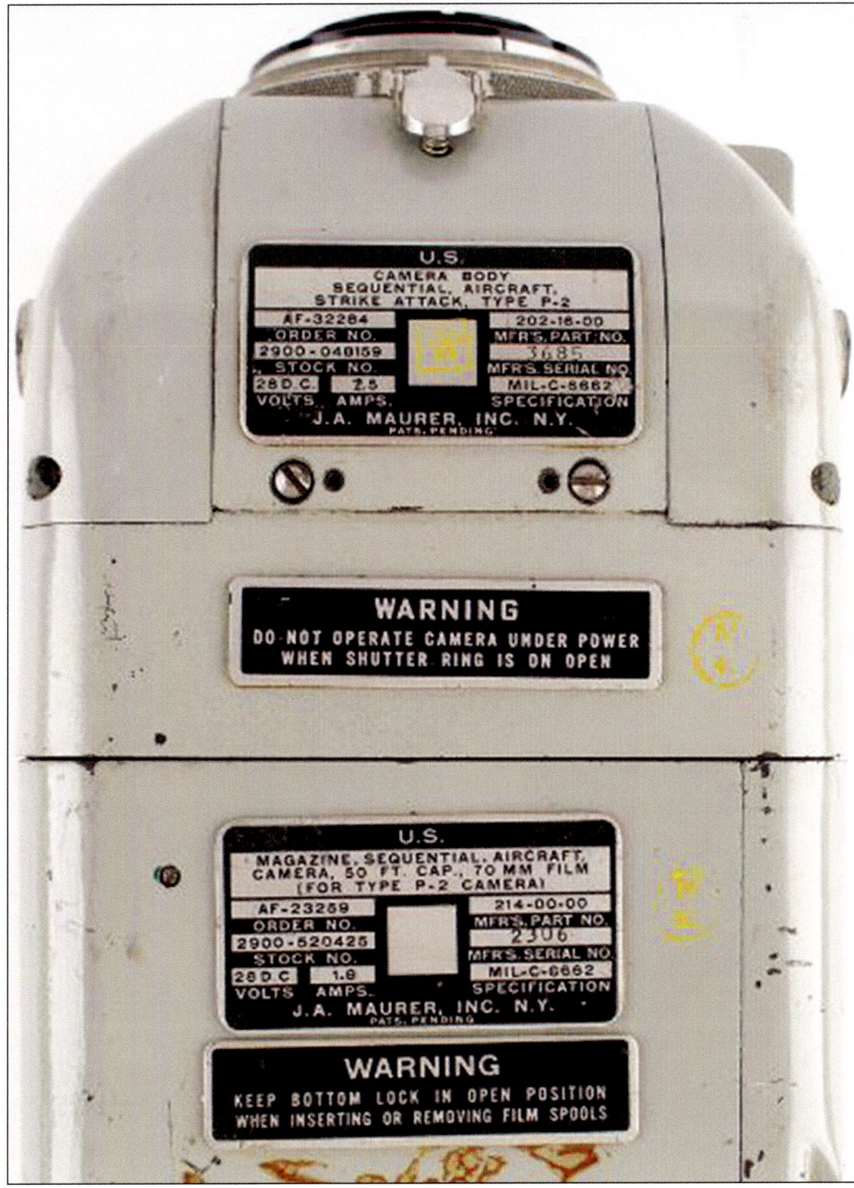

The Maurer P-2 Strike Attack camera, another high-speed device, was used to catch satellite retrievals. (Shinji Watanabe)

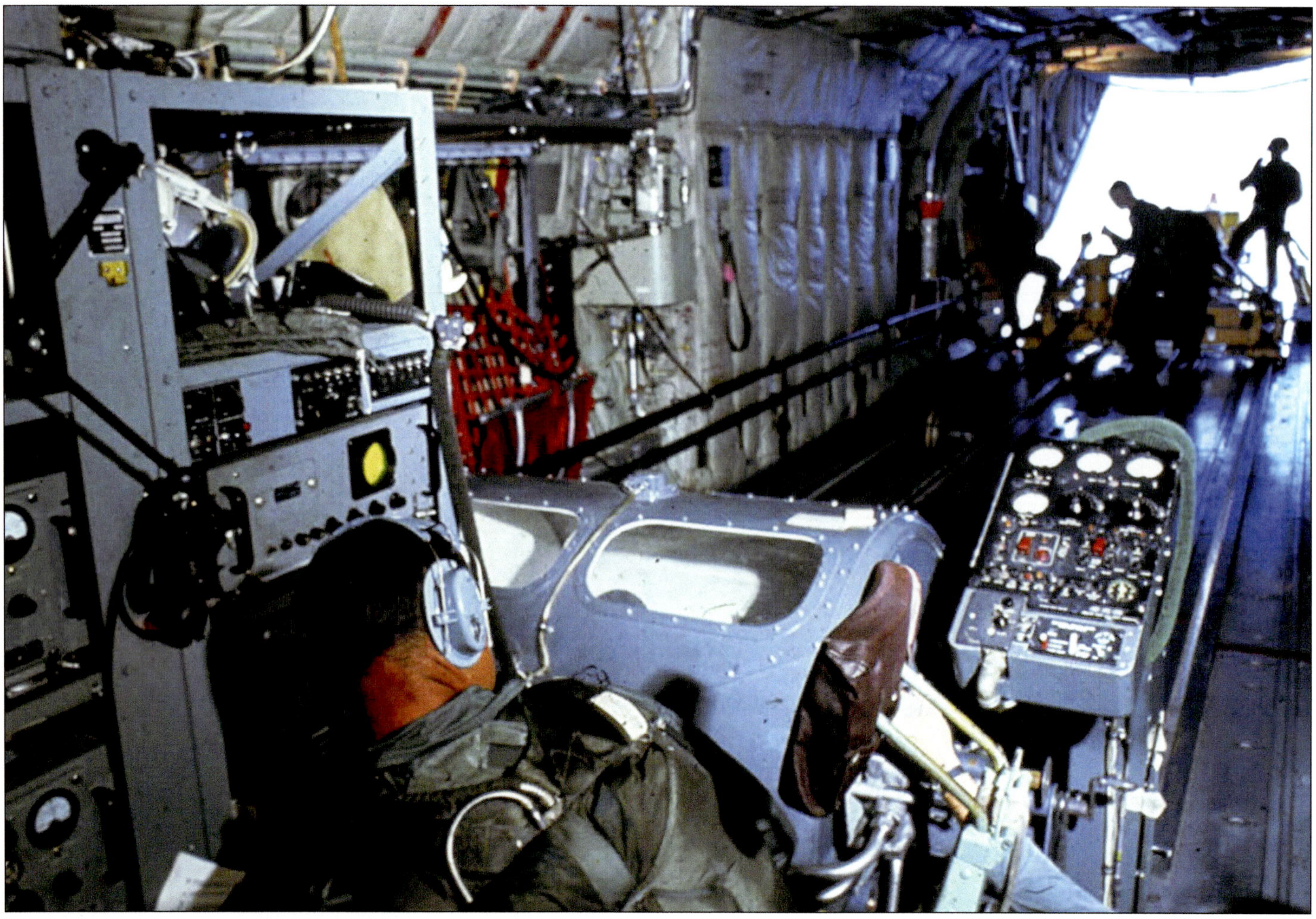

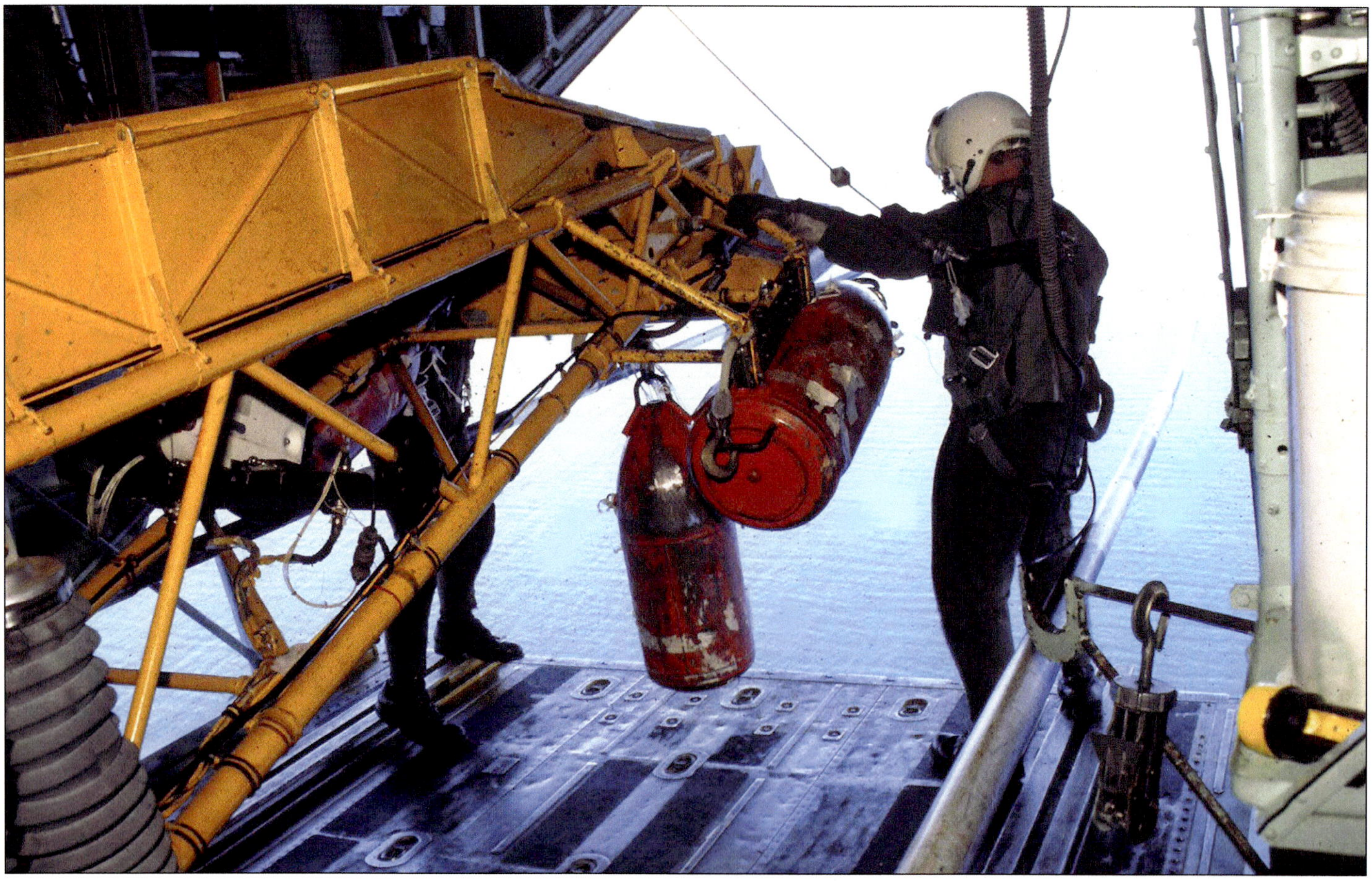

In the rear of the C-130, the crew was responsible for recovering the 'bucket' into the aircraft. Their work was filmed, sometimes using high-speed movie cameras, to check equipment function and devise possible improvements. (USAF)

6

WAR IN SOUTHEAST ASIA

Combat Camera Units were quickly inactivated at the end of World War Two, and the capability was not fully reconstructed during the Korean War. As the USAF became heavily committed to the war in Southeast Asia, it became clear that a more robust combat camera capability was necessary.

On 1 January 1966, the establishment of Military Airlift Command (MAC) replaced MATS. Its formation changed how the USAF's photographic operations were managed. The work of the APCS was reorganised, and the new Aerospace Audio-Visual Service was created, adopting some of the old organisation's tasks.

Into Vietnam

MAC's command history has outlined the evolution of AA-VS operations in SE Asia:

> The organisation began with a 19-person detachment and gradually grew to over 500 authorisations. Initially, finding enough qualified personnel to fill these slots was a major problem. In 1966, for example, although the service had 508 authorized spaces, just 151 audiovisual specialists were serving in Vietnam. To further exacerbate the situation, even units with adequate personnel often did not have enough audiovisual equipment.[1]

However, it was not just the number of people and their equipment that were problematic. There were more practical difficulties on the frontline. The combat documentation task for AA-VS was about to expand exponentially, and it was ill-prepared:

> Poor technique and the absence of a suitable camera pod also hampered early attempts to document air strikes. During the first years of the war, tactical fighter pilots were rotated to Southeast Asia for 90-day temporary duty (TDY) periods. This short-tour policy prevented adequate training in photographic requirements. Naturally, the pilots were more concerned with hitting their target and returning safely, than documenting the strike. Cameramen tried riding along in the backseat, taking pictures with hand-held cameras, but they could not hold their cameras steady enough to get useful photographs. Technicians improvised a camera pod that hung from the strike aircraft. This makeshift apparatus, however, vibrated excessively, and the pictures were of little value.

Through 1966, 'The Aerospace Audio-Visual Service began to overcome many of these technical difficulties and had begun processing large amounts of film in Southeast Asia'. Intelligence personnel used strike photography to analyse the effects of air attacks and recommend new targets. Co-locating AA-VS Detachments at the major air bases from where ground attack aircraft operated meant that the 'pilots reviewed the photos to assess their performances, while the missions were still fresh in their minds'.

AA-VS cameramen also provided ground photographs to supplement their aerial contributions. Technical shots depicting cargo handling, aircraft loading, refuelling, aerial port activities, airdrops, and air rescue operations helped supervisors and instructors train inexperienced personnel. Photographs often accompanied human interest stories. Film documentation of Air Force activities in Southeast Asia has proved invaluable to historians and other analysts interested in studying the war.[2]

The 600th Photo Squadron

There were soon changes in-theatre, too. The war's rapid escalation in SE Asia brought a sudden surge in demand for photographic and film services and increased demands for reconnaissance and battle damage imagery.

The growth of operations and the varying photographic demands created problems with the scope, quality, and scale of imagery, necessitating a much-improved response. Photographic requirements were mainly handled by personnel on a constantly revolving TDY basis rather than establishing a more stable presence. HQ USAF conducted a brief but detailed study of those changing needs. As a result of the review, responsibility for implementing its recommendations was passed on to AA-VS in December 1965. The 600th Photographic Squadron (PS) was activated on 8 February 1966, headquartered at Tan Son Nhut AB in South Vietnam. It was to become 'The single manager combat photo capability, including all photography except reconnaissance' for HQ USAF, PACAF and 7th Air Force.

The Squadron's tasks included handling all the Air Force's combat documentation and air-to-air gun camera photography film footage, and still imagery of air strikes. It processed some radar scope photography and panoramic KA-71A imagery, from F-105Ds to collect immediate post-strike battle damage assessment.

To handle all the tasks, detachments were created at bases across South Vietnam, and a further six in Thailand, subordinated to the 600th PS via the 601st Photo Flight, to manage them. Motion picture lab services were established at four locations to handle all the 16mm colour film processing and printing, with still photo processing labs at 10 locations. The 600th Photo Squadron Detachments were initially established at:

Det 4	Cam Ranh
Det 5	Phan Rang
Det 6	Bien Hoa
Det 7	Da Nang
Det 8	Tuy Hoa
Det 13	Nha Trang
Det 14	Pleiku
Det 15	Binh Thuy
Det 16	Phu Cat

The 601st Photo Flight was headquartered at Korat AB, Thailand, and was responsible for the in-country Detachments.

Det 1	Korat
Det 2	Takhli

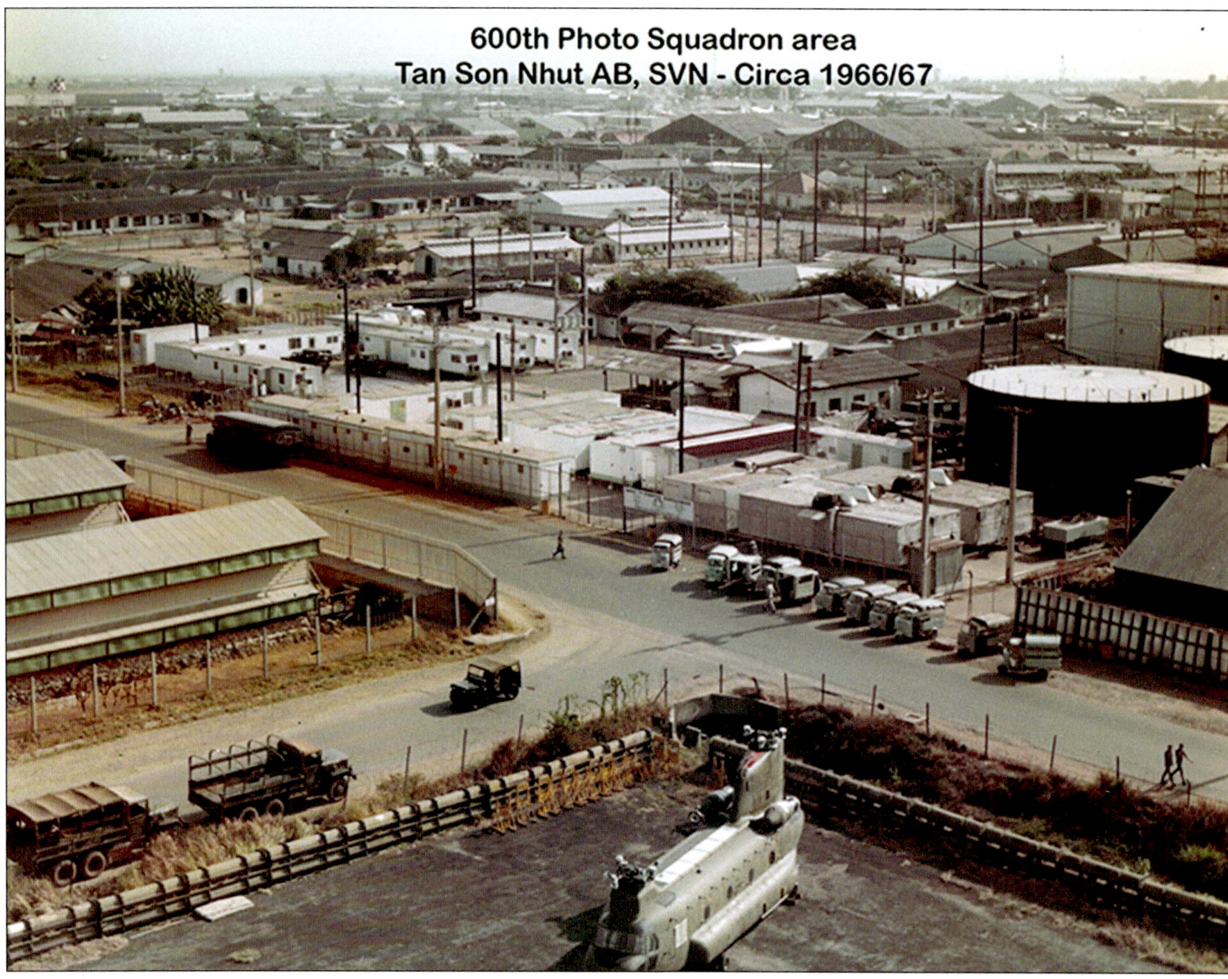

The 600th Photo Squadron compound at Tan Son Nhut AB in 1966–67. (Via usafcombat camera.org)

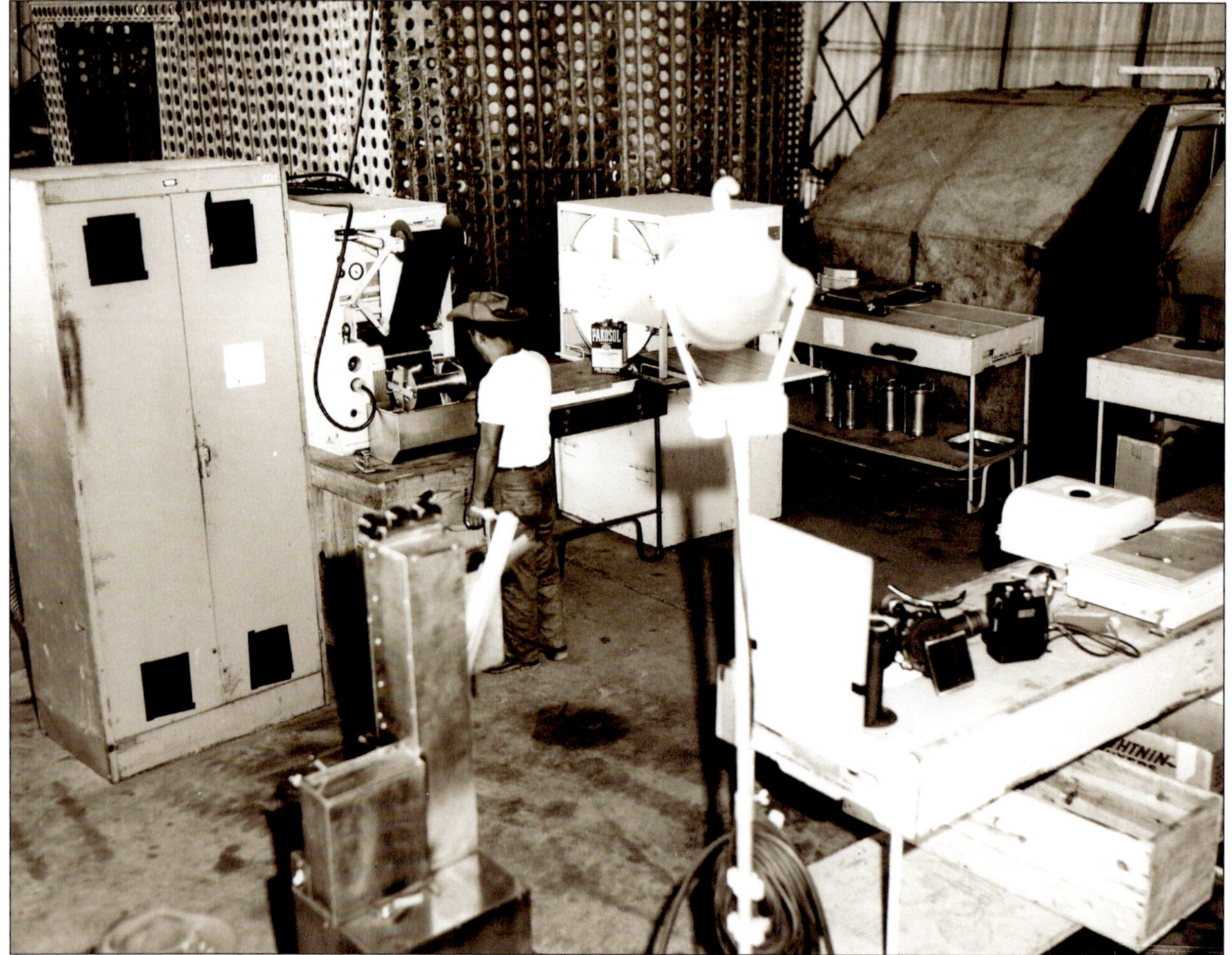

600th PS Airman drying film at Ben Hoa AB in 1962. (NARA)

Det 3   Ubon
Det 9   Udorn
Det 10   U-Tapao
Det 11   Don Muang
Det 12   Nakhon Phanom

To give a snapshot of the scale of operations, in January 1967, the 600th PS unit consisted of 16 officers and 374 enlisted men. Their camera equipment included one 16mm B1a, eight 16mm Arriflex, two 35mm Arriflex MP, seven Mamiya C-3, 12 Graflex XL, 16 Graflex 4X5 Super Speed, one Rolliflex, 120 SGIIIs and two Polaroid Pathfinders. In early 1967, the Squadron was staffed by 15 'mopic' cameramen, six still photographers, and two 'mopic' sound specialists.[3]

Combat Documentation

Fully gearing up the Squadron's combat documentation capabilities took some time. Cameramen began flying with and working alongside frontline aircrews and ground troops in operations against the Viet Cong. The early difficulties caused by the rapid expansion of activities and the lack of experienced personnel and specialised equipment were addressed.

However, the expansion of operations soon exerted a human cost. On 19 July 1966, AA-VS lost its first cameraman in combat, A1C Darryl Winters. He was 'flying as a backseat cameraman in an F-100F when it crashed during an attack on a Viet Cong position in South Vietnam'. This was Winter's second tour of Vietnam and was his 305th combat mission.[4] That was a vast number compared to the number of missions flown by aircrews during their tours.

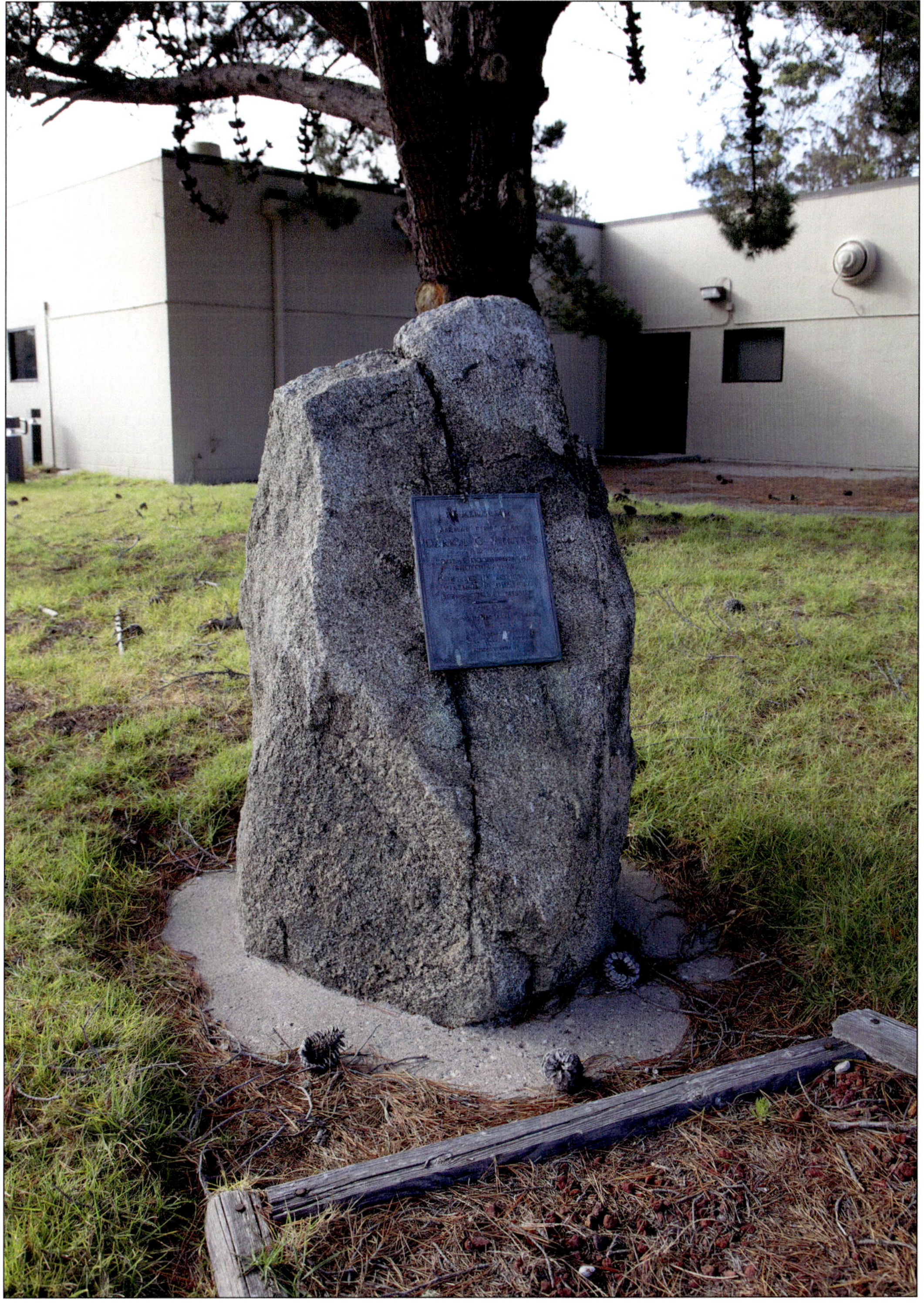

A memorial plaque to cameraman A1C Daryl Winters in a now partially abandoned part of Vandenberg AFB. (https://www.usafcombatcamera.org/the-darryl-gordon-winters-story/)

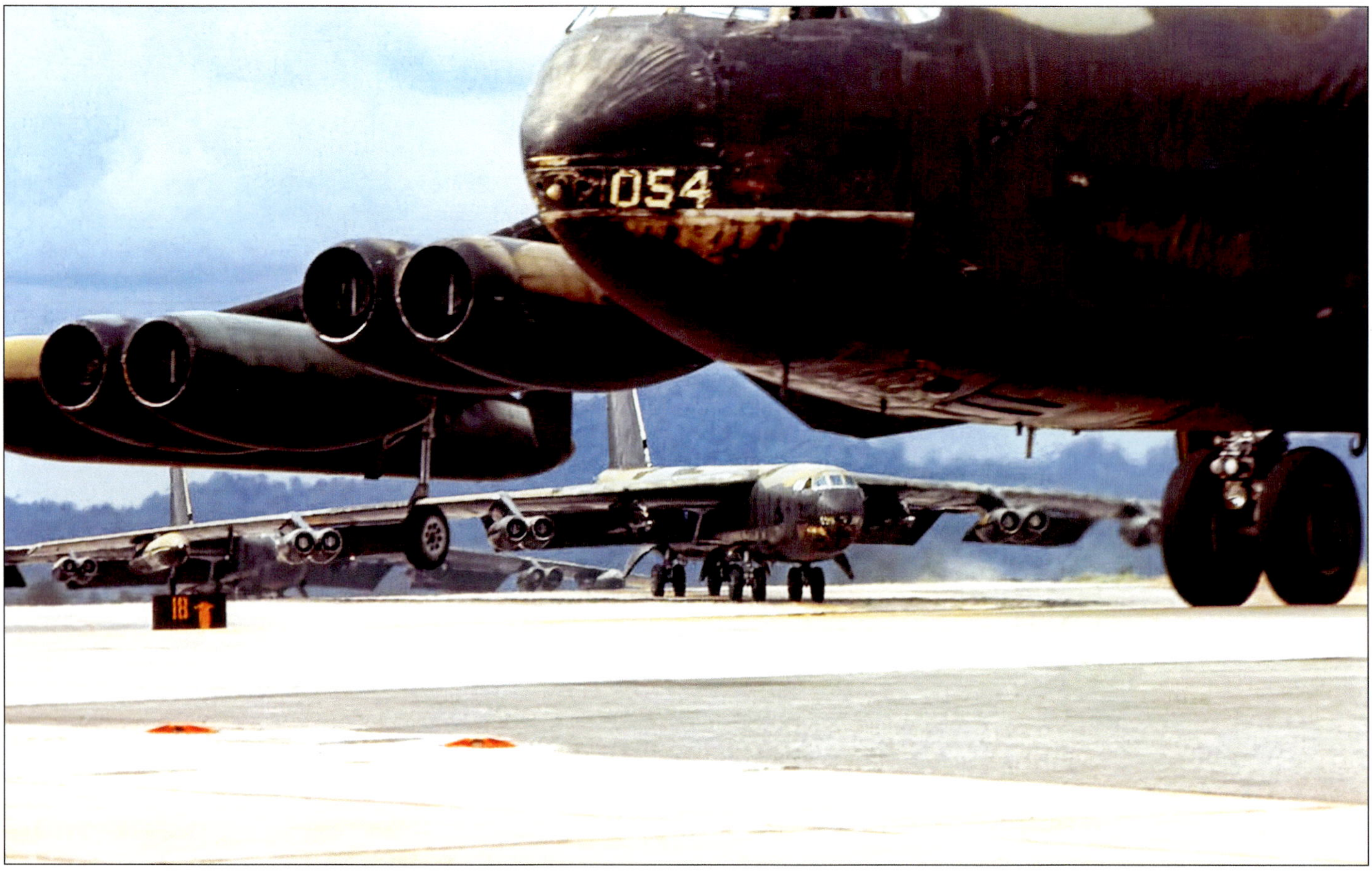

B-52Ds taxying at U-Tapao AB in Thailand for a Linebacker mission in 1972. (USAF)

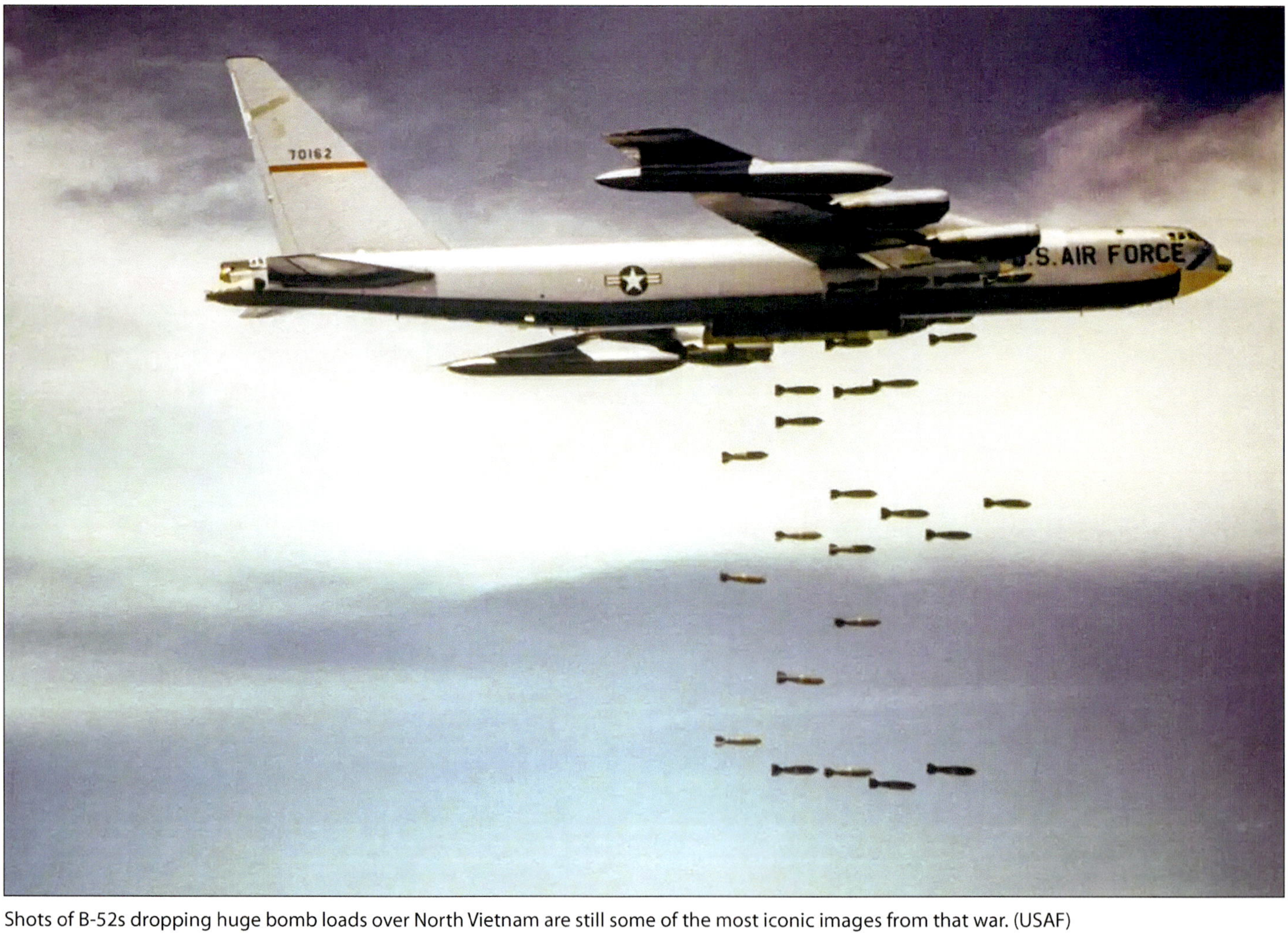

Shots of B-52s dropping huge bomb loads over North Vietnam are still some of the most iconic images from that war. (USAF)

Project Skypoint

Vital pre- and post-attack reconnaissance imagery was not the responsibility of AA-VS. However, senior commanders attached considerable importance to documenting US air strikes from the earliest days of the Air Force's involvement in Southeast Asia. Project Skypoint was intended to provide the means to do this more effectively.

The images of weapons being dropped by USAF aircraft are an enduring feature of regularly used video material in documentaries about the war in Southeast Asia. To produce this imagery, specialist camera modifications were required to enable their effective use during combat operations and sometimes put photographers into the air to film the attacks. Later, for the massive B-52 bombing raids that were flown from distant Guam and Thailand, cameras were rigged to show the bombs falling from the giant bombers' cavernous bomb bays. At the same time, other cameramen filmed the bombs dropping from adjacent aircraft in their formation, as during World War Two. To complete the scene, imagery was needed to show the bombs detonating on the ground targets.

In the 600th PS, the available airborne camera equipment supply grew rapidly. By the end of 1966, this included 22 Type IV camera pods and 321 N-9 gun cameras. The intention was to process all the camera pod and blister camera imagery locally and as rapidly as possible. Once processed, it was passed back to the aircraft's pilot/crew to give them immediate feedback on their attack. The ability to do this was said to have generated considerable enthusiasm for the project among the pilots and crews.

The pace of equipping aircraft with suitable cameras accelerated, too. In July 1966, only three aircraft were equipped with blister cameras, but by December, there were seven F-105s, three F-4Cs, and eight F-100s. Different blister installations were developed for each aircraft type but intended to achieve the same results. During the latter half of 1966, 16 of 23 podded cameras were lost due to the loss of the aircraft carrying them.[5]

The first six months of 1967 increased the pace, adding external blister cameras to the primary combat aircraft in-theatre, including the F-100, F-105, and F-4. These cameras were activated when ordnance was released. Facing rearwards, and when dropped from standard operating altitudes, they captured the fall of the weapons until detonation. Much of such imagery continues to be used in documentaries showing air strikes in Southeast Asia from these and similar cameras.

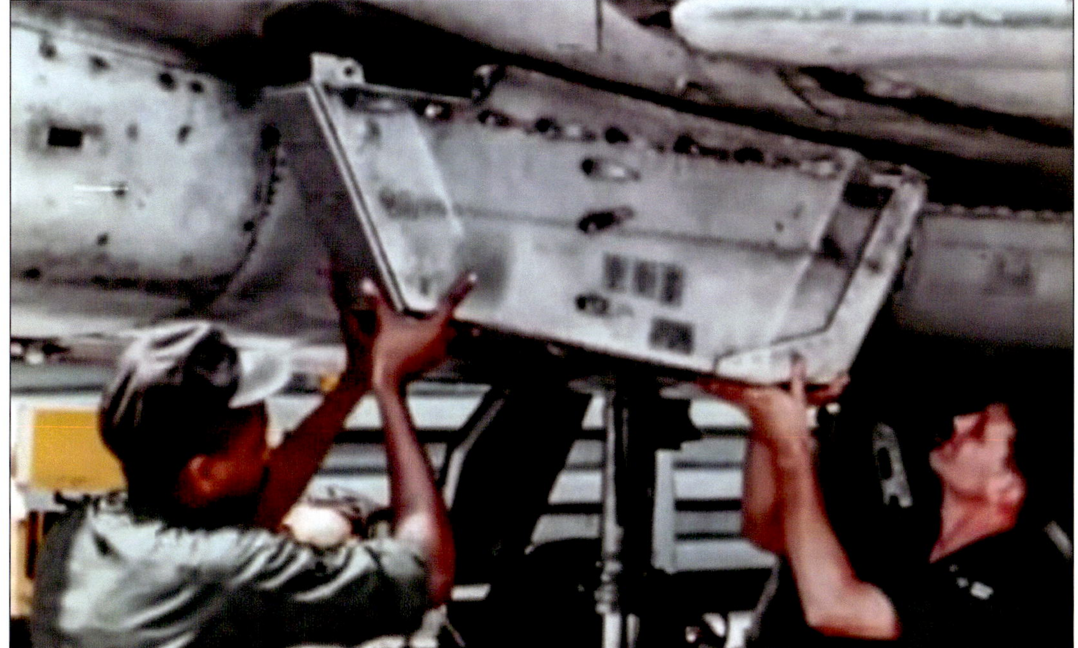

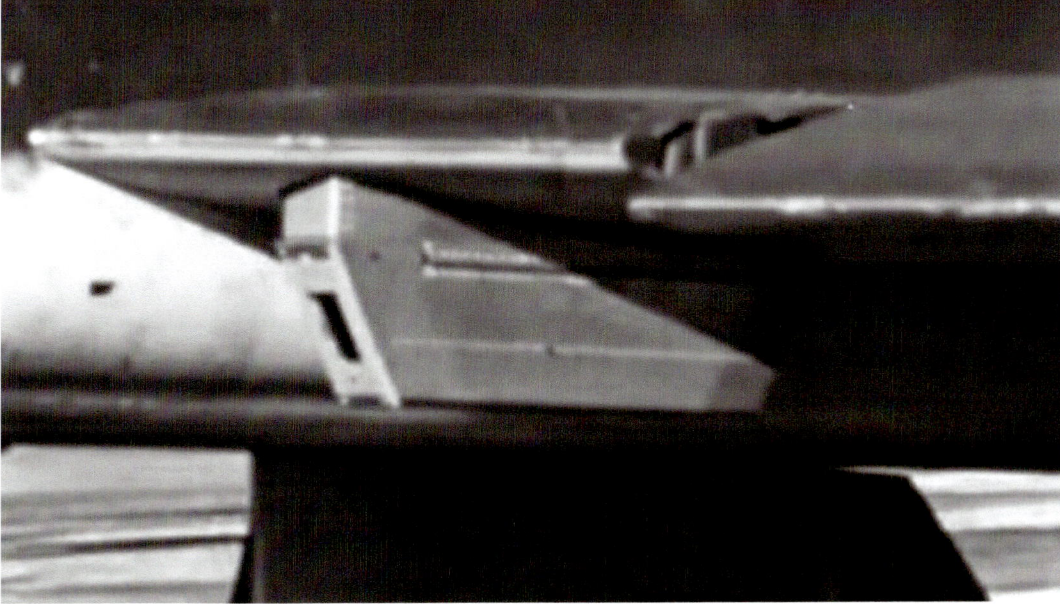

Early on, fitting an external forward-looking camera to the F-100 Super Sabre required using a vital weapons pylon. Soon, a fixed fuselage camera blister solution was developed to record weapons delivery. Good quality images of the arrangement have been challenging to locate. (USAF/NARA)

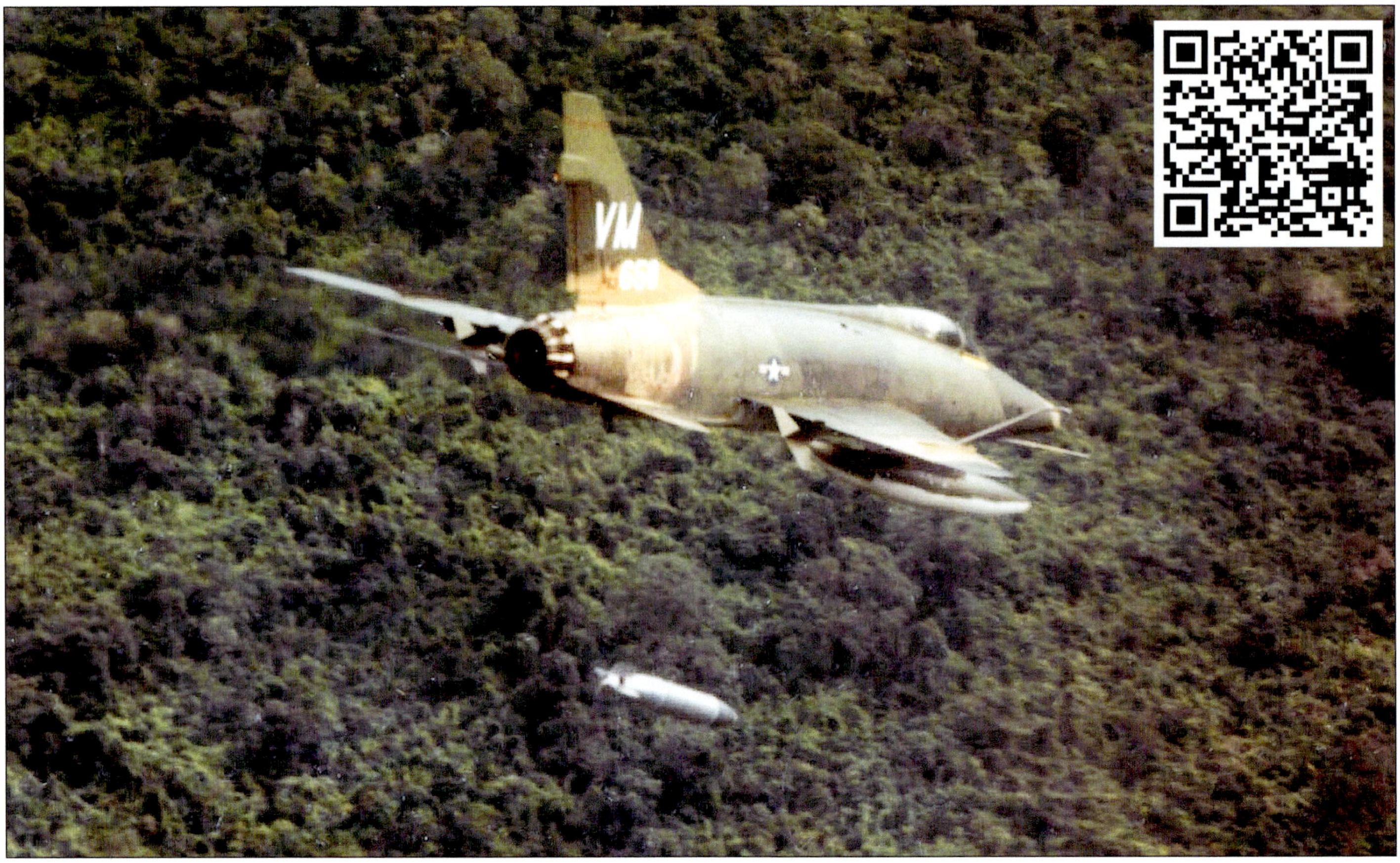

Produced by the 1352nd Photo Group, *Air Strikes Southeast Asia* (FR944), from 1968, documents a wide range of air strikes carried out by numerous aircraft types using different types of ordnance. The film includes rearward and forward-looking strafing imagery. (NARA) (YouTube/PeriscopeFilm)

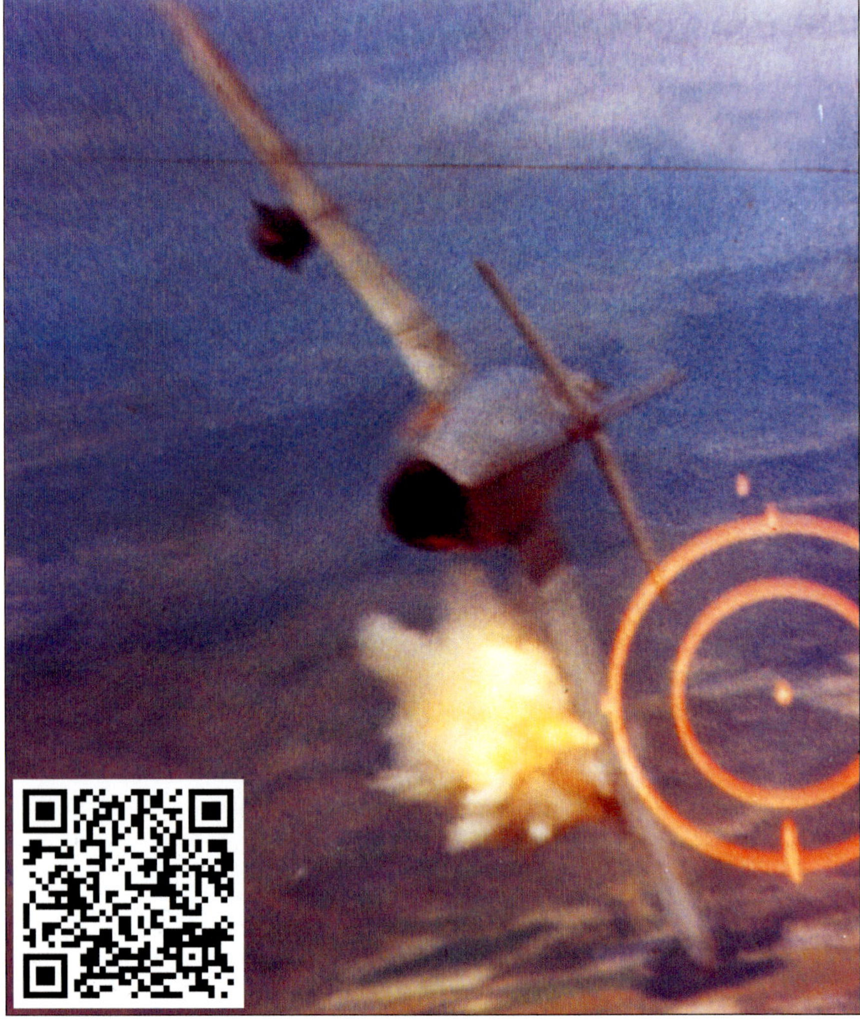

A rare colour image of a MiG-17 being hit over North Vietnam. USAF Film Report (FR879), *Air Strikes North 1966,* includes footage of the bombing of Hanoi and some rare air-to-air gun camera film showing the destruction of a Mig-17. (NARA) (YouTube/PeriscopeFilm)

External Camera Pods

The advent of externally carried podded cameras dramatically advanced combat documentation and weapon testing evaluation. A detailed 1966 article by Col William S Barksdale captured the then 'state of the art' as fixed and podded cameras were being developed for use on aircraft destined for SE Asia. It successfully illustrates many of the challenges AA-VS equipment and personnel faced.[6] He suggested that:

> Only under wartime conditions against a real enemy and hostile fire can the Air Force finally establish the superiority of one technique over another. Similarly, all weapons used by the Air Force are tested many times. But once they are committed to a war, they may not behave as they did under an exercise's controlled, simulated combat conditions.

He outlines how the technology for recording combat action had not significantly progressed since World War Two:

> The Air Force has attempted to use aerial motion-picture photography for combat documentation. During World War Two and the Korean War, it was necessary to rely on 16-mm gun cameras for this purpose; the results were extremely useful but left much to be desired. By the mid-1950s, the Air Force's variety of weapons further reduced the gun camera's utility.
>
> A workable system grew out of equipment designed by the Aerospace Audio-Visual Service (AA-VS) of Military Airlift Command (MAC) for another purpose: the production of training and orientation films. The two modes, combat documentation and production photography, employ completely different techniques, but certain requirements are common to both. For one thing, the pilot of an airplane is kept busy with just the flying routine, so the photographic system must be an automatic part of that routine. In addition, the photographic system cannot affect the aircraft's airworthiness. The system must be compatible with the aircraft and not vice versa.
>
> The pod imposed aerodynamic limitations on the aircraft. When the Cuban crisis developed in October 1962, the USAF Chief of Staff directed AA-VS's predecessor, the Air Photographic and Charting Service, to provide over-the-target documentation of air operations. The photographic headquarters immediately placed motion-picture cameramen in the rear seat of some Tactical Air Command (TAC) aircraft. They simultaneously asked the Aeronautical Systems Division (ASD), Air Force Systems Command, to construct six motion picture camera racks. Within 30 hours, a detachment based at Eglin AFB, Florida, had completed the racks, with both fore- and aft-facing cameras, and sent them to McCoy AFB, Florida. There photographic technicians installed them on F-100 aircraft.
>
> On October 30, 1962, during a rocket and bomb mission over the Avon Park Bomb Range in Florida, the F-100 squadron tested the camera system. It worked well, and the resulting photography was good. The following day, despite one camera's malfunction, another test further confirmed the system's capability.

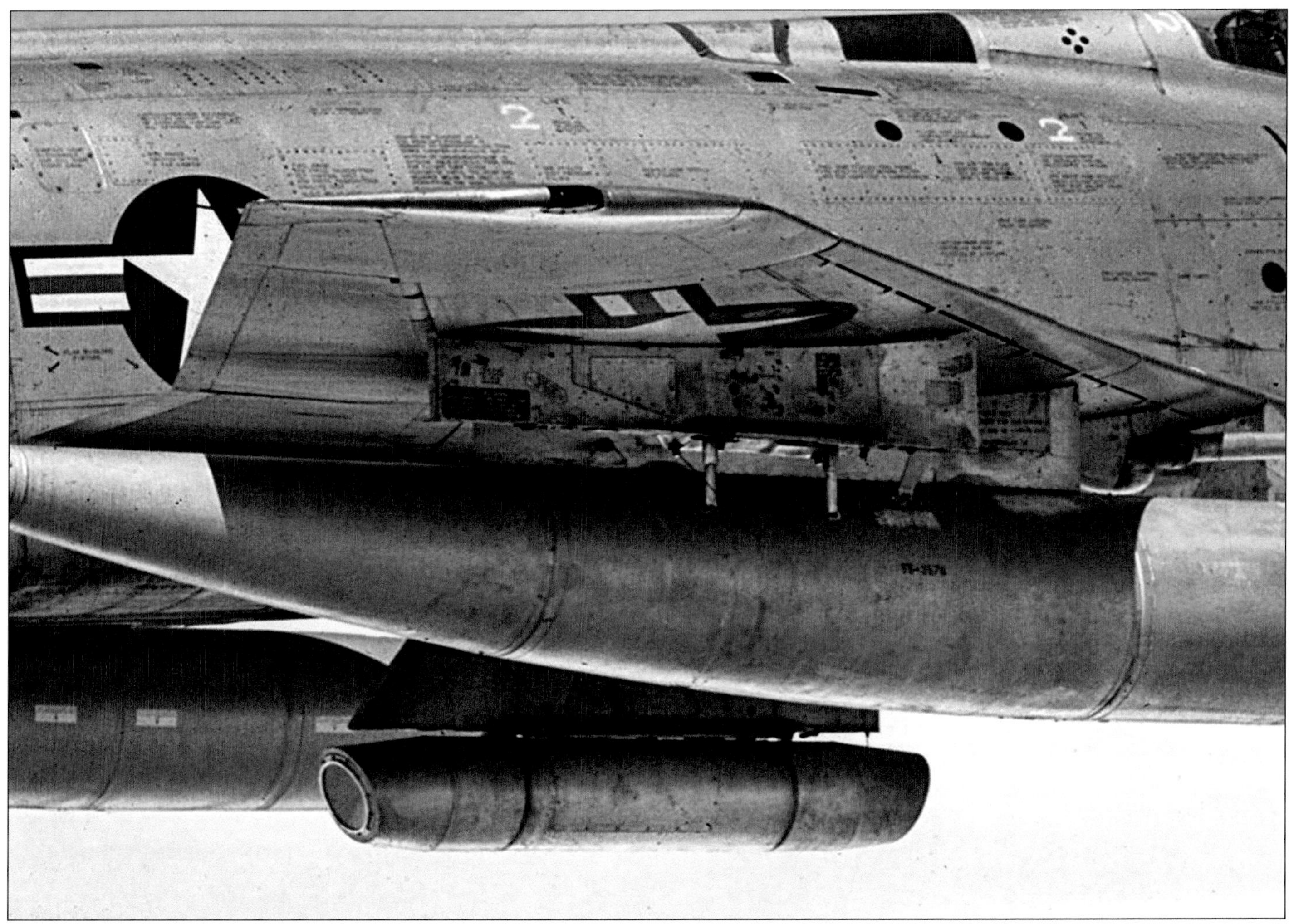

An early camera pod fitted under the fuselage of an F-100. (USAF)

Barksdale continued:

On 6 November, the commander of TAC's 2nd Air Division asked that a mount be installed on an RF-101. AA-VS and ASD made the modifications at Eglin AFB. Two days later, the aircraft returned to MacDill AFB, where test missions were flown on November 8 to 11. Only 10 per cent of the exposed film was accepted, but the first two tests proved the system's feasibility. The third, because of an operating error, was considered inconclusive. On 12 November, after viewing the test films, TAC Commander General W C Sweeney ordered the cameras to be used on an actual mission over Cuba. However, a fuelling mishap caused the aircraft to abort, so no over-target missions were flown with the system.

After the Cuban missile crisis, further developments took place. The simple racks to hold the cameras constructed during the crisis were crude, with the camera equipment exposed to the elements. A cover was necessary. During Project Full Scope, a TAC test after the missile crisis, an enclosed camera was used that permitted some angular adjustment of the camera to match the type of ordnance being delivered. However, although the modified napalm tanks worked, they did not allow sufficient camera angle depression. Further modifications and tests took place during 1963 for TAC exercises, and special tests at Nellis AFB brought some improvements. They also provided additional opportunities to assess the effectiveness of various lenses, film types, frame rates, and camera angles. However, none were said to have yielded consistently good results.

Meanwhile, during this period, photo personnel in Vietnam were working toward similar goals:

In late 1961, they had paid $35 to have a steel cylinder made, to which they added optical safety glass ports both fore and aft. Equipped with a 35-mm motion-picture camera carried internally and two 70-mm still cameras carried externally, it was mounted on an AT-28 and used to obtain aerial strike photography…By 1963, the Vietnam photo unit had built another pod. This enclosure had larger ports, fore and aft. It carried a 35mm motion-picture camera and a 70mm still camera internally.

Eventually, an aerodynamically acceptable pod was used based on the LAU-10 rocket launcher. Designated the 'Type IV', it carried two enclosed 16-mm cameras, one forward-looking and the other aft. In November 1963, TAC Test 63-77 began evaluation of the new pods on several TAC fighters. The initial tests of the Type IV started in January 1964, were attached to an F-100, and were completed in eight days. Although achieving good results, additional trials were conducted on an F-100 and F-105, resulting in two more significant modifications. 'The Type IVA, like the basic pod, had windows fore and aft; windows were introduced on both sides to allow side-looking photography. A further modification, designated Type IV B, added a bottom window'.

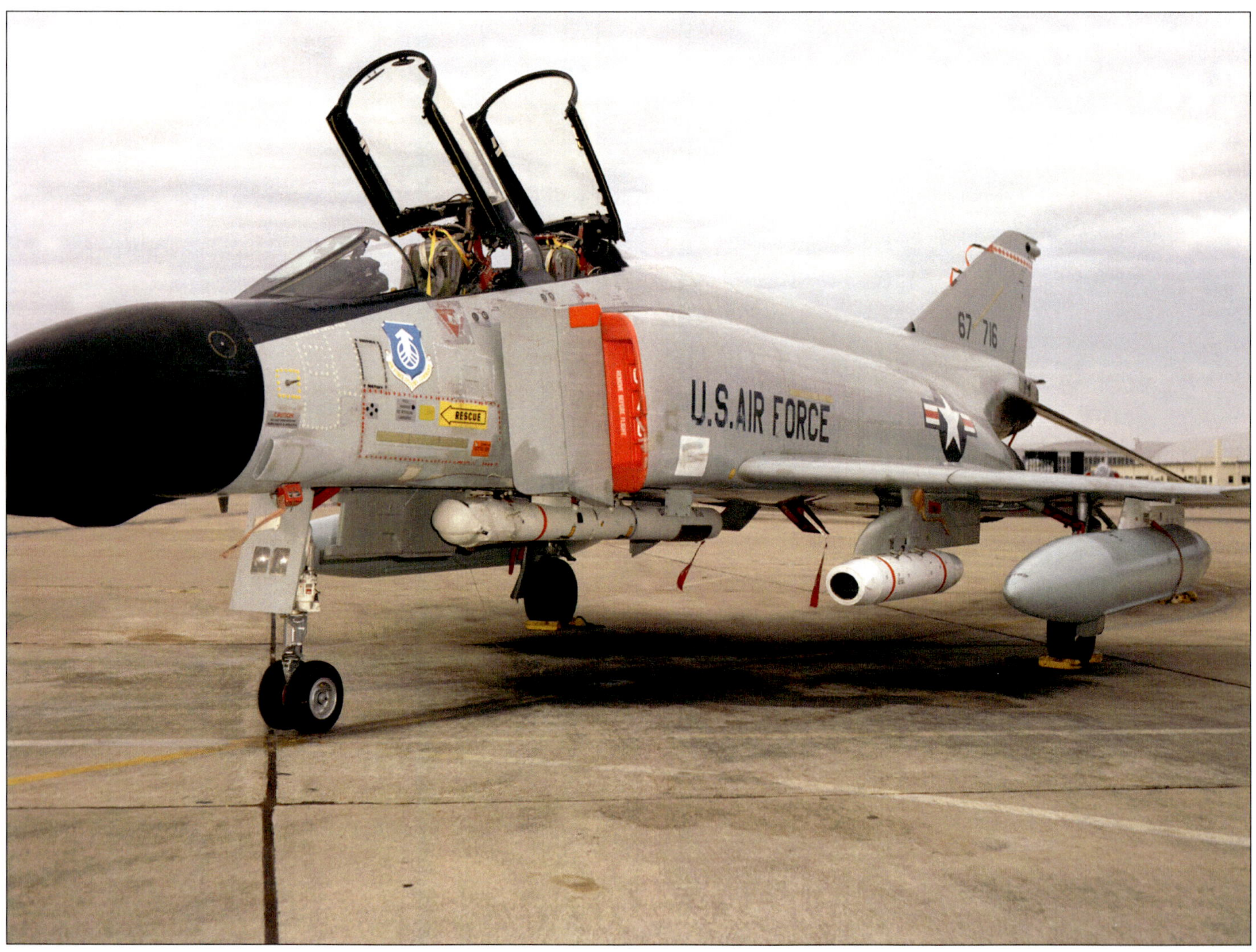

A wing-mounted Type IV camera pod, with a Pave Spike laser target designation pod under an F-4D forward fuselage in 1976. (USAF/NARA)

AA-VS also developed a closed-circuit television viewfinder to be installed in the pod when shooting production footage was required, and it was necessary to frame the film accurately. The viewfinder allowed the pilot, or backseat photographer, to see precisely what the camera saw.

Having completed the pod tests on the F-100 and F-105, the test team turned its attention to the use of the pod on the F-104 and F-4C aircraft. It began establishing the types of cameras to be used, various focal length lenses, camera speeds, and the depression angles required to meet varying altitudes, airspeeds, and ordnance types.

Barksdale explained:

By late 1964, in time for operation Gold Fire One, 23 Type IV pods were available. Six went to McConnell AFB, Kansas, and Olathe Naval Air Station, Kansas, for further testing, with the rest going to Joint Task Force Ozark. Camera pod photography took place from October 29 to November 11. Of the 30,000 feet of 16-mm colour film exposed, evaluators accepted 90 per cent as meeting data-collection requirements, a healthy improvement over the 10 per cent factor achieved in early tests.

However:

ASD had not completed exhaustive testing of the Type IV's aerodynamic characteristics, so the pods would not be used at airspeeds greater than 550 knots. This meant that if the pods were used in a combat environment, they could only be employed on non-jet aircraft.

A month-long trial at Eglin AFB during January and February 1965 determined the feasibility of mating the Type IV with A1E aircraft. As the test began, two pods were sent to Vietnam, and AA-VS specialists there began work to modify the wiring system of the A-1E Skyraider to allow the use of the pod. After completing the test at Eglin, AA-VS shipped more pods to Southeast Asia, and combat aircraft began carrying them. At about the same time, ASD cleared the pod for operation at speeds up to Mach 1.2.

Although the pods are performing exceptionally well, combat requirements had highlighted several drawbacks that were recognized when the first pod was put on an aircraft. The pod occupies an external store station that would otherwise be used for carrying ordnance. Since the pod is carried on the return leg of the mission, when the aircraft would normally be aerodynamically clean, its drag causes increased fuel consumption. Also, if hit by ground fire or attacked by

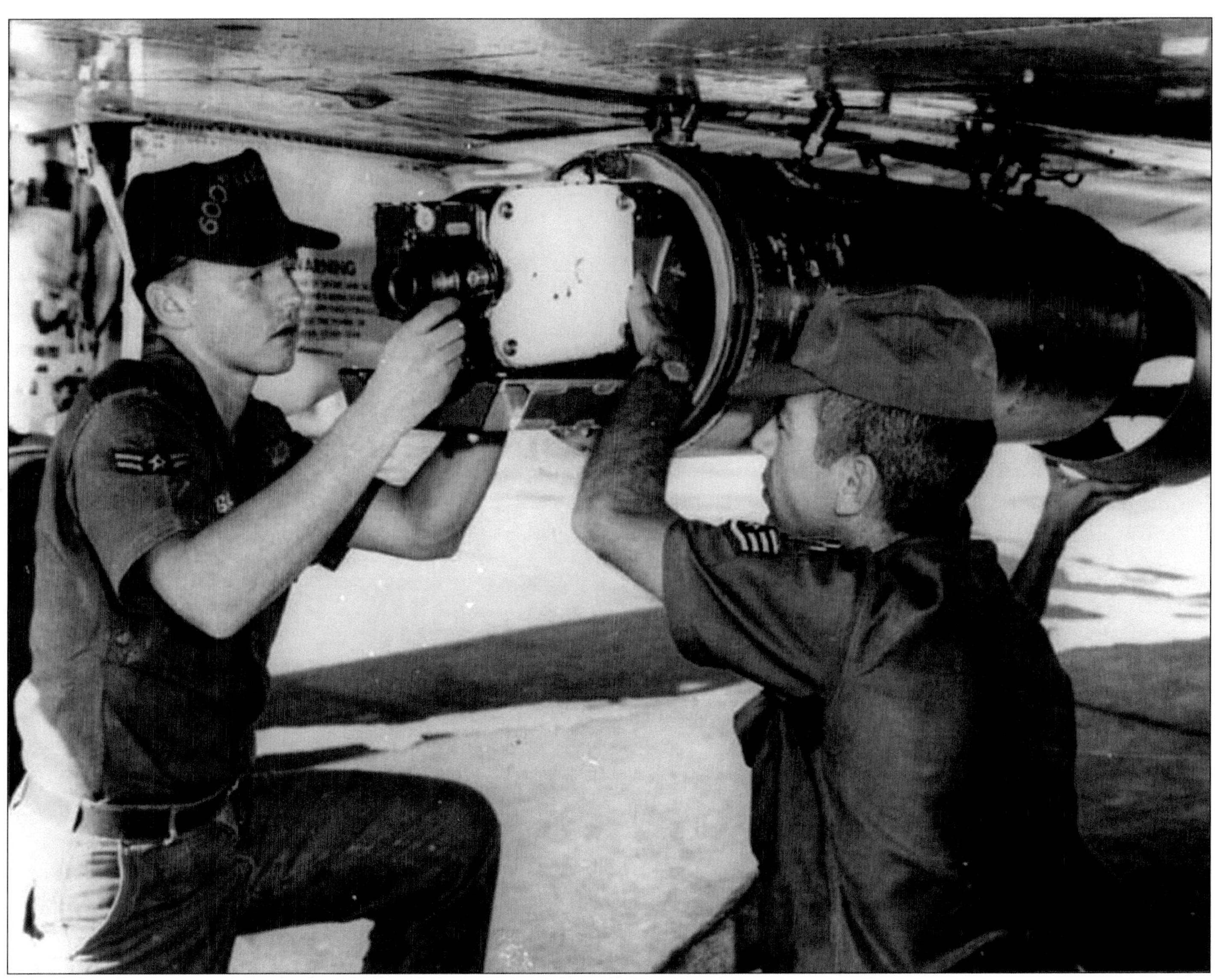

A 600th PS crew working on an under-fuselage camera on an F-4 (USAF/600th PS)

enemy fighters, the pilot must often jettison all external stores, including the pod and its precious film.

To eliminate some of these difficulties, AA-VS designed and Air Force Logistics Command (AFLC) engineered an internally mounted motion-picture camera system for the F-100, F-105, and F-4. It uses a 16-mm gun camera looking forward and slightly downward and a 16-mm high-speed instrumentation camera looking aft and down. Depending on the available space…the cameras have been either wholly or partly submerged in the aircraft fuselage or mounted beneath the wing. In each position, a smoothly faired blister has covered the camera protrusion to reduce aerodynamic drag.

On the F-4, the modification was relatively simple. A small radome on the bottom aft section of the main nose radome of US Navy F-4s was designed to house an electronic sensor. The Air Force did not require this particular type of sensor, as another electronic sensor was being engineered for this space in the Air Force version of the F-4. AFLC engineers combined the wiring for the camera installation with the electronic sensor. AA-VS and AFLC technicians developed a cylindrical camera housing for the necessary forward- and aft-looking camera windows.

On the F-105, the only available fuselage location that would provide a clear forward field of view was so close to the centreline multiple ejector rack that the ordnance loaded on the rack would obstruct the field of view of the aft camera. It was decided to house the cameras in two separate blisters, one on the lower right-hand part of the forward fuselage and one on the bottom of the fuselage aft section, just behind the tail hook.

No internal space was available in the F-100, so it was necessary to locate the cameras in a blister semi-sunk into the bottom of the aircraft's left wing, between the fuselage and the inboard external store station.

The blister camera system demonstrated the capability to produce good quality motion-picture coverage of conventional weapon strikes using 2.75-inch rockets, AGM-12 Bullpup missiles, 20-mm cannon strafing, and 750-pound general-purpose bombs. The camera system does not restrict the carriage of external ordnance or fuel stores and causes no measurable aerodynamic penalty.

Ronald Wayne Marshall served in Vietnam and has described how the gun camera film programme expanded. On the single-seat aircraft, 'They went with fitting cameras underneath the aircraft. The gunsight cameras were the only way to record images during World War Two and Korea. Now, by adding the pod to the aircraft, we could get a wider field of view than just the gunsight'.

Looking forward and aft with a camera was a vast improvement in capabilities:

When an aircraft did a strafing or bombing run, the pilot would push the button, starting the front camera. And as they came out of the dive after firing the guns or dropping the bombs, a mercury switch would turn the rear camera on. And then it was all automatic. The film ran 400 frames a second, which is high speed. Once the 100 or 200-foot roll of film ran through, that was it. It wouldn't take more than five minutes of film.[7]

David Hume Kennerly has described how it was then that the aircraft were most vulnerable: 'The NVA had a nasty habit of shooting a

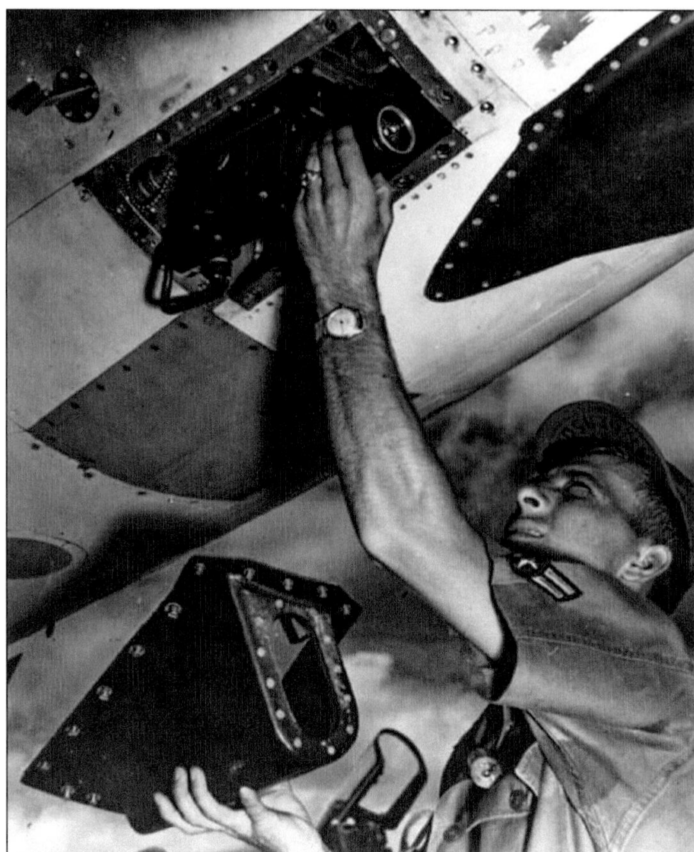

An early forward-looking camera fairing fitted to an F-105. (USAF/600th PS)

plane right after it pulled out of a rocket run. It was the only time the pilot couldn't see the enemy firing and call in an air strike on their position'.[8]

However, developments did not always go smoothly. Many F-105Ds were fitted with an aft-facing camera just behind the nose:

The aft blister installation on the F-105 fighter bombers consistently produced poor imagery due to fuel or hydraulic fluid collecting on the window surface. A suggestion from the 601st Photo Flight at Korat that a hole be cut in the window to eliminate the surface [build-up] proved a satisfactory solution. All F-105 blisters were modified in this way.[9]

One persistent problem for these cameras was that the aperture had to be set on the camera before take-off, which meant getting accurate exposures could be erratic. An automatic exposure control was developed for the N-9 gun camera. However, the control was sensitive to the g-forces experienced by the aircraft. It caused the camera shutter to close during g-generating manoeuvres.[10]

With the 600th Photo Squadron's air strike-related activities, there was an inevitable crossover into intelligence and mission planning actions. The 600th PS began working more closely with the 7th AF Intelligence staff. As the 7th AF planned their missions, the 600th PS recommended special photo-chase plane missions against some more lucrative targets.

As the 1966 unit history explained:

On 31 May 1966, the largest air raid against North Vietnam up to that time was carried out against the Yen Bay storage area. Riding in the rear of an F-4C equipped with two Type IV camera pods, A2C Virgil Siers recorded a portion of the air

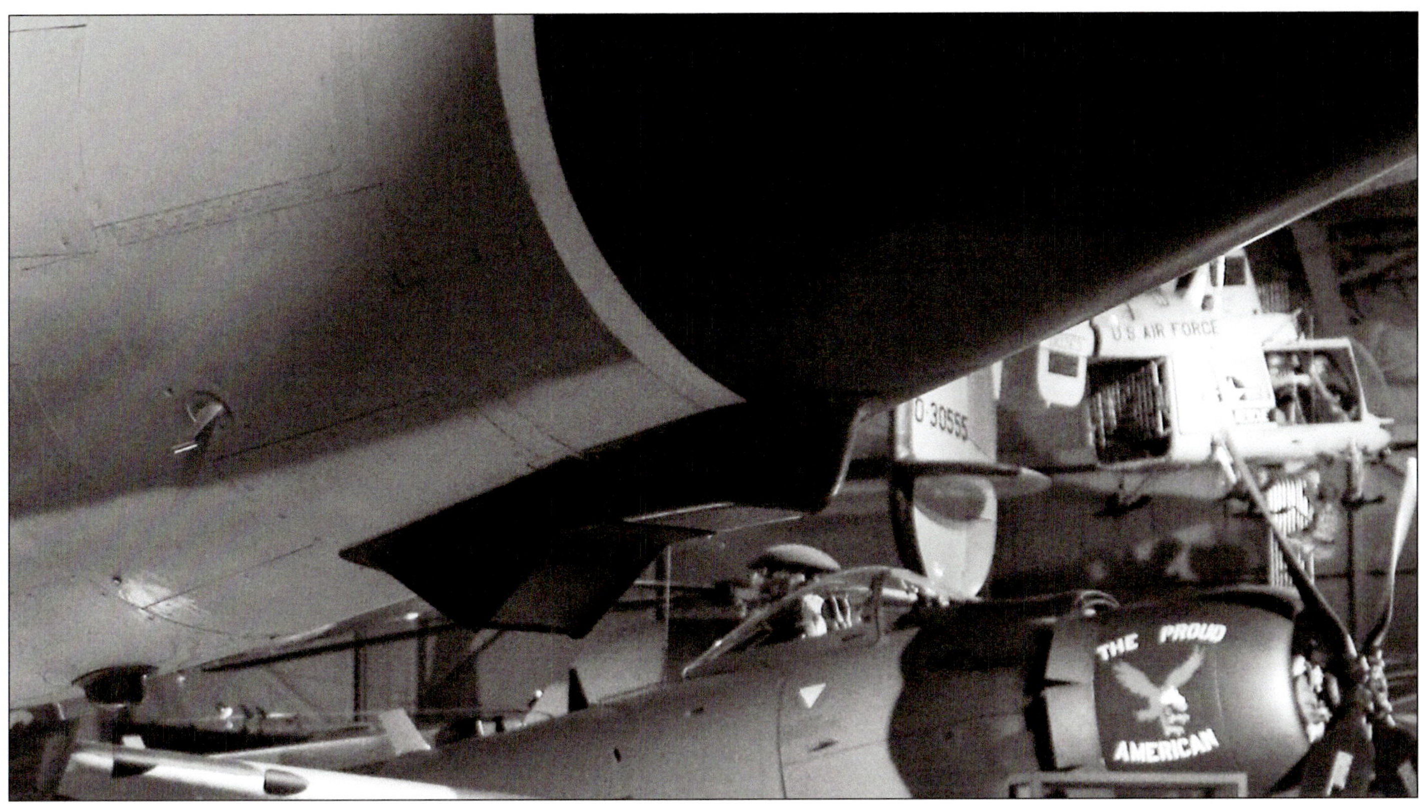

Aft-facing cameras were later fitted just behind the nose cone on the F-105s in Vietnam. (Kevin Wright)

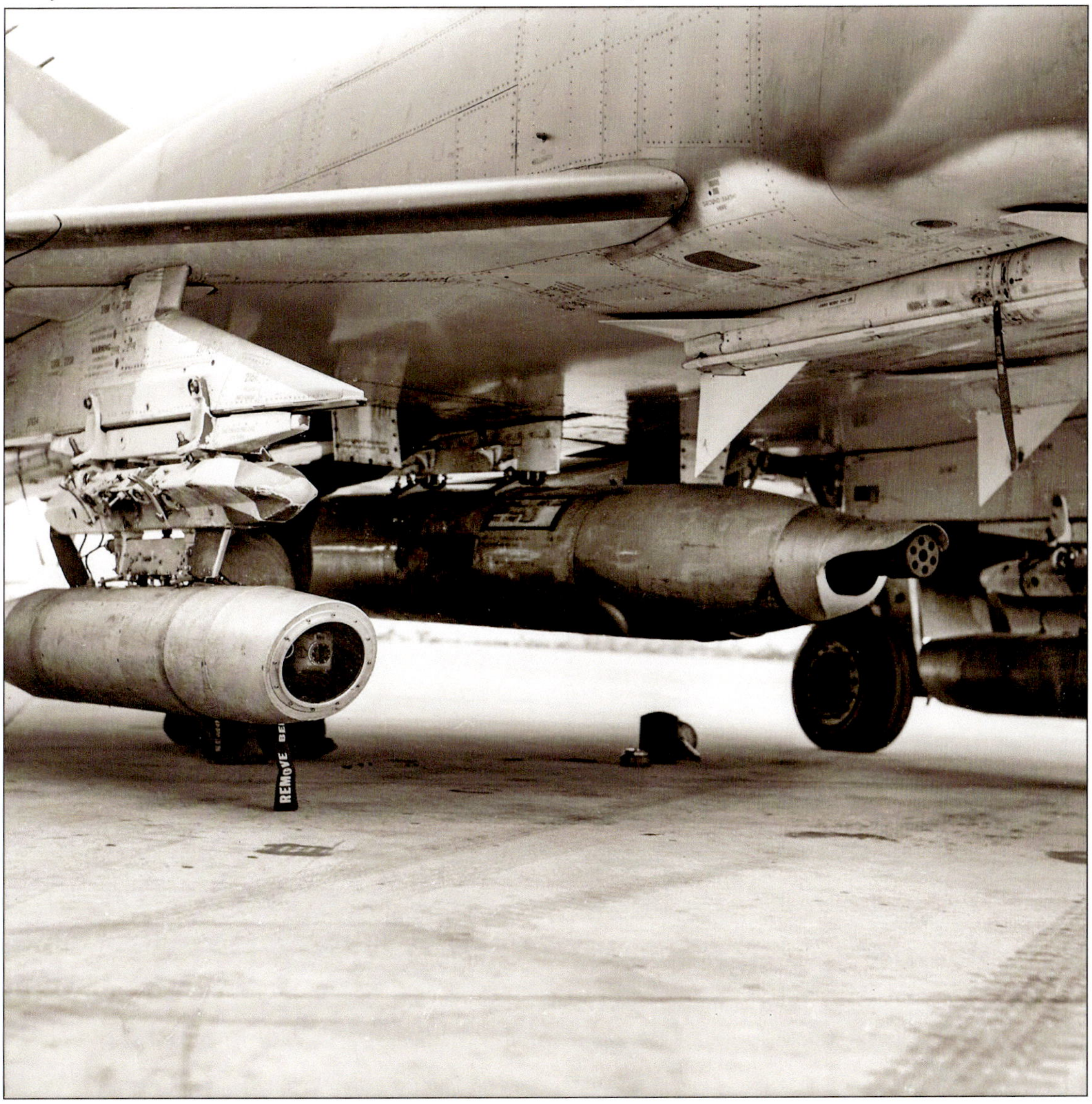

A clear shot of a camera pod fitted to the inner wing pylon on an armed F-4 on a multi-point ejector rack. (USAF-NARA)

strike. Two F-105 strike aircraft with pods also participated and recorded the launch of a SAM missile.

Although the footage of the strike was said to be poor, it paved the way for future involvement in operations that soon achieved much better photographic results.

To a significant extent, achieving good results from the backseat of a fighter depended on the attitude of the aircraft's pilot, as the 600th PS explained:

During the first week of June 1966, two pods [Type IV camera pods] were moved TDY to Cam Ranh Bay AB to obtain strike photography of F-4C fighters in support of [Operation] Tiger Hound…The 12th TFW was enthusiastic about the camera pod mission. As a result of their pilot's interest, the photographic results were excellent. Before June ended, the Wing asked that we continue on a permanent basis to fly pods and backseat missions with the F-4Cs.[11]

REAR SEAT PHOTOGRAPHER

In 1967, Ron Bogard was attached to the 601st Photo Flight at Royal Thai Air Force Base Korat. It was home to F-105 Thunderchief squadrons from the 388th Tactical Fighter Wing.

Ron explained: 'There was a 70mm camera just aft of the radar dome on the Thud. It held, I think, 50 or 100 feet of film. The photo maintenance guys loaded and unloaded the film from the aircraft and maintained the camera system'. Ron mainly worked processing film from strike missions over North Vietnam, using the Photo Flight's Kodak 'Bimat' processing machine. 'We took the negatives and made pictures of whatever the intelligence shop or squadron pilots wanted'. Bimat was a developing process designed to simplify chemical processing operations and make the finished images available more quickly than the existing processing techniques. Not assigned to flying duties, Ron was in the backseat of an F-105F sent 'up North' on six occasions, which he reasonably describes as having 'Scared the dickens out of me'. Later, in December 1967, Ron was assigned to an aerial Combat Camera Unit, where he spent most of his subsequent USAF career as a 'shooter'.

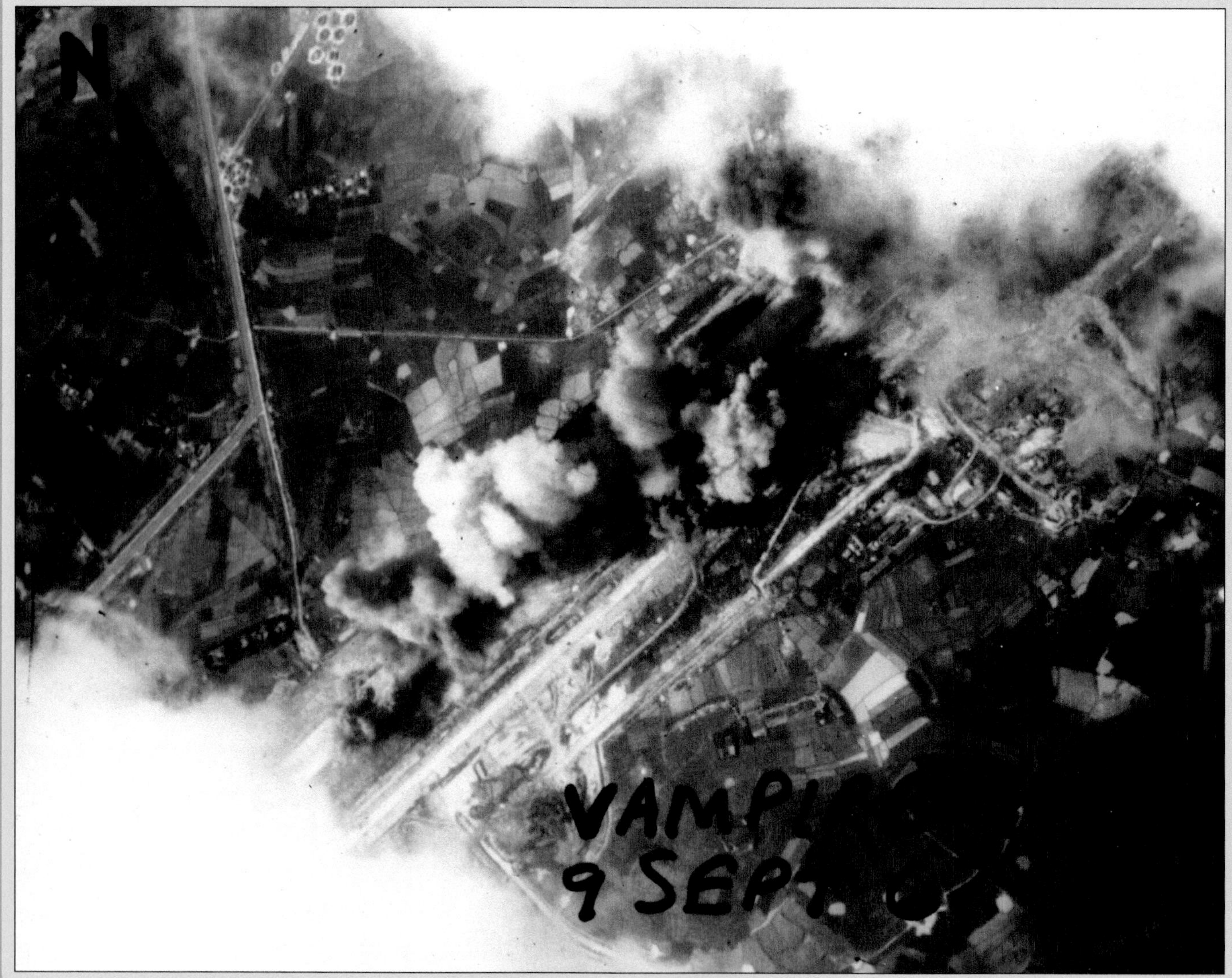

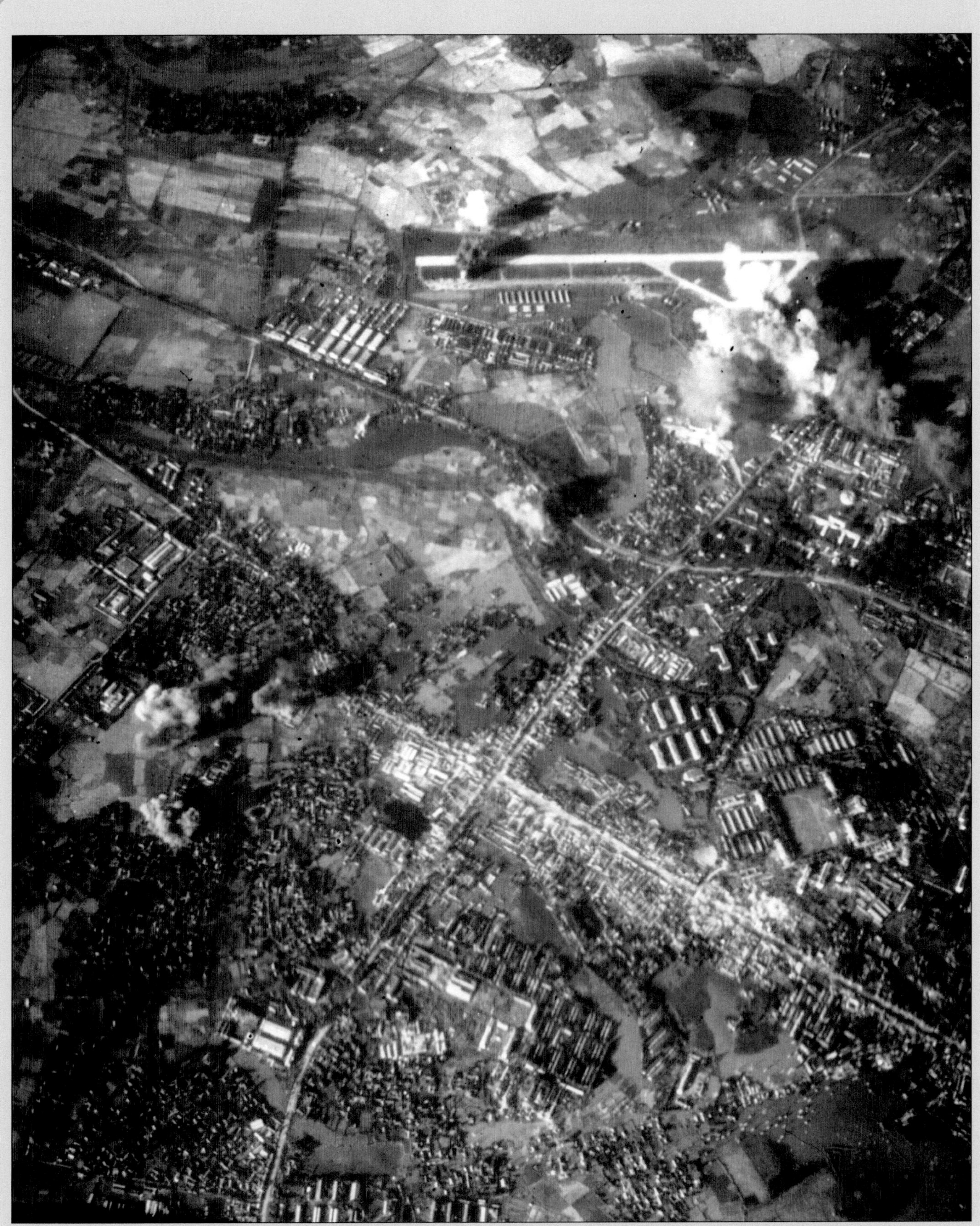

Above and previous page: Handheld images showing North Vietnamese airfields taken by Ron Bogard from the rear seat of an F-100F. (Ron Bogard)

Working with the Army

USAF Sargent Ronald Wayne Marshall was assigned to the 600th Photo Squadron at Tan Son Nhut AB in May 1967. He did not have flight status and was assigned to work with the Army on Operation Junction City, which involved working around Highway One, used by the North Vietnamese to re-supply the Viet Cong in the South.

He explained:

We were there trying to destroy all these strongholds and hiding areas and enemy caches for weapons, food, and stuff. The Army was there to do it, and the aircraft supported them. I was there to film the air support.

I would film the bombs dropping as we moved in, showing the actual damage on the ground and what we had hit. And then, every two weeks, I'd be sent back to base for a few days until another outfit picked me up, or I'd fly out by helicopter to another outfit. That's where I got the jungle [foot] rot from. I was out with a unit and was there longer than anticipated. I didn't have that many clothes and was in rice paddies. I ended up with 'Jungle rot' and had to be evacuated to Cam Ranh Bay Hospital and was there for about a week. They healed me up, and I returned to the same duty.

What was hard about being assigned to the Army was that I had to wear a super heavy flak jacket that everybody wore in Vietnam. I had a .38 pistol that I was trained to shoot, and I also had an M16. Plus, I had a camera and a tripod. The camera was a Hollywood Arriflex, which we shot movies on. The camera weighed about 25 pounds, and the tripod another 30 to 35 pounds. And then I still had the flak jacket, which weighed about 60 pounds.

The Army did an excellent job of protecting me. I usually had anywhere from 12 to 20 guys assigned to take care of me out there. And I had an armoured vehicle with me at all times and an APC with five or six soldiers in it, too, so I left my M16 back at base and just had my pistol.[12]

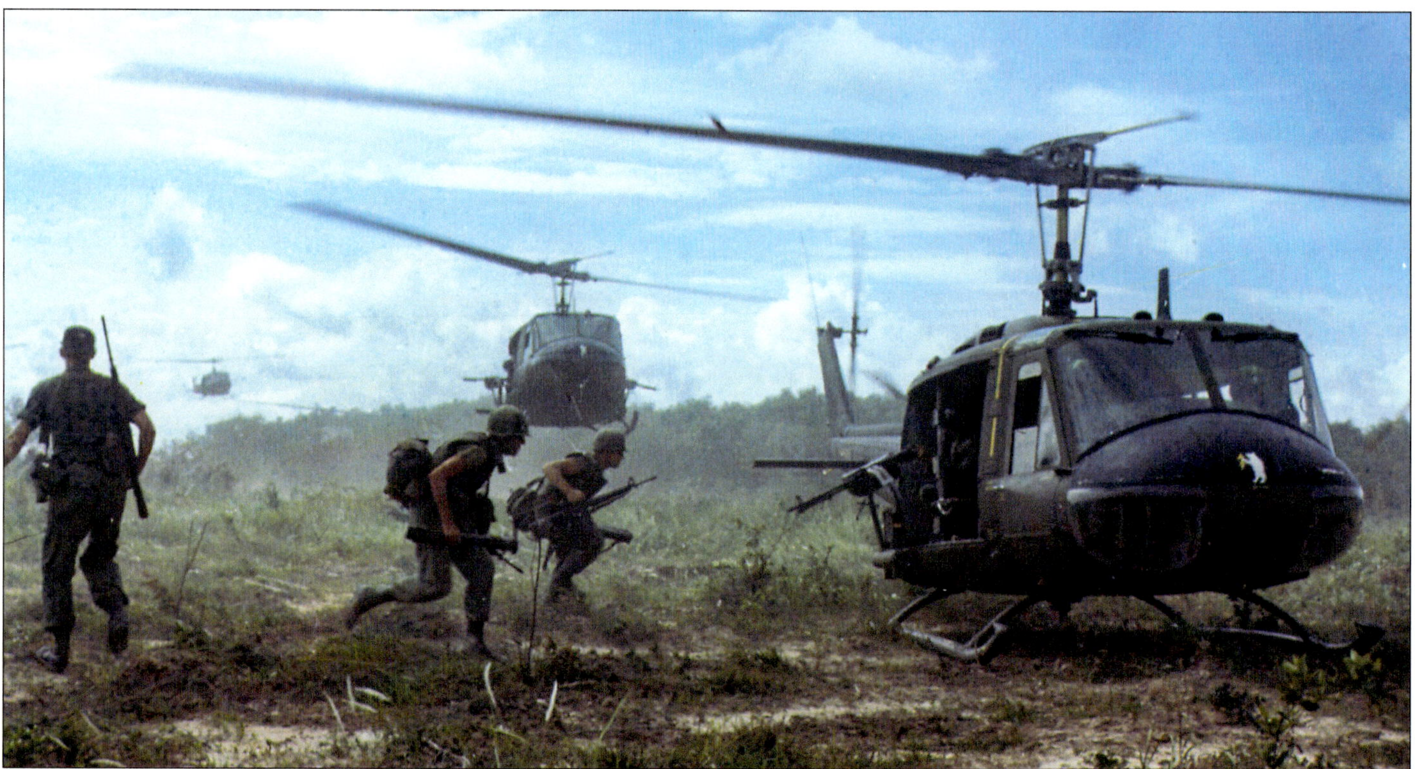

USAF Combat Cameraman Sgt Ronald Marshall was deployed with US Army soldiers, often helicoptered to different locations to film air strikes on Viet Cong and NVA positions from the ground. (NARA)

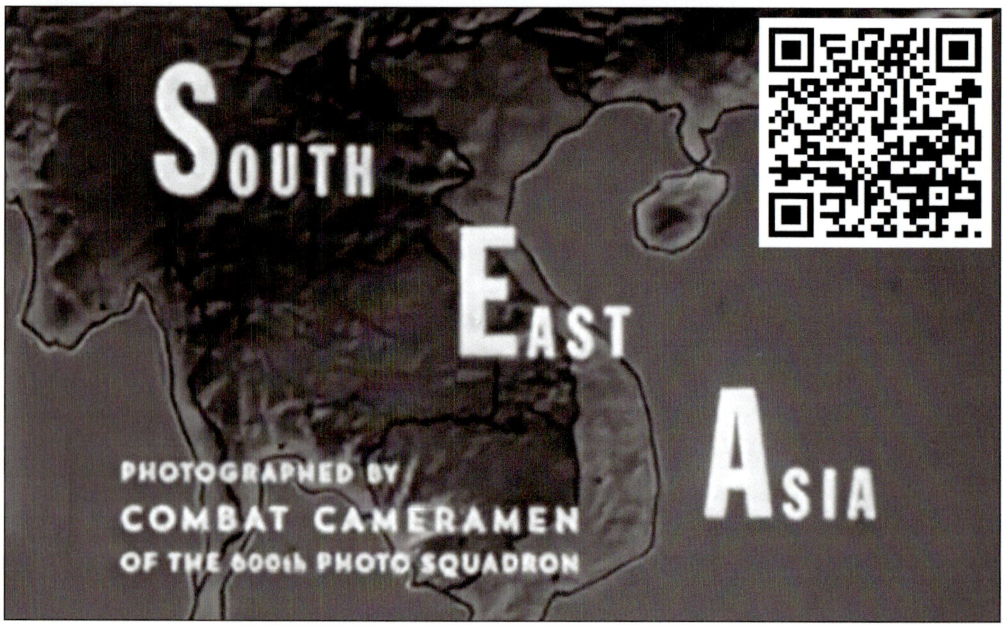

SEA Excerpts from Air Force News is in black and white and was filmed by the 600th PS in 1966. In addition to covering operations, it has segments about some of the less glamorous tasks performed by Air Force servicemen, including the work of cooks and postal services. The final part has coverage of Operation Attleboro, including air strikes shot from the ground by 600th AA-VS cameramen. (USAF/PeriscopeFilm)

USAF COMBAT PHOTOGRAPHY: SOUTHEAST ASIA (FR-885)

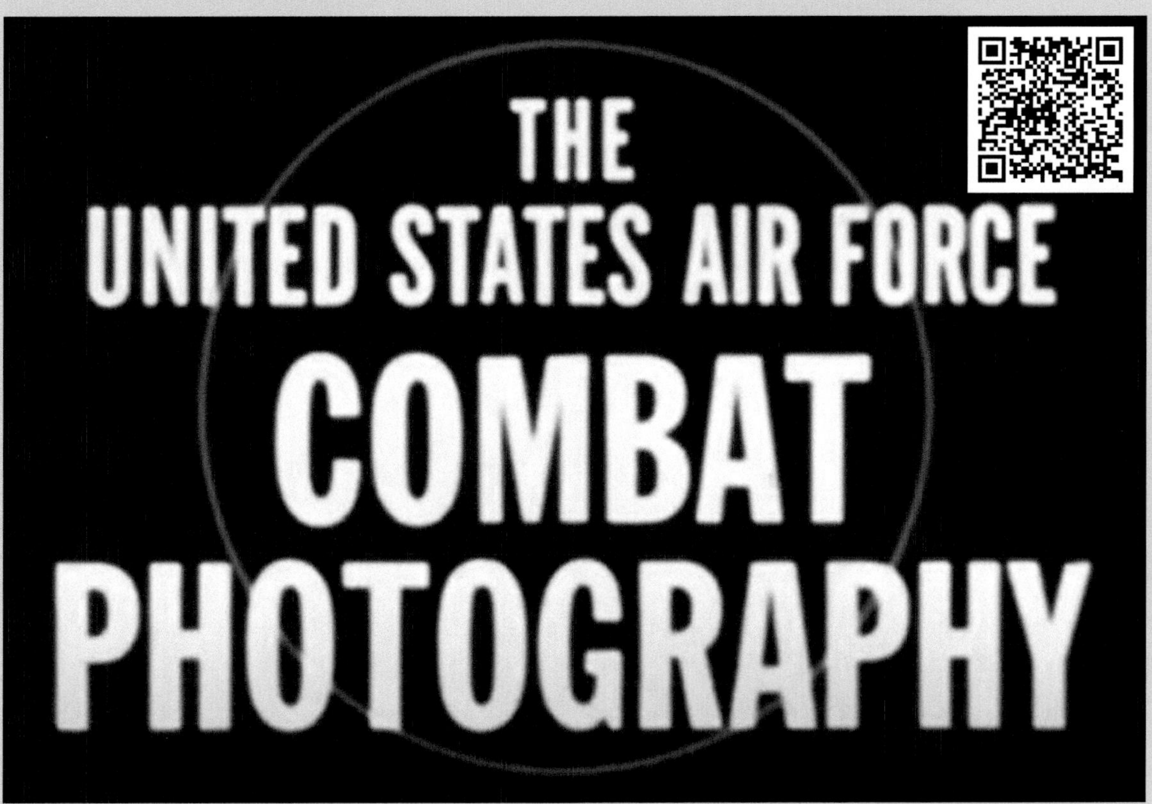

If a picture can capture a thousand words, this 1968 27-minute 'Film Report' produced by the 1352nd PS says so much more. Characteristic of its time, it illustrates the variety of work performed by the 600th Photo Squadron in Vietnam, including the daily tasks related to combat filming, such as editing and assessing photos in the lab. (USAF/NARA) (YouTube/NARA)

Civilian Media

In addition to the Army, Navy, Air Force and Marine Corps photographers and photojournalists working in Southeast Asia, there were many civilian ones. While some eschewed contact with the military, others worked more closely with their military counterparts. Moving any distance outside Saigon mainly required getting rides on military helicopters or travelling with US troops, either officially or unofficially. As Pulitzer Prize-winning API photographer David Hume Kennerly put it, 'Helicopters were the principal means of transportation at the time, ridden as casually as commuter trains in other parts of the world'.[13]

In addition to using their imagery within the Air Force and DoD, former Captain Richard Ruddy described an assignment working alongside civilian journalists and broadcasters during his year-long tour in Vietnam from early 1965. 'From time to time, television networks would also use our footage. On one occasion, CBS wanted to do a story on defoliation'. Known to the Air Force as Operation Ranch Hand, it was always a sensitive mission:

They used C-123s to defoliate whole areas, to deny the enemy a place to hide. There was an awful lot of defoliation that went on in Vietnam. CBS was doing a story about this; the reporter then was Dan Rather. I worked with Dan and his cameraman. They were inside one of the C-123s doing the defoliation.

We provided them with air-to-air coverage from another aircraft. So we were in the same formation as them, shooting from another plane toward the one that Dan Rather was in. So, in that story, most of the footage, other than that you saw

of Dan Rather inside the C-123, was shot by our guys, not by them. So we were helping the television networks in a situation like that.

He also drew an interesting comparison between civilian photographers' access during Vietnam with that in 1990 and Operations Desert Shield/Storm. 'I think in Vietnam, it was certainly very different from the way the first Iraq War went. The press in the first Iraq War was restricted in what they could do. Vietnam was quite different. We allowed, and even assisted, the media as much as we could in helping them get to tell the story'.

Operation Homecoming

On 12 February 1973, after a ceasefire began between US and North Vietnamese forces, an exchange of prisoners took place. Cameraman SSgt Herman Kokojan was present to record the exchange at Tan Son Nhut AB, overseen by representatives of the UN. The Americans were transported to Clark AB and repatriated to the United States.

A Tragic Conclusion

In July 1966, the AA-VS had suffered its first fatality in Vietnam when A1C Darryl Winters was lost. The rapid US withdrawal in the spring of 1975 would see another final tragic loss of AA-VS personnel. As the rout of South Vietnamese forces accelerated, the US began an operation to evacuate remaining US citizens and some orphaned Vietnamese babies and children. 'Operation Babylift' would eventually see around 2,500 babies and children evacuated from the country. However, the start of the operation was marred by tragedy.

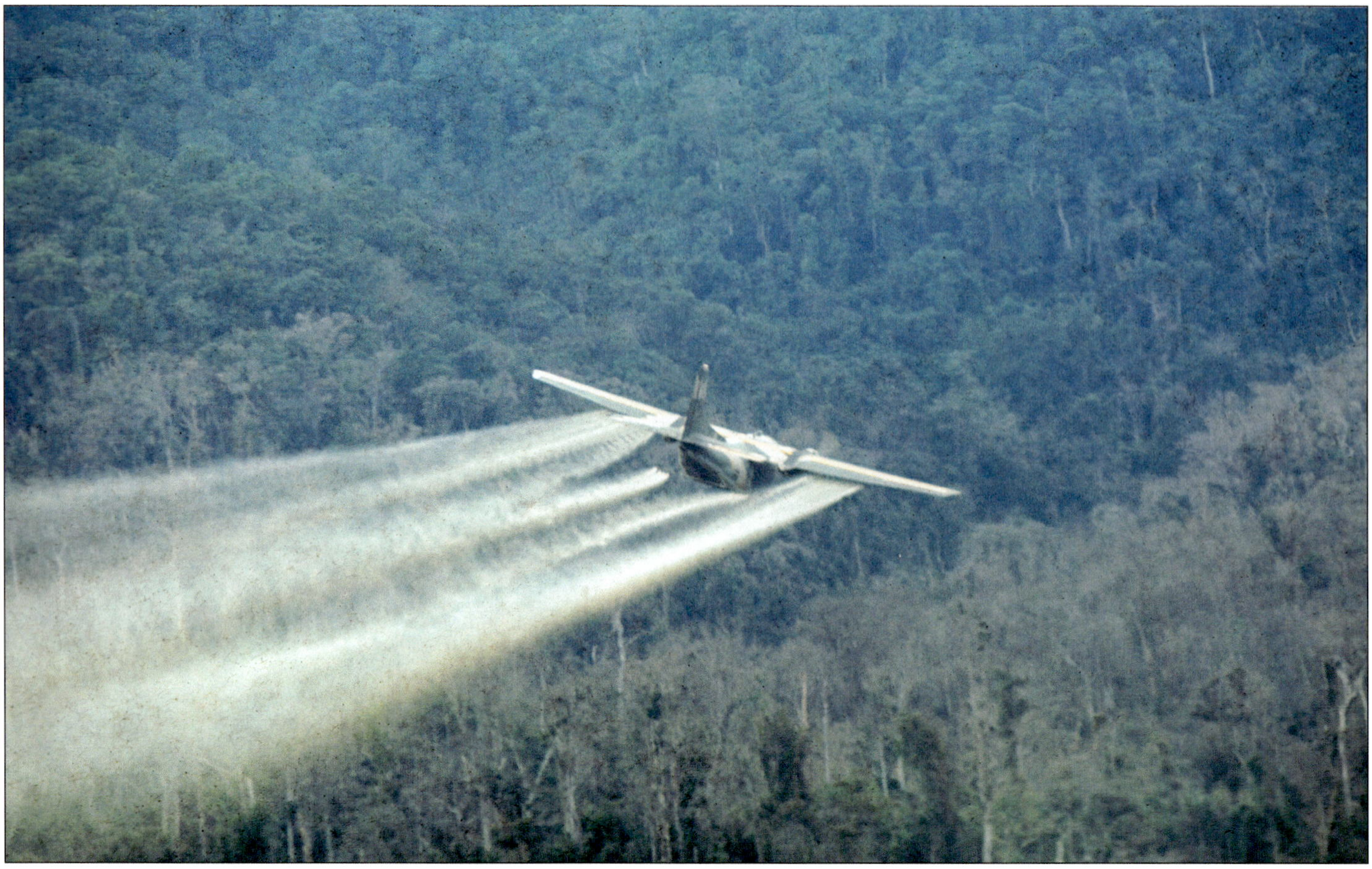

A modified C-123 defoliation mission spraying Agent Orange in North Vietnam. Operation Ranch Hand was intended to defoliate large areas of jungle to reduce the ability of North Vietnamese forces to hide their movements. It is most remembered now for deaths, sickness and deformities that it caused among the Vietnamese population and the US servicemen in contact with the chemicals, including some AA-VS personnel. (USAF)

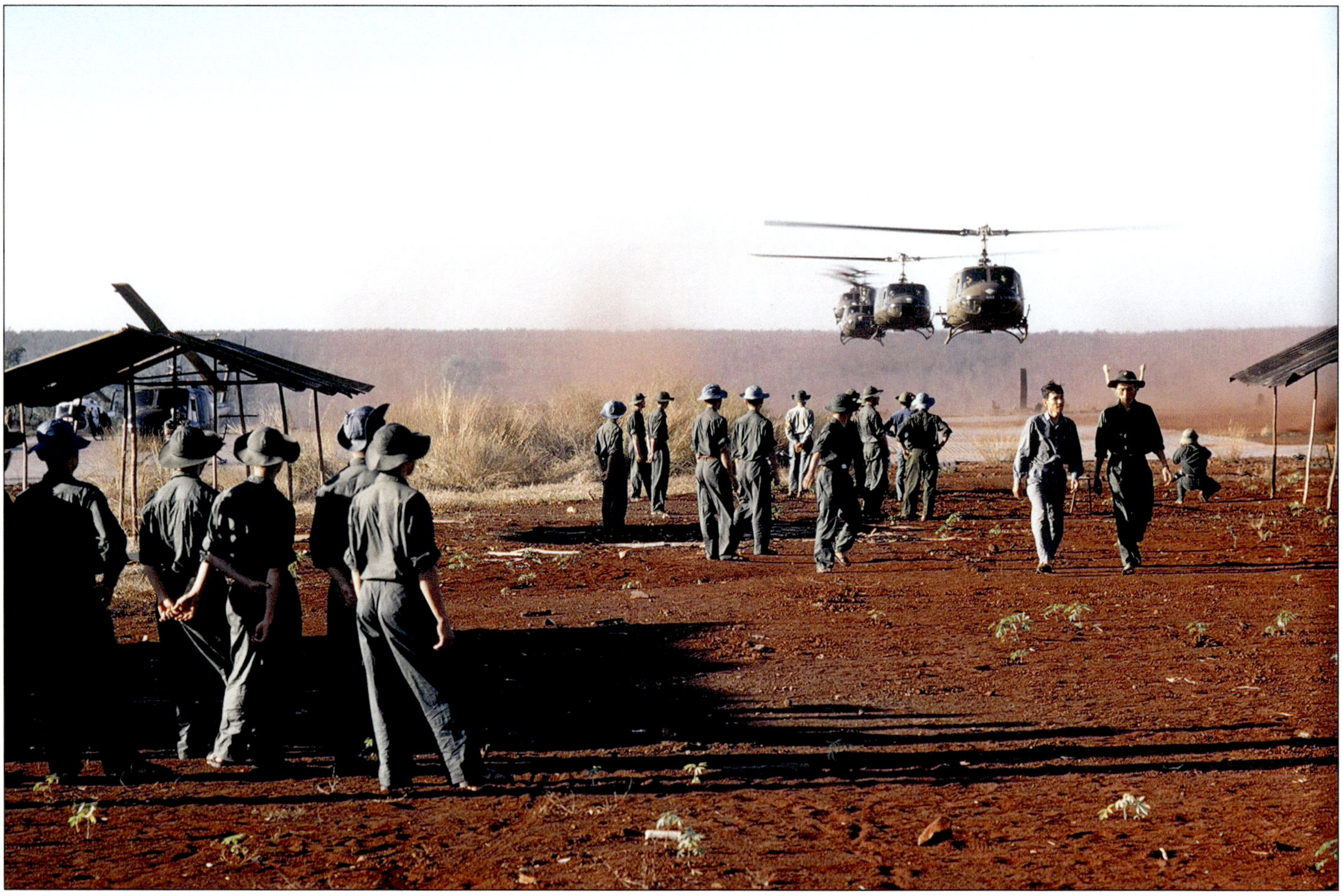

During Operation Homecoming, February 1973, US UH-1 helicopters arrive to transport released US PoWs. (USAF/SSgt Herman Kokojan)

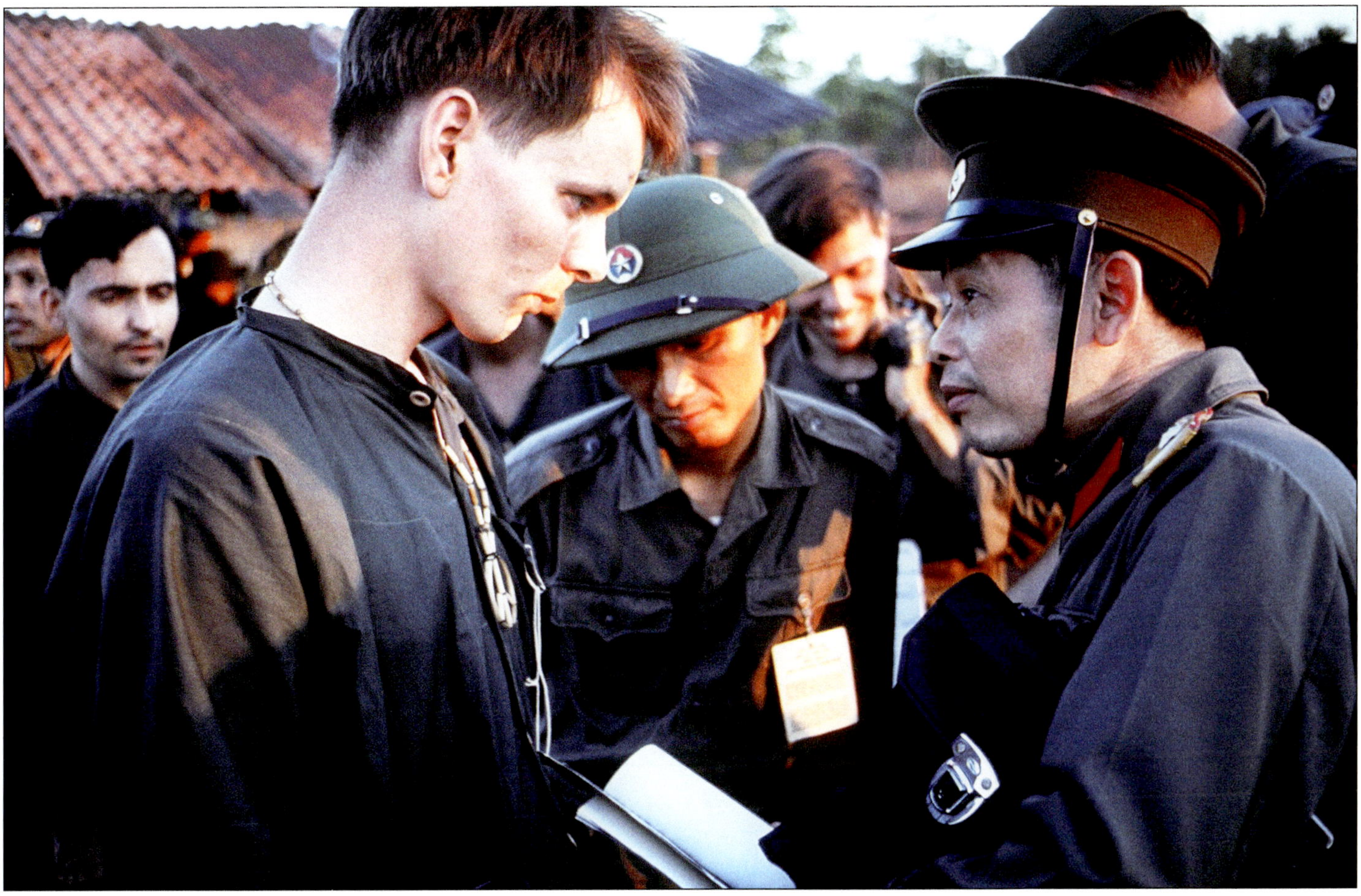

SPC-4 Richard Springman, captured on 25 May 1970, was one of 28 American PoWs released on 12 February 1973. (USAF/SSgt Herman Kokojan)

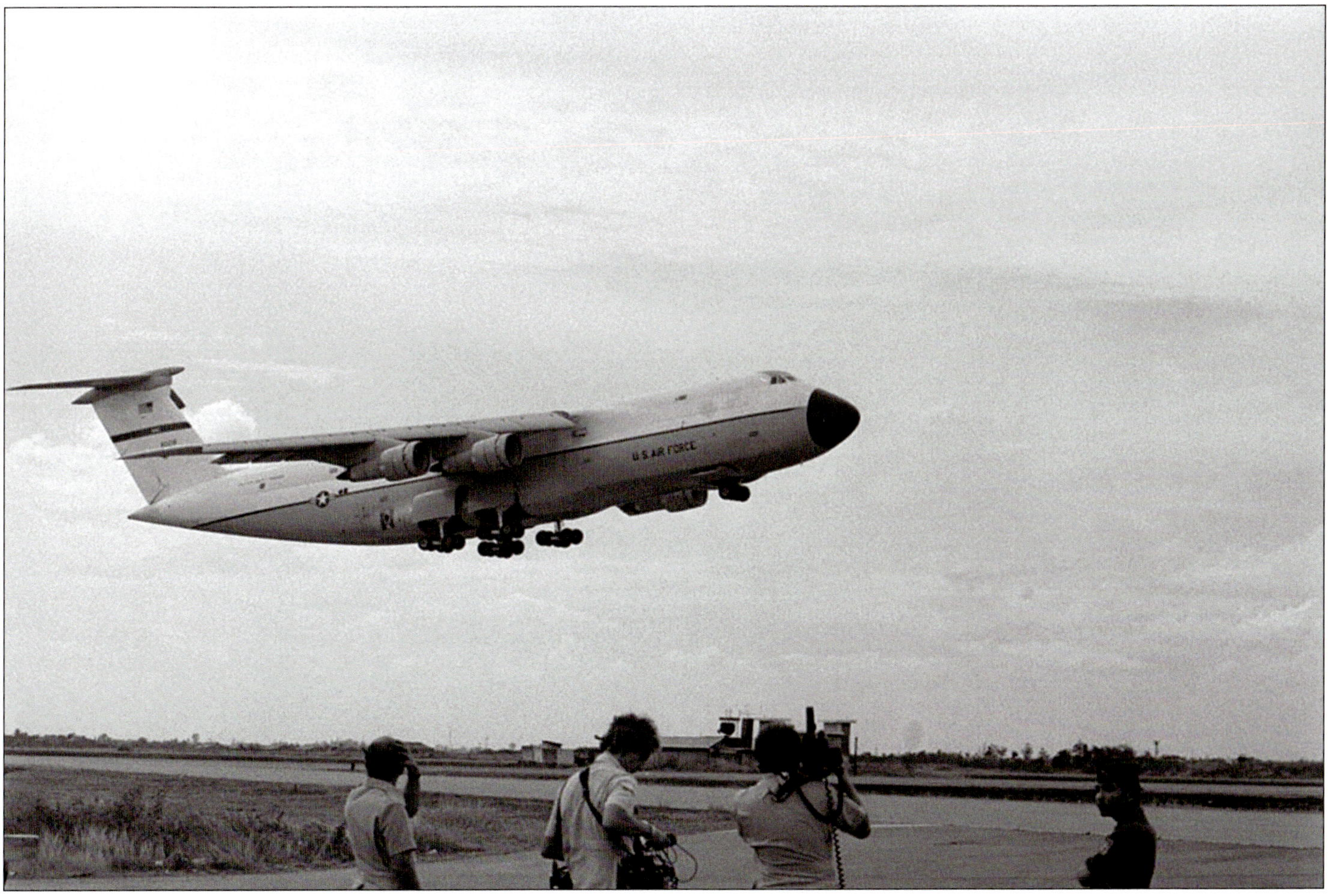

C-5A '0218' takes off from Tan Son Nhut AB on the first and fateful Operation Babylift flight on 4 April 1975. (UPI)

On 4 April 1975, a US Air Force C-5A (65-0218) took off from Tan Son Nhut Air Base carrying 314 children, carers, medics and service personnel. Among them were MSgt Joe Castro and SSgt Kenneth Nance, AA-VS photographers from the 1369th AVS. The aircraft successfully took off, but poorly installed locks on the massive C-5 rear loading door soon began to fail, eventually leading to rapid decompression and separation of the door from the C-5. The crew fought valiantly to get the aircraft back to Tan Son Nhut, having also lost much of its hydraulics. As the aircraft prepared for a possible crash landing, Castro and Nance 'Used their high-intensity lights to illuminate the area where [Flight Nurse] Captain Mary Klinker worked'.[14] The huge C-5A hit the ground, bounced and disintegrated around four kilometres short of the airfield's runway. Of the 330 crew and passengers onboard, amazingly, 159 survived. Joe Castro and Kenneth Nance were not among them.

The losses and conduct of the Vietnam War would haunt the US military for years to come. For the AA-VS, it left Vietnam in a very much more robust organisational condition than it had entered the conflict. Capabilities had been rebuilt, reinforced by the lessons of recent combat experience. In the following years, with more rapid technological advances and much more military funding, those experiences would be consolidated as the AA-VS moved into the final period of the Cold War.

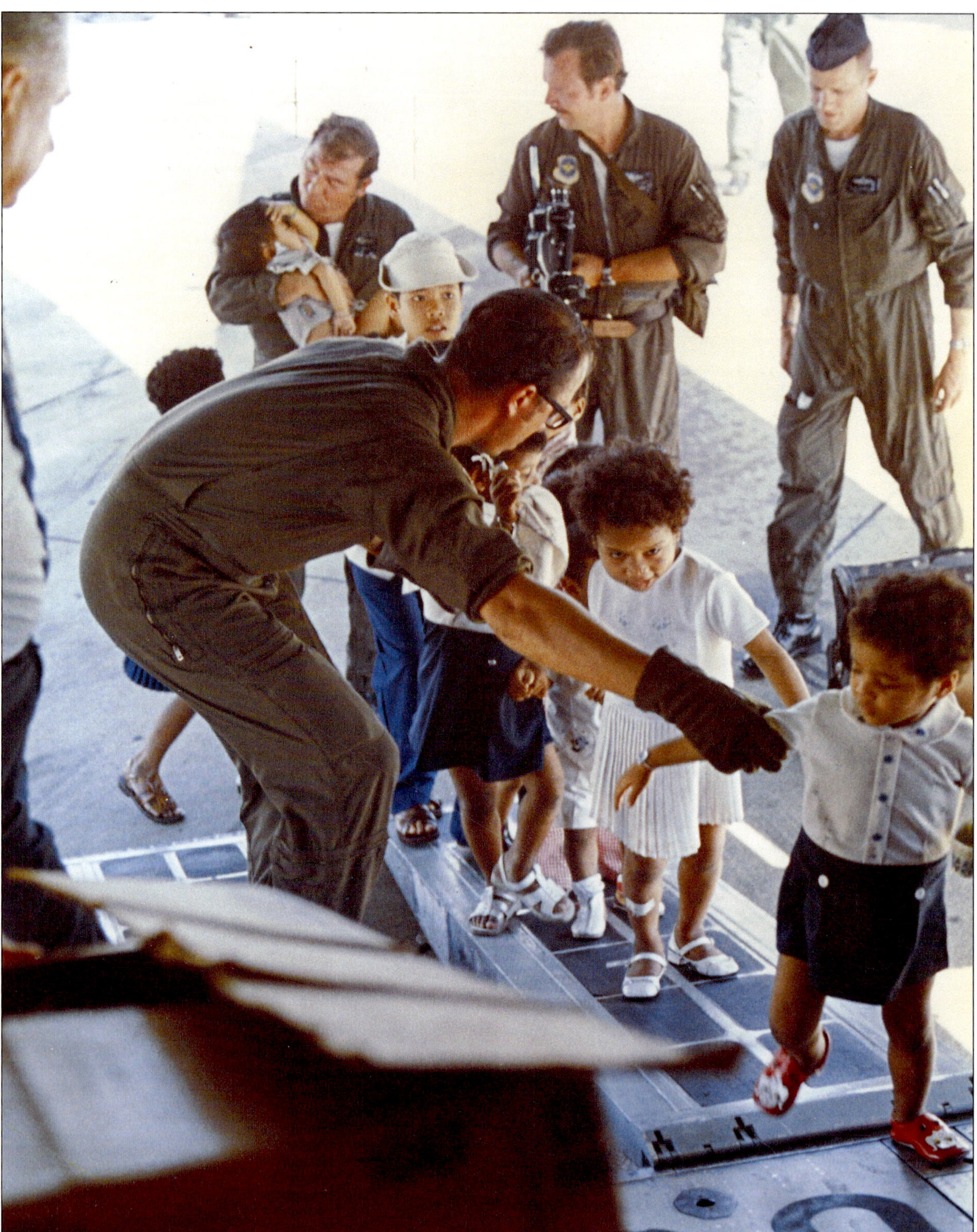

A Det 7 photographer from the 1369th PS pauses as an aircraft crew member helps young children board a C-141A for evacuation. Despite the tragedy of 4 April 1975, ultimately, Operation Babylift evacuated a large number of infants and children from Vietnam. (NARA)

Aircraft operations in-theatre were the centre of 600th Photo Squadron activities in Southeast Asia, but the large majority of footage never reached a wider audience. Below are links to three such film reels covering the activities of the F-100, RF-101, RF-4C, and F-105. All are unedited and without sound.

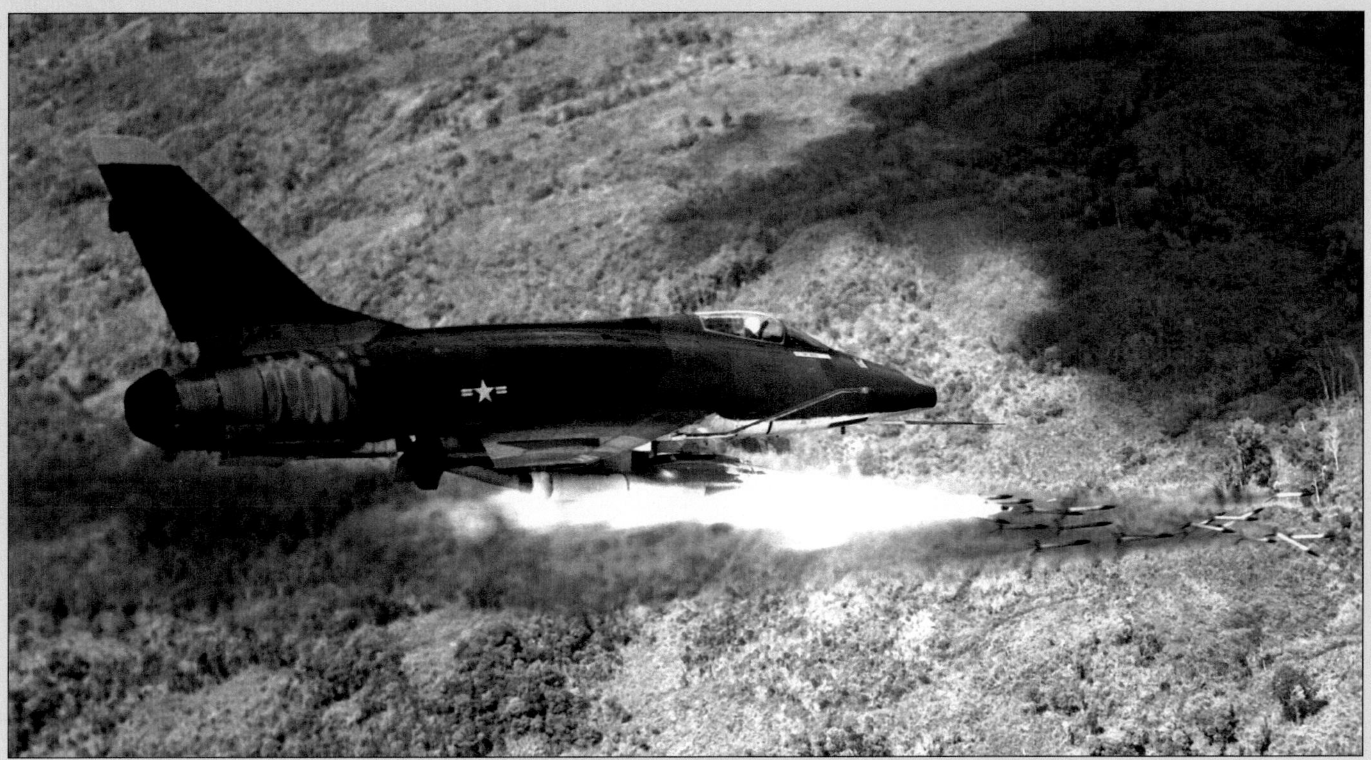

A USAF F-100D fires 2.75-inch rockets against a North Vietnamese position. (USAF)

F-100 Maintenance – 31 TFW Tuy Hoa AB (1968) shows the work of F-100 maintenance crews. (YouTube/ Christopher LaFrieda)

Very high-quality imagery from cameramen Aston and Sherill shows F-105 air and ground crews at Takhli AB preparing aircraft for their missions in mid-1967. (YouTube/ WWIIPublicdomain)

Mainly sequences of RF-4Cs and RF-101s, including airborne footage, but also take-off and landing imagery of C-130s, C-141s, C-47s A-1s, U-3s, C-123s, B-707s and others. (YouTube/Combat Camera Archive)

7

DOUG MORRELL, 'THE LEGEND'

While selecting an individual from the many men and women who have served in Combat Camera is undoubtedly invidious, Chief Master Sargent Doug Morrell is a worthy exception. He is a legendary character and an outstanding exemplar of the skills and character of his profession. His experiences span almost the entire period of USAF Combat Camera covered in this book. During World War Two, he was shot down twice. He served during the Korean War and spent time during the Cold War documenting Soviet 'Bears' over the North Atlantic. He was shot down again in Vietnam and, after retiring from the Air Force in 1973, continued serving as a civilian up to 1988. He died in 2017 at the age of 98.

The account below is an edited version but still in his own words, thanks to a wonderfully detailed interview he gave to 'Evergreen'.[1] Having been rejected by the Marines and the US Navy because of an eyesight colour deficiency, Doug Morrell joined the USAAF where they said: 'With a green-brown colour deficiency, you can spot camouflages'. He was placed on flying status almost two years before World War Two began.

As he explained:

When the war started, we went up and shot AT-6s, five of them. We travelled all over the United States, shooting those against the backgrounds of all the national monuments, the New York skyline, the Miami Skyline, and the San Francisco skyline. We went all over shooting this country, and the pictures were used for Air Force recruiting films.

They sent me to four different film studios. The Army Air Corps had become pretty technical and needed training films.

The need became so great that the studios couldn't handle the large influx of requests for training films.

The USAAF sent four people to rotate between four movie studios, spending three months at each.

I was not allowed to do anything, no camera work, no anything, just had to sit there and watch. But I learned so much because I wasn't doing anything; I could see everything that was happening. By that time, the war was starting to heat up.

High Above Nazi Germany

Morrell was posted to Britain as the build-up of the USAAF began after the United States entered the war. 'Most of our combat camera work was for operational evaluation. We were told mostly to shoot enemy fighter passes attacking our aircraft because the Germans were bringing down a lot of our bombers over Europe'. Morrell was flying in B-24 Liberators, four-engine bombers with open gun positions on both sides of the aircraft, from which they filmed:

The German fighters would come in from the sun and through the formation. And if they didn't shoot anybody then, and a lot of times they would, they would come around and hit us from behind where the crews weren't watching. We found this out from our films. We followed them as far as we could and would see them turn and follow them back in again, shooting at us all the way. At the time, you are so busy, you don't worry about it; you're just shooting.

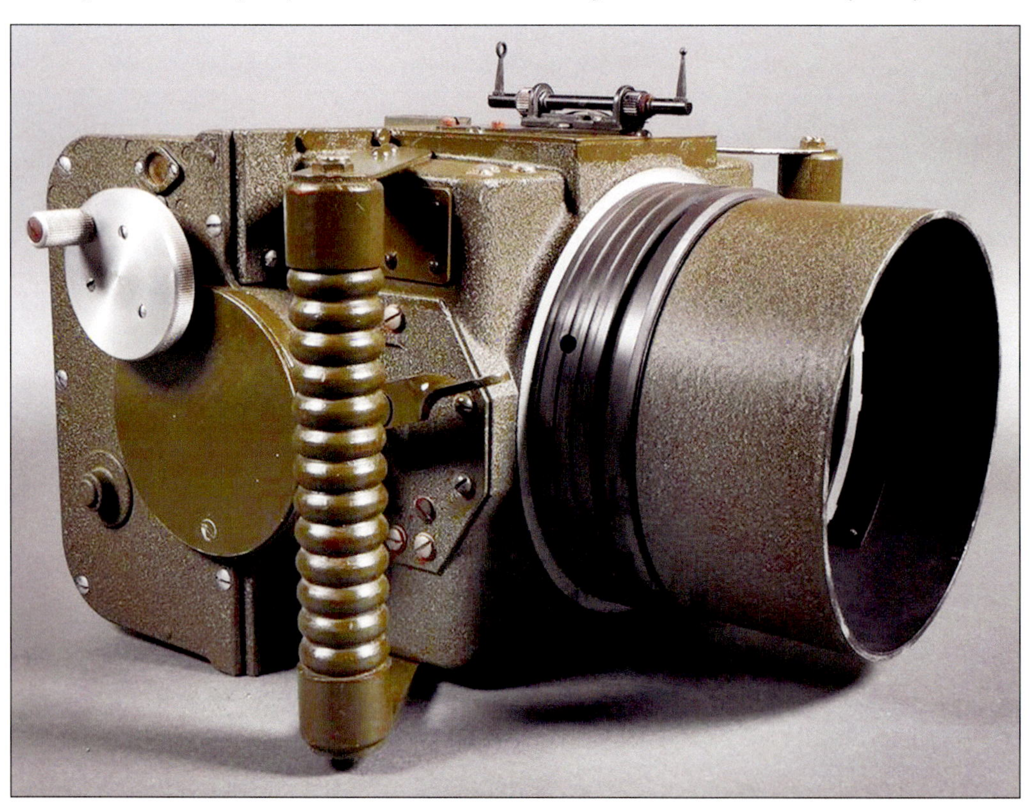

The Graflex K-21 camera was standard equipment for combat photographers on bomber aircraft. (NARA)

I had a still camera. It was a K-20 or a K-21. And I had a Bell and Howell Eyemo, which, at that time, was fitted with a single lens. Then, pretty soon, we went to the 'spider lens' on the turret. We shot 35mm film with a 50mm standard lens. We didn't have zooms or anything. If the subject did not fit, we had to back up until it did. Everything was set on infinity while we were up there, so there was little focussing.

The cameramen had to be very selective in what they filmed:

We had 100ft film loads. It was a hand-wound camera, and you had your own cranks, which were terrible. If you lost your crank, you were out of business. And you would get up there and have around 20 seconds or so of 35mm film going at 24 frames a second. You had about three minutes on a 100ft roll. So, we did not shoot indiscriminately at everything; we had to shoot what we thought would be the best. It was very different from shooting today, where they can sit and shoot forever. We had to pick out our shots carefully and almost anticipate what would happen.

You couldn't go out there and shoot documentation without knowing what was going to happen. You had to find out beforehand what was planned. They usually put you in as 'Tail-End Charlie', the last plane on the left-hand side or right-hand side of the formation. We could also sit up there with a still camera. When we approached a target, and the fighters did not come up, you went to another camera, an old K3B. It was a nine-inch square format with a 12-inch focal length lens. It was set in the bottom of the aircraft over the rear hatch, so when the bombs dropped, you could try to catch where the bombs hit. You were just guessing, mostly, where that would be.

We also had to shoot the bombs leaving the bomb bay with a motion picture camera. That was a little hairy because there was only a narrow catwalk, and you're out there on it. Of course, you have a parachute, but you don't want to go out with the bombs. Sometimes, we had to go and kick those bombs out because they became hung up.

I flew 32 and two half missions. These were in B-17 Flying Fortresses and B-24 Liberators. I flew over Austria, Italy, Germany, France, Romania and Yugoslavia on bombing missions. When it came to being afraid, you were too busy. You are afraid when you are not shooting. I'd be shooting pictures of the guns, the waist gunner shooting, and then over the waist gunner's shoulder, getting the fighters coming in, right over your head, and see the fire belching out of their guns. And it was kind of an 'Oh no, I wish I were somewhere else,' but not fear. I can't remember fear during combat because I was so busy. And as long as you kept busy, you did not feel so bad about it.

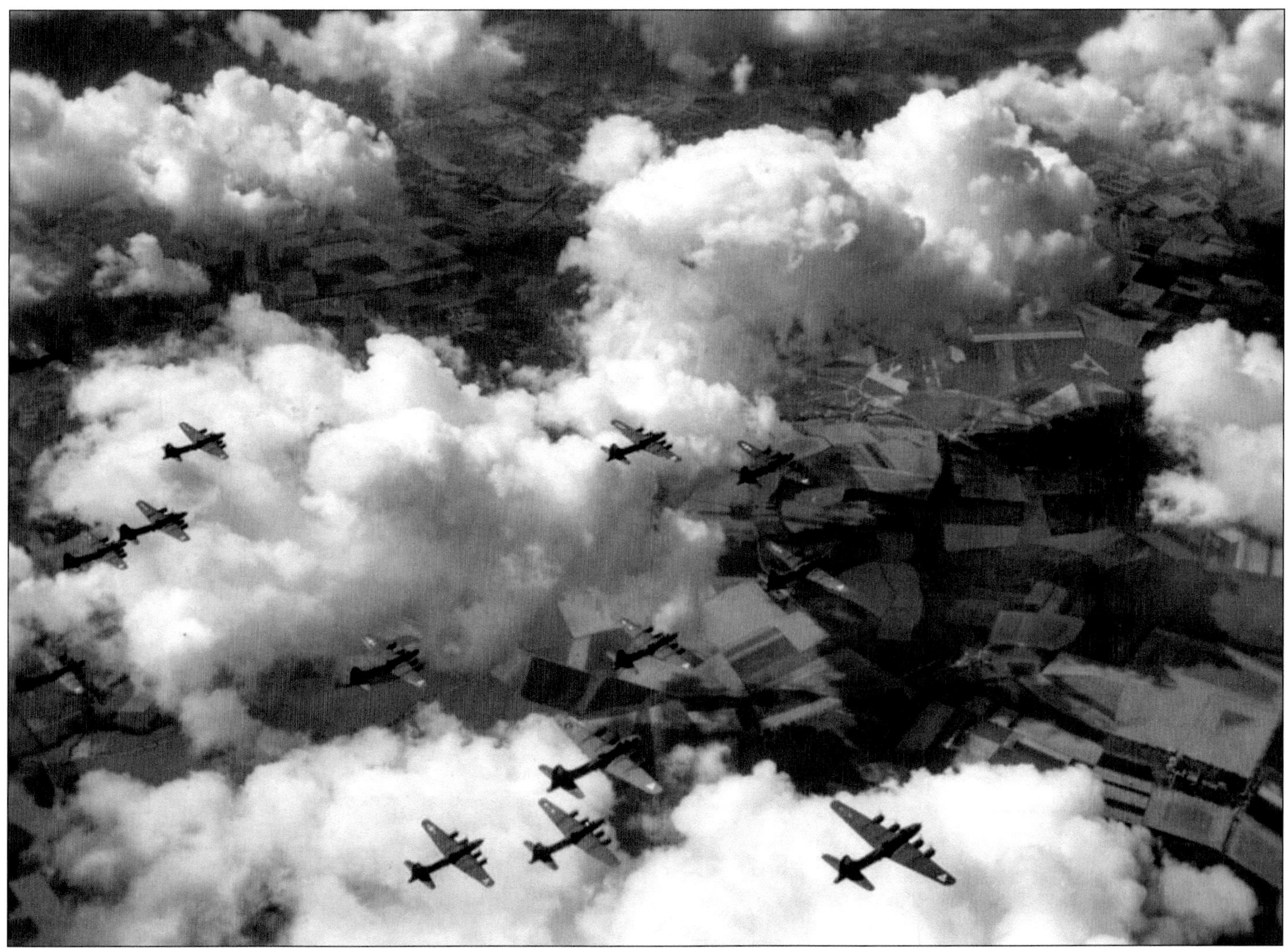

B-17s heading out on a mission from airfields in England. The combat photographer's position in the bomber formation was key to getting good shots of enemy fighter attacks. (NARA)

You would get an adrenaline rush, I'll tell you. That is another thing that counteracts any fear. You can do anything; you feel like you're indestructible. If something hits you, it is going to hit you. But there was an adrenaline rush, especially when the fighters came in, and you can see them blazing away, and they're going right over you like that. And with the flak out there you get a lot of adrenaline. I think some people got a blast out of it. I'll tell you that you feel good shooting an airplane down. You get a heck of a rush. But, of course, you don't see the guy you're shooting down. But, when you see it, as long as you see some smoke and some pieces of an airplane flying off, you get a rush out of it.

When the flak comes up, you know it, but the fighters are your main concern at first. The fighters aren't going to come in when the flak is coming up. They usually put up a different colour flak burst. It had red, black and some white, but the different colour bursts warned their fighters not to go in because they were about to throw a barrage up. While the flak was coming up, there was usually an FW190 sitting off to one side, just out of our gun range, flying parallel with us, radioing down our altitude and air speed. That made the gunners down below very happy and made us very unhappy. Now and then, our gunners fired off a burst at that guy, and he would move away a little, but he still knew your airspeed and altitude. If flak hits your airplane direct, you're going to go down. The flak has

proximity fuses set on the ground for our altitude, that the guy out there was calling it down.

You can see this big flak cloud and head straight into it. There is very severe turbulence from the flak bursts. And you will get shrapnel, about a 20 to 30-foot spread of it. I've had a couple of waist gunners and tail gunners shot out from under me, right there by the gun. And you can't help them immediately; you've got to get that gun going again, or the enemy will get the whole crew. And one of those guys, he was pretty well blown open. He got hit right in the chest with a 20mm through his flak suit. We had flak suits and heavy iron plates packed to make a vest. You had to take over the waist gunner position in that situation.

Morrell said his gunnery training was so thin that it was almost non-existent. But still, he would be credited with two Me109 kills and half of a Ju88.

Romania

The first time I was shot down, it was over the 'Iron Gates of Romania,' on the Danube River. It's at the northeastern tip of Yugoslavia, on the Romanian border. The current was so fast that they had to have tugs to pull the barges up. The oil barges were from the Ploesti area of Romania, and the Germans ran on that oil supply. Their whole war machine used that oil, so

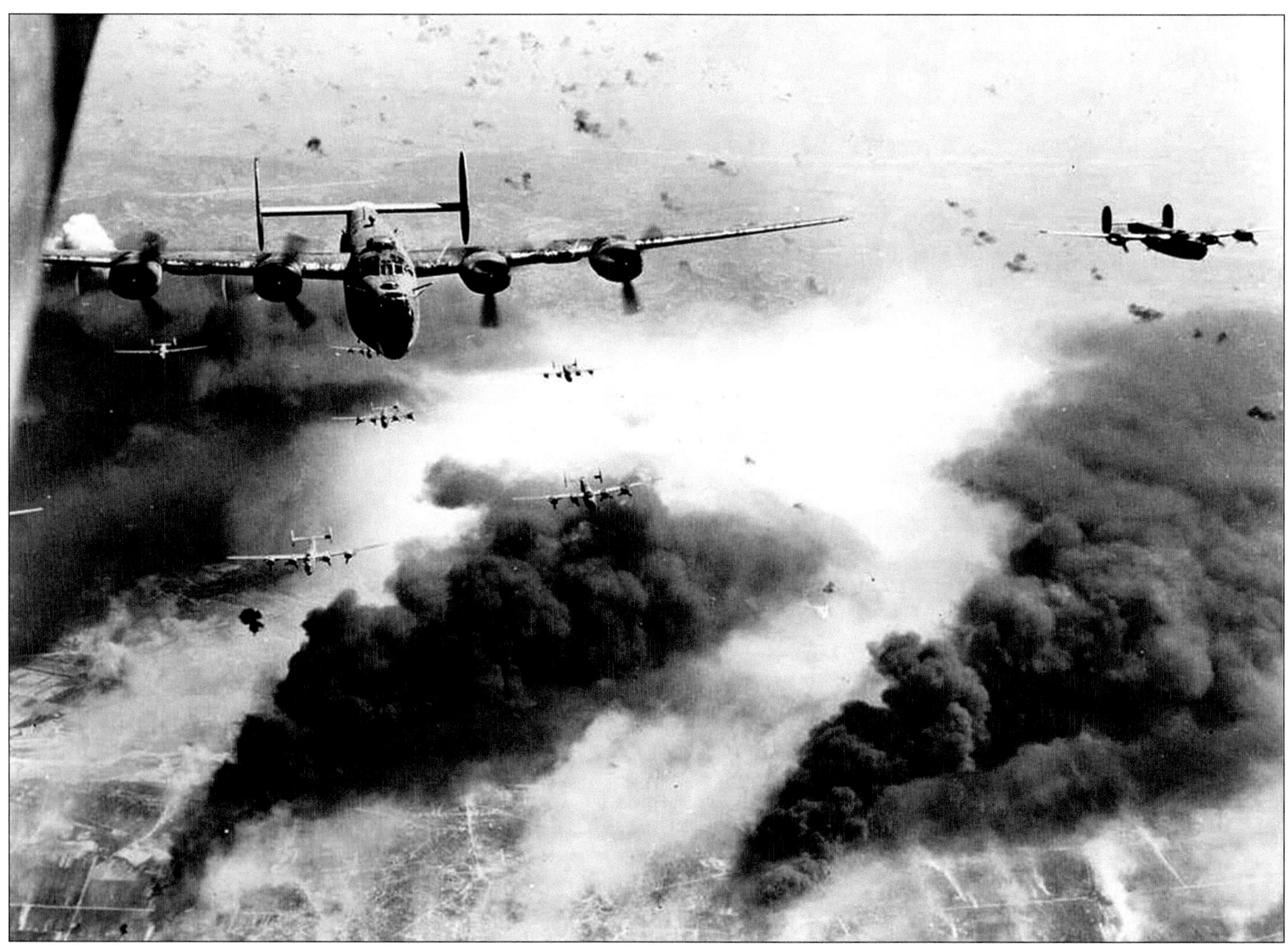

The B-24 Liberator was better suited to take the longest range missions over Eastern Europe launched from England. They could carry a larger bombload over greater distances than the B-17. (USAAF/NARA)

that was why we bombed the Ploesti refineries and the routes that they used to move the oil to Germany.

We lost one engine, and another was slightly damaged. We lost power, and we knew we couldn't make it back over the Yugoslav mountains. There was a designated safe area. We knew where these safe areas were. So, if we were in trouble, we could bail out over them and find underground members, partisans or somebody to help us there.

We bailed out two at a time. We weren't burning or anything; we were just disabled and knew we could not make it back. When they bailed me out with one of the gunners, they made a mistake and put us about five miles away from the rest of them. The partisans picked the others up that evening. A C-47 came over from Italy and took them back. However, we spent the next 26 days walking across the mountains, right across what is now modern Kosovo and Northern Albania, to reach the sea. I bribed a fisherman to take us across the Adriatic to Bari, Italy. Albanian fishing boats are not the sweetest smelling things in the world and stank terribly. It took us a couple of days to get the smell off us when we got to Italy.

The second time Morrell was shot down, it was on another mission against the Ploesti oil fields.

And this was one of the roughest missions in the whole war. We got hit by flak after we dropped our bombs. We had to drop out of formation because we couldn't keep up with it. Staying in formation was your greatest protection because the guns of the other 36 bombers in your Group could cover you. When you fell out of formation, you became far more vulnerable, and we got hit by about six ME109 fighters. They came in and repeatedly raked us with machine gunfire until they finally set us on fire.

As they supplied so much fuel to Germany, the Ploesti oil fields in Romania were a high-priority target for USAAF bomber missions throughout the war. On 1 August 1943, the USAAF mounted Operation Tidal Wave using B-24s equipped with new, low-level bomb sights.

All seven targets for the mission were near to one another. The five refineries located in the city of Ploesti were all within a 13-mile radius. The two outside Ploesti, Brazi (five miles away) and Campina (18 miles) were still relatively close. The bombs they dropped had time fuses, intended to detonate between 45 seconds and six hours after release. The 178 B-24s were launched from bases in Libya. The attack was disastrous, with 54 aircraft and nearly 500 men failing to return (310 killed and 186 captured). Sixteen photographers were onboard the aircraft to document the raid. Only TSgt Jerry Jostwick returned.[2]

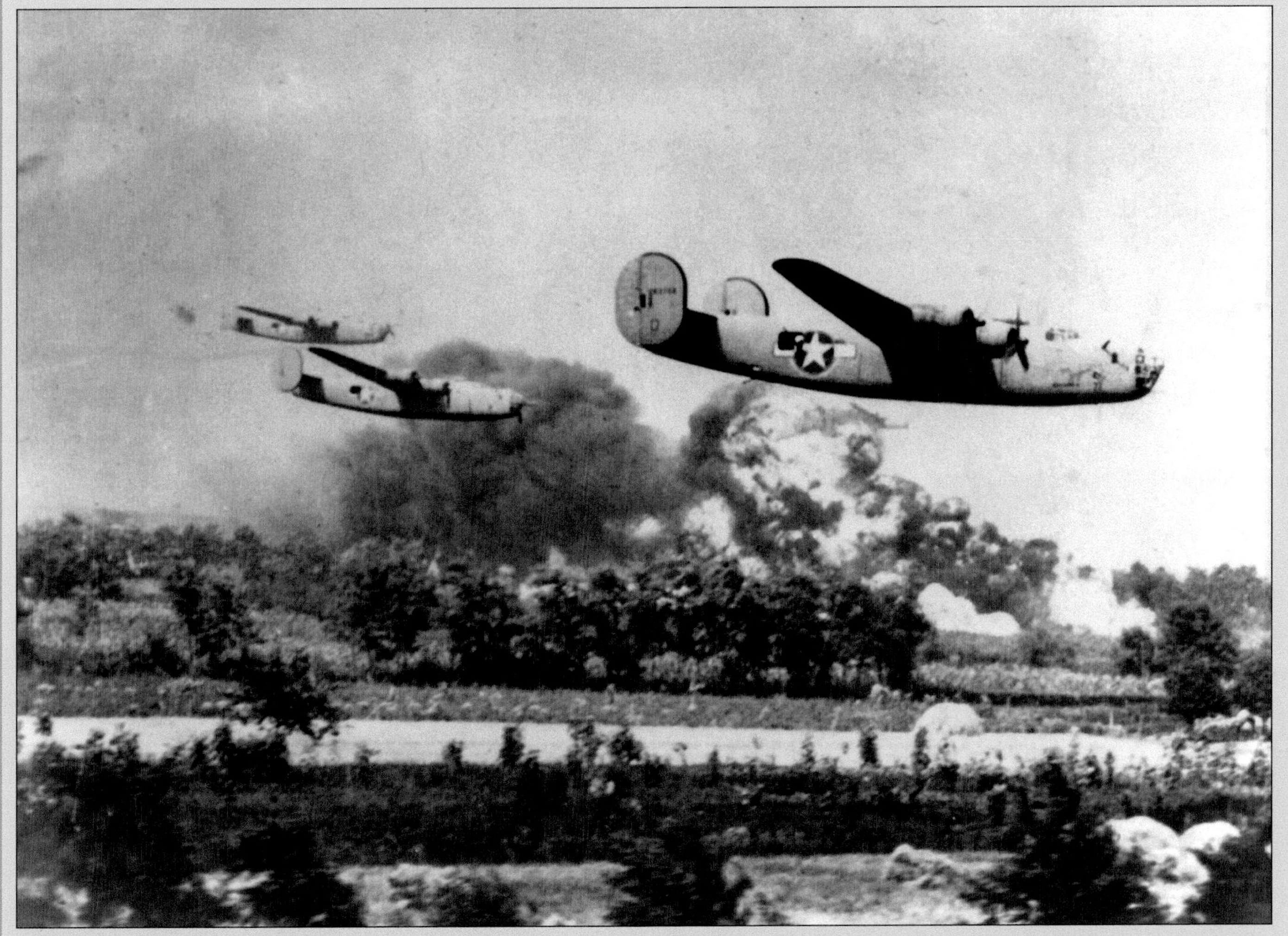

In addition to the danger, low-level flying posed extra challenges for combat photographers, not least increased turbulence, that made capturing good images even more difficult. (NMUSAF)

We noticed a couple of the guys up front had bailed out; we could see one below us on his 'chute, so we said, 'We better get out of here.' We got the two waist gunners out first, the tail gunner and I went out, and about two seconds later, the airplane exploded. I could feel the explosion when it blew. I was taking care of getting these guys out because this was their first mission.

They were hit at about 22,000 feet and bailed out at around 11,000 feet. Morell was immediately captured as he landed:

They put us in a prison camp. We stayed there for four and a half months until the advancing Russians released us. Of course, we went around town for a long time and had a ball. The Air Force tore the bomb bays out of about six or seven B-17s, put plywood floors in the bottom, and picked us up over there. I was on the last plane going out to Italy. I was lucky they found me because I was busy having a good time in the town.

While in that Romanian prison camp, Morrell had met other cameramen who had been captured from shot-down bombers:

I was terrified for a while; I didn't know what was going to happen to me. They had me in a one-metre square box, kept me in there for days at a time, and then dragged out to interrogate me. They knew I was a cameraman, therefore knew I worked for intelligence, and thought I knew something. Finally, they put me in a prison camp with the rest of the guys. But I spent the first 30 days in Luftwaffe headquarters.

Beating Camouflage

I was looking out the waist window at Wiener Neustadt, where we were bombing a Messerschmitt factory. I could see this regular shape in the woods, like a factory building or something. I said, 'I know a building was there because of my green-brown colour deficiency'. It was a camouflaged area, but they didn't believe me. The next day, I took a camera with me after readjusting the lens's focal length and took infrared pictures. I shot this Messerschmitt factory, and they got excited; it was exactly what I said it was. Another time, we were going up across Venice, and I saw, down along the shoreline, what looked like a couple of submarines. I asked one of the waist gunners, 'You see that sub down there?' but he couldn't. I took my infrared camera, shot the two submarines,

and got their coordinates from the navigator. The next day, a Wimpy [an RAF Wellington bomber] got them. So now I've two submarines, a Messerschmitt factory, two Me109s, and a Ju88 to my credit.

But that's combat documentation for you. It can be used for operational evaluation and reconnaissance in cases like these.

During wartime, many of the bomber crews were very superstitious and did not want anyone else onboard their aircraft who might bring them bad luck. They often did not want a cameramen around. 'They would say, sometimes when I would go to the briefing, "Oh, what do we need a cameraman up there for?" Or "What do we need all that for?" Sometimes, they had to be told, "Well, you're having a cameraman…". 'Historically, the pictures are invaluable, just priceless. Most of the best footage has been taken and used repeatedly in films. But it is very, very important to make people realize what the heck was going on'.

Korean War

Before being recalled for the Korean War in 1952, Morrell had a five-year break from the Air Force between 1947 and 1952. On his return:

I immediately went back on flying status, as an aerial photographer again. During the Korean War, I was in SAC RB-36s. That was a reconnaissance airplane; we had six pusher engines, two jets on each wing, and carried over 20 cameras. Our designated targets were all in Russia and China. We all had severe survival training – survival, survival, survival. Every time you changed crew, you would have to undergo survival training with the new crew. Crew integrity, they called it.

FICON

We also had the FICON system. This was used to carry a specialised reconnaissance parasite RF-84K under an RB-36D. The RF-84K had a hook on the front of the aircraft that helped secure it to the RB-36. It had two pins that retracted to release the mechanism, and the cameraman had to secure these. On the return from his mission, The RF-84 pilot would fly in between that and hook on. Then, we would lock him up and get him up inside our airplane and out of the cockpit. We had to reload his cameras, refuel him, and give him a walk-around oxygen bottle. It was quite a deal, but it wasn't in combat. But we were ready anytime.

THE PARASITE

One of the more exotic ideas that emerged during the early 1950s was one that ostensibly extended the range of escort fighters to provide SAC bombers with an organic fighter escort. Project Tip Tow was described as a 'floating wingtip' concept that saw two original straight-winged F-84s attached to the wingtip of a B-29. Following that was an idea from Convair called Project Tom Tom. It was a FICON (Fighter Conveyor) concept, designed to carry a 'parasite fighter' attached to a special compartment built into the underside of an adapted B-36. In reality, the intention was to extend SAC's long-range reconnaissance capabilities. Launched from one of the ultra-long-range specially modified RB-36s, the

parasite reconnaissance aircraft would have made a dash to cover its targets and returned to the GRB-36D.

After testing, the system saw limited service with SAC in 1955–56. Using 10 modified GRB-36D carriers from the 99th Strategic Reconnaissance Wing, they worked with 25 modified RF-84Ks from the 91st SRS. Whilst the idea ostensibly worked, it was challenging even for experienced test pilots in ideal conditions, with several RF-84Ks damaged in training flights. It would probably have proved nearly useless in more realistic operational situations with less-experienced pilots. It was quietly abandoned in April 1956.

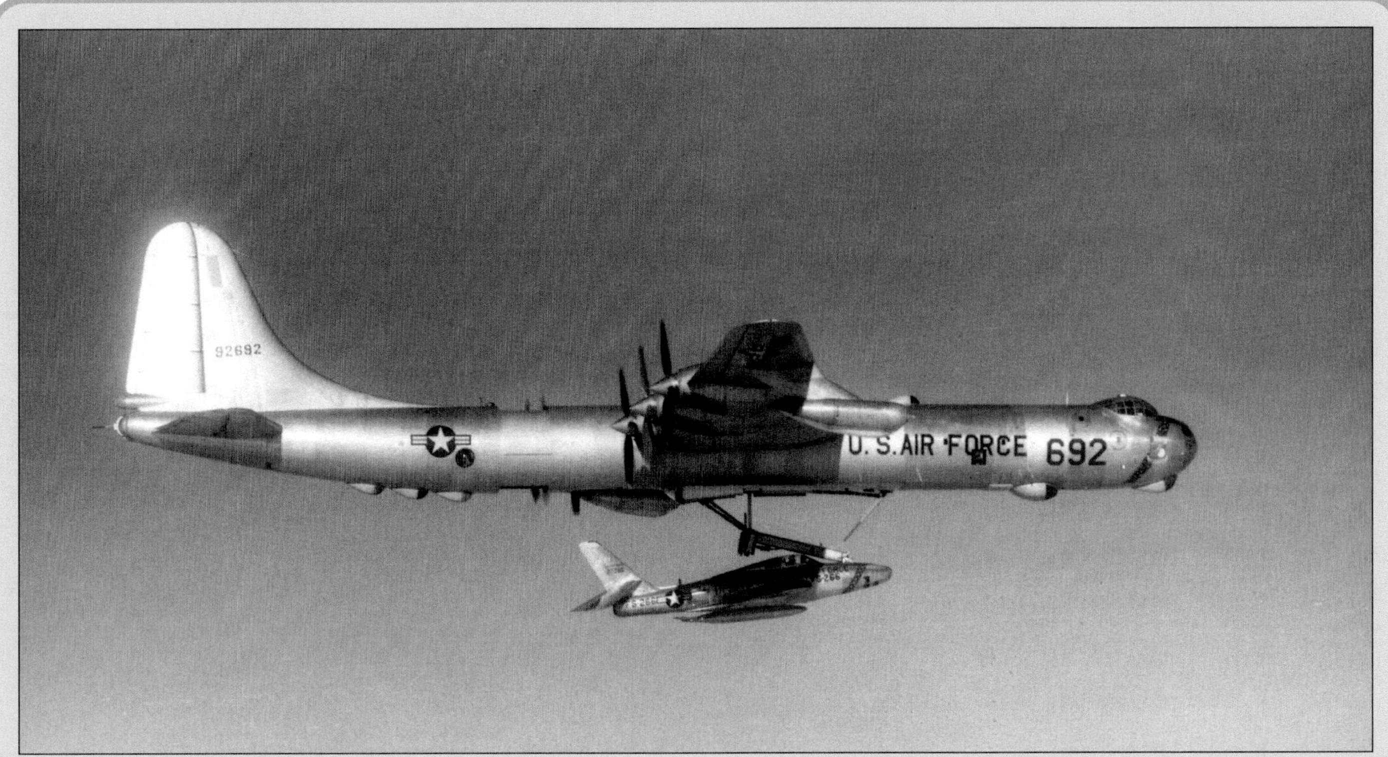

The FICON RF-84Ks were intended to be launched from the GRB-36Ds to make high-speed dashes to photograph targets behind the Iron Curtain. (NARA)

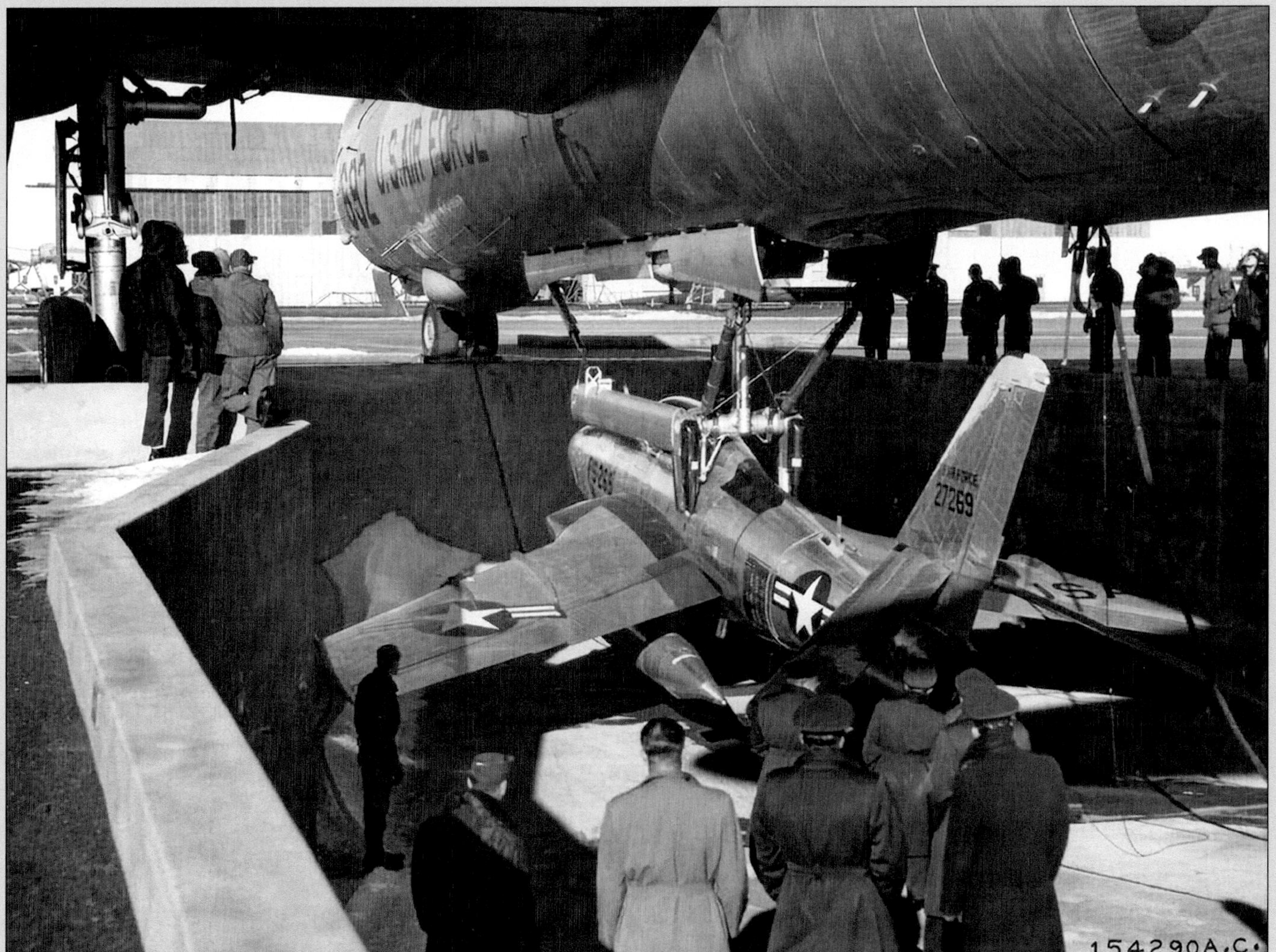

Installing the RF-84K into the bay of the GRB-36D on the ground was a very specialised effort, requiring a pit and dedicated handling equipment. Once fitted, the GRB-36D had minimal ground clearance. (NARA)

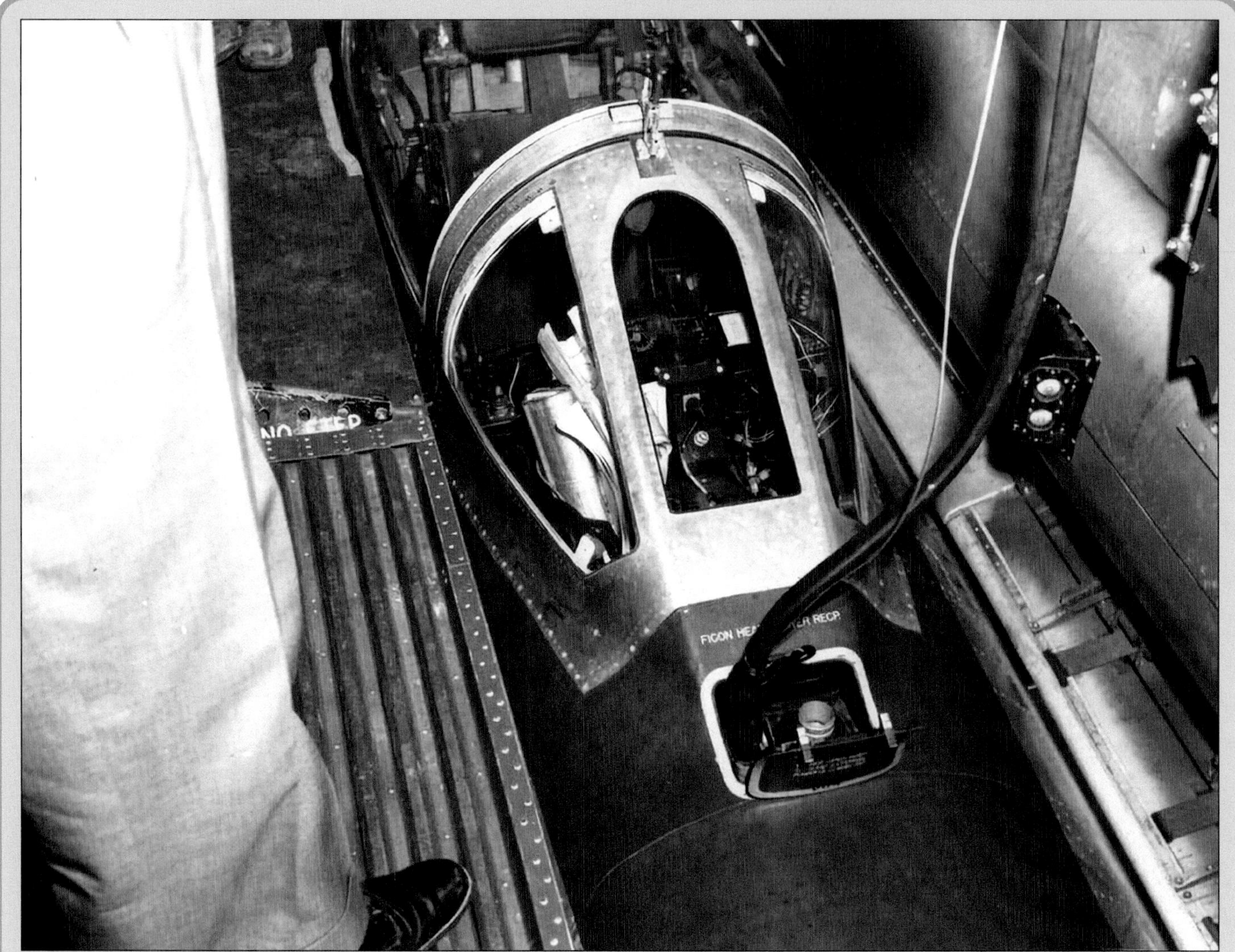

When flying in the FICON GRB-36D, part of Doug Morrell's job was to secure the aircraft and reload the cameras on its return. (NARA)

After I got out of RB-36s, they sent me to Panama. I spent five years in Panama documenting civic actions. We were trying to build rapport between the US and all these Central and South American countries. I visited every one of them down there. [After that]… They sent me to Colorado Springs, to Air Defense Command. They needed documentation of the Russian 'Bear' bombers coming down from the North on reconnaissance missions over our fleet. These were their electronic intelligence gatherers. They sent me to Iceland, and I documented about 25 to 30 intercepts over the next six months. We were flying in F-102B Delta Daggers, the two-seat side-by-side version of the aircraft.

We documented those aircraft. They kept sending the same airplanes but with different numbers painted on them. We knew that because we would go up close and photograph the aircraft's rivet pattern. We went right underneath them, and I'd shoot straight up to record the rivet pattern and aerials.

This was almost combat because once, the Russian bomber's tail gunner lowered his stowed tail guns. The minute he did that, my pilot prepared to fire a missile. The doors underneath our F-102 flew open; our missile rack went down, and it was ready to launch. Immediately, the Bear's tail gun returned to the stowed position.

Vietnam

From there, Morrell went to Vietnam:

I was sent to Clark AFB and through the Survival School there. Then, it was on to Thailand and Korat AFB. We were not getting good coverage from many bases, so I started to go around them all and check to see what they were doing and fly a few missions.

Shooting combat camera in Vietnam was an awful lot of chase stuff. We would get into the back of two-seat F-100s. The aircraft would always go in twos when they were making a bombing or a strafing attack, one ahead of the other. The cameraman would be in the second 'chase' plane, so we could show where the bombs fell, how they fell and get some quick bomb damage assessment and things like that. So we had a lot of guys on flying status in Vietnam. There were still and motion photographers, so it was way different from World War Two. And we had better equipment too. We shot 16mm in Vietnam, and the smaller cameras made filming much easier.

Shooting in World War Two was almost invariably in bombers. In Vietnam, we were the only enlisted men qualified to fly in high-performance jet aircraft as our shooting platforms. It wasn't all getting pictures from the angle of

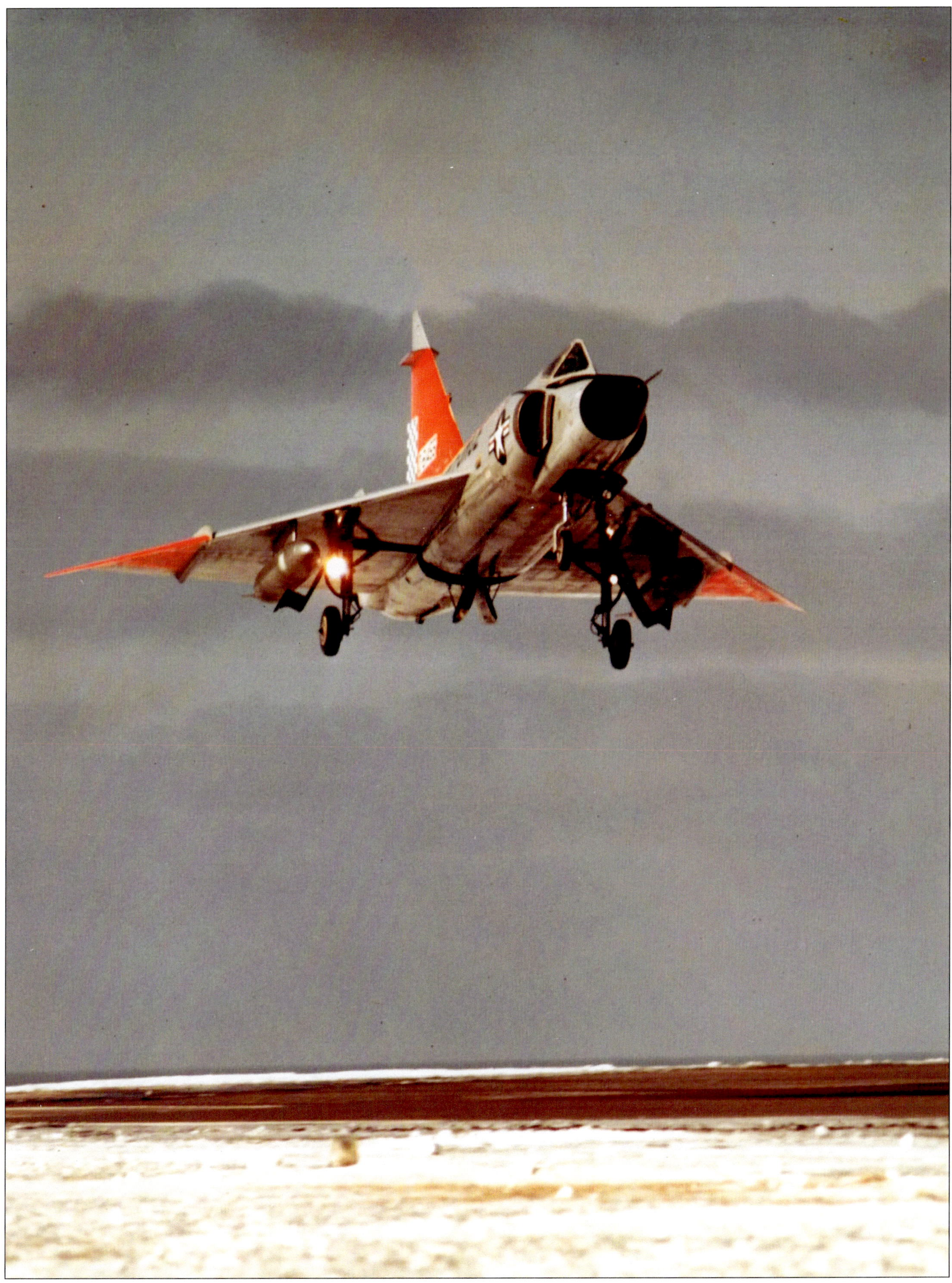

From Keflavik, Iceland, the 57th Fighter Interceptor Squadron was tasked with intercepting Soviet aircraft entering the North Atlantic between the UK and Iceland. Morrell got to fly 25–30 intercepts. (USAF)

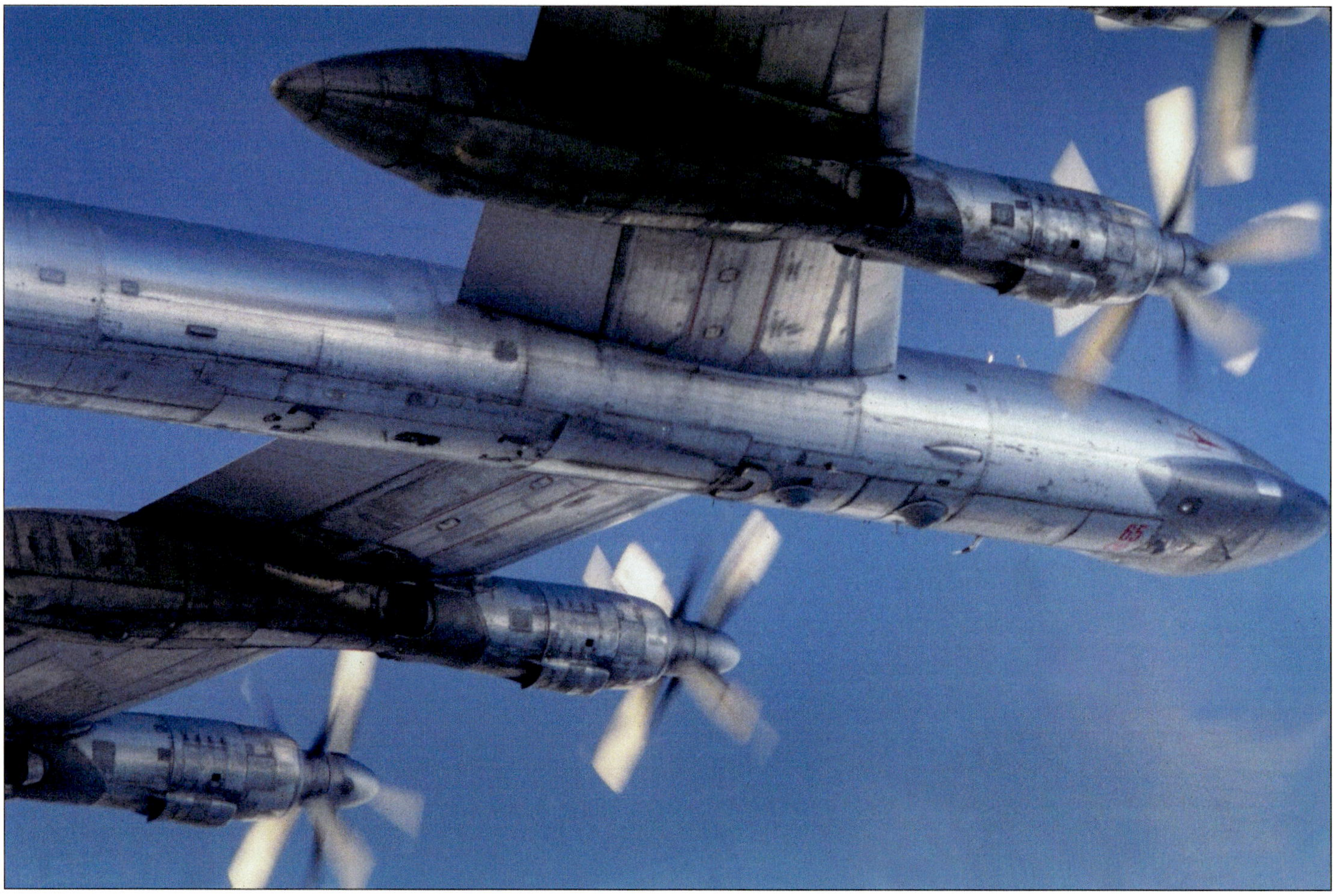

The identification numbers of Soviet bombers were regularly changed to confuse NATO intelligence. As the bombers were hand-built, by flying close underneath them and photographing the aircraft's rivet patterns, made it possible to identify individual airframes. (USAF)

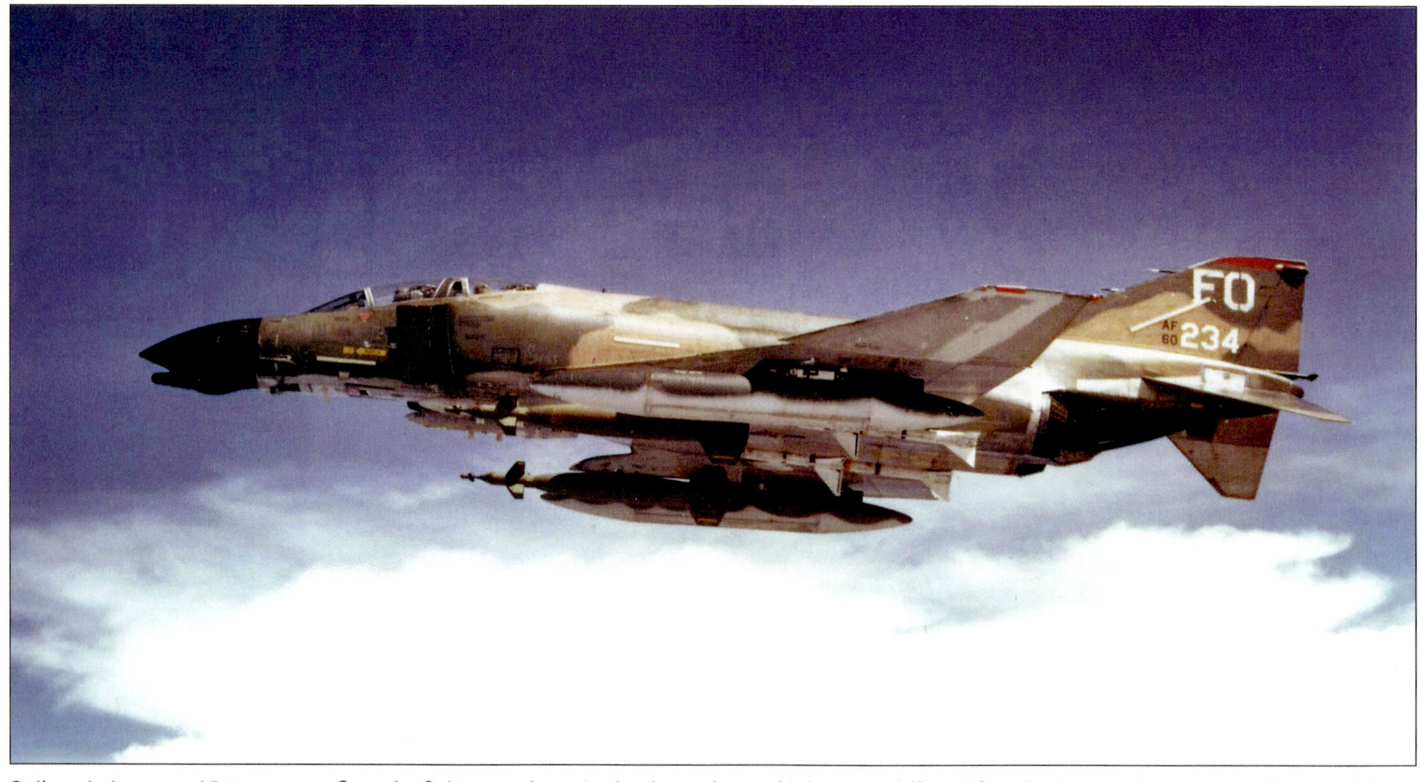

Strike missions over Vietnam were flown by fighters and required a chase plane, which is very different from being an extra crew member in a B-17 or B-24. In F-100s and F-105s, this meant flying in a two-seat version of the aircraft. In F-4s, it meant replacing the aircraft's navigator, which was not popular with crews. (USAF)

the guns firing and the bombs falling. It was shooting the action from another plane, which was completely different. It wasn't high-altitude bombing; this was low-altitude strafing, conventional bombing and the dropping of napalm.

We used Eastman Colour Negative colour film all the time. We did not use black and white, except for some instrumentation pictures. We had laboratories in trailers, so everything was all fixed up and raring to go. You got on the ground, and they would rush out, grab your film, and run with it to the lab. Within about an hour and a half, they would have turned around the pictures and had rough prints ready for intelligence, the fighter squadron commander, or whoever. So it was very fast.

Down in the Jungle

On 28 February 1969, just before his fiftieth birthday, Morrell was at Nakhon Phanom AB on the Mekong River, just across from Laos. Flown by pilot, Lt Stephen Long:

We went up from there in a Cessna O-2, used by Forward Air Controllers with a puller engine in the front and a pusher engine in the rear. We're up there about a half hour, flying over to Laos. We were going over to photograph these sensors that we would drop on the Ho Chi Minh trail. They were like javelins, two to three feet long. An airplane would fly directly over the trail, dropping a string of those. As this string went down, we were supposed to photograph it to see the actual position on the ground where they went in. After developing our film, the exact location of those sensors could be identified.

The sensors would start broadcasting if there was any activity on the Ho Chi Minh trail, even guys on bicycles. When the sensors buried themselves in the ground, they had a green tail. It looked like a leaf coming out, but it was the antenna. Any noise would start them operating and send us a beep signal.

We're flying around there in this O-2. Suddenly, we had four flak rounds, and it went bing, bing, bing, bing. The fourth hit us on the left wing, knocking the wing off and setting the stub on fire. The pilot says, 'Bail out!' I reached down, grabbed the handle, and the whole side of the O-2's cockpit came off. The pilot had to go out of my side of the airplane. We rolled out either side of the strut, connecting the fuselage to the wing. We were both rolling around; he was knocked out, and so was I temporarily, too. I woke up, I imagine, a couple of seconds afterwards. He went all the way down, and when he opened his 'chute, he only had about one swing. Then, he hit the ground and broke his legs. I don't know when I opened my parachute, but we were at 5,000 feet, and I opened it about two or three seconds after we bailed out. But I didn't even know it until I looked around and thought, 'Uh-oh, I better pull this.' When I had bailed out, I said to myself, 'Oh no, not again' almost that casually.

I opened my chute, and I could see a gun right below me. The gun that hit us was now firing at me. I looked down, and people were coming out of this truck park. It was the sleepy little village of Xepon, where more crews had been shot down than anywhere else. I saw all these people coming out, and it looked like I would land there. Pieces of the airplane were coming down all around me. So, just like I did in World War

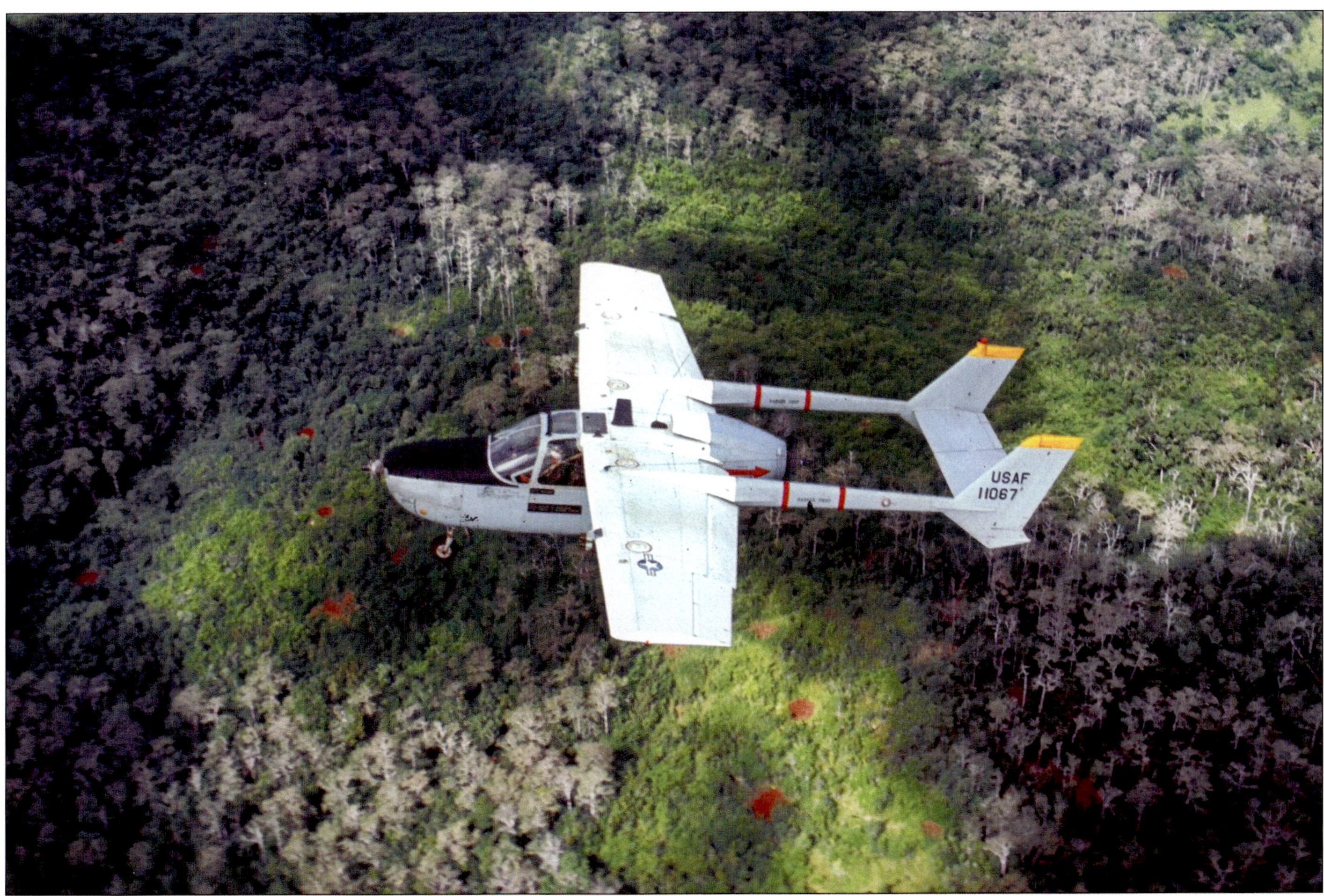

The Cessna O-2A was widely used as a Forward Air Control aircraft carrying a pilot and observer in Vietnam. The high wing gave good visibility. (USAF)

II, I pulled on my chute risers and sailed along. I saw a tree out there in the jungle sticking up by itself. I went into the tree fast, and my chute collapsed. I felt a momentary tug, and then I went down, straight down. It was a high jungle canopy of 40 or 50 feet, at least, maybe 80 feet. I went straight down, and on the way down, my right heel hit a tree limb, and it shattered my talus, the bone in your ankle that everything swivels on. I am all jarred up, but I got out of my outfit. The survival training says, "Go uphill. Go away from the people, go uphill, because that's where the helicopters can pick you up more easily".

I am going through the jungle, straight ahead, and I came on this truck park. I could see the trucks. I said to myself, 'I can't go there.' So I looked around, but there was no way to go up. It was just flat, level, all over. I finally saw a slight rise and headed out that way. And I walked on this broken ankle. You don't realise it, but the adrenaline makes a beautiful splint for you. I didn't even feel the leg hurting at all. I hid in some tall grass, got my radio out and called up. There was an OV-10 Bronco on forward air control that I contacted.

Morrell could not give a precise location to the OV-10 pilot, but eventually, he heard the aircraft.

I guided him in with my radio. 'Make a left turn.' And he came, and I said, 'Now you are over me, right now.' So he dipped his wing, and he says, 'Oh, you down there in that clearing?'

Remembering the enemy had Morrell's pilot and probably his radio equipment, too, he tried not to talk with him anymore. The OV-10 successfully passed above Morrell's location:

And the rescue force came in, and they had five A-1E 'Sandys.' They came in and sprayed all around the area. I told them where to go; the area was defended by six anti-aircraft guns, five 37 mm guns and a 'Quad 40' type weapon with four machine guns mounted together. I had to try to indicate to the Sandys where all these guns were situated by telling them over the radio. I called them in, and they put them out.

The US aircraft hit the area with miniguns and bombs. An F-100 came and dropped napalm as well. 'So we got rid of six guns'.

They sent in the Jolly Green Giant, the CH-53 rescue helicopter. I guided him in and over me. I waited until the jungle penetrator hit the ground to discharge the static electricity. I got onto the jungle penetrator, and they winched me right up. And we went up, no shots, no nothing. They had rescued me. On the way back, I drank plenty of cold water and an old 'rusty' cheeseburger left in the helicopter for three days. Best one I ever had. They dropped me back at Nakhon Phanom AB. Everybody was standing around congratulating me, and the doctor was checking me out; they put me on a stretcher finally and took me in an ambulance to the hospital. I spent three months in the hospital there, and then they sent me back to the States. And that was Vietnam.

Morrell's pilot that day was Lt Stephen Long, who was on his first tour as a Cessna O-2 Forward Air Controller with the 23rd TASS. He was captured that day and became a PoW. After spending 1,490 days in captivity, Lt Long was released during Operation Homecoming on 28 March 1973. He later flew F-4s, F-105s, and F-16s and was involved in the F-117 programme.

When Morrell retired as an active-duty serviceman in 1973, he continued working for combat camera as a civilian. Several AAVS cameramen from the early 1980s have recounted; still a little in awe, of meeting Morrell with a near-permanent cigar clamped in his mouth and being critiqued on their latest reel or their photographs that he had seen.

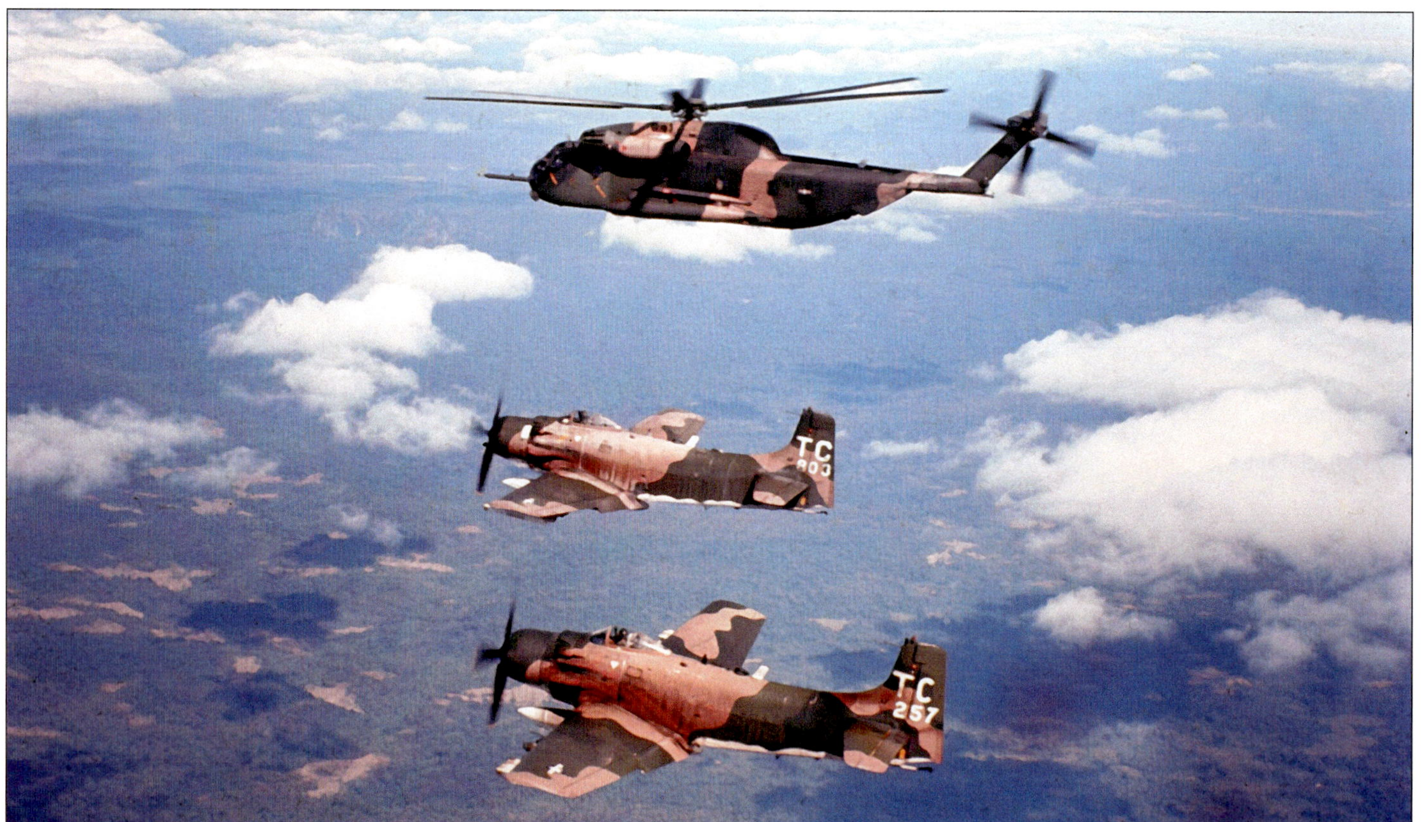

A-1E Skyraiders, often known as 'Sandys', went ahead of the CH-53 rescue helicopter to suppress enemy forces close to Morrell's pick-up point. (USAF)

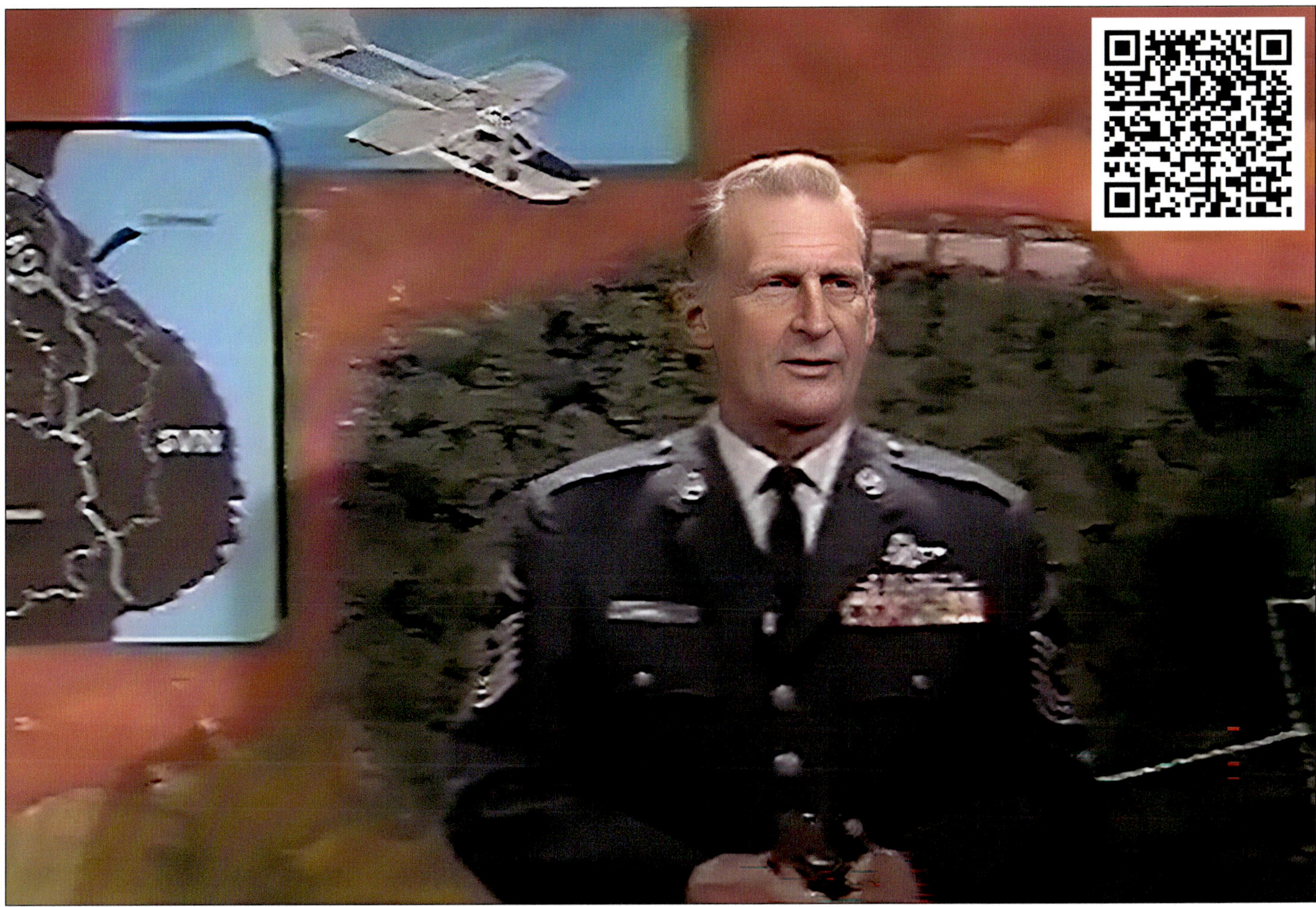

Third Time Down (AVA 297) is Doug Morrells own account of his shooting down in Vietnam given in a TV lecture intended for USAF personnel. It begins with a sequence of his pilot that day, Lt Stephen Long, on his flight back to the US after being released as a PoW. (DVIDS)

8

CONTINGENCY OPERATION: NICKEL GRASS

On 6 October 1973, in a coordinated attack, Syrian forces stormed Israeli positions on the Golan Heights, and Egyptian troops crossed the Suez Canal, streaming into the Sinai. Israeli forces were largely unprepared, and the first few days of the war went badly for them. Immediately on the defensive, they were quickly pushed back, suffered heavy losses and expended ordnance at an enormous rate. Prime Minister Golda Meir immediately turned to the United States for assistance. Under intense pressure, on 12 October 1973, President Nixon approved a massive but low-key US airlift led by the Military Airlift Command, codenamed Nickel Grass. MAC C-5As and C-141As began arriving in Israel on 14 October and continued beyond the war's end on 25 October 1973.

Personnel always had to be prepared for contingency operations, and Nickel Grass was one such event. Being a MAC-led operation, access to the activities was easier for personnel than for operations led by other commands. However, in the 50 years since then, publicly available images from this mostly secretive airlift have been remarkably sparse. However, a small number of unedited reels have been declassified and digitised by the US National Archive. The footage is unique. Apart from a brief press session at Lod International Airport and some UPI footage from the fence in the Azores, there are virtually no other still or video images publicly available.[1] Even in their unedited form, the films released to NARA give a unique insight into how this contingency operation was mounted.[2]

MAC boss, General Paul Carlton, had already begun preparing for the high-intensity operations Nickel Grass. He waived the standard crew rest requirements, aircraft weight limitations, daily flying hours and routine maintenance requirements. Supplies were funnelled through approximately 29 US airfields to just three East Coast US bases. From those locations, C-5s and C-141s flew to Lajes, with a refuelling stop and crew change, then on to Israel. Portugal's Lajes airfield, in the Azores, was the only overseas airfield available to the US. The C-5A Galaxy and C-141A Starlifters were the only aircraft capable of delivering the necessary supplies directly to Israel.

The Airlift Begins
The initial daily target was 4,000 tons of supplies. The average distance from the US East Coast departure points at McGuire AFB, NJ, Dover AFB, Delaware, and Charleston AFB, SC, to Lajes was

just under 3,300 miles. From the Azores, Lod Airport was another 3,163 miles. Aerial refuelling en route was out of the question because the C-141A was not equipped to do so, and to preserve their fatigue life, a decision was made not to use the C-5A's aerial refuelling capability.

A vast range of materials was airlifted, and the C-5A handled the large, oversized loads. These included over 3,600 tons of 105mm, 155mm and 175mm ammunition and rockets, from Little Rock AFB and Wright-Patterson AFBs. The munition loads were so heavy that the C-5s often reached their maximum payload weights while much of the cargo hold had to remain empty. Approximately 29 M-60 tanks and M-48 Chaparral mobile air defence systems came via Robins AFB; 25 were delivered after the ceasefire.

The recorded material from Dover AFB shows the C-141s and C-5s being prepared and loaded. Others show flight crew briefings, the main Air Operations Center at MAC headquarters and the cargo loads of 105mm shells and AGM-65 Maverick missiles being placed on aircraft. Personnel accompanied some of the flights. From Lajes, there are clips of the aircraft being refuelled and taking off again from the island airfield. Key to the operation was the establishment of a US 'Air Lift Coordination Element' (ALCE) at Lod Airport, commanded by Col Donald Strobaugh. Images show him and his senior staff, all in civilian attire, as they were ordered to be. There are significant sequences of aircraft handling and ramp operations at Lod Airport and the US aircrew 'lounge' established by El Al in the otherwise now deserted civilian air terminal.

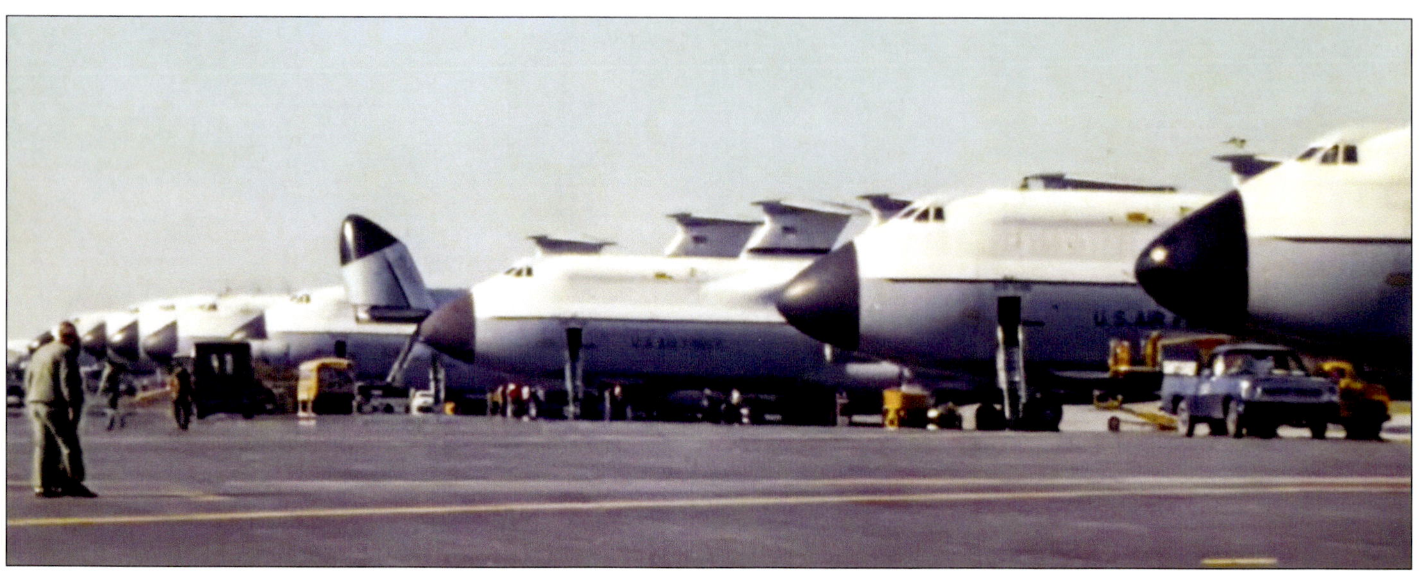

C-5s are being prepared at Dover AFB to airlift military equipment and supplies to Israel. (USAF/AAVS)

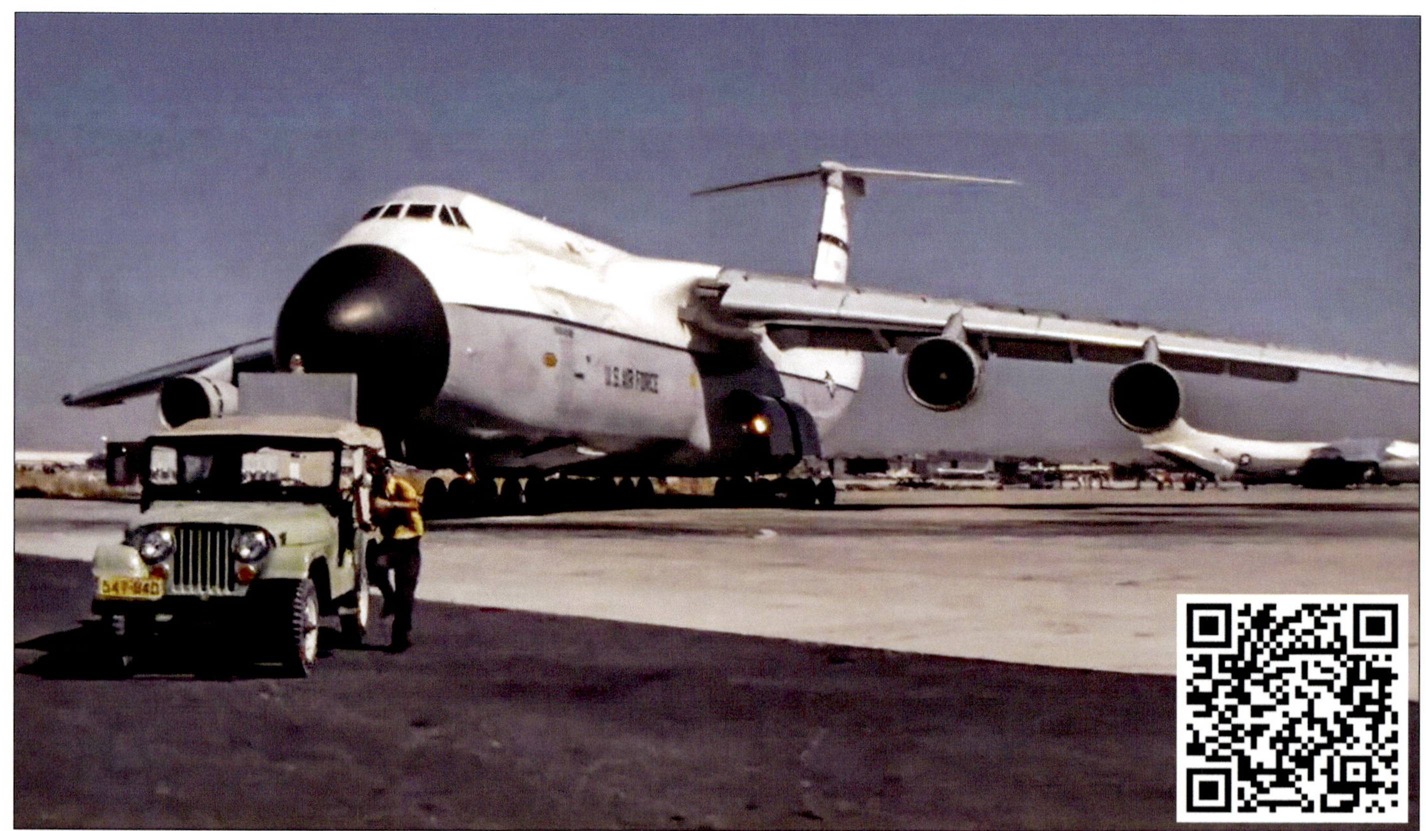

A C-5A guided into a parking space at Lod Airport. By the time Nickel Grass terminated on 14 November 1973, 145 C-5A flights had landed in Israel. (USAF/TSgt McConnell)

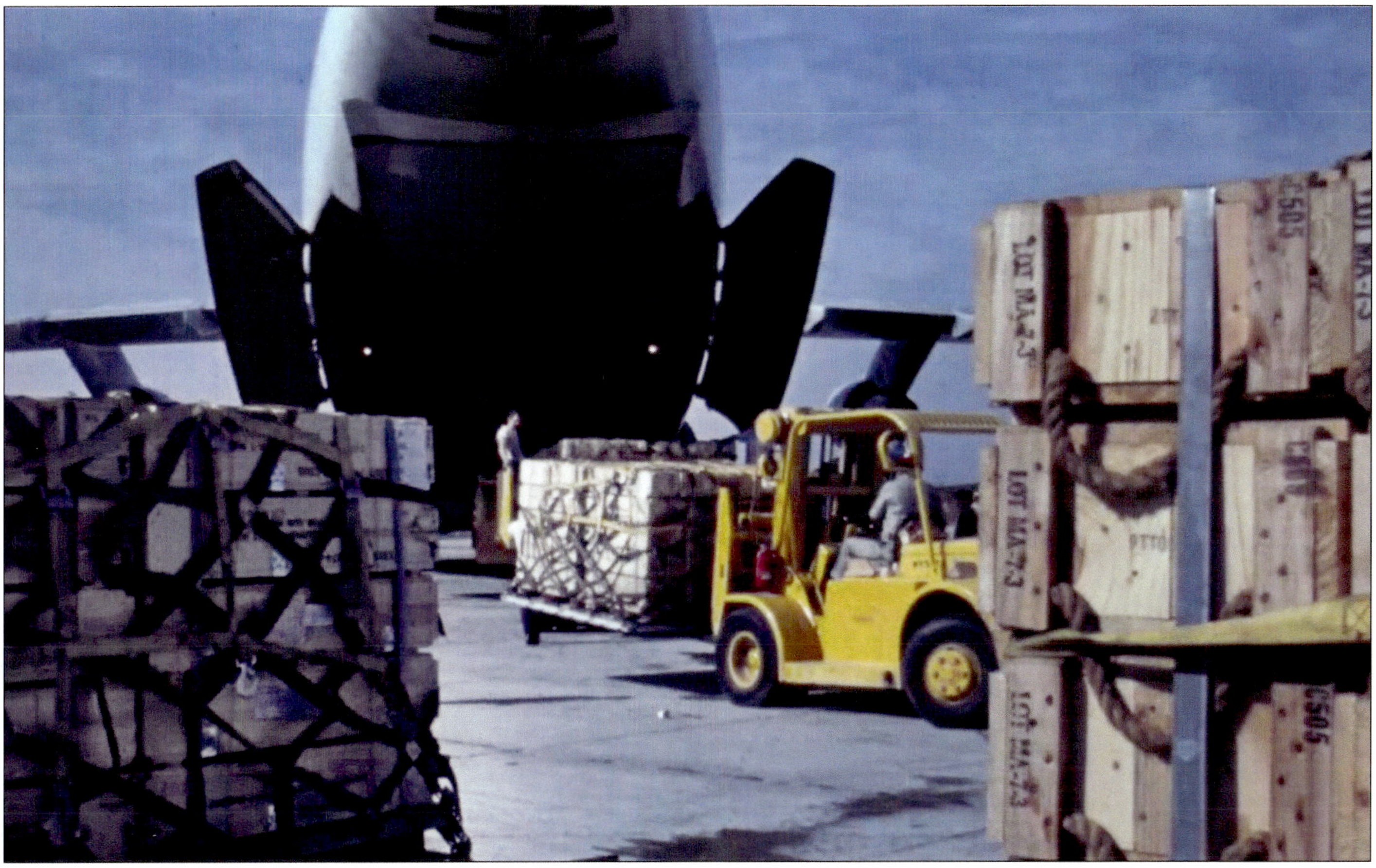

In the early stages of the airlift, before the arrival of specialist US handling equipment, the only way to unload aircraft was with forklift trucks, a much slower process. (USAF/TSgt PJ Lewis)

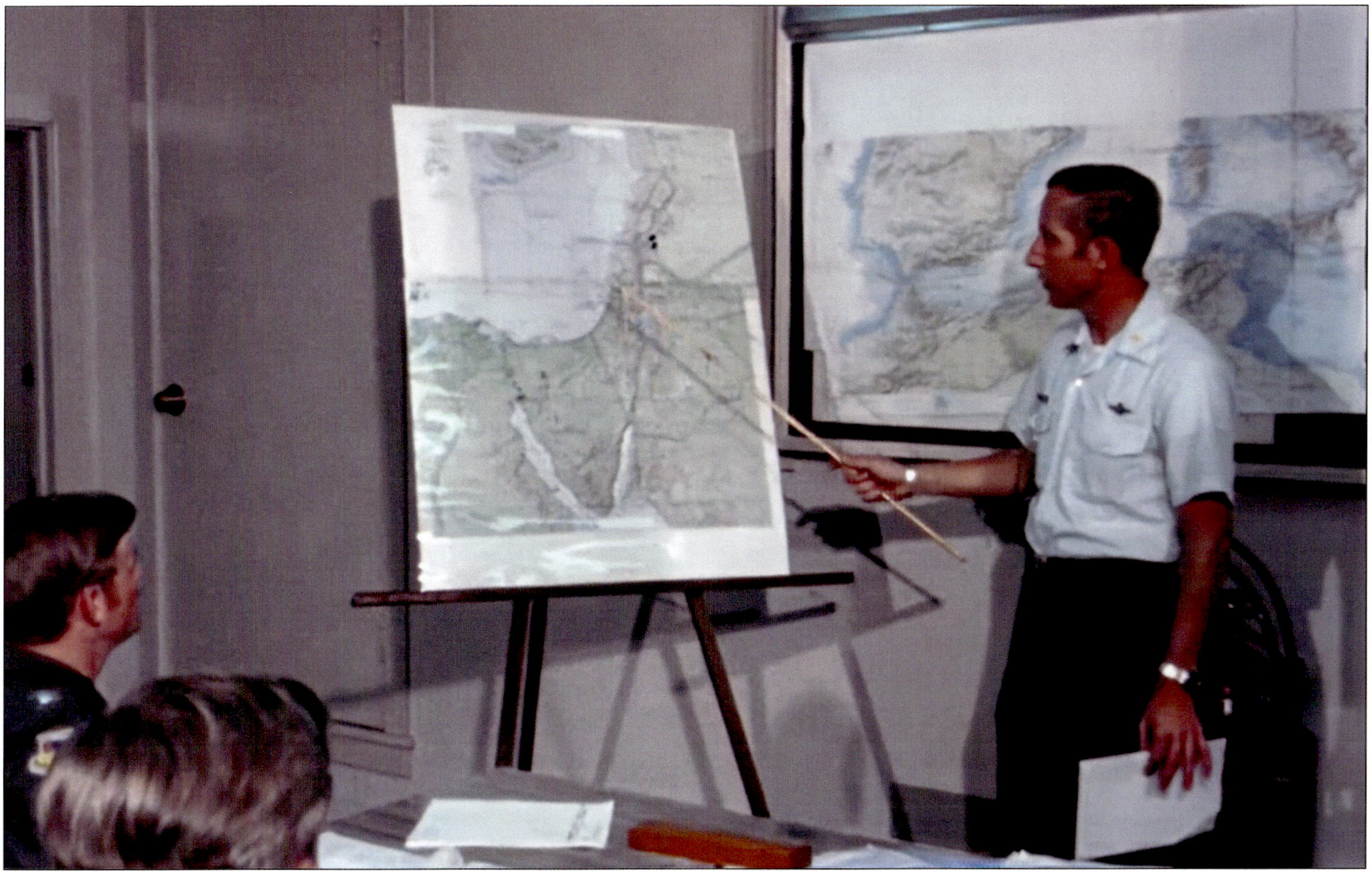

An aircrew briefing on the intricacies of reaching Lod Airport during wartime. (USAF)

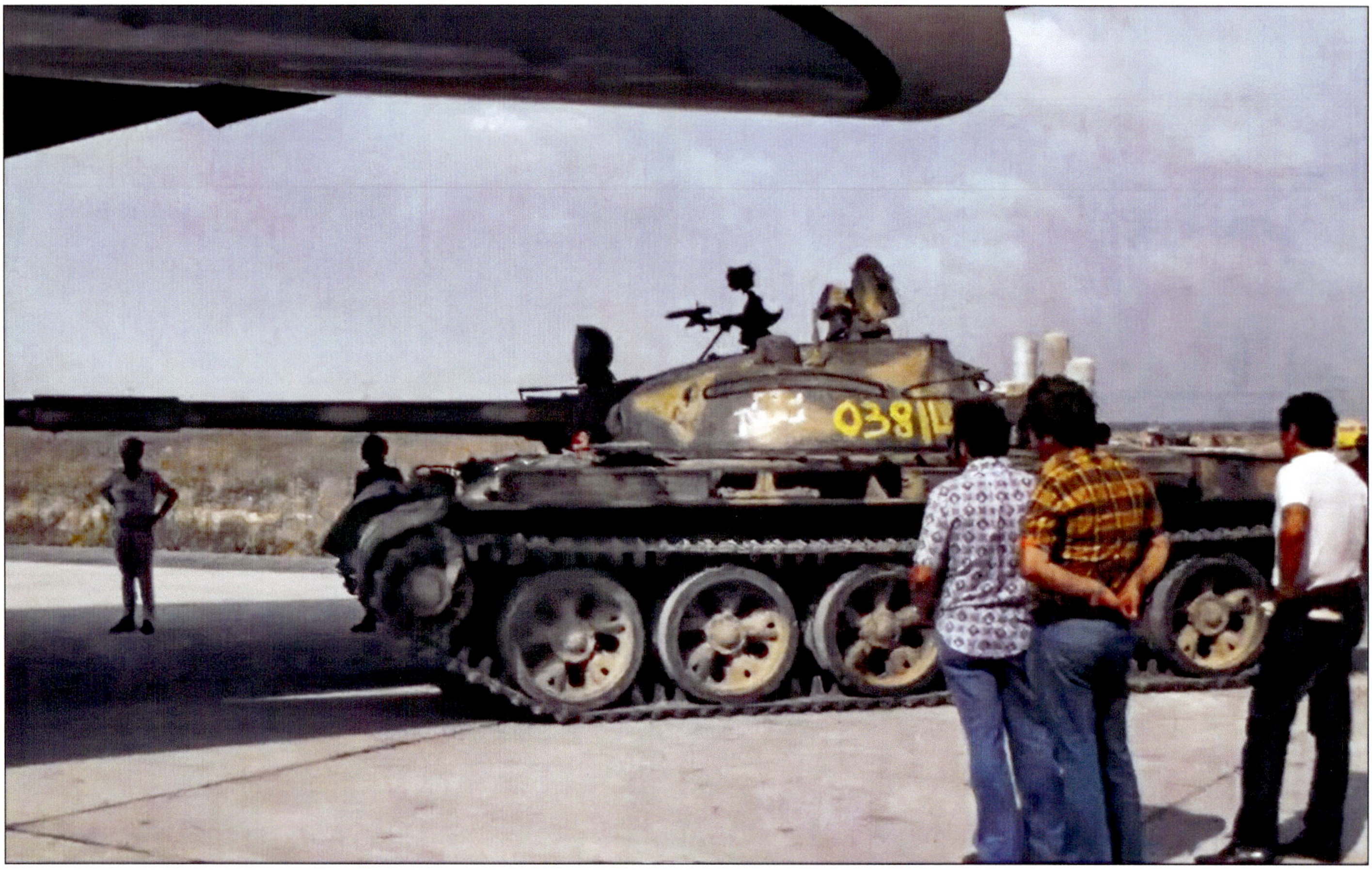

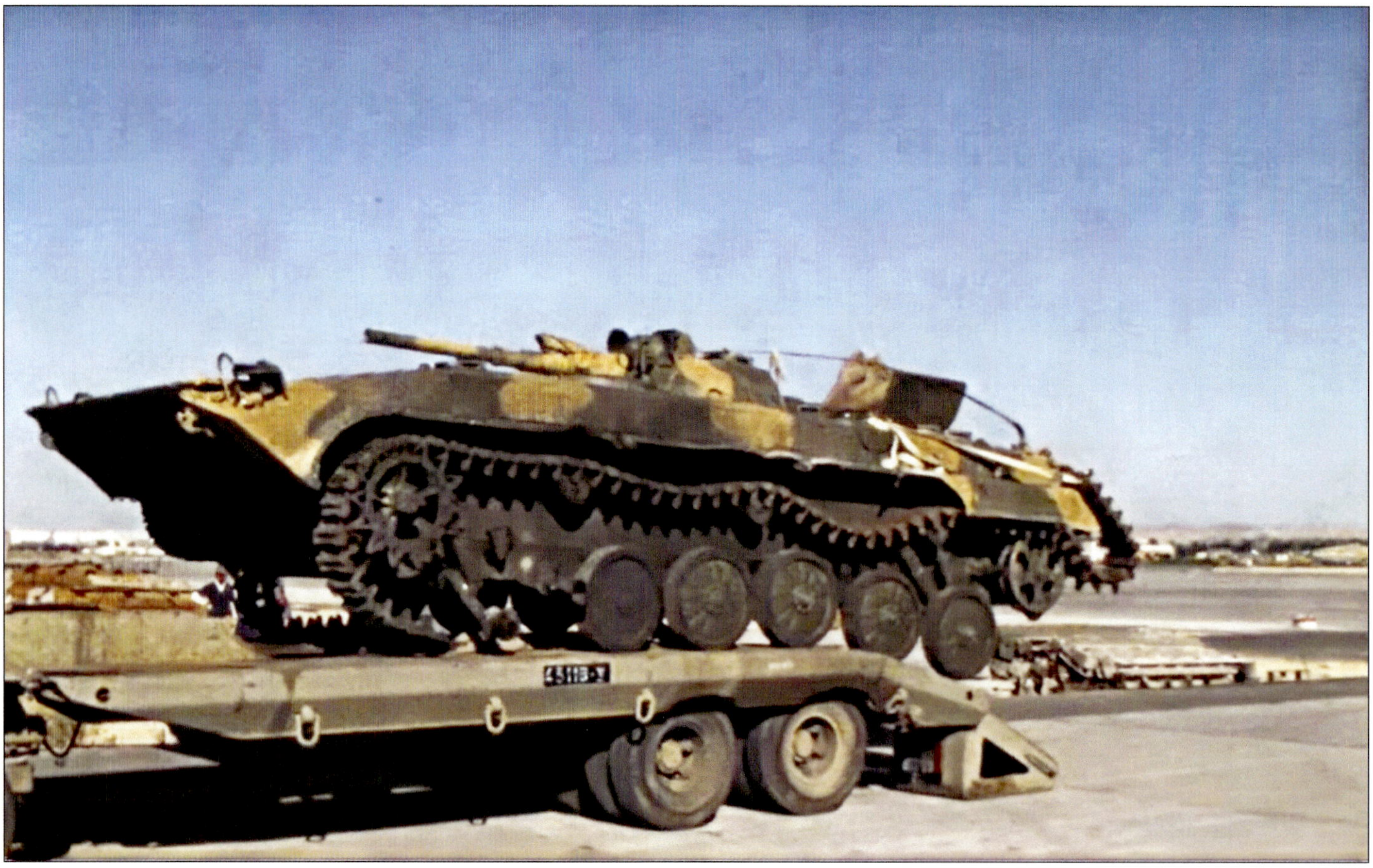

A captured Syrian T-62 tank and a damaged BMP-1 being loaded onto a C-5 at Lod Airport destined for the US. (USAF/TSgt McConnell)

The Tide Turns

As the tide of the Yom Kippur War turned and Israel gained the upper hand, among its successes, it began to capture Syrian and Egyptian-operated Soviet equipment. Some of these were of significant intelligence value to the US and its Western allies. With empty C-5s and C-141s on the Lod flight line ready to go home, some secretly carried captured equipment to the US and UK for detailed examination and analysis. One reel shows the loading of a damaged Syrian tank, a BMP-1 personnel carrier and an SA-3 missile onto C-5s for transport to the US and evaluation by the intelligence community.

By the time a ceasefire took effect on 25 October, just over 200 MAC flights had touched down at Lod, including 50 C-5As. However, the airlift continued until Nickel Grass officially ended on 14 November 1973. By then, MAC's 422 C-141A missions had delivered 11,632 tons of equipment and supplies, and the 145 C-5A flights another 11,645 tons. The C-5As delivered similar tonnage in roughly only a third of the C-141 flights. They consumed only about 75 percent of the Starlifters' fuel. Equally significant was that just over 2,264 tons of the C-5As cargo were outsize loads, which could only be carried by the Galaxy.

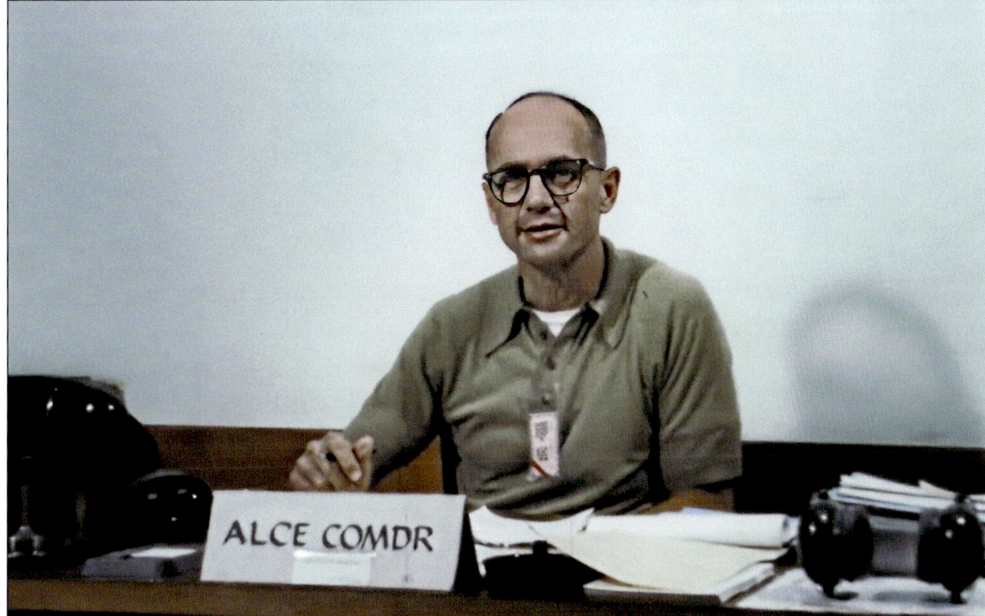

Col Donald Strobaugh was a key actor in the operation, heading the Airlift Coordination Element at Lod Airport. (USAF AAVS)

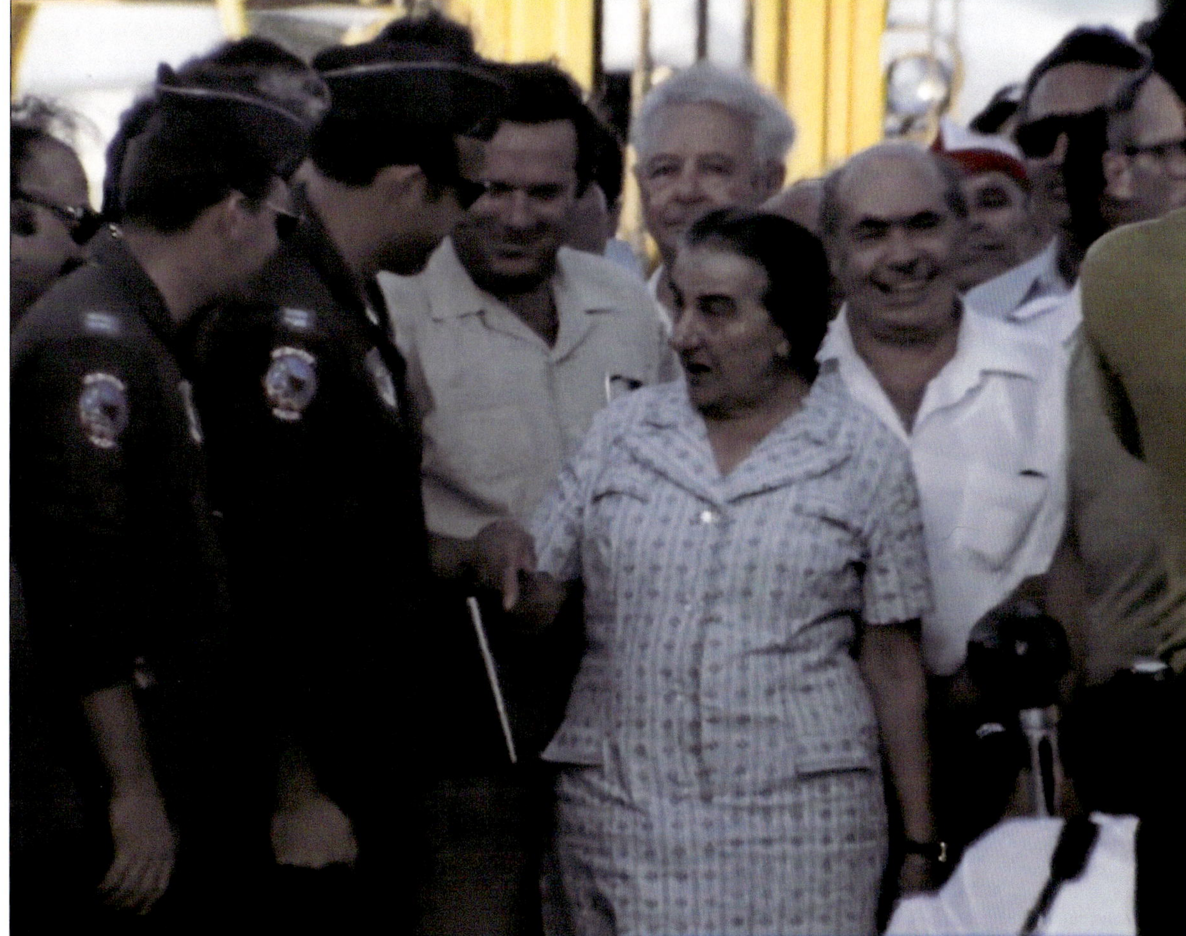

On 18 October 1973, Israeli premier Golda Meir visited Lod Airport to thank USAF airlift crews in person. (USAF/TSgt McConnell)

9

BACK TO THE COLD WAR

The mid-1970s oil crises and economic decline stretched US military spending and operations. Money was in short supply for facilities, maintenance, and training. During Jimmy Carter's presidency from 1977 to 1981, in the face of growing Soviet assertiveness worldwide, the foundations were laid for rectifying that difficult situation. Whilst President Carter may have advanced modernisation plans, the almost unlimited funding for the Pentagon during the Reagan years, between 1981 and 1989, allowed rapid renewal.

For the USAF, airfield facilities needed modernisation in Europe and at home, and a 'hardening' programme began to improve their wartime survivability. Comprehensive reinforcement plans were tested more frequently. There were huge acquisition programmes to replace the ubiquitous F-4 Phantom, which equipped nearly all of USAFE's and TAC's tactical fighter wings with brand-new F-16s, F-15s and A-10s. Most controversial of all was the introduction of intermediate-range Tomahawk GLCM and Pershing missiles in Europe to counter the Soviet deployment of SS-20s.

Analogous developments occurred in AAVS, too. News media was undergoing a technical revolution, and movie film cameras were being traded in for video cameras, videotape, and built-in microphones. Still cameras were becoming more versatile with

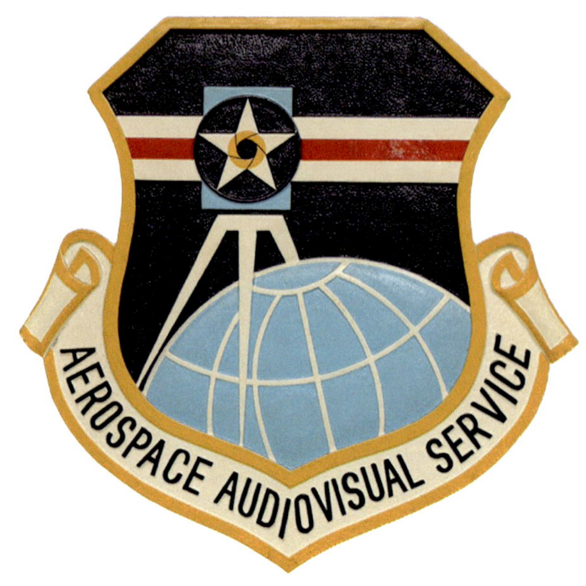

AA-VS became the Aerospace Audiovisual Service (AAVS) on 1 May 1981. (USAF)

more compact designs and better lenses. These changed image processing and later transmission methods as outputs moved from film to electronic media. The tempo of training and deployment steeply increased. All this meant more work for AAVS and its new equipment.

MOBILE PRODUCTION TRUCKS

The advent of TV presented new opportunities for production and distribution. Mobile production trucks could be airlifted to required locations. These included major Air Force and presidential events and sometimes to document civil disasters. Vehicle equipment became increasingly sophisticated, evolving through videotape and DVD formats.

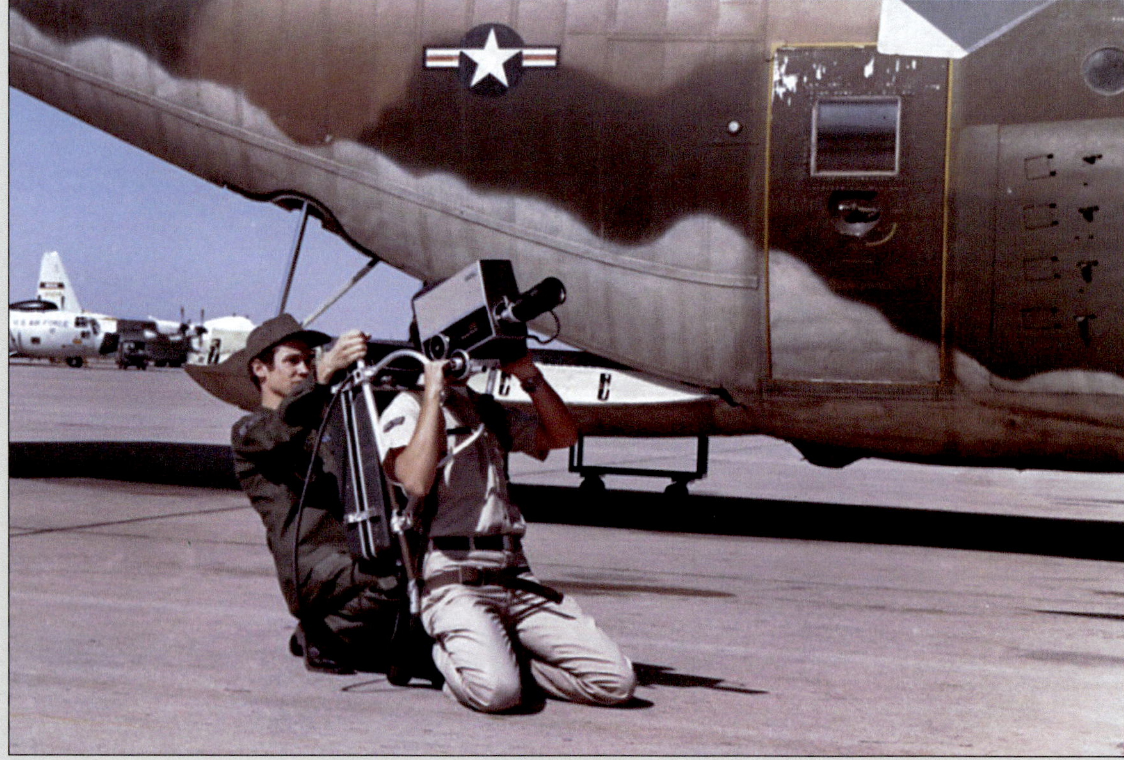

Filming with an early Air Force portable TV camera in the late 1960s. (USAF)

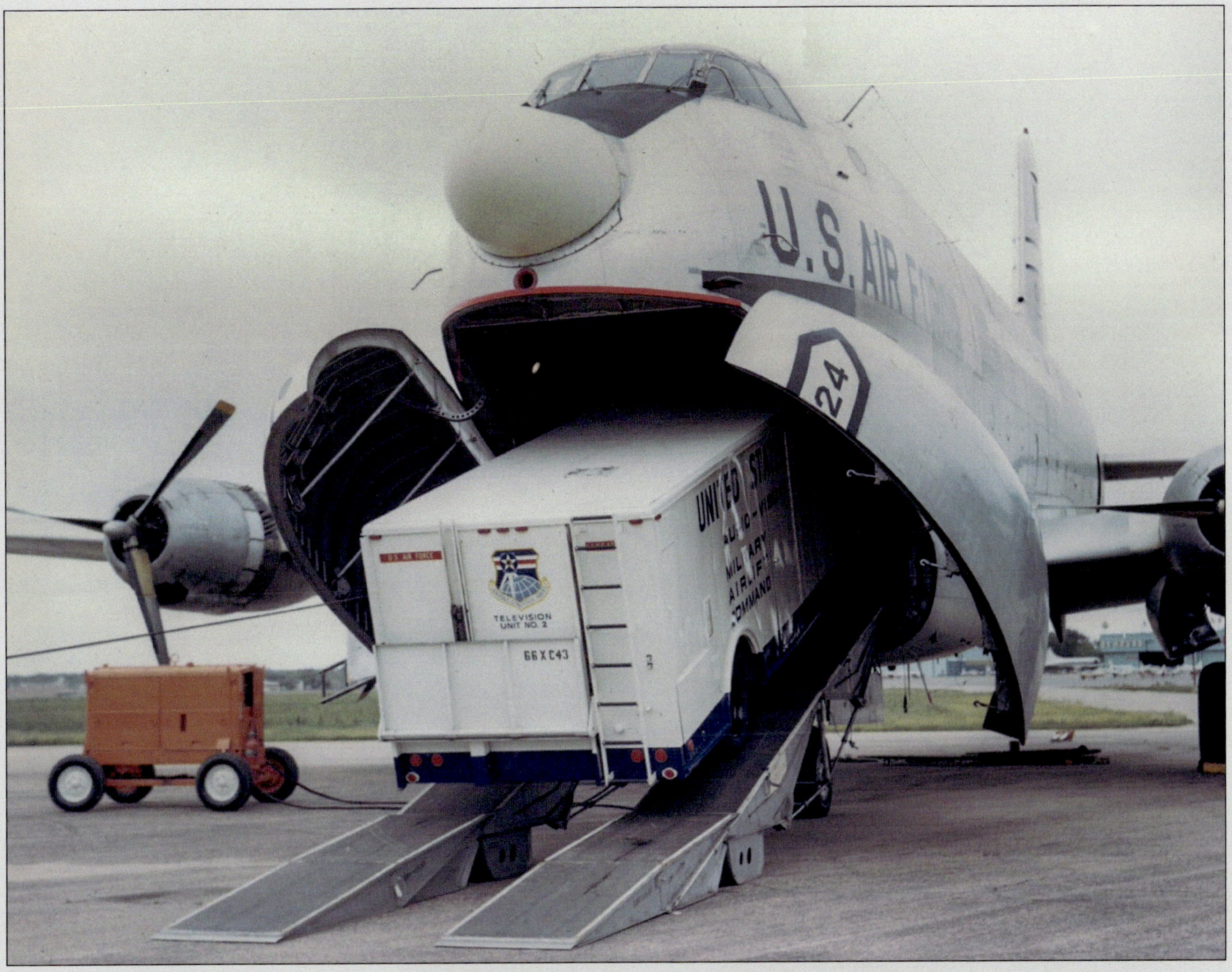

A very smartly turned-out AAVS mobile production truck is unloaded from a C-124 Globemaster. (USAF)

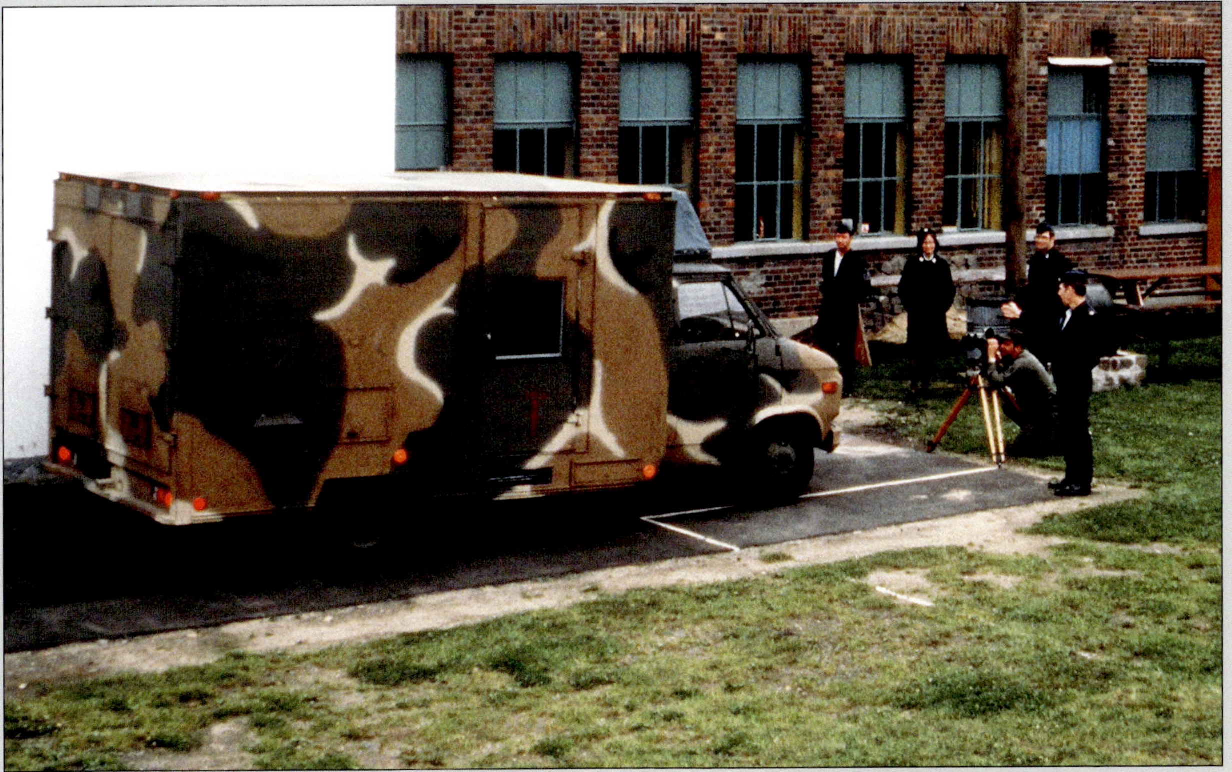

Now smaller and camouflaged, an AAVS mobile production truck at Rhien-Main AB in 1980. (USAF/CMSgt Don Sutherland)

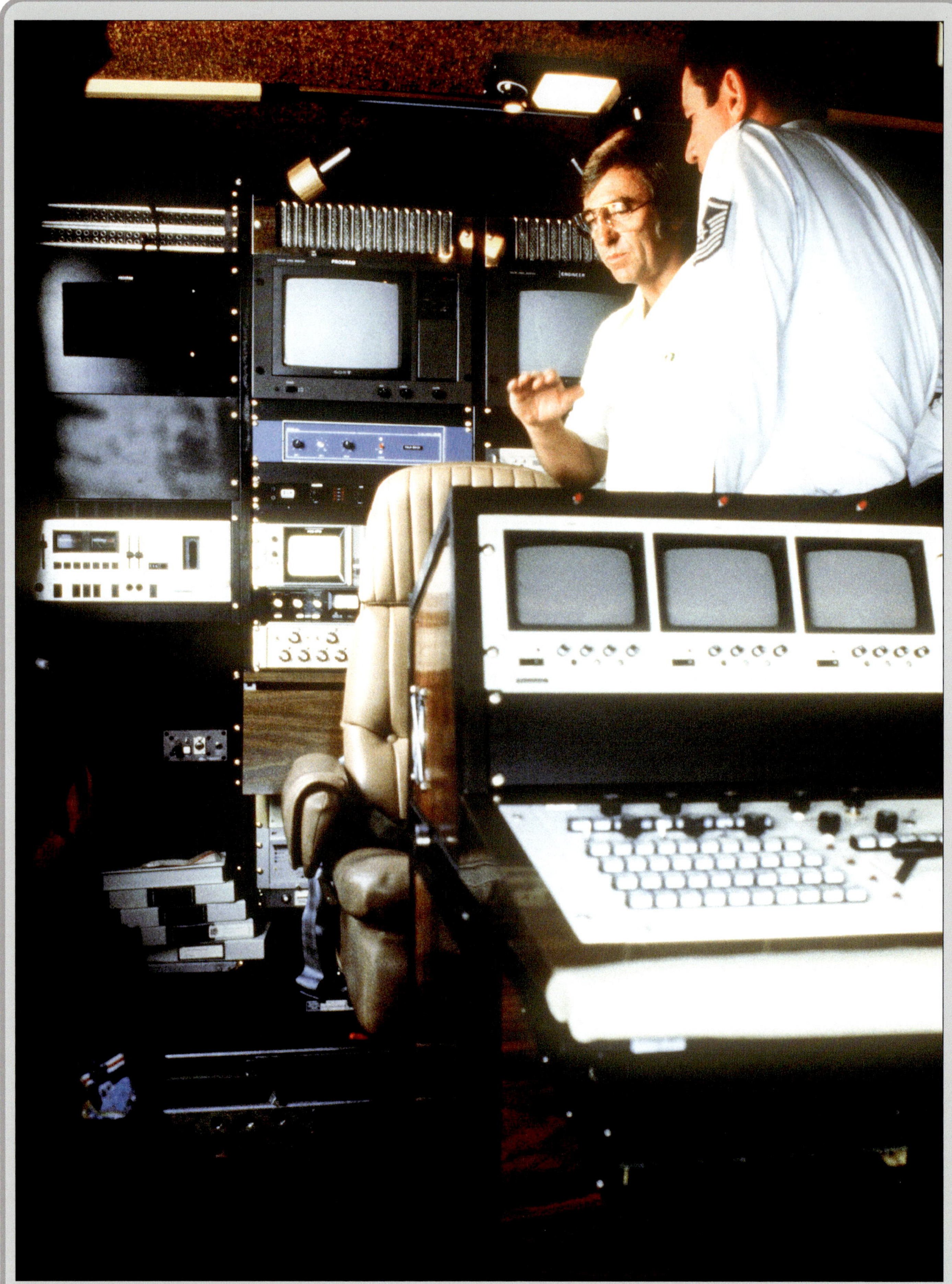

SMSgt Ralph Kelly and Al Merwitz inspecting the inside of the newly arrived AAVS mobile production truck at Rhien-Main AB. (USAF/CMSgt Don Sutherland)

By 1983, AAVS was headquartered at Norton AFB, CA, and had centralised responsibility for most overseas 'visual information activities', including those in Europe and Asia. The Service was organised into seven squadrons with subordinate detachments as required. The 1352nd Audiovisual Squadron (AVS) was at Norton AFB, CA; the 1360th AVS at Offutt AFB, NE; the 1361st AVS at Charleston AFB, SC; 1363d AVS at Yokota AB, Japan; 1365th AVS at Lackland AFB, TX, 1367th AVS at Ramstein AB, West Germany and 1369th AVS at Vandenberg AFB, CA.

Each squadron also maintained numerous detachments, often with a wide area of responsibility. For example, the 1367th AVS was at Ramstein Air Base in West Germany. It maintained its Det 1 at RAF Mildenhall (UK), Det 2 at Sembach AB in West Germany, and Det 3 at Rhein-Main AB in West Germany. Det 4 was at Torrejon AB in Spain, Det 5 at Aviano AB in Italy, and Det 6 at Lajes Field in the Azores.

Flight Training

Some AAVS photographers and videographers had opportunities to become flight-qualified. Dave 'Kiwi' Van De Brake joined the Air Force in 1980. He was posted to Charleston AFB, South Carolina, alongside Military Airlift Command's C-5s and C-141s. He soon earned an opportunity to gain his wings and undertook his Combat Camera flight training in 1983. It taught them how to become a contributing backseat crew member in assorted fighter and rotary-winged aircraft, from old F-105s to brand-new F-15s and through to HH-53 Jolly Green Giant helicopters.

As Dave described:

Early on, we had around three weeks of ground school. This stressed all aspects of air operations and safety, while learning to set up cameras, hang lights in an aircraft and attach camera

blister pods to different aircraft types. We also learned to assist with standard transport aircraft loading operations. We had to be able to do everything under scrutiny from our flight instructors and the Wing's life support division, to ensure there were no lapses in flightline procedures and radio and intercom protocols and to carry out our photo mission. Our NCOIC, MSgt Mitch Jenkins, used to tell us, 'Don't come back – without getting the shot!' We underwent a local survival training programme incorporating heavy weapons and small arms training. We were expected always to be ready for deployment.

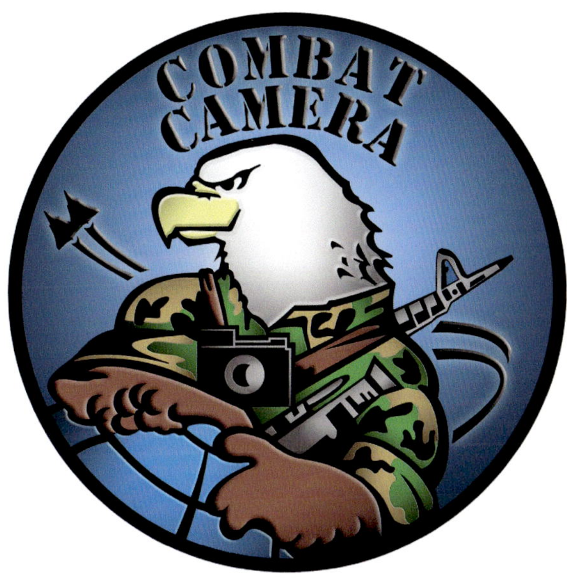

Variations of this patch became the mark of the flight-trained Combat Cameramen and women in the late 1980s. (USAF)

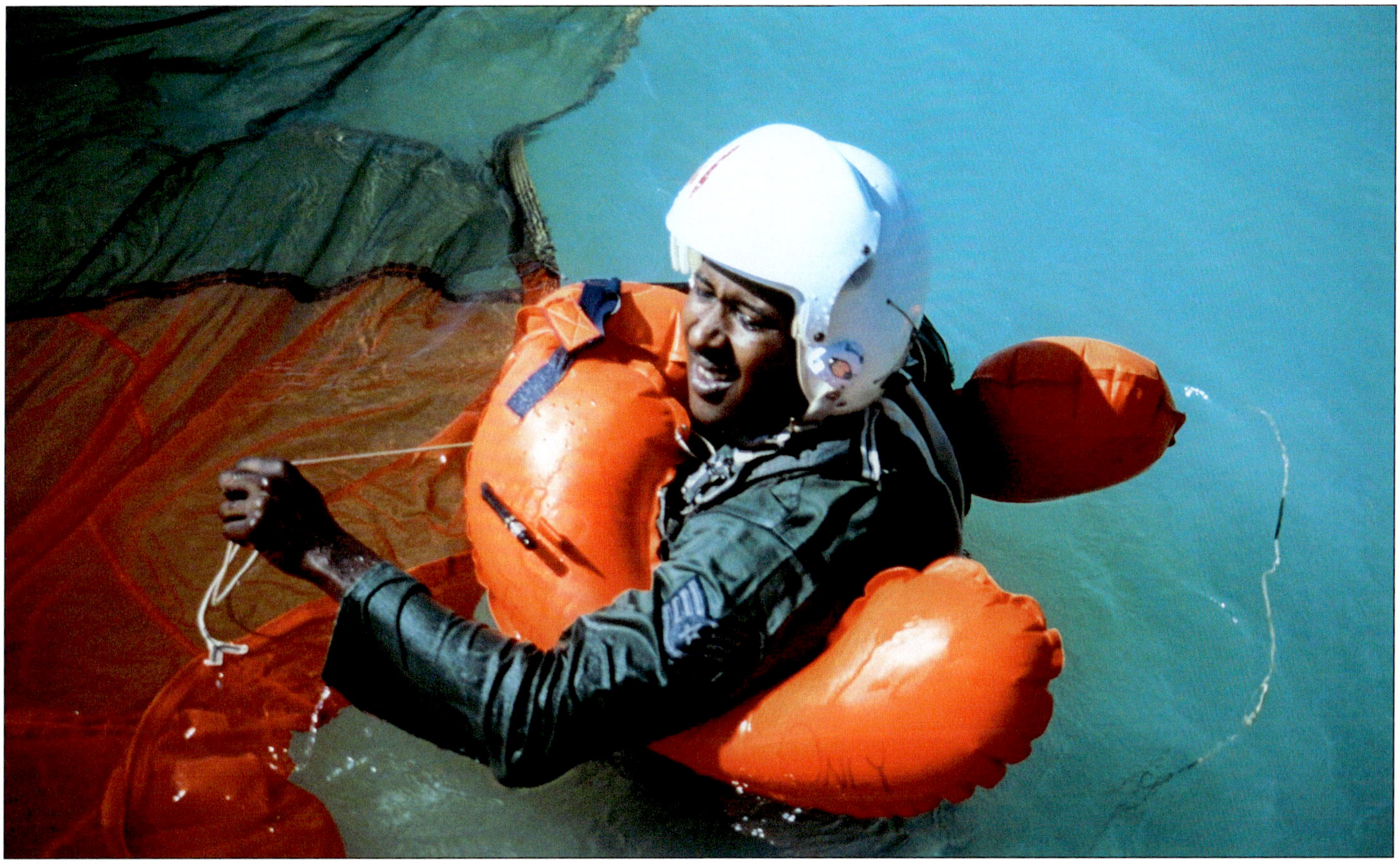

AAVS photographer SSgt Willie Dale undergoing a water survival training exercise at Hickam AFB in 1978. (USAF/TSgt Donald Bolender)

Towards the end of our training period, we were required always to keep an 'A-bag' of equipment and clothing so we were ready to go in any emergency. A Flight Instructor and Flight Examiner turned up for our no-notice final check ride one day. It was 'grab your trash, we've got a mission for you today, and your evaluation starts now.' For me, this involved going to Fort Lee with colleague Mark Rich to cover a US Army aeromedical 'dust off' and triage evacuation exercise. So we shot all the preparations, the helicopter crews getting ready, out on the flight line close-ups and medium distance shots, received briefings, coordinated with local Aviation Brigade commanders, the whole deal. After completing the exercise, our film was sent to Norton AFB in California for processing. There, it was edited and turned into an end product for Combat Camera legend CMSgt Doug Morrel to see and critique.

The Godfather of Modern Air Force Photojournalism

Professional training for AAVS camera operators was always a tricky subject. How much could be trained, and where did natural aptitude and individual ability come into play? Some members of AAVS benefited from external college-level programmes.

Ken Hackman is another legend within the Air Force Combat Camera community. A successful photographer in his own right and a civilian employee, he was the 'Chief Photographer of the Air Force'. He was instrumental in introducing high-quality professional photographic training to the Air Force.

He described how the programme began:

In the late 1960s, I worked for the Air Force. The Pentagon and the Air Force asked me to review the quality of Air Force still photography. There was nothing, and the photography sucked. Except for a very small select group of photographers, who incidentally were producing most of the images used by the Air Force, there was no corporate direction or entity to help maintain a viable source of good still photography.

In 1968, I wrote a note to the AAVS Director of Operations and suggested that we needed was a tiered system for photography. I suggested there should be four levels. Level One would be the apprentice, Level Two would be the competent technician, Level Three would be the documentary photographer, and Level Four would be the picture storyteller-photojournalist.

After the Air Force study, it was decided to emulate the US Navy's system, training a select group of photographers at a civilian university accredited in photography/photojournalism. The Navy's one-year programme at Syracuse had been long-running, with its first graduates in 1963. Their photojournalists followed an academic year-long training course to prepare them for their work. It was very successful; they did it very well. So, myself and a few others said we needed something like that.

Ed Michalski, from DoD Public Affairs, and a retired Air Force Lieutenant Colonel, and I decided to try to get the Air Force to establish a similar programme. We ran into a brick wall with the Air Force Training Command (ATC). Enlisted personnel were not allowed to be sent to universities for a year of training. Only officers were permitted to join advanced university-level training! Even though we had the support of the Secretary of Air Force Public Affairs (SAFPA), it made no difference to the established culture at ATC. So, the SAFPA,

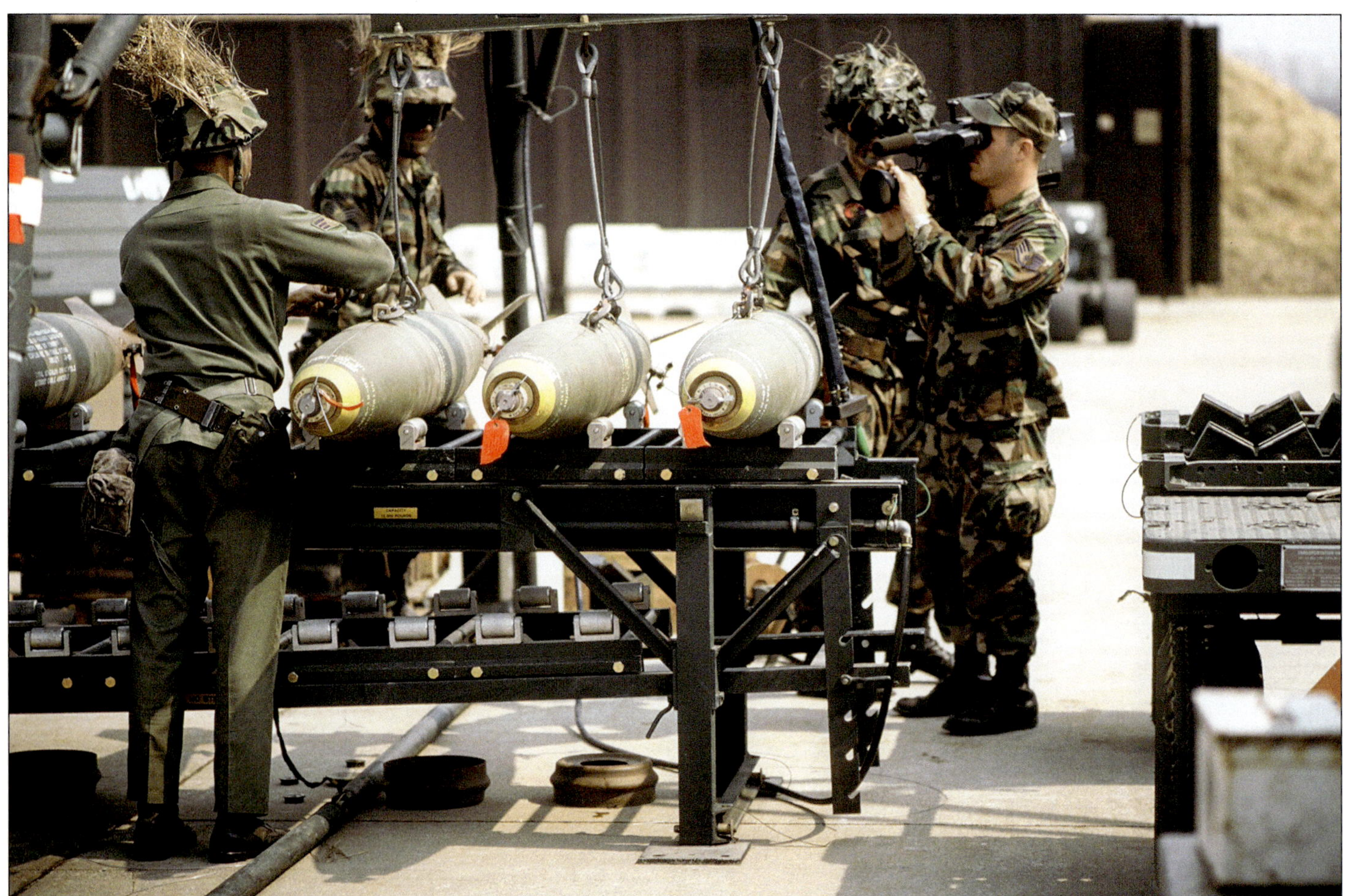

Dave 'Kiwi' Van De Brake's training partner, SSgt Mark Rich, videotapes munitions personnel handling 250lb bombs. (USAF)

which sent a number of its officers to university-level training programmes, negotiated with the Navy Public Affairs. 'Give us, the Air Force, one of your enlisted slots in the advanced photojournalism class at Syracuse University, and we will give you one of our officer slots at a university somewhere else.' The Navy agreed, and in 1972, a single Air Force photographer was sent to Syracuse University. The following year, we got two slots, and in the third year, we got four slots.

I established a system where people who wanted to go on the programme would submit portfolios. Professional civilian photographers, not Air Force officers, judged these for photographic quality and content. The top people would be selected to go to school. We worked with the Air Force Management and Personnel Center to establish a Special Experience Identifier (SEI). This would be applied to all graduates to assist in assigning these specially trained photographers to a location that ensured the Air Force was getting the most value from them.

I would then go up there twice a year just to check on them, and on the second visit, we asked them where they wanted

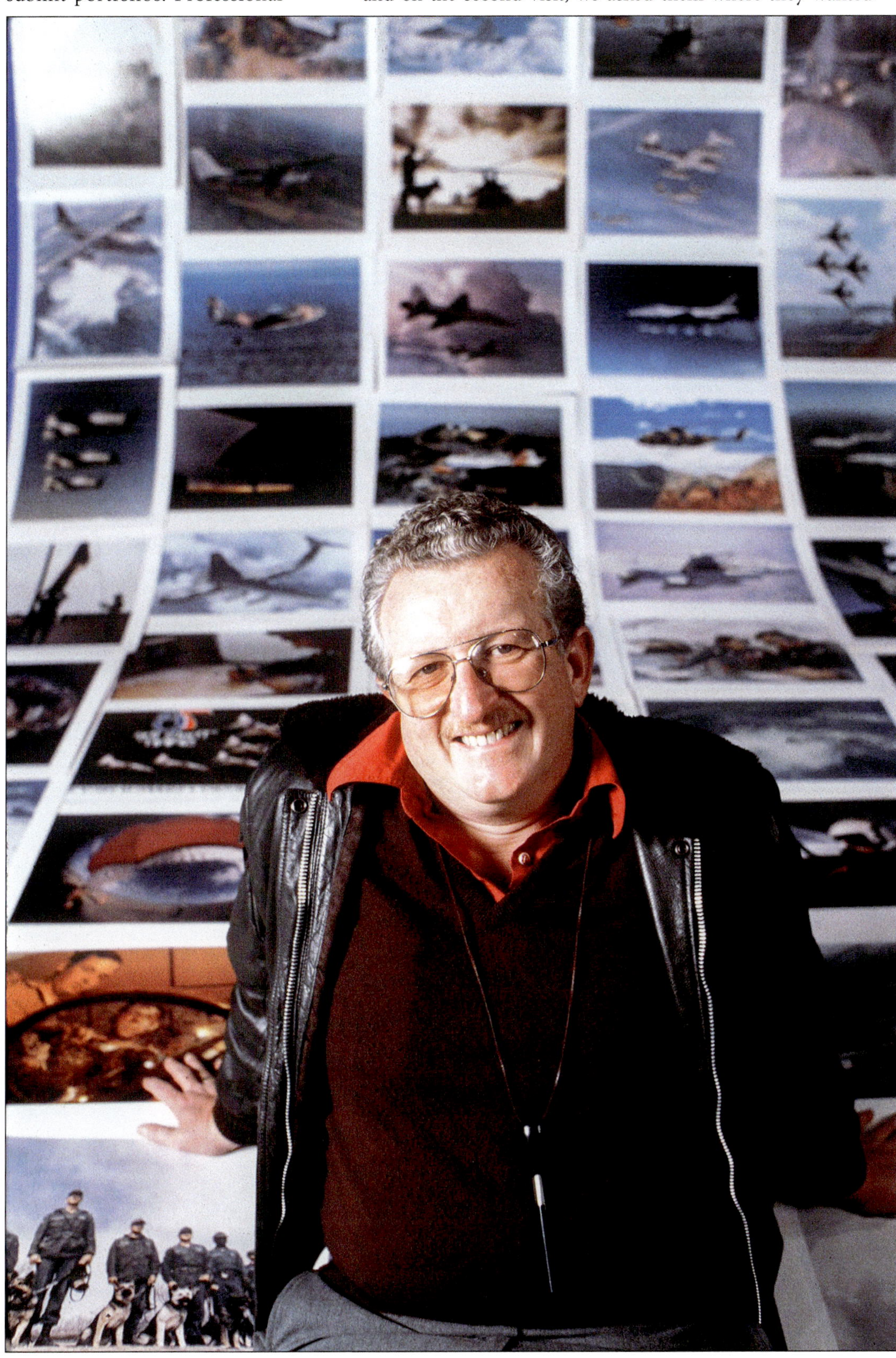

Chief Photographer of the US Air Force, Ken Hackman, pioneered the sending of selected AAVS cameramen and women to Syracuse University for professional training. (USAF/SSgt Steve Mcgill)

to go after leaving the college. If their preferences coincided with where we needed people, we sent them for their first tour there. I managed to negotiate with the personnel folks that graduates from the Syracuse programme would 'belong' to us at AAVS, and we could indicate where we wanted them assigned. That was intended to prevent them from being randomly dropped across the Air Force and ending up in non-productive slots where they could not utilise their new training. That worked out well, and I became the informal manager for the whole thing.

We got the right people in the right positions. I developed a good relationship with the personnel folks. Even after the graduates' first tour, we could often help people get their preferences for their second tour. If I sent a list of people and said, 'This is where I would like you to send them,' although there was no guarantee, I often got eight out of ten when my choices matched the Air Force's needs. I thought this was a pretty good record.

After a while, our Public Affairs said, 'This is not something we should be involved in,' and Air Force Training Command was instructed to handle it. However, the ideas got very complicated when we became involved in their bureaucracy. We ended up with a concept to start a programme at the Rochester Institute of Technology. The difficulty with that was that we were only sending five people a year, which was not viable from their perspective. In 1975-76, our students were dropped into selected second, third- and fourth-year modules without the benefit of having attended preliminary classes. It was a bad idea. It didn't work at all. So we went back and said, 'This is not working. We need to be where there's already a programme.' Syracuse had been running their course for 10 years and, having been working with the Navy was well used to the military. Eventually, we concluded negotiations with the Navy, and we ended up sending our people to Syracuse. That worked well up to 1988.

Then, the now combined Navy/Air Force contract was put out for bid and awarded to Rochester Institute of Technology for three years. However, there was a significant change, which I seriously disagreed with. It was now a 10-week course instead of a full academic year. My argument was you cannot educate people fully in ten weeks. If they failed or missed assignments, there was no time to allow a 're-shoot' or a 're-write.' It didn't work well for the trainees. I was vehemently displeased with the new programme and decided not to send any Air Force photographers to the 1990 class at RIT. However, I soon realised that was a mistake and that the whole Air Force photojournalism programme would dry up without some new input. I reconsidered, and we sent students to the third 10-week RIT class, which was the last in the ten-week format.

A new contract was written, and we returned to a complete academic year programme. The first five-year contract for photojournalism was awarded again to RIT. A new twist was, however, that after many years of trying, the Air Force and the Navy established a five-year contract for videographers. That contract was awarded to Syracuse University. The five-year contract was again put out for bidding. In 1997, the training for both photojournalism and video was awarded to Syracuse University for another five years.

Special Assignments

While Ken Hackman was involved in professional training for some AAVS personnel, his main job as Chief Air Force Photographer was taking pictures himself. He explained, 'I was doing a lot of aerial photography in the 1980s'. Ken became involved in several specialist shoots of selected aircraft. Many of the pictures he shot then were widely used in Air Force publicity materials and, having been digitised, are still available today. He described some of those special assignments:

I used Nikons throughout and stayed with them my whole career. I always took two camera bodies because I don't care how good the equipment is; things can go wrong. I usually had a 50mm lens on one and a 35mm lens on the other. I never used much longer lenses because you pick up some distortion from the aircraft's canopy with them. With the shorter focal length lens, you don't have that problem… Many guys who did the flying loved it. I didn't. If I want to fly, I like it to be comfortable, walking around on a Boeing 747.

California Recce Birds

Around 1985, I was requested by some of the different Air Force commands to do 'photo-essays' for them. I did one on Military Airlift Command and others including Air Defense Command, Training Command and Air Force Logistics Command. One of these ended up with me at SAC's Beale AFB to photograph the SR-71 and TR-1/U-2.

We set up for the U-2 flight and did all the briefings. The coastline nearby was always a good place to take pictures. As we were in Northern California, we decided to fly over San Francisco. Before we took off, the crews got the weather report that said San Francisco was fogged in. We had to go with that. I thought if we went there and the tops of the golden gate were visible sticking through the clouds, that would be something. Well, it turned out that when we got there, everything was clear. The weather report came from San Francisco Airport, about 15 miles south of the Bay. While they were clogged in, the Bay wasn't, so on this occasion, we were lucky, and I got the shots we originally planned.

Flying with the SR-71 was another remarkable opportunity. 'After it took off, the first thing it had to do after it got up to altitude, was hit the tanker and refuel. That's how I got the SR-71 photographs, during and just after he refuelled. Once he picked up speed, there was no way in hell we could stick with it in our T-38'.

Mount Rushmore

I don't like to be far away from my subject aircraft. If I am close to it and I want my pilot to accelerate so we can pull a little ahead to get a near head-on shot, if the distance between us is small, the manoeuvring is easier for the pilot and can be done quickly. If we're beside the target aircraft and I want to trail the subject, we don't have to drop back very far. But if we are far from the subject, it will take us much longer to get to the position I wanted. So close in is what I always did. The only time I ever varied from that was when I shot Air Force One over Mount Rushmore. On that occasion, I knew that Mount Rushmore, even though quite large, is not that large when you are up in the air. I knew that if I were close to the subject aircraft with a wide-angle lens, Rushmore would be minuscule. So, for that particular mission, we stood

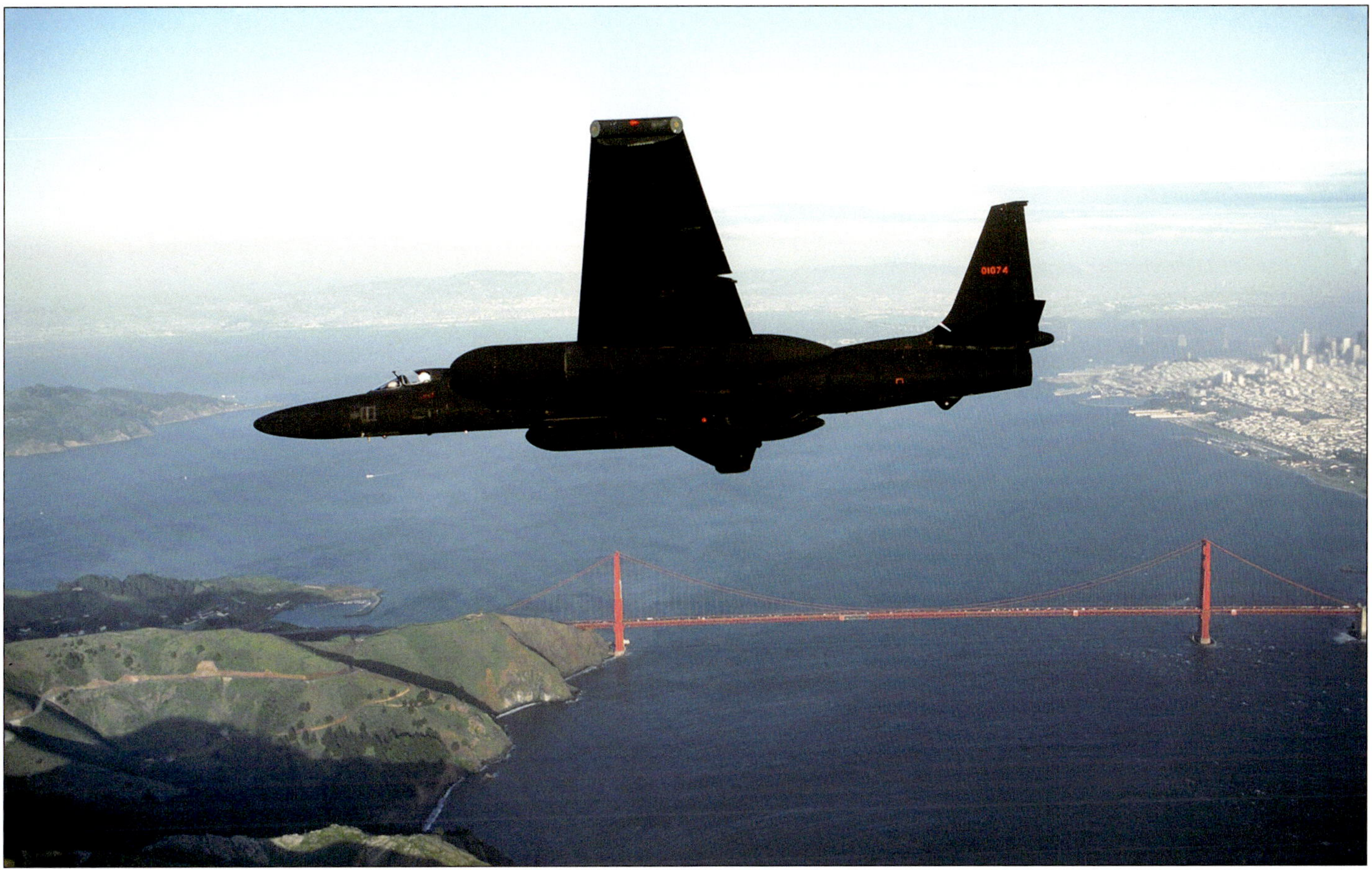

All clear over the Bay, Ken Hackman captures a USAF U-2R near the Golden Gate Bridge. (USAF/Ken Hackman)

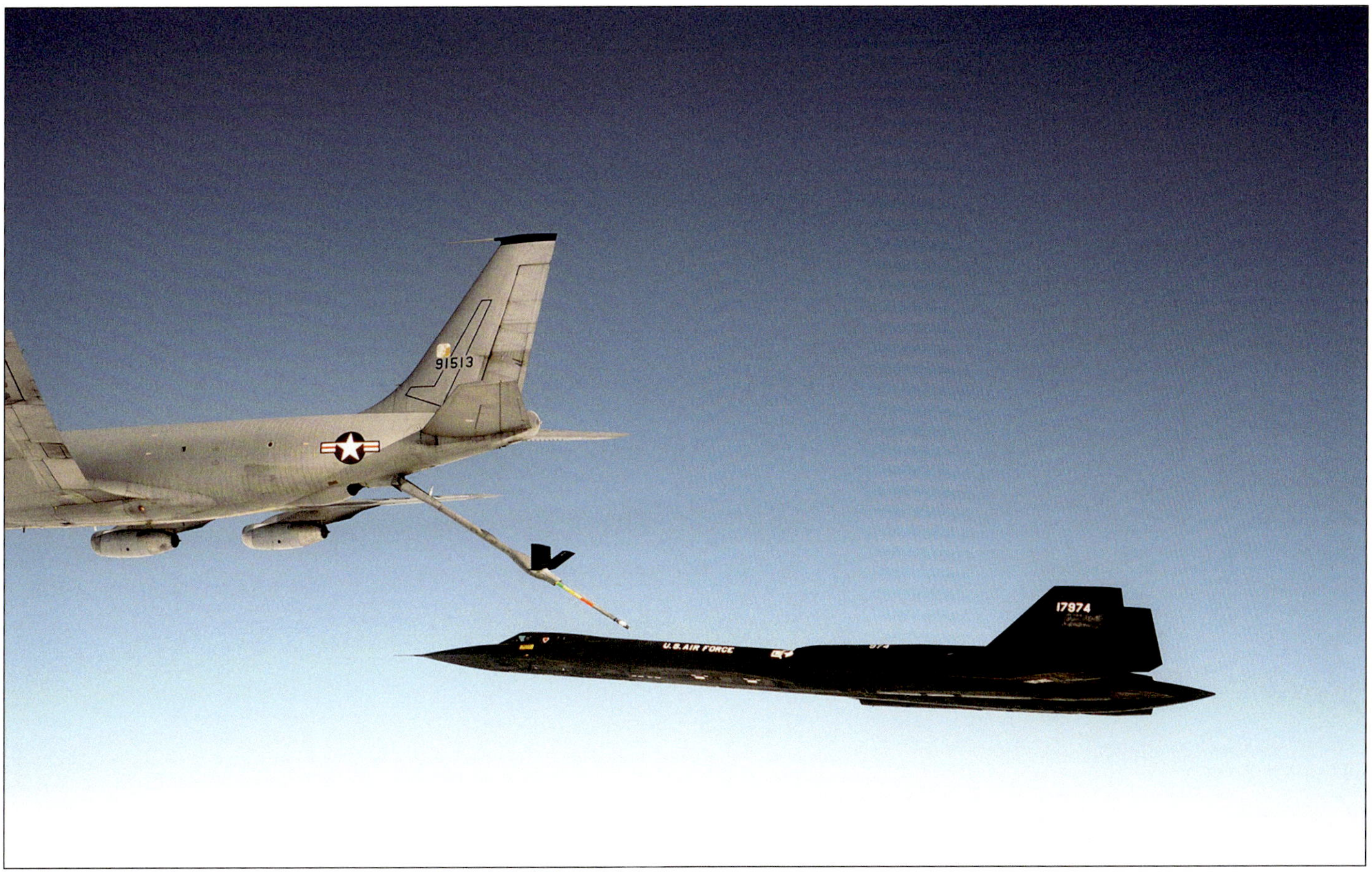

In 1983, a rare opportunity to photograph an SR-71 meant capturing it during aerial refuelling from a KC-135Q soon after take-off from Beale AFB. (USAF/Ken Hackman)

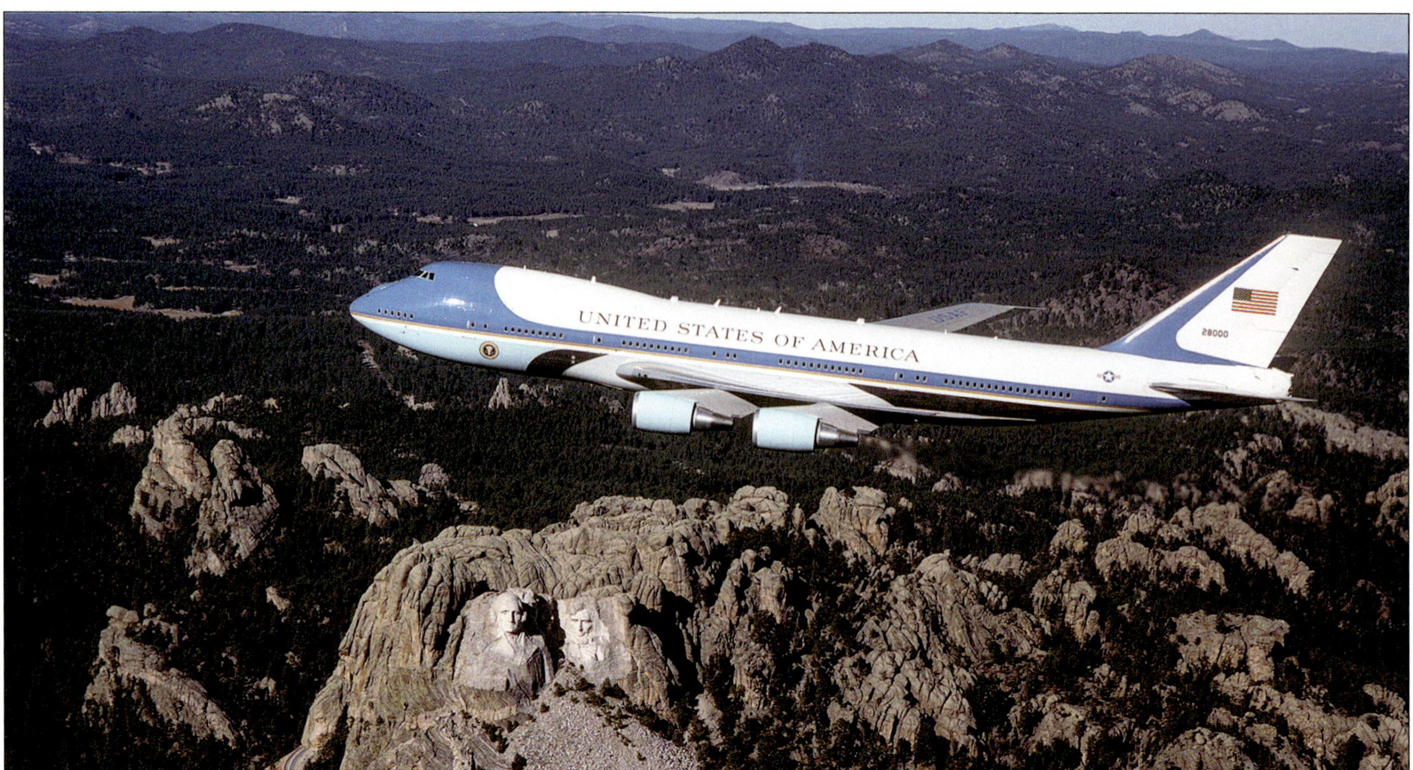

Two American icons. In 1990, Ken Hackman was tasked to capture a picture of VC-25A 'Air Force One' over Mount Rushmore in South Dakota. (USAF/Ken Hackman)

some distance away. And I shot most of those with a lens to compress the distance between the aircraft and the backdrop.

Camera Platforms and Wild Weasels

Ken also has an excellent series of shots taken with F-4G 'Wild Weasels' of the 35th TFW. As he explained:

I shot these from the rear seat of an F-4. I don't think I ever shot an F-4 when I wasn't in another one. It is much easier when you go to a unit and fly in the same aircraft type as they are operating. That has always worked for me. Otherwise, it means more coordination and bringing another aircraft in, probably from another airfield. The only aircraft I ever refused to take pictures from was the T-33 with its straight wings and the big fuel tank on the end, which severely limited the field of view.

We often just tried to find new ways of doing things because aerial photography gets pretty boring after a while unless you can figure out something new. And really, the only thing you can change is the viewpoint and lighting. One of my things was I would never fly when they said we would take off at noon. I would say, well, the angle of the light sucks then, and I am not interested in doing it.

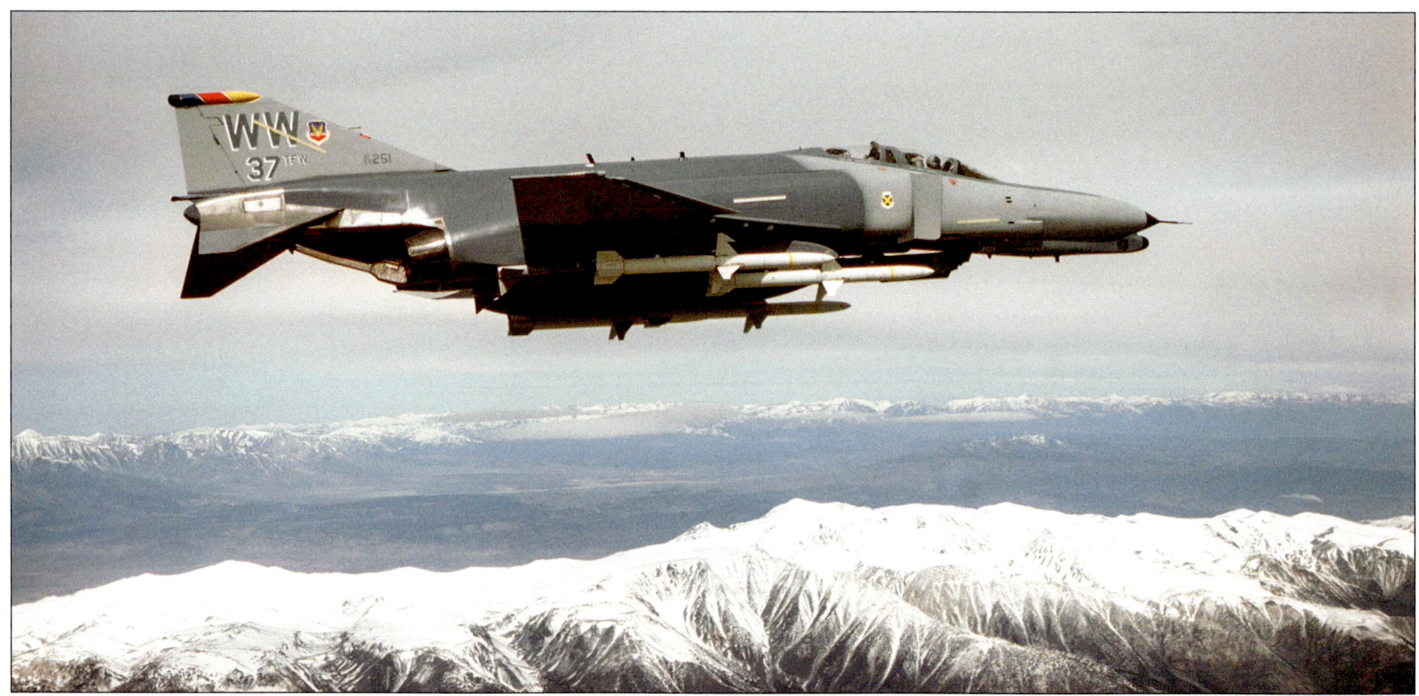

The 35th TFW's Commanders F-4G over the Californian mountains in 1988. (USAF/Ken Hackman)

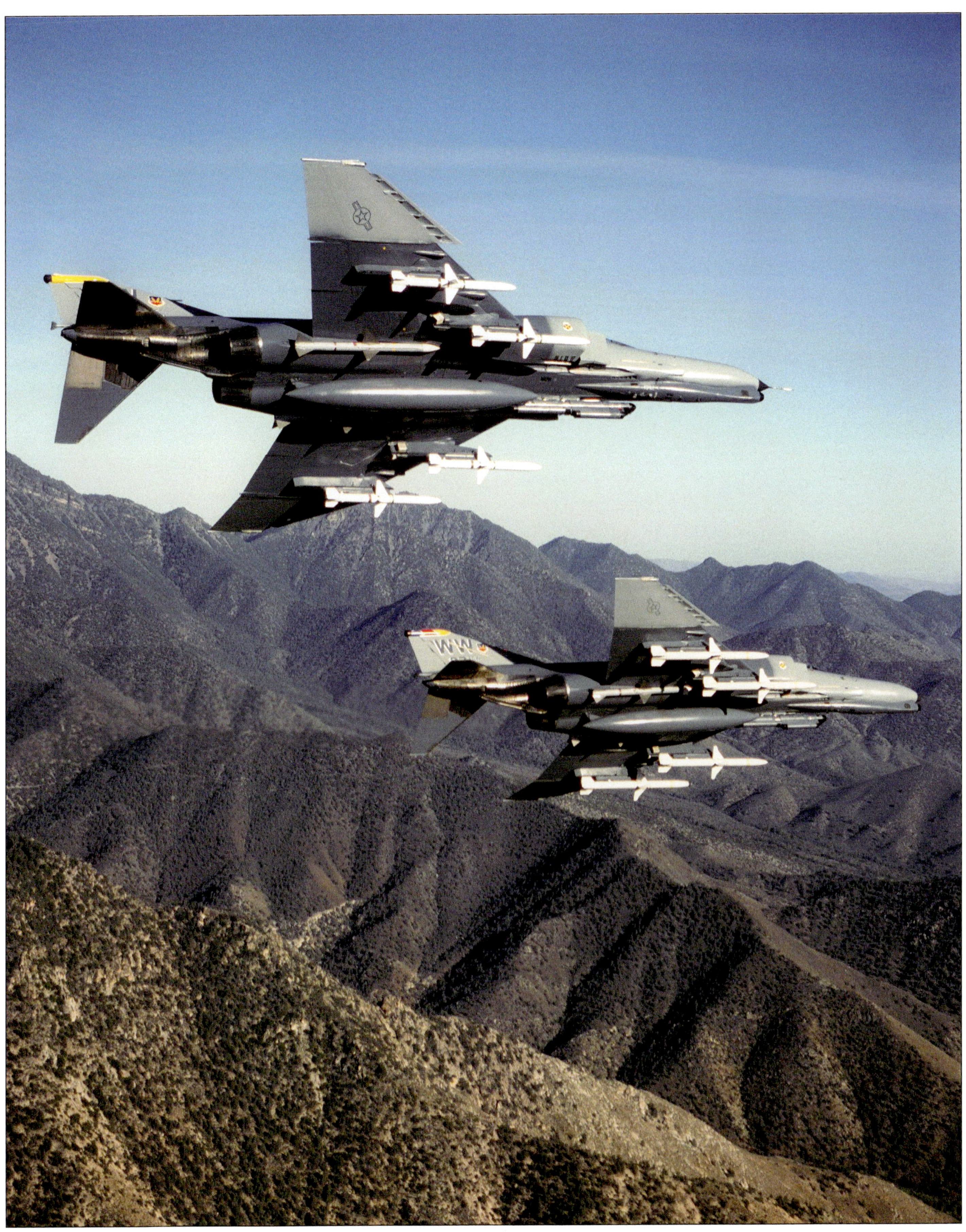

Shot from the rear seat of another F-4G, two 35th TFW 'Wild Weasels' bank away to show their war loads of AGM-88 HARMs. (USAF/Ken Hackman)

ANATOMY OF A SHOT: C-5 CLIMB OUT

In 1985, I had seen a Boeing-produced artist's impression of the C-17, then in development but not yet flying, that looked down on the aircraft as it climbed out steeply from a runway. I thought that was a fun idea, so I tore that page out of the magazine.

Ken was asked to provide new photography for Military Airlift Command the following year:

We went to Travis AFB to do some C-5 and C-141 pictures. At this big briefing, I showed the C-17 artist's impression to the commander there and said, 'I would like to do that, with a C-5 and Travis AFB in the background. Can we do that?' I knew how to do it. The Colonel said, 'Hell yes, we can do that. We will put you on a C-141, and then you'll fly over the C-5 as it's rolling down the runway. And you'll have it. How would that look?'

I had to say. 'Colonel, I have tried that before, and the timing is impossible.' What if we took off in the C-141 and the C-5 followed us? Then we lead him back around in a circuit passing over the runway? And then he pitches up into the climb as we pass back over the runway, and we make the picture? Can we do that?

And they did.

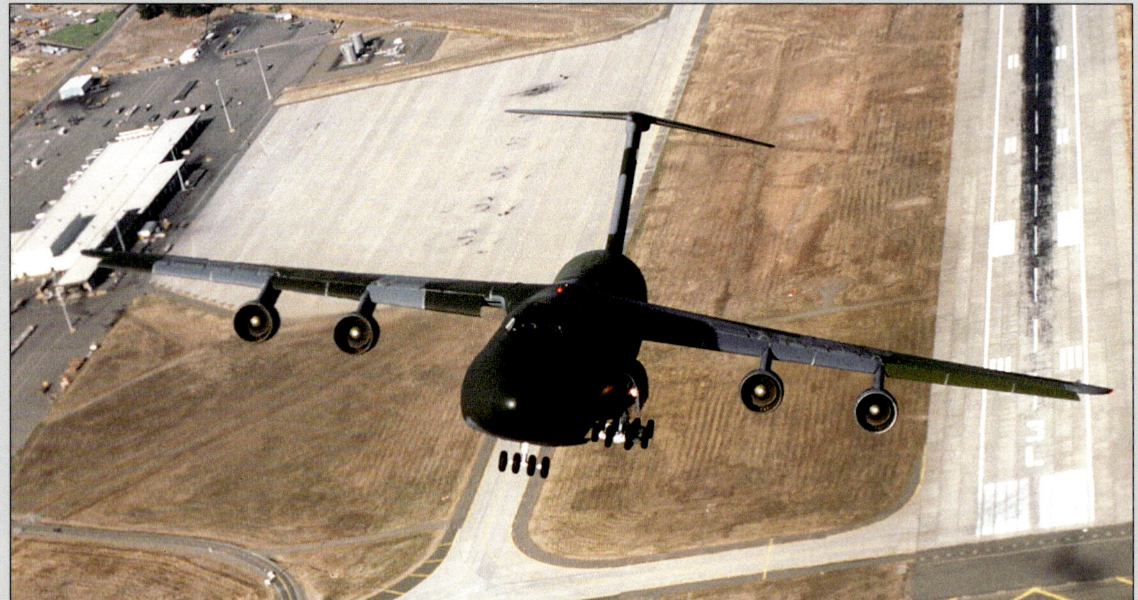

Taken from the open cargo ramp of a C-141, the 1986 head-on climb-out shot of the C-5 Ken Hackman had envisaged the previous year. (USAF/Ken Hackman)

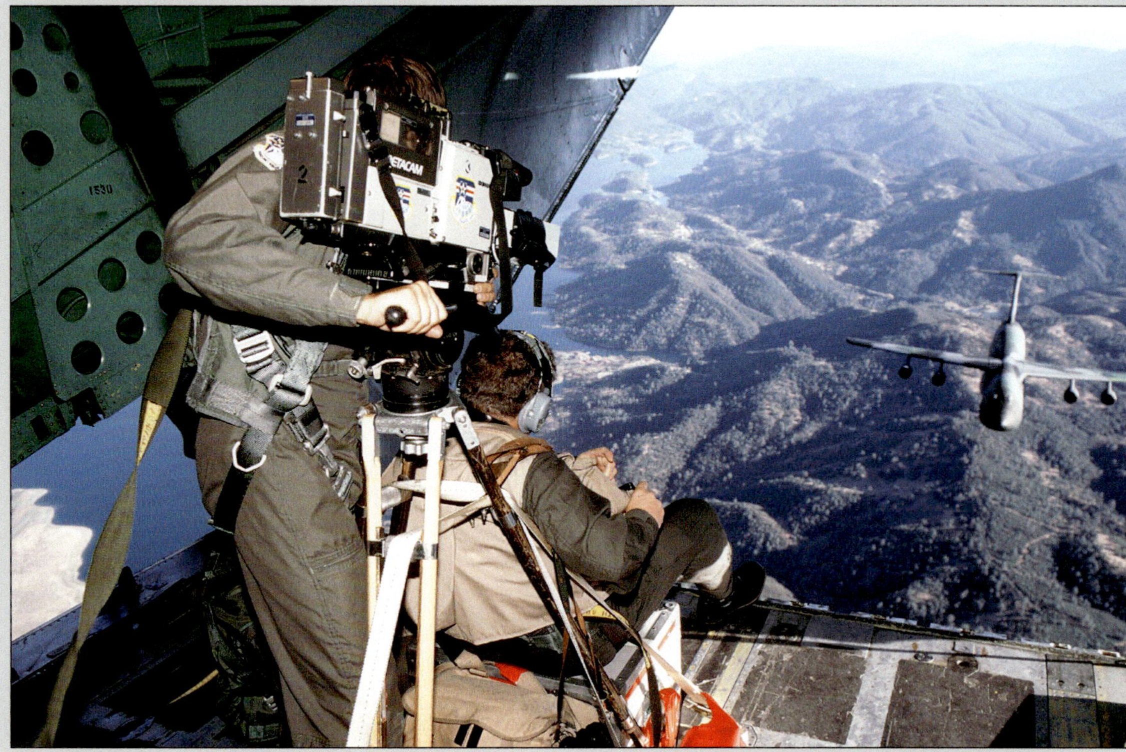

After the staged climb out of Travis AFB, Ken Hackman and a videographer begin an air-to-air photographic session with the C-5 Galaxy. (USAF/TSgt Steve Mcgill)

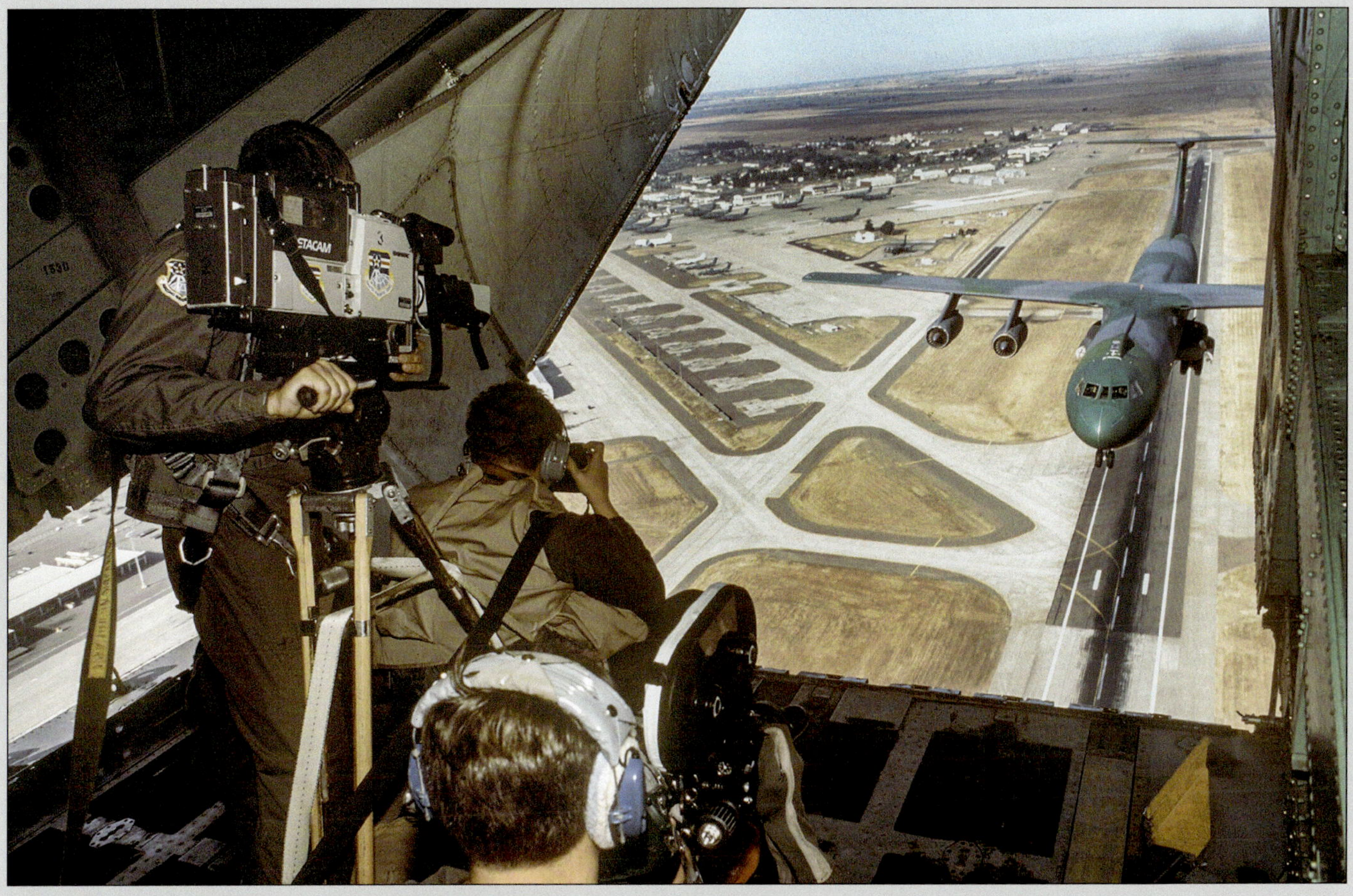

Similar photographs of a C-141B were taken on the same flight, over Travis AFB. Behind Ken Hackman on the ramp, the AAVS videographer shoots with his Betacam video camera. (USAF/TSgt Steve Mcgill)

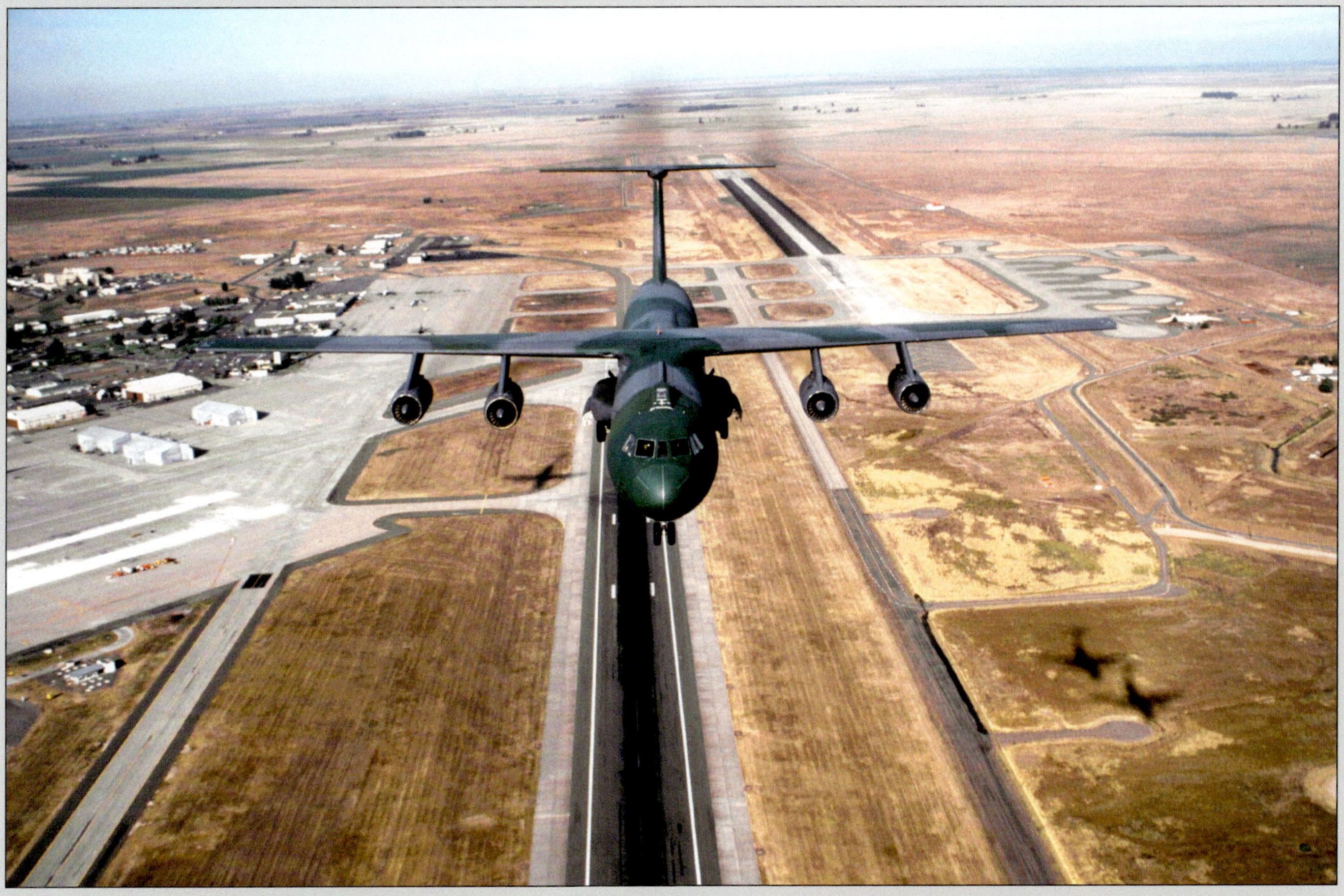

A 60th MAW C-141B circuits over the Travis AFB runway for a photographic run for some MAC publicity images. (USAF/SSgt Rose Reynolds)

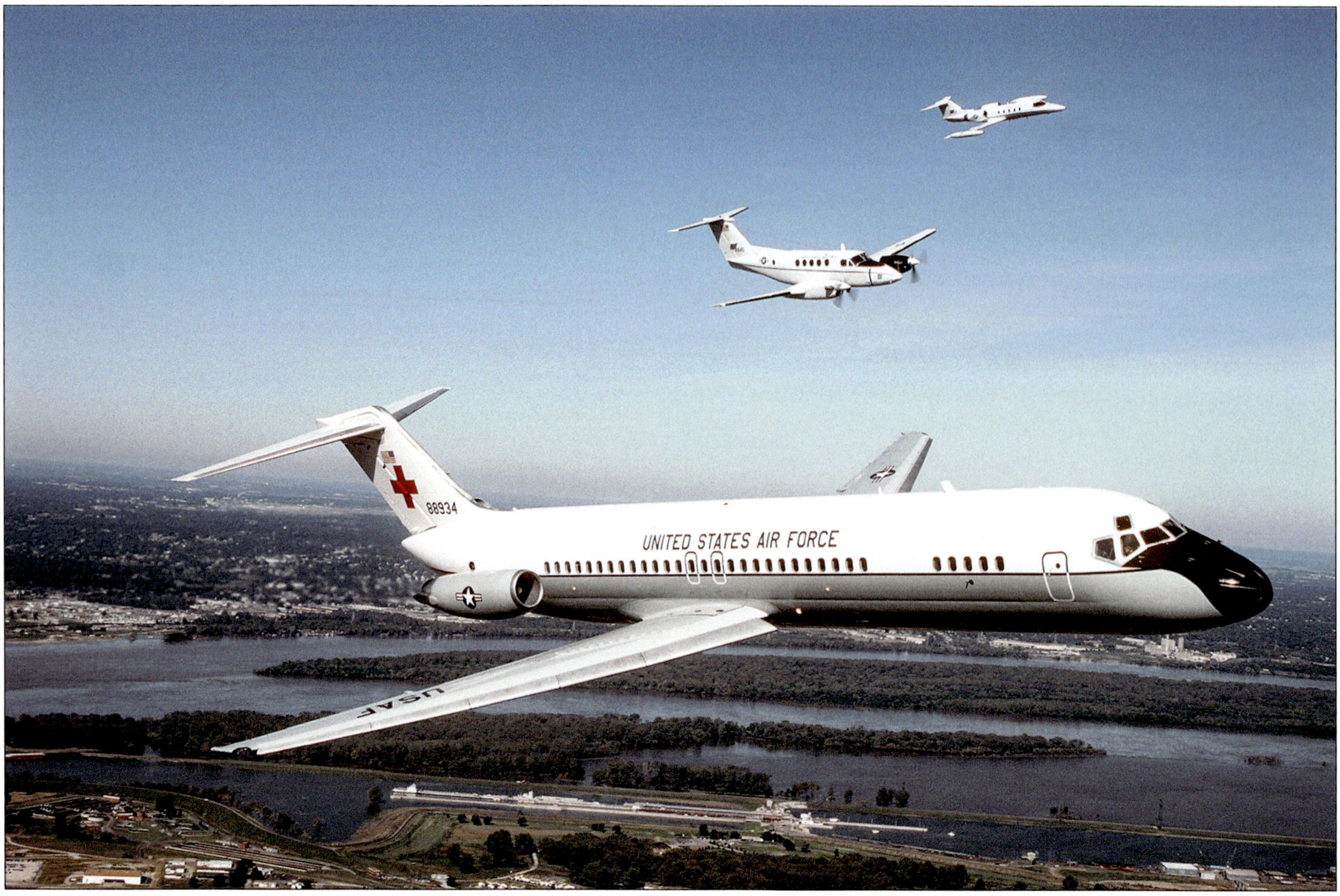

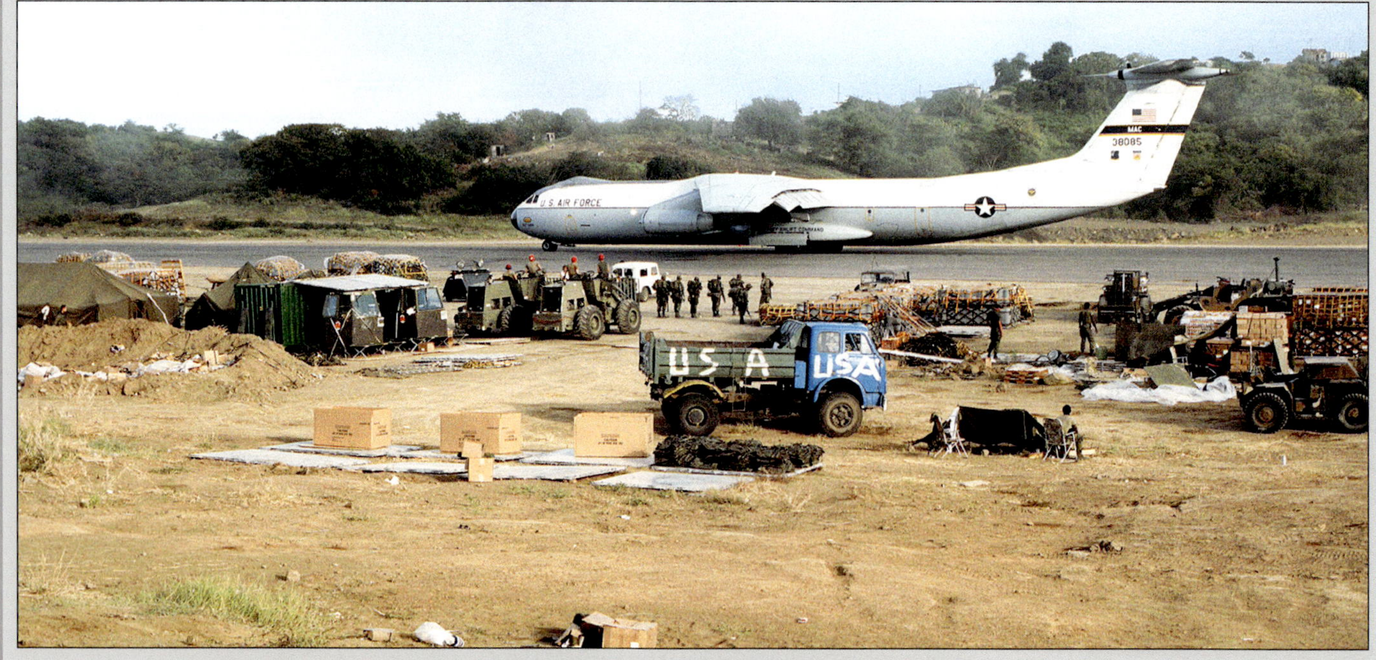

Images of a C-9A, C-12F and C-21A to be used by Military Airlift Command for publicity and briefing purposes taken close to HQ MAC at Scott AFB, Il. The key to success was to get the subject aircraft correctly stacked and in the sun at the same time. (USAF/Ken Hackman)

OPERATION URGENT FURY

On 25 October 1983, a large US force invaded Grenada and quickly occupied the island. The US 82nd Airborne Division and US Marines secured the Port Salines and Pearls Airports as key points. The airlift of US forces rapidly followed, and AAVS personnel documented many elements of the invasion and occupation.

Port Salines airfield was the main entry point for most US forces during Operation Urgent Fury. (USAF)

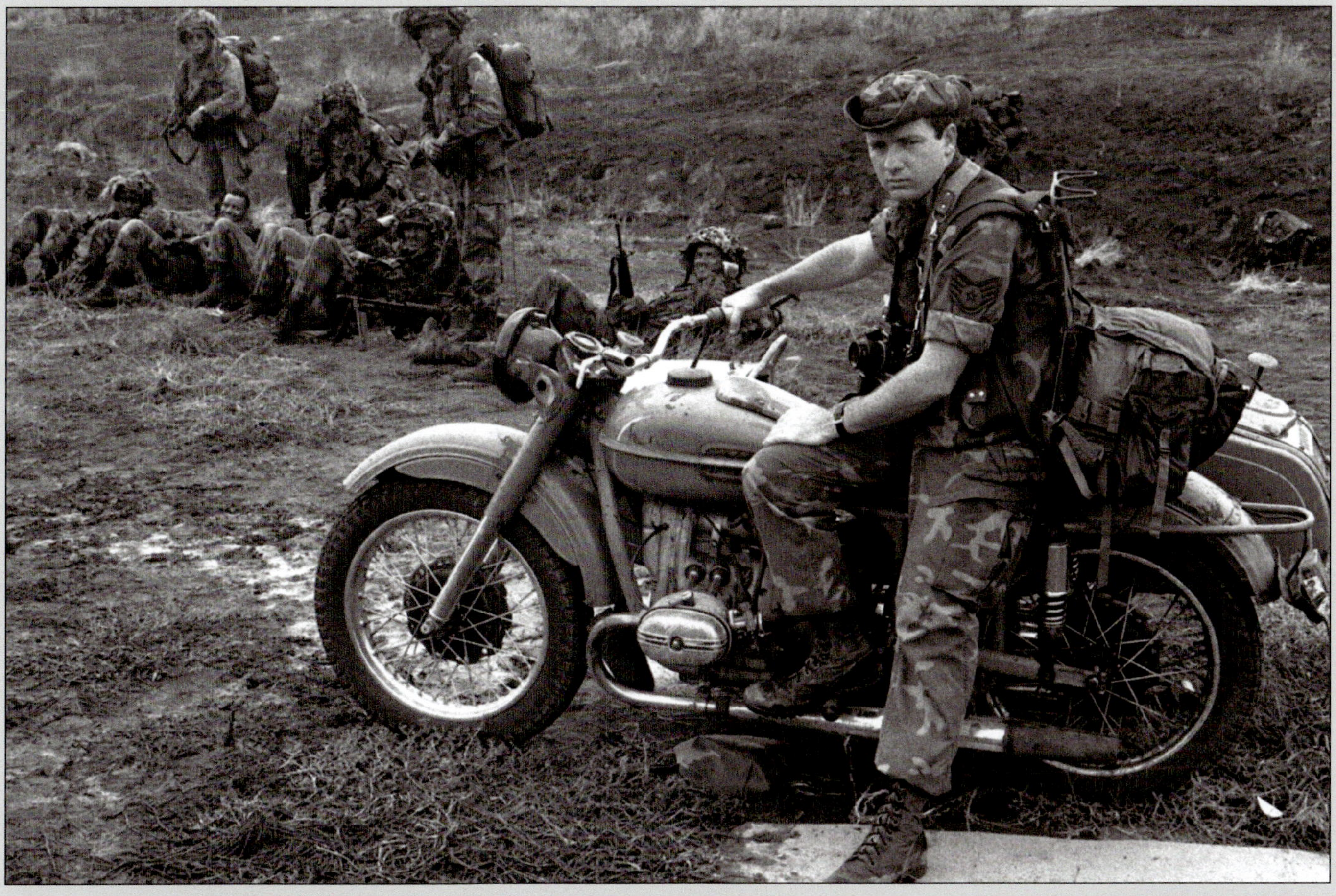

AAVS photographer SSgt Michael Haggerty poses on a locally owned motorcycle and sidecar for a picture in Grenada. (USAF/TSgt M Creen)

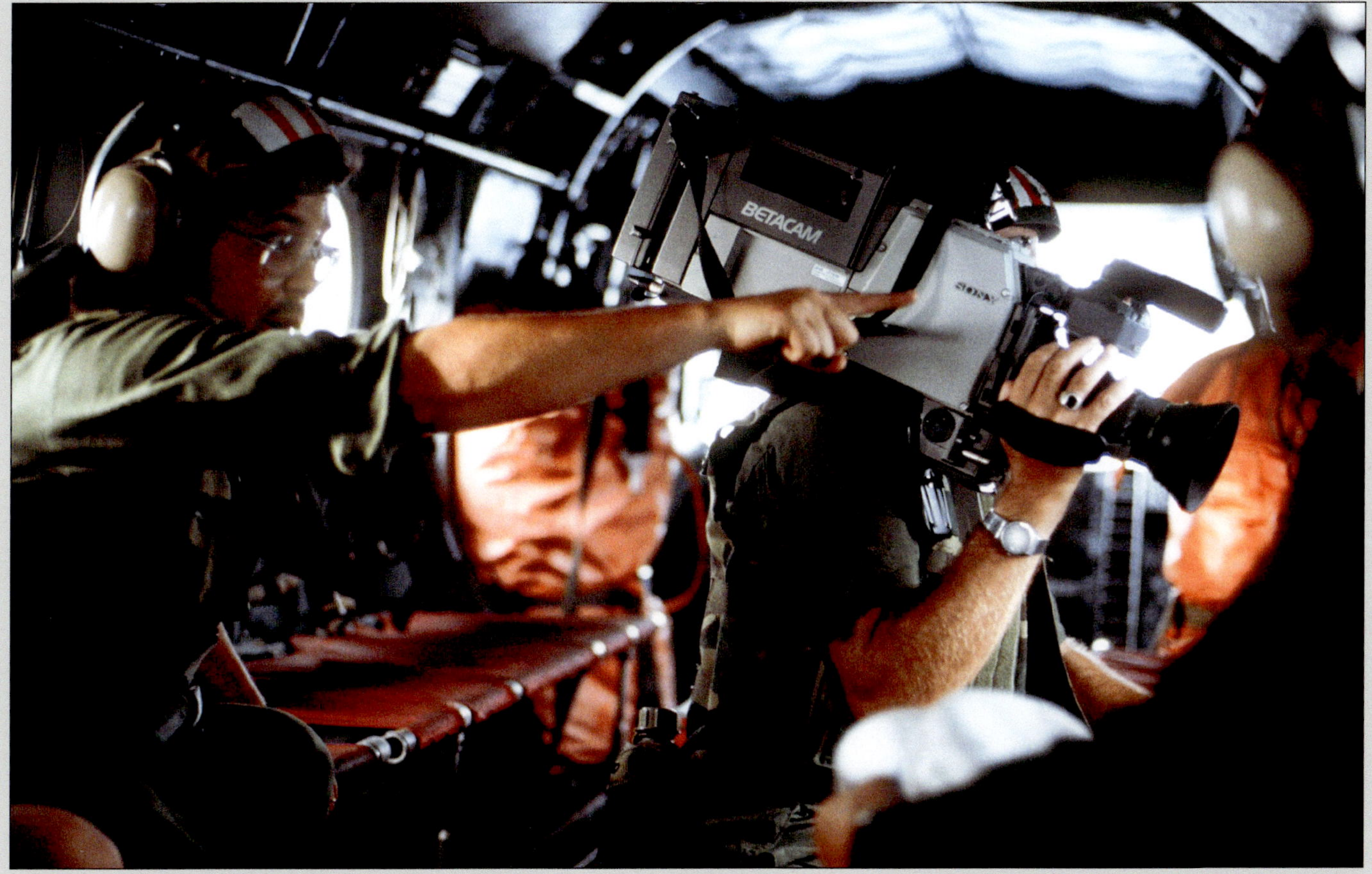

During Urgent Fury, an AAVS cameraman films the action with his Sony Betacam video camera from a helicopter window. (USAF/TSgt M Creen)

Stills Man

Hans Deffner had an interest in photography from a very young age. He explained:

When I was 16, my grandmother bought me a Canon AE 1; they're lovely cameras. I did high school yearbook stuff and some freelance sports photography in my hometown. My kind of hero at that time was David Hume Kennerly, a Pulitzer Prize-winning news photographer. His book *Shooter* chronicles his career as a newspaper photographer and photojournalist. He later became President Ford's photographer.

Air Force recruiters spoke at my high school, and something they said must have struck a chord with me because I signed up for a delayed enlistment, in the November of my senior year in high school. Then, I went into basic training 25 days after graduation in 1980. I had just turned 18.

I wanted to be a newspaper photographer, but it was by dumb luck that I did it in the Air Force. When I joined, that field was closed, but they gave me what they called a 'bypass test' to test my aptitude for photography. I scored high enough that I was able to come in as a photographer.

After an 18-month posting at Malmstrom AFB Force Base, I went to Korea for two years and loved it. There, I got to fly in fighter aircraft for the first time, including F-4 Phantoms, F-16s, OV-10 Broncos, and OA-37 Dragonflies. I was young and did not really know what I was doing, but I kinda liked it. At that time, I first heard about what was informally known as 'Combat Camera.' I started entering some photo contests and doing OK.

I first met Ken Hackman in 1982, and he inspired me and cajoled me a little into getting my portfolio together. After two years in Korea, I went to California in 1984. Then, I committed to getting a portfolio together and applying for the Syracuse programme. I graduated from that in 1988 and was sent to Charleston AFB.

I've been asked lots of times what I gained from the course. I didn't learn much about the technical side of photography there. I did learn a lot about its psychological side. The 'why' we make pictures the way we do, how to see things, and how to tell stories. You know, photography in the military is kind of unusual. For some, it was just a job, but it was what I wanted to do; I was very passionate about it. Plenty of people were competent, but to them, it was just a job.

I expressed an interest in flying, and a few opportunities arose. The pictures came out OK, so I got to do it again. I established a reputation for being reliable. Then, the squadron in Korea changed aircraft twice, so they wanted new pictures to hang on the wall each time. So it was just being in the right place at the right time with the right people.

I'm always fascinated by airplanes. So doing aerials, aircraft in flight, even on the ground, the pretty sunsets, and all that are enjoyable. I met a gentleman named Jim Pearson, who worked for Ken Hackman. He was an Air Force photographer who kind of mentored me and got me to focus more on the human side of 'air power.' And it's not just the planes. It's the people that fly and fix the aircraft, and it's all the thousands of tasks it takes to get an airplane off the ground.

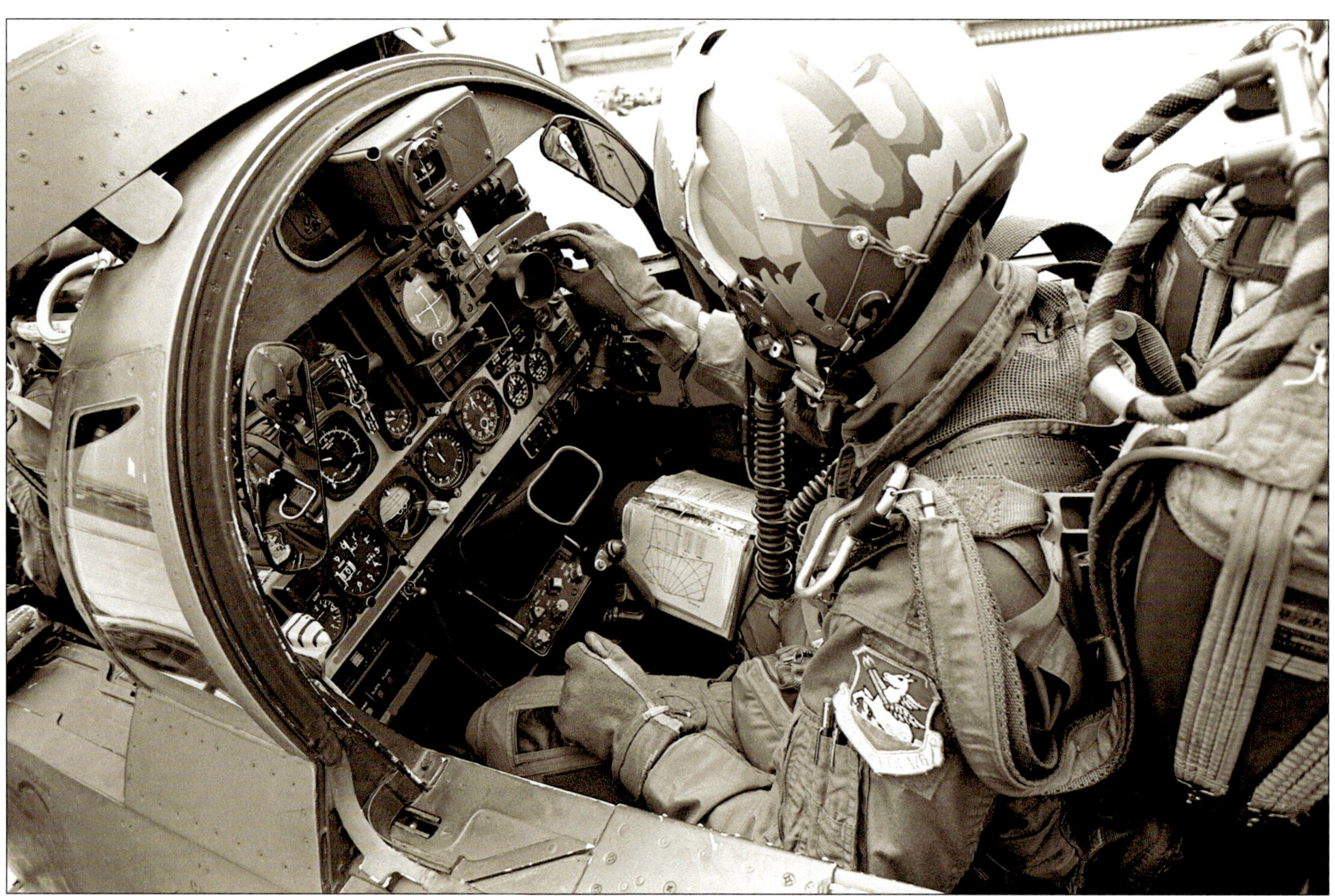

Taken at Osan AFB in 1983, Hans Deffner took this photograph of 1st Lt Scott Landis, a WSO, in the rear seat of his 51st TFW F-4E at Osan AB. (USAF/Hans Deffner)

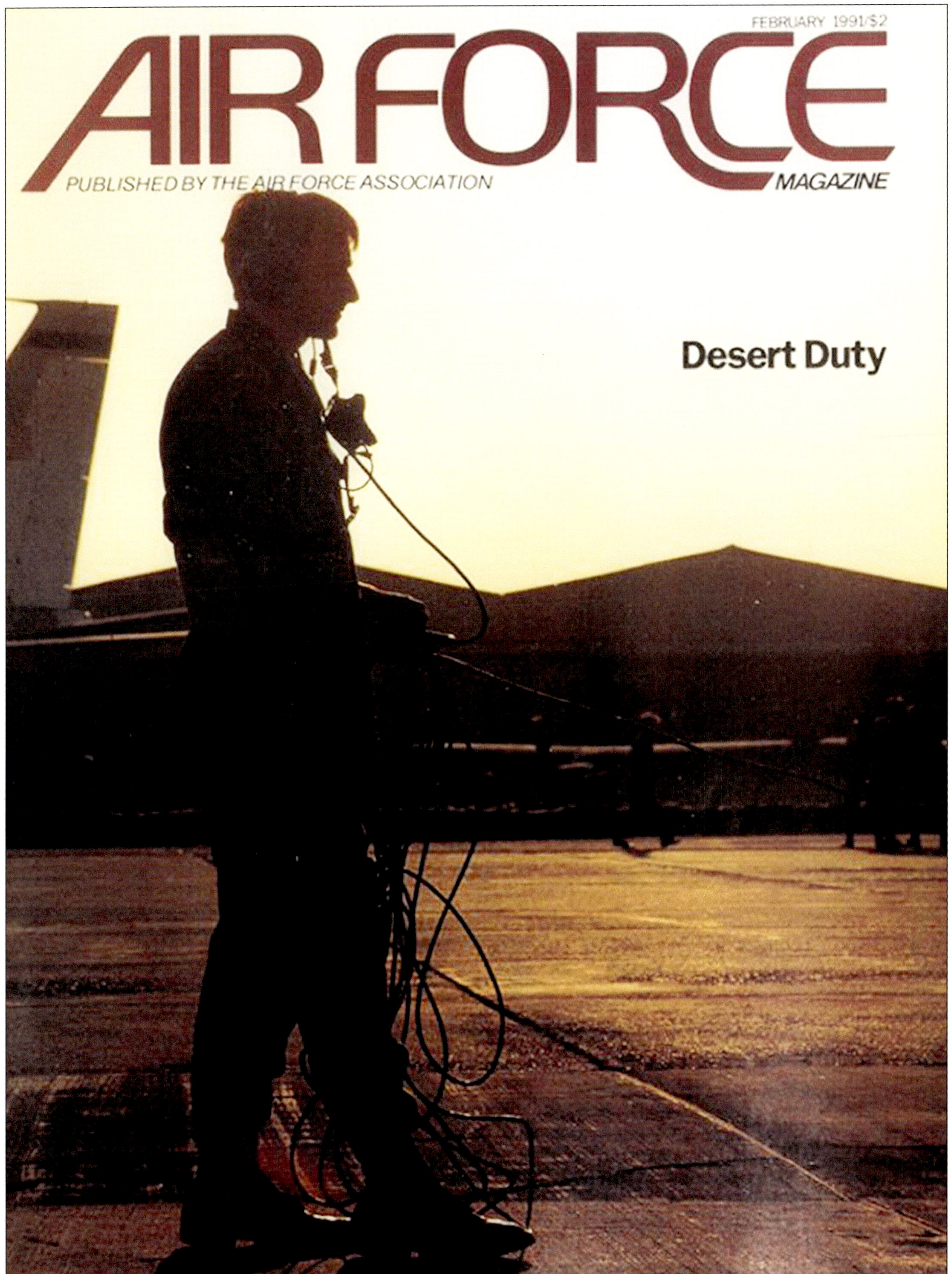

Good images told stories, and those by AAVS photographers were regularly used in *Air Force Magazine*. Getting a cover image was always a sign of professional achievement, including this one from February 1991 by Hans Deffner. (USAF/Hans Deffner)

When I was at Charleston, we went through formal aircrew training, essentially the same as the aircraft loadmasters. For aerial photography, we did five training flights with the instructor. They were primarily safety-focused, but they also taught you elements of techniques that were more specialised for taking pictures out of the aircraft. So, during these training flights, we practised to figure out what worked and what didn't. Remember that our primary medium was 100 ASA slide film back then.

If there was a large operation, everything we did went to the Joint Combat Camera Center in the Pentagon. We had a photojournalist on staff there, Steve McGill, another mentor and friend who also worked for Ken Hackman. He provided feedback, and there was more through Ken Hackman. So you got feedback through the leadership chain that you're doing good or perhaps not-so-good work.

Video Technology

The move to video from the film was an enormous jump in technology; it removed all the film processing, the tape could go straight to editing, and began to make sound-men redundant with the built-in microphones in these cameras. It took time to adjust to the new techniques that were now possible. The innovations introduced by new technology almost inevitably ruffled a few feathers along the way. Dave van de Brake explained that when he was at Charleston AFB in 1983, the Betacam video camera was just being introduced to AAVS. He and two colleagues in the unit were the first to use them.

As he described:

In 1983, I was sent to cover a large 82nd Airborne Division exercise involving a mass airdrop at Orangeburg, part of the Fort Bragg complex in South Carolina. I had my TV camera, and I had been trained well. I learned a lot by talking to Doug Morell and Mitch Jenkins. Doug Morrell told me, 'You do whatever works. Now you can tell a story in half the film.'

I am there waiting for the aircraft to come over the landing zone and drop this stick of men. An Army Major General is there, too, wearing an 82nd Airborne patch. He has a combat patch, too, and really looks the part. His boots are shiny, and you can see his attitude. I go up to him with my camera and explain who I am and that I am with the Aerospace Audiovisual Service to cover his operation. I had to explain that I was not with Public Affairs and was a combat documentation guy.

I asked him to talk about what was happening, and he gladly described the exercise. He spoke to me about what would happen, all the preparations, and the Division's role in the new US Rapid Deployment Force. The troops dropped; he walked out to where some of the guys were, getting their backpacks together, picking up their chutes and everything, and congratulating them on the drop. And I got it all. I got scooped. I got a general in the 'bank.' I'm loving it and thinking, you're here, you're doing TV, Dave. It's hot. It is on video, not film, so it can be used instantly.

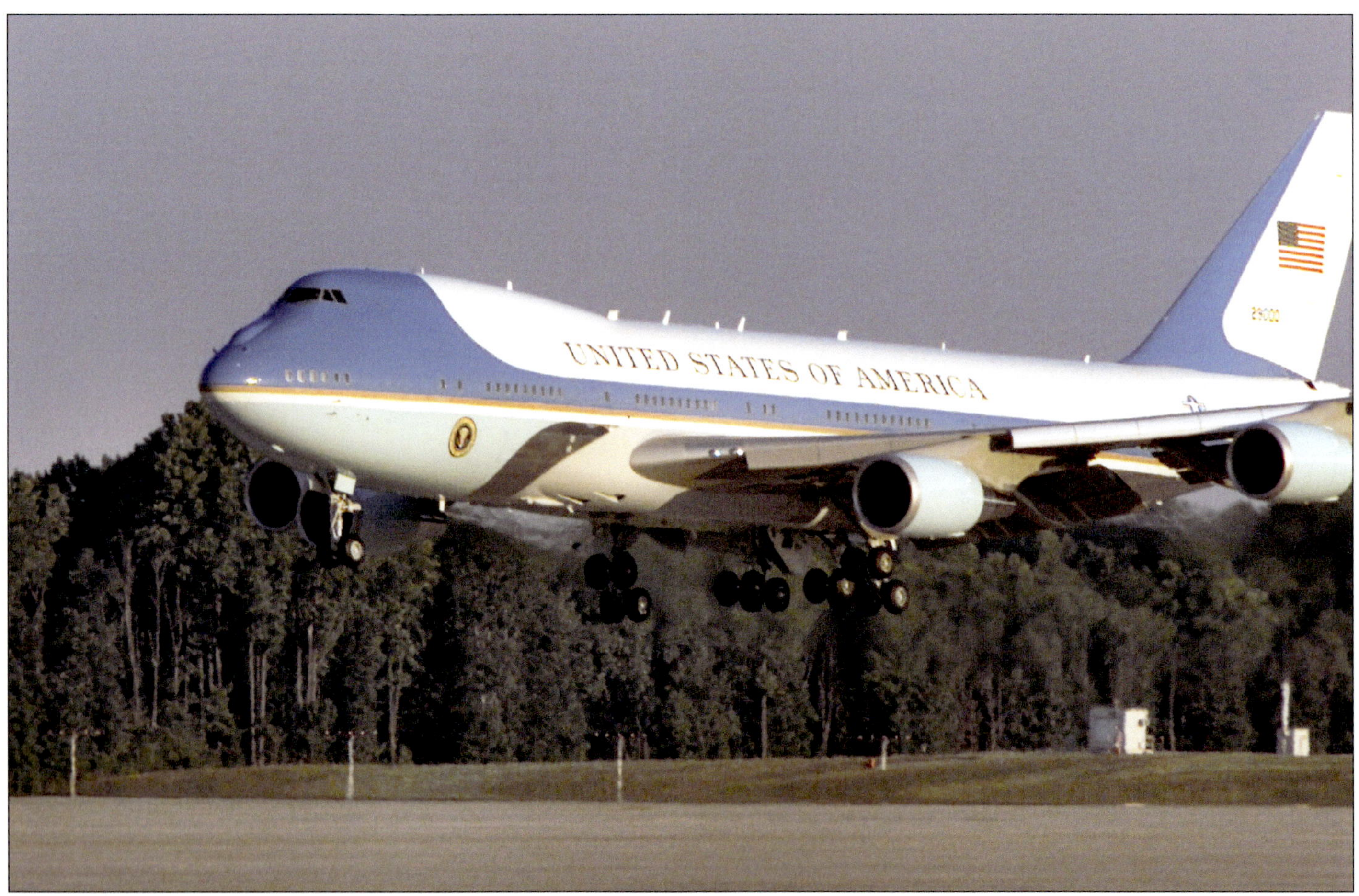

After leaving the Air Force, Hans Deffner continued working as a DoD civilian employee. He retired in 2001. 'The last official photo I had published was from September 11, 2001. I was stationed at Andrews AFB, and President Bush was off base. After all that transpired on that day, we shot Air Force One as it returned to Andrews. It was taken late afternoon with a 300mm lens with good light. We got a hint of how significant this day was, but we didn't know its ramifications'. (USAF)

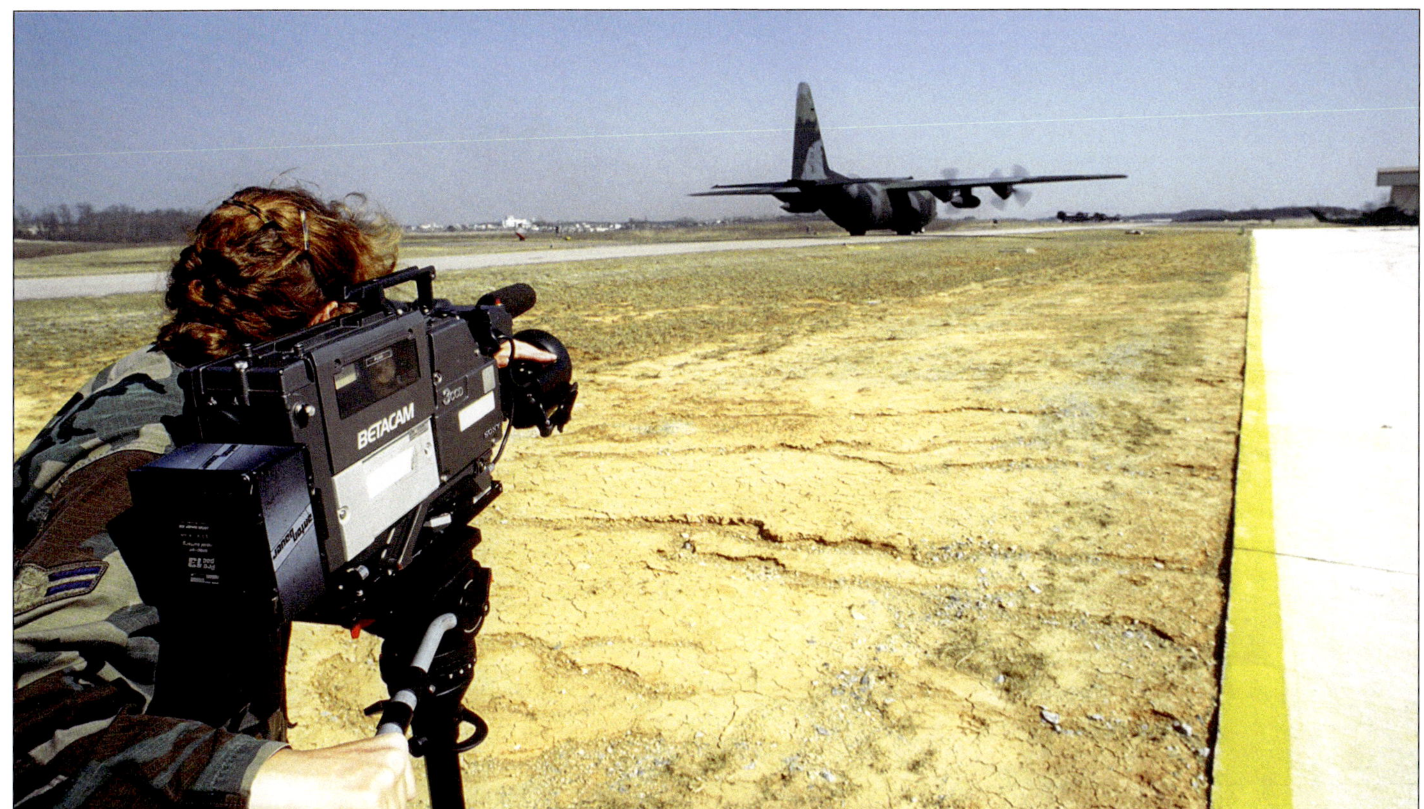

An AAVS camerawoman films a C-130E taxying at an airbase in South Korea in 1988. The Betacam video camera was large and unwieldy by later standards but revolutionised filming within AAVS. (USAF/SSgt Moo H Han)

I took the tape over to the Joint Information Bureau when I returned to base and gave it to them. One of the more senior NCOs, a motion picture guy, comes over and says, 'Van de Brake, come over here. What the hell are you doing? We don't do that in film.' He didn't like that I had just done the whole thing as a movie. I pointed to the microphone built into the Betacam and clicked the two switches that go from line-in to my hot mic. I told him, 'With your Airflex, you don't have a microphone; you can't do anything without a soundman'. The guy gave me a puzzled look; he didn't realise this video camera had a built-in microphone. We suddenly made a big jump in our ability to cover stories. By then, my supervisor, Mitch Jenkins, stepped in and said to the guy who had just rebuked me, 'See this guy? He's thinking. He's just grabbed a prime interview that we would've missed.'

Combat Documentation

TSgt Robert Zoucha joined AAVS in 1987, having previously flown with the 7405th Operations Squadrons on reconnaissance missions from Rhein-Main AB along the Berlin Air Corridors. His first posting with AAVS was with the Detachment at Nellis AFB in 1987. He described some of the weapons documentation work that was going on at the Nellis ranges:

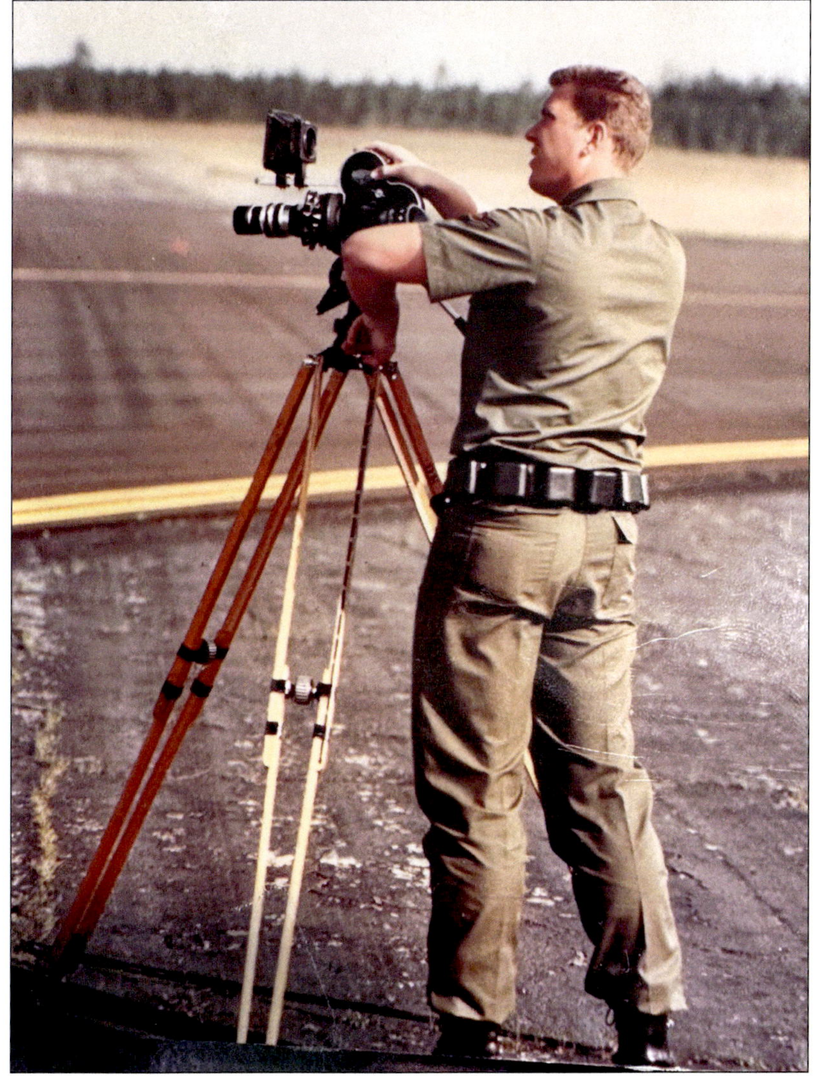

Dave van de Brake sets up a film camera. The video cameras, with their built-in microphones, vastly improved the ability of Air Force cameramen to capture events without the need for a soundman. (Dave van de Brake)

On the documentation side, we did bomb testing there, and there was a lot of work filming cluster bombs. When you filmed from ground level, you could not tell where the individual cluster bomblet hits were because their coverage area was so big. The only way to observe the spread properly was from the air. So we would launch in a helicopter. When I started, we flew in UH-1Ns from Det 1, 57th Tactical Training Wing, out of Indian Springs Auxiliary Airfield. We would drive over to Indian Springs, get on a helicopter, and do these missions.

Later, the work was contracted out, so we flew in these civilian helicopters. We shot through the open door or took the door off the helicopter to look down and shoot where the bombs hit. Analysts could then go back and look at the film and say, OK. 'On this drop, we did a 20-degree dive or a 20-degree toss-bomb release where they pulled up in a 20-degree climb and released the bomb. We were aiming at this point, and this is where it hit.' That sort of thing. We would hover about 3,000 feet offset at 1,500 to 2,000 feet altitude. It was never so close as to be dangerous; we didn't have to be that precise. We did a lot of those flights. Wayne Evans and I probably did 500 of those – a lot between us. There were times when it was several times a day, every day for four or five days a week.

Robert continued:

We had a good relationship with the Fighter Weapons School (FWS) at Nellis. Sometimes, we would go and fly with them. When I first arrived, we had one flying position for an aerial photographer, and Wayne Evans was my predecessor. When he moved to Norton AFB, I was put in that position. Now and then, probably five times a year, they would call me up and go, 'Hey. We got a seat going in a tub next Tuesday, you wanna go?' and of course it was, oh, yeah. Absolutely and we would go and fly with them. And as long as the ranges were up and it didn't interfere with them doing their primary work when airborne, they let us fly with them. We would shoot videos or stills, and then, of course, we always shared the results with them because they wanted the imagery for their internal use. That was mostly in two-seat F-15s and F-16s, but we would fly with anybody that offered us the opportunity.

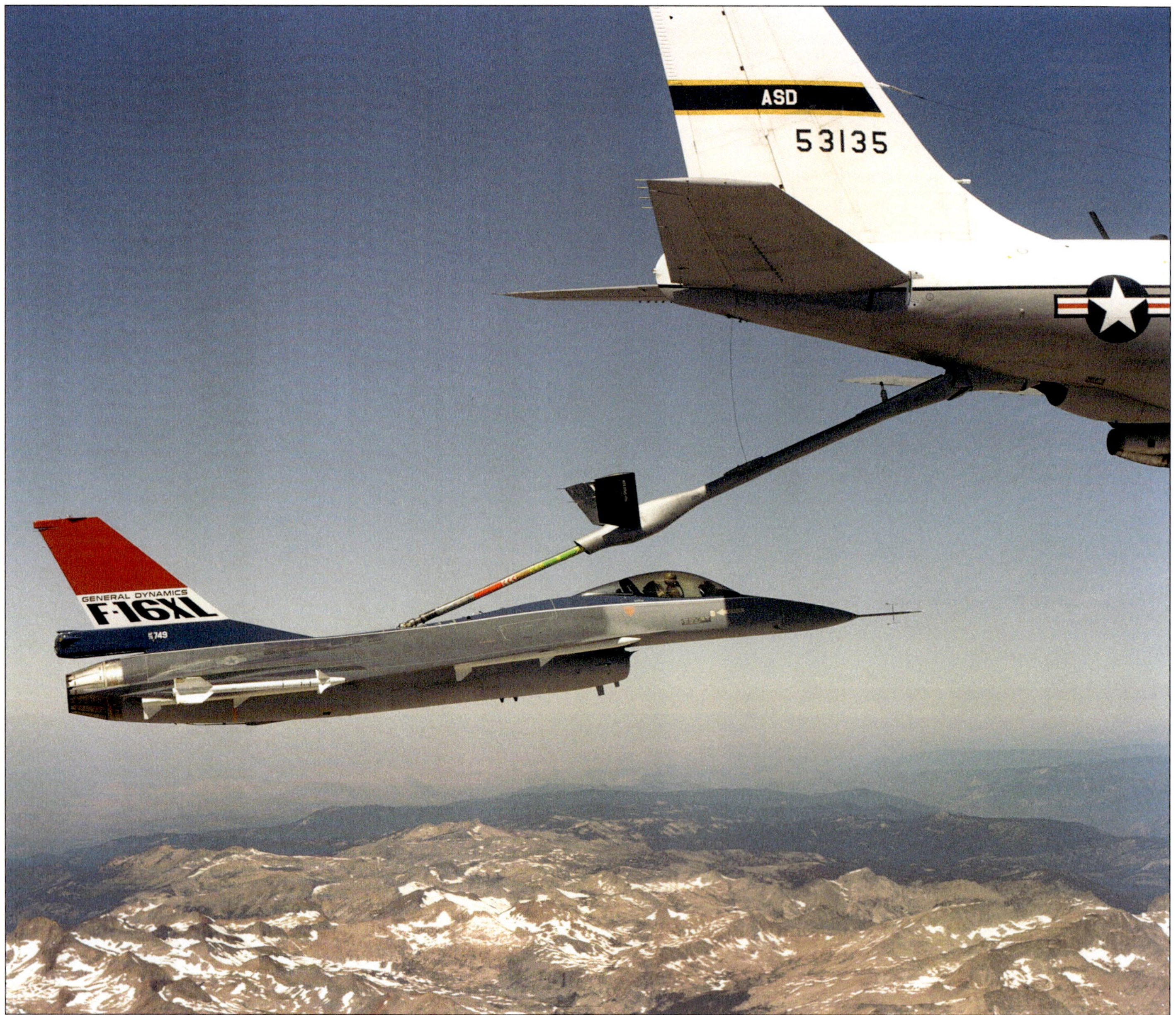

Filming aircraft for test, evaluation, training or publicity purposes, such as this F-16XL, was all part of the work for combat cameramen assigned to test units. (USAF/Sgt D Thompson)

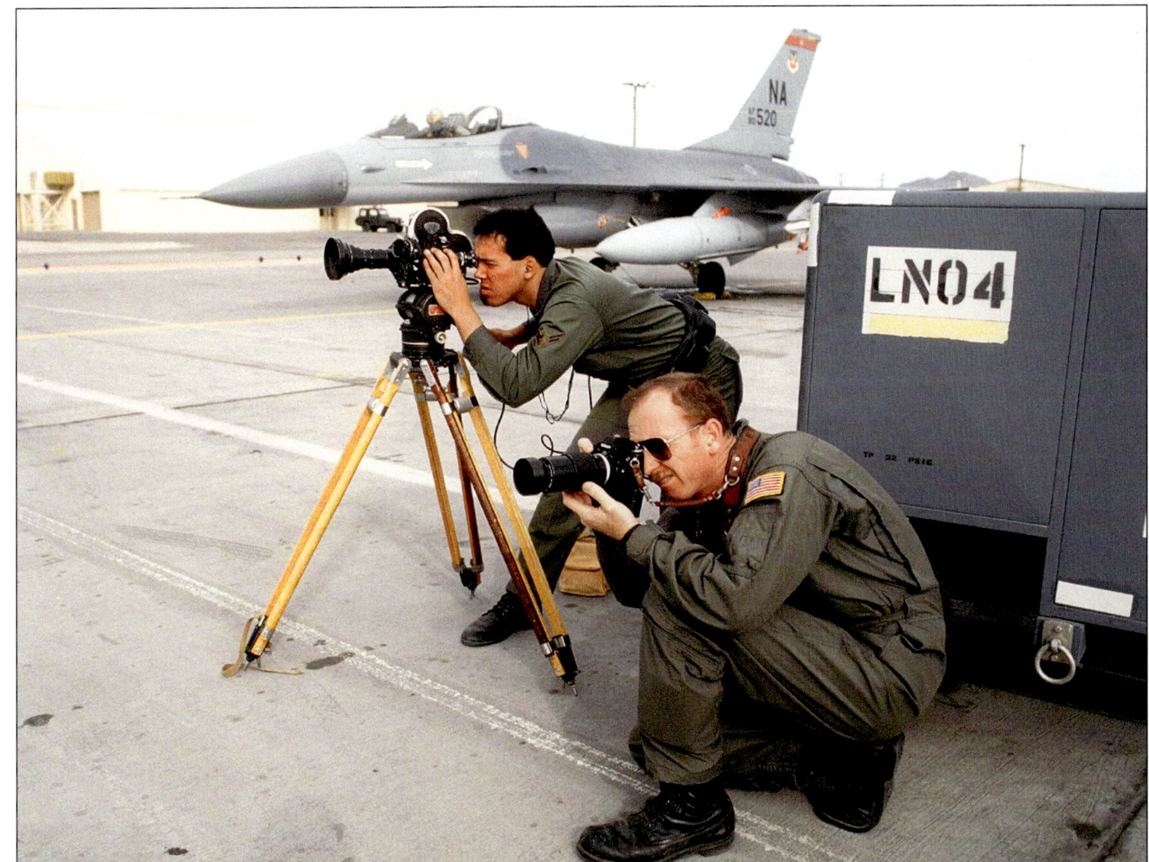

Right: TSgt Boyd Belcher at the tripod with an Arriflex 16mm camera and TSgt Wayne Evans with a still camera documenting flightline activity at Nellis AFB. (USAF)

Below: Opportunities to fly with the many different aircraft types operated at Nellis AFB were always seized upon by the AAVS personnel based there. (USAF/SSgt Mike Hinson)

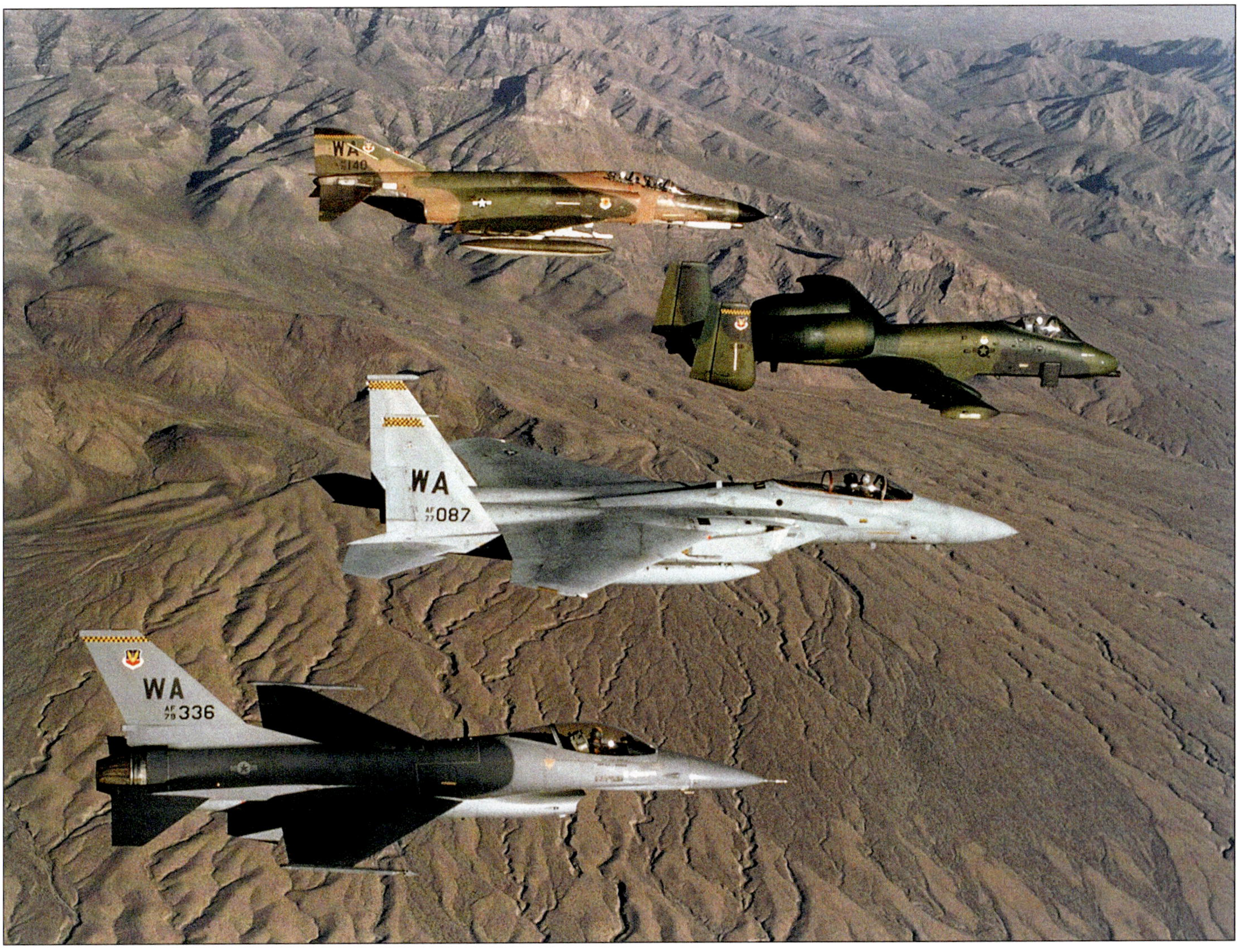

Nellis also had other needs, as Robert explained:

The FWS wanted us to come over and record some of their ground classes. We filmed their instructors at work, and they used the footage to evaluate themselves and each other. They also had archival footage so they could go back and look at how they had taught a particular class in the past. So some days, we would get a call and go to the Fighter Weapons School the next day, using a tripod, camera, and enough tapes for a few hours of recording.

There were times when we might be working on several documentation projects at once, and there were many of them. We probably spent 75% of our time working on production stuff. At the time, there were five or six of us, all Staff or Technical Sergeants, with an NCOIC in charge of everybody. But as we all were the same rank, as the work would come in, we would allocate the tasks between ourselves. One of us would become the producer for the whole thing, go and talk to the 'customer', find out what they wanted, write the script and ask one of the others to come and help shoot the scene or assist with whatever else was needed. So we all got a taste of being camera operators, audio guys, lighting, producers, editors etc. You did everything involved with production, which was cool because we learned a lot. That was kinda how things worked there.

One of us was always the 'alert photographer'. They had to carry a beeper with them because, in those days, all we had was a beeper, no cell phones. And for that week, you were on-call. If the beeper went off and was always the same thing, it was, 'This is the Nellis Air Force Base Command Post; please contact us immediately'. So you went and found a phone and called them up to ask, 'What's going on?'

All too often, it was 'an aircraft accident' or 'there's been a natural disaster', and we needed to assemble a team to cover it. When I first got to Nellis, airplanes were going into the ground about once a month for the first few months. So we would have to go and document what had happened. You would grab your stuff, go to the command post, and then drive up to the crash site or be helicoptered wherever the accident or incident

had happened. Then we would go and document what was going on, look over all the pieces and parts and the bodies and so on.

On the edge of Las Vegas, on 4 May 1988, several large explosions occurred at the Pacific Engineering and Production Company of Nevada (PEPCON). It was a major chemical plant in Henderson, Nevada, just over 10 miles from Nellis AFB and produced chemicals for missile fuel. Robert explained, 'I was the alert photographer that week. We got the beep and had to head out. We were in the desert, in the middle of nowhere, waiting hours before they decided what they wanted us to do. Nellis AFB went out there, provided light hauls and some security forces, and assisted around where the explosion happened, which we covered'.

REFORGER, BRIGHT STAR and TEAM SPIRIT

Annual, large-scale exercises and deployments were a regular feature of USAF and US military life, especially with the increased tempo from the late 1970s to the end of the Cold War. Tactical Air Command, in particular, deployed aircraft from its bases in the continental United States to locations worldwide, supported by MAC to airlift personnel and equipment. In Europe, these were the 'REFORGER' reinforcement exercise series each autumn. In Korea, these were known as 'TEAM SPIRIT', and in Egypt, from 1980, there were bilateral US-Egyptian 'BRIGHT STAR' exercises. Within these overarching series were many smaller exercises for the units involved. These, and many others, were major tests of their deployment plans, capabilities, and training events that demonstrated the US military's resolve and commitment. There were also large Air Force and NATO competitions like Giant Voice, William Tell, Volant Rodeo, Tiger Meets and many others.

These activities were often heavily documented by teams of video cameramen and photographers for senior commanders and sometimes for publicity purposes. Actions included documenting almost every activity from prior logistic preparations to the units arrival home. The frequent 'Coronet' deployments of Air National Guard and TAC units to Europe for two to four weeks were regular AAVS coverage subjects.

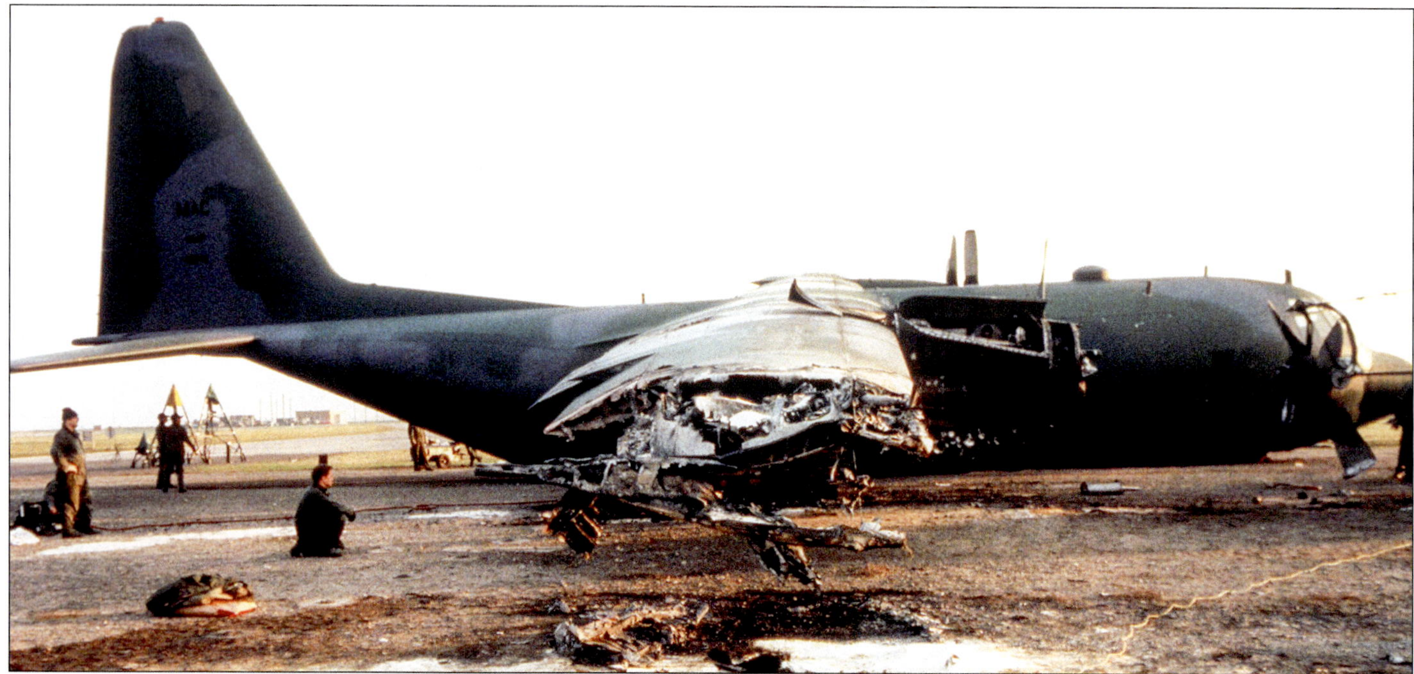

A 37th TAS C-130E crash-landed at Biebelstadt Army Airfield in Germany. AAVS duty photographers would be called to such accidents and some civil disasters to produce imagery for later investigations. (USAF/SSgt Dave Nolan)

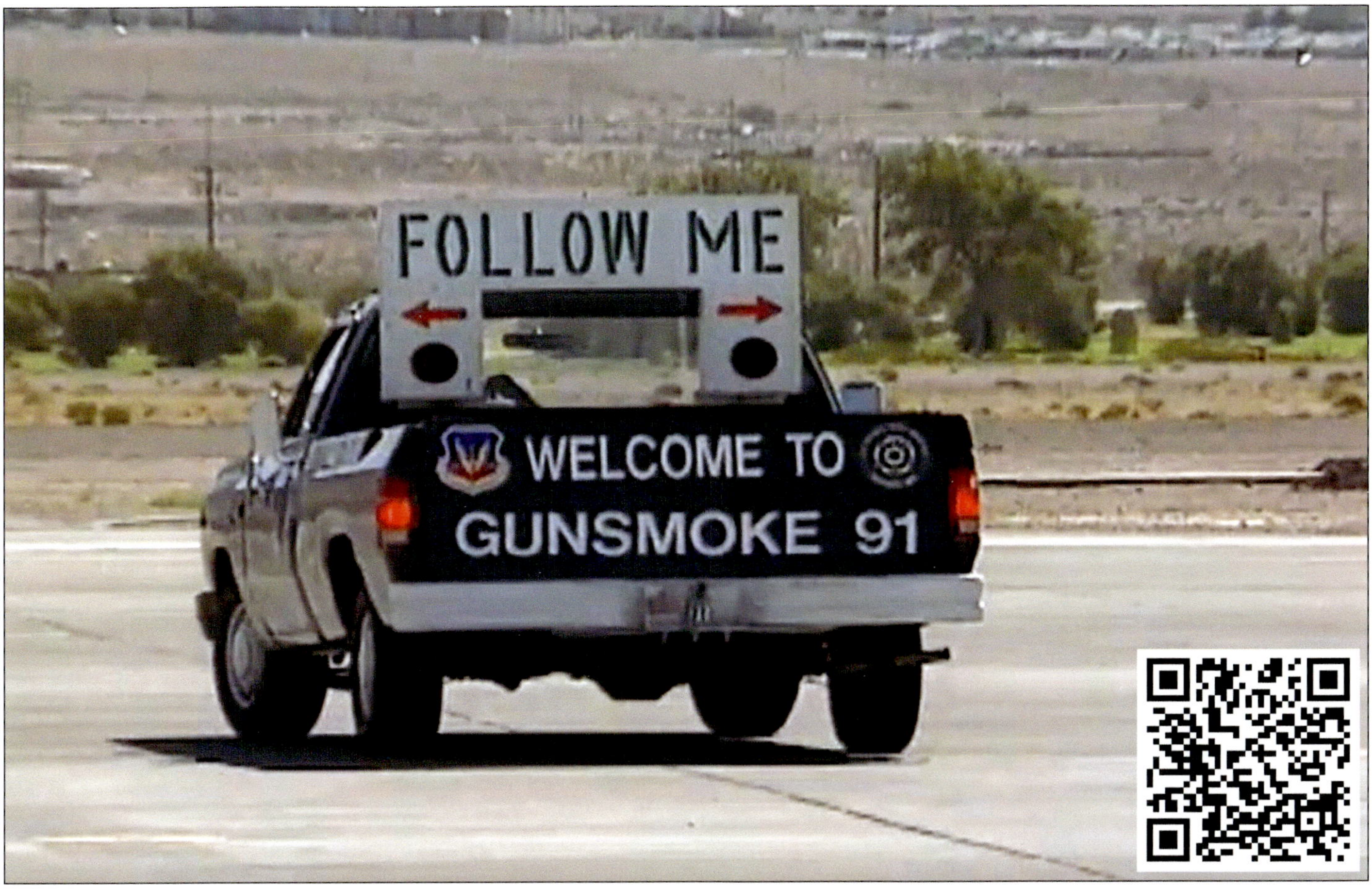

AAVS covered many major USAF and international events. In 1991 the USAF's 'Gunsmoke' competition was held at Nellis AFB. This nine-minute video shows many aspects of the event and well illustrates the innovations that video cameras and editing offered. (YouTube/Flying Z Customs)

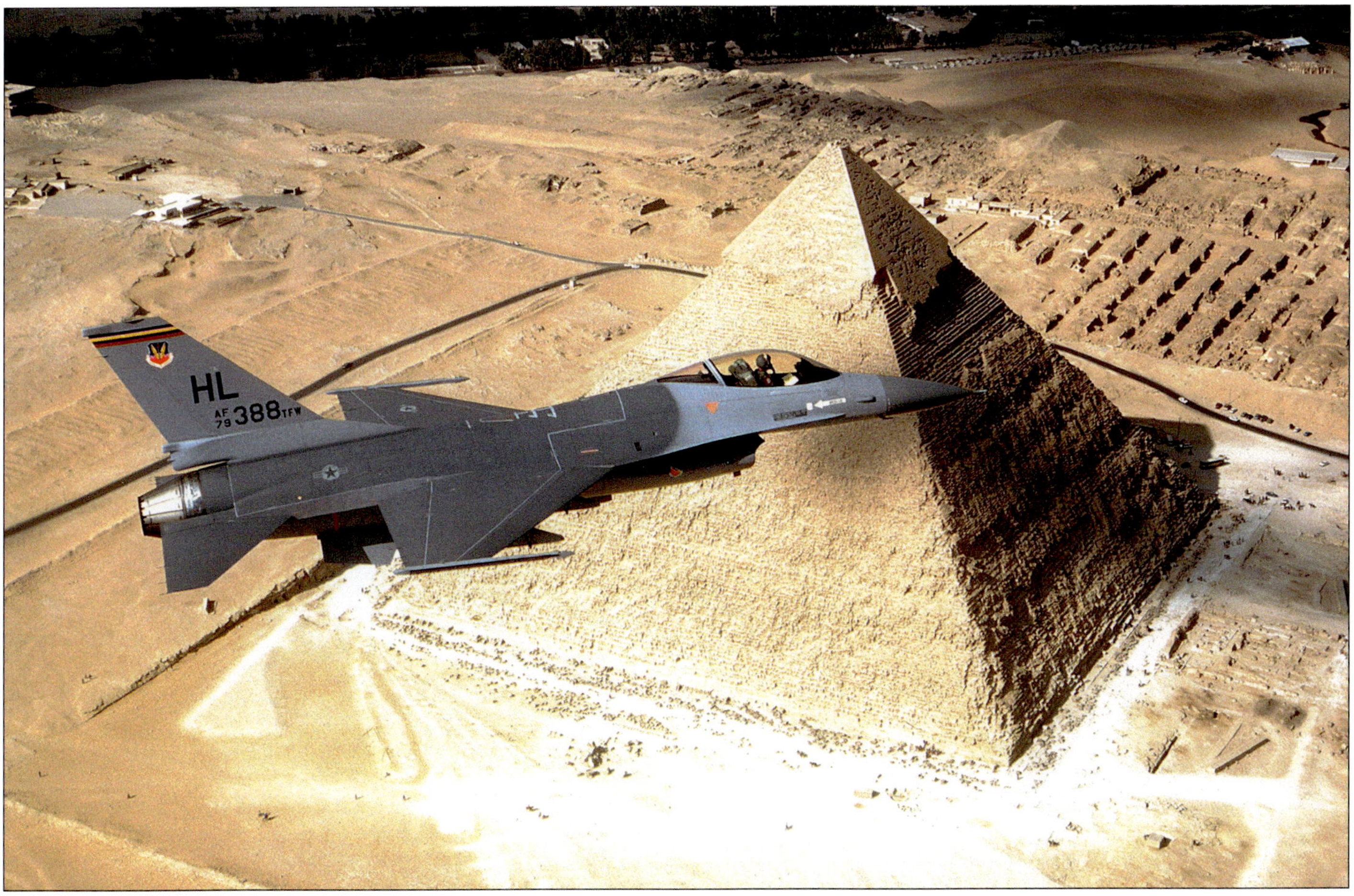

In his F-16A, the CO of the 388th TFW overflies a pyramid near Cairo during 'Bright Star 82'. (USAF/MSgt Don Sutherland)

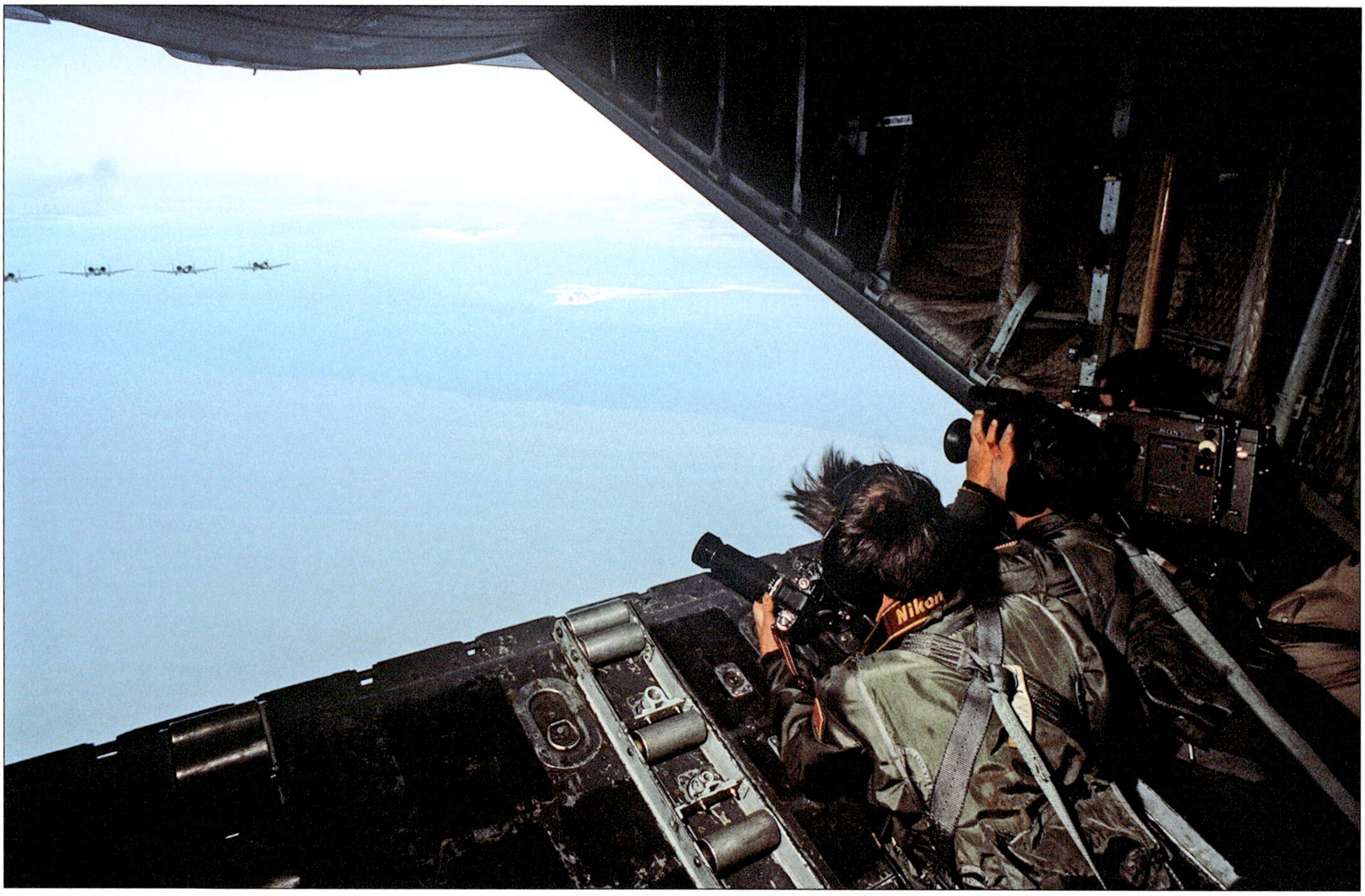

AAVS still and video cameramen waiting to photograph an approaching formation of A-10s during TEAM SPIRIT '86. (USAF)

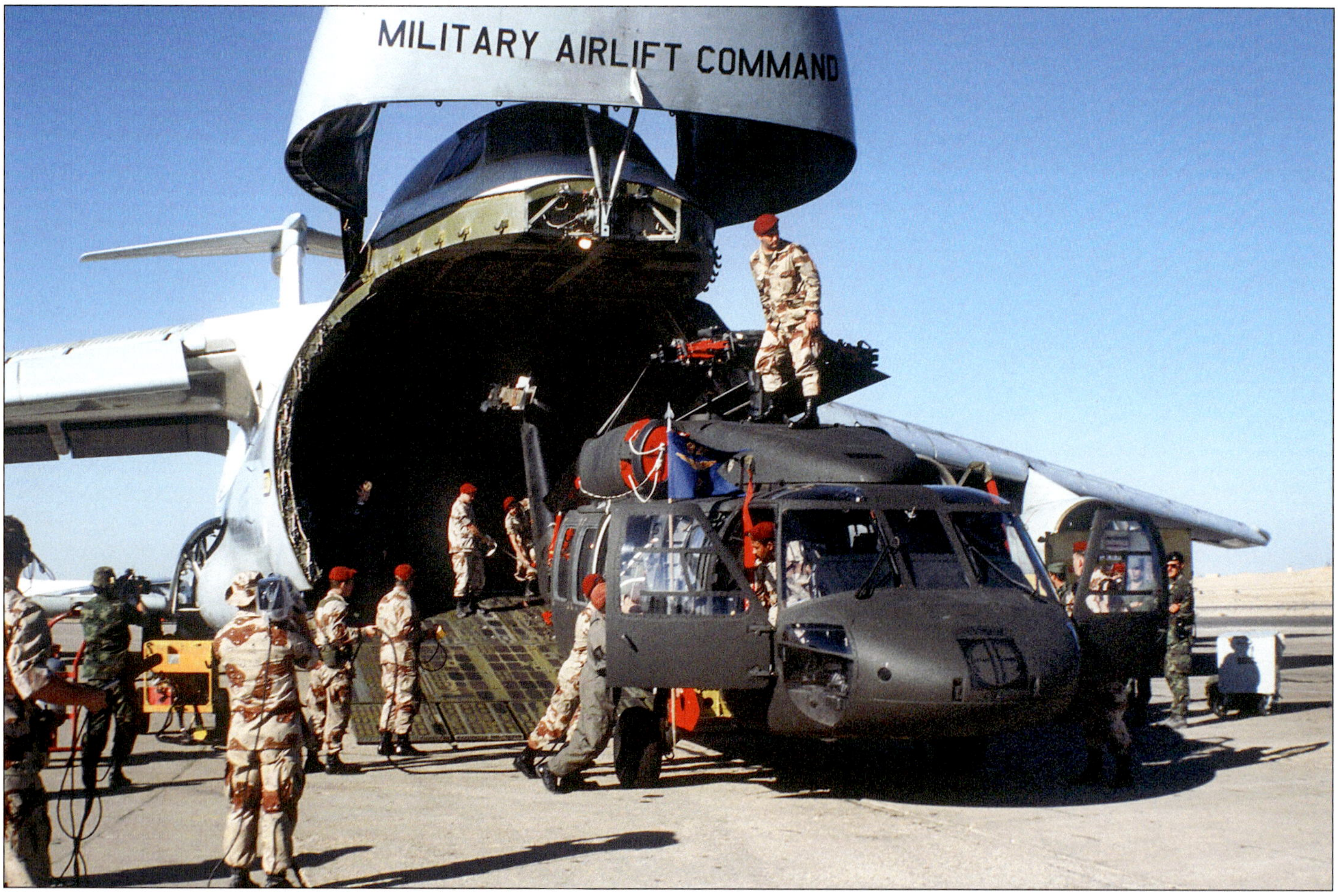

From 1980, 'Bright Star' saw US forces annually deploy to Egypt to participate in joint exercises. AAVS videographers filmed a US Army UH-60A helicopter being unloaded from a C-5A during 'Bright Star 82'. (USAF/TSgt Frank Garzelnick)

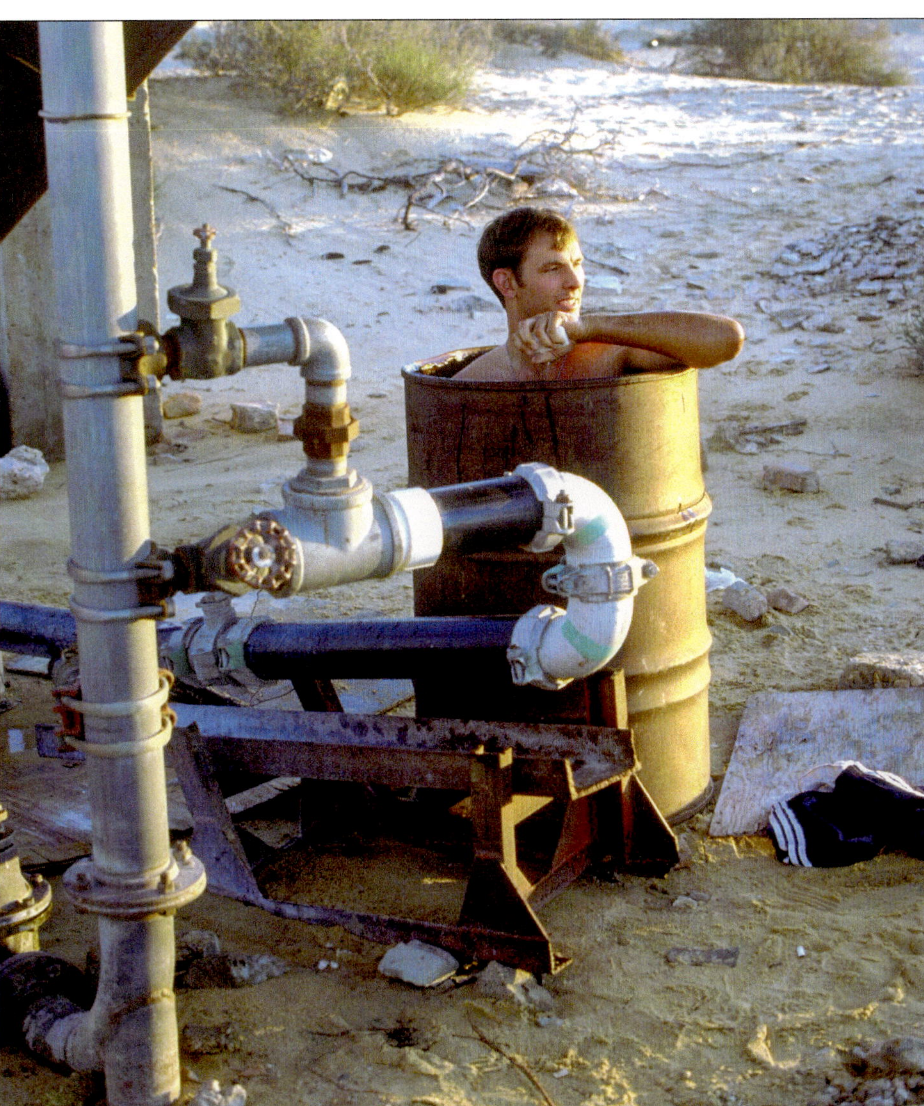

Right: AAVS personnel on assignment often had to work with local solutions. SSgt Carl Black of the 1365th AVS bathes in a 55-gallon oil drum in the Egyptian desert during Bright Star '82. (USAF)

Below: 'Getting the shot' two F-15As from the 33rd TFW overfly Hohenzollern Castle during autumn 1987, part of REFORGER deployment 'Coronet Phaser' to West Germany. (USAF/SSgt Fernando Serna)

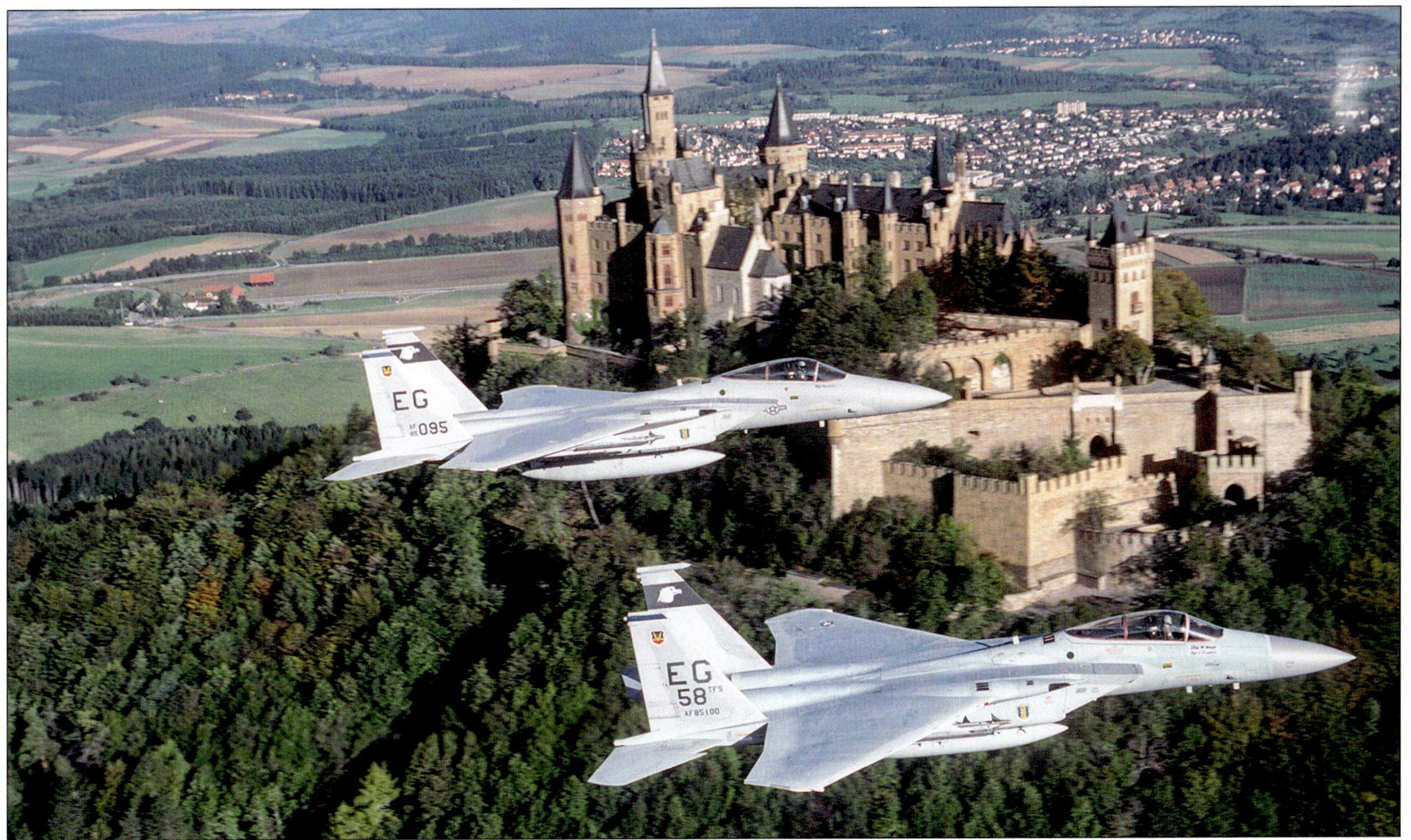

NEW TO THE JOB

Greg Krager described what AAVS was like when he joined it as a young officer in 1989:

When I first got to Norton AFB in California, I was assigned to work on a film production called *Air Force Now*. That was motion picture film production, a monthly news magazine distributed across the Air Force. It was all on film; they were getting rid of wet processing just about when I arrived in 1989 and moved me into video documentation. I was a 'Project Officer', like a team leader.

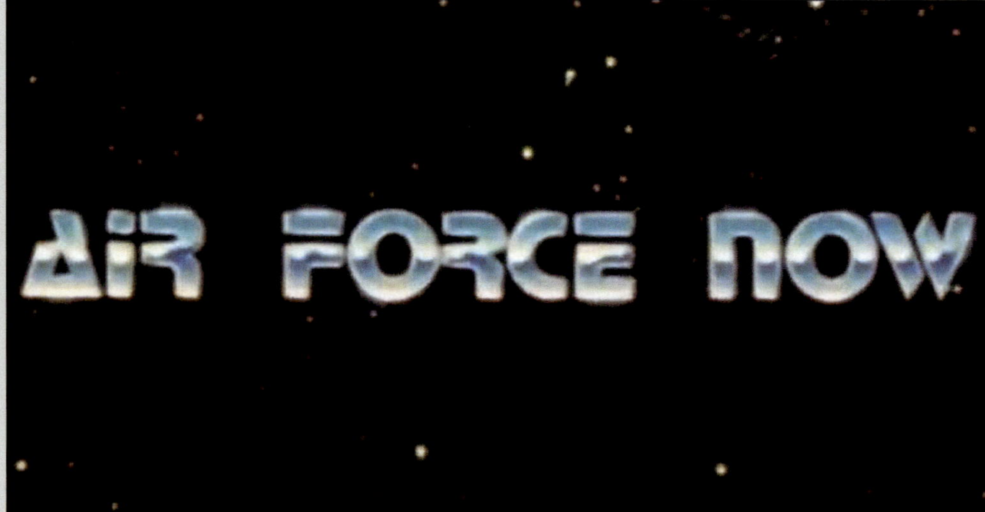

This is an episode of *Air Force Now*, a monthly AAVS video news production. This 15-minute edition (#192) is from 1986. It has a historic segment on USAF uniforms, the introduction of the C-23A to USAFE, and the USAF's Arctic Survival School. (YouTube/PeriscopeFilm)

You have various ongoing projects for documentation. I could be doing a story on Chuck Yeager or one on the SR-71's last flights or the first flight of the C-17. What you were doing was kind of varied. Sometimes, we might write a story about security forces or cooks. Everybody was important in the Air Force, and we wanted to show that. We didn't want an airman sitting there guarding a jet on the flight line feeling like his job was not important. We aimed to bring light to what people were doing, that no matter how small you think it is, it was all part of a greater picture, a link in the chain, and that's important in a huge organisation.

We did a lot of training within our organisation. We had to be ready to move at very short notice, virtually anywhere. I had my Arctic, Desert, and Jungle bags for field gear. I had a bag for everything, so many bags. We did physical training every day and regular combat arms training because if you're documenting something and you get pinned down, guess what? You're gonna have to drop your camera and shoot back.

Operation Just Cause

Panamanian President Manuel Noriega resorted to increasingly desperate measures to remain in power during the late 1980s. His criminal activities, political thuggery, and the importance of the Canal eventually provoked a US invasion. Beginning on 20 December 1989, over 27,000 troops and hundreds of aircraft took part in Operation Just Cause which occupied Panama and deposed Noriega.

For AAVS, Just Cause was a significant event, with personnel deployed to cover many aspects of the operation. Robert Zoucha described his experience.

We were tasked with assembling a combat camera crew and going to Panama. Nine or ten of us went down there in a C-5 in the middle of the night, along with some Marines. We had our cameras ready to go when we landed, jumped off the airplane, and documented the unloading of the Marine Corps troops on the ramp at Howard AFB. We never stopped from there on for the next month.

I was only supposed to be gone for about six days. Still, I spent 34 days in Panama, documenting everything down there. That included flying with OA-37s as air support to the convoy missions we ran between the Atlantic and Pacific entrances to the Canal. Officially, we were there to enforce the Canal Treaty, but we were trying to provoke the Panamanians to start a fight. We loaded up convoys of M35 Deuce-and-a-Half trucks and Humvees, with just troops in the back armed with light machine guns, M16s, grenades and other weapons.

The top priority for transport back to the US was the evacuation of US casualties. The second priority was the tapes we shot. When we were running those convoys back and forth, there were A-37s, A-10s and AC-130s flying overhead as top cover to provide close air support for us if something happened. The cameramen might fly for two days and then run a convoy for two or four days, and then you might get pulled off to do something else. That was how things happened in AAVS.

We started using digital cameras in Panama, including an early Sony Mavica video camera. The whole thing was about 14 inches long, with camera and lens and recorded onto a two-inch disk. We had this backpack and satellite rigs that you could set up on the ground with a generator, and you could uplink photos. They could be back in Washington in like 17 minutes or so. Everybody was all googly-eyed about it because it had never been possible before.

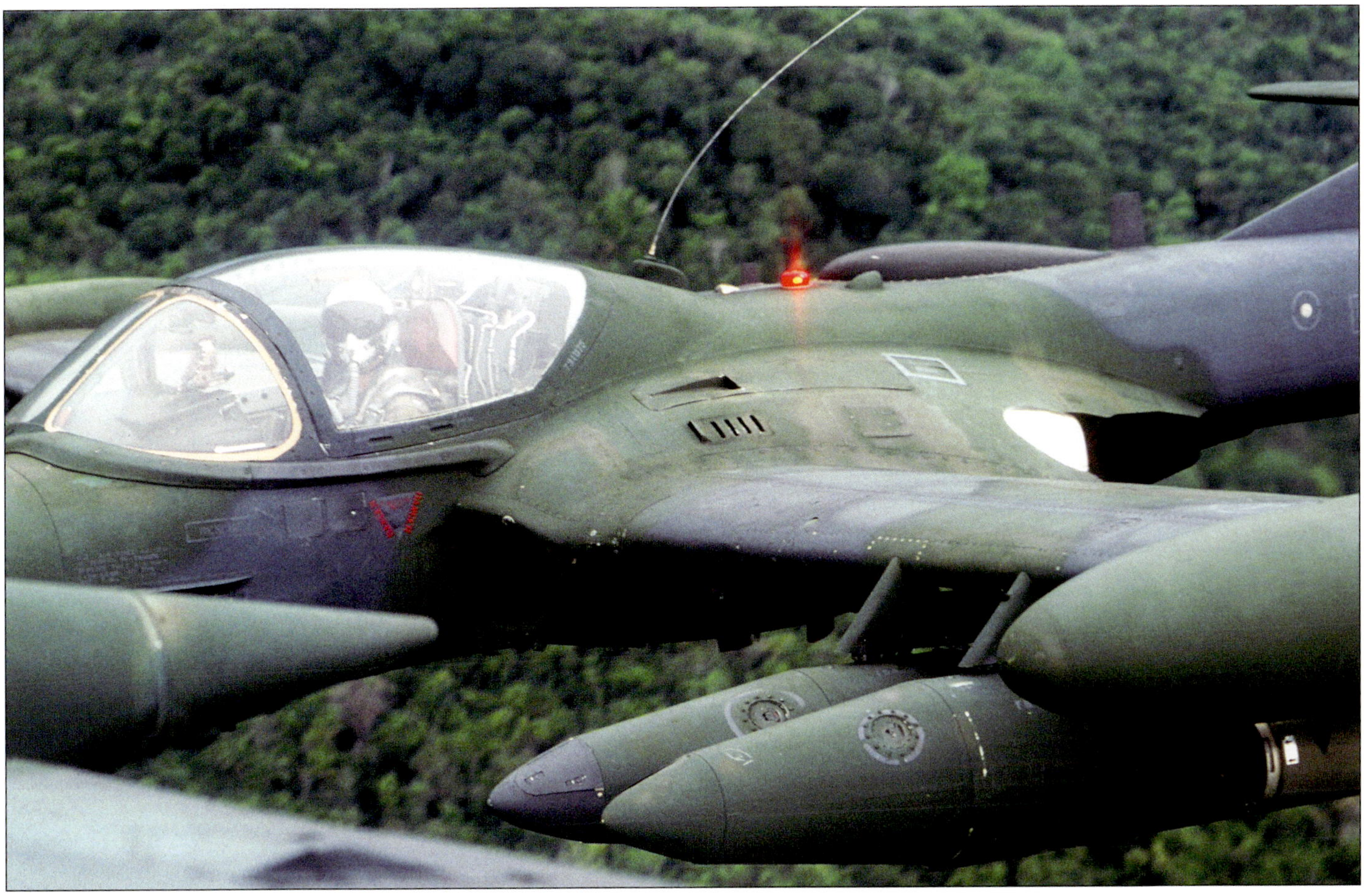

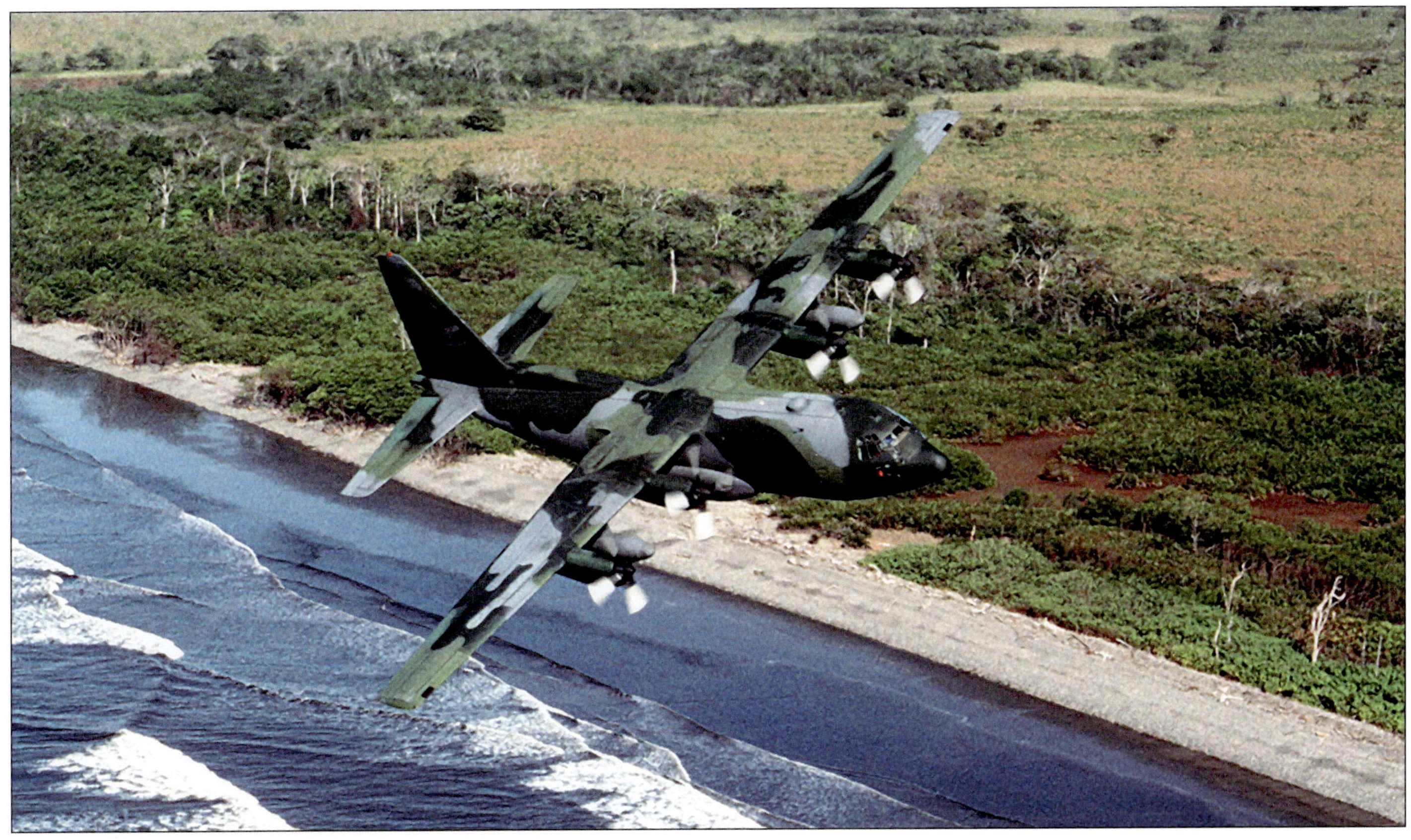

Flying air support for a convoy patrol during Just Cause, an OA-37 Dragonfly from the 24th Tactical Air Support Squadron based at Howard AFB in Panama. (USAF/MSgt Donald Wetterman)

A 934th TAG C-130E has some 'fun time' returning to Howard AFB, flying along the Panamanian coast after dropping paratroopers during a Just Cause training exercise. AAVS photographer MSgt Ken Hammond was on the rear ramp of another C-130 to record the event. (USAF/MSgt Ken Hammond)

The Rendition of Noreiga

SSgt Charles Reger went to Panama during Operation Just Cause as an Air Force photographer:

You know, we were doing air assaults with the Army Rangers. And then we were with the Marine Corps kicking in doors downtown, putting in buildings and doing all that stuff.

Manuel Noriega hid out in the Papal Nuncio compound in Panama. The PSYOPS guys were down there blasting music at him, trying to get him to surrender. We were on 'Noriega watch' 24/7, wanting to photograph the moment he surrendered. We would go out during the day, do missions, come back to base, get a cot, and catch a cat nap, while we waited for notification that he was ready to surrender.

He came out before I could get to the Papal Nuncio for my shift. Instead, we met him on the airfield flight line, escorted by several other guys. When they brought him off the helicopter and threw him on the C-130 to fly him out of Panama, we took pictures of him being taken into custody after he was changed out of his Panamanian uniform into a jumpsuit.

He continued:

An Army videographer and I collected all the film taken during the event. We returned it to the photo lab at Howard AFB. We needed to get the film and video back to DC immediately. There were just two aircraft leaving Howard AFB that night. Unable to stop a C-130 at the end of the runway, the remaining aircraft

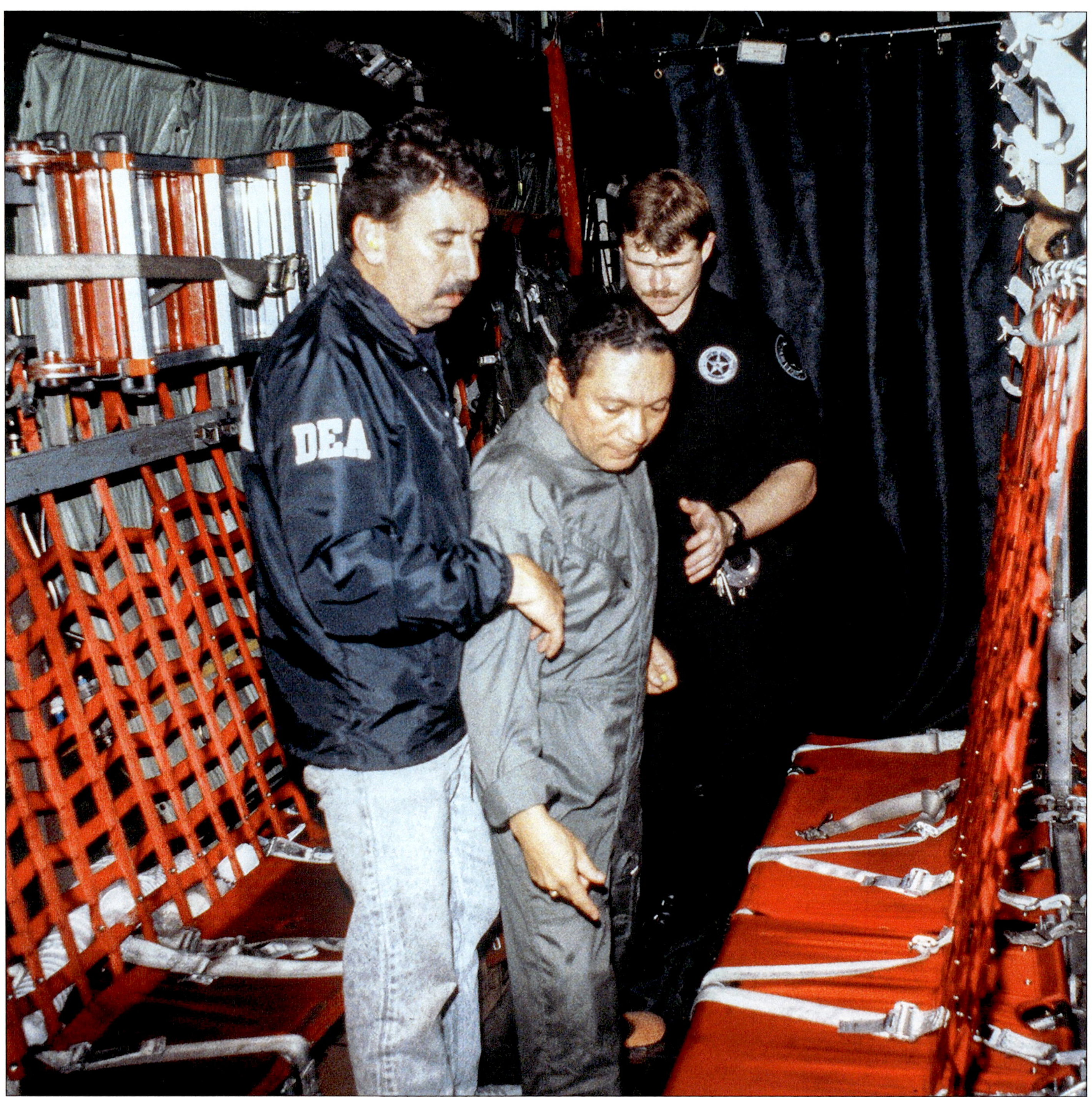

Manuel Noriega was detained by US troops and placed on a USAF C-130 by DEA Agents for transport to the United States. The pictures of him on the aircraft were widely used in the news media. (USAF/SSgt Charles Reger)

was a C-5 with Cdr Richard Marchenko and his SEAL team returning home with the bodies of four of their comrades. They really did not want us on the aircraft, but after several frantic calls to the Pentagon to try and get us thrown off, we took off.

The next thing I know, we're landing in Virginia. They threw me off of the plane into a blacked-out panel van with all my film and gear. I'm still filthy because I have been out in the field all day in Panama. The van pulls around to the other side of the base, right in front of this C-21, with the steps down and its engines running. I'm told to get on that plane right there. As I run up the steps, the pilot hands me a cell phone and asks where we are going?

We head to Andrews AFB, and I am met on the ramp by a driver who takes me directly to the Pentagon and the Office of the Secretary of Defense for Public Affairs (OSDPA). I meet with Betty Spriggs and Louis 'Pete' Williams, then the Assistant Secretary of Defense for Public Affairs. He asks, 'What have you got?' After handing over the material to be fully processed, someone took me to get breakfast, showered and gave me a clean uniform.

Returning to the OSDPA offices, we did a swift edit with Pete Williams. I told him what pictures could be used and which could not, because undercover people were in the shots and had to be kept out of the picture. Then, I was standing in the back of the Pentagon briefing room that morning when they showed the pictures when briefing the Secretary of Defense on Noriega's being taken into custody.

The pictures and video that came into the public domain were released that morning; our material was run on every newscast, CBS, NBC, CNN, Time, Newsweek, and the New York Times. Every major newspaper ran with the images of Noriega being taken into custody. It was not a perfect picture, but it had excellent news value; it was my million-dollar photo.

Top Secret Clearances

Some personnel, particularly cameramen and videographers, with previous experience in the reconnaissance or intelligence field before joining AAVS, held high-level Top Secret (TS) security clearances. This could be both a blessing and a curse when within AAVS. Robert Zoucha explained:

> When a classified project came up while I was at Nellis, I was the first one considered for the work, because my supervisor, Wayne Robinson, and I were the only ones with a TS or higher clearance. Even my Squadron detachment commander didn't have a clearance as high as we did. So, there were projects we did when I was at Nellis that my detachment commander couldn't look at, which upset him.

Holding a TS clearance meant uncleared personnel could not work on the filmed material or even be in the room when the footage was edited. 'So that was good, but it was bad because whenever something like that came up, I got stuck doing it. Some of them were interesting tasks, others were not'. Other AAVS personnel with

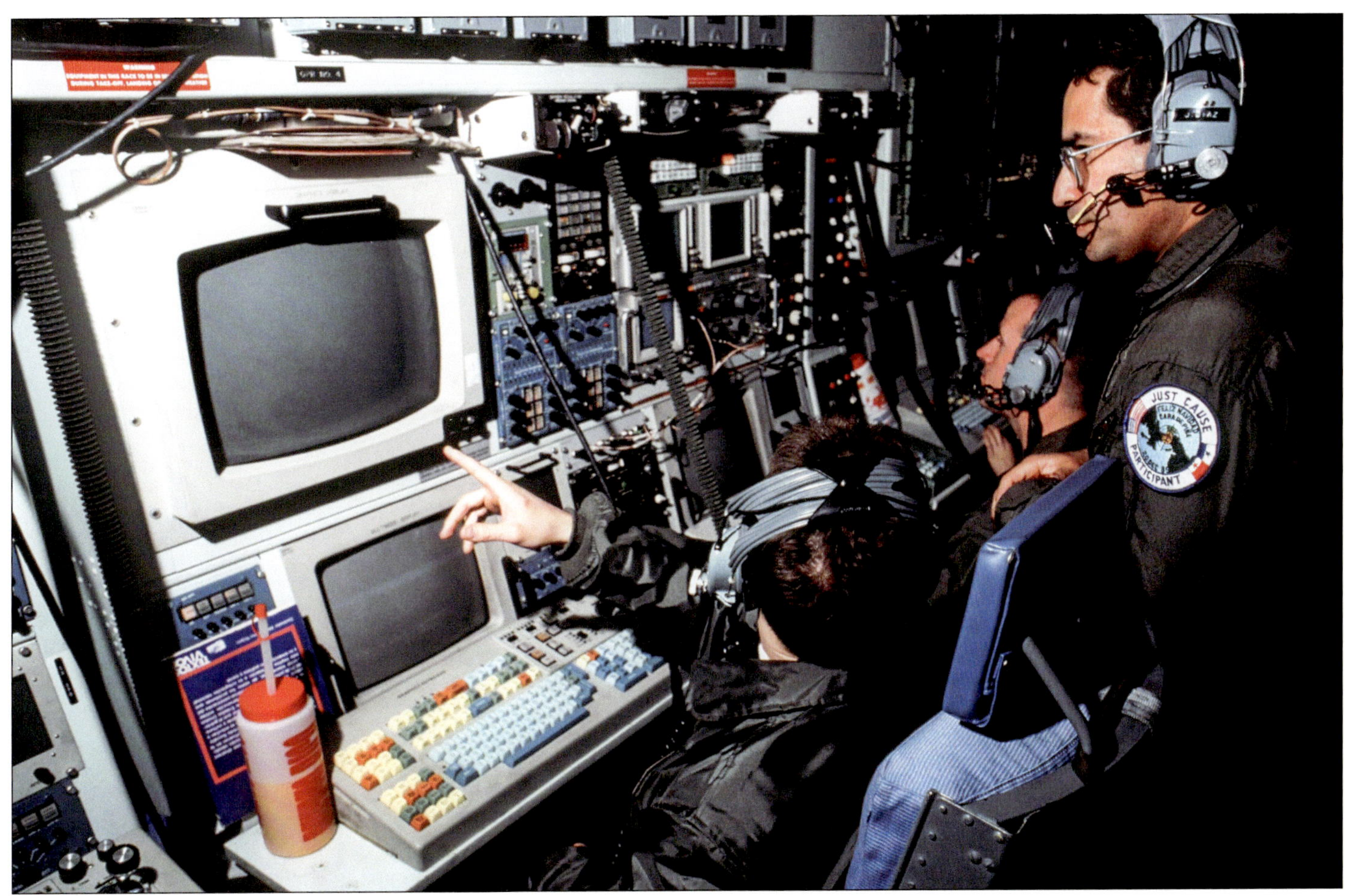

Taking pictures inside an RC-135 has always been sensitive work. The most crucial secret equipment on the aircraft is either out of shot or discreetly concealed. (USAF)

TS clearances got to document Special Forces training exercises and rehearsals for real-world operations. For others, it could be filming the testing of new secret weaponry and equipment before they were introduced to frontline service.

Greg Krager highlighted one experience during Operation Desert Shield in early 1991:

We sometimes received specific taskings. One was from the Commander in Chief of Strategic Air Command. For such tasks, the cameramen and imagery editors had to have adequate special security clearances to photograph inside extremely sensitive platforms like the RC-135s and EC-130Hs. He requested we film some newly installed equipment onboard an RC-135 deployed to Ryadh. Because of its secret nature, the RC-135 Squadron Commander, who was deployed with the aircraft, refused to let us board until the access issue was resolved. Ultimately, this was solved by CinC SAC, who definitely wanted the images.

When imagery was likely to be used for unclassified purposes, for public and non-cleared personnel, the problem was solved primarily by carefully selecting camera angles or discreetly positioned people or objects to hide the classified items.

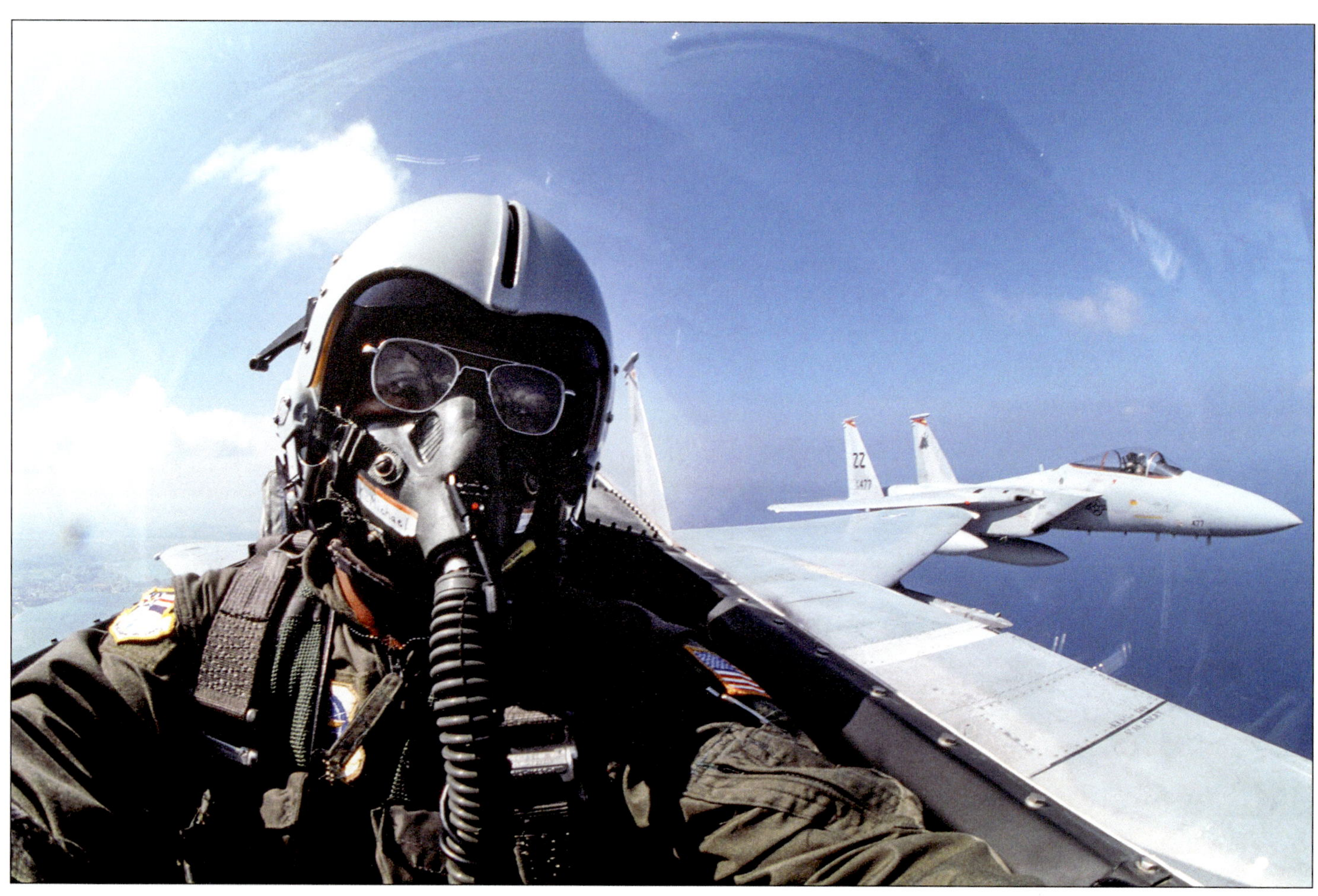

A perk of being an AAVS flight-trained photographer. If you are having a great time, why not take a 'selfie?' SSgt Donald McMichael in the back seat of an 18th TFW F-15D during the 'William Tell 84' weapons meet at Tyndall AFB. (USAF/SSgt Donald McMichael)

10

COMBAT CAMERA AND THE 1990–91 GULF WAR

After the major operation in Panama from late December 1989, AAVS was looking at the transformations taking place in the Soviet Union. The thaw in the Cold War was well advanced and showed no signs of slowing. At that stage, AAVS's organisation remained largely unchanged, but in January 1990, 'Combat Camera' was officially added to their AAVS squadron designations.

After the Iraqi invasion of Kuwait in August 1990, the US-led coalition's Operation Desert Shield and Desert Storm became a landmark in the history of Combat Camera. The AAVS and much of the US military soon embarked on a vast expeditionary mission centred on Saudi Arabia. With operating locations scattered around the region, it was later characterised by some military commentators as 'the first video war'. As Greg Krager described, AAVS 'Created an Air Force-led organisation in the Gulf with the other service branches incorporated into it. Those in-theatre became part of the 1615th Audiovisual Squadron (Provisional) Combat Camera. We had photo and video journalists, an editing team, plus photo maintenance technicians who operated a wet film-processing photo lab'.

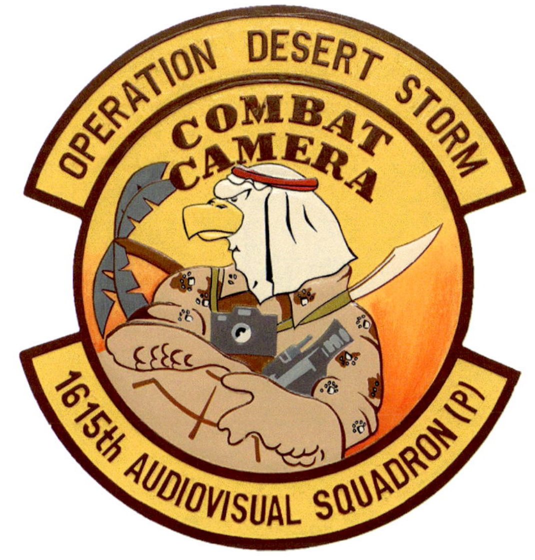

The 1615th Audiovisual Squadron (Provisional) Combat Camera was created to manage AAVS operations during Desert Shield and Desert Storm. It incorporated US Army, Navy and Marine photographers and videographers. (USAF)

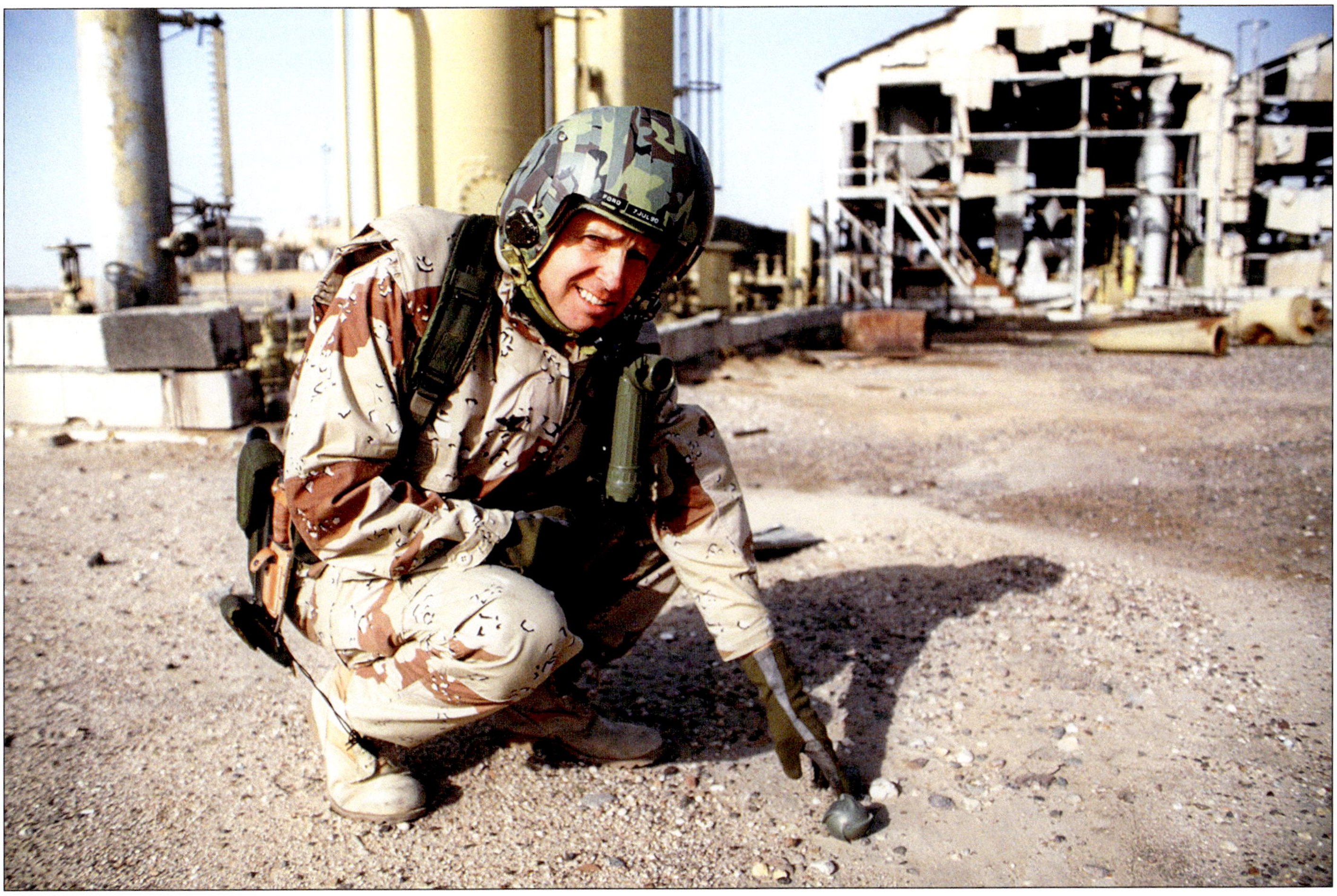

Col John Ford III, commander of the 1615th AVS (P), points to a cluster bomblet at a gas/oil separation plant in South Rumalia. (USAF/MSgt Jose Lopez)

Into Theatre

Lt Col David Gephardt was the Operations Officer for the Desert Shield deployment in 1990. He explained that for Desert Shield/ Storm, the USAF AAVS had 162 Combat Camera personnel in-theatre, the Army 37, Marines 41 and US Navy 100 – most onboard ships. These were formed into Joint Combat Camera Team (JCCT) Detachments spread across the region. Det 2 was at Dhahran Air Base, Det 3 at King Fahd IAP, Jeddah, and Det 4 at Sheikh Isa in Bahrain, with an operating location at Doha in Qatar. Det 5 was at New Jeddah, Det 6 at Al Jubail supporting the US Marines, Det 7, a US Navy and Coastguard unit in Bahrain and Det 8 at Al Minhad, with Operating Locations at Al Dhafra at Al Ain, all in the UAE. Det 9 operated from Al Karj, Det 10 from King Khalid Military City and Det 11 from Riyadh AB in Saudi Arabia.

In 1990, Greg Krager was a Project Officer with the 1352nd AVS at Norton AFB, California. He described the higher command structure:

> The National Command Authority (NCA) was our first and biggest customer. We had a permanent Joint Camera Center (JCC) in the Pentagon to collect information from all the armed services. We assembled the still and video imagery and passed it through to the JCS and the National Command Authority, including the White House, when appropriate. This was our primary job; we were their eyes and ears in the field.

For the Gulf conflict, Greg Krager commanded Detachment 1 in Riyadh, with 16 USAF personnel and one member from the US Army:

> We had another editing team operating out of Riyadh's Saudi Ministry of Defense building. Early during Desert Shield, the NCA demanded information about the ongoing bare base construction programme taking place across the theatre. We had deployed to many locations where there was absolutely nothing. USAF Red Horse and US Army engineers had to

build all the infrastructure required for future operations, so we needed to get images back to show their progress. We also identified challenges being faced by personnel in the field. We didn't want to sugarcoat things; we needed to highlight problems and successes. For example, we interviewed a fast jet maintenance technician, and he demonstrated the problem he and his colleagues were having with a particular wrench when working on fighter aircraft. Someone in the Pentagon picked up the video and quickly contracted for a redesigned, better piece of equipment that was rushed to the Gulf.

In-theatre, a C-130 shuttle service operated between several bases every few days, collecting films and videos and dropping them back to AAVS HQ before being transported to the US:

> Our material was edited by the JCC and passed onto those who needed to see it. The classified items we collected went to specific individuals or offices, and the more general material went to an internal Pentagon pool for broader access. A small amount of imagery was released to the public domain. Still, the main goal was to inform the Chairman of the Joint Chiefs Office; it was responsible for briefing the President on developments.

Short clips were even used for the all-important Presidential Daily Brief for George Bush.

By 1990, Hans Deffner was an experienced photojournalist and probably the first stills photographer to arrive in-theatre:

> When we left the US in early August 1990, we were not told precisely where we were going. As we were getting ready to land in Saudi, we were instructed to insert our war filters into our gas masks, and that was when we suddenly realised things were real. Over the next few weeks, we did a lot of moving around, sleeping in backrooms and on floors.

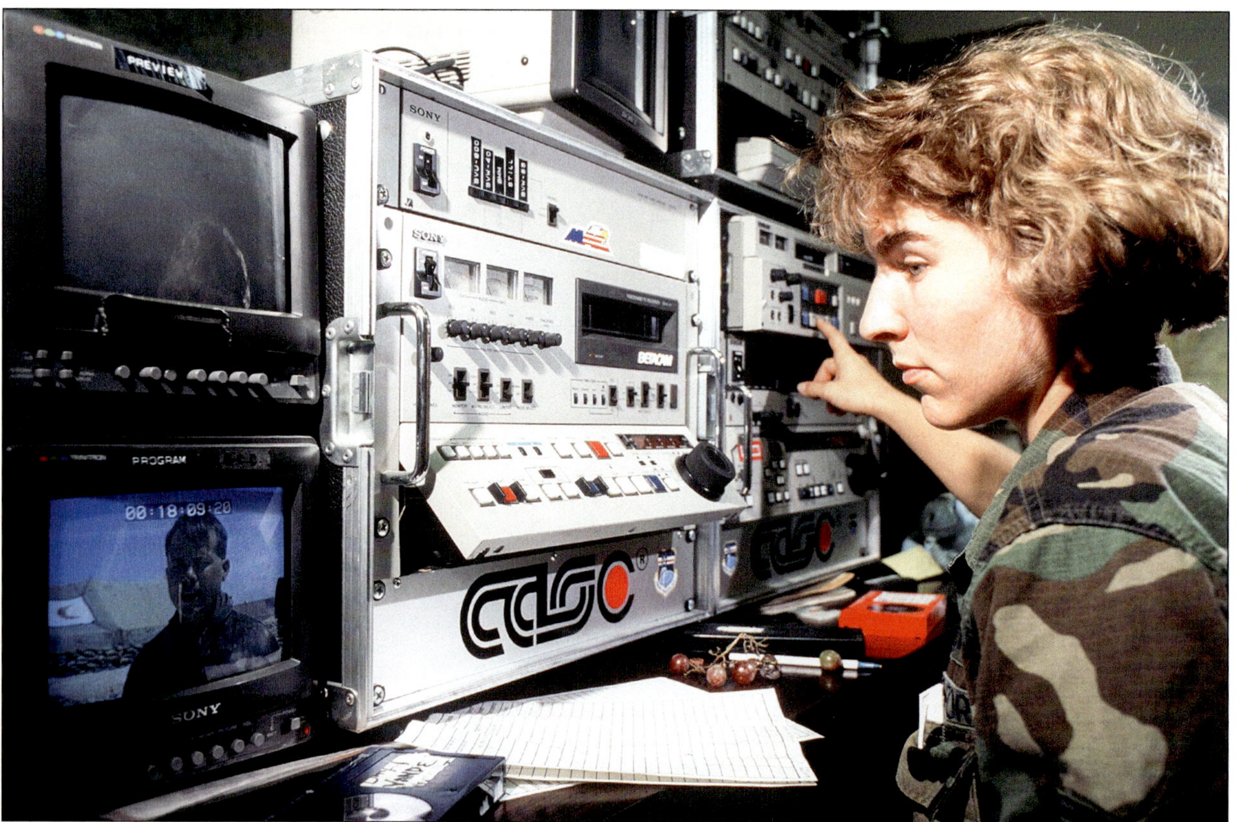

From deep underground in the Saudi Ministry of Defense building, Riyadh, the AAVS team edited and passed material back to the Pentagon. (USAF)

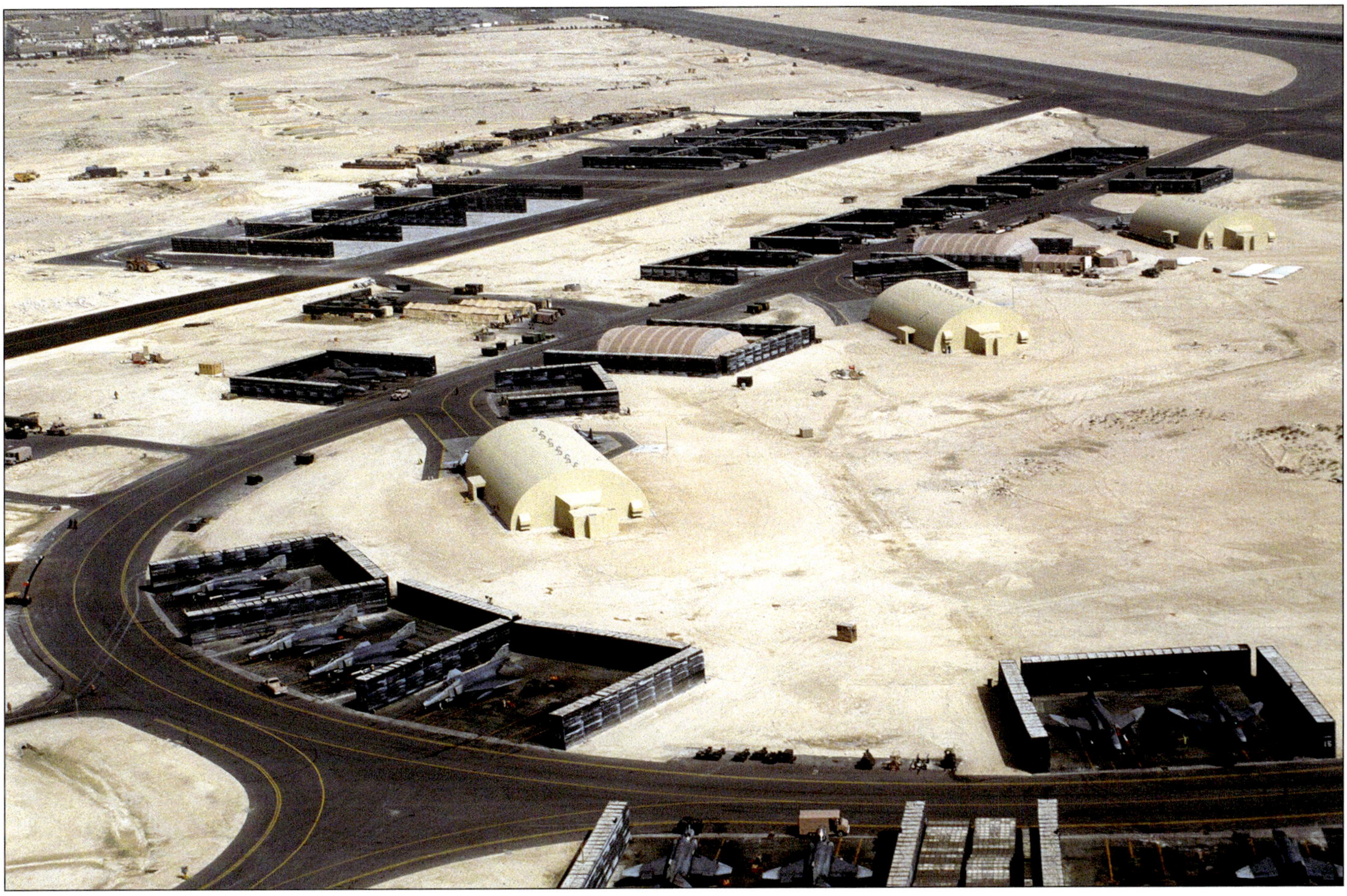

Great efforts were made to document the progress of infrastructure construction such as these revetments prepared for the 35th TFWs F-4Gs at Shaikh Isa AB. (USAF/TSgt Paul Page)

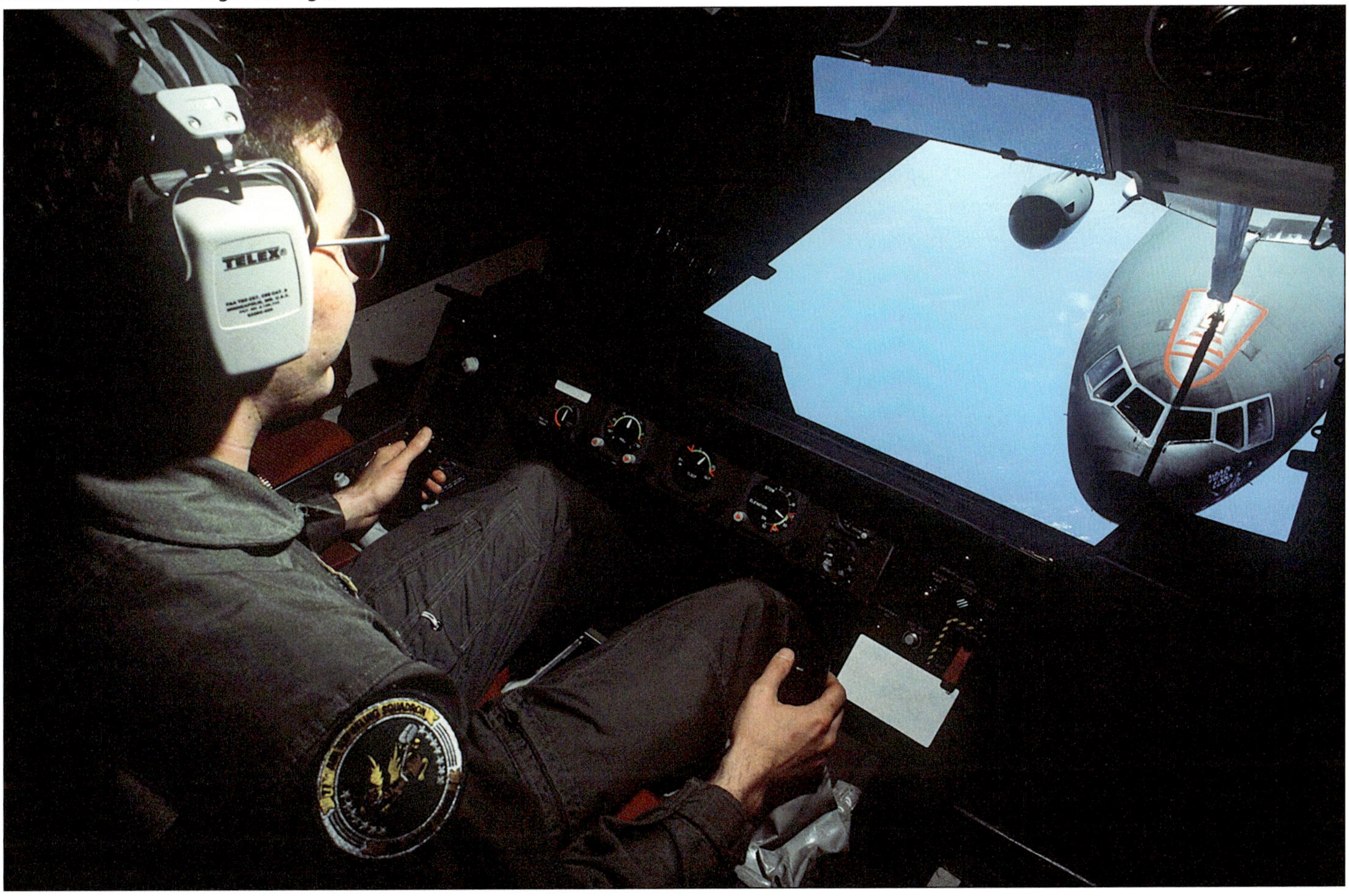

AAVS Photographers were assigned to regularly work from KC-135 and KC-10 tankers in the Gulf during 1990–91. (USAF/TSgt Hans Deffner)

He continued:

> In the build-up to the war, I was based at Riyadh, where a tanker squadron was based. I flew with them multiple times each week and soon developed a good working relationship with their Operations Officer. The unit wanted pictures of their KC-135s refuelling as many different aircraft as possible, so I flew with them all the time and got some awesome images.
>
> Our primary medium was 100 ASA slide film, but we were asked to shoot more black and white and colour negative images for a while. I took two lots of Kodak Ektachrome 100 Plus1 36 exposure slide film, one pack of Kodak T-MAX 100 black and white film and another of colour negative, put them in a big film bag, shook it up and pulled films out randomly. Each roll we used had to be slated at the start with our name, date, location and subject. In the early part of Desert Shield, we did not even see the pictures we had taken. It was just bagged and sent to the Pentagon for processing, so there was always a bit of trepidation from shooting stuff and sending it to DC without ever seeing it.

Black Jets

Hans was one of the first photographers to be given access to photograph the then Top Secret F-117 'Stealth Fighters'.

> It was kept very cloak and dagger when the F-117s arrived in the Gulf. We got a call one day, and with a videographer, we were told to go to a specific location and photograph their operations. We got there in a roundabout fashion and were just dropped out on the flight line in the darkness. To say the F-117 wing commander was not pleased to see us was an understatement. To his credit, he was very professional; he called our leadership and chewed them out but was extremely courteous to us, well aware we had not just turned up on our own initiative. We were granted permission to take pictures of the F-117s. However, the Saudis had not given their permission for us to take pictures on their airfield, so, unable to wait for their agreement, we drove around the air base for the next two days in the back of a maintenance truck. We positioned it where we wanted to take pictures, opened the back doors, quickly took pictures, closed them and moved off. All done as covertly as possible.
>
> The day the air war was to start, I got a call from the KC-135 squadron Ops Officer who told me they had a real-world mission and we needed to be there that night. I got on the tanker with the videographer, and we filmed F-117s refuelling on their way to Baghdad. Our night vision equipment was cumbersome and produced poor-quality images. At the time, it was just another mission; we didn't appreciate just what a historic event we were documenting.

Fighter Forays

Dave 'Kiwi' van de Brake was one of the first cameramen selected to use video cameras when they were introduced to AAVS. Their new Sony Broadcast Betacam cameras weighed around 23 pounds. They had an inbuilt two-channel shotgun microphone and were sometimes mistaken as a 'shoulder-mounted rocket launcher'.

Van de Brake was based in Germany, and it was there, on his birthday in August 1990, that he heard the news of Saddam Hussein's invasion of Kuwait. Within five days, he was on the ground at Dhahran AB in Saudi Arabia, covering the F-15C-equipped 1st

TFW's air defence missions. The Wing was among the first to be rushed to Saudi Arabia to establish a US presence in case Saddam Hussein decided to roll on and invade Saudi Arabia:

> In the extreme Saudi heat, we started documenting operations. It took a while for the communications and intelligence infrastructure to catch up. For about the first month, we slept in the hallways of an aircraft hanger alongside the US Army's 82nd Aviation Brigade. We became friendly with them and accompanied them when they began setting up forward operating areas, documenting their activities.

Soon, Dave was moved to Shaikh Isa AB in Bahrein. 'We were there when the 35th TFW and their F-4G 'Wild Weasels' arrived. They were a very professional unit, ready to go from day one. We thoroughly covered their highly specialised mission, telling everyone's story'. Dave was working alongside AAVS colleague Chief Ed Scavio, 'We were a two-man team that created goodwill. We spent three months going to forward bases and isolated posts and setting up Media Operations at Jeddah, from where we covered the secret arrival of the B-52s in theatre'. At these often remote locations, they took pictures and 'messages to the family' videos of the troops and did 'on-scene' reports talking with troops and commanders, mainly collecting human interest stories.

> Using the mobile photo printers and video editing equipment, we brought along; we gave the troops individual prints and unit videos that they could send home to their families, home stations, squadrons and wings back in the US or Germany. These efforts earned us a lot of appreciation from the troops, on-scene commanders, and Riyadh. It also gave senior staff in Washington additional information on the 'real-time' situation at isolated forward units in the Gulf. Overall, this

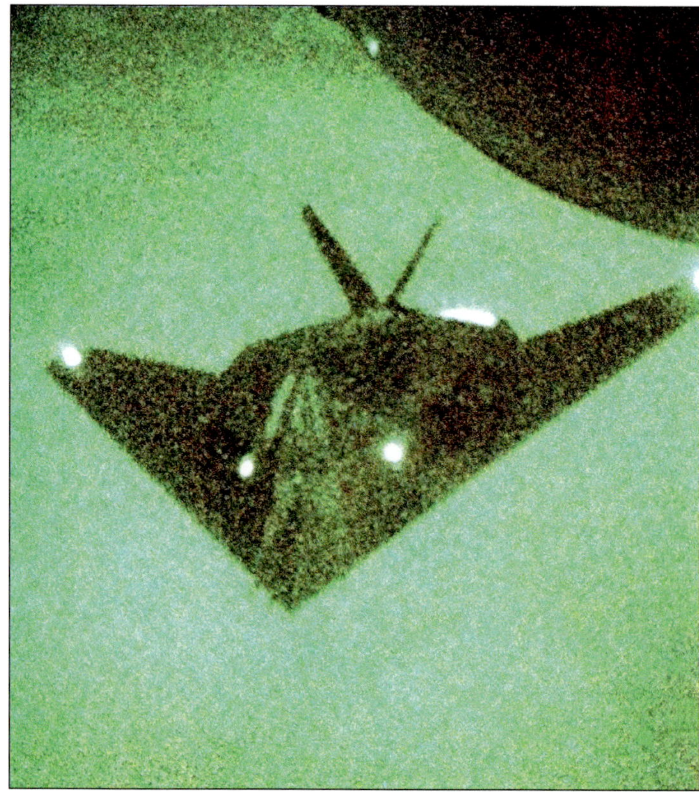

Camera night vision equipment was still in its infancy in 1991. Still, when the Desert Storm offensive started, it was possible to capture this image as an F-117 refuelled from a KC-135. (USAF/Hans Deffner)

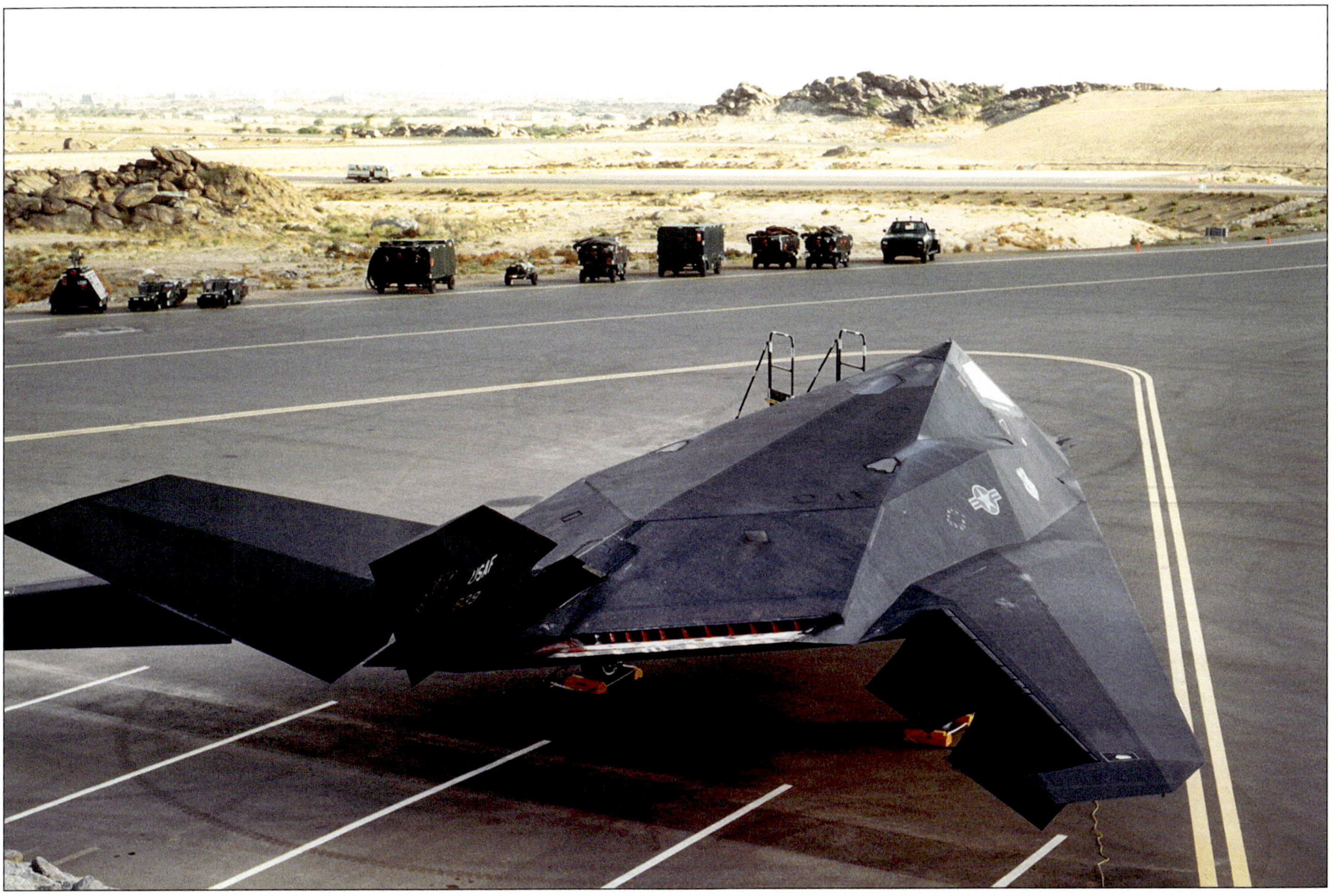

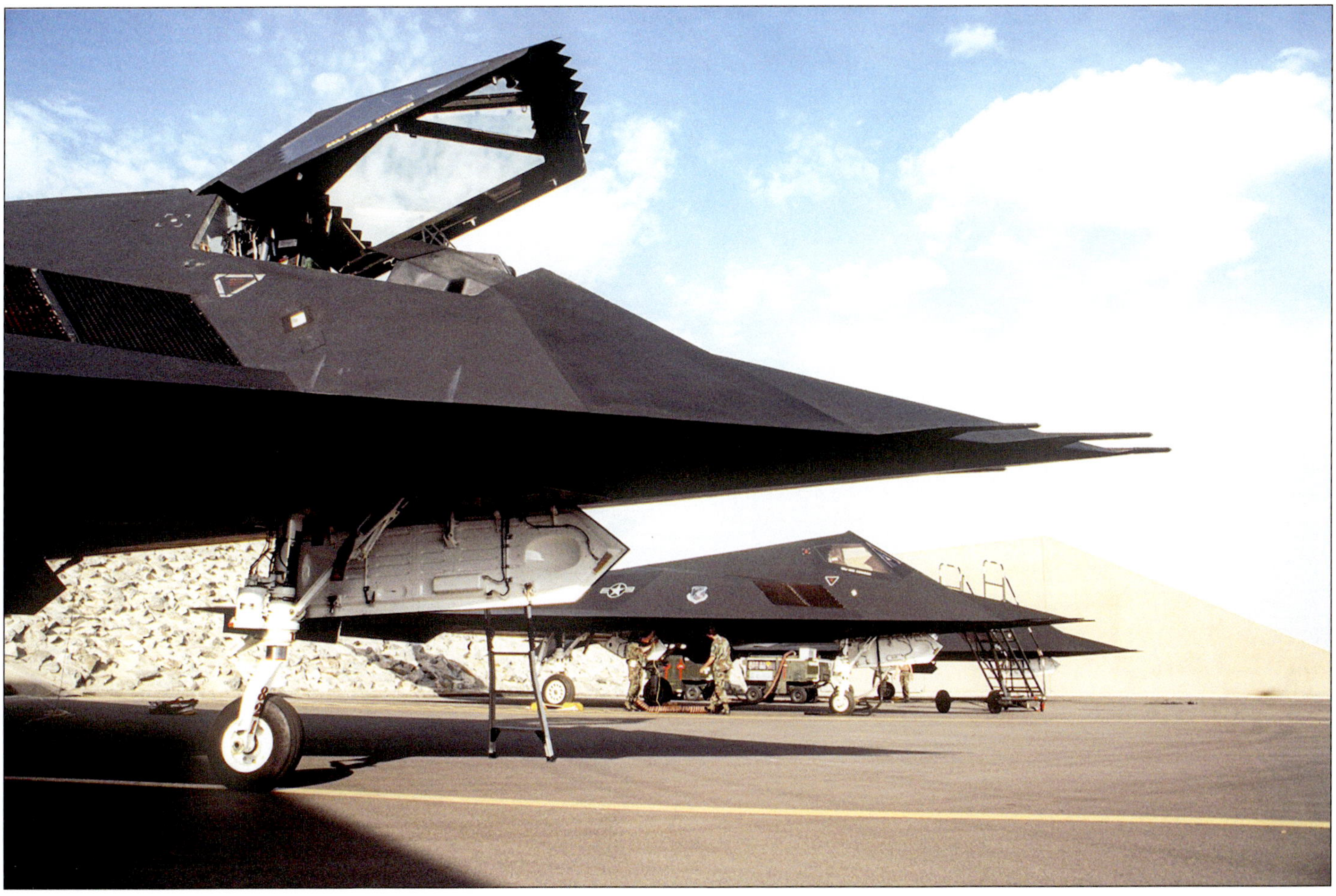

Discretion meant that taking pictures of the USAF's F-117s at their Saudi base had to be done surreptitiously. (USAF/Hans Deffner)

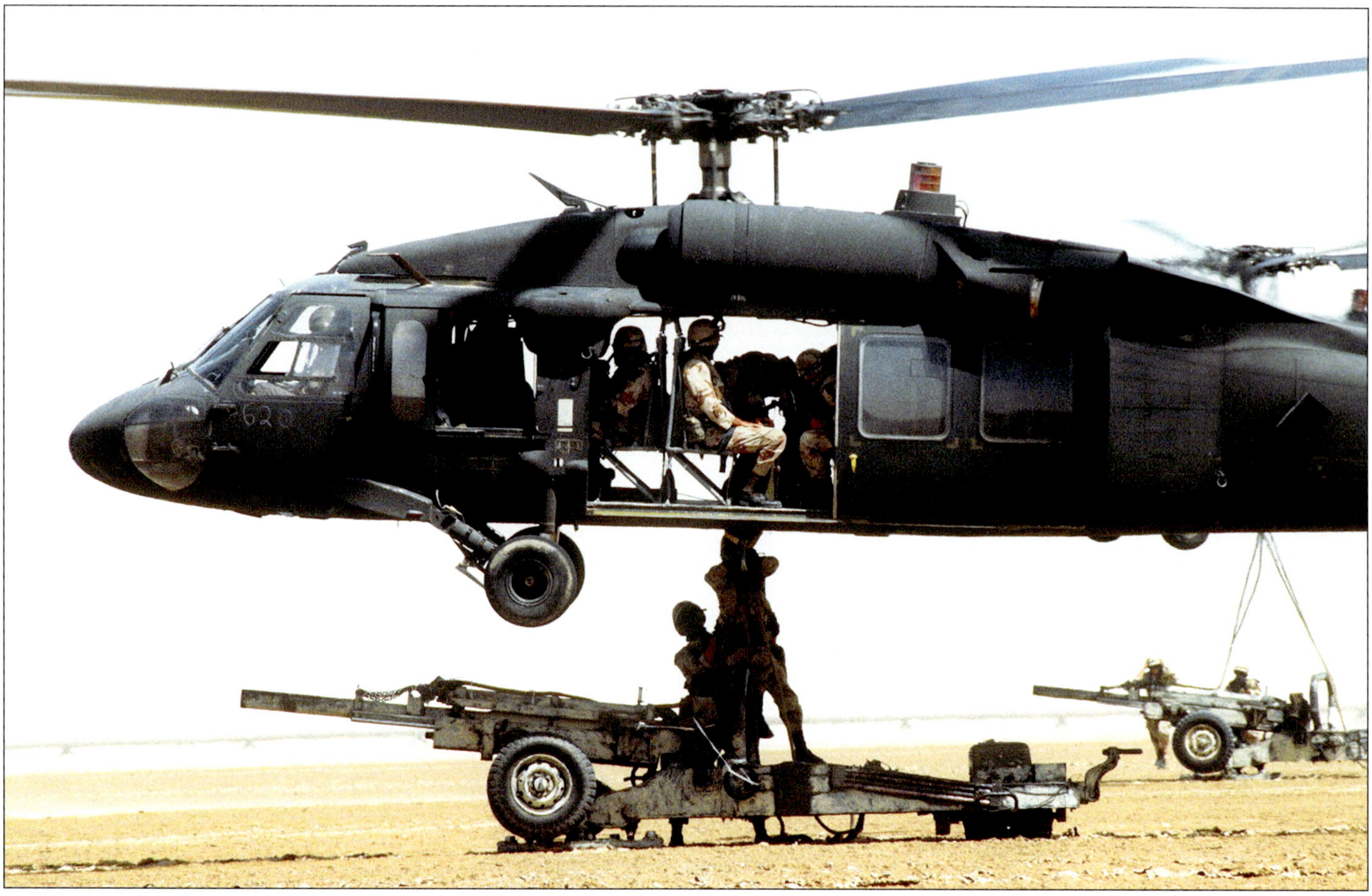

In the early days following their arrival in Saudi Arabia, Dave van de Brake and his colleagues spent time moving around with and filming the 82nd Aviation Brigade and their UH-60s. (USAF/Sgt Brian Cumper)

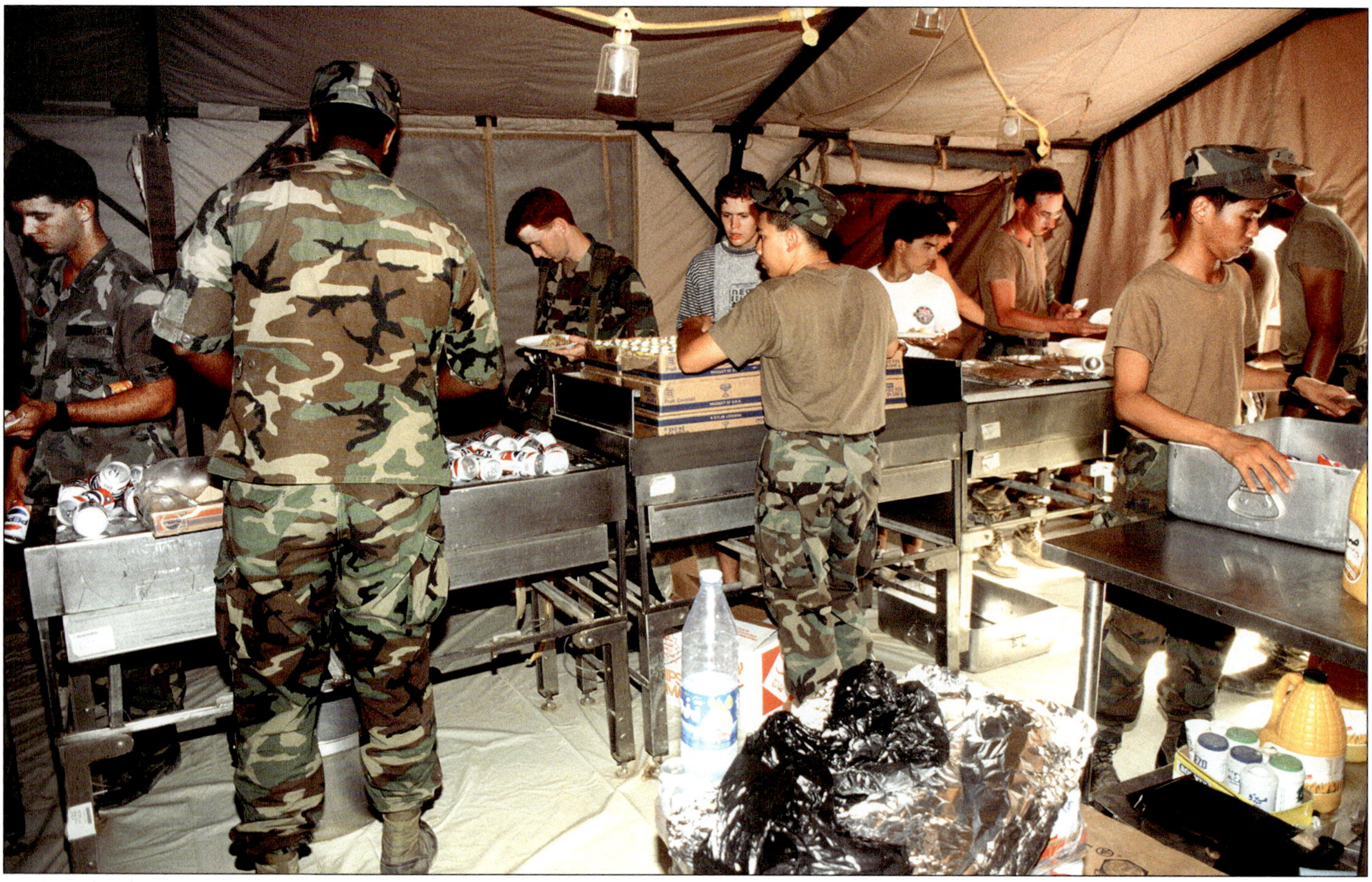

Photographers and videographers made a significant effort to visit small and remote units, doing the less glamorous but still vital jobs to take images for their units and families back home. (USAF/Sgt Brian Cumper)

was very successful. It often helped to mend hurt feelings for troops working far from the frontline in distant outposts or doing widely undervalued jobs.

Dave got to fly several times in the backseat of F-15Ds and F-15Es:

I was grateful being more used to flying in F-4s, where at six feet five inches, I was almost too tall to fit in. [But as he said], Loving aviation and getting paid to fly was perfect. The F-15 was the 'Cadillac' aircraft to fly in, with enough space to move your camera around to use photo angles I knew worked well. I got some very nice stuff…I always remembered the 'Don't Come Home without the Shot!'

I also got to fly with the Marine Corps and the tankers and did a few special operations flights. Early in the air war, several of the missions lasted 12 hours. We flew for a while, hit the refueller, then got shots of A-10s striking ground targets with black blossoms of smoke erupting below and then back to the tanker. I heard General Buster Glossom liked how I captured the Air Force story and interviewed the pilots about all aspects of escorting flight packages to the target and our later surveys of airfields we had recently hammered.

Partway through the air war:

We were requested to see if more Iraqi fighter aircraft could be drawn out. In an F-15, our formation was sent to fly over the mountains that marked the Iraq-Iran border. As the lead aircraft pushed up and across the mountains, I asked

my pilot, Lt Col Van Pelt, 'What is the expectation?' He responded, 'It's either going to be Battle of Britain Two or will signal there will be no more engagements.' [Everything stayed quiet.] The footage was transmitted by satellite back to Washington immediately when we returned. I received a call from the Secretary of Defense's Office, saying it had gone down extremely well with senior Air Force commanders and the JCS, demonstrating we had achieved full air superiority.

Dave van de Brake continued:

The newer, smaller Sony Hi8 camcorders began replacing our much bulkier but superior quality Betacams. During the squadron briefs for specific flights, we pre-briefed a few specific formations to fly for the photography. I also asked the crews if there was anything they wanted to try and capture, and we would factor that in, too. This often worked the best. The 45-degree-over-the-shoulder camera angle looked good, but as it was impossible to see the viewfinder, it was sometimes just a Hail Mary shot.

I had a great time filming as we did barrel rolls. During those, I had to brace myself against the aircraft sides to steady the camera as we rolled over the top. But still, as you began pulling higher g-forces, the camera became challenging to handle. I tried to rest part of the camera on the aircraft canopy rail to take some of the extra weight. The high 'g' manoeuvres and high-speed action stuff were real, and on the videos, you can hear the pilot or me grunting as the 'g' increased.

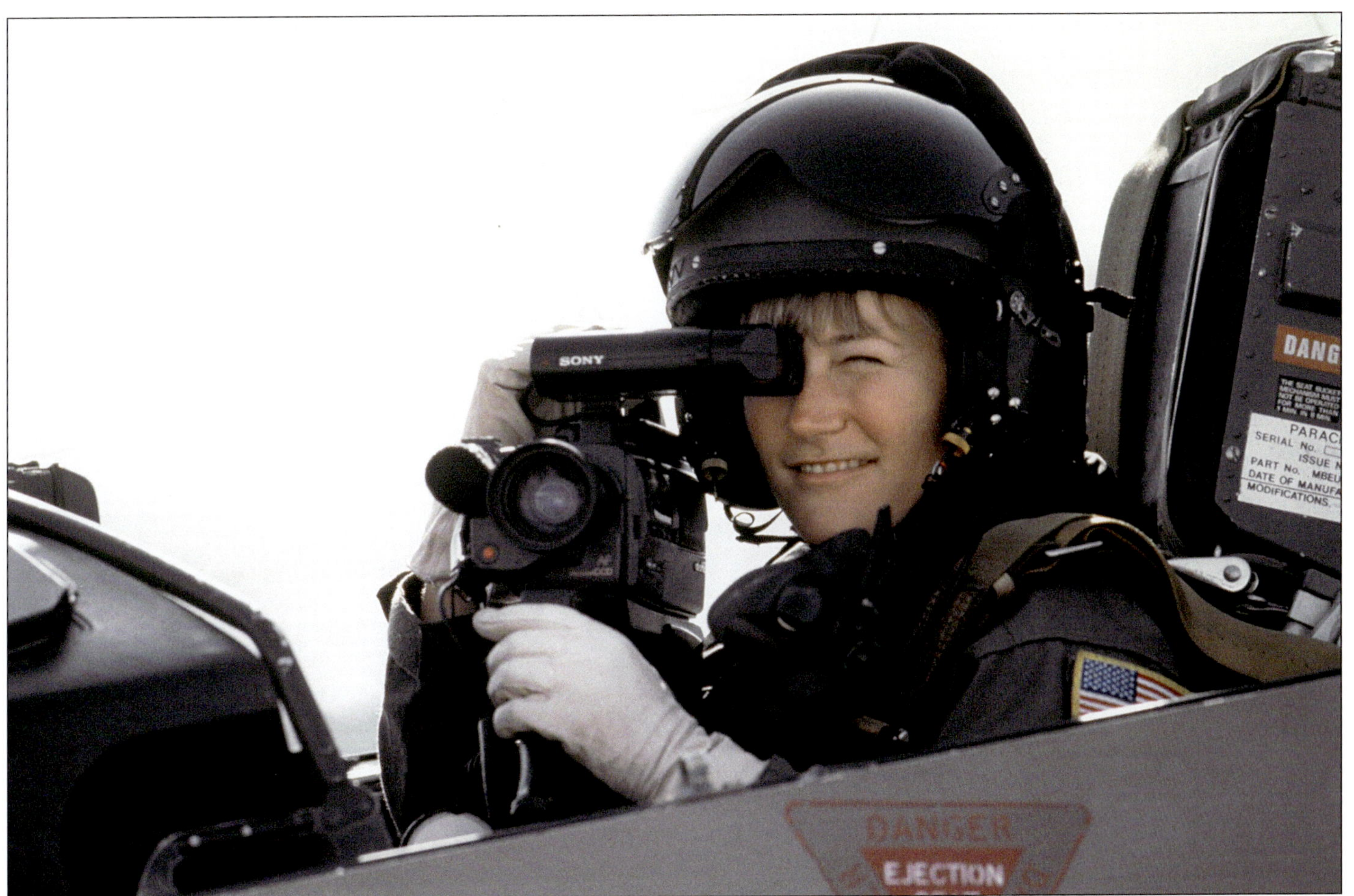

AAVS videographer in the rear seat of an F-4 during Desert Shield with a Sony Hi-8 camera. Some said it was inferior to the Betacam. Still, its compact size made it far easier to use in confined spaces like aircraft cockpits. (USAF)

Women in the Gulf

For female AAVS personnel, life during Desert Shield and Desert Storm was far more complicated. Angela Marie was an electronic specialist with AAVS. She was responsible for maintaining and repairing the cameras and associated equipment, keeping them free of the ever-present sand. Her technical skills saw her also involved in setting up special camera rigs, including fixing a camera in a B-52 bomb bay, activated by the copilot when its bombload was released.

In Jeddah, personnel were sometimes allowed to go off base to relax, but not in uniform. Female personnel had to wear culturally 'appropriate' clothing, including headdresses and be escorted. However, even then, they were not always safe from harassment by some Saudi citizens, who believed them to be Saudi women in the obvious and forbidden company of foreigners.

TSgt Rose Reynolds had joined the Air Force in July 1977 as a B-52 reconnaissance camera maintainer but switched to become a photographer in 1982. She graduated from the competitive specialist Military Photojournalism course at Syracuse University in 1985 and soon became flight-qualified. At the time, the Air Force only permitted women to become 'operational support flyers' and were not allowed to fly on combat missions. She said, 'I did get to fly with helos, fastburners, cargo and refuelers'. Her first working flight was in an F-4 at George AFB, supporting the development of a new podded system for the Wild Weasel F-4Gs.

When the Kuwait invasion occurred, Rose explained, 'I was at Norton AFB when word came down from Headquarters to prepare Combat Camera crews for departure to the Gulf. SSgt Jimmy Kemplin, an aircrew videographer and I teamed up to fly out and soon arrived in theatre on a KC-135 from Seymour Johnson AFB'.

Rose took on the additional duties of 'crew chief', coordinating the flights for the men permitted to fly combat missions. She did fly on numerous tanker flights, producing remarkable airborne images of A-10s, F-15Es, and US Navy A-6E, A-7E, and F-18s. On one occasion, 'I was allowed to fly in the navigator's seat with four F-111s on a dedicated photo mission. With the F-111's side-by-side seating and the formation on the pilot's side most of the time, shooting across the cockpit from the navigator's seat made photography tricky'.

On her broader experiences in the Gulf, Rose said that working with other US personnel posed few problems. With the Saudis, it was an entirely different matter. She explained:

I was a female and a 'photographer', so I'm not sure what could have been worse from their viewpoint! Saudi security people were assigned to us everywhere we photographed. In the beginning, we framed the shots, and then our escort looked through the lens to ensure nothing prohibited was in the shot. But after a couple of months, as we became more familiar, we were eventually allowed to coordinate our photo shoots over the phone.

As crew chief, it was difficult because the Saudis wouldn't speak or even look directly at me initially. Over the following months, I began to get a side eye from them, later a full-on look, and eventually, SSgt Kemplin and SSgt Brown didn't even have to 'translate' our conversations. It eventually got to the point where we were all invited to tea before starting our day's work. When our team left, the head of Saudi security even came to the airport and hugged us all goodbye.

In the end, it was the professional relationships and eventual friendships I was able to form with the Saudis that remain one of my most memorable takeaways from the Gulf.

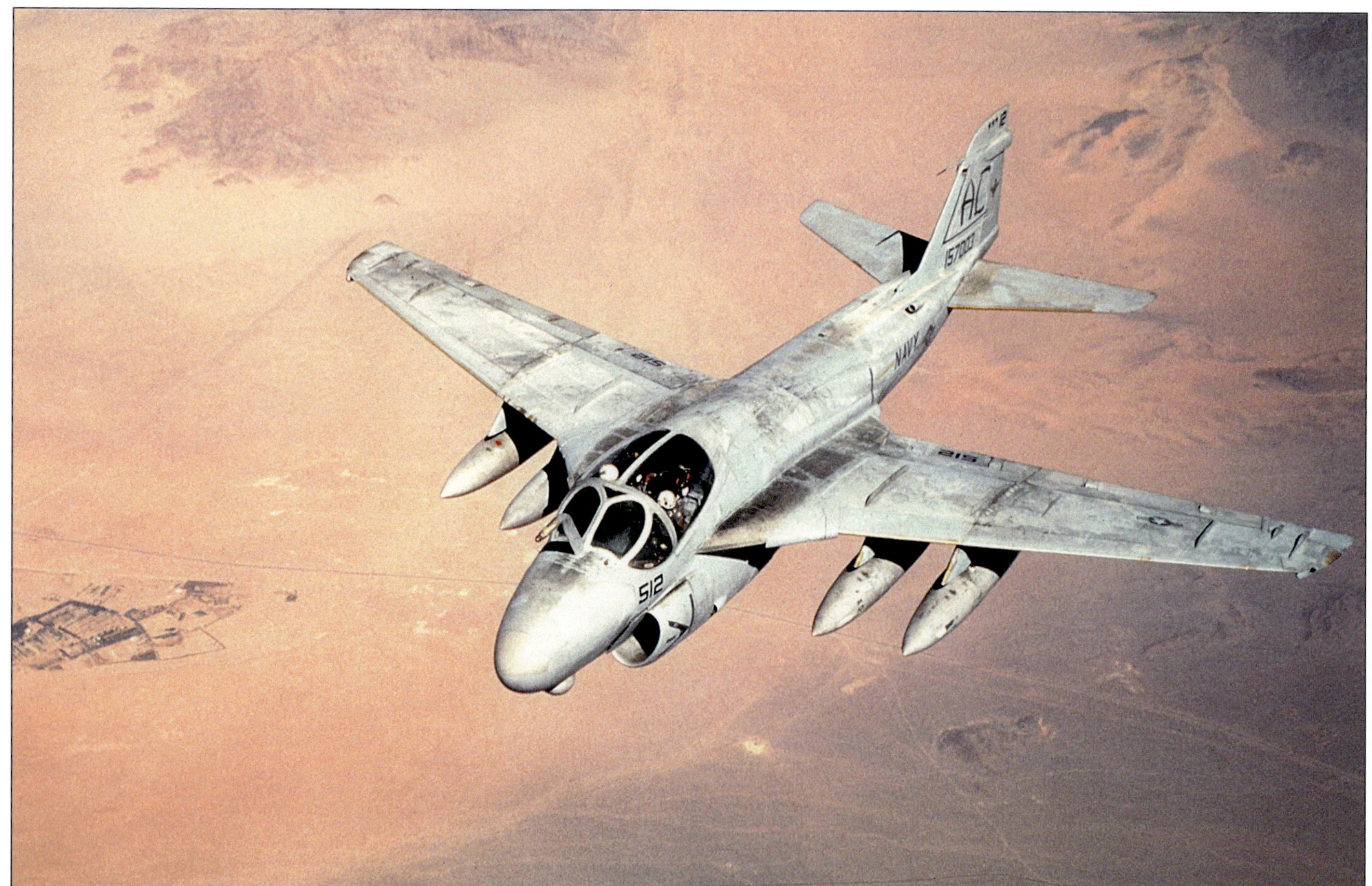

Many air-to-air images from the Gulf War came from AAVS personnel flying in USAF KC-135 and KC-10 tankers during refuelling operations, including this US Navy A-6E Intruder. (USAF/TSgt Rose Reynolds)

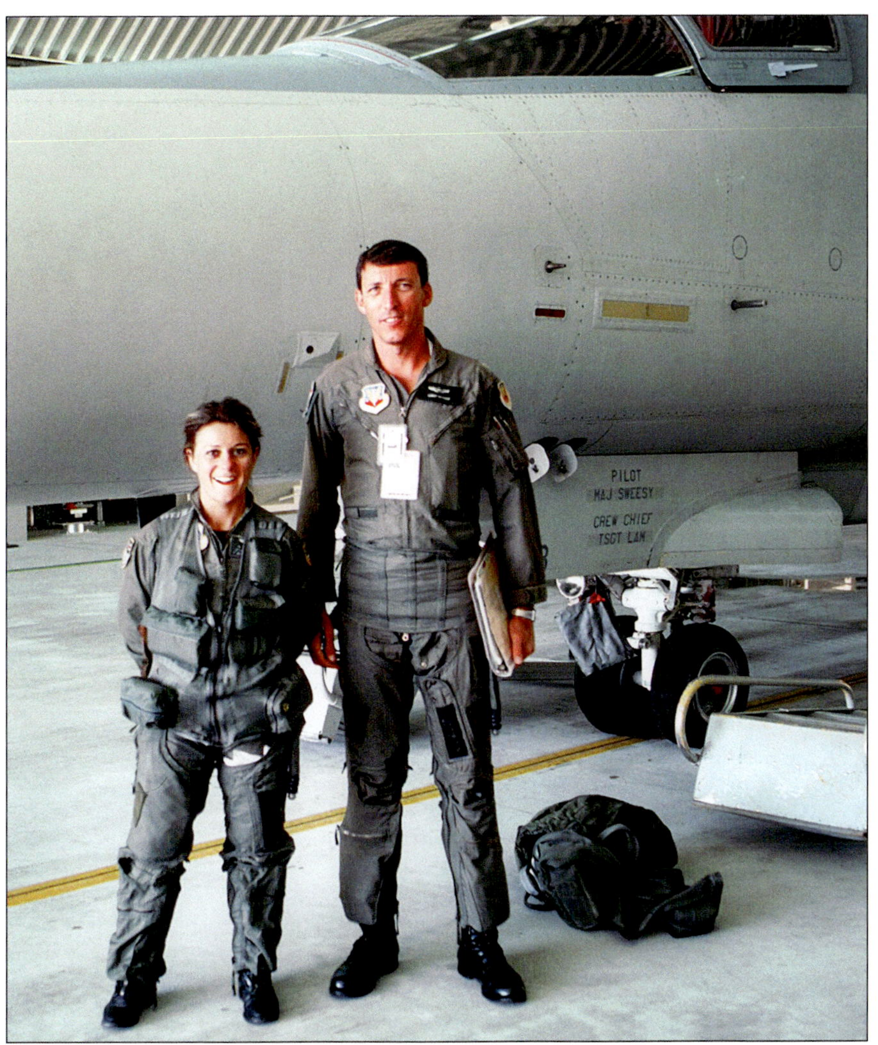

TSgt Rose Reynolds became the first female flight-qualified Combat Camera photojournalist. From an EF-111A, she captured this formation of 48th TFW F-111Fs and another EF-111A during Desert Shield. (USAF)

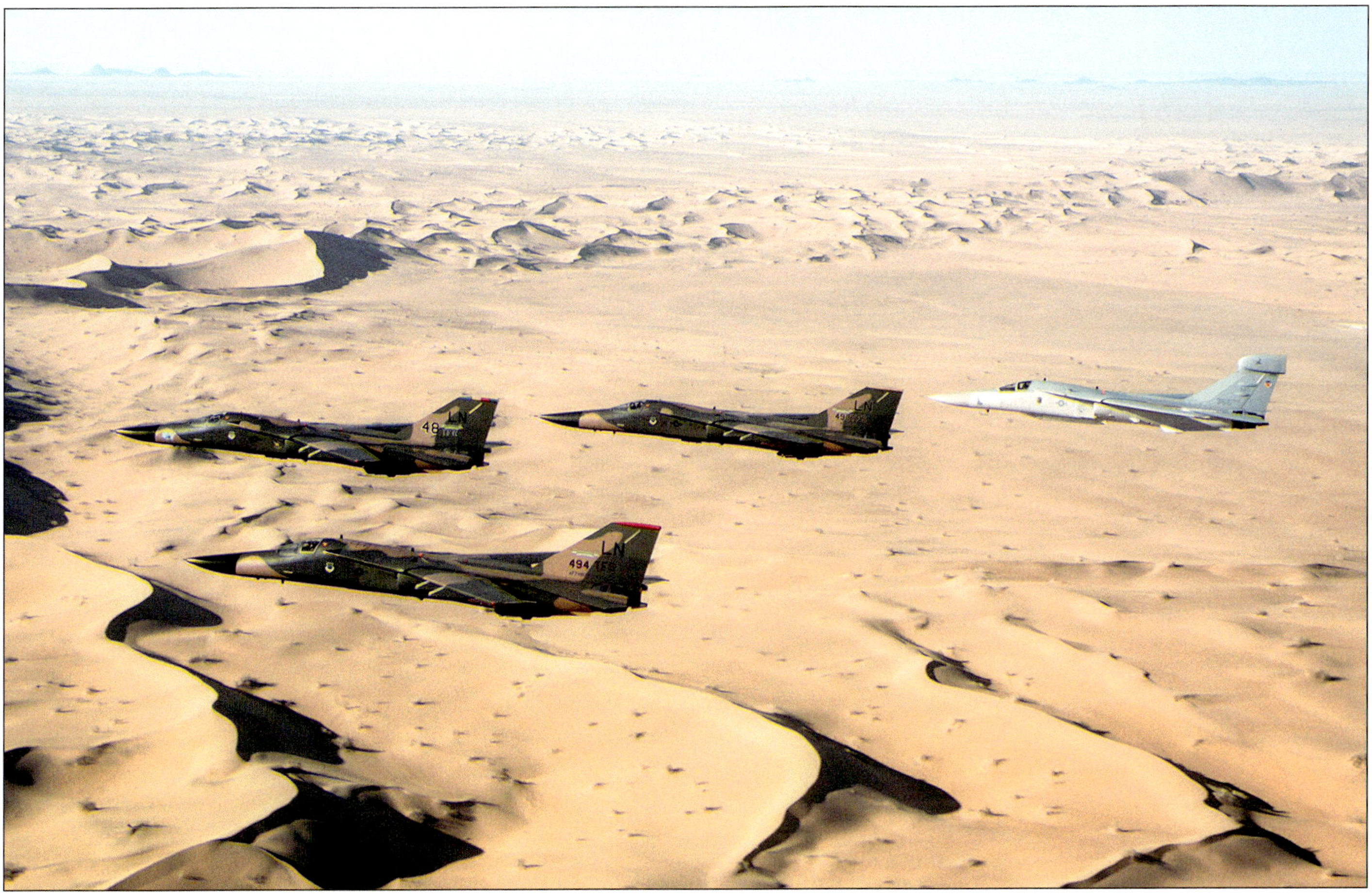

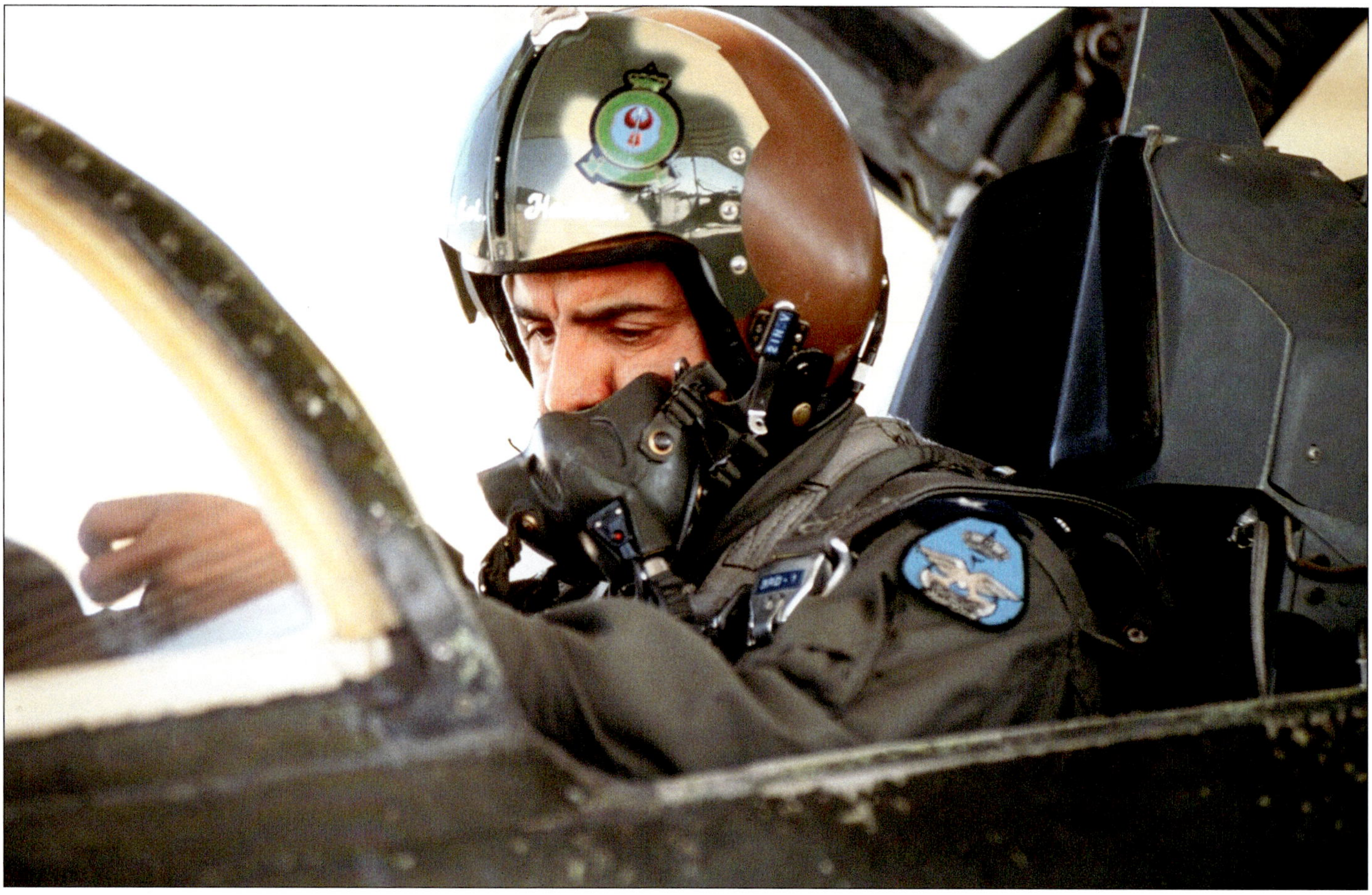

Lt Col Hassoon, the CO of 3 Squadron Royal Saudi Air Force, prepares for a flight in an F-5. For female US service members, working with Saudi military personnel imposed an extra layer of difficulty and frustration. (USAF/TSgt Rose Reynolds)

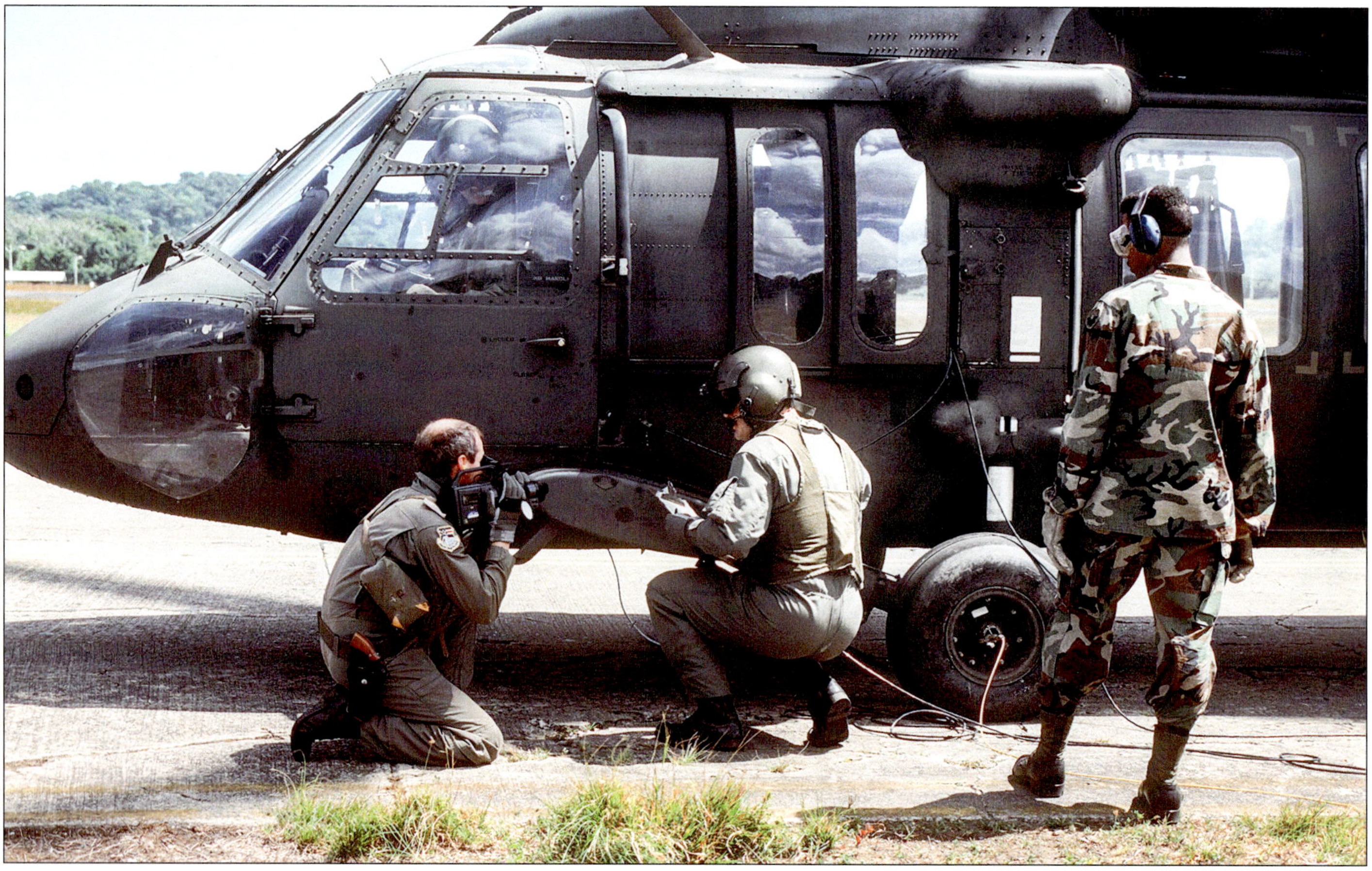

SSgt Jimmy Kemplin films a field operation with a US Army UH-60 during Operation Just Cause in Panama. Just over a year later, like many AAVS personnel, he worked in Saudi Arabia during Operation Desert Shield/Desert Storm. He had to interface with Saudi personnel for Crew Chief colleague TSgt Rose Reynolds because of Saudi restrictions on US servicewomen. (USAF/MSgt Ken Hammond)

Satellite Man

Chuck Reger explained:

During the Gulf War, I was a 'shooter,' but I was a shooter who had a technical ability that a lot of the other guys hadn't yet acquired. We were trying to maximize our capability as quickly as possible. At that moment, I was of more use as a troubleshooter than as a cameraman, I guess. In the middle of all the operations for Desert Shield, we did this amphibious landing exercise, 'Imminent Thunder' with Marines, right before things were ready to happen. Unknown to everyone then, it was a diversionary operation to deflect the Iraqis from the actual plan.

I went from Riyadh with a set of equipment to what was essentially just a grid location. I set up in the desert with an INMARSAT, laptop and computer equipment. Then, all the guys filming the amphibious landing and exercise came to me with their cameras. I quickly edited their stuff, picked three to five images, and transmitted them directly to the Pentagon. It was pretty cool stuff at the time.

It also told me how vulnerable we were when doing this. Every time I would fire up the INMARSAT and start transmitting, the British Tornados, the French Mirages and our F-15s and F-16s would pick up on the signal and scream right over the top of us at low level. We were emitting signals that could be easily located and targeted, and we might have gone 'boom' pretty quickly. And it's like, okay, I'm glad this is just an exercise, but do I really want to be doing this? It hit home how vulnerable we were.

Non-combat Photo-missions

As Greg Krager recalled:

We had people fly on B-52 operations and did lots of refuelling coverage from the KC-135s and KC-10s tankers. We also filmed from two-seat trainer versions of the F-15 and F-16s, acting as chase planes. Most of the time, when we got actual combat footage of the planes loaded with weapons flying their missions, they were filmed from the chase planes as they headed out. However, the chase planes had no operational combat role. The Air Force was reluctant to risk its jets and cameramen to accompany combat missions, so much of the fast jet filming away from the tankers was using specially set up photo-flights or training missions.

Our still photographers were shooting relatively high-resolution digital imagery for the time. Some were using adapted Nikon still cameras fitted with Kodak digital sensors. So it was weird because the front of the camera said Nikon, but the back with the hard drive said Kodak, and these also had a night vision capability.

We ended up with tons of support stuff, but obviously, we wanted more combat tactical fighter stuff, but we were pretty limited in what we could get. We even had to take some 'hero shots' because we lacked so much of the real stuff that we could release. We would get cargo planes to fly with their rear ramp down and have the fighters form up behind them. Often, the cargo planes maxed out on speed, but the willing fighter planes sometimes had to fly at very low speeds, close to stalling.

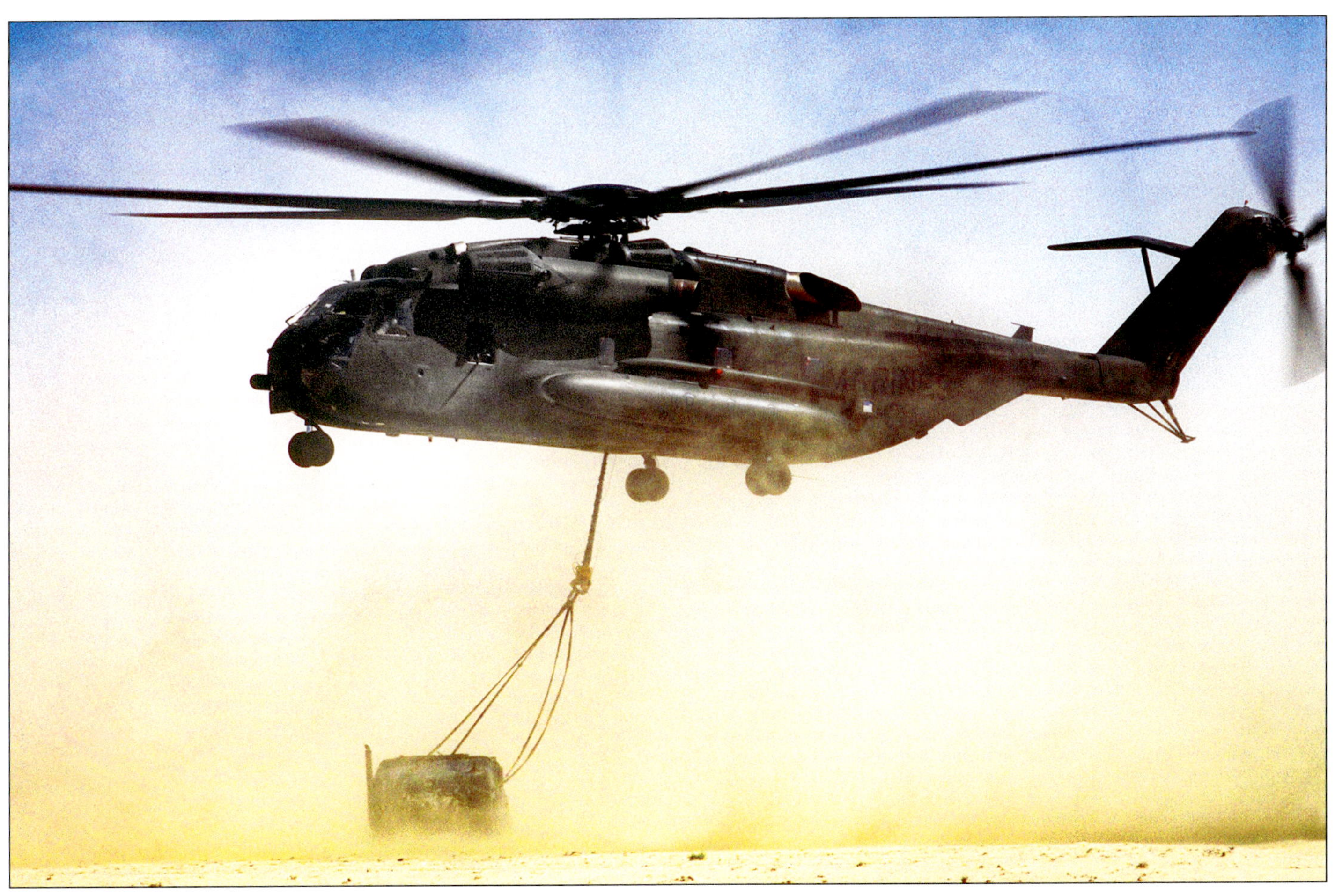

A US Marine CH-53 places a Humvee at a landing zone during Exercise 'Imminent Thunder' (USAF/SSgt Charles Reger)

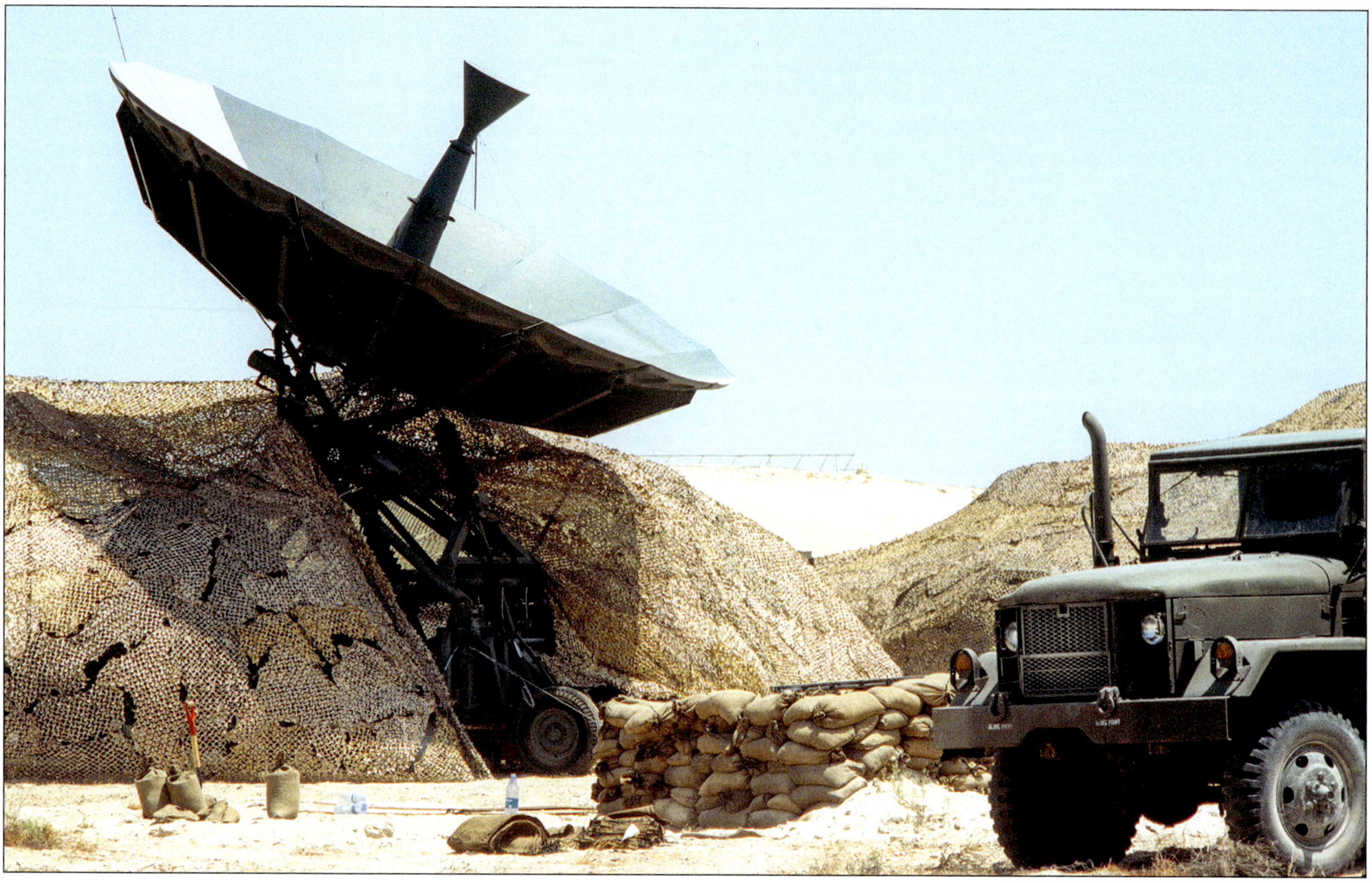

In 1990, digital imaging and data transmission were still in their comparative infancy with AAVS. The highest priority material was sent to the US via the Saudi government-managed commercial system in Riyadh. (USAF/Greg Krager)

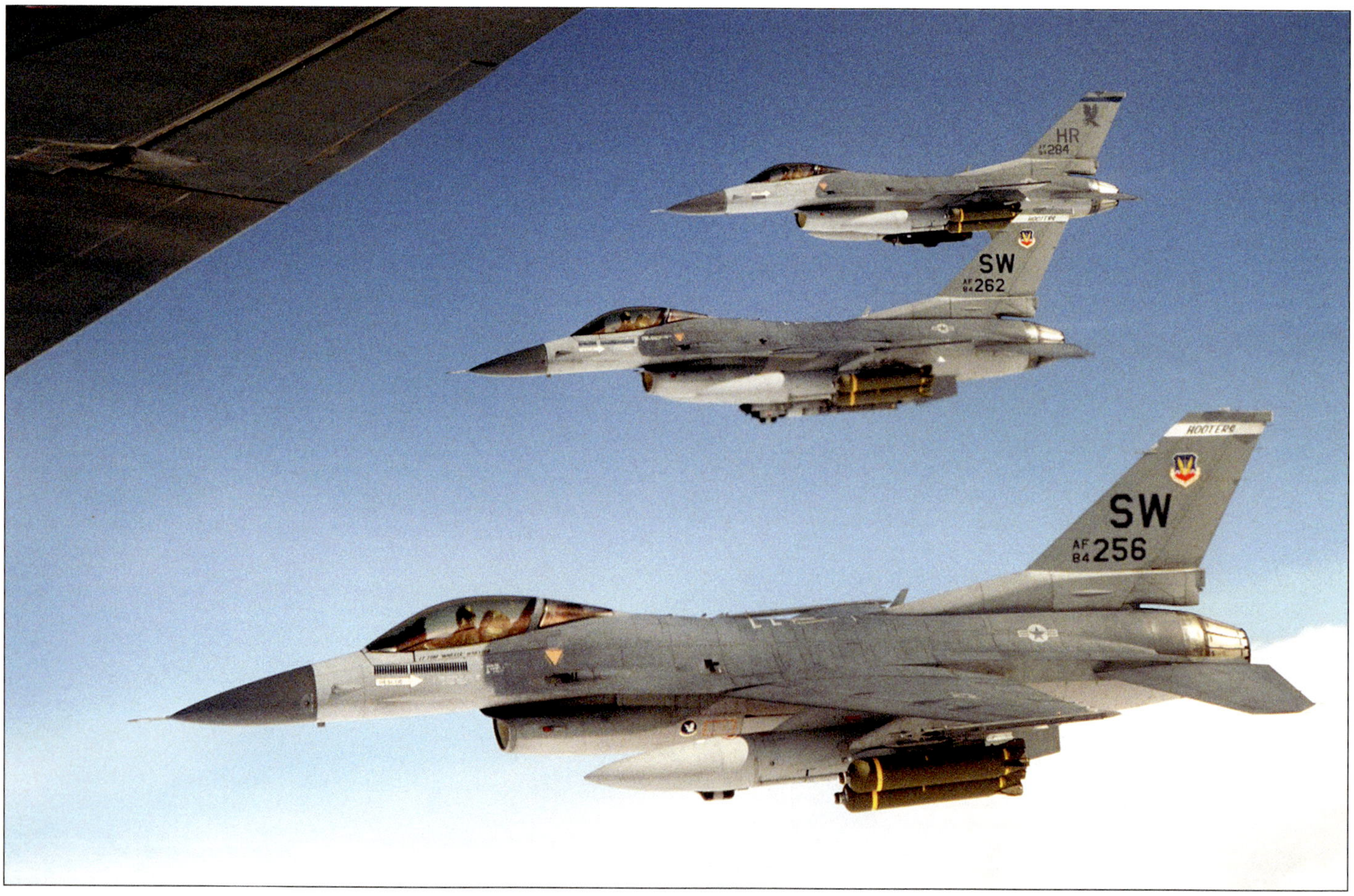

AAVS was reluctant to risk its personnel to fly on combat missions, so aircraft like these F-16s were filmed from a KC-135 tanker as they headed out on their missions. (USAF/TSgt Marvin Lynchard)

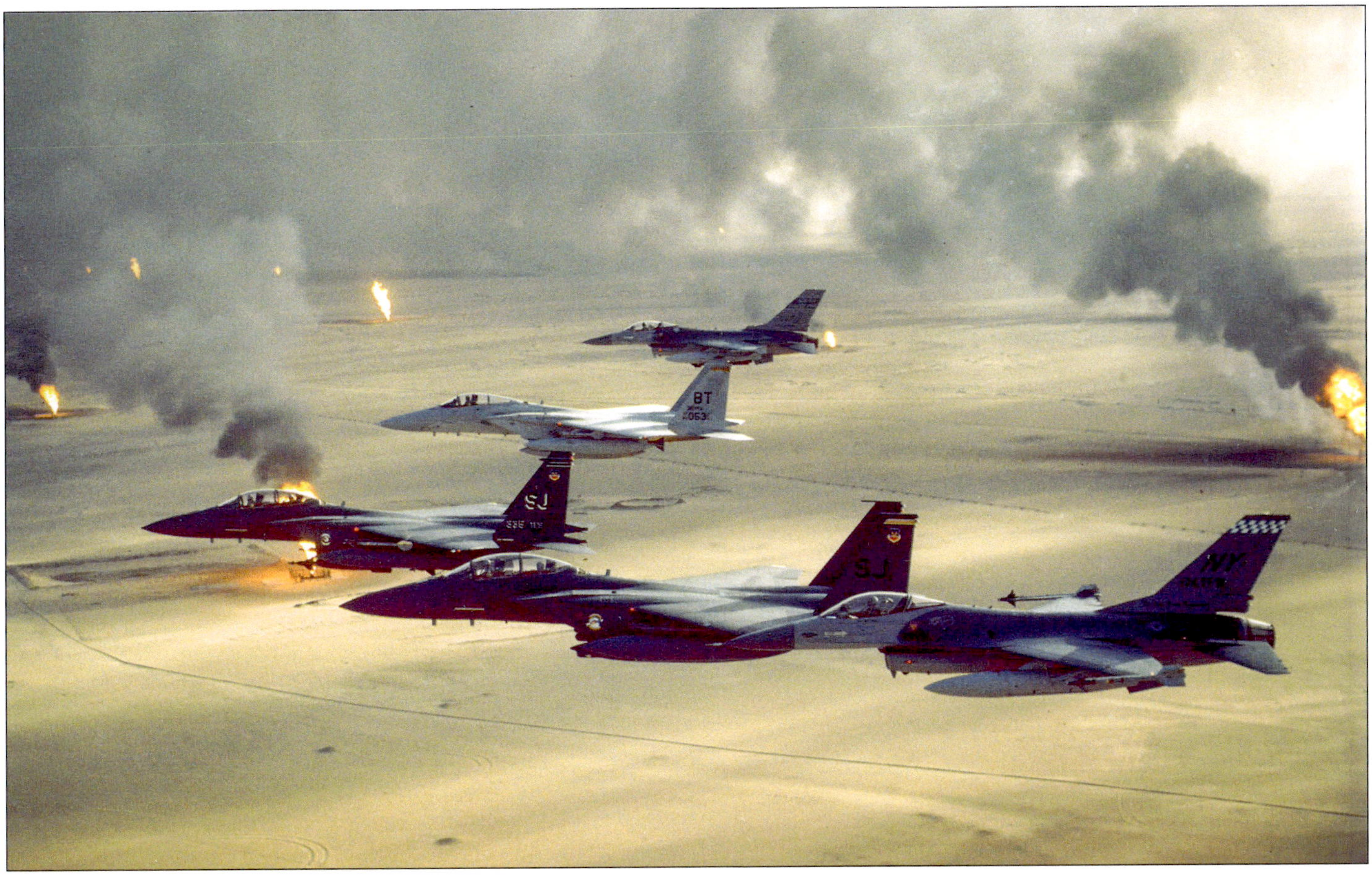

One of the more widely used aircraft shots from the Gulf War, staged using F-15s and F-16s from selected units, fly over burning oil wells in Kuwait. (USAF)

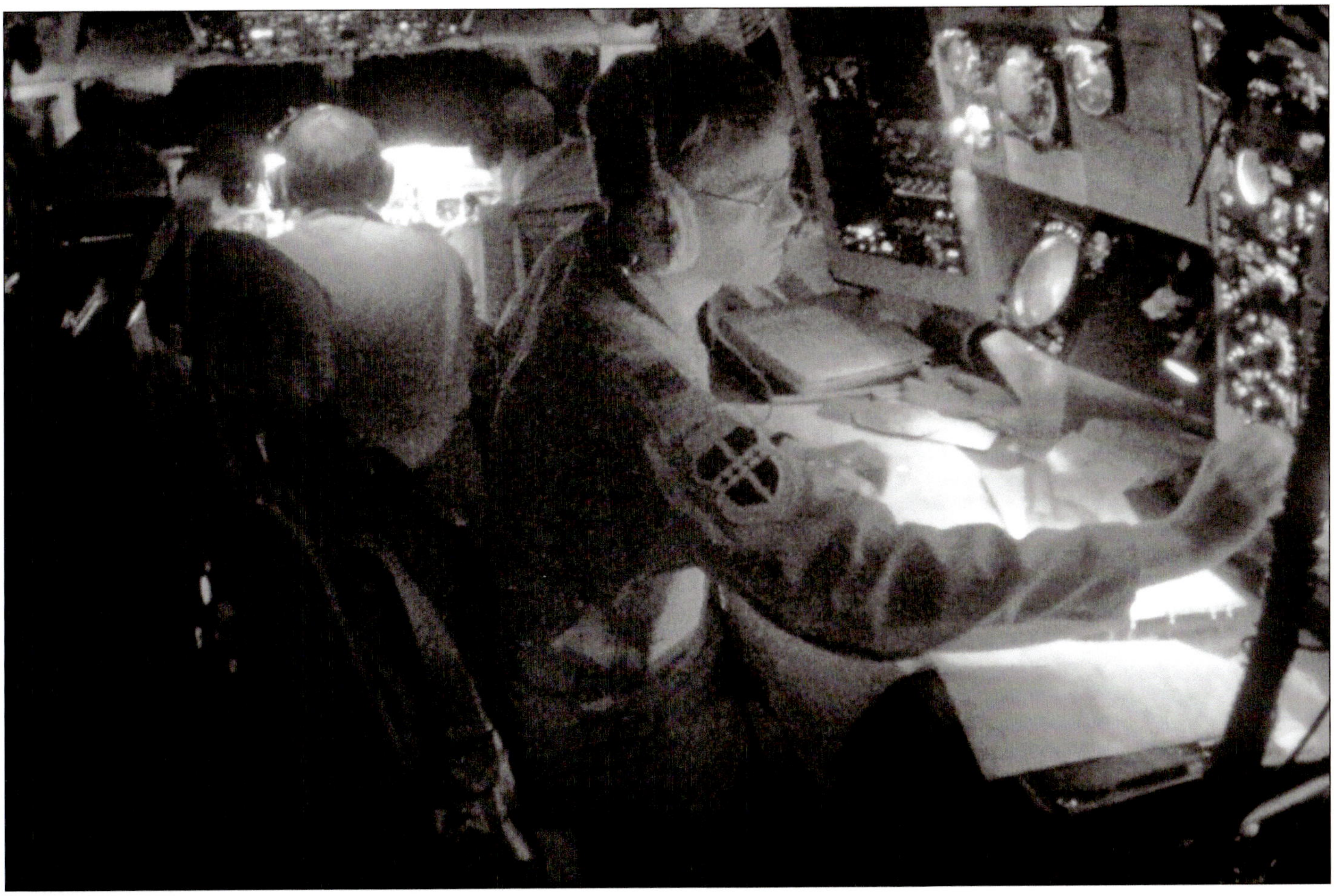

The flight deck of a USAF KC-135 during night refuelling operations during Desert Storm photographed using night vision equipment. (USAF/ TSgtHans Deffner)

Operating at night posed additional challenges, as Greg explained:

The F-117 stealth fighters were flying at night. It was always an impressive sight because they operated in blackout conditions without any lights. So you're just there waiting for it, and they don't reflect much light. When there was insufficient ambient light behind them, they were difficult to photograph.

We had early night vision cameras. They were the first generation and were not even close to modern performance. We put them on the still cameras and got some cool stuff. I remember these cameras were pretty rudimentary night vision systems, big and heavy. But then this company, Night Owl Optics, came out with a night vision system that we could put on smaller and single-lens reflex cameras for the still photographers out there.

On the Ground in Kuwait

On the second day of the ground war, Greg Krager and his team were dispatched in a convoy with an Army Reserve Civil Affairs Team to head into Kuwait. Even by that second day, the Army had penetrated much further than was expected:

There were Iraqi vehicles just littered both sides of the highway, with tanks still on fire and some pretty gruesome sights. Our Humvee was taken by someone else, so my team of eight was split between two civilian Isuzu Troopers, and there was no radio. Our vehicles got punctures and the convoy left us behind.

Once we got rolling again, we headed for the airport because I knew the Marines were there; I had no idea where the Army convoy went. They didn't even know where they were going. They thought they would set up in one of the hotels downtown, but didn't know where.

On that first night, we rolled up at Kuwait City airport. Because we were travelling at night in Isuzu Troopers, the Marines were ready to shoot at us. I'm just arriving there with my headlights on, and all these guys are there with their guns. I had my hands out the window and shouted we are Air Force. After some discussion, they helped us out, and we stayed the night with the Marines camped by their Light Armoured Vehicles.

After a day at the airport, there was a ceasefire, and I managed to find the rest of the Army Civil Affairs Team at the Kuwait International Hotel. There were oil well fires everywhere. You could hardly sleep at night because it was super bright with all the oil well fires around us. The fire's light reflected off the underside of the smoke clouds they were creating. It was a very eerie effect.

Any Air Force, Army, Navy or Marine assets that had still footage brought it to us, and I sent it back for processing. We had couriers moving around to get the video back to Riyadh for editing. That was a five-plus hour drive until they started the C-130 service, which took a week to get going.

We were there to try to get war crimes footage of the Iraqi torture devices because we had heard all these horrendous stories. We needed to document evidence. So I sent my still and video photographer to this ice rink, where the refrigeration units were used to store the bodies, including those of some children. I stayed outside as security to make sure no one attacked us. Seeing that naturally affected my guys, especially

those with young families at home. We were not prepared to get mentally wrecked by seeing that. But it had happened, and our job was to document it.

When we got back, I had to go through the video and still photos, which was the worst thing, trying to figure out what we would keep or discard. There was some pretty horrendous stuff. But we were there and documented some of their stories, interviewed families and determined what had happened to them. That work was not great, but we did it for a month. We handed over the footage for others to do further investigation.

Frustrations

SSgt Robert Zoucha was posted to the JCC at the Pentagon immediately following the start of Operation Desert Shield. He reviewed the cameramen's footage received overnight, edited it, and prepared the finished video materials for distribution:

I came in at nine in the morning because that was when we got the satellite feed from the Middle East. In Saudi Arabia, they did preliminary editing, went to a satellite uplink point in Riyadh, and sent the video material to us. It was downloaded near Washington and brought over to the Pentagon. We sorted it for the JCS, White House and the external news media. We tried to meet the external news media requests for footage with current material as it came from Saudi, or our archives if we didn't have contemporary materials.

Two months later:

As operations in theatre expanded further, my counterpart in Saudi wanted to go and film in the field. He sort of tricked me into replacing him deep underground at the Saudi Military Operation Defense Agency building in Riyadh. Nevertheless, I was happy to leave the Pentagon. I spent the next six and a half months in Saudi as chief of video editing for the theatre.

For me, the overall experience was frustrating, as I had spent the last 10 years on flying duties, and now I was sitting deep underground and unable to do the job I had been trained for. I found my experience of Desert Storm rewarding but stressful. It felt like a lot of weight for a 26-year-old Staff Sergent, with four people working for me, to be responsible for video editing in the entire theatre.

However, Robert did get occasional opportunities to film special features, including interviews with General Norman Schwarzkopf and USAF air boss General Charles Horner. 'After the war finished, on March 5, 1991, at the last moment, I was sent on a C-141 to Amman in Jordan as the videographer, with US Navy stills photographer PH2 Susan Carl. We filmed the return of the first 10 PoWs, who had arrived in Jordan by bus'.

In addition to combat documentation, other USAF photojournalists worked for the Armed Forces *Stars and Stripes* newspaper and *Airman Magazine*, and videographers collecting material for the *Air Force Now* video magazine. Their role was different from that of the AAVS COMDOC personnel. They would arrive at a location, complete a specific story for their publication, and move on to their next assignment.

In a later 'after action' analysis, Dave Gephardt identified shortcomings in the Joint Combat Camera Teams' operations during Desert Storm. These included the lack of wet processing equipment and just how high the demand for photographic printing

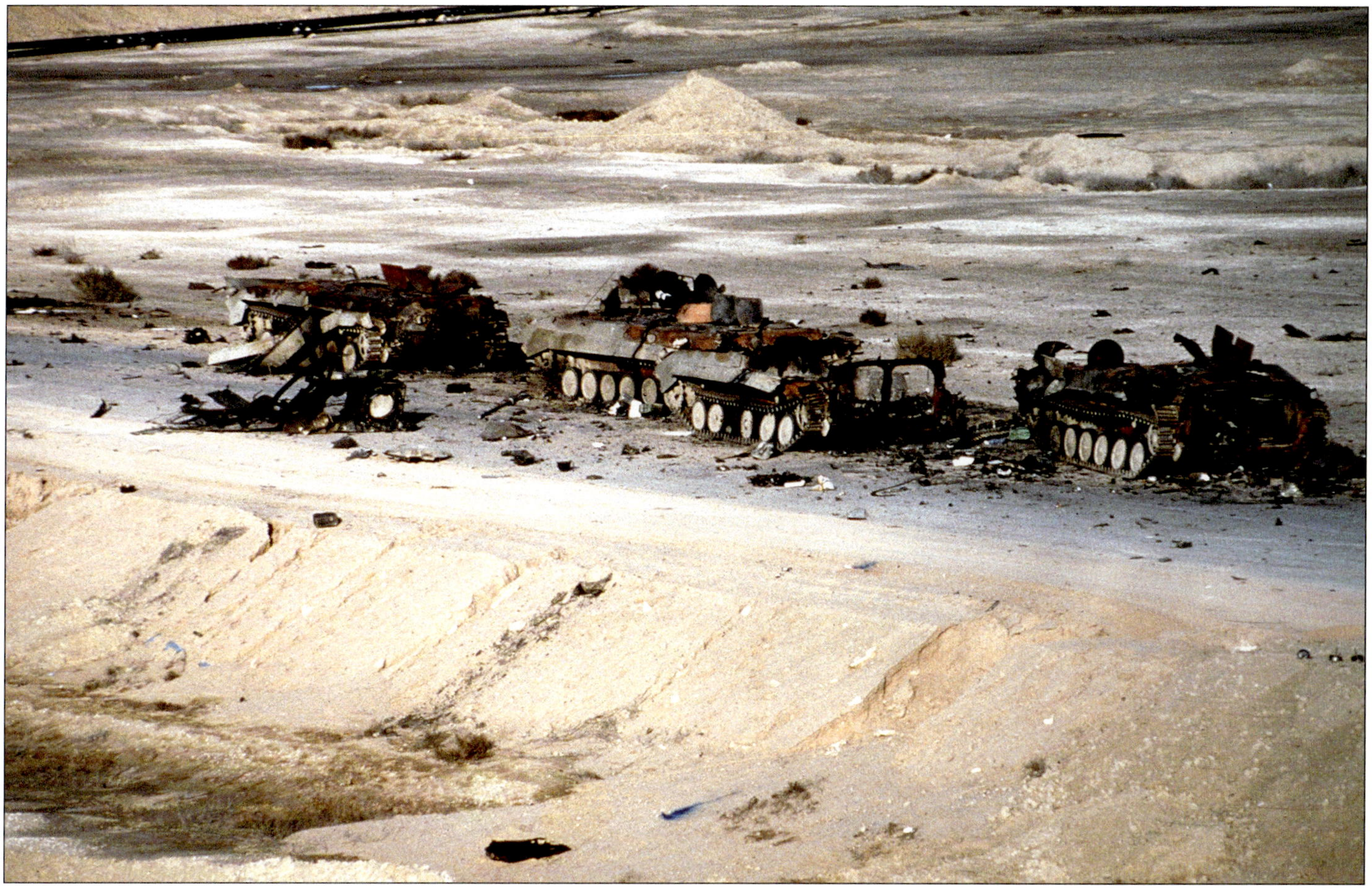

For Greg Krager and his team, the drive from Saudi Arabia to Kuwait City was strewn with destroyed Iraqi vehicles, including trucks, cars and armour like these BMP-1s. (USAF/Sgt Dean Wagner)

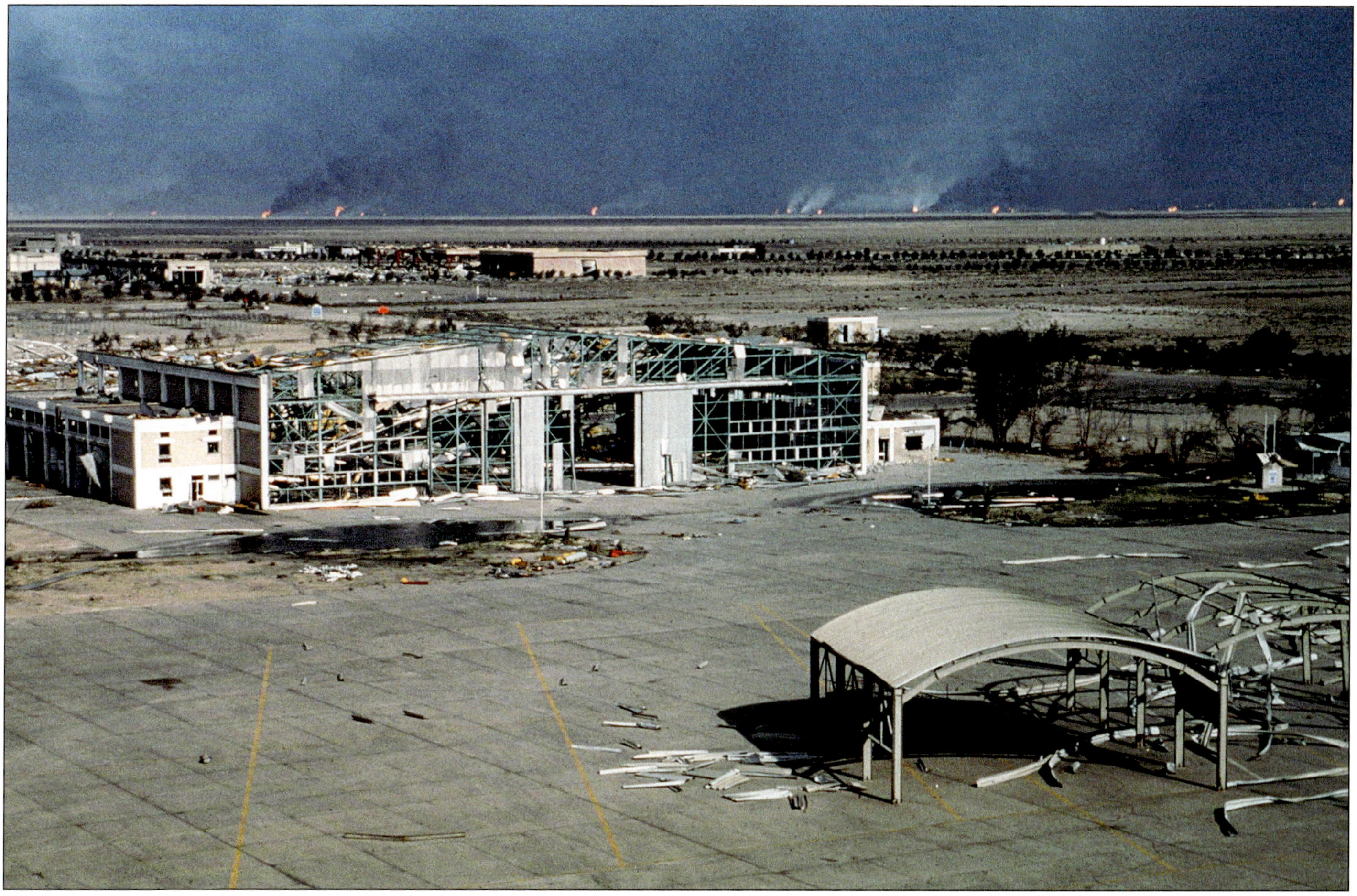

Kuwait City Airport was heavily damaged during the Iraqi invasion. (USAF/TSgt Perry Heimer)

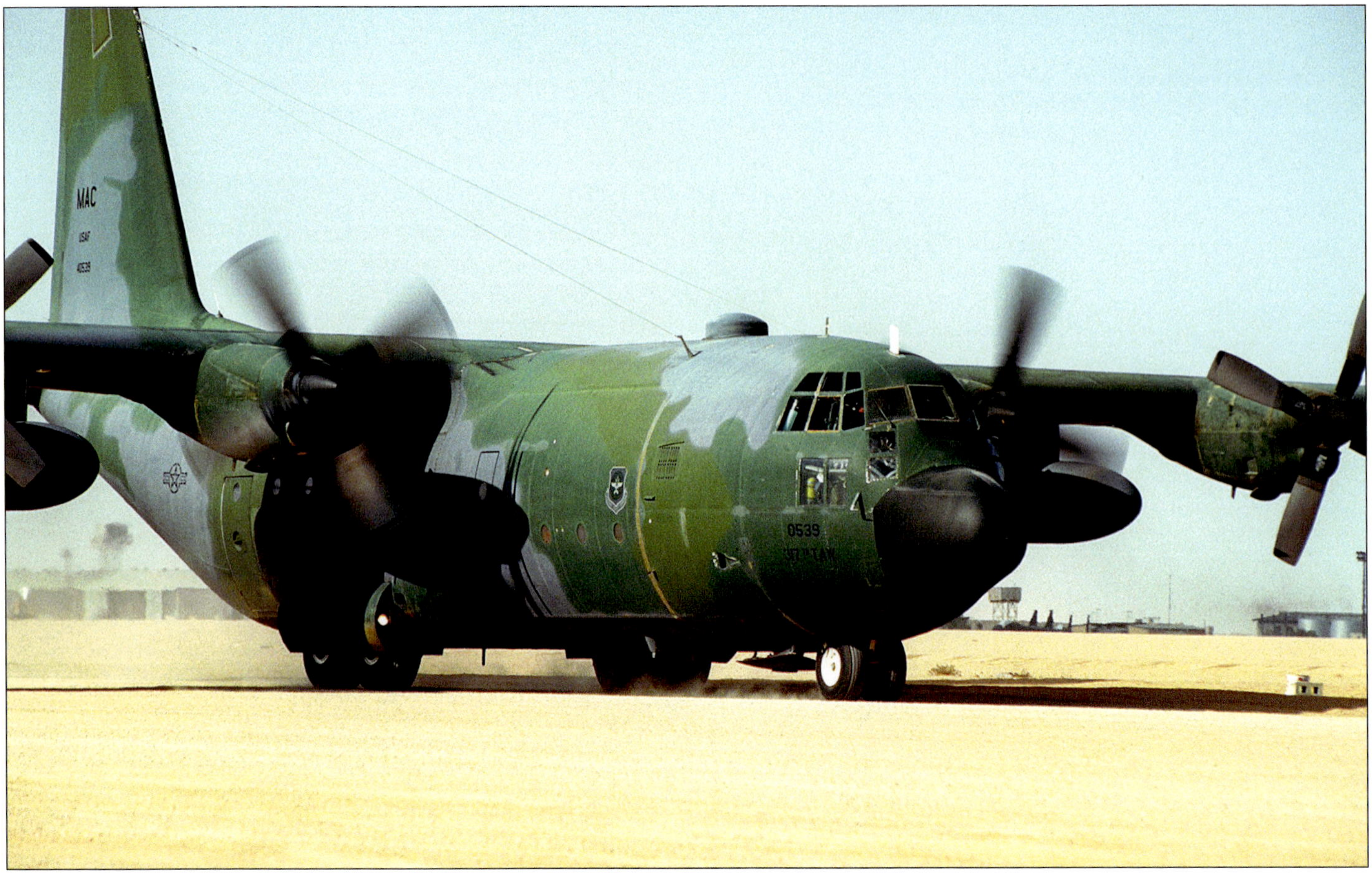

The AAVS regularly used a C-130 shuttle service to collect film and video materials from its remote Detachments. A 317th TAW C-130E taxies at a desert location. (USAF/TSgt Rose Reynolds)

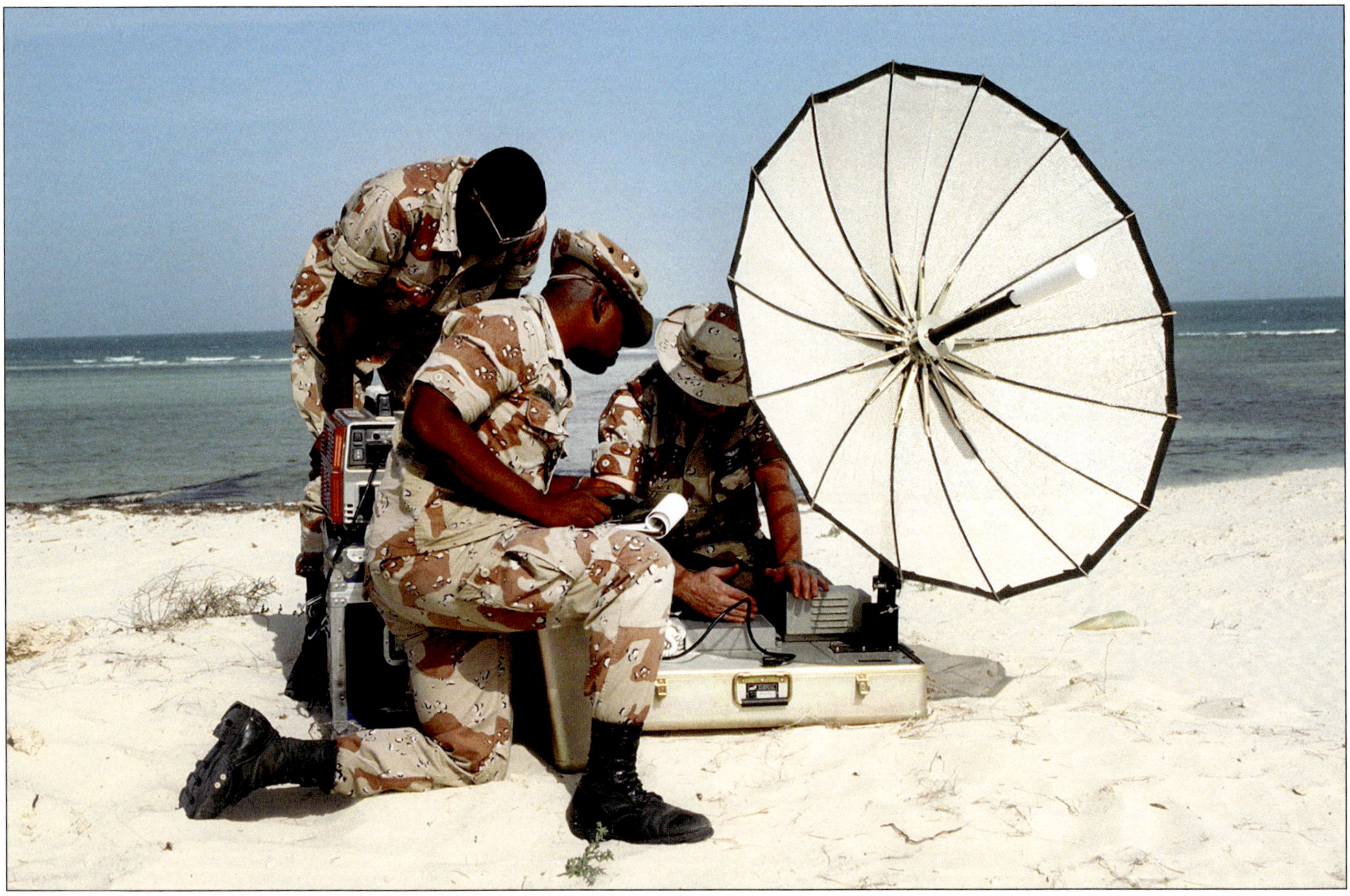

Man-portable satellite image transmission, still in its early stages, transformed the passing of video and still images. A Joint Combat Camera Team set up a TCS-9200 Lite International Marine Satellite System during a Desert Shield training exercise. (USAF/TSgt Rose Reynolds)

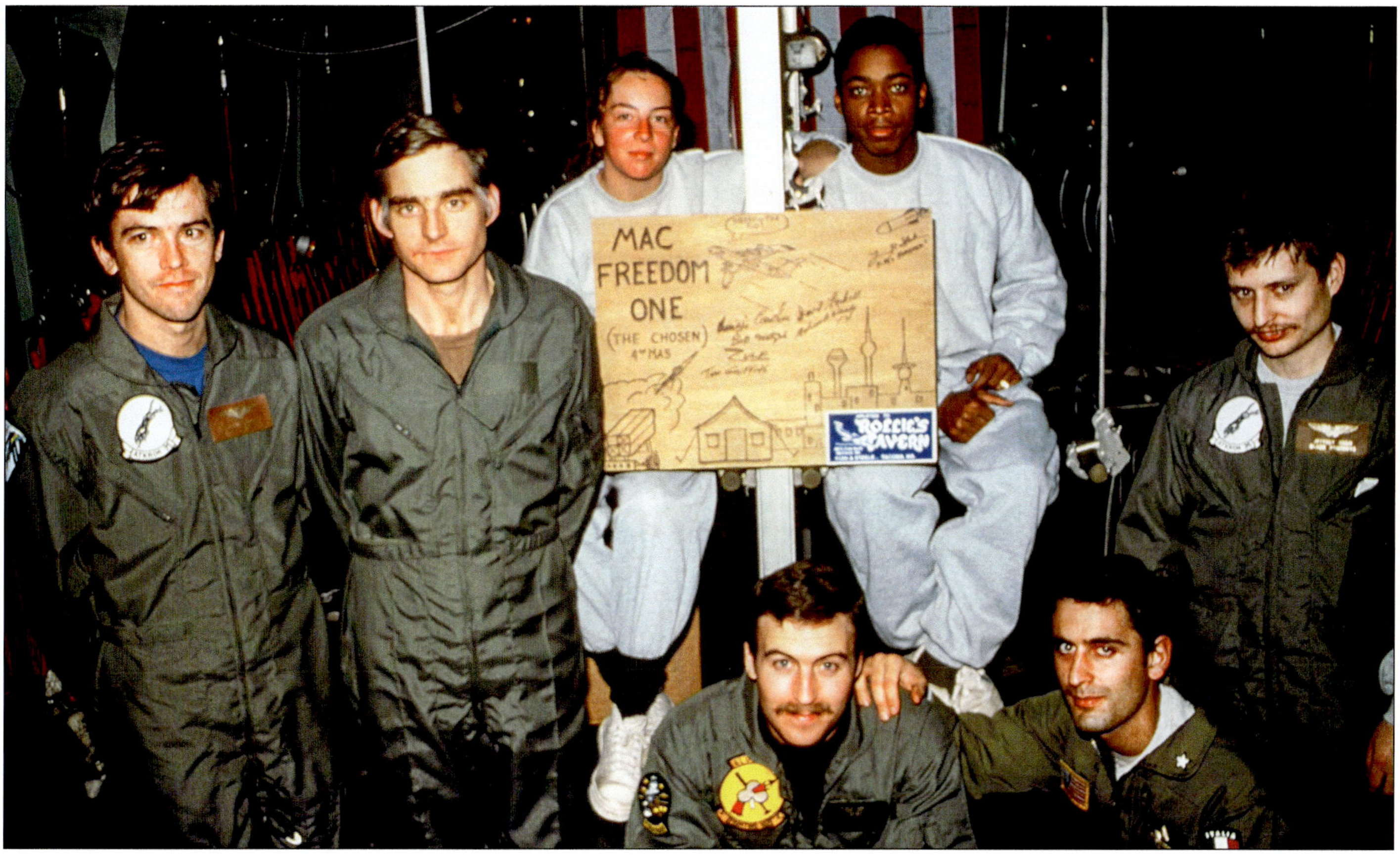

Released on 4 March 1991, heading for freedom on a C-141B from Jordan, the first Allied POWs released by the Iraqis. They included (from left) Lt Robert Wetzel, Maj Thomas Griffith, Spc Melissa Rathburn-Nealy, Spc David Lockett, Lt Jeffrey Zahn, Lt Slade and Italian Air Force Tornado navigator Capt Maurizio Cocciolone. (USN/PH2 Susan Carl)

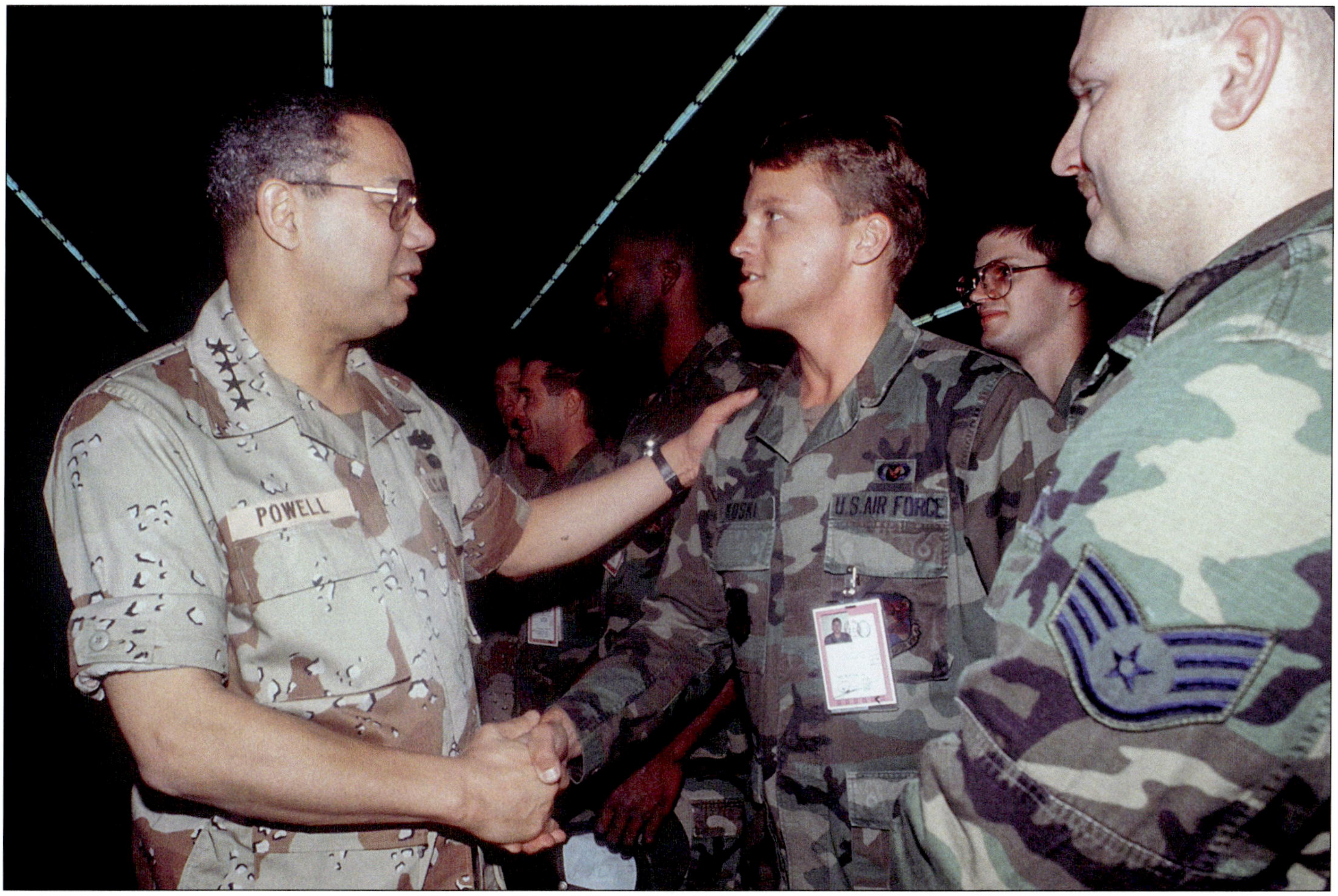

Covering visits from senior commanders or other VIPs was a regular task for AAVS cameramen and technicians, such as this visit by General Colin Powell to members of the 37th TFW during Desert Storm. (USAF/Rose Reynolds)

was in-theatre. During normal operations in the US, the AAVS was regularly asked to provide Armament Delivery Recording (ADR). Those missions provided imagery to document how successfully weapon releases worked from different aircraft types. AAVS had not expected that there would be a high demand for this service during actual wartime operations. There were also significant delays in returning some materials to the US for processing and ensuring there was a subsequent wider distribution around the armed forces.

After the Gulf

Soon after the end of the Gulf War, the US Air Force was significantly restructured. On 1 April 1992, AAVS was re-designated as the Air Combat Camera Service (Air CCS). US military doctrine underwent a radical rethink as it attempted to adapt to a new international environment. The emphasis became on 'Military Operations Other Than War' (MOOTW). The result was a high operational tempo for AAVS. Combat cameramen and women were increasingly assigned to participate in multinational operations that included peacekeeping missions in the Balkans and working with US and UN forces in Somalia. They supported humanitarian and disaster relief operations at home and abroad, and their work continued to reflect a determination to 'get the shot' firmly established by the Combat Cameramen ever since World War Two.

While the story stops here, Combat Camera did not. The final 10 years of the twentieth century, and especially after September 11, 2001, have seen the biggest changes of all. Equipment has transformed from bulky, heavy cameras that required specialised training to operate, to devices we all now carry and use every day. This can capture events in much finer detail than was ever conceivably possible with the best film equipment of World War Two.

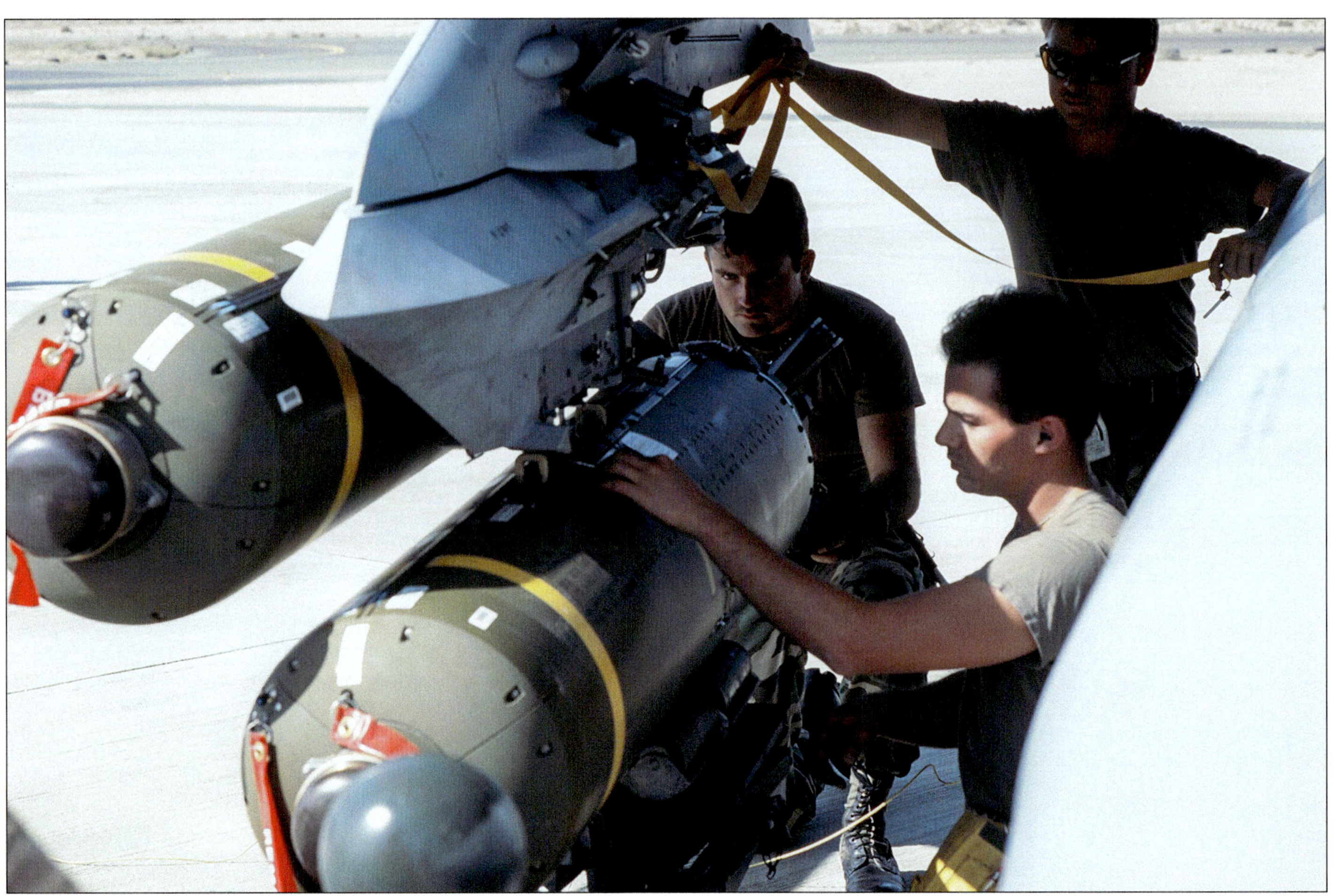

SUU-65/B weapons dispensers are loaded onto an aircraft during Desert Storm. AAVS was surprised by the number of requests to document armament delivery, to demonstrate how well individual weapons performed. (USAF/TSgt Marvin Lynchard)

On 22 August 2014, a black granite memorial bench was dedicated to the members of Combat Camera from World War Two to the present day in the Memorial Park grounds at the National Museum of the US Air Force at Wright-Patterson AFB.

Retired Maj Gen John Spiegel, who spent part of his career as a combat camera detachment commander, was the main speaker. He referenced the many conflicts combat camera photographers have participated in and their involvement in photographing events like the flights of the hypersonic X-15, the Mercury space programme and the Cuban missile crisis in 1962.

Two quotes on the reverse side of the bench immortalise the work of the men and women of combat camera. The first is from Robert Capa, a famous war photographer and photojournalist for *Life Magazine*, who produced some iconic World War Two images and says, 'If your pictures aren't good enough, you're not close enough'. The second inscription is from Joe Longo, the World War Two motion picture cameraman and post-war founder of the International Combat Camera Association. It aptly says, 'The brave ones shot bullets, the crazy ones shot film'.

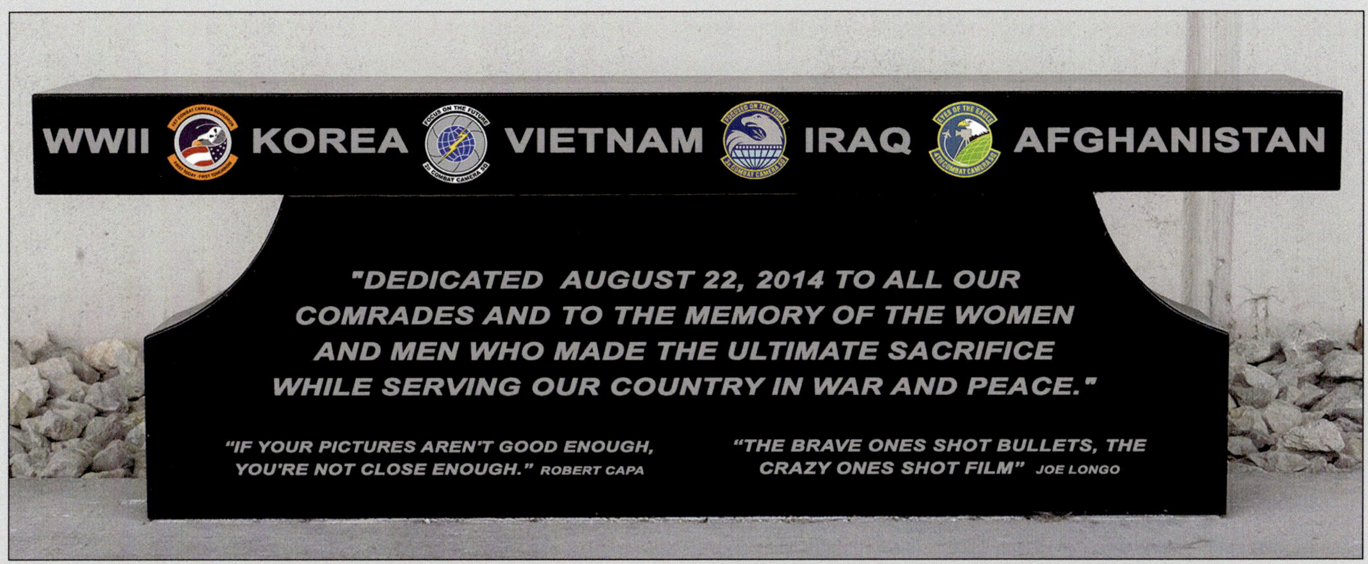

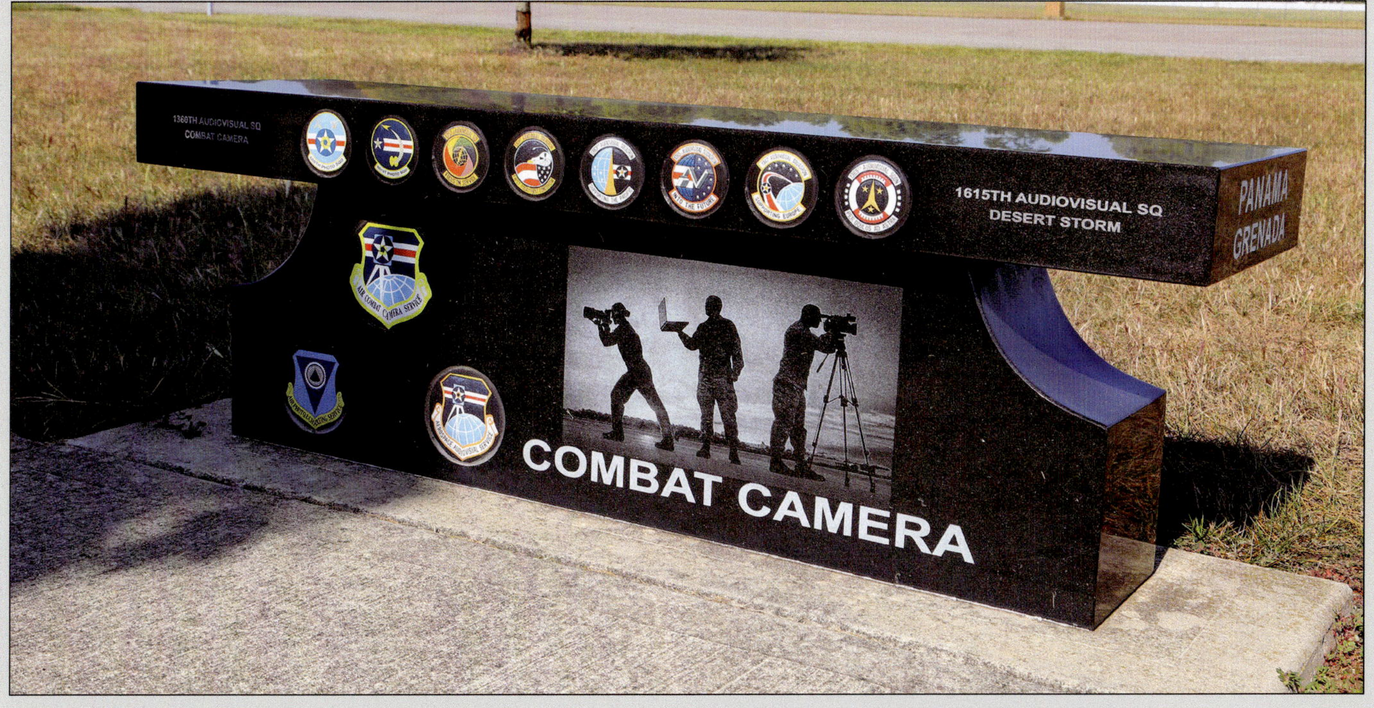

(USAF and Kevin Wright)

BIBLIOGRAPHY

Alcine, W, 'Camera Action', *Yank Down Under*, (April 7, 1944), Vol 1, No. 36, pp.2–3.

Barksdale, WS, 'Aerial Combat Photography', *Air Force Review*, July-August 1966, pp.60–69.

O'Connor, R, 'AAF Film Unit', *Flying Magazine*, April 1945, pp.54–55, 106.

Correll, JT, ' The Poltava Debacle', *Air and Space Forces Magazine*, March 1, 2011, pp.64–68.

Cross, CF, *MAC and Operation BABYLIFT* (MAC, Scott AFB: 1989)

Glines, CV, 'Hollywood Without the Ulcers', *Air Force Magazine*, May 1960, pp.100–102.

Hamilton, K, O'Gorman, N, *Lookout America! The Secret Hollywood Studio at the Heart of the Cold War* (Dartmouth College Press: 2019)

Kennerly, D, *Shooter* (Newsweek Books, NY: 1979)

McCabe, J, *Rebels to Reels: A Biography of Combat Cameraman Daniel A McGovern* (Carrickmacross, Co Monaghan: Gallowglass, 2023)

Schlosser, E, *Command And Control: Nuclear Weapons, the Damascus Accident, and the Illusion of Safety* (Penguin Books, London: 2013)

USAAF, *4th Combat Camera Unit History, 1941-45*, https://www.416th.com/SupportUnits/A0484_4thCCU_History.pdf p.5.

USAF, *Air Photographic and Charting Service History* (1951-62)

USAF, *Anything, Anywhere, Anytime: An Illustrated History of the Military Airlift Command. 1941-1991* (HQ MAC, Scott AFB:1992)

USAF, *History of 600th Photo Squadron, 1 July 1966 to 31 December 1966*

USAF, *History of 600th Photo Squadron, January 1967 to June 1967*

USAF, *History of the 1352nd Photographic Group, 1 July to 31 December 1962*

USAF, *History of the 1352nd Photographic Group, 1 January to 30 June 1963*

USAF, *History of the 1352nd Photographic Group, 1 January to 31 July 1964*

USAF, *History of the 1352nd Photographic Group, 1 July to 31 December 1964*

USAF, *History of 1352nd Photographic Group, 1 January thru 30 June 1969*

Wright, K, 'Catch a Falling Star', *Aeroplane Monthly*, Vol. 48, No. 5, (May 2019), pp.58–64.

Wright, K, *Danger Zone: US Clandestine Reconnaissance Operations Along the West Berlin Air Corridors, 1945-1990* (Warwick: Helion, 2023)

ENDNOTES

Chapter 1

1 Richard O'Connor, 'AAF Film Unit', *Flying Magazine*, April 1945, pp.54–55, p.106

2 Richard O'Connor, 'AAF Film Unit', *Flying Magazine*, April 1945, p.106. An example of a cartoon production on in-flight disorientation is at https://www.youtube.com/watch?v=cUBzs3cq9DM (Accessed 29 January 2025).

3 4th Combat Camera Unit History, 1941-45, https://www.416th.com/SupportUnits/A0484_4thCCU_History.pdf, p.5. (Accessed 29 January 2025).

4 McCabe, J, *Rebels to Reels: A biography of Combat Cameraman Daniel A McGovern* (Carrickmacross, Co Monaghan: Gallowglass, 2023), pp.124–132.

5 McCabe, pp.136–37.

6 4th CC Unit History, 1941-45, op cit, p.50.

7 NARA has a list of 34 *Memphis Belle* out take reels and links at https://www.youtube.com/playlist?list=PLugwVCjzrJsX_s9uHyFxYygX-LPvI8H-_ (Accessed 29 January 2025).

8 McCabe, op cit p.141.

9 Data from American Air Museum.

10 4th CC Unit History, 1941-45, p.60.

11 4th CC Unit History, 1941-45, p.63.

12 John T Correll, ' The Poltava Debacle', *Air and Space Forces Magazine*, March 1, 2011. https://www.airandspaceforces.com/article/0311poltava/ (Accessed 30 January 2025).

13 4th CC Unit History, 1941-45, p.86 and p.91.

14 4th CC Unit History, 1941-45, pp.94–95.

15 4th CC Unit History, 1941-45, pp.91–99.

16 4th CC Unit History, 1941-45, pp.100–101.

17 4th CC Unit History, 1941-45, p.111.

18 K. Wright, *Danger Zone: US Clandestine Reconnaissance Operations along the West Berlin Air Corridors, 1945-1990* (Warwick: Helion, 2023), pp.10–11.

Chapter 2

1 Bill Alcine, 'Camera Action', *Yank Down Under*, (April 7, 1944), Vol 1, No. 36, pp.2–3.

2 Alcine, p.3.

3 5th CC Unit History, 1941-45, p.87.

4 5th CC Unit History, 1941-45, p.3.

5 5th CC Unit History, 1941-45, pp.91–92.

6 https://evergreenpodcasts.com/warriors-in-their-own-words/s-sgt-joe-longo-combat-cameraman (Accessed 30 January 2025).

7 A simple externally mounted viewfinder aid to help the cameraman capture fast moving objects more quickly as seen on some images of cameras in this chapter.

Chapter 3

1 McCabe, pp.279–284.

2 McCabe, pp.362–365.

3 McCabe, pp.362–385.

4 McCabe, pp.418–421.

5 https://www.governmentattic.org/22docs/DoDfilmOfferNARA_1990-1996.pdf (Accessed 2 February 2025)

6 Eric Schlosser, *Command And Control: Nuclear Weapons, the Damascus Accident, and the Illusion of Safety* (Penguin Books, London: 2013), pp.307–308.

7 https://nsarchive2.gwu.edu/nukevault/ebb304/index.htm

Chapter 5

1   *Air Photographic and Charting Service History*, p.2. https://www. nro.gov/Portals/65/documents/foia/declass/WS117L_Records/275. PDF (Accessed 4 February 2025)
2   *Air Photographic and Charting Service History*, p.19.
3   W S Barksdale Jr, "Aerial Combat Photography", *Air Force Review*, July-August 1966, pp.60–69.
4   Lt Col Carroll V Glines, 'Hollywood without the ulcers', *Air Force Magazine*, May 1960, pp.100–102
5   *History of the 1352nd Photographic Group, 1 January to 30 June 1963*, p.36. https://www.lookoutamerica.org/items/show/153 (Accessed 3 February 2025)
6   The images donated to the San Diego Air & Space Museum Archives are available https://www.flickr.com/photos/ sdasmarchives/albums/72157649485000247/ (Accessed 3 February 2025)
7   *History of the 1352nd Photographic Group, 1 January to 30 June 1963*, p.36. https://www.lookoutamerica.org/items/show/153, (Accessed 3 February 2025)
8   *History of the 1352nd Photographic Group, 1 January to 30 June 1963*, p.37.
9   Library of Congress interview with Eddie W Carroll, https://www. loc.gov/item/afc2001001.106313/#item-service_history, (Accessed 3 February 2025)
10 *Secret Film Studios: Lookout Mountain*, https://nnss.gov/wp-content/uploads/2023/04/DOENV_1142-1.pdf (Accessed 4 February 2025)
11 *History of the 1352nd Photographic Group, 1 July to 31 December 1962*, pp.53–66. https://lookoutamerica.org/files/ original/1499ed5b1a08e979dc7d6bc179a49e19.pdf (Accessed 4 February 2025)
12 *History of 1352nd MPS, Lookout Mountain AFS, 1 January to 30 June, 1960.* https://www.lookoutamerica.org/files/ original/5009bf569f6a9c90fba03ec23f60e7da.pdf, pp.14–15. (Accessed 4 February 2025)
13 K. Wright, (2020), 'Catch a Falling Star', *Aeroplane Monthly*, Vol. 48, No. 5, (May 2019), pp.58–64.
14 *History of the 1352nd Photographic Group, 1 July to 31 December 1962*, p.62 https://lookoutamerica.org/files/ original/1499ed5b1a08e979dc7d6bc179a49e19.pdf (Accessed 4 February 2025)
15 *History of the 1352nd Photographic Group, 1 January to 31 July 1964*, p.69. https://www.lookoutamerica.org/items/show/160 (Accessed 4 February 2025)
16 *History of the 1352nd Photographic Group, 1 July to 31 December 1964*, pp.102–103. https://www.lookoutamerica.org/items/show/162 (Accessed 4 February 2025)
17 *History of 1352nd Photographic Group, 1 January thru 30 June 1969*, pp.52–54, pp.38–41. https://www.lookoutamerica.org/files/ original/fc86b7a2d588580c7e6b3d8b922d0bf8.pdf

Chapter 6

1   *Anything, Anywhere, Anytime: An Illustrated History of the Military Airlift Command. 1941-1991* (HQ MAC, Scott AFB:1992), pp.142–43. https://www.amc.af.mil/Portals/12/documents/AFD-131018-047.pdf (Accessed 5 February 2025).
2   *Anything, Anywhere, Anytime*, pp.142–43.
3   USAF, *History of 600th Photo Squadron, January 1967 – June 1967*, pp.7–10. http://tijil.org/pcat/history600thps_jan-jun67.pdf600ps history p.14 pdf (Accessed 5 February 2025).
4   USAF, *History of 600th Photo Squadron, 1 July 1966 – 31 December 1966*, p ii (Foreword), http://tijil.org/pcat/history600thps_jul-dec66.pdf (Accessed 5 February 2025).
5   *History of 600th Photo Squadron, 1 July 1966 – 31 December 1966*, p.13. (Accessed 5 February 2025).
6   William S Barksdale, J r, "Aerial Combat Photography", *Air Force Review*, July-August 1966, pp.60–69.
7   Ronald Wayne Marshall interview. https://www.loc.gov/ collections/veterans-history-project-collection/serving-our-voices/ creative-expressions-of-service/military-photographers-framing-the-shot/item/afc2001001.34472/ (Accessed 5 February 2025).
8   DH Kennerly, *Shooter* (Newsweek Book, NY: 1979) p.95.
9   *History of 600th Photo Squadron, January 1967 – June 1967*, op cit p.20.
10 USAF, *History of the 600th Photographic Squadron 1 July to December 1967*, pp.13–15 *An Illustrated Parts Breakdown for the Gun Camera Type N-9* is available at https://www.cia.gov/ readingroom/docs/CIA-RDP70B00198R000700010008-1.pdf (Accessed 5 February 2025).
11 USAF, *History of 600th Photo Squadron, 1 July 1966 – 31 December 1966*, pp.12–13.
12 Ronald Wayne Marshall interview op cit.
13 Kennerly, op cit p.47.
14 CF Cross, *MAC and Operation BABYLIFT* (MAC, Scott AFB: 1989), p.37. https://media.defense.gov/2012/Aug/31/2001330018/-1/-1/0/MAC%20AND%20OPERATION%20BABYLIFT.pdf (Accessed 6 February 2025).

Chapter 7

1   The interview has been lightly edited for clarity. Part 1: https:// evergreenpodcasts.com/warriors-in-their-own-words/chief-master-sergeant-doug-morrell-part-i-the-legend-in-wwii (Accessed 6 February 2025) Part 2: https://evergreenpodcasts.com/ warriors-in-their-own-words/chief-master-sergeant-doug-morrell-part-ii-the-legend-in-vietnam (Accessed 6 February 2025)
2   Sean M Miskimins, *Operation Tidal Wave* (Airmen Memorial Museum: Washington DC, undated), p.5. https://media.defense. gov/2016/May/18/2001540805/-1/-1/0/AFD-160518-001-011.PDF

Chapter 8

1   https://www.youtube.com/watch?v=I5cO15keOdg
2   https://catalog.archives.gov/search-within/62003?availableOnline= true (Accessed 6 February 2025).

ABOUT THE AUTHOR

Having taught Cold War history, international security and politics at the University of Essex from where he gained a PhD, Kevin is a regular contributor to several UK aviation magazines and is an aviation photographer. Publications have included books on the U-2, Cold War aerial intelligence and contemporary military topics.